14 Days

FEB. 4 1983

AUG. 9 1983

JUN. 1 3 1986

NOV. 2 8 1986

APR. 1 1 1987

MAY 5 1989

JAN. 1 3 1990

MAR. 2 0 1990

DEC. 1 2 1992

DEC 1 4 1994

MAR 1 7 1995

APR 2 3 1997

OCT 2 7 1998

WITHDRAWN

Y0-CRU-894

Akron Carnegie Public Library
205 E. Rochester Street
Akron, IN 46910

Practical
Record Keeping

FOURTH EDITION

HAROLD BARON
Chairman, Accounting Department
Lafayette High School, Brooklyn, New York

SOLOMON C. STEINFELD
Chairman, Accounting Department
Flushing High School, Flushing, New York

COURSE 1

Published by

BO4 SOUTH-WESTERN PUBLISHING CO.

CINCINNATI   WEST CHICAGO, ILL.   DALLAS   PELHAM MANOR, N.Y.
PALO ALTO. CALIF.   BRIGHTON, ENGLAND

Copyright © 1975

Philippine Copyright 1975
by
SOUTH-WESTERN PUBLISHING CO.
Cincinnati, Ohio

All Rights Reserved

The text of this publication, or any
part thereof, may not be reproduced or
transmitted in any form or by any means,
electronic or mechanical, including
photocopying, recording, storage in an
information retrieval system, or otherwise, without the prior written per-
mission of the publisher.

ISBN: 0-538-02040-7

Library of Congress Catalog Card Number: 73-91287

6 7 8 K 2 10 9

Printed in the United States of America

657
B

PREFACE

The Fourth Edition of PRACTICAL RECORD KEEPING, COURSE I retains those basic features of the previous editions that have made the book an effective tool of learning, and introduces new features to increase its proven effectiveness.

The new size of the book permits a greater utilization of space to make for more readable copy. Frequent marginal comments, made possible by this new size, summarize and emphasize key facts. Key ideas are given further emphasis by the strategic use of color.

An important innovation introduced in the previous edition has been expanded. The psychological benefit of reinforcing learning by providing students with the means of verifying their work is recognized. Wherever feasible, interim and final answers are provided in the practice problems to serve as check points to reassure the student in the solution of the problems.

Sample problems, illustrations, cartoons, and practice problems have been updated to reflect current prices, current tax rates, and current business and office procedures.

The increased use of machine and electronic equipment to process data is reflected in the frequent references to this equipment at the points in the book where its application can be shown.

The organization of the book remains unchanged. The year's work is divided into ten units. Each unit is subdivided into a series of jobs. Each job is constructed around a directed lesson plan, including (1) related arithmetic drill; (2) the aims of the job; (3) an explanation of the job, including motivation and recall of related learning; (4) a sample problem, shown with a step-by-step solution; and (5) practice problems.

Two workbooks are available for PRACTICAL RECORD KEEPING, COURSE I. Workbook I contains the forms for completing the jobs in textbook Units 1–6, together with supplementary problems and forms paralleling those in the book. Similarly, Workbook II contains the forms for completing the jobs in the textbook Units 7–10 and supplementary problems and forms. A series of eight tests (four tests for each semester) is available. The tests may be used for evaluating student skills and understanding. Also available, and new to this edition, is a self-contained teacher's manual with expanded teaching suggestions and a set of transparency masters to supplement the illustrations in the book. As in the past, a teacher's edition for each of the two workbooks is provided to assist in the checking of student work.

This edition evolved from the wide experience of teachers and students with the previous editions. Their comments and advice have guided the authors. The authors have also been guided by the editors of South-Western Publishing Co. who supervised the entire edition and provided valuable assistance in the preparation of the manuscript. The authors appreciate this guidance and welcome suggestions for improving the next edition.

Baron-Steinfeld

34359

TABLE OF CONTENTS

UNIT 1

RECORD KEEPING BASIC SKILLS

UNIT 1

JOB 1 | COMPARING NAMES, NUMBERS, AND ADDRESSES

AIM

To introduce you to the study of record keeping.

EXPLANATION

What kind of starting job will you get after being graduated? The chances are that no matter where you find yourself working — in an office, in a supermarket, behind a sales counter, in a stockroom, in an automobile service station or in your own small business — you will need to know how to keep clerical records and you will have to understand the language of business. Data processing! Accounts receivable! Invoices! Checks! Petty cash! These are just a few of the business terms you will hear many times on the job.

Job preparation

When you apply for your first job, how will you match up against your competition for that job? Will you know how to keep a record of cash received and paid out? Will you know how to write checks and keep an accurate checkbook balance? Will you know how to keep a record of purchases and sales of merchandise? Will you be able to prepare a payroll and keep payroll records? Will you know how to keep a record of business income and expenses? Will you know how to keep a record of the amounts owed by customers?

These are some of the valuable skills you will acquire through the study of record keeping. Through your study of record keeping you will be better prepared to compete for a job and better able to handle your own personal business affairs.

Record-keeping tools

All good artists sharpen the tools of their trade before tackling a job. If you are to be successful in your study of record keeping, there are certain tools or skills you should sharpen and improve. On the job, much attention is given to

Spelling makes the difference

correct spelling, neatness in writing, and accuracy in arithmetic. These are some of the record-keeping tools you will have to sharpen.

Throughout your record-keeping work, in addition to learning about many business activities, you will be asked to write clearly and carefully. In addition, you will be given practice in arithmetic.

When you apply for a job, the employer may test your record-keeping skill. One way of doing this is to test your ability to find errors in lists of names, addresses, and numbers. Samples from employment tests are given below and on the following pages. First, examine the sample problem; then, see how accurate you are in making similar comparisons.

SAMPLE PROBLEM

Find the errors in the following lists of names by comparing the names in Column A with the names in Column B. If the names are exactly the same, place a check mark in the column headed "Alike." If there is an error, place a check mark in the column headed "Not Alike."

Item	Column A	Column B	Alike	Not Alike
1)	Jim Brown	James Brown		√
2)	Tony Ricco	Tony Ricca		√
3)	Raymond McGrath	Raymond McGrath	√	

Notice that only in Item 3 of the sample problem are the names exactly alike.

Now, test your own accuracy by doing the following problems.

PRACTICE PROBLEMS

Working papers are available for completing the problems of each record-keeping job in this textbook. When the working papers are used, it is not necessary for the student to copy headings and prepare forms on separate papers.

Problem 1

Comparing personal names

You apply for an office position with the Gordon Trucking Company. To test your accuracy, the personnel manager gives you the lists of names shown on the next page and the following directions.

Directions:
a) If working papers are not provided, copy the following headings at the top of a sheet of paper:

Item	Alike	Not Alike

b) Indicate whether the names shown in Columns A and B are alike or not alike by placing a check mark under the proper heading. To help you get started, the answers for the first two pairs of names are shown below:

Item	Alike	Not Alike
1		√
2	√	

Number each answer carefully under the heading "Item."

Item	Column A	Column B
1)	Samuel Ackerman	Sam Ackerman
2)	James Porter	James Porter
3)	Lynda Secchia	Lynda Secchia
4)	Patricia Gray	Patricia Gray
5)	Miguel Gonzalez	Miguel Gonzalez
6)	Greg Lombardi	Gregory Lombardi
7)	Dominick Rizzo	Domonick Rizzo
8)	Calvin Byrnes	Calvin Burns
9)	Jeffrey Laskowski	Jeffrey Laskowski
10)	Keith Ainsworth	Keith Ainsworth, Jr.
11)	Alan Kornstein	Alan Korstien
12)	Aaron Knopf	Aaron Knopf
13)	Thos. A. Goldstone	Thos. A. Goldstein
14)	Harry McNeil	Harry MacNeil
15)	Catherine Di Benedetto	Catherine Di benedetto
16)	Stephen Perrone	Steven Perrone
17)	Robert Gray	Roberta Gray
18)	R. C. Mannheimer	R. C. Mannheimer
19)	Phylis Kessler	Phylis Kessler
20)	Charles Hanson	Charles Hansen

Problem 2

You apply for an office position with the National Steel Company. To test your accuracy, the office manager gives you the lists of names shown below and the following directions.

Comparing business names

Directions:

a) Copy the following headings at the top of a sheet of paper:

Item	Alike	Not Alike

b) Indicate whether the names shown in Columns A and B are alike or not alike by placing a check mark under the proper heading. Number each answer carefully under the heading "Item."

Item	Column A	Column B
1)	Terrill Mfg. Co.	Terrill Mfg. Co.
2)	Parker Paint Store	Parker Paint Stores
3)	Data Processing Center	Data Processing Central
4)	Wood Consultant Co.	Woods Consultant Co.
5)	Neighborhood Theater	Neighborhood Theatre

6)	John E. Mauro & Son	John E. Mauro & Son
7)	Carlisle Construction Co.	Carlisle Construction Co.
8)	Gelber Hair Stylist	Gelber Hair Stylists
9)	Lee Modernization Co.	**Lee Modernization, Inc.**
10)	Macrose Corporation	MacRose Corporation
11)	Rivera Bros.	Rivera Bros.
12)	Fast Vacuum Co.	Fast Vacuum Co.
13)	John Marchionne Co.	John Marchionné Co.
14)	Twin-City Freight	Twin City Freight
15)	Casey & Ryan Co.	Casey & Ryun Co.
16)	Jones Drilling Corp.	**Jones Drilling, Inc.**
17)	Vignola Dress Co.	Vingola Dress Co.
18)	Browne Electric Assn.	Brown Electric Assn.
19)	Scanlon Office Supplies	Scanlon Office Supplies
20)	Lefkowitz & Reisner	Lefkowitz & Reisner

Problem 3

Comparing personal and business names

You apply for an office position with the Lee Construction Company. To test your accuracy, the manager gives you the lists of names shown below and the following directions.

Directions:

a) Copy the following headings at the top of a sheet of paper:

Item	Alike	Not Alike

b) Indicate whether the names shown in Columns A and B are alike or not alike by placing a check mark under the proper heading. Number each answer carefully under the heading "Item."

Item	Column A	Column B
1)	Jose Torres	Jose Torres
2)	Olga Brandquist	Olga Brandquist
3)	Anderson Corporation	Anderson Corp.
4)	Philadelphia Electric	Philadelphia Electric
5)	Cohen Bros., Inc.	Cohan Bros., Inc.
6)	Smith & Lane Co.	Smith & Lane, Co.
7)	Minnesota Telephone	Minneola Telephone
8)	Burke Contracting Co.	Burke Contracting Company
9)	Higgins Bros. Co.	Higgins Bros. & Co.
10)	Carmela Rapaglio	Carmela Rappaglio
11)	Mark Apparel Shops	Mark Apparel Shops
12)	James J. Kelley	James J. Kelly
13)	Sea Cliff Iron Works	Sea Cliff Iron Works
14)	Robert J. Russell	Roberto J. Russell
15)	Breitman & Bisogni	Breitman & Besogni
16)	Lewis Maintenance Co.	Lewis Maintenence Co.
17)	Feschetti Designers	Fischetti Designers
18)	Miguel Jiminez	Migual Jiminez
19)	Ron's Discount Fabrics	Ron Discount Fabric
20)	Corey Reyes	Corey Reyes

Problem 4

You apply for a position in the accounting department of the Soma Products Company. To test your accuracy, the head accountant gives you the lists of amounts shown below and the following directions.

Comparing amounts

Directions:
a) Copy the following headings at the top of a sheet of paper:

Item	Alike	Not Alike

b) Indicate whether the amounts shown in Columns A and B are alike or not alike by placing a check mark under the proper heading. Number each answer carefully under the heading "Item."

Item	Column A	Column B
1)	$4,721.18	$4,721.18
2)	1,934.32	1,934.23
3)	8,617.15	8,671.15
4)	15,346.27	15,346.27
5)	31,492.85	31,492.85
6)	19,563.46	19,563.46
7)	93,218.34	93,128.34
8)	64,767.89	64,767.98
9)	76,531.25	76,531.25
10)	23,457.73	23,475.73
11)	56,384.26	56,384.26
12)	41,119.30	41,191.30
13)	12,856.14	12,586.14
14)	37,472.56	37,472.65
15)	19,616.60	19,616.06
16)	86,941.37	86,941.37
17)	24,331.43	24,313.43
18)	92,724.82	92,724.82
19)	38,227.71	38,227.71
20)	14,202.90	14,202.90

Problem 5

You apply for a position in the mailing room of Acme Printing Company. To test your accuracy, the chief mail clerk gives you the lists of addresses shown on the next page and the following directions.

Comparing addresses

Directions:
a) Copy the following headings at the top of a sheet of paper:

Item	Alike	Not Alike

b) Indicate whether the addresses shown in Columns A and B are alike or not alike by placing a check mark under the proper heading. Number each answer carefully under the heading "Item."

Item	Column A	Column B
1)	217 North Franklin Ave.	212 North Franklin Ave.
2)	385 Route 110, Huntington	385A Route 110, Huntington
3)	65 Chespeake Road	65 Chesepeake Road
4)	1785 Milburne Ave.	1785 Milburn Ave.
5)	18 Ridgedale Street	18 Ridgdale Street
6)	4816 Washington Blvd.	4186 Washington Blvd.
7)	92 **Plandome St.**	92 Plandome St.
8)	16 Nortern Blvd.	16 Northern Blvd.
9)	1891 Eagle Street	1891 Eagle Street
10)	24 Shanley Ave.	24 Shanley Ave.
11)	3745 Miami Drive	3475 Miami Drive
12)	418 Bonita Street	418 Bonito Street
13)	6495 Tiffany Ave.	6495 Tifany Ave.
14)	116 Jericho Tpke.	116 Jericko Tpke.
15)	270 Apple Valley Ave.	270 Apple Valley St.
16)	35 Beach Channel Drive	35 **Beach Chanel Drive**
17)	1415 Parallel Avenue	1415 Parallel Avenue
18)	90 Herricks Road	90 Herrick Road
19)	265 Woodfield St.	265 Woodfeild St.
20)	541 Shawmut Ave.	541 Shawmut Ave.

Problem 6

Comparing names and addresses

You apply for a position in the customer service department of the County Electric Company. To test your accuracy, the personnel director gives you the lists of names and addresses shown below and the following directions.

Directions:

a) Copy the following headings at the top of a sheet of paper:

Item   **Alike**   **Not Alike**

b) Indicate whether the names and addresses shown in Columns A and B are alike or not alike by placing a check mark under the proper heading. Number each answer carefully under the heading "Item."

Item	Column A	Column B
1)	Robert A. Brumby 73 Westbury Ave.	Robert A. Brumby 73 Westbury Ave.
2)	Harold Klein 37 Nottingham Rd.	Harold Klein 37 Nottingahm Rd.
3)	Federal Pump Corp. 119 Kentucky Street	Federel Pump Corp. 119 Kentucky Street
4)	Otto Ranzweiser 1410 Telegram Place	Otto Ranzweiser 1410 Telegram Place
5)	Victor La Fuente 450 Devonshire Ave.	Victor Di La Fuente 405 Devonshire Ave.
6)	McKeon Auto Repair 121 Millington Road	McKeon Auto Repair 121 Millingten Road

7)	La Mair Medical Labs 4916 Jackson Street	La Mar Medical Labs 4916 Jackson Street
8)	John Falcone 325 Poplar Ave.	John Falcone 325 Poplar Ave.
9)	Diaz & Baines 31 Michigan Street	Diaz & Baines 31 Michigan Street
10)	Wilson Plumbing Co. Inc. 1021 Hillside Ave.	Wilson Plumbing Co., Inc. 1021 Hillside Ave.
11)	Reuben Berris 34 Lexington Ave.	Reuben Berris 43 Lexington Ave.
12)	Slattery Corporation 3516 Riverview Rd.	Slattery Corporation 3516 Riverveiw Rd.
13)	Skor-Hi Bowling Alley 45 No. Main Street	Skor Hi Bowling Alley 45 North Main Street
14)	Kings Petroleum Co. 31 Veterans Hwy.	Kings Petroleum Co. 31 Veterans Hwy.
15)	Lamm & Rubin 815 Pimlico Parkway	Lamm & Rubin 815 Pimlico Parkway
16)	Brunswick Center 2251 Mohegan Rd.	Brunswick Center 2251 Mohegan Rd.
17)	Richard C. Hothersall 171–10 Jamaica Ave.	Richard C. Hothersale 171–10 Jamaica Ave.
18)	Margaret D'Amato 2661 Essex Court	Margaret D'Amato 2661 Essex Court
19)	Stanley Bobkowski 149 Sampson Ave.	Stanley Bobkowski 149 Simpson Ave.
20)	Nova Air Freight Co. 8161 Coolidge St.	Nova Air Freight Co. 8161 Coolidge St.

	Copy and complete the following problems:			
	(1)	(2)	(3)	(4)
Practicing Related Arithmetic	Add $413.52	Add $727.84	Add $324.70	Add $684.12
	392.58	641.19	773.42	813.77
	634.19	432.11	512.68	492.31
	275.34	978.76	375.13	548.65
	127.76	356.57	687.96	725.84

AIM

To test your accuracy and record-keeping skill.

EXPLANATION

You have learned that business firms may test your accuracy when you apply for a job by asking you to locate errors in lists of names, numbers, and addresses. They may also test your record-keeping skill by asking you to arrange numbers or dates in proper order. Find out if you would get the job if the following problems were given to you.

PRACTICE PROBLEMS

Problem 1

Arranging numbers

You apply for a position in the credit department of Rudd Instrument Company. To test your record-keeping skill, the credit manager asks you to do the following problem.

Directions: Copy each group of numbers shown on the next page, arranging the numbers in each group so that the lowest number is first and the highest number is last.

Example	Answer
3,826	3,358
3,718	3,718
3,942	3,826
3,358	3,942

a)	b)	c)	d)	e)
4,651	6,392	2,705	7,226	3,901
4,670	6,185	2,392	6,981	3,898
4,419	6,910	2,921	6,895	4,005
4,298	6,573	2,615	7,139	4,010
4,532	6,060	2,846	7,005	3,890
f)	g)	h)	i)	j)
14,827	64,384	59,117	40,165	38,541
15,061	63,817	59,096	40,109	37,817
15,105	63,709	58,874	39,818	38,486
14,962	64,178	59,103	40,181	37,798
14,836	64,295	58,952	39,662	38,492

Problem 2

You apply for an office position with Wilson Mfg. Co. To test your record-keeping skill, the office manager asks you to do the following problem.

Directions: Copy each group of numbers shown below, arranging the numbers in each group so that the lowest number is first and the highest number is last.

a)	b)	c)	d)	e)
3,846	5,492	1,817	8,116	6,857
3,714	5,981	1,768	8,109	6,735
3,981	5,318	1,892	7,985	6,918
3,658	5,679	1,506	7,891	7,086
3,792	5,501	1,685	7,996	7,112
f)	g)	h)	i)	j)
5,692	78,648	52,687	81,140	46,712
4,817	78,195	52,742	81,137	46,685
4,763	77,721	53,060	80,651	45,784
5,105	78,062	53,019	81,099	45,612
5,078	77,854	53,126	80,713	45,967

Problem 3

You apply for a position with the Doral Machine Company. To test your record-keeping skill, the placement director asks you to do this problem.   Arranging dates

Directions: Copy each group of dates shown on the next page, arranging the dates in each group so that the earliest date is first and the latest date is last. *(The year is the same for all the dates.)*

Example	Answer
April 24	March 10
March 13	March 13
March 10	April 24
May 6	May 6

S M T W T F S
JANUARY
1 2 3 4 5
6 7 8 9 10 11 12
13 14 15 16 17 18 19
20 21 22 23 24 25 26
27 28 29 30 31
FEBRUARY
1 2
3 4 5 6 7 8 9
10 11 12 13 14 15 16
17 18 19 20 21 22 23
24 25 26 27 28
MARCH
1 2
3 4 5 6 7 8 9
10 11 12 13 14 15 16
17 18 19 20 21 22 23
24/31 25 26 27 28 29 30
APRIL
1 2 3 4 5 6
7 8 9 10 11 12 13
14 15 16 17 18 19 20
21 22 23 24 25 26 27
28 29 30
MAY
1 2 3 4
5 6 7 8 9 10 11
12 13 14 15 16 17 18
19 20 21 22 23 24 25
26 27 28 29 30 31
JUNE
1
2 3 4 5 6 7 8
9 10 11 12 13 14 15
16 17 18 19 20 21 22
23/30 24 25 26 27 28 29
JULY
1 2 3 4 5 6
7 8 9 10 11 12 13
14 15 16 17 18 19 20
21 22 23 24 25 26 27
28 29 30 31
AUGUST
1 2 3
4 5 6 7 8 9 10
11 12 13 14 15 16 17
18 19 20 21 22 23 24
25 26 27 28 29 30 31
SEPTEMBER
1 2 3 4 5 6 7
8 9 10 11 12 13 14
15 16 17 18 19 20 21
22 23 24 25 26 27 28
29 30
OCTOBER
1 2 3 4 5
6 7 8 9 10 11 12
13 14 15 16 17 18 19
20 21 22 23 24 25 26
27 28 29 30 31
NOVEMBER
1 2
3 4 5 6 7 8 9
10 11 12 13 14 15 16
17 18 19 20 21 22 23
24 25 26 27 28 29 30
DECEMBER
1 2 3 4 5 6 7
8 9 10 11 12 13 14
15 16 17 18 19 20 21
22 23 24 25 26 27 28
29 30 31

a)	b)	c)	d)
February 11	August 16	May 31	October 10
March 8	July 17	April 28	February 8
January 23	June 23	June 29	April 19
April 15	September 9	March 17	May 21

e)	f)	g)	h)
November 3	January 20	July 8	March 6
September 24	August 31	May 25	January 20
December 11	March 9	June 17	August 12
October 31	January 12	September 16	April 30

i)	j)	k)	l)
July 9	September 3	April 12	December 29
May 14	June 15	February 21	October 16
August 27	October 24	May 1	August 4
May 21	April 30	March 3	November 30

Problem 4

You apply for a position with the Prime Furniture Company. To test your record-keeping skill, the personnel interviewer asks you to do this problem.

Directions: Copy each group of dates shown below, arranging the dates in each group so that the earliest date is first and the latest date is last. *(The year is the same for all the dates.)*

a)	b)	c)	d)
May 18	April 30	August 16	November 8
February 27	June 23	July 10	September 6
July 9	May 4	October 26	December 11
January 29	March 18	April 4	October 29

e)	f)	g)	h)
March 4	September 23	October 15	July 18
September 10	June 16	April 2	September 6
August 26	February 28	November 11	March 17
November 12	May 13	December 16	November 9

i)	j)	k)	l)
January 31	June 28	November 11	August 28
April 2	February 3	April 29	May 31
January 29	October 16	December 21	November 8
August 6	April 27	July 10	September 23

JOB 3 | IMPROVING HANDWRITING

Practicing Related Arithmetic	Copy and rearrange each group of numbers shown below so that the lowest number is first and the highest number is last.				
	(1)	(2)	(3)	(4)	(5)
	6,392	4,025	8,350	18,732	31,152
	6,215	4,941	7,612	19,016	30,984
	7,806	3,726	7,838	19,009	31,416
	7,328	3,630	7,736	18,684	31,012
	6,287	4,813	8,279	18,893	30,817

AIM

To help you improve your handwriting skill.

EXPLANATION

Your ability to write words and numbers clearly and accurately is a skill that is necessary for successful record-keeping work. It is for this reason that employers often will test your handwriting when you apply for a job.

Your handwriting can be improved by continuous practice and by following the four simple guides in the following pages.

Guide 1. Size of Letters and Numbers

Let us first examine a penmanship chart which you have probably seen before in some of your classes. Although the size and appearance of your writing may vary a bit from that of others, you should use the following chart as a guide to help improve the size and style of the letters and figures you write.

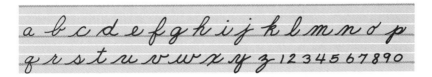

If you were asked to examine this chart and to group the letters and numbers according to size, you would discover that all the letters and numbers shown in the chart fall into three groups.

In **Group 1** are the letters and numbers that take up about one-third the space between the heavy lines. Most of the letters and all the numbers shown in the penmanship chart fall into this group, as shown below:

Group 1
⅓ space

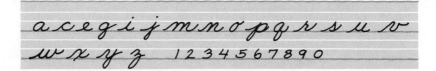

In **Group 2** are the letters that take up about one-half the space between the heavy lines. The following letters fall into this group, as shown below:

Group 2
½ space

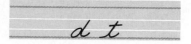

In **Group 3** are the letters that take up about two-thirds the space between the heavy lines. The following letters fall into this group, as shown below:

Group 3
⅔ space

Compare the size of the letters taken from each of the three groups:

Group 1	Group 2	Group 3

Notice the following facts:
1. Letters in *Group 1* take up about one-third the space between lines.
2. Letters in *Group 2* take up about one-half the space between lines.
3. Letters in *Group 3* take up about two-thirds the space between lines.

Guide 2. Spacing of Letters and Numbers

Business forms usually provide a minimum of space for the words and numbers to be recorded. It is important to adjust your writing to the space allowed on the printed business form. Avoid leaving too much space between the letters of a word or between numbers.

Good Form   **Poor Form**

Fit writing to
space provided

Guide 3. Form of Letters and Numbers

a) The writing on business forms must be clear so that these records can be read and understood by many different people. It is a good practice to keep numbers and letters as simple in appearance as possible. For example, compare the penmanship samples shown below:

Simple and Businesslike	Fancier, but Less Clear
i	i
c	e
t	t
5	5
4	4
2	2

Clear not fancy

b) If you were asked to examine the penmanship chart shown on page 13 and select all letters that are formed with a loop *above* the line, here are the letters you would find: *b, f, h, k,* and *l*. Notice in the illustration shown below that the loops in these letters are formed with two strokes: a curved upstroke and a straight downstroke. If the loop in the letter is *below* the line, as in the letters *f, g, j, p, q, y,* and *z*, the same rule is used: The downstroke is a straight line, and the upstroke is a curved line to form the loop, as in the letter *g*. Notice that the curved upstroke joins the straight downstroke at the ruled line, as shown in the letter *g*.

Loop Above the Line

Curve upstroke
Straight downstroke

Loop Below the Line

c) Be sure that letters such as *m* and *n* are rounded at the top and not pointed. Compare the illustrations shown below:

Good Form   Poor Form

moving   moving

Guide 4. Slant of Letters and Numbers

All letters and numbers should slant in the same direction, as shown in the illustration below. Pay particular attention to the slant of the straight down-strokes in the loops of the letters *b, f, g, h, j, k, l, p, q, y,* and *z.*

Correct Slant for Letters and Numbers

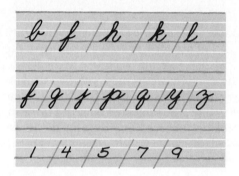

PRACTICE PROBLEMS

Problem 1

You apply for a position with The Rapid Computer Company. To test your handwriting skill, the office manager asks you to do the following:

Directions:
a) In your best handwriting, copy each of the items shown below. Be sure to pay particular attention to the size and slant of your writing. Try to use not more than one line for each item.

    Item 1: it is wise to learn
    Item 2: buy 451 yards of cloth
    Item 3: dictated data must be clear
    Item 4: record keepers must be accurate

b) Examine the letters and numbers shown in Group 1 below:

Group 1

a c e g i j m n o p q r s u v
w x y z 1 2 3 4 5 6 7 8 9 0

Now examine Item 1, which you copied in Part a) of this problem. Pick out all the letters and numbers from Item 1 that belong in Group 1. ⅓ Space

Write each letter as many times as it occurs. Remember that the letters and numbers in this group should take up about one-third the space between the heavy lines.

c) Now examine Item 2, which you copied in Part a) of this problem. Again, pick out all the letters and numbers from this item that belong in Group 1. Write each letter as many times as it occurs. Remember that the letters and numbers in this group should take up about one-third the space between the heavy lines. ⅓ Space

d) Examine the letters shown in Group 2 below. Now examine Item 3, which you copied in Part a) of this problem. Pick out all the letters from Item 3 that belong in Group 2. ½ Space

Group 2

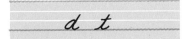

Write each letter as many times as it occurs. Remember that the letters in this group should take up about one-half the space between the heavy lines.

e) Now examine Item 4, which you copied in Part a) of this problem. Again, pick out all the letters from this item that belong in Group 2. Write each letter as many times as it occurs. Remember that the letters in this group should take up about one-half the space between the heavy lines. ½ Space

Problem 2

You apply for a position in the office of the Coast Import Company. To test your handwriting skill, the head bookkeeper asks you to do the following.

Directions:

a) In your best handwriting, copy each of the items shown below. Be sure to pay particular attention to the size and slant of your writing. Try to use not more than one line for each item.

Item 1: 164 checks were received
Item 2: improvement comes with practice
Item 3: addresses must be written clearly
Item 4: seat belts do save lives

b) Examine the letters and numbers shown in Group 1 below:

Group 1

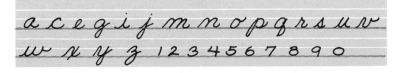

Now examine Item 1, which you copied in Part a) of this problem. Pick out all the letters and numbers from Item 1 that belong in Group 1. ⅓ Space

Write each letter as many times as it occurs. Remember that the letters and numbers in this group should take up about one-third the space between the heavy lines.

⅓ Space

c) Now examine Item 2, which you copied in Part a) of this problem. Again, pick out all the letters and numbers from this item that belong in Group 1.

Write each letter as many times as it occurs. Remember that the letters and numbers in this group should take up about one-third the space between the heavy lines.

d) Examine the letters shown in Group 2 below. Now examine Item 3, which you copied in Part a) of this problem. Pick out all the letters from Item 3 that belong in Group 2.

Group 2

½ Space

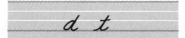

½ Space

Write each letter as many times as it occurs. Remember that the letters in this group should take up about one-half the space between the heavy lines.

e) Now examine Item 4, which you copied in Part a) of this problem. Again, pick out all the letters from this item that belong in Group 2. Write each letter as many times as it occurs. Remember that the letters in this group should take up about one-half the space between the heavy lines.

Problem 3

You apply for a position in the credit department of the Allen Baking Company. In order to test your handwriting skill, the department manager asks you to do the following.

Directions:

a) In your best handwriting, copy each of the items shown below. Be sure to pay particular attention to the size and slant of your writing. Try to use not more than one line for each item.

Item 1: hold the line for our school
Item 2: keep the home fires burning
Item 3: follow the rules of the game
Item 4: writing habits can be improved

b) Examine the letters in Group 3 below. Now examine Item 1, which you copied in Part a) of this problem. Pick out all the letters from Item 1 that belong in Group 3.

Group 3

⅔ Space

Write each letter as many times as it occurs. Remember that the letters in this group should take up about two-thirds the space between the heavy lines.

c) Now examine Item 2, which you copied in Part a) of this problem. Again, pick out all the letters from this item that belong in Group 3. Write each letter as many times as it occurs. Remember that the letters in this group should take up about two-thirds the space between the heavy lines.

d) Examine Item 3, which you copied in Part a) of this problem. Pick out all the letters from Item 3 that are formed with a loop.

Letters Formed with a Loop

⅔ Space

Curve upstroke
Straight
downstroke

Write each letter as many times as it occurs. Remember, each loop consists of a curved upstroke and a straight downstroke. All downstrokes should slant in the same direction.

e) Now examine Item 4, which you copied in Part a) of this problem. Again, pick out all the letters from this item that are formed with a loop. Write each letter as many times as it occurs. Remember, each loop consists of a curved upstroke and a straight downstroke. All downstrokes should slant in the same direction.

Curve upstroke
Straight
downstroke

Problem 4

You apply for a position in the public relations department of Levy & Walsh. To test your handwriting skill, the placement director asks you to do the following.

Directions:

a) In your best handwriting, copy each of the items shown below. Be sure to pay particular attention to the size and slant of your writing. Try to use not more than one line for each item.

Item 1: look before you leap
Item 2: find a good book to read
Item 3: be honest with yourself
Item 4: business papers must be filed

b) Examine the letters in Group 3 below. Now examine Item 1, which you copied in Part a) of this problem. Pick out all the letters from Item 1 that belong in Group 3.

Group 3

Write each letter as many times as it occurs. Remember that the letters in this group should take up about two-thirds the space between the heavy lines.

⅔ Space

c) Now examine Item 2, which you copied in Part a) of this problem. Again, pick out all the letters from this item that belong in Group 3. Write each letter as many times as it occurs. Remember that the letters in this group should take up about two-thirds the space between the heavy lines.

⅔ Space

d) Examine Item 3, which you copied in Part a) of this problem. Pick out all the letters from Item 3 that are formed with a loop.

Curve upstroke
Straight
downstroke

Letters Formed with a Loop

b f h k l g j p q y z

Write each letter as many times as it occurs. Remember, each loop consists of a curved upstroke and a straight downstroke. All downstrokes should slant in the same direction.

e) Now examine Item 4, which you copied in Part a) of this problem. Again, pick out all the letters from this item that are formed with a loop. Write each letter as many times as it occurs. Remember, each loop consists of a curved upstroke and a straight downstroke. All downstrokes should slant in the same direction.

Practicing
Related
Arithmetic

Copy each group of dates shown below, arranging the dates in each group so that the *earliest date is first and the latest date is last* (January 8, February 11, etc.). The year is the same for all the dates.

(1)	(2)	(3)	(4)
April 17	December 18	August 15	July 7
August 20	July 23	May 6	June 12
January 8	November 5	February 19	March 19
September 24	March 20	January 22	June 9
July 15	October 14	September 10	December 15
February 11	June 4	May 13	June 5

AIM

The purpose of this job is to introduce you to some simple rules of filing which will help you in your everyday affairs and will also serve you in your record-keeping work.

EXPLANATION

"Where do I file it?"

In very large business firms the job of filing is done by a person known as a file clerk who has been specially trained to arrange and store business papers in an orderly way. The file clerk can locate papers quickly and easily whenever they are needed. The business papers *(documents)* may be processed by hand by the file clerk or they may be located and selected *(retrieved)* within a few seconds using special equipment known as *automated data processing equipment*.

Illustration 4a on page 22 shows an operator facing a special TV screen and rows of mechanized files. By merely pressing the proper buttons or control keys, she can locate and select from among hundreds of thousands of documents, which have been put on microfilm, the required document instantaneously. She can view the document and, if desired, can have a paper copy of the document printed in seconds.

It is quite possible, however, that you may get a job with a firm that does not employ specially trained file clerks or use automated data processing equipment. As an employee in such a firm, you will find many occasions when it will be necessary for you to file or locate a business paper. Therefore, your employer will expect you to be familiar with basic filing rules and procedures which all office workers should know.

Courtesy
Eastman Kodak

Illustration 4a — An Information Retrieval System

Business papers may be filed in many different ways. The three most common systems of filing which you as a record keeper will have occasion to use are numeric filing, chronological filing, and alphabetic filing.

Numeric
1
2
3
4
5
etc.

NUMERIC FILING

Examine the numeric file shown on the next page. Note that the first guide reads 101–110; the second guide, 111–120; the third guide, 121–130, etc.

If you had to locate a business paper numbered "116," you would refer to the guide 111–120. Behind it you would find that the paper numbered "116" follows the one numbered "115."

657
B

If you had to locate a business paper numbered "129," you would refer to the card guide labelled "121–130." Behind it you would find that the paper numbered "129" follows the one numbered "128."

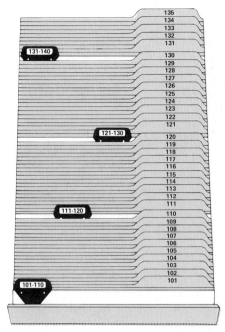

Illustration 4b — Numeric File

This method of filing is called numeric filing because, as you can see, each paper to be filed has a number and the papers are arranged in numerical sequence: "2" follows "1," "3" follows "2," and so on.

CHRONOLOGICAL FILING

The word "chronological" means that happenings or events are arranged in proper order of time. Therefore, chronological filing means filing business papers based on dates.

You have probably borrowed books from public and school libraries many times and have been allowed to use the books for a limited time without charge. Have you ever thought about how the librarian knows which books have to be returned by a certain date? Have you also wondered how a record keeper remembers which bills have to be paid on a certain date?

Look at the chronological file shown on page 24 and perhaps you can get a clue to how the librarian and the record keeper solve their problems. The chronological file (often called a *follow-up* or *tickler* file) is used to help these people "remember" what is due on a certain date.

Chronological	
January	1
	2
	3
	4
	5
	etc.
February	1
	2
	3
	4
	5
	etc.

34359

Notice that there is a card guide for each month. Behind the card guide headed "January" can be found guides arranged in numerical sequence by date, from 1 to 31. If you received a business paper on January 10 which had to be attended to on January 20, you would place this paper behind the guide numbered "20." This means that you can forget about it until January 20. On January 20 you would remove all papers filed behind the card guide numbered "20" and take care of them that day.

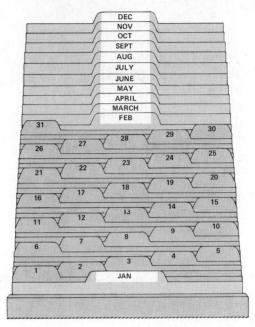

Illustration 4c — Chronological File

Since you would have no further use of the guide numbered "20" during the month of January, you would place it behind the card guide labelled "February." Of course, as each day goes by, the numbered card guide for that day would be shifted to the next month. Therefore, by the end of the month, all card guides would have been shifted behind the card guide headed "February." That is the reason there is only one set of card guides numbered 1 to 31 in the illustration.

Alphabetic

A
B
C
D
E
etc.

ALPHABETIC FILING

Look at the alphabetic file shown on the next page. Notice that there is a separate guide for each letter of the alphabet and that each guide is arranged in strict alphabetic order: "B" follows "A"; "C" follows "B"; and so forth. Now you will see how this system of filing operates by getting acquainted with a few simple rules.

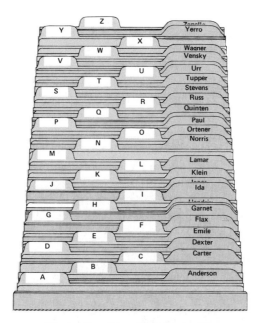

Illustration 4d — Alphabetic File

Rule 1: File papers by the last name (surname).

Suppose you had to locate a business paper sent to your company by *ALAN BROWN.* Would you look for the paper behind the guide "A" because his first (given) name "ALAN" begins with the letter "A"? Or would you look for the paper behind the guide "B" because his last name (surname) "BROWN" begins with the letter "B"?

Since Rule 1 states that you file according to the last name (surname), you would look behind the guide "B," the first letter of the name (BROWN), to find the business paper.

In a similar manner, a paper from *BERT COLBY* would be found behind the card guide "C" and one from *JOHN ACE* would be found behind the card guide "A."

Rule 2: When the last names of two or more persons begin with the same first letter, use the second letter in the names to decide which name is to be filed in front of the other. If the second letter is the same, use the third, and so on.

Suppose you had to locate a paper from *LOUIS DAMON* and also one from *PAUL DOBBS.* According to Rule 1, you would look first at the last names. Since both last names begin with the letter "D," you would refer to the card guide "D." According to Rule 2, you would then look at the second letter in the last name of each person. Since the second letter in DAMON is an "a"

Alphabetic Filing

Rule 1

Surname   Given Name

Ace,   John
Brown,   Alan
Colby,   Bert

Rule 2

Surname

Damon
Dobbs

Eagle
Evans

Ferris
Fuller

Gray
Grice

and the second letter in DOBBS is an "o," you would find the paper from "DAMON" filed *before* the paper from *DOBBS*. Similarly, the surname EAGLE would be filed before EVANS and FERRIS before FULLER.

Which of the two surnames "GRICE" and "GRAY" would be filed in front of the other?

Look at Rule 2 again, and you find that if the second letter is the same in both names, you must refer to the third letter. Since the second letter in "GRICE" is the same as the second letter in "GRAY," you must look at the third letter of each name. The third letter in "GRICE" is "i" and the third letter in "GRAY" is "a." Since "a" comes before "i" in the alphabet, *GRAY* would be filed before *GRICE*.

Rule 3

Surname	Given Name
Hale,	Mary
Haley,	Mary
Iver,	Al
Iverg,	Al
Jud,	Cathy
Judd,	Cathy

Rule 3: File "nothing" before "something."

Suppose you had to locate a paper from MARY HALE and one from MARY HALEY. Which would be found in the files ahead of the other? If you apply Rule 3, you would find that MARY HALE comes first since *nothing* follows the "e" in MARY HALE, but a "y" follows the "e" in MARY HALEY.

Likewise, AL IVER would be filed in front of AL IVERG and CATHY JUD would be filed in front of CATHY JUDD.

Rule 4: If the last names (surnames) of two or more persons are the same, compare the first letters in the first names to decide the order of filing. If the first letters in the first names (given names) are the same, compare the second letters in the given names, and so forth.

Rule 4

Surname	Given Name
Kibbs,	Jack
Kibbs,	Louis
Lorer,	Ralph
Lorer,	Victor
Moore,	Beth
Moore,	Carrie
Nielson,	F.
Nielson,	Frank
Ober,	E.
Ober,	Ethel
Perez,	A.
Perez,	Alex

If you had to locate a paper from Jack Kibbs and one from Louis Kibbs, you would find the one from Jack Kibbs in front of the one from Louis Kibbs. Rules 1, 2, and 3 do not apply because the last names are alike. Rule 4, however, states that you must now look at the *first* names since the last names are the same. Since the "J" in "Jack" comes before the "L" in "Louis" in the alphabet, the paper from Jack Kibbs is filed in front of that from Louis Kibbs. Similarly, a paper from Ralph Lorer would be filed in front of one from Victor Lorer, and one from Beth Moore would be filed in front of one from Carrie Moore.

If you had to locate a paper from F. Nielson and one from Frank Nielson, which would be found in the file ahead of the other? Using Rule 3 (nothing before something), you would find F. Nielson filed ahead of *Frank* Nielson because no letter follows the "F" in F. Nielson while the letter "r" follows the "F" in Frank Nielson. Likewise, E. Ober would come before Ethel Ober, and A. Perez would come before Alex Perez.

Rule 5: When a name contains a first name and a middle name or initial, use the middle name or initial to decide alphabetical order only if the surnames and the first names or initials are alike.

If you had to locate papers in the files from John George Quinn and from Mary Agnes Quinn, you would find the paper from John George Quinn filed before the paper from Mary Agnes Quinn. Remember that according to Rule 5, you do not consider the middle name or initial until you have compared the first names or initials. Since the "J" in John comes before the "M" in Mary in the alphabet, you must file John George Quinn before Mary Agnes Quinn.

If you had to locate a paper from Elliot Charles Reade and one from Elliot David Reade, which would be ahead of the other in the files? The Elliot Charles Reade paper would appear before the Elliot David Reade. Because both first and last names are the same, you must consider the middle names, and the "C" in Charles comes before the "D" in David in alphabetic order.

In what order would papers from Betty *Ruth* Satin and Betty *R.* Satin be filed? According to Rule 3 (nothing before something), you would find the paper from Betty *R.* Satin ahead of the paper from Betty *Ruth* Satin. Likewise, Judy *A.* Thorne would be before Judy *An*ne Thorne, and Roy *M.* Uhl would appear in front of Roy *Mi*chael Uhl.

Rule 5

Sur-names	Given Names	Middle Names
Quinn,	John	George
Quinn,	Mary	Agnes
Reade,	Elliot	Charles
Reade,	Elliot	David
Satin,	Betty	R.
Satin,	Betty,	Ruth
Thorne,	Judy	A.
Thorne,	Judy	Anne
Uhl,	Roy	M.
Uhl,	Roy	Michael

Rule 6: The complete name of a person in a business name is considered in the same order as if the name of the person appeared by itself.

If you had to file a paper from Larry Vaile Company, behind which guide would you file it? According to Rule 6, you would file it behind the "V" guide. Rule 6 tells us to use Rules 1 through 5 for names of individuals. You learned in Rule 1 that the first thing to be considered is the last name (surname), which in this case is *Vaile*.

A bill from Arthur Walsh Company would be filed behind the guide "W." If you had a bill from Arthur Walsh, would you place it in front of the one from Arthur Walsh Company or after it? You would place it in front. Do you know why? If you refer to Rule 3 (nothing before something), you will understand. Notice that Arthur Walsh *Company* has the added word "Company."

Rule 6

Sur-names	Given Names	
Vaile,	Larry	Company
Walsh,	Arthur	
Walsh,	Arthur	Company

Rule 7: Names of business firms which do not contain complete names of persons are filed according to their first words. If the first words are the same, the second words are considered, and so forth.

If you had to file a letter from the Yorkville Oil Company, you would file it behind the guide "Y" because the first word "Yorkville" begins with a "Y." A letter from the Z A Company would be filed behind the guide "Z" because the initial "Z" takes the place of the first name. Would you file a letter from the

Rule 7

Yorkville	Auto	Company
Yorkville	Oil	Company
Z	A	Company

Yorkville <u>O</u>il Company in front of or behind a Yorkville <u>A</u>uto Company letter? Because the first word, Yorkville, is the same, you must look at the second word. The word "*Auto*" begins with the letter "A" and the word "*Oil*" begins with the letter "O"; therefore, you now have your answer. The letter from the Yorkville <u>A</u>uto Company would be placed in front of the letter from the Yorkville <u>O</u>il Company.

PRACTICE PROBLEMS

You apply for a position in the office of a collection agency. Since the work requires you to locate quickly the records of both individuals and businesses, you are tested on the following problems.

Problem 1

Directions:

a) Copy on separate pieces of paper each name listed below. You can use a small piece of paper for each name. Write the *surnames first* (last names) *followed by* a comma and the *first name or initial;* for example, Abate, John.

John Abate	Peter Sulo
Mary Brille	James Degan
Arnold Crafte	Doris Feller
Laura Weill	Richard Kaplan
Leon Rauch	Philip Grogan
Clyde Evans	George Tyler

b) Refer to Rule 1 on page 25 and arrange the slips of paper alphabetically according to the last names (surnames).

c) Using the slips of paper, make a list of the names in strict alphabetic order. The first name listed should be *Abate, John,* and the last name listed should be *Weill, Laura.*

Problem 2

Directions:

a) Copy on separate pieces of paper each name listed below. You can use a small piece of paper for each name. Write the surnames first, followed by a comma and the first name or initials.

Mark Addis	Robert Bruno
Grace Alfano	Otis Hollman
Paul Rieller	Judy Riellman
Harold Ennis	Victor Enteen
Linda Holler	Tony Riellora
Karen Brown	Edna Hollnor

b) Refer to Rules 1 and 2 on page 25 and arrange the slips in strict alphabetic order.

c) Make an alphabetic list of the names. The first name listed should be *Addis, Mark,* and the last name listed should be *Riellora, Tony.*

Problem 3

Directions:

a) Copy on separate pieces of paper each name listed below. You can use a small piece of paper for each name. Write the surnames first, followed by a comma and the first name or initials.

Henry Auer	Joel Grosse
Andy Auero	Cindy Klemm
Ruth Tower	Emma Towers
Peggy Gross	Frank Maddena
Peter Klemma	Walter Klemmat
Robert Madd	Alice Madden

b) Refer to Rules 1 through 3 on pages 25 and 26 and arrange the slips in strict alphabetic order.

c) Make an alphabetic list of the names.

Problem 4

Directions:

a) Copy on separate pieces of paper each name listed below. You can use a small piece of paper for each name. Write the surnames first, followed by a comma and the first name or initials.

Albert Caine	W. Sancheze
Frank Caine	James Jackson
Rual Sanchez	Lester Miller
John Jackson	Harry Felton
Bruce Felton	Barry Miller
L. Miller	Vito Sancheze

b) Refer to Rules 1 through 4 on pages 25 and 26 and arrange the slips in strict alphabetic order.

c) Make an alphabetic list of the names.

Problem 5

Directions:

a) Copy on separate pieces of paper each name listed below. You can use a small piece of paper for each name. Write surnames first followed by a comma and first and middle names and initials (Deulin, Cathy M.); write business names in the order given unless they contain the full name of an individual, in which case the surname must be written first (Ryder, Charles Company).

Cathy Deulin	L E A Corporation
Cathy M. Deulin	Sixteenth Avenue Corporation
George H. Quine	A. Harris Electric Company
R W Company	Charles Ryder Company
Harrison Electric Company	George H. Quin
George R. Quine	L A B Corporation

b) Refer to Rules 1 through 7 on pages 25 through 27 and arrange the slips in strict alphabetic order.

c) Make an alphabetic list of the names.

Problem 6

Directions:

a) Copy on separate pieces of paper each name listed below. You can use a small piece of paper for each name. Write the surnames first, followed by a comma and the first name or initials.

A. Chan Company	C R Company
Royal Corporation	A. R. Greco Company
A. Victor Mackie	Albert Chan Company
Anthony Greco	R C M Corporation
Mark G. Abbeye	A. Herbert Mackie
R C P Corporation	Mark G. Abbey

b) Refer to Rules 1 through 7 on pages 25 through 27 and arrange the slips in strict alphabetic order.

c) Make an alphabetic list of the names.

Problem 7

Directions:

a) Copy on separate pieces of paper each name listed below. You can use a small piece of paper for each name. Write the surnames first, followed by a comma and the first name or initials.

David S. White	C. Bennett Company
Recea Express Company	Henry A. Fait
Central Island Gas Company	Stewart Service Company, Inc.
C T Bennett Company	David R. White
Stewart Service Company	Recee Express Company
Henry Albert Fait	Central High School

b) Refer to Rules 1 through 7 on pages 25 through 27 and arrange the slips in strict alphabetic order.

c) Make an alphabetic list of the names.

Problem 8

Directions:

a) Copy on separate pieces of paper each name listed below. You can use a small piece of paper for each name. Write the surnames first, followed by a comma and the first name or initials.

H G Pizza Company	James D. Datz
Meade Knit Company	Acme Flower Company
James E. Datz	H L Pizza Company
Acme Wire Company	Louis Meade
H L Record Company	Datz Shipping Company
Louis Meade Company	Louis Meade Company, Inc.

b) Refer to Rules 1 through 7 on pages 25 through 27 and arrange the slips in strict alphabetic order.

c) Make an alphabetic list of the names.

UNIT 2

RECORD KEEPING FOR CASHIERS

UNIT 2

Copy and complete the following problems:

(1)
(2)

Add across and then add down

	Practicing Related Arithmetic		$ 2.75

$ 2.75
5.80
6.95
27.38
72.92
+38.70

Practicing
Related
Arithmetic

(a) 7 + 3 + 20 + 40 =
(b) 60 + 30 + 70 + 80 =
(c) 35 + 25 + 55 + 75 =
(d) 42 + 62 + 82 + 12 =
(e) 36 + 46 + 66 + 26 =

(f) ___ + ___ + ___ + ___ =

AIMS

1. To learn how to prepare receipts when you receive money.
2. To learn how to record the receipts systematically.

EXPLANATION

A *cashier* is a person whose job includes the tasks of receiving and paying out money. Depending upon the size of the business, a person may be hired to do either of these tasks or both of them. Occasionally, a person who is hired as a salesclerk in a small retail store also acts as cashier. You have seen clerks in many shops who make the sale and also handle the cash.

People are considered to be efficient cashiers if they:
a) figure and make change rapidly and accurately,
b) write legibly,
c) recognize counterfeit money, and
d) show a sense of responsibility by always checking their work.

"You forgot my receipt!"

Cashier

SAMPLE PROBLEM

Now that you have been given a brief description of the cashier's job, you will learn how to handle the records of a cashier. Assume that you have been chosen by the school treasurer to act as a cashier in the office during the home room period. The work is divided among a number of cashiers. The school treasurer has assigned you to handle all the money received for class dues from the rooms on the third floor. Money is brought to you by the class treasurer of each of the following rooms on Monday, October 6, 19--:

From Room	Amount	Class Treasurer
301	$4.25	Carl Amato
310	6.50	Jean Poggi
307	9.75	Jules Croll

Here is how you would handle your job as you receive money from each of these rooms.

Step 1: Count the money.

When you are handed the money by the class treasurer from Room 301, you count the money to make certain that it amounts to $4.25.

Step 2: Make out a receipt.

After you have made certain that you have received the correct amount, you make out a receipt. For this purpose you will have been supplied with a *receipt book*. Office supply stores sell many different kinds of receipt books. The most commonly used are the forms shown below.

Stub
(Remains in Receipt Book)

Receipt
(Given to Carl Amato)

NO. _1_
DATE: _Oct 6, 19--_
RECEIVED FROM: ____
Carl Amato
ROOM: _301_
FOR: _Class dues_
AMOUNT: _$4.25_

Clarke HIGH SCHOOL
NO. _1_   DATE: _Oct 6_ 19 _--_
RECEIVED FROM: _Carl Amato_ $ _4 25/100_
Four 25/100 ———————————————— DOLLARS
FOR: _Class dues_
Juan Ruaez
CASHIER

Amount written in Words   Amount written in Figures

Illustration 5a — A Receipt with Stub

Clarke HIGH SCHOOL
NO. _1_   DATE: _Oct 6_ 19 _--_
RECEIVED FROM: _Carl Amato_ $ _4 25/100_
Four 25/100 ———————————————— DOLLARS
FOR: _Class dues_
Juan Ruaez
CASHIER

Duplicate copy remains
in Receipt Book

Illustration 5b — Duplicate Receipt Form

If the form in Illustration 5a is used, the receipt part is handed to Carl Amato, the class treasurer of Room 301, and the stub part remains attached in the receipt book.

If the form in Illustration 5b is used, you will find that each original receipt can be torn out and a duplicate of this will remain in the book. Naturally, carbon paper is used to get the duplicate. You will use receipts similar to the form shown in Illustration 5a. However, the important point to remember is that the cashier must have a record of every receipt issued. You will learn what to do with this information in a short while.

Step 3: Put the money in a cash box.

After the receipt has been issued, put the $4.25 in a cash box. Cash boxes have separated compartments so that you can keep the various coins and bills arranged neatly. This reduces the possibility of giving out the wrong change. A typical cash box is shown in the picture at the right.

Always make certain that the money is put in the cash box before you take care of the next student.

Step 4: Record the amounts shown on the stubs daily in a Record of Cashier's Collections.

After you have issued all the receipts for the day, your next job is to make a record of certain information found on each stub on a separate sheet known as a "Record of Cashier's Collections."

This record is pictured in Illustration 5c, page 36.

Assume that you have issued the following receipts:

Receipt No.	Room No.	Amount
1	301	$4.25
2	310	6.50
3	307	9.75

Illustration 5c on page 36 shows how the form would look at the end of the day on Monday, October 6, 19––, after these receipts were recorded.

Notice that amounts appear for only three rooms on Monday. This means that you, the cashier, have received money from only three different rooms and you must have $20.50 in your cash box.

Also, notice that the total, $20.50, has been written twice. Writing it the first time in small pencil figures is known as "pencil footing the column." The second total is written in ink. It is a sound business practice to write all totals in pencil before writing them in ink so that if you find an error after checking the work, the totals can be easily erased and corrected. In order to write these pencil footings in small, clear figures, use a well-sharpened pencil.

RECORD OF CASHIER'S COLLECTIONS

CASHIER _Juan Ruaez_   WEEK OF _Oct. 6, 19--_

ROOM	MON	TUES	WED	THURS	FRI	TOTALS
301	4 25					
302						
303						
304						
305						
306						
307	9 75					
308						
309						
310	6 50					
TOTAL	20 50					

Pencil footing — 20 50
Inked in total — TOTAL 20 50

Illustration 5c — Partially Completed Record of Cashier's Collections

Step 5: Turn over all records and cash to the school treasurer.

Before you leave, you will turn over to the school treasurer the cash box, the receipt book, and the Record of Cashier's Collections. Each morning, the school treasurer will give back to you the cash box, your receipt book, and your Record of Cashier's Collections so that you can handle the day's business.

Step 6: Find the weekly total for each room.

Each day during the week, you will issue many additional receipts for money received. At the end of the week, the completed form should look like the one illustrated below.

RECORD OF CASHIER'S COLLECTIONS

CASHIER _Juan Ruaez_   WEEK OF _Oct. 6, 19--_

ROOM	MON	TUES	WED	THURS	FRI	TOTALS	
301	4 25	7 75	8 00			20 00	— Crossfooting
302		5 25		4 75		10 00	
303		9 00		7 00	5 25	21 25	
304			11 00		7 50	18 50	
305		6 75			8 25	15 00	
306			5 75		12 50	18 25	
307	9 75			6 25		16 00	
308		10 00			3 75	13 75	
309			4 00	5 50		9 50	
310	6 50			9 50	3 25	19 25	
TOTAL	20 50	38 75	28 75	33 00	40 50	161 50	— Grand Total

Illustration 5d — Completed Record of Cashier's Collections

Look at the first room number, which is 301. You will note that you have collected $20.00 for the week from this room. The $20.00 was found by adding across or, to use the business expression, by "crossfooting." The $161.50 is known as the *grand total* because it is the sum of all the separate total figures in the column headed *Totals*. This figure can be checked by crossfooting the penciled totals of the columns for each day. The answer should agree with the grand total. If you compare what was just done with what you did in Practicing Related Arithmetic Problem 2 on page 33, you will notice that you did the same kind of arithmetic problem when you crossfooted and then added down.

Now that you have learned some of the duties of a cashier, see how well you can handle the following problems.

PRACTICE PROBLEMS

Problem 1

You are the cashier in charge of collecting dues from the following rooms on the second floor:

201	203	205	207	209
202	204	206	208	210

Directions:

a) Refer to the Record of Cashier's Collections, Illustration 5d, on page 36. Open a similar one, recording in the proper column the room numbers 201–210. Be sure to record the numbers in numerical sequence (201, 202, 203, etc.).

Open Record of Cashier's Collections

b) You received money on Monday, March 3, 19––, as shown below.

Room No.	Amount	Class Treasurer
201	$ 4.50	Ruth Lang
202	6.25	James Maro
208	12.75	Maria Gomez
206	9.00	Henry Barnes

Make a receipt for each room, using the forms your teacher has distributed or those provided in the workbook. *Be sure to make out the stub first.* The starting number for your receipts will be "1." Use the name of your school, and sign your own name as cashier.

Record stub information

c) Enter the information found on the stubs in the Record of Cashier's Collections which you opened in accordance with direction a).

d) Pencil foot the column headed "Monday."

Record total

e) To give you additional practice, you are asked to fill in the Record of Cashier's Collections for the balance of the week as follows:

Tuesday, March 4, 19––

At the end of the day, the stubs show the information given on the next page:

Receipt No.	Room No.	Amount
5	210	$14.50
6	207	11.75
7	203	7.25
8	209	13.25
9	204	10.00

Since you have had enough practice writing receipts for Monday's collections, you have not been requested to write Tuesday's receipts.

Directions:
a) Enter in the column headed "Tuesday" the information found on Tuesday's receipts. Be sure to use the same report you prepared for Monday's collections.
b) Pencil foot the column headed "Tuesday."

Wednesday, March 5, 19—

At the end of the day, the stubs show the information given below.

Receipt No.	Room No.	Amount
10	208	$ 5.25
11	203	4.75
12	209	7.00
13	206	6.25
14	205	15.00
15	201	8.25
16	210	9.50

Directions:
a) Enter in the column headed "Wednesday" the information found on Wednesday's receipts. Be sure to use the same report you prepared for the two previous days.
b) Pencil foot the column headed "Wednesday."

Thursday, March 6, 19—

The stubs showed this information at the end of the day:

Receipt No.	Room No.	Amount
17	204	$ 8.25
18	202	10.75
19	209	9.25
20	201	11.00
21	210	3.00
22	206	4.25
23	203	6.50
24	207	5.00
25	205	7.50

Directions:

a) Enter in the column headed "Thursday" the information found on Thursday's receipts.

b) Pencil foot the column headed "Thursday."

Friday, March 7, 19——

The stubs showed this information at the end of the day:

Receipt No.	Room No.	Amount
26	202	$12.50
27	207	15.25
28	205	10.25
29	201	3.25
30	209	7.00
31	210	5.25
32	208	8.50
33	204	6.25

Directions:

a) Enter in the column headed "Friday" the information found on Friday's receipts.

b) Pencil foot the column headed "Friday."

c) Find the total collected from *each room* for the entire week by crossfooting the column (adding across).

d) Find the *grand total* for the week. In order to do this, you must add the last column. (Is your answer $279.00?)

e) Check your addition by crossfooting the totals for each day. The answer should agree with the *grand total* found in direction d). After the totals have been found to agree, ink them in. If the totals do not agree, the error should be found by re-adding all the columns (crossfooting and then adding down).

Problem 2

You are the cashier in charge of collecting dues from the following rooms on the third floor:

301	303	305	307	309
302	304	306	308	310

Directions:

a) Refer to the Record of Cashier's Collections, Illustration 5d on page 36. Open a similar form, recording in the proper column the room numbers 301–310. Be sure to record the numbers in numerical sequence (301, 302, 303, etc.).

b) Make the necessary entries on the form from the receipt stubs which are listed on the next page on a *day by day basis*. Be sure to pencil foot each column daily.

Monday, April 14, 19--

Receipt No.	Room No.	Amount
41	301	$ 9.00
42	310	6.75
43	305	4.25
44	302	3.25
45	307	8.25
46	303	7.00
47	309	5.25
48	304	5.50

Thursday, April 17, 19--

Receipt No.	Room No.	Amount
65	305	$13.50
66	309	9.00
67	308	7.75
68	306	8.25
69	307	2.50
70	302	14.00
71	310	12.75
72	301	5.75

Tuesday, April 15, 19--

Receipt No.	Room No.	Amount
49	310	$ 7.25
50	304	6.25
51	301	12.25
52	308	10.25
53	302	8.00
54	305	5.75
55	303	9.25
56	306	9.00

Friday, April 18, 19--

Receipt No.	Room No.	Amount
73	306	$10.00
74	301	11.00
75	310	5.00
76	303	8.75
77	309	7.25
78	302	12.00
79	307	6.75
80	304	9.50

Wednesday, April 16, 19--

Receipt No.	Room No.	Amount
57	301	$ 6.00
58	308	13.25
59	303	5.00
60	306	12.50
61	304	8.25
62	309	7.50
63	307	11.75
64	310	4.25

Now that you have recorded all the necessary information from the receipt stubs, complete the following steps:

c) Find the total collected from *each room* for the entire week by crossfooting the column (adding across).

d) Find the *grand total* for the week by adding the last column. (Is your answer $329.50?)

e) Check your addition by crossfooting the totals for each day. The answer should agree with the *grand total* found in direction d). After the totals have been found to agree, ink them in. If the totals do not agree, the error should be found by re-adding all the columns (crossfooting and then adding down).

JOB 6 | RECORDING RECEIPTS

**Practicing
Related
Arithmetic**

Copy this drill on a sheet of paper and find the answers. Crossfoot (add across) and then add down.

(a)	$ .51	+	$ .70	+	$ .81	+	$ .90	= $
(b)	.40	+	.55	+	.70	+	.85	=
(c)	.33	+	.40	+	.63	+	.50	=
(d)	.17	+	.37	+	.50	+	.27	=
(e)	.29	+	.50	+	.49	+	.79	=
(f)	$	+	$	+	$	+	$	= $

AIM

To give you additional practice in the use of cashiers' records.

EXPLANATION

In Job 5, you learned how to keep a record of receipts systematically. Now, you will have an opportunity to get more practice in recording receipts and in proving your work.

PRACTICE PROBLEMS

Problem 1

You are the cashier in charge of collecting dues from the following rooms on the first floor:

101	103	105	107	109
102	104	106	108	110

Directions:
a) Refer to the Record of Cashier's Collections, Illustration 5d on page 36. Open a similar form, recording in the proper column the room numbers given above. Be sure to record the numbers in numerical sequence (101, 102, 103, etc.).

Open Record of Cashier's Collections

b) Make the necessary entries on the form from the receipt stubs which are listed on the following page on a *day by day basis*. Be sure to pencil foot each column daily.

Record stub information

Monday, May 19, 19—

Receipt No.	Room No.	Amount
221	101	$ 8.00
222	110	6.50
223	105	4.00
224	103	3.75
225	109	7.00
226	107	9.25

Tuesday, May 20, 19—

Receipt No.	Room No.	Amount
227	108	$ 8.25
228	104	4.75
229	110	7.25
230	105	3.50
231	102	5.00
232	107	2.75
233	106	10.25

Wednesday, May 21, 19—

Receipt No.	Room No.	Amount
234	106	$14.00
235	101	6.75
236	109	8.50
237	104	10.75
238	108	5.25
239	110	9.50
240	103	13.25

Thursday, May 22, 19—

Receipt No.	Room No.	Amount
241	106	$15.75
242	102	12.25
243	110	2.50
244	103	7.25
245	107	8.00
246	105	14.50
247	101	9.00
248	109	5.75

Friday, May 23, 19—

Receipt No.	Room No.	Amount
249	107	$12.25
250	104	9.25
251	110	5.25
252	101	11.00
253	108	7.75
254	102	4.50
255	109	6.75
256	105	13.25

Find totals

c) Find the total collected from *each room* for the entire week by crossfooting the column (adding across).

d) Find the *grand total* for the week by adding the last column. (Is your answer $293.25?)

Crossfoot to check your figures

e) Check your addition by crossfooting the totals for each day. The answer should agree with the *grand total* found in direction d). After the totals have been found to agree, ink them in. If the totals do not agree, the error should be found by re-adding all the columns (crossfooting and then adding down).

f) Find which room handed in the *most* money this week.

g) Find which room handed in the *least* amount of money this week.

Problem 2

You are the cashier in charge of collecting dues from the following rooms on the fourth floor:

| 401 | 403 | 405 | 407 | 409 |
| 402 | 404 | 406 | 408 | 410 |

Directions:

a) Open a new Record of Cashier's Collections and record in the proper column the room numbers given above. Be sure to record them in numerical sequence.

b) Make the necessary entries on the form from the receipt stubs which are listed below on a *day by day basis*. Pencil foot each column.

Monday, September 22, 19--

Receipt No.	Room No.	Amount
57	406	$ 8.00
58	402	3.75
59	410	16.00
60	404	7.50
61	408	9.00
62	405	12.00
63	409	4.25

Thursday, September 25, 19--

Receipt No.	Room No.	Amount
79	403	$ 6.50
80	408	8.00
81	405	16.50
82	410	7.50
83	402	7.25
84	409	9.25
85	407	5.25
86	401	10.00
87	406	6.00

Tuesday, September 23, 19--

Receipt No.	Room No.	Amount
64	407	$ 7.25
65	403	5.25
66	409	3.50
67	405	6.00
68	401	8.25
69	410	4.00
70	406	4.50

Friday, September 26, 19--

Receipt No.	Room No.	Amount
88	401	$ 5.25
89	408	16.25
90	404	14.50
91	406	4.50
92	402	9.00
93	407	12.00
94	403	7.75
95	409	13.00
96	405	11.25

Wednesday, September 24, 19--

Receipt No.	Room No.	Amount
71	403	$ 7.75
72	408	12.25
73	404	6.25
74	407	14.00
75	401	11.00
76	409	15.25
77	402	10.25
78	406	13.25

c) Find the total collected from *each room* for the entire week by crossfoot-ing the column (adding across).

d) Find the *grand total* for the week by adding the last column. (Is your answer $359.00?)

e) Check your addition by crossfooting the totals for each day. The answer should agree with the *grand total* found in direction d). After the totals have been found to agree, ink them in. If the totals do not agree, the error should be found by re-adding all the columns (crossfooting and then adding down).

f) Find which room handed in the *most* money this week.

g) Find which room handed in the *least* amount of money this week.

Problem 3

You are the cashier in charge of collecting dues from the following rooms:

201	203	205	207	209
202	204	206	208	210

Directions:

a) Open a new Record of Cashier's Collections and record in the proper column the room numbers given above. Be sure to record them in numerical sequence.

b) Make the necessary entries on the form from the receipt stubs which are listed below on a *day by day basis*. Pencil foot each column daily.

Monday, October 20, 19--

Receipt No.	Room No.	Amount
128	203	$ 7.00
129	201	5.00
130	210	4.25
131	202	9.00
132	209	5.75
133	205	8.25
134	207	10.25
135	206	6.50

Tuesday, October 21, 19--

Receipt No.	Room No.	Amount
136	206	$10.50
137	204	9.75
138	201	6.00
139	208	11.25
140	202	13.00
141	210	14.00
142	203	8.25
143	209	10.25
144	205	7.75

Wednesday, October 22, 19--

Receipt No.	Room No.	Amount
145	209	$ 5.50
146	203	9.50
147	210	12.75
148	205	6.25
149	208	7.50
150	206	8.75
151	204	10.75
152	207	12.00

Thursday, October 23, 19--

Receipt No.	Room No.	Amount
153	202	$15.75
154	207	8.00
155	209	9.25
156	201	14.25
157	210	4.75
158	205	5.50

Friday, October 24, 19--

Receipt No.	Room No.	Amount
159	201	$ 9.50
160	209	10.00
161	205	7.25
162	203	10.75
163	207	13.25
164	204	16.00
165	210	7.50
166	206	11.50
167	208	16.50

c) Find the total collected from *each room* for the entire week by crossfooting the column (adding across).

d) Find the *grand total* for the week (add the last column).

e) Check your addition by crossfooting the totals for each day. The answer should agree with the *grand total* found in direction d). After the totals have been found to agree, ink them in. If the totals do not agree, the error should be found by re-adding all the columns (crossfooting and then adding down).

f) Find which room handed in the *most* money this week.

g) Find which room handed in the *least* amount of money this week.

Problem 4

You are the cashier in charge of collecting dues from the following rooms:

301	303	305	307	309
302	304	306	308	310

Directions:

a) Open a new Record of Cashier's Collections and record in the proper column the room numbers given above. Be sure to record them in numerical sequence.

b) Make the necessary entries on the form from the receipt stubs which are listed below and on the following page on a *day by day basis*. Pencil foot each column daily.

Monday, December 1, 19--

Receipt No.	Room No.	Amount
141	308	$11.00
142	305	9.25
143	301	7.00
144	307	10.50
145	304	5.75
146	310	6.50
147	303	8.00

Tuesday, December 2, 19--

Receipt No.	Room No.	Amount
148	306	$13.00
149	302	9.00
150	310	8.50
151	303	6.00
152	309	5.75
153	307	3.75
154	305	10.75
155	304	7.25

Wednesday, December 3, 19—   ### Friday, December 5, 19—

Receipt No.	Room No.	Amount	Receipt No.	Room No.	Amount
156	310	$11.25	173	308	$ 9.25
157	301	12.75	174	304	11.75
158	306	8.75	175	310	5.00
159	302	4.50	176	302	10.00
160	309	13.25	177	307	12.50
161	303	9.50	178	301	11.25
162	308	7.00	179	309	16.25
163	307	6.25	180	306	5.25
			181	303	5.75
			182	305	7.00

Thursday, December 4, 19—

Receipt No.	Room No.	Amount
164	302	$ 8.50
165	308	16.00
166	303	7.50
167	307	14.00
168	304	9.25
169	305	13.75
170	301	10.25
171	306	6.75
172	309	12.50

c) Find the total collected from *each room* for the entire week by crossfooting the column (adding across).

d) Find the *grand total* for the week (add the last column).

e) Check your addition by crossfooting the totals for each day. The answer should agree with the *grand total* found in direction d). After the totals have been found to agree, ink them in. If the totals do not agree, the error should be found by re-adding all the columns (crossfooting and then adding down).

f) Find which room handed in the *most* money this week.

g) Find which room handed in the *least* amount of money this week.

Copy and complete the following problem:

	Quantity	×	Value (Denomination)	=	Amount
	5	×	$20 bills	=	$
	8	×	$10 bills	=	
Practicing	4	×	$ 5 bills	=	
Related	39	×	$ 1 bills	=	
Arithmetic	22	×	Half dollars	=	
	16	×	Quarters	=	
	32	×	Dimes	=	
	15	×	Nickels	=	
	57	×	Pennies	=	
			Total Amount		$

AIM

To learn how to prove that the amount of money in the cash register at the end of a day's business is correct.

EXPLANATION

In Jobs 5 and 6 you learned one method used by the cashier to keep a record of the money received each day. You also learned that the cashier may keep the money collected in a cash box like the one shown on page 35. If, however, the cashier handles a large amount of money, businesses find it desirable to use a *cash register*.

A cash register is helpful in reducing the possibility of errors, and it helps to safeguard the cash. You have seen these registers usually at the checkout counters in self-service stores. The next time you visit a retail store to buy something, watch how the cashier depresses the keys and how the figures are printed on *tapes*. The cashier may give you a tape which lists the various amounts charged for each item and then shows the final total.

Cash registers reduce errors and safeguard money

In addition to being recorded on the tape, the figures are also recorded in a device inside the machine known as a *register*. Each time a sale is made, the amount of this sale is automatically recorded in the register and added to the total sales which have been accumulated up to that time. This register looks like the speedometer on a car which tells how many miles the car has traveled since it was bought. If you want to know how many miles you have traveled on

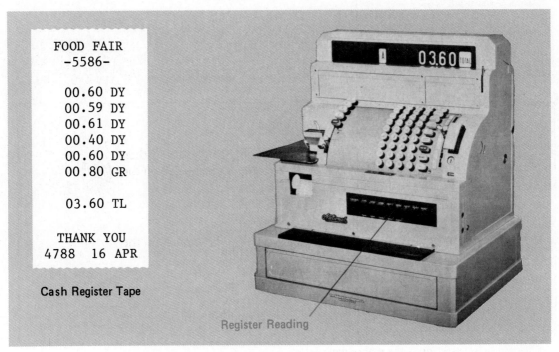

```
    FOOD  FAIR
    -5586-

    00.60 DY
    00.59 DY
    00.61 DY
    00.40 DY
    00.60 DY
    00.80 GR


    03.60 TL

    THANK  YOU
  4788   16 APR
```

Cash Register Tape

Register Reading

a particular day, you will note the speedometer reading at the time you leave home and compare this with the speedometer reading at the end of the day. For example, if the reading was 3,000 at the beginning of the day and 3,100 at the end of the day, you have traveled 100 miles.

End of day reading		3,100
Start of day reading	−	3,000
Number of miles traveled that day	=	100

In a similar manner, a cashier notes the register reading at the beginning of the day to be $200.00. At the end of the day the register reading is $360.00. The cashier knows that $160.00 in sales has been rung up.

Register Reading, end of day		$360.00
Register Reading, start of day	−	200.00
Sales for the day	=	$160.00

You may also have seen registers recording the number of passengers passing through a turnstile in a stadium or in a subway station. The next time you go through a turnstile, watch what happens to the *register reading* (the figures in the register).

Every time a business buys a cash register, the owners are given a key which allows them to turn back the register to zero. It is customary for the owners to keep possession of this key themselves or make one employee responsible for it. It is not usual for the cashier to be able to turn back the register.

SAMPLE PROBLEM

In order to understand clearly how the cashier checks the work at the end of the day, look in on a cashier whose name is Cindy. Cindy works in a retail store. Each morning she is given $40.00 in assorted coins and bills by the owner of the store. She will use this $40.00 as a change fund. Here are the steps Cindy will follow each day to check her work:

Step 1: Take register reading at beginning of day.

She puts the money in the drawer in various compartments and then takes a reading of the register. Assume that the register reads $500.00 on the morning of May 1.

Step 2: Take register reading at end of day.

As each customer makes a purchase, Cindy rings up the money on the register. At the end of the day the reading shows $700.00.

Step 3: Find sales for the day.

In order to find out how much was sold, Cindy subtracts the reading at the beginning of the day from the reading at the end of the day. For example:

Reading at the end of day		$700.00
Reading at beginning of day	−	500.00
Total sales for the day	=	$200.00

Step 4: Find total cash to be accounted for.

Although Cindy's total sales amount to $200.00 (Step 3), she must account for $240.00 because:

Sales for the day		$200.00
Plus: Change fund in register, start of day	+	40.00
Equals: Total cash to be accounted for	=	$240.00

Step 5: Count actual cash in register at end of day.

Since Cindy knows how much cash she is supposed to have, she empties all the compartments in the register and this is what she finds:

Quantity	Denomination
6	$20 bills
7	$10 bills
2	$ 5 bills
31	$ 1 bills
10	Half dollars
8	Quarters
9	Dimes
12	Nickels
50	Pennies

She enters the quantities of each denomination in the form shown below and does the necessary multiplication just the way you did when you solved the problem for the Practicing Related Arithmetic on the first page of this job.

Quantity	X	Value (Denomination)	= Amount	
6		$20 Bills	120	00
7		10 Bills	70	00
2		5 Bills	10	00
31		1 Bills	31	00
10		.50 Coins	5	00
8		.25 Coins	2	00
9		.10 Coins		90
12		.05 Coins		60
50		.01 Coins		50
		Total in Cash Drawer	240	00

Illustration 7a — Actual Cash Count

Step 6: Prepare proof of cash.

Cindy now compares the amount of cash she should have (Step 4) with the amount of cash she actually has (Step 5) and prepares the following Proof of Cash which she turns in daily with her actual cash.

Proof of Cash

Date *May 1, 19--*

Register reading, end of day	700	00
Register reading, start of day	500	00
Sales for the day	200	00
Cash in register at start of day	40	00
Cash that should be in register, end of day	240	00
Cash in register, end of day	240	00
Cash short or over	0	00

Illustration 7b — Proof of Cash

Note that since the cash in Cindy's register agreed with the amount she was supposed to have, the cash was neither short nor over.

But occasionally, even with the greatest of care, the cashier will find that the cash in the register at the end of the day does not agree with the cash that should be in the register. If the cash in the register at the end of the day had been $239.00, the cashier would have completed the last 3 lines of the Proof of Cash form as follows:

Cash that should be in register, end of day	$240.00
Cash in register, end of day	239.00
Cash short ~~or over~~	$ 1.00

Finding a cash shortage

Since Cindy does not have enough money, she draws a line through the words "or over." This is called a *cash shortage*.

On the other hand, if the cash in the register at the end of the day had been $241.00, the cashier would have completed the Proof of Cash form as follows:

Cash that should be in register, end of day	$240.00
Cash in register, end of day	241.00
Cash ~~short or~~ over	$ 1.00

Finding a cash overage

Since Cindy has too much money, she draws a line through the words "short or." This called a *cash overage*.

Since you now know how to prepare this form, see if you can do the following problems.

PRACTICE PROBLEMS

Problem 1

On June 5, 19--, you started with a change fund of $25.00 at the beginning of the day. The register reading at the beginning of the day was $1,000.00. At the end of the day, the register reading was $1,300.00. You had $325.00 in actual cash in the register.

If cash in register checks out, cash is neither short nor over

Directions: Prepare a Proof of Cash similar to Illustration 7b on page 50.

Problem 2

On July 17, 19--, you started with a change fund of $50.00 at the beginning of the day. The register reading at the beginning of the day was $3,100.00. At the end of the day, the register reading was $3,900.00. You had $847.00 in actual cash in the register.

Less cash in register than there should be = cash short

Directions: Prepare a Proof of Cash form as you did in Problem 1.

Problem 3

On March 5, 19--, you started with a change fund of $35.00 at the beginning of the day. The register reading at the beginning of the day was

More cash in register than there should be = cash over

$589.50. At the end of the day the register reading was $1,015.40. You had $461.00 in actual cash in the register.

Directions: Prepare a Proof of Cash form as you did in Problems 1 and 2.

Problem 4

On September 12, 19––, you started with $60.00 in the cash drawer as change for the day. At the start of the day's business, the register reading showed $1,537.20. At the end of the day, the register reading was $1,968.55. You counted the following cash in the drawer at the end of the day:

Quantity	Denomination
10	$20 bills
12	$10 bills
20	$ 5 bills
42	$ 1 bills
30	Half dollars
16	Quarters
50	Dimes
60	Nickels
235	Pennies

Directions:
a) Find how much money you have according to the information given above by preparing an Actual Cash Count form as shown in Illustration 7a, page 50. (Is your answer $491.35?)
b) Now that you know how much money you actually have, prepare a Proof of Cash form.

Problem 5

On December 19, 19––, you started with $15.00 in the cash drawer as change for the day. At the start of the day's business the register reading showed $829.35. At the end of the day, the register reading was $1,037.17. You counted the following cash in the drawer at the end of the day:

Quantity	Denomination
2	$20 bills
7	$10 bills
11	$ 5 bills
39	$ 1 bills
14	Half dollars
28	Quarters
26	Dimes
13	Nickels
47	Pennies

Directions:
a) Find how much money you have according to the information given above by preparing an Actual Cash Count form as shown in Illustration 7a, page 50. (Is your answer $221.72?)

b) Now that you know how much money you actually have, prepare a Proof of Cash form.

Problem 6

On January 29, 19--, you started with $20.00 in the cash register as change for the day. The register reading at the start of the day was $1,807.43. The register reading at the end of the day was $2,123.51. You counted the following cash in the drawer at the end of the day:

Quantity	Denomination
3	$20 bills
14	$10 bills
17	$ 5 bills
33	$ 1 bills
16	Half dollars
10	Quarters
24	Dimes
19	Nickels
23	Pennies

Directions:
a) Find how much money you have according to the information given above by preparing an Actual Cash Count form.
b) Now that you know how much money you actually have, prepare a Proof of Cash form.

Problem 7

On April 3, 19--, you started with $10.00 in the cash register as change for the day. The register reading at the start of the day was $708.29. The register reading at the end of the day was $971.70. You counted the following cash in the drawer at the end of the day:

Quantity	Denomination
17	$10 bills
11	$ 5 bills
41	$ 1 bills
7	Half dollars
9	Quarters
6	Dimes
13	Nickels
66	Pennies

Directions:
a) Find how much money you have according to the information given above by preparing an Actual Cash Count form.
b) Now that you know how much money you actually have, prepare a Proof of Cash form.

Practicing Related Arithmetic

Copy and complete the following problem:

Quantity	×	Value (Denomination)	=	Amount
21		$20 bills	=	$
19		$10 bills	=	
14		$ 5 bills	=	
51		$ 1 bills	=	
42		Half dollars	=	
36		Quarters	=	
27		Dimes	=	
82		Nickels	=	
17		Pennies	=	
			+	_____
		Total Amount		$_____

AIM

To give you additional practice in preparing a Proof of Cash form.

PRACTICE PROBLEMS

Problem 1

On November 1, 19--, you started with $10.00 in the cash drawer as change for the day. The register reading at the start of the day was $600.50. The register reading at the end of the day was $799.22. At the end of the day you have cash in the drawer as listed below:

Quantity	Denomination
2	$20 bills
13	$10 bills
3	$ 5 bills
17	$ 1 bills
5	Half dollars
12	Quarters
9	Dimes
4	Nickels
18	Pennies

Directions:

a) Prepare an Actual Cash Count form. (Refer to Illustration 7a, page 50.) Is your answer $208.78?

b) Prepare a Proof of Cash form. (Refer to Illustration 7b, page 50.)

Problem 2

On July 15, 19--, you started with $15.00 in the cash drawer as change for the day. The register reading at the start of the day was $1,091.70. The register reading at the end of the day was $1,321.78. You have the following cash in the drawer at the end of the day:

Quantity	Denomination
5	$20 bills
4	$10 bills
6	$ 5 bills
59	$ 1 bills
14	Half dollars
7	Quarters
49	Dimes
36	Nickels
12	Pennies

Directions:

a) Prepare an Actual Cash Count form. (Is your answer $244.57?)

b) Prepare a Proof of Cash form.

Problem 3

On August 13, 19--, you started with $40.00 in the cash drawer as change for the day. The register reading at the start of the day was $914.85. The register reading at the end of the day was $1,388.69. You have the following cash in the drawer at the end of the day:

Quantity	Denomination
18	$20 bills
8	$10 bills
7	$ 5 bills
25	$ 1 bills
9	Half dollars
16	Quarters
30	Dimes
43	Nickels
19	Pennies

Directions:

a) Prepare an Actual Cash Count form.

b) Prepare a Proof of Cash form.

Problem 4

On September 30, 19--, you started with $20.00 in the cash drawer as change for the day. The register reading at the start of the day was $2,013.41. The register reading at the end of the day was $2,313.43. You have the following cash in the drawer at the end of the day:

Quantity	Denomination
6	$20 bills
11	$10 bills
8	$ 5 bills
21	$ 1 bills
15	Half dollars
76	Quarters
13	Dimes
22	Nickels
23	Pennies

Directions:
a) Prepare an Actual Cash Count form.
b) Prepare a Proof of Cash form.

Problem 5

On March 26, 19--, you started with $60.00 in the cash drawer as change for the day. The register reading at the start of the day was $2,479.13. The register reading at the end of the day was $3,419.30. You have the following cash in the drawer at the end of the day:

Quantity	Denomination
30	$20 bills
23	$10 bills
16	$ 5 bills
73	$ 1 bills
4	Half dollars
14	Quarters
7	Dimes
35	Nickels
21	Pennies

Directions:
a) Prepare an Actual Cash Count form.
b) Prepare a Proof of Cash form.

Problem 6

On June 11, 19--, you started with $35.00 in the cash drawer as change for the day. The register reading at the start of the day was $1,296.89. The register reading at the end of the day was $1,800.02. You have the following cash in the drawer at the end of the day:

Quantity	Denomination
14	$20 bills
16	$10 bills
17	$ 5 bills
9	$ 1 bills
2	Half dollars
3	Quarters
15	Dimes
10	Nickels
38	Pennies

Directions:

a) Prepare an Actual Cash Count form.

b) Prepare a Proof of Cash form.

PREPARING THE CASHIER'S DAILY REPORT FORM

Practicing Related Arithmetic

Copy and complete the following problem:

Quantity	×	Value (Denomination)	=	Amount
34		$20 bills	=	$
41		$10 bills	=	
27		$ 5 bills	=	
80		$ 1 bills	=	
12		Half dollars	=	
23		Quarters	=	
19		Dimes	=	
55		Nickels	=	
16		Pennies	=	
			+	
		Total Amount		$

AIM

To learn how the cashier for a self-service market proves cash at the end of the day.

EXPLANATION

In Jobs 7 and 8 you learned how cashiers in charge of cash registers prove their work at the end of a day.

Now you will learn how a cashier at a check-out counter in a self-service food market proves the cash at the end of each day. You will also learn how to prepare a report of the various sales made during the day. This report will help the businessperson keep a record of sales in the different sections or departments in the store.

The next time you go shopping in a self-service market, watch the checker (the person at the register) ring up the items you have purchased.

When the keys on the register are depressed to record the selling price of butter, the checker will also depress a key which reads "Dairy." If you watch the register, you will note that the selling price of the butter appears and also the word "Dairy." When the keys for the selling price of frankfurters are depressed, a key which reads "Seafood & Meats" is also depressed. Notice that the checker must depress not only the keys for the selling price of each individual item, but also a key for the name of the department in which this

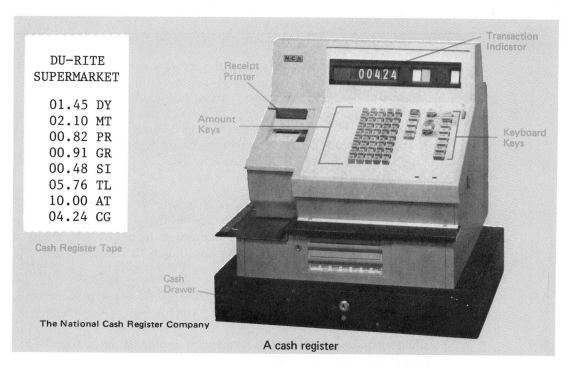

DU–RITE
SUPERMARKET

01.45 DY
02.10 MT
00.82 PR
00.91 GR
00.48 SI
05.76 TL
10.00 AT
04.24 CG

Cash Register Tape

The National Cash Register Company

A cash register

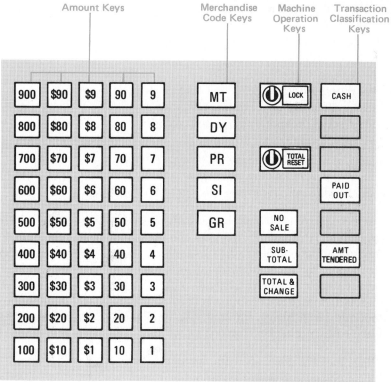

item is found. When each individual item has been rung up, a "Total" key is depressed, which gives the total amount of the entire sale.

Cash registers can be purchased with special keys for each department. Usually, self-service stores are interested in cash registers with special keys to separate sales of seafood and meats (various fish and meat products), dairy products (butter, cheese, cream, eggs, milk, etc.), produce (fresh vegetables and fruits), and groceries (canned foods, cereals, bread, etc.). Items which cannot be included in these four departments are rung up as "Sundry Items." The heading "Sundry Items" includes miscellaneous items such as soaps, powders, paper napkins, brushes, and beverages.

Another helpful feature of many cash registers is a device to show the cashier the amount of change that must be given to the customer. When the customer hands the cashier a sum of money larger than the total amount of the sale, the cashier needs to know how much "change" to give the customer.

For example, if the total sale amounted to $5.76 and the customer gave the cashier $10.00, the cashier would enter the $10.00 on the keyboard and the register would now show $4.24 as the change to be given. Thus, the possibility of making a mistake in subtraction is eliminated. The cashier would now hand the customer $4.24 consisting of 4 pennies, two dimes, and four one-dollar bills. Handing the money to the customer, the cashier will usually say, "$5.76" (the amount of the sale), "$5.80" ($5.76 plus the 4 pennies), "$6.00" ($5.80 plus two dimes), "$7.00, $8.00, $9.00, $10.00" ($6.00 plus the four one-dollar bills).

Note that:

the amount of the sale		$ 5.76
plus the change given to the customer	+	4.24
must equal the money given to the cashier	=	$10.00

Cashiers make it a practice not to put paper money in the cash register until after they have given the change to the customers. In this way, if the customer above claims to have given the cashier more than $10.00, the cashier can show the customer the actual $10 bill.

At the close of each day's business the cashier will prepare a report. This report will help the cashier check out the amount of money that should be in the register at the end of the day. In addition, the cashier will be able to find the total sales for each department rung up on the register that day. This report is called a "Cashier's Daily Report." Illustration 9a, page 61, shows a blank report form for keeping a record of the sales of groceries, produce, seafood and meats, dairy, and sundry (miscellaneous) items. Study it careful-ly. Each cashier (checker) fills out a report.

Now that you have seen the form, see how this would be used by the cashier at the end of a day's business.

Part 1   Cashier's Daily Report

Cashier_____ Register No._____ Date_____

1) Register reading, end of day		
2) Register reading, start of day		
3) Sales for the day *(See Summary of Sales)- Part 2*		
4) Add: Change fund in register, start of day		
5) Total cash to be accounted for		
6) Less: Refunds		
7) Total Cash that should be in register, end of day		
8) Actual Count of money in register, end of day *(See Part 3)*		
9) Cash Short or Over *(Cross out one)*		

Part 2   Departmental Sales

	Grocery		Produce		Seafood and Meat		Dairy		Sundry		Total	
Register reading, end of day												
Register reading, start of day												
Sales for the day												

Summary of Sales for Day for All Departments

Grocery		
Produce		
Seafood and Meat		
Dairy		
Sundry		
Total *(Enter in Part 1 - Item 3)*		

Part 3   Actual Cash Count

Quantity	X	Value *(Denomination)*	= Amount	
		$20 Bills		
		10 Bills		
		5 Bills		
		1 Bills		
		.50 Coins		
		.25 Coins		
		.10 Coins		
		.05 Coins		
		.01 Coins		
Total in Cash Drawer *(Enter in Part 1 — Item 8)*				

Illustration 9a — Cashier's Daily Report

SAMPLE PROBLEM

Jim Gates is a cashier (checker) at the By-Rite Self-Service Market. He handles Register 2 and begins each day's business with a change fund of $50.00 in assorted coins and bills. When Jim began his work as a "checker" on Monday, May 5, 19--, he started with a "total" register reading of $4,400.00. At the end of the day, the "total" register reading was $7,500.00. The separate departmental register readings are shown below.

Items	Register reading start of day	Register reading end of day
Grocery	$1,000.00	$1,900.00
Produce	1,100.00	1,300.00
Seafood & Meat	500.00	1,800.00
Dairy	600.00	900.00
Sundry	1,200.00	1,600.00
Totals	$4,400.00	$7,500.00

At the end of each day, Jim turns in to his employer the cash from his register and a completed Cashier's Daily Report. To prepare the report, which is illustrated on page 63, he follows eight simple, but very important, steps each day. As you study each step, notice how it is done in the illustration.

Step 1: Record the amount for the change fund.

Jim recorded $50.00 for Item 4 in Part 1 of Illustration 9b on page 63.

Step 2: Record the register readings at the start of each day.

Jim recorded all the register readings at the beginning of the day's business. In Part 1, Item 2, he entered $4,400.00.

In Part 2, on the line for "Register reading, start of day," Jim made entries for each department:

Grocery..............................	$1,000.00
Produce..............................	1,100.00
Seafood & Meat....................	500.00
Dairy	600.00
Sundry	1,200.00
Total	$4,400.00

Step 3: Record the register readings at the end of each day.

At the end of the day, Jim recorded all the register readings. In Part 1, Item 1, he entered $7,500.00, the "total" register reading at the end of the day. In Part 2, on the line for "Register reading, end of day," he entered the register readings listed on page 64.

Part 1   Cashier's Daily Report

Cashier_____ Register No. _2_ Date _May 5, 19--_

1) Register reading, end of day	7500 | 00
2) Register reading, start of day	4400 | 00
3) Sales for the day (See Summary of Sales)- Part 2)	3100 | 00
4) Add: Change fund in register, start of day	50 | 00
5) Total cash to be accounted for	3150 | 00
6) Less: Refunds	10 | 00
7) Total Cash that should be in register, end of day	3140 | 00
8) Actual Count of money in register, end of day (See Part 3)	3140 | 00
9) Cash Short or Over (Cross out one)	0 | 00

Part 2   Departmental Sales

	Grocery	Produce	Seafood and Meat	Dairy	Sundry	Total
Register reading, end of day	1900 | 00	1300 | 00	1800 | 00	900 | 00	1600 | 00	7500 | 00
Register reading, start of day	1000 | 00	1100 | 00	500 | 00	600 | 00	1200 | 00	4400 | 00
Sales for the day	900 | 00	200 | 00	1300 | 00	300 | 00	400 | 00	3100 | 00

Summary of Sales for Day for All Departments

Grocery	900 | 00
Produce	200 | 00
Seafood and Meat	1300 | 00
Dairy	300 | 00
Sundry	400 | 00
Total (Enter in Part 1 - Item 3)	3100 | 00

Part 3   Actual Cash Count

Quantity	X	Value (Denomination)	= Amount
90		$20 Bills	1800 | 00
80		10 Bills	800 | 00
100		5 Bills	500 | 00
30		1 Bills	30 | 00
4		.50 Coins	2 | 00
20		.25 Coins	5 | 00
15		.10 Coins	1 | 50
5		.05 Coins	| 25
125		.01 Coins	1 | 25
Total in Cash Drawer (Enter in Part 1 — Item 8)			3140 | 00

Illustration 9b — Cashier's Daily Report Completed

Grocery.............................	$1,900.00
Produce.............................	1,300.00
Seafood & Meat....................	1,800.00
Dairy.................................	900.00
Sundry	1,600.00
Total	$7,500.00

Step 4: Find the sales for the day.

In order to find how much was sold (Part 1, Item 3), Jim subtracted the reading at the beginning of the day from the reading at the end of the day, just the way you learned to do it in Jobs 7 and 8. For example:

Register reading, end of day	$7,500.00
Register reading, start of day	− 4,400.00
Total sales for the day	$3,100.00

That is why you see $3,100.00 entered as Item 3.

The amount in Part 1, Item 3, which in this case was $3,100.00, must always agree with the *total* of all the departmental sales as shown in Part 2, "Summary of Sales for Day." To find the sales for each department Jim subtracted the register reading at the start of day from the register reading at end of day. For example, look at the column headed *Grocery* at the top of Part 2. You will note that the sales for the day were $900.00 because:

How to find the
sales for a
department

Register reading, end of day	$1,900.00
Register reading, start of day	− 1,000.00
Sales for the day	$ 900.00

This same process was completed for every other department.

You will note that Jim entered the sales for each department in the "Summary of Sales for Day of All Departments." Also note that the total of all departments is $3,100.00, which agrees with the figure entered in Part 1, Item 3.

If the totals had not agreed, Jim would have re-checked his work, because either he had made a mistake in copying his figures, or he had made a mistake in arithmetic.

Step 5: Find total cash to be accounted for.

Although Jim has recorded $3,100.00 in sales, he must account for $3,150.00 because:

Sales for the day	$3,100.00
Plus: Change fund in register, start of day	+ 50.00
Gives: Total cash to be accounted for	=$3,150.00

In Part 1, Item 5, Jim entered $3,150.00.

Step 6: Find total cash that should be in the register.

You know that many stores require deposits when certain bottled beverages are sold. When the empty bottles are brought back, the deposits are refunded (returned). That is the reason you see $10.00 entered for Item 6. To find the total cash that should be in the register at the end of the day, Jim did the following:

Total cash to be accounted for (Item 5)	$3,150.00	
Less: Refunds	− 10.00	Handling refunds
Gives: Total cash that should be in register at end of day	= $3,140.00	

Jim entered $3,140.00 in Part 1, Item 7.

Step 7: Count actual cash in register at end of day.

Since Jim now knew how much cash he was supposed to have, he emptied all the compartments in the register and this is what he found:

Quantity	Denomination	
		To find the amount in each compartment:
90	$20 bills	
80	$10 bills	
100	$ 5 bills	a) Empty compartment
30	$ 1 bills	
4	Half dollars	b) Find the quantity (total number)
20	Quarters	
15	Dimes	
5	Nickels	c) Amount = quantity × value (denomination)
125	Pennies	

He entered the quantities of each denomination in Part 3 and did the necessary multiplication, just the way you did when you solved the problem for the related drill on the first page of this job. When he found the total sum of $3,140.00, he entered it in Part 1, Item 8.

Step 8: Find shortage or overage.

Jim compared the actual count of money recorded in Item 8 ($3,140.00) with the total cash that should have been in the register according to Item 7 ($3,140.00) to see if he had a *shortage* or an *overage*. Since they agreed, cash was neither "short" nor "over"; and he entered "0" for Item 9.

Compare actual amount of cash with the amount that should have been in the register

If there had been a shortage, Jim would have put a line through the words "or over" on line 9 and would have entered the amount of shortage. For example, if the cash in the register at the end of the day had been $3,136.00, Jim would have completed lines 7 through 9 of Part 1 as follows:

7) Total cash that should be in register, end of day		$3,140.00
8) Actual count of money in register		3,136.00
9) Cash short ~~or over~~		$ 4.00

If there had been an overage, Jim would have put a line through the words "short or" on line 9 and would have entered the amount. For example, if the cash in the register at the end of the day had been $3,144.00, Jim would have completed lines 7 through 9 of Part 1 as follows:

7) Total cash that should be in register, end of day $3,140.00
8) Actual count of money in register 3,144.00
9) Cash short or over .... $ 4.00

Each cashier will go through the same steps that Jim did.

It is customary for the manager in charge of the entire store to take all these reports and combine them into one report. This shows the total sales of each department and the total sales of the entire store for that day. At the end of each week, the manager combines the figures for each day. Then this *weekly* sales figure is compared with the sales figures of other weeks.

PRACTICE PROBLEMS

Problem 1

a) Use a Cashier's Daily Report form similar to Illustration 9b. Copy all the figures you find in Illustration 9b. Use your name in place of Jim Gates as the cashier. Now that you have copied the figures for Monday's business, you are ready to handle the cashier's job for Tuesday, May 6, 19--.

Step 1: Record
the amount for
the change fund
(Item 4, Part 1)

b) Use another form. Write your name and the date in the proper places. Your register is still #2. You start the day with a $50.00 change fund.

Step 2: Record
the register
readings at the
start of the day

The individual departmental register readings at the *start* of the day are (Record these amounts in Part 2):

Grocery	$1,900.00
Produce	1,300.00
Seafood & Meat	1,800.00
Dairy	900.00
Sundry	1,600.00

The "Total" register reading at the *start* of the day is $7,500.00 (Record this amount in Part 1, Item 2)

Step 3: Record
the register
readings at the
end of the day

(Notice! These are the same figures that you showed as the register readings at the close of Monday's business. Do you know why?)

Step 4: Find the
sales for the day
(Part 2 and Part 1,
Item 3)

The individual departmental readings at the *end* of the day are (Record these amounts in Part 2):

Grocery	$ 2,600.00
Produce	1,600.00
Seafood & Meat	2,700.00
Dairy	1,400.00
Sundry	2,200.00

Step 5: Find total
cash to be
accounted for
(Part 1, Item 5)

The "Total" register reading at the *end* of the day is $10,500.00 (Record this amount in Part 1, Item 1)

The refunds are $5.00 (Record in Part 1, Item 6). You count the money at the end of the day and find you have:

Quantity	Denomination
75	$20 bills
71	$10 bills
60	$ 5 bills
510	$ 1 bills
24	Half dollars
28	Quarters
25	Dimes
64	Nickels
30	Pennies

Step 6: Find total cash that should be in register (Part 1, Item 7)

Step 7: Count actual cash in register at end of day (Part 3; Part 1, Item 8)

Step 8: Find cash short or cash over (Part 1, Item 9)

Directions: Prepare all three parts of the Cashier's Daily Report. (Do you find that the total cash in Part 3 is $3,045.00?)

Problem 2

Use a new Cashier's Daily Report. You are ready to handle the cashier's job for Wednesday, May 7, 19--. You start the day with a $50.00 change fund.

Step 1: Record the amount for the change fund (Part 1, Item 4)

The individual departmental register readings at the *start* of the day are (Record these amounts in Part 2):

Grocery	$ 2,600.00
Produce	1,600.00
Seafood & Meat	2,700.00
Dairy	1,400.00
Sundry	2,200.00

Step 2: Record the register readings at the start of day

The "Total" register reading at the *start* of the day is $10,500.00 (Record this amount in Part 1, Item 2)

(Notice! These are the same figures that you should have shown as the register readings at the close of Tuesday's business. Do you know why?)

The individual departmental readings at the end of the day are (Record these amounts in Part 2):

Grocery	$ 3,150.00
Produce	1,700.00
Seafood & Meat	3,550.00
Dairy	1,850.00
Sundry	2,550.00

Step 3: Record the register readings at the end of day

The "Total" register reading at the *end* of the day is $12,800.00 (Record this amount in Part 1, Item 1)

Step 4: Find the sales for the day (Part 2 and Part 1, Item 3)

The refunds are $7.00. You count the money at the end of the day and find you have:

Step 5: Find total cash to be accounted for (Part 1, Item 5)

Step 6: Find total
cash that should
be in register
(Part 1, Item 7)

Step 7: Count
actual cash in
register at end of
day (Part 3; Part
1, Item 8)

Quantity	Denomination
80	$20 bills
21	$10 bills
55	$ 5 bills
231	$ 1 bills
9	Half dollars
40	Quarters
73	Dimes
56	Nickels
140	Pennies

Step 8: Find cash
short or cash over
(Part 1, Item 9)

Directions: Prepare all three parts of the Cashier's Daily Report. (Do you find that your total cash in Part 3 is $2,342.00?)

Problem 3

Step 1: Record
the amount for
the change fund
(Part 1, Item 4)

Step 2: Record
the register
readings at the
start of day

Use a new Cashier's Daily Report. You are ready to handle the cashier's job for Thursday, May 8, 19--. You start the day with the $50.00 change fund.

The individual departmental register readings at the *start* of the day are (Record these amounts in Part 2):

Grocery	$ 3,150.00
Produce	1,700.00
Seafood & Meat	3,550.00
Dairy	1,850.00
Sundry	2,550.00

The "Total" register reading at the *start* of the day is $12,800.00 (Record this amount in Part 1, Item 2)

(Notice! These are the same figures that you should have shown as the register readings at the close of Wednesday's business.)

Step 3: Record
the register
readings at the
end of day

Step 4: Find the
sales for the day
(Part 2 and Part 1,
Item 3)

The individual departmental readings at the *end* of the day are (Record these amounts in Part 2):

Grocery	$ 3,775.00
Produce	2,025.00
Seafood & Meat	4,275.00
Dairy	2,190.25
Sundry	2,840.15

The "Total" register reading at the *end* of the day is $15,105.40 (Record this amount in Part 1, Item 1)

Step 5: Find total
cash to be
accounted for
(Part 1, Item 3)

The refunds are $8.10. You count the money at the end of the day and find you have:

Step 6: Find total
cash that should
be in register
(Part 1, Item 7)

Quantity	Denomination
53	$20 bills
49	$10 bills
106	$ 5 bills
243	$ 1 bills

17	Half dollars
48	Quarters
37	Dimes
19	Nickels
40	Pennies

Step 7: Count actual cash in register at end of day (Part 3; Part 1, Item 8)

Directions: Prepare all three parts of the Cashier's Daily Report. (Do you find that your total cash in Part 3 is $2,348.55?)

Step 8: Find cash short or cash over (Part 1, Item 9)

Problem 4

Use a new Cashier's Daily Report. You are ready to handle the cashier's job for Friday, May 9, 19--. You start the day with the $50.00 change fund.

The individual departmental register readings at the *start* of the day are (Record these amounts in Part 2):

Grocery	$ 3,775.00
Produce	2,025.00
Seafood & Meat	4,275.00
Dairy	2,190.25
Sundry	2,840.15

The "Total" register reading at the *start* of the day is $15,105.40 (Record this amount in Part 1, Item 2)

(Notice! These are the same figures that you should have shown as the register readings at the close of Thursday's business.)

The individual departmental readings at the *end* of the day are (Record these amounts in Part 2):

Grocery	$ 4,481.30
Produce	2,406.45
Seafood & Meat	5,081.92
Dairy	2,564.61
Sundry	3,249.38

The "Total" register reading at the *end* of the day is $17,783.66 (Record this amount in Part 1, Item 1)

The refunds are $12.60. You count the money at the end of the day and find you have:

Quantity	Denomination
62	$20 bills
102	$10 bills
46	$ 5 bills
196	$ 1 bills
38	Half dollars
24	Quarters
13	Dimes
14	Nickels
16	Pennies

Directions: Prepare all three parts of the Cashier's Daily Report. (Do you find that your total cash in Part 3 is $2,713.16?)

Problem 5

Use a new Cashier's Daily Report. You are ready to handle the cashier's job for Saturday, May 10, 19--. You start the day with the $50.00 change fund.

The individual departmental register readings at the *start* of the day are (Record these amounts in Part 2):

Grocery	$ 4,481.30
Produce	2,406.45
Seafood & Meat	5,081.92
Dairy	2,564.61
Sundry	3,249.38

The "Total" register reading at the *start* of the day is $17,783.66 (Record this amount in Part 1, Item 2)

(Notice! These are the same figures that you showed as the register readings at the close of Friday's business.)

The individual departmental readings at the *end* of the day are (Record these amounts in Part 2):

Grocery	$ 5,291.55
Produce	2,821.62
Seafood & Meat	6,012.00
Dairy	3,065.74
Sundry	3,798.30

The "Total" register reading at the *end* of the day is $20,989.21 (Record this amount in Part 1, Item 1)

The refunds are $14.70. You count the money at the end of the day and find you have:

Quantity	Denomination
98	$20 bills
57	$10 bills
68	$ 5 bills
354	$ 1 bills
6	Half dollars
21	Quarters
31	Dimes
24	Nickels
29	Pennies

Directions:
a) Prepare all three parts of the Cashier's Daily Report. (Do you find that your total cash in Part 3 is $3,236.84?)
b) Answer each of the following questions on a sheet of paper, numbering each answer, or use the sheet from your workbook.

1. What is the total amount of sales rung up on your register for Groceries for the week? (Do you get an answer of $4,291.55?)
2. What is the total amount of sales rung up for Produce for the week? (Do you get an answer of $1,721.62?)
3. What is the total amount of sales rung up for Seafood & Meat for the week?
4. What is the total amount of sales rung up for Dairy for the week?
5. What is the total amount of sales rung up for Sundry Items for the week?
6. What is the total amount of *all sales* rung up for the week?

Practicing Related Arithmetic

Copy and complete the following problem:

Quantity	×	Value (Denomination)	=	Amount
28		$20 bills	=	$
81		$10 bills	=	
13		$ 5 bills	=	
48		$ 1 bills	=	
36		Half dollars	=	
52		Quarters	=	
65		Dimes	=	
74		Nickels	=	
99		Pennies	=	
			+	
		Total Amount		$

AIM

To give you additional practice in the preparation of a Cashier's Daily Report form for a self-service market.

EXPLANATION

In your previous job you learned that cashiers in self-service markets fill out a Cashier's Daily Report, which gives in detail a breakdown of the day's business. You also learned that this report is arranged so that the store manager can get valuable information about the departmental business carried on in a store. In Job 10 you will have an opportunity to become more skillful in handling these reports.

PRACTICE PROBLEMS

You are a cashier in the Elite Self-Service Market in charge of Register 3. *You start each day with a change fund of $40.00.* At the end of the day you prepare a Cashier's Daily Report form similar to the form shown in Illustration 9b, page 63. Listed below is the information needed to prepare the report for each day:

Monday — July 14, 19--

The individual departmental register readings at the *start* of the day are:

Grocery	$ 244.25
Produce	157.65
Seafood & Meat	538.40
Dairy	109.55
Sundry	247.16
The "Total" register reading at the *start* of the day is	$1,297.01

The individual departmental readings at the *end* of the day are:

Grocery	$ 503.00
Produce	266.95
Seafood & Meat	959.20
Dairy	276.80
Sundry	452.26
The "Total" register reading at the *end* of the day is	$2,458.21

The refunds are $16.25. You count the money at the end of the day and find you have:

Quantity	Denomination
15	$20 bills
47	$10 bills
69	$ 5 bills
41	$ 1 bills
19	Half dollars
56	Quarters
9	Dimes
37	Nickels
65	Pennies

Directions: Prepare all three parts of the Cashier's Daily Report. (Do you find that your total cash in Part 3 is $1,182.90?)

Tuesday — July 15, 19--

The individual departmental register readings at the *start* of the day are:

Grocery	$ 503.00
Produce	266.95
Seafood & Meat	959.20
Dairy	276.80
Sundry	452.26
The "Total" register reading at the *start* of the day is	$2,458.21

The individual departmental readings at the *end* of the day are:

Grocery	$ 799.00
Produce	378.25
Seafood & Meat	1,465.95
Dairy	459.73
Sundry	667.80
The "Total" register reading at the *end* of the day is	$3,770.73

The refunds are $13.15. You count the money at the end of the day and find you have:

Quantity	Denomination
25	$20 bills
32	$10 bills
74	$ 5 bills
108	$ 1 bills
20	Half dollars
80	Quarters
95	Dimes
9	Nickels
142	Pennies

Directions: Prepare all three parts of the Cashier's Daily Report. (Do you find that your total cash in Part 3 is $1,339.37?)

Wednesday — July 16, 19--

The individual departmental register readings at the *start* of the day are:

Grocery	$ 799.00
Produce	378.25
Seafood & Meat	1,465.95
Dairy	459.73
Sundry	667.80

The "Total" register reading at the *start* of the day is $3,770.73

The individual departmental readings at the *end* of the day are:

Grocery	$1,004.35
Produce	476.05
Seafood & Meat	1,897.60
Dairy	603.41
Sundry	907.30

The "Total" register reading at the *end* of the day is $4,888.71

The refunds are $8.45. You count the money at the end of the day and find you have:

Quantity	Denomination
31	$20 bills
18	$10 bills
25	$ 5 bills
187	$ 1 bills
30	Half dollars
64	Quarters
22	Dimes
10	Nickels
78	Pennies

Directions: Prepare all three parts of the Cashier's Daily Report. (Do you find that your total cash in Part 3 is $1,146.48?)

Thursday — July 17, 19--

The individual departmental register readings at the *start* of the day are:

Grocery	$1,004.35
Produce	476.05
Seafood & Meat	1,897.60
Dairy	603.41
Sundry	907.30
The "Total" register reading at the *start* of the day is	$4,888.71

The individual departmental readings at the *end* of the day are:

Grocery	$1,286.05
Produce	600.72
Seafood & Meat	2,281.12
Dairy	801.67
Sundry	1,159.24
The "Total" register reading at the *end* of the day is	$6,128.80

The refunds are $6.20. You count the money at the end of the day and find you have:

Quantity	Denomination
45	$20 bills
26	$10 bills
12	$ 5 bills
33	$ 1 bills
10	Half dollars
50	Quarters
41	Dimes
3	Nickels
35	Pennies

Directions: Prepare all three parts of the Cashier's Daily Report. (Do you find that there is a cash overage of $1.21?)

Friday — July 18, 19--

The individual departmental register readings at the *start* of the day are:

Grocery	$1,286.05
Produce	600.72
Seafood & Meat	2,281.12
Dairy	801.67
Sundry	1,159.24
The "Total" register reading at the *start* of the day is	$6,128.80

The individual departmental readings at the *end* of the day are:

Grocery	$1,613.87
Produce	768.82
Seafood & Meat	2,792.30
Dairy	1,019.06
Sundry	1,453.37
The "Total" register reading at the *end* of the day is	$7,647.42

The refunds are $9.25. You count the money at the end of the day and find you have:

Quantity	Denomination
16	$20 bills
94	$10 bills
40	$ 5 bills
76	$ 1 bills
7	Half dollars
11	Quarters
14	Dimes
6	Nickels
32	Pennies

Directions: Prepare all three parts of the Cashier's Daily Report. (Do you find that there is a shortage of $5.10?)

Saturday — July 19, 19--

The individual departmental register readings at the *start* of the day are:

Grocery	$1,613.87
Produce	768.82
Seafood & Meat	2,792.30
Dairy	1,019.06
Sundry	1,453.37
The "Total" register reading at the *start* of the day is	$7,647.42

The individual departmental readings at the *end* of the day are:

Grocery	$2,043.22
Produce	1,086.40
Seafood & Meat	3,400.51
Dairy	1,433.31
Sundry	1,817.27
The "Total" register reading at the *end* of the day is	$9,780.71

The refunds are $7.25. You count the money at the end of the day and find you have:

Quantity	Denomination
50	$20 bills
70	$10 bills
80	$ 5 bills
45	$ 1 bills

11	Half dollars
30	Quarters
51	Dimes
35	Nickels
116	Pennies

Directions:

a) Prepare all three parts of the Cashier's Daily Report. (Do you find that there is a shortage of $.03?)

b) Answer each of the following questions on a sheet of paper, heading your answers "Saturday" and then numbering them.

1. What is the total amount of sales rung up on your register for Groceries for the week? (Do you get an answer of $1,798.97?)

2. What is the total amount of sales rung up for Produce for the week? (Do you get an answer of $928.75?)

3. What is the total amount of sales rung up for Seafood & Meat for the week?

4. What is the total amount of sales rung up for Dairy for the week?

5. What is the total amount of sales rung up for Sundry Items for the week?

6. What is the total amount of sales you have rung up for *all departments* for this week?

Problem 2

You are a cashier in the Jiffy Self-Service Market in charge of Register 6. *You start each day with a change fund of $75.00.* At the end of the day's business you must prepare a Cashier's Daily Report form just the way you did in Problem 1. Listed below and on the following pages is the information you need to prepare the report for each day:

Monday — August 25, 19--

The individual departmental register readings at the *start* of the day are:

Grocery	$ 2,605.10
Produce	1,328.15
Seafood & Meat	3,107.25
Dairy	1,714.80
Sundry	1,130.60
The "Total" register reading at the *start* of the day is	$9,885.90

The individual departmental readings at the *end* of the day are:

Grocery	$ 2,874.92
Produce	1,445.53
Seafood & Meat	3,418.15
Dairy	1,820.27
Sundry	1,286.31
The "Total" register reading at the *end* of the day is	$10,845.18

The refunds are $11.30. You count the money at the end of the day and find you have:

Quantity	Denomination
35	$20 bills
15	$10 bills
16	$ 5 bills
77	$ 1 bills
13	Half dollars
4	Quarters
70	Dimes
28	Nickels
8	Pennies

Directions: Prepare all three parts of the Cashier's Daily Report. (Do you find that your total cash in Part 3 is $1,022.98?)

Tuesday — August 26, 19--

The individual departmental register readings at the *start* of the day are:

Grocery	$ 2,874.92
Produce	1,445.53
Seafood & Meat	3,418.15
Dairy	1,820.27
Sundry	1,286.31
The "Total" register reading at the *start* of the day is	$10,845.18

The individual departmental readings at the *end* of the day are:

Grocery	$ 3,083.10
Produce	1,592.34
Seafood & Meat	3,761.12
Dairy	1,994.20
Sundry	1,421.40
The "Total" register reading at the *end* of the day is	$11,852.16

The refunds are $21.90. You count the money at the end of the day and find you have:

Quantity	Denomination
42	$20 bills
19	$10 bills
2	$ 5 bills
4	$ 1 bills
8	Half dollars
6	Quarters
39	Dimes
2	Nickels
58	Pennies

Directions: Prepare all three parts of the Cashier's Daily Report. (Do you find that your total cash in Part 3 is $1,054.08?)

Wednesday — August 27, 19--

The individual departmental register readings at the *start* of the day are:

Grocery	$ 3,083.10
Produce	1,592.34
Seafood & Meat	3,761.12
Dairy	1,994.20
Sundry	1,421.40

The "Total" register reading at the *start* of the day is $11,852.16

The individual departmental readings at the *end* of the day are:

Grocery	$ 3,334.15
Produce	1,792.51
Seafood & Meat	4,173.85
Dairy	2,096.74
Sundry	1,607.61

The "Total" register reading at the *end* of the day is $13,004.86

The refunds are $10.05. You count the money at the end of the day and find you have:

Quantity	Denomination
33	$20 bills
20	$10 bills
57	$ 5 bills
38	$ 1 bills
32	Half dollars
12	Quarters
50	Dimes
21	Nickels
245	Pennies

Directions: Prepare all three parts of the Cashier's Daily Report. (Do you find that your total cash in Part 3 is $1,210.50?)

Thursday — August 28, 19--

The individual departmental register readings at the *start* of the day are:

Grocery	$ 3,334.15
Produce	1,792.51
Seafood & Meat	4,173.85
Dairy	2,096.74
Sundry	1,607.61

The "Total" register reading at the *start* of the day is $13,004.86

The individual departmental readings at the *end* of the day are:

Grocery	$ 3,651.73
Produce	1,990.64
Seafood & Meat	4,556.47
Dairy	2,240.55
Sundry	1,909.36
The "Total" register reading at the *end* of the day is	$14,348.75

The refunds are $6.15. You count the money at the end of the day and find you have:

Quantity	Denomination
52	$20 bills
16	$10 bills
29	$ 5 bills
58	$ 1 bills
14	Half dollars
3	Quarters
18	Dimes
3	Nickels
24	Pennies

Directions: Prepare all three parts of the Cashier's Daily Report. (Do you find that there is a cash overage of $.20?)

Friday — August 29, 19--

The individual departmental register readings at the *start* of the day are:

Grocery	$ 3,651.73
Produce	1,990.64
Seafood & Meat	4,556.47
Dairy	2,240.55
Sundry	1,909.36
The "Total" register reading at the *start* of the day is	$14,348.75

The individual departmental readings at the *end* of the day are:

Grocery	$ 4,067.55
Produce	2,284.66
Seafood & Meat	5,173.63
Dairy	2,559.95
Sundry	2,185.73
The "Total" register reading at the *end* of the day is	$16,271.52

The refunds are $18.85. You count the money at the end of the day and find you have:

Quantity	Denomination
29	$20 bills
91	$10 bills
83	$ 5 bills
62	$ 1 bills

15	Half dollars
9	Quarters
8	Dimes
36	Nickels
7	Pennies

Directions: Prepare all three parts of the Cashier's Daily Report. (Do you find that there is a cash overage of $.50?)

Saturday — August 30, 19--

The individual departmental register readings at the *start* of the day are:

Grocery	$ 4,067.55
Produce	2,284.66
Seafood & Meat	5,173.63
Dairy	2,559.95
Sundry	2,185.73

The "Total" register reading at the *start* of the day is $16,271.52

The individual departmental readings at the *end* of the day are:

Grocery	$ 4,661.61
Produce	2,663.04
Seafood & Meat	5,990.42
Dairy	3,002.08
Sundry	2,520.77

The "Total" register reading at the *end* of the day is $18,837.92

The refunds are $13.25. You count the money at the end of the day and find you have:

Quantity	Denomination
68	$20 bills
82	$10 bills
43	$ 5 bills
200	$ 1 bills
23	Half dollars
60	Quarters
16	Dimes
82	Nickels
55	Pennies

Directions:
a) Prepare all three parts of the Cashier's Daily Report. (Do you find that there is a cash shortage of $.40?)
b) Answer each of the following questions on a sheet of paper, heading your answers "Saturday" and then numbering them.
   1. What is the total amount of sales you have rung up for Groceries for this week? (Do you get an answer of $2,056.51?)
   2. What is the total amount of sales you have rung up for Produce for this week? (Do you get an answer of $1,334.89?)

3. What is the total amount of sales you have rung up for Seafood & Meat for this week?
4. What is the total amount of sales you have rung up for Dairy for this week?
5. What is the total amount of sales you have rung up for Sundry Items for this week?
6. What is the total amount of sales you have rung up for *all departments* for this week?

Copy and complete the following problem:

Practicing Related Arithmetic

Quantity	×	Value (Denomination)	=	Amount
14		$20 bills	=	$
11		$10 bills	=	
28		$ 5 bills	=	
67		$ 1 bills	=	
18		Half dollars	=	
25		Quarters	=	
53		Dimes	=	
32		Nickels	=	
138		Pennies	=	
			+	
		Total Amount		$

AIM

To learn how to prepare a deposit slip so you can deposit in the bank the money you receive each day.

EXPLANATION

It is the usual practice for a cashier to prepare daily deposits of the money received.

Step 1: Separate and wrap bills.

Mark packages which do not contain the required number of bills

Illustration 11a — Wrapped Bills

Place bills face up

Use proper bank
wrappers

The cashier removes from the register all the bills that are to be deposited. They are then arranged according to denominations so that the $20 bills, the $10 bills, the $5 bills, and the $1 bills are all in separate stacks. The bills are placed face up and then counted in stacks of a hundred bills to a package. (Some banks prefer fifty bills to a package.) The cashier now uses paper wrappers supplied by the bank to wrap the money.

Very often the cashier will find that there are not enough bills of a special denomination to make one complete package. For example, the cashier may have 127 $1 bills. Since only 100 of these are needed to make a complete package, 27 $1 bills remain. These bills are put in a $1 wrapper and marked $27.00. The same procedure is followed with all other denominations.

Step 2: Separate and wrap coins.

The cashier removes from the register all the coins that are to be deposited. The table below helps the cashier sort out the coins and insert them in the wrappers correctly.

Coin	Color of Wrapper	Number of Coins in Full Wrapper	Value of Coins in Full Wrapper
Half Dollars	Tan	20	$10.00
Quarters	Orange	40	10.00
Dimes	Green	50	5.00
Nickels	Blue	40	2.00
Pennies	Red	50	.50

Mark rolls which do not
contain the required
amount of coins

Illustration 11b — Wrapped Coins

Again (as happened when the cashier packaged the bills in Step 1), it is likely that there will not be enough coins of a special denomination to make one complete roll of coins. For example, if there are 16 half dollars, the cashier is not able to prepare a full roll of half dollars. As you can see by the illustration and table above, 20 half dollars are needed to make one roll. It is necessary to put the 16 half dollars in a wrapper marked "Half Dollars" and write $8.00 on the wrapper, to show how much money is inside. The same procedure is followed for coins of other denominations.

Step 3: Tally the money to be deposited.

After the cashier has sorted the money, the next job is to get the total. Careful cashiers make a list, or *tally*, of the money that they have sorted so that they can recheck their totals. Each of the related arithmetic drill problems that you completed during the past few days gave you practice in making a tally. You will now learn how to set up this information in a more organized way.

Let us assume that Roy, a cashier who works for Mr. Gene Conti of 30 Center St., New York, has packaged and sorted out his bills and coins and this is what he now finds on his desk on June 2, 19--:

6	loose **$5 bills**	=	$ 30.00
8	packages of **$1 bills** (Remember, each package contains 100 $1 bills)	=	800.00
35	loose $1 bills	=	35.00
5	rolls of **half dollars** (Each roll contains 20 half dollars, or $10 worth)	=	50.00
12	loose half dollars	=	6.00
4	rolls of **quarters** (Each roll contains 40 quarters, or $10 worth)	=	40.00
16	loose quarters	=	4.00
9	rolls of **dimes** (Each roll contains 50 dimes, or $5.00 worth)	=	45.00
15	loose dimes	=	1.50
3	rolls of **nickels** (Each roll contains 40 nickels, or $2.00 worth)	=	6.00
11	loose nickels	=	.55
10	rolls of **pennies** (Each roll contains 50 pennies, or $.50 worth)	=	5.00
42	loose pennies	=	.42

On page 86 all this information is shown by Roy in an orderly manner on a sheet known as a tally sheet. Roy lists the highest denomination first, second highest denomination second, and so forth. Notice how he shows the loose bills and coins on his tally sheet. This tally sheet is prepared for his own use. After he is certain that he has counted his cash correctly, he is ready for the next step, preparing a deposit slip.

Record on tally sheet

Step 4: Prepare the deposit slip.

Supplies of bank deposit slips are obtained free of charge from the bank in which the deposit is to be made. A deposit slip for the money tallied above is shown at the bottom of page 86.

Notice that the values of the bills and coins are separated. You must be wondering what will be put in the boxes to the right of the word "checks." This will be discussed when you learn about checks in later jobs. Now you can get some practice in completing the steps you have been studying.

TALLY SHEET

BILLS

List highest denomination first — 6 loose $5 bills	30	00	
8 pkgs. of $1 bills (100 per pkg.)	800	00	
List loose bills separately from corresponding packaged bills — 35 loose $1 bills	35	00	
Total bills to be deposited			865 00

COINS

List highest denomination first — 5 rolls of half dollars (20 per roll)	50	00	
12 loose half dollars	6	00	
4 rolls of quarters (40 per roll)	40	00	
List loose coins separately from corresponding rolled coins — 16 loose quarters	4	00	
9 rolls of dimes (50 per roll)	45	00	
15 loose dimes	1	50	
3 rolls of nickels (40 per roll)	6	00	
11 loose nickels		55	
10 rolls of pennies (50 per roll)	5	00	
42 loose pennies		42	
Total coins to be deposited			158 47
Total cash to be deposited			1023 47

Illustration 11c — Tally Sheet

For DEPOSIT to the Account of

GENE CONTI

Date *June 2* 19 – –

Lenox Bank
New York, NY

Subject to the Terms and Conditions of this Bank's Collection Agreement

	Dollars	Cents
BILLS	865	00
COINS	158	47
Checks as Follows Properly Endorsed		
TOTAL DEPOSIT	1023	47

The totals are copied from the "Tally Sheet"

⑈128⑈ ⑈1⑈929 4

Illustration 11d — Deposit Slip

PRACTICE PROBLEMS

Problem 1

Directions: Write the answers to the following questions on a sheet of paper or in the workbook spaces provided:

a) You have 22 half dollars.
   1. How many full packages of half dollars would you wrap?
   2. How many loose half dollars would you have?
b) You have 43 quarters.
   1. How many full packages of quarters would you wrap?
   2. How many loose quarters would you have?
c) You have 104 dimes.
   1. How many full packages of dimes would you wrap?
   2. How many loose dimes would you have?
d) You have 86 nickels.
   1. How many full packages of nickels would you wrap?
   2. How many loose nickels would you have?
e) You have 173 pennies.
   1. How many full packages of pennies would you wrap?
   2. How many loose pennies would you have?

Problem 2

Directions: Write the answers to the following questions on a sheet of paper or in the workbook spaces provided:

a) You have 49 half dollars.
   1. How many full packages of half dollars would you wrap?
   2. How many loose half dollars would you have?
b) You have 90 quarters.
   1. How many full packages of quarters would you wrap?
   2. How many loose quarters would you have?
c) You have 203 dimes.
   1. How many full packages of dimes would you wrap?
   2. How many loose dimes would you have?
d) You have 135 nickels.
   1. How many full packages of nickels would you wrap?
   2. How many loose nickels would you have?
e) You have 86 pennies.
   1. How many full packages of pennies would you wrap?
   2. How many loose pennies would you have?

Problem 3

Assume you are working as a cashier for Perry Wayne who has an account in the Union Bank. At the close of the day's business on July 1, 19--, you have the money shown below and on the next page to be deposited:

Quantity	Denomination
17	$ 5 bills
362	$ 1 bills

30	Half dollars
79	Quarters
110	Dimes
52	Nickels
124	Pennies

Directions:
a) Prepare a tally sheet like that on page 86, Illustration 11c.
b) Prepare a deposit slip like that on page 86, Illustration 11d. (Does your total deposit amount to $496.59?)

Problem 4

You are still working for the Perry Wayne mentioned in Problem 3. At the close of the day's business on July 2, 19--, you have the following money to be deposited:

Quantity	Denomination
43	$10 bills
507	$ 1 bills
100	Half dollars
211	Quarters
158	Dimes
125	Nickels
149	Pennies

Directions:
a) Prepare the tally sheet just as you did in Problem 3.
b) Prepare the deposit slip. (Does your total deposit amount to $1,063.29?)

Problem 5

You are still working for the Perry Wayne mentioned in Problem 3. At the close of the day's business on July 3, 19--, you have the following money to be deposited:

Quantity	Denomination
9	$20 bills
35	$ 5 bills
733	$ 1 bills
128	Half dollars
120	Quarters
137	Dimes
160	Nickels
304	Pennies

Directions:
a) Prepare the tally sheet just as you did in Problem 3.
b) Prepare the deposit slip. (Does your total deposit amount to $1,206.74?)

JOB 12 | MAKING BANK DEPOSITS

You have the following bills and coins to be deposited:

Quantity	Denomination
653	$1 bills
78	Half dollars
47	Quarters
259	Dimes
300	Nickels
906	Pennies

Write the answers to the following questions on a sheet of paper:

Practicing Related Arithmetic

1. (a) How many $1 bill packages would you wrap?
   (b) How many loose $1 bills would be left over?

2. (a) How many packages of half dollars would you wrap?
   (b) How many loose half dollars would be left over?

3. (a) How many packages of quarters would you wrap?
   (b) How many loose quarters would be left over?

4. (a) How many packages of dimes would you wrap?
   (b) How many loose dimes would be left over?

5. (a) How many packages of nickels would you wrap?
   (b) How many loose nickels would be left over?

6. (a) How many packages of pennies would you wrap?
   (b) How many loose pennies would be left over?

7. What would be the total amount that you would deposit?

AIM

To give you additional practice in preparing a tally sheet and a deposit slip for money to be deposited in the bank.

PRACTICE PROBLEMS

Problem 1

You are working for John Fiske and he has a bank account in the Trenton Bank. Mr. Fiske wants the money listed on the next page deposited on November 3, 19--:

Quantity	Denomination
12	$20 bills
814	$1 bills
27	Half dollars
100	Quarters
38	Dimes
91	Nickels
103	Pennies

Directions:
a) Prepare a tally sheet such as the one shown in Job 11 on page 86.
b) Prepare a deposit slip such as the one shown in Job 11 on page 86. Be sure to check your arithmetic carefully. (Does your total deposit amount to $1,101.88?)

Problem 2

Mr. Fiske wants the following cash deposited in his account on November 4, 19--:

Quantity	Denomination
5	$20 bills
36	$10 bills
203	$ 1 bills
44	Half dollars
72	Quarters
161	Dimes
59	Nickels
607	Pennies

Directions:
a) Prepare a tally sheet.
b) Prepare a deposit slip. (Does your total deposit amount to $728.12?)

Problem 3

Mr. Fiske wants the following cash deposited in his account on November 5, 19--:

Quantity	Denomination
18	$5 bills
523	$1 bills
180	Half dollars
360	Quarters
196	Dimes
320	Nickels
65	Pennies

Directions:
a) Prepare a tally sheet.
b) Prepare a deposit slip. (Does your total deposit amount to $829.25?)

Problem 4

Mr. Fiske wants the following cash deposited in his account on November 6, 19--:

Quantity	Denomination
17	$10 bills
40	$ 5 bills
311	$ 1 bills
122	Half dollars
115	Quarters
200	Dimes
103	Nickels
134	Pennies

Directions:
a) Prepare a tally sheet.
b) Prepare a deposit slip. (Does your total deposit amount to $797.24?)

Problem 5

Mr. Fiske wants the following cash deposited in his account on November 7, 19--:

Quantity	Denomination
40	$10 bills
11	$ 5 bills
142	$ 1 bills
116	Half dollars
127	Quarters
352	Dimes
160	Nickels
414	Pennies

Directions:
a) Prepare a tally sheet.
b) Prepare a deposit slip. (Does your total deposit amount to $734.09?)

Problem 6

Mr. Fiske wants the following cash deposited in his account on November 10, 19--:

Quantity	Denomination
10	$20 bills
49	$ 5 bills
1,113	$ 1 bills
25	Half dollars
178	Quarters
101	Dimes
402	Nickels
377	Pennies

Directions:
a) Prepare a tally sheet.
b) Prepare a deposit slip. (Does your total deposit amount to $1,648.97?)

UNIT 3

RECORD KEEPING FOR BANKING

UNIT 3

JOB 13 | WRITING CHECKS

In your best handwriting, copy and answer the following problems:

	(1)	(2)	(3)	(4)
Practicing Related Arithmetic	$ 629.18	$4,352.73	$3,168.40	$1,832.59
	134.22	− 746.35	− 481.21	− 692.46
	96.45	Ans. $	Ans. $	Ans. $
	347.86	+ 531.64	+ 916.57	+ 858.71
	3,818.37	Ans. $	Ans. $	Ans. $
	+ 1,582.73			
	Ans. $			

AIM

To learn how to open a checking account and how to write checks.

EXPLANATION

During the month of May, Mr. Fred Mead had to pay the following bills:

$75.00 to be paid to the Allen Tire Co. for automobile tires.

$25.00 to be paid to the Central Electric Co. for the month's electric bill.

$136.45 to be paid to the Fareway Insurance Co. for a life insurance premium.

The safest and most convenient way for Mr. Mead to pay these bills is by writing a check for each amount and mailing it to the company or individual to whom he owes money.

Checks are safe and convenient

In order for Mr. Mead to pay his bills by check, he must open a *checking account* in a bank. Many students know something about savings accounts because they have money deposited in these accounts on which they earn interest. However, not many students have had an opportunity to become familiar with checking accounts. Here is how a checking account is started.

When Mr. Mead opens a checking account in a bank, he will be asked to fill out a *signature card* like the one on the next page.

Authorized Signature For:

$\underline{\text{Fred Mead}}$

Address: $\underline{\text{350 W. 24 Street}}$
$\underline{\text{New York, NY 10011}}$
Telephone $\underline{\text{833-2200}}$

County National Bank   New York City

Account Number: $\underline{\text{1243-666}}$

Signature $\underline{\textit{Fred Mead}}$
Date $\underline{\text{May 1, 19--}}$

Illustration 13a — Signature Card

The signature card will be used by the bank to compare Fred Mead's signature on any check he issues with the signature he used to open the account. It is important for the bank to compare these signatures because the bank will be held responsible by Mr. Mead if it makes payment on a forged signature.

After the signature card is completed, Mr. Mead will be given a checkbook containing pages of checks like the one below.

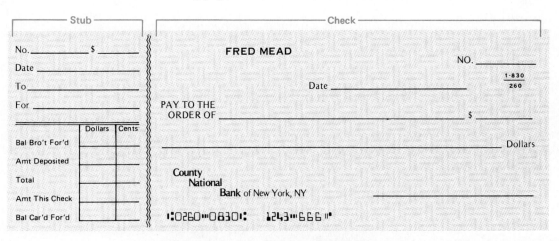

Illustration 13b — Page of a Checkbook

Notice that there are two parts to each check in Mr. Mead's checkbook:

1) the *stub* which remains in the checkbook, and

2) the *check* which will be detached from the stub and sent to the person to whom Mr. Mead is mailing the money.

The purpose of the stub is to provide a record of the important facts about any check that is written. Careful people always fill out the stub before writing the check; otherwise, they may mail the check and then find they have no record of the details about it.

| No. _____ $ _____ |
| Date _____ |
| To _____ |
| For _____ |

	Dollars	Cents
Bal Bro't For'd		
Amt Deposited		
Total		
Amt This Check		
Bal Car'd For'd		

When Mr. Mead wants to deposit money, he will prepare a deposit slip just like the deposit slips you practiced preparing in previous jobs. When Mr. Mead makes a deposit, the bank will give him a receipt for the money deposited. Most large banks today use electronic equipment and give the depositor a printed receipt similar to Illustration 13c.

Your Deposit Receipt

C
N
B

County
National
Bank

New York, NY

May 1 $600.00

Illustration 13c — Deposit Receipt

SAMPLE PROBLEM

On May 1, Mr. Fred Mead opened a checking account at the County National Bank. He was asked to complete the signature card as shown on page 96. Then he deposited $600.00 in the bank. The bank teller gave Mr. Mead a supply of deposit slips and a checkbook containing a supply of blank checks. (Some checkbooks are printed with one check to a page and others are printed with three checks to a page. Mr. Mead preferred to use the one with three checks to a page.)

On May 4, Mr. Mead issued check #1 to the Allen Tire Co. for $75.00 for auto tires. The completed check and check stub for check #1 are shown in the checkbook on page 98.

	Dollars	Cents
No. __1__ $ 75 00/100		
Date _May 4, 19--_		
To _Allen Tire Co._		
For _Auto Tires_		
Bal Bro't For'd		
Amt Deposited	600	00
Total	600	00
Amt This Check	75	00
Bal Car'd For'd	525	00

FRED MEAD   NO. __1__
                                                              1-830
                                                              260
                          Date _May 4, 19--_

PAY TO THE
ORDER OF _Allen Tire Company_ $ 75 00/100

Seventy-five 00/100 _____ Dollars

County
   National
     Bank of New York, NY   _Fred Mead_

⑆0260⑈0830⑆ 1243⑈666⑈

	Dollars	Cents
No. _____ $ _____		
Date _____		
To _____		
For _____		
Bal Bro't For'd	525	00
Amt Deposited		
Total		
Amt This Check		
Bal Car'd For'd		

FRED MEAD   NO. _____
                                                              1-830
                                                              260
                          Date _____

PAY TO THE
ORDER OF _____ $ _____

_____ Dollars

County
   National
     Bank of New York, NY   _____

⑆0260⑈0830⑆ 1243⑈666⑈

	Dollars	Cents
No. _____ $ _____		
Date _____		
To _____		
For _____		
Bal Bro't For'd		
Amt Deposited		
Total		
Amt This Check		
Bal Car'd For'd		

FRED MEAD   NO. _____
                                                              1-830
                                                              260
                          Date _____

PAY TO THE
ORDER OF _____ $ _____

_____ Dollars

County
   National
     Bank of New York, NY   _____

⑆0260⑈0830⑆ 1243⑈666⑈

Illustration 13d — Properly Written Check and Stubs

There are three parties involved in each check. In check #1 the three parties are:

1) *Fred Mead*, called the *drawer*. The drawer writes the check and draws against his checking account. In check #1 Mr. Mead has, in effect,

ordered the County National Bank to draw $75.00 out of his account and pay it to the Allen Tire Co.

2) *The County National Bank*, called the *drawee*. The drawee is the party who is ordered to pay. In check #1 the County National Bank has been ordered by Mr. Mead to pay $75.00 out of his account.

3) *The Allen Tire Co.*, called the *payee*. The payee is the one who receives the money. In check #1 the Allen Tire Co. will receive $75.00 when this check is presented at the County National Bank.

Illustration 13e — Parties to a Check

Look at the stub for check #1 shown in Illustration 13d. Notice that the top half of this stub contains the following information:

a) Check number: No. 1

b) Amount: $75.00

c) Date: May 4, 19--

d) Payee's name: Allen Tire Co.

e) Purpose for which check is issued: Auto Tires

Look at the bottom half of the stub for check #1. Notice that this part of the stub contains the following information:

a) *Balance Brought Forward (Bal Bro't For'd)*

Usually, this space shows the amount of money remaining in the checking account after the previous check. Since this is a new account, there was no previous balance to be brought forward, so no amount was written in this space.

b) *Amount Deposited (Amt Deposited)*

The $600.00 recorded in this space is the amount deposited by Mr. Mead on May 1.

c) *Total*

The total is found by adding the balance brought forward to the deposit of $600.00. Since there was no amount to be brought forward, the total is $600.00.

d) *Amount of This Check (Amt This Check)*

The amount, $75.00, is written neatly in this space.

e) *Balance Carried Forward (Bal Car'd For'd)*

This amount is found by subtracting the amount of the check from the total as follows:

Total	$600.00
Less Amt. This Check	− 75.00
Bal Car'd For'd	$525.00

Notice that this amount, $525.00, is shown as the Balance Brought Forward on the stub of check #2. Before issuing check #2, Mr. Mead will look at this amount to see whether or not there is enough money left in the bank to cover this check. After each check stub has been completed, the new balance is carried forward to the next check stub.

Look at check #1 shown on page 101.

Here are the important points to notice:

a) The amount of the check is written in figures: $75 $\frac{00}{100}$;

and in words: *Seventy-five* $\frac{00}{100}$ _____ Dollars.

b) The amount of dollars in figures is written close to the printed dollar sign ($75), and the amount of cents is written as a fraction:

$\frac{(00)}{(100)}$ No decimal point is used.

c) The amount of the check in words starts at the left margin of the check. The number of cents is written as a fraction. The unused space is filled with a line to the printed word "Dollars."

Illustration 13f — Amount Written on a Check

Seventy-five $\frac{00}{100}$ _____ Dollars

In writing the amount in words, remember that the numbers twenty-one through ninety-nine are written with a hyphen and that only the first letter of the amount is capitalized.

d) Fred Mead signed the check in exactly the same way that he had signed his signature card shown in Illustration 13a on page 96.

e) The numbers $\frac{1-830}{260}$, shown in the upper right-hand corner of the check, are called *ABA numbers*. They are assigned to banks by the American Bankers Association and are used to help separate the checks according to banking districts and the different banks to which the checks must be presented for collection.

ABA number

f) The numbers in the lower left-hand corner of the check, 0260-0830 and 1243-666, are the bank's code number and the code number assigned to Fred's account. These numbers are printed in magnetic ink in a special style of printing so that the bank's electronic bookkeeping equipment can recognize the check as one made by Mr. Mead on his bank account. The numbers also appear on all deposit slips.

Bank code number

On May 7, Mr. Mead issued check #2 to the Central Electric Company for $25.00 for service for the previous month. The check and check stub for check #2 are shown on page 102 as they appear in the checkbook. (Notice that the check stub for check #1 remains in the checkbook even though check #1 has been mailed to Allen Tire Co.)

Notice that the balance of $500.00 shown on check stub #2 is carried forward to the stub of check #3.

No. _1_ $ _75 00/100_
Date _May 4, 19--_
To _Allen Tire Co._
For _Auto Tires_

	Dollars	Cents
Bal Bro't For'd		
Amt Deposited	600	00
Total	600	00
Amt This Check	75	00
Bal Car'd For'd	525	00

No. _2_ $ _25 00/100_
Date _May 7, 19--_
To _Central Electric Co._
For _Monthly bill_

	Dollars	Cents
Bal Bro't For'd	525	00
Amt Deposited		
Total	525	00
Amt This Check	25	00
Bal Car'd For'd	500	00

FRED MEAD   NO. _2_

Date _May 7, 19--_   1-830/260

PAY TO THE ORDER OF _Central Electric Company_ $ _25 00/100_

Twenty-five 00/100 _____ Dollars

County National Bank of New York, NY   _Fred Mead_

⑆0260⑈0830⑆ 1243⑈666⑈

No. _____ $ _____
Date _____
To _____
For _____

	Dollars	Cents
Bal Bro't For'd	500	00
Amt Deposited		
Total		
Amt This Check		
Bal Car'd For'd		

FRED MEAD   NO. _____

Date _____   1-830/260

PAY TO THE ORDER OF _____ $ _____

_____ Dollars

County National Bank of New York, NY

⑆0260⑈0830⑆ 1243⑈666⑈

Illustration 13g — Properly Written Check and Stubs

On May 8, Mr. Mead issued check #3 to the Fareway Insurance Co. for $136.45 for the premium due on his life insurance policy. The check and check stub for check #3 are shown on page 103 as they appear in the checkbook. (Notice that the check stubs for checks #1 and #2 remain in the checkbook even though the checks have been mailed to those being paid.)

No. _1_ $ 75 00/100
Date _May 4, 19--_
To _Allen Tire Co._
For _Auto Tires_

	Dollars	Cents
Bal Bro't For'd		
Amt Deposited	600	00
Total	600	00
Amt This Check	75	00
Bal Car'd For'd	525	00

No. _2_ $ 25 00/100
Date _May 7, 19--_
To _Central Electric Co._
For _Monthly bill_

	Dollars	Cents
Bal Bro't For'd	525	00
Amt Deposited		
Total	525	00
Amt This Check	25	00
Bal Car'd For'd	500	00

No. _3_ $ 136 45/100
Date _May 8, 19--_
To _Fareway Insurance_
For _Life Ins. Premium_

	Dollars	Cents
Bal Bro't For'd	500	00
Amt Deposited		
Total	500	00
Amt This Check	136	45
Bal Car'd For'd	363	55

FRED MEAD

NO. _3_

1-830 / 260

Date _May 8, 19--_

PAY TO THE ORDER OF _Fareway Insurance Company_ $ 136 45/100

One hundred thirty-six 45/100 ———————— Dollars

County National Bank of New York, NY

Fred Mead

⑆0260⑈0830⑆ 1243⑈666⑈

Illustration 13h— Properly Written Check and Stubs

As on the other check stubs, the balance shown on check stub #3 would be carried forward to the stub of check #4.

Here are some suggestions you should follow when you write a check stub and a check:

Hints for writing
checks

1. Use ink.

2. Complete the stub *before* writing the check.

3. Use your best handwriting. Write clearly and legibly. Checks that are not clear will not be accepted or paid by the bank.

4. Learn to spell correctly all the amounts you will need to write on checks. Use the following spelling list to see if you have spelled these words correctly. It is important for you to know how to spell all of these words.

Spelling list for
checks

Spelling List for Amounts Written on Checks		
one	eleven	ten
two	twelve	twenty
three	thirteen	thirty
four	fourteen	forty
five	fifteen	fifty
six	sixteen	sixty
seven	seventeen	seventy
eight	eighteen	eighty
nine	nineteen	ninety

5. If an error is made in writing a check, the stub and the check must be marked "VOID" in large letters and a new stub and check must be written. This is necessary because a check with an erasure or correction will be questioned by the bank. Most people destroy voided personal checks, but businesspeople usually keep all voided checks for their records.

Businesspeople who have many checks to issue and who wish to prevent any possible change in the amounts shown on their checks use a machine known as a *check writer* or *check protector*. This machine prints the amount on the check in a way that make changes impossible. A check writer and a machine-written check are shown below.

Illustration 13i — Check and Check Writer

PRACTICE PROBLEMS

Problem 1

On May 1, Fred Mead opened a checking account with the County National Bank with a deposit of $600.00.

Directions:
a) Since this is a new account, there is no balance to be brought forward. Enter the deposit of $600.00 in the space for "Amt Deposited" on the stub for check #1.
b) Fill in the total.
c) Assume that you are Mr. Mead and write check #1 on May 4 for $75.00 to the Allen Tire Co. to pay for auto tires. *Remember, first complete the stub, and then write the check.* When you have finished writing the check, compare the stub and check with check #1 shown in Illustration 13d on page 98.

Stub first

d) Bring the balance of $525.00 forward to the stub of check #2 as shown in Illustration 13d on page 98.
e) Write the stub and check #2 on May 7 for $25.00 to the Central Electric Company to pay the monthly bill. When you have finished writing the check, compare the stub and check with check #2 shown in Illustration 13g on page 102.
f) Bring the balance of $500.00 forward to the stub of check #3.
g) Write the stub and check #3 on May 8 for $136.45 to the Fareway Insurance Company for a life insurance premium. When you have finished writing the check, compare the stub and check with check #3 shown in Illustration 13h on page 103.

Problem 2

On October 1, Louis Gray opened a checking account with the County National Bank with a deposit of $800.00.

Directions:
a) Enter the deposit of $800.00 in the space for "Amt Deposited" on the stub of check #1. Fill in the total.
b) Write the stub and check #1, dated October 4, for $83.45 to Charlie's Service Station for auto repairs. Find the new balance.
c) Write the stub and check #2, dated October 9, for $31.15 to the New York Telephone Company for the monthly bill. Find the new balance.
d) Write the stub and check #3, dated October 17, for $149.20 to the Loft Department Store for the balance due on Mr. Gray's charge account. Find the new balance.
e) If you did your arithmetic correctly your *balance carried forward* shown on the stub of check #3 should be $536.20.

Problem 3

On April 1, Ruth Owens opened a checking account with the County National Bank with a deposit of $940.00.

Directions:

a) Enter the deposit of $940.00 in the space for "Amt Deposited" on the stub of check #1. Fill in the total.

b) Write the stub and check #1, dated April 6, for $14.90 to the Glover Supply Store for hardware supplies. Find the new balance.

c) Write the stub and check #2, dated April 10, for $218.00 to the Town Realty Company for rent for the month of April. Find the new balance.

d) Write the stub and check #3, dated April 23, for $194.75 to the Ebony Insurance Company for auto insurance. Find the new balance.

e) Your *balance carried forward* on the stub of check #3 should be $512.35.

Problem 4

On March 1, Ann Oliva opened a checking account with the County National Bank with a deposit of $875.00.

Directions:

a) Enter the deposit of $875.00 in the space for "Amt Deposited" on the stub of check #1. Fill in the total.

b) Write the stub and check #1, dated March 5, for $368.60 to the Gold Appliance Store for a television set. Find the new balance.

c) Write the stub and check #2, dated March 16, for $13.09 to Lou's Stationery Shop for stationery supplies. Find the new balance.

d) Write the stub and check #3, dated March 22, for $119.12 to Macy's Department Store for an arm chair. Find the new balance.

e) Your *balance carried forward* on the stub of check #3 should be $374.19.

Problem 5

On November 1, Louis Fried opened a checking account with the County National Bank with a deposit of $695.00.

Directions:

a) Enter the deposit of $695.00 in the space for "Amt Deposited" on the stub of check #1. Fill in the total.

b) Write the stub and check #1, dated November 5, for $311.95 to the Kings Discount House for a refrigerator. Find the new balance.

c) Write the stub and check #2, dated November 13, for $57.80 to the Globe Health Plan for medical insurance. Find the new balance.

d) Write the stub and check #3, dated November 20, for $12.84 to the Rios Service Station for gasoline. Find the new balance.

e) Your *balance carried forward* on the stub of check #3 should be $312.41.

In your best handwriting, copy and answer the following problems:

<table>
<tr><td></td><td>(1)</td><td>(2)</td><td>(3)</td><td>(4)</td></tr>
<tr><td rowspan="2">Practicing Related Arithmetic</td><td>$2,873.45
+ 2,745.78</td><td>$6,247.35
+ 1,875.06</td><td>$5,739.21
− 2,825.73</td><td>$8,392.56
− 5,298.40</td></tr>
<tr><td>Ans. $
− 3,107.64</td><td>Ans. $
+ 3,768.92</td><td>Ans. $
+ 1,962.32</td><td>Ans. $
+ 7,342.76</td></tr>
<tr><td></td><td>Ans. $_____</td><td>Ans. $_____</td><td>Ans. $_____</td><td>Ans. $_____</td></tr>
</table>

AIM

To get more experience in writing checks and to learn how to find the checkbook balance when additional deposits are made.

"I hope I have enough money in my account."

REMINDER

Complete the check stub *before* writing the check.

EXPLANATION

As you have learned, it is necessary to know the exact amount of money left in the checking account before issuing a check. The bank will not pay any check unless there is enough money in the account. For this reason, people using checking accounts must keep an up-to-date record of the balance of the account on the check stubs. In the previous job you learned how to find the checkbook balance when a new account was started. The following sample problem shows how to find the checkbook balance when additional deposits are made in a checking account.

SAMPLE PROBLEM

Joseph Duffy has a checking account in the City National Bank. On March 1, there was a balance of $300 in his checking account. On March 5, Mr. Duffy deposited the following cash which totals $85.00:

> 6 — $10 bills
> 3 — $ 5 bills
> 14 — Half dollars
> 12 — Quarters

Mr. Duffy filled out the deposit slip on the following page:

For DEPOSIT to the Account of		Dollars	Cents
Joseph Duffy	BILLS	75	00
	COINS	10	00
Date *March 5* 19—	Checks as Follows Properly Endorsed		
City National Bank NEWARK, NJ			
Subject to the Terms and Conditions of this Bank's Collection Agreement	TOTAL DEPOSIT	85	00

⑆1416⑉182⑈

Examine the stub for check #21 shown below. The deposit of March 5 was entered on it by recording one amount, $85.00, the *total* shown on the deposit slip.

No._____ $_____	JOSEPH DUFFY	NO._____
Date _____		1-830 / 260
To_____	Date _____	
For_____	PAY TO THE ORDER OF _____ $_____	
	_____ Dollars	
	Dollars	Cents
Bal Bro't For'd	300	00
Amt Deposited	85	00
Total	385	00
Amt This Check		
Bal Car'd For'd		

City National **Bank** of New York, NY

⑆0260⑉0830⑆ 1416⑉182⑈

Now look at the total line on the check stub. The total of $385.00 was found by adding the *balance brought forward* of $300.00 to the *deposit* of $85.00.

	Bal Bro't For'd	$300.00
Plus:	Amount of Deposit	85.00
Equals:	Total	$385.00

Mr. Duffy wrote checks and made deposits as follows:

March 8 — check #21 for	$ 35.00
13 — check #22 for	60.00
15 — deposit of	100.00
19 — check #23 for	140.00

Study the check stubs for the checks he wrote and the deposit he made shown on page 109.

No. __21__ $ 35⁰⁰⁄₁₀₀
Date _March 8, 19--_
To _Time T.V. Center_
For _Repair T.V. Set_

	Dollars	Cents
Bal Bro't For'd	300	00
Amt Deposited	85	00
Total	385	00
Amt This Check	35	00
Bal Car'd For'd	350	00

No. __22__ $ 60⁰⁰⁄₁₀₀
Date _March 13, 19--_
To _Allen Dept. Store_
For _Balance Due_

	Dollars	Cents
Bal Bro't For'd	350	00
Amt Deposited		
Total	350	00
Amt This Check	60	00
Bal Car'd For'd	290	00

No. __23__ $ 140⁰⁰⁄₁₀₀
Date _March 19, 19--_
To _Tony's Auto Body Co._
For _Auto repairs_

	Dollars	Cents
Bal Bro't For'd	290	00
Amt Deposited	100	00
Total	390	00
Amt This Check	140	00
Bal Car'd For'd	250	00

PRACTICE PROBLEMS

Problem 1

On July 1, Mr. Carter had a balance of $1,683.42 in his checking account. He issued checks and made a deposit as follows:

July 2	Issued check #51	$376.84
12	Deposited	612.92
16	Issued check #52	847.26
19	Issued check #53	238.15

Directions: Find the balance in Mr. Carter's checking account by copying and completing the form below, which shows the checks issued and the deposit made by Mr. Carter.

Subtract checks
Add deposits

Balance July 1	$1,683.42
Less check #51	376.84
Balance	
Add deposit	612.92
Balance	
Less check #52	847.26
Balance	
Less check #53	238.15
Balance July 19	

Problem 2

On April 1, Mr. Berris had a balance of $1,648.21 in his checking account. He issued the following checks and made the following deposit:

April	3 Issued check #31	$316.18
	9 Deposited	275.39
	12 Issued check #32	468.45
	18 Issued check #33	193.87

Directions: Find the balance in Mr. Berris' checking account by copying and completing the form below:

Subtract checks
Add deposits

Balance April 1	$1,648.21
Less check #31	316.18
Balance	
Add deposit	275.39
Balance	
Less check #32	468.45
Balance	
Less check #33	193.87
Balance April 18	

Problem 3

On October 1, you opened a checking account in the County National Bank with a deposit of $1,400.00.

Directions:

a) Start your checkbook record by entering the October 1 deposit on the first check stub.

b) Write check #1, dated October 5, for $18.50 to the New York Telephone Co. for the bill dated September 30. (Don't forget to write the stub first.) Find the new balance carried forward.

c) Write check #2, dated October 10, for $315.90 to Kay Audio Shop for a television set. Find the new balance carried forward.

d) On October 16, you deposit the following cash:

> 8 — $10 bills
> 14 — $ 5 bills
> 21 — $ 1 bills
> 7 — Half dollars
> 16 — Quarters
> 23 — Dimes
> 19 — Nickels

Prepare the deposit slip. Enter the *total* amount of the deposit on the stub of check #3 and enter the new balance on the total line.

e) Write check #3, dated October 23, for $24.16 to the Lite Co., Inc. for a desk lamp. Find the new balance carried forward. If your work is correct, the new balance should be $1,223.19.

Problem 4

On May 1, you opened a checking account in the County National Bank with a deposit of $965.80.

Directions:
a) Start your checkbook record by entering the May 1 deposit on the first check stub.
b) Write check #1, dated May 4, for $108.60 to the Mart Furniture Co. for a desk. Find the new balance carried forward.
c) On May 10, you deposit the following cash:

> 5 — $10 bills
> 7 — $ 5 bills
> 32 — $ 1 bills
> 9 — Half dollars
> 17 — Quarters
> 27 — Dimes
> 14 — Nickels

Prepare the deposit slip. Enter the *total* amount of the deposit on the stub of check #2 and enter the new balance on the total line.
d) Write check #2, dated May 14, for $217.90 to the Fair Insurance Co. for auto insurance. Find the new balance carried forward.
e) Write check #3, dated May 18, for $325.85 to the Key Appliance Co. for a washing machine. Find the new balance carried forward. If your work is correct, the new balance should be $442.60.

Practicing Related Arithmetic

In your best handwriting, copy and answer the following problems:

(1)	(2)	(3)	(4)
$4,065.32	$1,498.76	$2,461.65	$ 893.45
+ 914.78	+ 355.90	− 239.75	− 285.76
+ 753.24	+ 587.47	Ans. $	Ans. $
Ans. $	Ans. $	+ 87.32	+ 514.29
− 2,184.75	− 846.75	+ 643.96	+ 128.60
Ans. $	Ans. $	Ans. $	Ans. $

AIM

To gain more experience in writing checks and finding the checkbook balance.

EXPLANATION

Payments of less than one dollar are usually made by using coins. Occasionally, however, it is necessary to write a check for less than one dollar. For example, Sarah Sutton wished to buy a pamphlet from the Garden Publishing Company. The cost of the pamphlet was 75 cents. She wrote a check for this amount.

Illustration 15a — A Check for Less Than One Dollar

Notice that the 75 cents is written as a fraction. It is written again in words on the next line, with the word "Only" before it and the word "Dollars" crossed out.

PRACTICE PROBLEMS

Problem 1

Directions: On a sheet of paper, in your best handwriting, write out the following amounts in words as you would when writing a check. (Remember the hyphens in numbers from twenty-one to ninety-nine. Check your spelling by referring to page 104.)

a) _____ $18\frac{25}{100}$
   _____Dollars

b) _____ $94\frac{16}{100}$
   _____Dollars

c) _____ $67\frac{50}{100}$
   _____Dollars

d) _____ $119\frac{00}{100}$
   _____Dollars

e) _____ $\frac{45}{100}$
   _____Dollars

See check spelling list on page 104

Problem 2

Directions: On a sheet of paper, in your best handwriting, write out the following amounts in words as you would when writing a check. (Watch your spelling and remember the hyphens in numbers from twenty-one to ninety-nine.)

a) _____ $28\frac{60}{100}$
   _____Dollars

b) _____ $214\frac{75}{100}$
   _____Dollars

c) _____ $113\frac{00}{100}$
   _____Dollars

d) _____ $512\frac{30}{100}$
   _____Dollars

e) _____ $\frac{85}{100}$
   _____Dollars

See check spelling list on page 104

Problem 3

You have a checking account in the County National Bank. On November 1 you have a balance of $416.92 in your account.

Directions:
a) Enter the November 1 balance on the first stub as *Bal Bro't For'd*.
b) On November 5, prepare a deposit slip for the money shown on the next page.

Add deposits
Subtract checks

Quantity	Denomination
3	$20 bills
5	$ 5 bills
21	Half dollars
9	Quarters
41	Dimes
16	Nickels
72	Pennies

c) On the first stub enter the total amount of the deposit and enter the new balance on the total line.

d) On November 9, write check #51 for $65.00 to Dr. R. Cole for a dental bill. Find the new balance carried forward.

e) On November 12, write check #52 for $168.90 to the Firm Loan Co. for the monthly payment on an auto loan.

See Illustration
15a on page 112

f) On November 16, write check #53 for 95¢ to the State Farm Bureau for a pamphlet. Find the new balance carried forward. If you did your work correctly, your new balance should be $285.44.

Problem 4

You have a checking account in the County National Bank. On April 1, you have a balance of $1,138.40 in your account.

Directions:

a) Enter the April 1 balance on the first stub as *Bal Bro't For'd.*

b) On April 9, write check #101 for $129.00 to the Dow Department Store for the balance due. Find the new balance carried forward.

c) On April 17, prepare a deposit slip for the following money:

Quantity	Denomination
11	$10 bills
12	$ 5 bills
17	Half dollars
25	Quarters
42	Dimes
34	Nickels

d) On the stub for check #102 enter the total amount of the deposit and enter the new balance on the total line.

See Illustration
15a on page 112

e) On April 20, the Dow Department Store informs you that the check you sent on April 9 should have been $129.85 instead of $129.00. Write check #102 for 85¢ to correct the error. Find the new balance carried forward.

f) On April 23, write check #103 for $65.40 to the A. C. Plumbing Co. for plumbing repairs. Find the new balance carried forward. If you did your work correctly, your new balance should be $1,133.80.

Problem 5

You have a checking account in the County National Bank. On September 1, you have a balance of $869.24 in your account.

Directions:

a) Enter the September 1 balance on the first stub as *Bal Bro't For'd*.

b) On September 4, you made a deposit of $217.10. Enter this amount on the first stub and enter the new balance on the total line.

c) On September 10, write check #91 for 65¢ to the West Publishing Co. for a pamphlet on sports. Find the new balance carried forward.

See Illustration 15a on page 112

d) On September 14, write check #92 for $35.95 to the City Electric Co. for their bill dated September 1. Find the new balance carried forward.

e) On September 17, write check #93 for $275.00 to the New Realty Co. for the monthly rent. Find the new balance carried forward. If you did your work correctly, your new balance should be $774.74.

JOB 16 | ENDORSING CHECKS

	(1)	(2)	(3)	(4)
Practicing Related Arithmetic	$2,354.72	$1,649.20	$3,461.38	$2,953.27
	+ 3,721.28	+ 915.35	− 292.29	− 876.35
	+ 5,189.31	+ 2,387.58	Ans. $ _____	Ans. $ _____
	Ans. $ _____	Ans. $ _____	+ 2,105.36	+ 1,468.92
	− 6,738.47	− 1,674.83	+ 576.84	+ 735.46
	Ans. $ _____	Ans. $ _____	Ans. $ _____	Ans. $ _____

In your best handwriting, copy and answer the following problems:

AIM

To learn how checks are used to transfer money from one person to another person.

EXPLANATION

In the previous jobs you have written checks to pay out money. You have also prepared deposit slips for money to go into the bank. These deposits consisted of currency (bills and coins) only. Many times checks are received instead of currency. (For example, you may receive your salary in the form of a paycheck.) If these checks are to be deposited, they must be listed on the deposit slip along with any currency to be deposited.

Let us assume that John Daley, who has a checking account in the Main National Bank, works for Fred Boyer and that he receives his salary by check. The salary check Mr. Daley received from his employer is shown below.

FRED BOYER AND SONS

No. _178_

Date _May 11_ 19 _--_   1-315 / 260

Pay to the order of _John Daley------------------------------_ $ 215 100/00

Two hundred fifteen 100/00 ---------------------------- Dollars

FORT NATIONAL BANK OF LONG ISLAND, NY

Fred Boyer
PRESIDENT

⑆0260⑆0315⑈   424⑆52373

Illustration 16a — A Salary Check

You probably have noticed the phrase "Pay to the order of " that appears on each check. You may have wondered why the simpler phrase "Pay to" is not used. The words "Pay to *the order of* " make the check transferable, or, to use the business word, "negotiable."

Checks are negotiable

When Fred Boyer signed the check and gave it to John Daley, he really was saying, "I, Fred Boyer, order my bank, the Fort National Bank, to pay $215.00 from my account to John Daley or anyone to whom John Daley *orders my bank* to pay the money."

In other words, John Daley has the right to transfer or negotiate this check. Since John Daley wants his bank, the Main National Bank, to collect the $215.00 for him, he will transfer the check to his bank by signing his name on the back of it, at the end that was attached to the stub. This is called *endorsing the check*.

Endorsing checks

Mr. Daley can transfer the check to his bank by using either one of the following two endorsements.

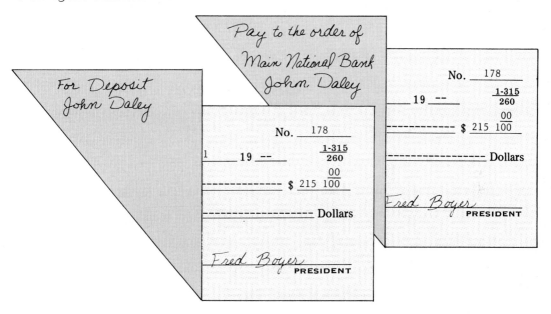

Illustration 16b — Check Endorsements

Mr. Daley prefers the endorsement, "For deposit, John Daley."

After endorsing the check, Daley deposits it in *his* checking account at the Main National Bank, listing the check on the deposit slip as shown in Illustration 16c on the next page.

The endorsement allows *only* the Main National Bank to present the check to the Fort National Bank and collect the $215.00. The Fort National Bank will take the check, mark it "Paid," and later return it to Fred Boyer, the drawer. Such checks are referred to as "canceled checks." At some future time, if there is any question about this payment, Boyer can use the canceled check, which now contains Daley's endorsement, as proof that he paid Daley.

Canceled checks

For DEPOSIT to the Account of		Dollars	Cents
JOHN DALEY	BILLS		
	COINS		
Date May 12 19—	Checks as Follows Properly Endorsed	215	00
MAIN NATIONAL BANK NEW YORK, NY			
Subject to the Terms and Conditions of this Bank's Collection Agreement	TOTAL DEPOSIT	215	00

203⑈011611⑈

Illustration 16c — A Deposit Slip with a Listed Check

It is for this reason that canceled checks should be saved for a reasonable length of time. Below are illustrations of the back and front of a canceled check.

Illustration 16d — Back of a Canceled Check

FRED BOYER AND SONS   No. 178

Date May 11 19 --   1-315/260

Pay to the order of John Daley---------------------------- $ 215 00/100

Two hundred fifteen 00/100---------------------------- Dollars

FORT NATIONAL BANK OF LONG ISLAND, NY

Fred Boyer PRESIDENT

⑈0260⑈0315⑈ 424⑈52373 ⑈000021500

Illustration 16e — Face of a Canceled Check

If you compare Illustration 16e with Illustration 16a, you will see that the amount of the check has been encoded (printed with special magnetic ink characters — 000021500) in the lower right-hand corner so that the bank's automated data processing equipment can recognize the amount of the check.

Encoding checks

It is not practical for the Main National Bank to take the check directly to the Fort National Bank to collect the $215.00. If the Main National Bank tried to do this, they would need a large staff of messengers to deliver the thousands of checks deposited each day. In addition, large sums of money would have to be mailed back and forth each day.

In all large cities the banks arrange a central meeting place called a *clearing house* where they distribute and exchange checks deposited with them each day. The numerical symbol $\frac{1\text{-}315}{260}$ shown in the upper right-hand corner of the check (Illustration 16a) is reprinted in the lower left-hand corner of the check by using magnetic ink characters (0260-0315) so that automated data processing machinery can sort the checks according to the various banks to which the checks must be presented.

Clearing house

If we were to draw a diagram to show what happened to the $215.00 check Mr. Boyer issued to Mr. Daley, it would look like this:

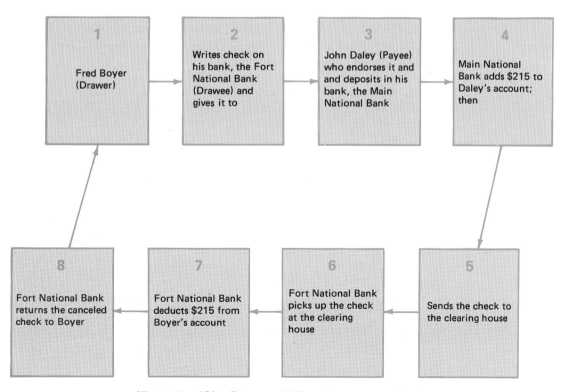

1	2	3	4
Fred Boyer (Drawer)	Writes check on his bank, the Fort National Bank (Drawee) and gives it to	John Daley (Payee) who endorses it and and deposits in his bank, the Main National Bank	Main National Bank adds $215 to Daley's account; then

8	7	6	5
Fort National Bank returns the canceled check to Boyer	Fort National Bank deducts $215 from Boyer's account	Fort National Bank picks up the check at the clearing house	Sends the check to the clearing house

Illustration 16f — Diagram of What Happens to a Check

SAMPLE PROBLEM

David Nelson received a check from Mary Post:

Mary Post	No. _87_

Date _March 5_ 19 __ $\frac{1\text{-}315}{260}$

Pay to the
order of _David Nelson_ $ _96 \frac{00}{100}$

Ninety-six $\frac{00}{100}$ ——————————————— Dollars

FORT NATIONAL BANK
OF LONG ISLAND, NY   _Mary Post_

⑆260⑈0315⑈   3344⑈9800

Mr. Nelson wants to deposit this check in his bank, the Main National Bank, along with $350.00 in bills, $40.00 in coins, and two other checks he has received for $90.00 and $20.00.

Step 1: Endorse checks.

Mr. Nelson would have to endorse the check he received from Ms. Post before depositing it in order to give his bank the right to collect the money from the Fort National Bank for him.

Mr. Nelson would endorse the check as shown at the left. Of course, Mr. Nelson would also have to endorse any other checks that he wants to deposit. He would therefore use the same endorsement on the $90 and the $20 checks he had received.

*Pay to the order
of
Main National Bank
David Nelson*

Step 2: Prepare deposit slip.

The bills, the coins, and the checks to be deposited would then be listed on a deposit slip as shown below. Notice that this deposit slip was printed for

For DEPOSIT to the Account of		Dollars	Cents
DAVID NELSON	BILLS	3 50	00
	COINS	40	00
Date _March 7_ 19 —	Checks as Follows Properly Endorsed	96	00
		90	00
MAIN NATIONAL BANK NEW YORK, NY		20	00
Subject to the Terms and Conditions of this Bank's Collection Agreement	TOTAL DEPOSIT	5 96	00

203⑈046⑈

Mr. Nelson by his bank and that his account number, 203-0116, is encoded (printed with special magnetic ink characters) at the bottom of the slip. The bank's electronic data processing equipment will now be able to automatically recognize that this deposit is to be added to Mr. Nelson's account.

Step 3: Record deposit in checkbook.

Mr. Nelson would enter the total amount of the deposit, $596.00, on the checkbook stub and add it to the old balance to find his new checkbook balance as shown at the right.

	Dollars	Cents
No. _____ $ _____		
Date _____		
To _____		
For _____		
Bal Bro't For'd	713	12
Amt Deposited	596	00
Total	1309	12
Amt This Check		
Bal Car'd For'd		

PRACTICE PROBLEMS

Problem 1

Arthur Mayer has a checking account in the Grand National Bank. He has the following currency and the following two checks to be deposited:

Quantity	Denomination
15	$10 bills
24	$ 5 bills
40	Quarters

JOSE PEREZ NO. 406 70-12/711

Date October 26, 19--

PAY TO THE ORDER OF Arthur Mayer $ 275 00/100

Two hundred seventy-five 00/100 Dollars

Peoria National Bank Main Street Branch Peo

⑆0711⑆0012⑆985⑆695

Jerry Santora No. 137 5-76/110

October 28 19--

Pay to the order of Arthur Mayer $ 91 60/100

Ninety-one 60/100 Dollars

BOSTON NATIONAL BANK Liberty Branch Boston, Massachusetts   Jerry Santora

⑆0110⑆0076⑆5312 6631

Directions:
a) Show the endorsement Mr. Mayer would use on both checks before depositing them. Use the full endorsement as shown in Illustration 16b on page 117.
b) Prepare the deposit slip, dated October 31, listing both currency and checks. List each check separately on the deposit slip. Compare your deposit slip with the slip shown on page 120.

Problem 2

You have a checking account in the Grand National Bank, and on September 1 you have a balance of $738.42 in your account.

Directions:
a) Enter the September 1 balance on the first check stub as *Bal Bro't For'd.*
b) On September 5, prepare a deposit slip for the following deposit:

Quantity	Denomination
4	$20 bills
31	$ 5 bills
53	Half dollars
27	Nickels
A check for $84.65	
A check for $279.51	

c) Enter the deposit on the first stub, and enter the new balance on the total line.
d) On September 10, write check #431 for $117.70 to the Audio Shack for a tape recorder. Find the new balance carried forward.
e) On September 14, write check #432 for $100.00 to the order of "Cash" so that you can withdraw this amount from your checking account and use it for personal living expenses. The bank will ask you to endorse the check as proof that you have received the money. Find the new balance carried forward. If your work is correct, your new balance should be $1,147.73.

Problem 3

You work in the office of Grove Bros., and part of your job is to prepare the deposit slips and keep the checkbook. Grove Bros. deposits its money in the Grand National Bank.

Directions:
a) July 1 — Enter the checkbook balance of $1,469.30 on the first check stub.
b) July 5 — Write check #401 to the Pitt Steel Company for $572.80 for their bill of June 25. Find the new balance carried forward.
c) July 10 — Prepare a deposit slip for the following deposit:

Quantity	Denomination
14	$10 bills
7	Half dollars
A check for $114.30	
A check for $371.25	

Enter the total amount of the deposit on check stub #402. Enter the new balance on the total line.

d) July 16 — Write check #402 to the Range Corporation for $318.50 for their bill of July 6. Find the new balance carried forward. If your work is correct, your new balance should be $1,207.05.

Problem 4

You are employed to assist the bookkeeper for Rural Builders, Inc. This business has a checking account in the Grand National Bank.

Directions:

a) March 1 — Enter the checkbook balance of $2,861.15 on the first check stub.

b) March 2 — Write check #621 to the Condon Lumber Company for $800.00 as part payment on the bill of February 20. Find the new balance carried forward.

c) March 6 — Prepare a deposit slip for the following deposit:

Quantity	Denomination
17	$10 bills
15	Quarters
A check for $920.00	
A check for $45.65	

Enter the total amount of the deposit on stub #622, and enter the new balance on the total line.

d) March 9 — Write check #622 to Cohen & Russo for $814.00 for their bill dated February 27.

e) March 14 — Write check #623 to Central Realty for $340.00 for rent for the month. Find the balance carried forward. If your work is correct, the new balance should be $2,046.55.

Practicing Related Arithmetic

Copy and complete the following problems:

(1)		(2)		(3)	
Balance	$615.35	Balance	$837.40	Balance	$534.25
+Deposit	903.48	−Check #1	349.71	−Check #1	157.30
Balance		Balance		Balance	
−Check #1	584.62	+Deposit	783.25	−Check #2	89.34
Balance		Balance		Balance	
−Check #2	327.16	−Check #2	962.37	+Deposit	621.18
Balance	$	Balance	$	Balance	$

AIM

To learn about bank statements and how they are used to check the accuracy of the checkbook balance.

EXPLANATION

In the previous job you learned that after a bank pays a check drawn by one of its depositors, it marks the check "Paid" and returns the canceled check to the depositor. In other words, if you have a checking account, the bank will return to you all the checks that you have issued after they have been paid by the bank.

Actually, the bank does not return each canceled check as it is paid. Instead, most banks hold all the canceled checks until the end of the month and return all of them at one time along with a statement showing the checks paid out during the month, the deposits made during the month, and the amount of money in the account at the end of the month (see Illustration 17a on page 125). The amount of money in the bank account at the end of the month is called the *bank balance*. It should be compared with the *checkbook balance* to see if any error has been made.

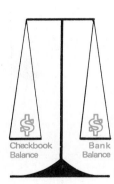

Checkbook Balance   Bank Balance

Although most banks prepare the bank statements at the end of the month, some banks prefer to send statements to their depositors on dates other than the end of the month. Other banks prefer to prepare statements covering longer periods of time; for example, every two months.

SAMPLE PROBLEM

Let us assume that you have been keeping a checkbook for Harry West and at the end of the month of June the stubs in the checkbook contained the facts shown on the next page.

	Dollars	Cents
No. _1_ $ _300 00_		
Date _June 4, 19—_		
To _Dolan & Kelly_		
For _legal fee_		
Bal Bro't For'd	4475	00
Amt Deposited		
Total	4475	00
Amt This Check	300	00
Bal Car'd For'd	4175	00

	Dollars	Cents
No. _2_ $ _250 00_		
Date _June 9, 19—_		
To _Dean Realty_		
For _office rent_		
Bal Bro't For'd	4175	00
Amt Deposited		
Total	4175	00
Amt This Check	250	00
Bal Car'd For'd	3925	00

	Dollars	Cents
No. _3_ $ _125 00_		
Date _June 13, 19—_		
To _L. Weitz & Co._		
For _bill of June 3_		
Bal Bro't For'd	3925	00
Amt Deposited		
Total	3925	00
Amt This Check	125	00
Bal Car'd For'd	3 800	00

	Dollars	Cents
No. _4_ $ _100 00_		
Date _June 23, 19—_		
To _Brown Stores Inc._		
For _deposit on office furniture_		
Bal Bro't For'd	3800	00
Amt Deposited	460	00
Total	4260	00
Amt This Check	1 00	00
Bal Car'd For'd	4160	00

	Dollars	Cents
No. _5_ $ _160 00_		
Date _June 27, 19—_		
To _R. Wood, Inc._		
For _auto repair_		
Bal Bro't For'd	4160	00
Amt Deposited		
Total	4160	00
Amt This Check	160	00
Bal Car'd For'd	4000	00

	Dollars	Cents
No. _6_ $ _500 00_		
Date _June 30, 19—_		
To _Mason & Co._		
For _bill of June 1_		
Bal Bro't For'd	4000	00
Amt Deposited		
Total	4000	00
Amt This Check	500	00
Bal Car'd For'd	3500	00

Stubs of checks issued

This is the bank statement Mr. West received from his bank on July 1.

County National Bank

Account of
Harry West
1091 Grand Avenue
Hempstead, NY 11550

Account Number
202--03056

Statement Date
June 30, 19--

Total Deposits	Total Checks Cleared	Current Balance
$460.00	$775.00	$4160.00

Checks Paid	Deposits	Date	Balance
Balance Brt. Forward		June 1	$4475.00
$300.00		6	4175.00
250.00		10	3925.00
125.00		16	3800.00
	$460.00	23	4260.00
100.00		27	4160.00

Illustration 17a — A Bank Statement

The following canceled checks were returned in the same envelope with the bank statement:

Canceled checks

Check #1	Dolan & Kelly	$300.00
" 2	Dean Realty	250.00
" 3	L. Weitz & Co.	125.00
" 4	Brown Stores, Inc.	100.00

Mr. West notices that the bank balance of $4,160.00 on June 30 does not agree with the June 30 checkbook balance of $3,500.00. He asks you to find out why there is a difference and to see if the two balances can be brought into agreement, or *reconciled*. Here are the steps you would follow:

Step 1: Compare deposits.

Compare the amount of the deposit listed on the bank statement with the amount shown on check stub #4 on page 125. Notice that the deposit of $460.00 was recorded properly on the bank statement on June 23.

Step 2: Arrange canceled checks.

Arrange the canceled checks in numerical order.

Step 3: Compare canceled checks with stubs.

Compare the canceled checks with the check stubs. Make a small check mark on stub if its canceled check has been returned. Those stubs for which you do not have check marks are for checks *not* returned by the bank.

Outstanding checks

Step 4: Find outstanding checks.

Notice that check #5 for $160.00 issued to R. Wood, Inc. on June 27 and check #6 for $500.00 issued to Mason & Co. on June 30 have not been returned by the bank. Do you know why these checks have not been returned? The probable reason is that R. Wood, Inc. and Mason & Co. did not deposit these checks in their banks by June 30. The checks are called *outstanding checks*, because they have been issued but not yet cashed at the bank.

Step 5: Prepare bank reconciliation statement.

Subtract outstanding checks

Because check #5 and check #6 have been subtracted from our checkbook balance, it is necessary to subtract these outstanding checks of $160.00 and $500.00 from the bank balance of $4,160.00 to see if that will make it agree with the checkbook balance. A special form called a *bank reconciliation statement* is prepared for this purpose.

If you examine the bank reconciliation statement shown in Illustration 17b, you will see that the heading contains the answers to three questions:

Who? Harry West
What? Bank Reconciliation Statement
When? June 30, 19--

Notice also that the outstanding checks are listed separately and their total of $660.00 is subtracted from the bank balance of $4,160.00.

Harry West
Bank Reconciliation Statement
June 30, 19—

Checkbook Balance	$ 3,500.00	Bank Balance	$4,160.00
		Less: outstanding checks	
		#5 $160.00	
		#6 500.00	
		Total outstanding checks	660.00
Adjusted balance	$ 3,500.00	Adjusted balance	$ 3,500.00

Illustration 17b — Bank Reconciliation Statement

Harry West now knows that although the bank statement shows that he has $4,160.00 in his checking account, he must not withdraw more than the $3,500.00 shown in his checkbook balance, since $660.00 must be left in the bank for the two outstanding checks.

PRACTICE PROBLEMS

Problem 1

On May 31, your checkbook balance is $600.00. Your bank statement shows a balance of $1,500.00. After comparing the canceled checks returned by the bank with the check stubs, you determined that the following checks were outstanding:

#72	$500.00
#74	250.00
#75	150.00

Directions: Prepare the bank reconciliation statement as of May 31. Follow the form shown in Illustration 17b above.

Problem 2

On February 28, your checkbook balance is $1,700.00. The bank statement on that date shows a balance of $2,800.00. The outstanding checks are:

#86	$235.00
#88	500.00
#90	115.00
#91	250.00

Directions: Prepare the bank reconciliation statement as of February 28.

Problem 3

The checkbook balance on October 31 is $1,627.35. The bank balance on October 31 is $2,730.40. The outstanding checks are:

#211	$434.65
#214	325.00
#216	189.30
#217	154.10

Directions: Prepare the bank reconciliation statement as of October 31.

Problem 4

The checkbook balance on August 31 is $872.50. The bank balance on August 31 is $1,462.73. The outstanding checks are:

#318	$114.25
#320	67.34
#323	210.80
#325	197.84

Directions: Prepare the bank reconciliation statement as of August 31.

Problem 5

The checkbook balance on June 30 is $592.20. The bank balance on June 30 is $1,648.80. The outstanding checks are:

#154	$241.35
#157	57.20
#159	486.25
#160	271.80

Directions: Prepare the bank reconciliation statement as of June 30.

Problem 6

The checkbook balance on November 30 is $1,736.40. The bank balance on November 30 is $2,816.30. The outstanding checks are:

#232	$307.50
#236	264.35
#238	189.90
#239	318.15

Directions: Prepare the bank reconciliation statement as of November 30.

Copy and complete the following problems:

Practicing Related Arithmetic

	(1)		(2)		(3)
Balance	$4,264.27	Balance	$1,762.85	Balance	$3,846.20
+Deposit	2,176.83	+Deposit	5,319.25	−Check #1	1,078.45
Balance		Balance		Balance	
−Check #1	1,785.92	+Deposit	782.73	−Check #2	734.83
Balance		Balance		Balance	
−Check #2	876.46	−Check #1	995.21	+Deposit	2,851.76
Balance	$	Balance	$	Balance	$

AIM

To gain experience in preparing bank reconciliation statements.

PRACTICE PROBLEMS

Problem 1

Your check stubs show that the following checks were issued during the month of October:

Check stubs

Check Number	Amount	Check Number	Amount
#161	$113.80	#165	$ 87.30
#162	92.70	#166	364.70
#163	284.10	#167	61.20
#164	109.40	#168	175.00

Your checkbook balance on October 31 is $1,876.30. The bank balance on October 31 as shown on your bank statement is $2,302.20.

The following canceled checks were returned with your bank statement:

Canceled checks

#161	$113.80	#164	$109.40
#162	92.70	#165	87.30
#163	284.10	#168	175.00

Directions:
a) Find which checks were outstanding on October 31 by matching each canceled check with the stub for each check issued. (You should find two outstanding checks.)
b) Prepare the bank reconciliation statement as of October 31.

Problem 2

Your check stubs show that the following checks were issued during the month of May:

Check stubs

Check Number	Amount	Check Number	Amount
#225	$226.35	#229	$431.83
#226	127.14	#230	189.70
#227	98.40	#231	236.15
#228	314.55	#232	81.90

The checkbook balance on May 31 is $2,914.85

The bank balance on May 31 as shown on the bank statement is $3,664.73. The following canceled checks were returned with your bank statement:

Canceled checks

#225	$226.35	#228	$314.55
#226	127.14	#230	189.70
#227	98.40		

Directions:
a) Find which checks were outstanding on May 31 by matching each canceled check with the stub for each check issued. (You should find three outstanding checks.)
b) Prepare the bank reconciliation statement on May 31.

Problem 3

Directions: Prepare a bank reconciliation statement on January 31 from the following facts:

Checkbook balance	$3,738.71
Bank balance per statement	4,652.01

Outstanding checks:	
#248	$317.20
#250	194.60
#253	401.50

Problem 4

Directions: Prepare a bank reconciliation statement on April 30 from the following facts:

Checkbook balance	$1,892.25
Bank balance per statement	3,369.79

Outstanding checks:			
#347	$812.30	#351	$212.00
#348	357.14	#354	96.10

Problem 5

Directions: Prepare a bank reconciliation statement on February 28 from the following facts:

Checkbook balance			$2,407.90
Bank balance per statement			3,244.70

Outstanding checks:

#107	$265.80	#111	$322.45
#110	72.95	#115	175.60

Problem 6

Directions: Prepare a bank reconciliation statement on August 31 from the following facts:

Checkbook balance			$3,640.95
Bank balance per statement			4,425.35

Outstanding checks:

#562	$186.30	#566	$ 74.20
#563	318.90	#568	205.00

Copy and complete the following problems:

Practicing Related Arithmetic

	(1)		(2)		(3)
Balance	$3,615.24	Balance	$7,241.30	Balance	$5,824.50
+Deposit	1,973.92	−Check #1	982.96	−Check #1	3,915.95
Balance		Balance		Balance	
−Check #1	2,368.45	−Check #2	857.23	+Deposit	2,824.12
Balance		Balance		Balance	
−Check #2	857.50	+Deposit	418.78	−Check #2	782.25
Balance	$_____	Balance	$_____	Balance	$_____

AIM

To learn how to prepare a bank reconciliation statement when the bank statement shows a service charge.

EXPLANATION

Bank service charge

Many banks charge their depositors for certain bank services. If you have a regular checking account, the bank may make a small charge for each check it pays for you and for each item you deposit. A charge made by a bank for maintaining a checking account is called a *service charge*. The bank statement will show a deduction for the service charge.

You have already learned that one reason the checkbook balance and the bank statement balance may not agree is because of outstanding checks. A second reason the checkbook balance and bank balance may not agree is the service charge.

It is necessary, therefore, to consider the bank service charge when preparing a bank reconciliation statement. Let us see how this is done.

SAMPLE PROBLEM

Your bank statement shows a balance on March 31 of $796.00 after the bank has taken out a $4.00 service charge.

Your checkbook shows a balance on March 31 of $800.00. The reason the checkbook balance does not agree with the bank balance is that you have not known about the $4.00 service charge. Since the bank has already subtracted the $4.00 service charge, it is now necessary for you to subtract this amount from the checkbook balance.

Here is how you would reconcile the two amounts:

Checkbook Balance	$ 800.00	Bank Balance	$796.00
Less: Service Charge	4.00		
Adjusted balance	$796.00	Adjusted balance	$796.00

Illustration 19a — Bank Reconciliation Statement

You have now learned that there are two reasons why the checkbook balance may not agree with the bank balance. One reason may be outstanding checks. The second reason may be the bank service charge. Here is how both of these items would appear in a bank reconciliation statement:

Subtract service charge from checkbook balance

Checkbook Balance	$926.00	Bank Balance		$1,370.00
Less: Service charge	6.00	Less: Outstanding checks		
		#176	$150.00	
		#179	300.00	
		Total outstanding checks		$450.00
Adjusted balance	$920.00	Adjusted balance		$920.00

Illustration 19b — Bank Reconciliation Statement

The bank service charge is subtracted from the *checkbook* balance; the outstanding checks are subtracted from the *bank* balance.

PRACTICE PROBLEMS

Problem 1

Directions: Prepare a bank reconciliation statement on May 31 from the following facts:

Checkbook balance			$3,696.00
Bank balance per statement			4,260.00
Service charge			6.00

Outstanding checks:			
#191	$160.00	#195	$120.00
#192	80.00	#198	210.00

Problem 2

Directions: Prepare a bank reconciliation statement on January 31 from the following facts:

Checkbook balance			$2,935.00
Bank balance per statement			3,784.00
Service charge			5.00

Outstanding checks:			
#101	$240.00	#106	$104.00
#104	195.00	#108	315.00

Problem 3

Directions: Prepare a bank reconciliation statement on October 31 from the following facts:

Checkbook balance			$3,564.00
Bank balance per statement			4,192.00
Service charge			7.00

Outstanding checks:			
#412	$ 95.00	#417	$150.00
#415	330.00	#418	60.00

Problem 4

Directions: Prepare a bank reconciliation statement on September 30 from the following facts:

Checkbook balance			$2,488.00
Bank balance per statement			3,075.00
Service charge			9.00

Outstanding checks:			
#414	$270.00	#418	$180.00
#417	96.00	#420	50.00

Copy and complete the following problem:

Quantity	×	Denomination	=	Amount
18		$10 bills	=	$
15		$ 5 bills	=	
32		$ 1 bills	=	
27		Half dollars	=	
33		Quarters	=	
110		Dimes	=	
24		Nickels	=	
69		Pennies	=	
			+	_____
		Total Amount		$ _____

Practicing Related Arithmetic

AIM

To gain more experience in preparing bank reconciliation statements.

PRACTICE PROBLEMS

Problem 1

Directions: Prepare the bank reconciliation statement on November 30 from the following facts:

Checkbook balance	$3,577.33
Bank balance per statement	4,163.60
Service charge	7.25

Outstanding checks:

#308	$187.25	#314	$103.14
#311	215.62	#315	87.51

Problem 2

Directions: Prepare the bank reconciliation statement on April 30 from the following facts:

Checkbook balance	$3,249.53
Bank balance per statement	3,814.15
Service charge	8.65

Outstanding checks:			
#151	$217.83	#156	$107.08
#154	184.19	#158	64.17

Problem 3

Directions: Prepare the bank reconciliation statement on December 31 from the following facts:

Checkbook balance	$4,794.73
Bank balance per statement	5,618.74
Service charge	12.50

Outstanding checks:			
#612	$371.87	#616	$258.21
#613	96.25	#618	110.18

Problem 4

Directions: Prepare the bank reconciliation statement on February 28 from the following facts:

Checkbook balance	$1,604.08
Bank balance per statement	2,017.56
Service charge	10.35

Outstanding checks:			
#87	$ 93.46	#93	$61.80
#90	182.57	#95	86.00

Problem 5

Directions: Prepare the bank reconciliation statement as of June 30 from the following facts:

Checkbook balance	$2,947.07
Bank balance per statement	3,624.18
Service charge	11.45

Outstanding checks:			
#144	$276.40	#148	$ 43.30
#147	151.26	#149	217.60

Copy and complete the following problem:

Quantity	×	Denomination	=	Amount
76		$10 bills	=	$
59		$ 5 bills	=	
48		Half dollars	=	
39		Quarters	=	
115		Dimes	=	
23		Nickels	=	
146		Pennies	=	
			+	
		Total Amount		$_____

AIM

To review keeping a checkbook.

EXPLANATION

You will practice the skills involved in keeping a checkbook, preparing deposit slips, writing endorsements and checks, finding the checkbook balance, and preparing bank reconciliation statements.

PRACTICE PROBLEMS

Problem 1

On October 1, Louis Jason opened a checking account at the County National Bank with a deposit of $882.25 consisting of:

Bills	$384.00
Coins	27.25
Checks	218.00
	253.00

Directions:
a) Prepare a deposit slip.
b) Show the endorsement Mr. Jason would write on the two checks to be deposited. (Use a full endorsement.) See Illustration 16b on page 117.
c) Start a checkbook with check #101 and record the total amount of the deposit on check stub #101.

d) October 5 — Write check #101 to Spears & Co. for $224.70 for an office desk. Find the new balance.

e) October 16 — Write check #102 to Ramirez Bros. for $115.80 in payment of their bill of October 6. Find the new balance.

f) October 29 — Write check #103 to Gold & Co. for $86.35 for office stationery. Find the new balance. If your work is correct your new balance carried forward should be $455.40. If it is not, recheck your work.

g) October 31 — Prepare the bank reconciliation statement using the facts in Mr. Jason's checkbook and the following information:

Mr. Jason's bank statement for October showed that the bank service charge for the month was $2.60, the bank statement balance was $654.95, and the bank returned canceled check #101 for $224.70. (Remember to find the outstanding checks.)

Problem 2

On July 1, Frank Smith opened a checking account at the County National Bank with a deposit of $1,125.80 consisting of:

Bills	$624.00
Coins	23.80
Checks	286.00
	192.00

Directions:
a) Prepare the deposit slip.

b) Show the endorsement Mr. Smith would write on the two checks to be deposited. (Use a full endorsement.) See Illustration 16b on p. 117.

c) Start a checkbook with check #301 and record the total amount of the deposit on check stub #301.

d) July 10 — Write check #301 for $217.90 to the Acme Insurance Co. for the fire insurance premium. Find the new balance.

e) July 27 — Write check #302 for $345.00 to the Low Realty Co. for the office rent for the month. Find the new balance.

f) July 30 — Write check #303 for $84.70 to the Bell Telephone Company for the office telephone bill. Find the new balance. If your work is correct your balance carried forward should be $478.20. If it is not, recheck your work.

g) July 31 — Prepare the bank reconciliation statement using the facts in Mr. Smith's checkbook and the following information:

Mr. Smith's bank statement for July showed that the bank service charge for the month was $1.90, the bank statement balance on July 31 was $906.00, and the bank returned canceled check #301 for $217.90. (Remember to find the outstanding checks.)

JOB 22 | MAINTAINING A CHECKING ACCOUNT

Copy and complete the following problem:

Quantity	×	Denomination	=	Amount
26		$20 bills	=	$
107		$ 5 bills	=	
25		Half dollars	=	
86		Quarters	=	
125		Dimes	=	
29		Nickels	=	
217		Pennies	=	
			+	_____
		Total Amount		$_____

Practicing Related Arithmetic

AIM

To review the job of keeping a checkbook.

PRACTICE PROBLEMS

Problem 1

You work in the office of the Acme Supply Company. The company has a checking account in the County National Bank.

Directions:

a) November 1 — Enter the checkbook balance of $2,076.28 on the first check stub.

b) November 9 — Write check #521 to Mars Realty, Inc. for $415.00 for the business rent. Find the new balance.

c) November 14 — Prepare a deposit slip for the following deposit:

Quantity	Denomination
15	$10 bills
31	Half dollars
A check for $296.40	
A check for $314.80	

Enter the total amount of the deposit on check stub #522.

d) November 26 — Write check #522 to the Ward Equipment Company for $454.75 for an electronic calculator. Find the new balance.

e) November 28 — Write check #523 to Platt Bros. for $348.20 for their bill of November 1. Find the new balance. Your new balance should be $1,635.03. If it is not, recheck your work.

Problem 2

The Acme Supply Company, whose checkbook you worked on in Problem 1, received its bank statement for the month of November.

The bank service charge for the month was	$ 2.30
The bank statement balance on November 30 was	2,435.68
The bank returned canceled check #521	415.00

Directions: Prepare the bank reconciliation statement on November 30 using the facts in Problems 1 and 2.

Problem 3

You work in the office of Carson & Company, Inc.

Directions:
a) April 1 — Enter the checkbook balance of $2,658.10 on the first check stub.
b) April 12 — Write check #311 to the Dow Corporation for $482.60 for their bill of April 2. Find the new balance.
c) April 26 — Write check #312 to Tom Alvarez for $260.00 for legal services. Find the new balance.
d) April 27 — Prepare a deposit slip for the following deposit:

Quantity	Denomination
21	$10 bills
37	Quarters
A check for $471.20	
A check for $186.50	

Enter the total amount of the deposit on check stub #313.
e) April 29 — Write check #313 to R. Davis for $319.75 for repair of the business automobile. Find the new balance. Your new balance should be $2,472.70. If it is not, recheck your work.

Problem 4

Carson & Company, Inc., whose checkbook you worked on in Problem 3, received its bank statement for the month of April.

The bank service charge for the month was	$ 3.70
The bank statement balance on April 30 was	3,048.75
The bank returned canceled check #311	482.60

Directions: Prepare the bank reconciliation statement on April 30 using the facts in Problems 3 and 4.

UNIT 4

RECORD KEEPING FOR PETTY CASH

UNIT 4

JOB 23 | WRITING PETTY CASH VOUCHERS

	Copy and complete the following problems:			
	(1)	(2)	(3)	(4)
Practicing Related Arithmetic	$2,471.80 − 268.93	$1,607.84 − 898.15	$ 168.43 379.82 214.55 64.18 + 171.76	$ 418.76 291.30 543.84 190.45 + 73.28

AIM

To learn how to keep a record of payments made from a petty cash fund.

EXPLANATION

Businesspeople must keep careful records of all money they spend. This is true for payments made by check and also for payments made by currency. When you speak of *currency* you mean actual bills and coins.

"A check! For two stamps?"

Although businesspeople prefer to make payments by check, very often it is more convenient and sometimes necessary to make payments by currency. Can you imagine paying for bus fare by check? You would, of course, have to use currency.

There are many other situations, such as purchasing postage stamps or paying for the taxi fare of an employee delivering a package, in which currency must be used. Usually these payments are made in small, or petty, amounts and they are therefore referred to as *petty cash* payments.

Petty = small

Since all the cash of the business is kept in a checking account, the currency needed for these petty cash payments is obtained by writing and cashing a check. The businessperson estimates an amount of money that will be enough for a certain period of time, a week or a month, perhaps. The currency is then placed in a box called a *petty cash box*. In this way, a *petty cash fund* has been started.

So that a record can be kept of each payment from the petty cash fund, each person who receives money must sign a printed receipt form called a *petty cash voucher*, shown in Illustration 23a. The petty cash cashier approves each voucher by initialling it.

Be Sure To Use The Correct Compartment

PETTY CASH VOUCHER

No._____

Date_____ 19_____

Pay to _____ $ ¢

For _____

Approved by   Payment Received

_____   _____
cashier

Illustration 23a — Petty Cash Voucher

SAMPLE PROBLEM

Assume that you are working for Carol Gallo, a designer. On June 1, Ms. Gallo starts a petty cash fund with $50.00 in the petty cash box and places you in charge of the fund. The procedure you would follow as petty cash cashier is explained on the following pages.

Step 1: Prepare the petty cash voucher.

Prepare a petty cash voucher for each payment made from the petty cash fund. Have the voucher signed by the person receiving the money.

On June 4, you gave an employee, John Holder, $3.50 to buy first-aid supplies from the drug store. The voucher would look like this:

PETTY CASH VOUCHER

No. _1_

Date _June 4_ 19____

Pay to _John Holder_ $ ¢

For _first-aid supplies_   3   50

Approved by   Payment Received

_H.B._   _John Holder_
cashier

Illustration 23b — Completed Petty Cash Voucher

Step 2: Attach the bill to the voucher.

When John returns, attach the bill from the drug store to the petty cash voucher you prepared. The bill is additional proof of payment. There are, of course, some petty cash payments where it is impossible to get a bill. For example, if you had given John bus fare to deliver a package, his signature on the petty cash voucher would have been sufficient proof of payment.

Step 3: Check the balance of the fund.

At the end of each day, check the balance in your petty cash box by counting the currency in the box and by finding the total of the petty cash vouchers in the box. If at the end of the first day there were three vouchers in the box totalling $8.00, you should have currency in the amount of $42.00 in the box. Remember, you started with $50.00. The total of the petty cash vouchers plus the cash in the box should equal the original fund of $50.00.

Total of vouchers in box	$ 8.00
plus	
Cash in box	42.00
equals	———
Original fund	$50.00

Step 4: Replenish the fund.

Replenishing the petty cash fund

When the fund is running low, remove all the vouchers from the box, total them, and give them to Ms. Gallo. Ms. Gallo will give you enough money to bring the fund back to $50.00. If these vouchers total $45.00, for example, Ms. Gallo will cash a check for this amount so that you will again have $50.00 in the petty cash fund. Replacing the money spent in this way is called *replenishing the fund*.

PRACTICE PROBLEMS

Problem 1

Frank Booth, a private detective, starts a petty cash fund on September 1 with $80.00 in the petty cash box. He puts you in charge of the fund and instructs you to prepare a petty cash voucher for each of the payments made from the fund. You are to fill in all the information called for on the voucher except the signature.

Directions:

a) Prepare a petty cash voucher for each of the following payments made from the petty cash fund. Start with Voucher #1.

Sept. 4 Paid $2.25 to J. & J. Bros. for a typewriter ribbon.
6 Paid $16.00 to the post office for stamps.
7 Paid $30.00 to Nick DiMarco, the office manager, for entertaining some clients at lunch.
12 Paid $4.80 to Al Berman for taxi fare to deliver a package.
14 Paid $12.60 to David Hecker for waxing the office floor.

b) Now that you have prepared the vouchers, answer the following questions on a sheet of paper. Number your answers carefully.

Original balance
minus
Total of vouchers
equals
Balance of fund

1) How much money has been spent so far?
2) How much money should you have in the petty cash on the morning of September 15? If your answer is $14.35, you are correct.
3) How much money does Mr. Booth have to add to the balance of the fund so that he can again have $80.00 in the petty cash box? (*Reminder:* Restoring the fund to its original balance of $80.00 is called *replenishing the fund*.)
4) How will Mr. Booth get the money to add to the fund?

Problem 2

You started with $75.00 in the petty cash box.

Directions:

a) Fill out a petty cash voucher for each of the following payments made from the petty cash fund. Start with Voucher #1.

> May 1 Paid $24.00 to the post office for stamps.
> 3 Paid $15.65 to Van's Gift Shop for a gift for an employee who was ill.
> 4 Paid $12.60 to Jack Weiss, an employee, for travel expenses.
> 7 Paid $18.00 to Sam Green for repairing an office window.

b) Answer the following questions on a sheet of paper. Number each answer.

Total of vouchers equals amount needed to replenish

1) How much money have you spent so far?
2) How much money is left in the fund on the morning of May 8? If your answer is $4.75, you are correct.
3) How much is needed to replenish the fund — to bring it up to $75.00 again?

Problem 3

You started a petty cash fund with $90.00.

Directions:

a) Fill out a petty cash voucher for each of the following payments made from the fund. Start with Voucher #1.

> Oct. 2 Paid $12.45 to the Fast Freight Co. for a delivery charge.
> 5 Paid $35.00 to the Elkay Service Co. for cleaning the office.
> 10 Paid $16.00 to the post office for stamps.
> 15 Paid $9.75 to Bianco Bros. for file folders.

b) Answer each of the following questions on a sheet of paper. Number each answer.

1) How much money has been spent so far?
2) How much is left in the fund on the morning of October 16? If your answer is $16.80, you are correct.
3) How much is needed to replenish the fund — to bring it up to $90.00 again?

	(1)	(2)	(3)	(4)
Copy and complete the following problems:				
Practicing Related Arithmetic	$2,418.70 − 765.21	$1,014.70 − 462.85	$1,317.52 3,641.88 752.70 2,065.37 + 1,878.19	$1,846.23 1,491.87 915.64 3,783.72 + 674.50

AIM

To learn how to classify business expenses.

EXPLANATION

A person in charge of a petty cash fund pays out money for various business items and prepares a petty cash voucher as a record of each payment.

The businessperson finds it useful to know how much has been spent on various types of business expenses. To learn this, expenses of the same type may be grouped together, or *classified*, under one heading. For example, money spent for pencils, postage, typewriting paper and similar office supplies would be grouped under the heading "Office Expenses." Money spent for wrapping paper, twine, labels, cartons, and similar shipping supplies would be grouped under the heading "Shipping Expenses." There are many group headings or classifications used in business. Some typical ones are:

Office Expenses include office postage and stationery.
Shipping Expenses include wrapping and shipping supplies.
Delivery Expenses include gas, oil, and repairs for the delivery truck; bus and taxi fare for employees making deliveries.
Telephone and Telegraph include the cost of telegrams and telephone calls.
General Expenses include miscellaneous, minor expenses such as washing windows, or first-aid supplies.

Classifying
business
expenses

SAMPLE PROBLEM

At the end of the week you find the petty cash vouchers on page 148 in the petty cash box:

Voucher Number	Paid for	Amount
1	File folders for office	$ 7.30
2	Gas for truck	6.90
3	Repair office window	14.50
4	Postage for office	16.00
5	Taxi fare for delivery	4.25
6	First aid supplies	3.70
7	Repair truck tire	6.50
8	Repair chairs in reception room	21.80
9	Postage for office	8.00

Your employer asks you to find the total amount taken out of the petty cash box and also the total amount spent for each of the following groupings, or to use the business word for groupings, "classifications."

> Office Expenses
> Delivery Expenses
> General Expenses

Using a *Petty Cash Record* is one way of doing this job. Notice that there is a special column in the Petty Cash Record for each classification listed above.

PETTY CASH RECORD

PAID FOR	Vo. No.	Total Payments	Office Expenses	Delivery Expenses	General Expenses
File folders	1	7 30	7 30		
Gas for truck	2	6 90		6 90	
Repair office window	3	14 50			14 50
Postage	4	16 00	16 00		
Taxi fare for delivery	5	4 25		4 25	
First-aid supplies	6	3 70			3 70
Repair truck tire	7	6 50		6 50	
Repair chairs in reception room	8	21 80			21 80
Postage	9	8 00	8 00		
		88 95	31 30	17 65	40 00

Illustration 24 — Petty Cash Record

Follow these steps in completing a petty cash record:

Step 1: Record vouchers in numerical order.

In the petty cash record shown in Illustration 24, the petty cash vouchers were listed in numerical order. The abbreviation "Vo. No." stands for voucher number.

Vo. No. (Voucher Number)

Step 2: Record payments in proper columns.

The amount of each voucher was entered twice on the same line. Look at the entry made in the petty cash record for Voucher #1. First, the $7.30 was recorded in the "Total Payments" column. (All vouchers must be entered in this column, since it is the *total* column.) Then the petty cash clerk had to select one of the expense columns to record the fact that $7.30 was spent for file folders. The petty cash clerk knows that the folders will be used in the office, so $7.30 was entered in the "Office Expenses" column.

Amounts are entered twice on the same line

In the same way, for Voucher #2, the $6.90 spent for gas for the truck was also entered twice: first, in the "Total Payments" column; and second, in the "Delivery Expenses" column.

The petty cash clerk recorded Voucher #3 in the same way. Again, the amount was entered twice and again the clerk had to decide which of the expense columns to use. The clerk used the "General Expenses" column because the $14.50 spent to repair the office window was considered to be a miscellaneous expense. You may wonder why this amount was not recorded in the "Office Expenses" column, since the window was in the office. "Office Expenses" usually mean postage and stationery used in the office.

Notice that two lines were needed in Illustration 24 to write the explanation "Repair chairs in reception room." Whenever possible, use only one line for each explanation. Occasionally, when you *must* use two lines, write the amounts on the second line used for this explanation.

Step 3: Pencil foot all columns.

All columns were pencil footed and the column totals checked *before* the amounts were written in ink. (Remember to use a well-sharpened pencil so that the numbers can be written in small, clear figures.)

Step 4: Check totals by crossfooting.

The total of $88.95 was checked by adding the totals of each expense column.

Total of Office Expenses............................	$31.30
Total of Delivery Expenses	17.65
Total of General Expenses	40.00
Total of Expense columns........................	$88.95

Totals of expense columns equal Total Payments column

Finding errors

If the totals do not agree, the error can be found by:

a) re-adding each column; and

b) making sure that each amount entered in the "Total Payments" column has been extended correctly into one of the expense columns.

Step 5: Record totals in ink and rule them.

Single rule
indicates
addition; double
rule indicates
completed record

After the totals have been checked, they are inked in and single and double rulings are drawn *with a ruler* as shown in the petty cash record. The single ruling shows that all the amounts above this line have been added, and the double ruling shows the inked totals have been checked and that the record has been completed.

Notice that the single ruling is a continuous line through all money columns, beginning after the "Vo. No." column. The double ruling is drawn below all the money columns and also under the "Vo. No." column.

PRACTICE PROBLEMS

Problem 1

Directions:

a) Enter the following petty cash vouchers in a petty cash record. Use the same headings as shown in Illustration 24.

Voucher Number	Paid for	Amount
1	Stationery for office	$12.60
2	Delivery truck repairs	15.50
3	First-aid supplies (General Expenses)	3.00
4	Gas for delivery truck	7.15
5	Stamps for office	8.00
6	Cleaning windows (General Expenses)	23.40
7	Bus fare to deliver package	.70
8	Stamps for office	16.00

b) Pencil foot the columns.
c) Prove that your addition is correct (crossfoot).
d) Record the column totals in ink and rule the petty cash record.

Problem 2

Directions:

a) Enter the petty cash vouchers at the top of page 151 in a petty cash record. Use the same headings as shown in Illustration 24.

Voucher Number	Paid for	Amount
9	Gas for delivery truck	$ 6.30
10	Stamps for office	24.00
11	Envelopes for office	7.25
12	Cleaning supplies (General Expenses)	18.00
13	Taxi fare to deliver package	4.10
14	Typing paper for office	6.40
15	Paper towels (General Expenses)	3.20
16	Delivery truck repairs	15.65

b) Pencil foot the columns.
c) Check totals by crossfooting.
d) Record the column totals in ink and rule the petty cash record.

Problem 3

Directions:
a) Prepare a petty cash record with the following headings:

PAID FOR	Vo. No.	TOTAL PAYMENTS	OFFICE EXPENSES	SHIPPING EXPENSES	DELIVERY EXPENSES	GENERAL EXPENSES

b) Enter the following petty cash vouchers in the petty cash record:

Voucher Number	Paid for	Amount
1	Shipping labels	$ 6.35
2	Stamps for office	24.00
3	Twine for shipping	7.50
4	Repair window (General Expenses)	16.90
5	Typing paper for office	4.90
6	Cartons for shipping	19.80
7	First-aid supplies (General Expenses)	5.25
8	Delivery truck repairs	8.70
9	Gas for delivery truck	11.80
10	Typewriter ribbons (Office Expenses)	7.45

c) Pencil foot the columns.
d) Check totals by crossfooting.
e) Record the column totals in ink and rule the petty cash record.

Problem 4

Directions:
a) Prepare a petty cash record with the same headings shown in Problem 3.
b) Enter the petty cash vouchers on the next page in the petty cash record.

Voucher Number	Paid for	Amount
11	Stationery for office	$14.45
12	Tire for delivery truck	21.60
13	Wrapping paper for shipping	9.80
14	Gas for delivery truck	12.75
15	Envelopes for office	8.35
16	Stamps for office	16.00
17	Paper towels (General Expenses)	4.25
18	Cartons for shipping	17.50
19	Cleaning supplies (General Expenses)	6.10
20	Pencils for office	4.20

c) Pencil foot the columns.

d) Check totals by crossfooting.

e) Record the column totals in ink and rule the petty cash record.

Copy the following problem. Add and crossfoot all columns.

Practicing
Related
Arithmetic

$43.10 + $20.30 + $10.20 = $ _____
14.60 + 12.15 + 31.10 = $ _____
25.72 + 33.34 + 9.30 = $ _____

Totals $ _____ + $ _____ + $ _____ = $ _____

AIM

To learn how to record petty cash vouchers in a *Petty Cash Book*.

EXPLANATION

You have learned that at certain times the businessperson likes to know how much has been spent from the petty cash fund on each type of business item. You know that to get this information a record is made on a form with special columns for various types of payments. In business this record is often kept in a book called a Petty Cash Book. (See Illustration 25a on page 154.) The Petty Cash Book is similar to the petty cash record you used in Job 24. When you compare Illustration 24 on page 148 with Illustration 25a, however, you see several differences. The new form has a date column, a column headed "Receipts," and a column headed "Other Items." The date column is used to record the date of each transaction. The "Receipts" column is used to record any money added to the petty cash fund, amounts which replenish the fund, and also the balance of the fund. You will see how the "Other Items" column is used by studying the sample problem in this job.

Petty Cash Book

SAMPLE PROBLEM

On June 1, your employer cashed check #221 for $60.00 to start a petty cash fund. Listed below are the amounts which were spent from the petty cash fund and the vouchers which were issued.

Date	Voucher Number	Paid For	Amount
June 4	1	Stamps for office	$16.00
7	2	Shipping cartons	24.50
11	3	Paper towels	2.50
13	4	Cleaning supplies	3.00
14	5	Stamps for office	8.00

Here is how these petty cash vouchers would be recorded in a Petty Cash Book:

PETTY CASH BOOK

DATE	EXPLANATION	Vo. No.	RECEIPTS	PAYMENTS	OFFICE EXPENSES	GENERAL EXPENSES	OTHER ITEMS ITEM	AMT.
19-- June 1	Cashed check #221		60 00					
4	Stamps	1		16 00	16 00			
7	Shipping cartons	2		24 50			Shipping expenses	24 50
11	Paper towels	3		2 50		2 50		
13	Cleaning supplies	4		3 00		3 00		
14	Stamps	5		8 00	8 00			
			60 00	54 00	24 00	5 50		24 50
			60 00	54 00	24 00	5 50		24 50
15	Balance		6 00					

Illustration 25a — Petty Cash Book

Step 1: Record the opening balance.

Study the Petty Cash Book shown in Illustration 25a. Notice that before any of the payments were entered, the $60.00 used to start the fund was recorded in the "Receipts" column and "Cashed check #221" was written in the "Explanation" column. Since this was the first entry in the Petty Cash Book, the month, day, and year were written once at the top of the Date column. The complete date will be repeated only when a new page is started or when the year changes.

The month is written only once, in the first of the two columns set aside for the date. The month is written again only when starting a new page or when the month changes. The second of the two columns set aside for the date is used to write the day of the month on which an entry is recorded.

Step 2: Record the payments.

Record amounts twice for each payment

After the petty cash vouchers were arranged in order by voucher numbers, they were entered in the "Payments" column and extended to a second column which showed the type of business expense for which the payment was made. For example, on June 4 the $16.00 spent for stamps was recorded in the "Payments" column. It was recorded again in the "Office Expenses" column because the purchase of stamps is classified under that heading.

Recording the payment of $24.50 for shipping cartons presented a special problem. In Job 24 you learned that shipping cartons are classified under the heading "Shipping Expenses." Since none of the columns in the Petty Cash Book had this heading, it was necessary to use the column "Other Items." In other words, whenever there was no *special column* for a payment, the column "Other Items" was used. Of course, if you continued to make frequent payments for shipping expenses, you would add a column headed "Shipping Expenses" to the Petty Cash Book.

Notice that there are two columns under the heading "Other Items." The first column headed "Item" is for recording the group heading or classification used for a particular type of payment. If you refer to the list of business payments shown on page 147, you will see that payments for shipping cartons are grouped or classified under the heading "Shipping Expenses." That is why you see "Shipping expenses" listed in the "Item" column of the Petty Cash Book when money was spent for shipping cartons. In listing a payment in the "Item" column, you must decide which of the group headings shown on page 147 you are to use. For example, suppose the following payments were made from the petty cash fund:

Date	Voucher Number	Paid for	Amount
June 16	6	Delivery truck repairs	$18.50
18	7	First-aid supplies	4.00
21	8	Wrapping paper for shipping	9.50

Here is how these items would appear in the "Explanation" column and in the money columns of the Petty Cash Book shown on page 154:

PETTY CASH BOOK

DATE	EXPLANATION	Vo. No.	RECEIPTS	PAYMENTS	OFFICE EXPENSES	GENERAL EXPENSES	OTHER ITEMS ITEM	AMT.
16	Truck repairs	6		18 50			Delivery expenses	18 50
18	First-aid supplies	7		4 00		4 00		
21	Wrapping paper	8		9 50			Shipping expenses	9 50

Illustration 25b — Petty Cash Book

Step 3: Pencil foot all columns.

All columns were totaled by using small pencil figures which you can see at the foot of each column. Do you remember why it is a good idea to pencil foot the columns before inking in the totals?

Step 4: Check the totals by crossfooting.

Total of expense
columns equals
total payments

The totals were checked by adding the pencil footings for the columns headed "Office Expenses," "General Expenses," and "Other Items" and comparing this total with the total of the "Payments" column. In other words, it was necessary to do this addition problem:

Total of Office Expenses	$24.00
Total of General Expenses	5.50
Total of Other Items	24.50
Total of Expense columns	$54.00

If the totals had not agreed, then the error could have been found by:

a) re-adding each column; and

b) making sure that every amount entered in the "Payments" column had been repeated or extended correctly into one of the expense columns.

Step 5: Ink in the totals.

After the pencil footings were found to be correct, all the totals were inked in. After the totals were inked in, the Petty Cash Book was ruled by drawing a single line above the totals and a double ruling under the totals. Notice that the double ruling is repeated in the date column and is extended into the "Vo. No." column.

Step 6: Find the new balance.

The new balance of $6.00 was found by doing this following subtraction problem on a scratch pad:

Finding the new
balance

Total of Receipts column	$60.00
Minus total of Payments column	54.00
Equals: new balance	$ 6.00

The balance of $6.00 was recorded in the "Receipts" column, after the double rulings, and dated June 15. This balance of $6.00 must be checked by comparing it with the actual currency in the petty cash box on the morning of June 15.

PRACTICE PROBLEMS

Problem 1

Directions:

a) Prepare a Petty Cash Book with the same headings shown in Illustration 25a on page 154.

b) Record the receipt of $100.00 (cashed check #201) on December 1, 19--, to start the fund.

c) Enter the following petty cash vouchers in the Petty Cash Book:

Date	Voucher Number	Paid for	Amount
Dec. 3	1	Stamps for office	$24.00
7	2	Paper cups (General Expenses)	3.15
8	3	Envelopes for office	13.75
11	4	Wrapping paper (Shipping Expenses)	7.30
14	5	Christmas decorations (General Expenses)	10.00
16	6	Carbon paper for office	7.60
18	7	Towel service (General Expenses)	9.85
21	8	Pencils for office	4.90

d) Pencil foot all columns.

e) Prove your addition by crossfooting.

f) If your totals are correct, ink them in and rule the Petty Cash Book according to the model form shown in Illustration 25a on page 154.

g) Find the new balance and record it in the "Receipts" column on December 22. The new balance should be $19.45.

Total receipts minus total payments equals new balance

Problem 2

Directions:

a) Prepare a Petty Cash Book with the same headings shown in Illustration 25a on page 154.

b) Record the receipt of $150.00 (cashed check #411) on May 1, 19--, to start the fund.

c) Record the following petty cash vouchers in the Petty Cash Book:

Date	Voucher Number	Paid for	Amount
May 2	1	Cleaning supplies (General Expenses)	$ 6.35
4	2	Typing paper for office	12.40
7	3	Twine for shipping	8.75
8	4	Stamps for office	32.00
10	5	Paper towels (General Expenses)	4.55
11	6	Repair delivery truck	27.90
14	7	Waxing office floors (General Expenses)	18.70
16	8	Stamps for office	16.00

d) Pencil foot all columns and check addition by crossfooting.

e) Ink in totals and rule the Petty Cash Book.

f) Enter the new balance in the "Receipts" column on May 17. The new balance should be $23.35.

Problem 3

Directions:

a) Prepare a Petty Cash Book with the following headings:

DATE	EXPLANATION	Vo. No.	RECEIPTS	PAYMENTS	DELIVERY EXPENSES	GENERAL EXPENSES	OTHER ITEMS	
							ITEM	AMT.

b) Record the receipt of $125.00 (cashed check #215) on July 1, 19--, to start the fund.

c) Enter the following petty cash vouchers in the Petty Cash Book:

Date	Voucher Number	Paid for	Amount
July 3	1	Tire for delivery truck	$29.30
6	2	Cleaning office (General Expenses)	18.00
9	3	Memo pads for office	8.50
16	4	Gas for delivery truck	11.65
18	5	Repair water cooler (General Expenses)	12.40
21	6	Tape for office	3.15
27	7	Paper cups (General Expenses)	2.85
31	8	License for truck	34.00

d) Pencil foot all columns and check addition by crossfooting.

e) Ink in totals and rule the Petty Cash Book.

f) Enter the new balance in the "Receipts" column on August 1. The new balance should be $5.15.

Problem 4

Directions:

a) Prepare a Petty Cash Book with the same headings used in Problem 3.

b) Record the receipt of $120.00 (cashed check #161) on March 1, 19--, to start the fund.

c) Enter the following petty cash vouchers in the Petty Cash Book:

Date	Voucher Number	Paid for	Amount
March 5	1	Windshield wipers for truck	$ 8.00
8	2	Wax office floors (General Expenses)	10.70
12	3	Shipping labels	5.65
15	4	First aid supplies (General Expenses)	8.25
19	5	Repairs on delivery truck	29.85
23	6	Service typewriters (Office Expenses)	17.00
28	7	Gas for delivery truck	9.40
30	8	Bulbs for ceiling lamps (General Expenses)	12.60

d) Pencil foot all columns and check addition by crossfooting.

e) Ink in totals and rule the Petty Cash Book.

f) Enter the new balance in the "Receipts" column on April 1. The new balance should be $18.55.

Practicing Related Arithmetic

Copy the following problem. Add and crossfoot all columns.

$41.60	+ $30.20	+ $14.10	= $	
14.50	+ 21.50	+ 33.70	= $	
26.40	+ 45.60	+ 15.80	= $	_____
Totals $ ____	+ $ ____	+ $ ____	= $	_____

AIM

To gain more experience in recording information in the Petty Cash Book from petty cash vouchers.

EXPLANATION

It is important to remember that information recorded in the Petty Cash Book does not come from a written list of payments but is taken from the actual petty cash vouchers that were prepared as each payment was made. As a petty cash cashier, you probably would not stop after each voucher to record the information in the Petty Cash Book. Instead, you would follow the more sensible practice of waiting until you had a number of vouchers before recording them in the Petty Cash Book.

In this job you will practice recording information in the Petty Cash Book from the vouchers themselves. You will also practice using Petty Cash Books with special headings for different types of businesses. This practice is important because different types of businesses will require different headings in the Petty Cash Book.

PRACTICE PROBLEMS

Problem 1

Nick Gatti runs a long distance moving and storage business. He keeps a petty cash fund for miscellaneous expenses and to reimburse drivers for emergency expenses they may have to pay while on the road. On May 1, Mr. Gatti has $135.00 in the petty cash box. He asks you to record the petty cash vouchers in a Petty Cash Book.

Directions:
a) Prepare a Petty Cash Book with the following headings:

DATE	EXPLANATION	Vo. No.	RECEIPTS	PAYMENTS	TRIP EXPENSES	VAN EXPENSES	OTHER ITEMS	
							ITEM	AMT.

b) Enter the balance of $135.00 in the "Receipts" column as of May 1. Here are the vouchers you find in the petty cash box:

No. 1 Date *May 2, 19--*			No. 2 Date *May 4, 19--*		
Paid to *G. Wood*	$	¢	Paid to *E. Hoerig*	$	¢
For *Tolls & meals*	24	50	For *Align van wheels*	16	05
U.R.S. *G. Wood*			U.R.S. *E. Hoerig*		
No. 3 Date *May 7, 19--*			No. 4 Date *May 10, 19--*		
Paid to *Roxy Uniforms*	$	¢	Paid to *G. Wood*	$	¢
For *Laundry service*	10	70	For *Tolls & meals*	14	25
U.R.S. *K. Roxy*			U.R.S. *G. Wood*		
No. 5 Date *May 11, 19--*			No. 6 Date *May 14, 19--*		
Paid to *E. Hoerig*	$	¢	Paid to *Miller Supplies Inc.*	$	¢
For *Gas for van*	12	80	For *Office stationery*	8	10
U.R.S. *E. Hoerig*			U.R.S. *J. J. Miller*		
No. 7 Date *May 15, 19--*			No. 8 Date *May 16, 19--*		
Paid to *Carlin Co.*	$	¢	Paid to *E. Hoerig*	$	¢
For *Cleaning windows*	17	00	For *Gas for van*	19	15
U.R.S. *T. Carlin*			U.R.S. *E. Hoerig*		

c) On May 16, you record in the Petty Cash Book the petty cash vouchers issued from May 1 to May 16. You are instructed to record payments in the different columns as follows:

Trip Expenses

Vouchers for meals for drivers while on the road and vouchers for bridge and road tolls.

Van Expenses

Vouchers for emergency repairs of vans or gas purchases for vans while on the road.

Other Items

All other vouchers such as:
>waxing office floors (General Expenses)
>cleaning office windows (General Expenses)
>laundry for uniforms and towels (Laundry Expenses)
>stationery and stamps (Office Expenses)
>telephone calls from pay stations (Telephone Expenses)

d) Pencil foot, ink in totals, and rule the Petty Cash Book. (Did you prove that the totals were correct by crossfooting?)

e) Enter the May 17 balance in the "Receipts" column. The new balance should be $12.45.

Receipts minus payments equals balance

Problem 2

Directions:

a) Open a Petty Cash Book for George Bailey who operates a moving and storage business. Copy the headings used in Problem 1. Review the instructions given in Problem 1 for classifying the various items. Here are the vouchers you find in the petty cash box:

No. 1 Date Oct. 4, 19--	No. 2 Date Oct. 5, 19--
Paid to M. Ahern $ ¢	Paid to H. Webb $ ¢
For Gas for van 12 40	For Tolls and meals 21 90
S.M.B. M. Ahern	S.M.B. H. Webb
No. 3 Date Oct. 9, 19--	No. 4 Date Oct. 10, 19--
Paid to J. Levy $ ¢	Paid to M. Ahern $ ¢
For Stamps for office 16 00	For Repair van tire 7 60
S.M.B. J. Levy	S.M.B. M. Ahern
No. 5 Date Oct. 15, 19--	No. 6 Date Oct. 16, 19--
Paid to H. Webb $ ¢	Paid to S. Kelly $ ¢
For Outside telephone calls 4 15	For Waxing office floors 15 50
S.M.B. H. Webb	S.M.B. S. Kelly
No. 7 Date Oct. 18, 19--	No. 8 Date Oct. 19, 19--
Paid to M. Ahern $ ¢	Paid to H. Webb $ ¢
For Gas for van 18 30	For Tolls and meals 12 75
S.M.B. M. Ahern	S.M.B. H. Webb

b) Enter the balance of $120.00 in the "Receipts" column as of October 1.
c) From the information appearing on the petty cash vouchers on page 161, complete the record in the Petty Cash Book.
d) Pencil foot, ink in the totals, and rule the Petty Cash Book.
e) Find the new balance and enter it in the "Receipts" column as of October 20. The new balance should be $11.40.

Problem 3

Harry Regan owns a pizza parlor. He keeps a petty cash fund for miscellaneous expenses and emergency purchases. On January 1, Mr. Regan has $100.00 in the petty cash fund. He asks you to record the petty cash vouchers in a Petty Cash Book.

Directions:
a) Prepare a Petty Cash Book with the following headings:

DATE	EXPLANATION	Vo. No.	RECEIPTS	PAYMENTS	KITCHEN EXPENSES	MAINTENANCE EXPENSES	OTHER ITEMS	
							ITEM	AMT.

b) Enter the balance of $100.00 in the "Receipts" column as of January 1.
c) On January 17 you record in the Petty Cash Book the petty cash vouchers issued from January 1 to January 17. You are instructed to record payments in the different columns as follows:

Kitchen Expenses

Vouchers for repairs of kitchen and cooking equipment; also, vouchers for the purchase of sponges, steel wool, cleaning powders, and similar supplies used in the kitchen.

Maintenance Expenses

Vouchers for cleaning and waxing the floor; washing and repairing windows; repairing chairs, tables, and counters; and vouchers for keeping the parking lot in good condition.

Other Items

All other vouchers such as:

stationery (Office Expenses)
laundry service (Laundry Expenses)
signs and advertisements (Advertising)

Here are the vouchers you find in the petty cash box:

No. 1 Date *Jan. 3, 19—*			No. 2 Date *Jan. 5, 19—*		
Paid to *Kay Supply House*	$	¢	Paid to *M. G. Corp.*	$	¢
For *Steel wool for kitchen*	6	15	For *Repair stove*	14	00
K.S.K. *Kay Supply House*			K.S.K. *M. G. Corp.*		

No. 3 Date *Jan. 8, 19—*			No. 4 Date *Jan. 10, 19—*		
Paid to *L. Jones*	$	¢	Paid to *The Bugle*	$	¢
For *Waxing floor*	11	60	For *Newspaper advertise-ment*	16	50
K.S.K. *L. Jones*			K.S.K. *S. Brown*		

No. 5 Date *Jan. 12, 19—*			No. 6 Date *Jan. 15, 19—*		
Paid to *M. Dobler*	$	¢	Paid to *S. Gelber*	$	¢
For *Repair coffee urn*	18	70	For *Snow removal parking lot*	10	70
K.S.K. *M. Dobler*			K.S.K. *S. Gelber*		

No. 7 Date *Jan. 16, 19—*			No. 8 Date *Jan. 17, 19—*		
Paid to *Klein Laundry*	$	¢	Paid to *L. C. Stores*	$	¢
For *Laundry service*	12	80	For *Envelopes for office*	4	40
K.S.K. *R. Klein*			K.S.K. *L. C. Smith*		

d) Pencil foot, ink in the totals, and rule the Petty Cash Book.

e) Find the new balance, and enter it in the "Receipts" column as of January 18. The new balance should be $5.15.

Problem 4

Directions:

a) Open a Petty Cash Book for Helen Marcus who operates a steak house. Copy the same headings used in Problem 3. Review the instructions given in Problem 3 for classifying the various items.

b) Enter the balance of $130.00 in the "Receipts" column as of March 1.

c) From the information appearing on the petty cash vouchers on page 164, complete the record in the Petty Cash Book.

No. 1 Date *March 3, 19--*			No. 2 Date *March 6, 19--*		
Paid to *Ford Supplies*	$	¢	Paid to *J. K. Paving Co.*	$	¢
For *Sponges for kitchen*	4	80	For *Repair parking lot*	30	00
R.M.H. *A. Ford*			R.M.H. *J. K. Gallo*		
No. 3 Date *March 7, 19--*			No. 4 Date *March 9, 19--*		
Paid to *Orient Laundry*	$	¢	Paid to *Bay Cleaning Co.*	$	¢
For *Laundry service*	14	30	For *Washing windows*	16	50
R.M.H. *H. King*			R.M.H. *M. Jones*		
No. 5 Date *March 12, 19--*			No. 6 Date *March 13, 19--*		
Paid to *J. Sert*	$	¢	Paid to *M. & M. Stationers*	$	¢
For *Display signs*	15	00	For *Typing paper*	9	80
R.M.H. *J. Sert*			R.M.H. *M. Morris*		
No. 7 Date *March 15, 19--*			No. 8 Date *March 16, 19--*		
Paid to *D. Palk*	$	¢	Paid to *Ford Supplies*	$	¢
For *Repair kitchen oven*	19	70	For *Cleaning supplies for kitchen*	7	75
R.M.H. *D. Palk*			R.M.H. *A. Ford*		

d) Pencil foot, ink in the totals, and rule the Petty Cash Book.

e) Find the new balance, and enter it in the "Receipts" column as of March 17. The new balance should be $12.15.

Practicing Related Arithmetic

Copy and answer the following problems:

1) 28 × \$.50 = \$ _____   5) 41 × \$.25 = \$ _____
2) 30 × \$.25 = \$ _____   6) 129 × \$.10 = \$ _____
3) 65 × \$.10 = \$ _____   7) 76 × \$.05 = \$ _____
4) 23 × \$.05 = \$ _____   8) 317 × \$.01 = \$ _____

AIM

To gain additional experience in keeping petty cash records and to learn how to continue the Petty Cash Book after the fund has been replenished.

EXPLANATION

In this job you will practice using a Petty Cash Book for more than one month for the same business. In the illustration below notice particularly how the balance of the previous month is used as the starting figure for the next month. Also notice how the check cashed to replenish the fund is recorded. At the end of the month when the Petty Cash Book is pencil footed the two amounts in the Receipts column will add up to the original balance of the fund of \$100.00.

PETTY CASH BOOK

DATE	EXPLANATION	Vo. No.	RECEIPTS	PAYMENTS	TRIP EXPENSES	VAN EXPENSES	OTHER ITEMS	
							ITEM	AMT.
19— Dec. 1	Balance		2 70					
1	Cashed check #536		97 30					

Balance of previous month   Check to replenish

Illustration 27 — A Petty Cash Book

PRACTICE PROBLEMS

Problem 1

Mr. Curtis, the owner of the OK Equipment Co., started a petty cash fund on November 1 by cashing check #461 for \$100.00.

Directions:

a) Record the opening balance of $100.00 in a Petty Cash Book with the following columns:

DATE	EXPLANATION	Vo. No.	RECEIPTS	PAYMENTS	GENERAL EXPENSES	OFFICE EXPENSES	DELIVERY EXPENSES	OTHER ITEMS	
								ITEM	AMT.

b) Record the vouchers which were issued during the month of November:

Date	Voucher Number	Paid for	Amount
Nov. 5	1	Stamps for office use	$16.00
8	2	Repair door lock (General Expenses)	12.70
12	3	Gas for delivery truck	9.15
14	4	Shipping cartons (Shipping Expenses)	18.60
19	5	Adding machine tape for office	6.50
23	6	Repair delivery truck	21.80
28	7	Paper towels (General Expenses)	4.20
30	8	Envelopes for office use	8.35

c) Pencil foot all columns and check addition by crossfooting.

d) Ink in the totals and rule the Petty Cash Book.

Total receipts minus total payments equals new balance

e) Enter the new balance in the "Receipts" Column on December 1. The new balance should be $2.70.

f) How much money should be added to the fund to bring it up to its original balance of $100.00?

Problem 2

On December 1, Mr. Curtis cashed check #536 for $97.30 to replenish the petty cash fund as a result of the payments made in November.

Directions:

a) Continue using the same Petty Cash Book used in Problem 1 by copying the same headings on a new page and by copying the December 1 balance of $2.70 on the first line in the "Receipts" column.

b) Record the $97.30 in the "Receipts" column. Compare your work with Illustration 27 on page 165. Notice that the $97.30 when added to the starting balance of December 1 of $2.70 equals the original fund of $100. (If you counted the money in the petty cash box at this time, what amount would you expect to find?)

c) Record the following vouchers issued during December:

Date	Voucher Number	Paid for	Amount
Dec. 3	9	Stationery for office use	$ 7.10
7	10	Gas for delivery truck	6.85
14	11	Removal of rubbish (General Expenses)	12.50
17	12	Calendars for customers (Advertising)	24.20

Dec. 26	13	Stamps for office use	8.00
27	14	Repair truck tire	5.90
28	15	Repair time clock (General Expenses)	9.40
31	16	Carbon paper for office use	3.00

d) Pencil foot, ink in totals, and rule the Petty Cash Book.

e) Enter the new balance in the "Receipts" column on January 1. Your new balance should be $23.05.

Problem 3

On January 1, Mr. Curtis asks you to compare your Petty Cash Book balance with the actual currency in the petty cash box. On January 1, your Petty Cash Book shows a balance of $23.05, and the petty cash box contains the cash listed below:

> 3 — $5 bills
> 2 — $1 bills
> 5 — half dollars
> 19 — dimes
> 25 — nickels
> 40 — pennies

Directions: Answer the following questions on a sheet of paper.

a) What is the total amount of money in the petty cash box?

b) Copy and complete the following form:

Balance in petty cash box	$_____
Balance recorded in Petty Cash Book	_____
Short or over (cross one out)	$_____

Problem 4

Mr. Stone, the owner of an auto supply shop, started a petty cash fund on May 1 by cashing check #401 for $90.00.

Directions:

a) Enter the opening balance of $90.00 in a Petty Cash Book with the following columns:

DATE	EXPLANATION	Vo. No.	RECEIPTS	PAYMENTS	OFFICE EXPENSES	DELIVERY EXPENSES	OTHER ITEMS	
							ITEM	AMT.

b) Enter the vouchers below and on page 168 which were issued during the month of May:

Date	Voucher Number	Paid for	Amount
May 2	1	Pencils for office use	$ 2.25
7	2	Gas for delivery truck	7.30
10	3	Stamps for office use	8.00

May 14	4	Paper cups (General Expenses)	1.90
17	5	Replace truck windshield wipers	8.70
22	6	Rubbish removal (General Expenses)	15.00
29	7	Typing paper	12.45
31	8	Ad in school paper (Advertising)	20.00

c) Pencil foot all columns and check addition by crossfooting.
d) Ink in totals and rule the Petty Cash Book.
e) Enter the new balance in the "Receipts" column on June 1. The new balance should be $14.40.
f) How much money does Mr. Stone have to add to the fund to bring it up to its original balance of $90.00?

Total payments equals amount needed to replenish fund

Problem 5

On June 1, Mr. Stone cashed check #491 for $75.60 to replenish the petty cash fund as a result of the payments made in May.

Directions:
a) Continue using the same Petty Cash Book used in Problem 4 by copying the same headings on a new page and by copying the June 1 balance of $14.40 on the first line of the "Receipts" column.
b) Enter the $75.60 on the second line in the "Receipts" column. See Illustration 27 on page 165 as a guide. Notice that the $75.60, when added to the June 1 starting balance of $14.40, equals the original fund of $90.00.
c) Enter the following vouchers issued during the month of June:

Date	Voucher Number	Paid for	Amount
June 4	9	File folders for office	$ 3.60
8	10	Replace truck headlight	14.50
12	11	Repair light switch (General Expenses)	6.25
18	12	Stamps for office use	16.00
21	13	Twine for packages (Shipping Expenses)	4.10
25	14	Gas for delivery truck	5.50
28	15	Rubber bands for office use	2.15
29	16	Taxi fare for delivery (Delivery Expenses)	4.75

d) Pencil foot, ink in totals, and rule the Petty Cash Book.
e) Enter the new balance in the "Receipts" column on July 1. The new balance should be $33.15.

Problem 6

On July 1, Mr. Stone asks you to compare your Petty Cash Book balance with the actual currency in the petty cash box. On July 1, the Petty Cash Book shows a balance of $33.15 and the petty cash box contains the following:

> 3 — $5 bills
> 12 — $1 bills
> 5 — half dollars
> 27 — dimes
> 13 — nickels
> 30 — pennies

Directions:
a) Find the total amount of money in the petty cash box.
b) Copy and complete the following form:

Balance in petty cash box $_____
Balance recorded in Petty Cash Book   _____
Short or over (cross one out) $_____

Problem 7

On September 30, the Petty Cash Book of the Rainey Co. shows a balance of $41.70. At the same time, the petty cash box contains the currency listed below:

> 4 — $5 bills
> 10 — $1 bills
> 11 — half dollars
> 9 — quarters
> 23 — dimes
> 31 — nickels
> 30 — pennies

Directions:
a) Find the total amount of money in the petty cash box.
b) Copy and complete the following form:

Balance in petty cash box $_____
Balance recorded in Petty Cash Book   _____
Short or over (cross one out) $_____

Problem 8

On July 31, the Petty Cash Book of the Savoy Co. shows a balance of $38.60. At the same time the petty cash box contains the currency listed below:

> 3 — $5 bills
> 8 — $1 bills
> 20 — half dollars
> 11 — quarters
> 15 — dimes
> 12 — nickels
> 15 — pennies

Directions:

a) Find the total amount of money in the petty cash box.

b) Copy and complete the following form:

Balance in petty cash box $_____

Balance recorded in Petty Cash Book   _____

Short or over (cross one out) $_____

UNIT 5

RECORD KEEPING FOR STUDENTS AND FAMILIES

UNIT 5

JOB 28 | KEEPING PERSONAL RECORDS OF INCOME AND EXPENSES

Practicing Related Arithmetic

Copy these problems on a sheet of paper and find the answers. (Crossfoot and then add down.)

1) $ 4.55 + $ 8.00 + $ 9.75 + $ 7.00 = $_____
2)   6.75 +   5.25 +   4.00 +   2.50 = $_____
3) 11.30 + 10.70 +   6.55 +   8.60 = $_____
4) 14.25 + 21.65 + 45.40 + 31.85 = $_____

5) $_____ + $_____ + $_____ + $_____ = $_____

AIM

1. To learn the importance of keeping a budget.

2. To learn how budgets are prepared.

3. To learn how to keep a simple record of one's receipts of income and payments of expenses.

EXPLANATION

Each week many of you receive an allowance from your parents to meet your school and personal needs.

"Ever hear of a budget?"

Some of you have spent your allowance within a few days and are waiting impatiently for the next week's allowance. Others try to get an advance from their parents or attempt to borrow from friends who have been a bit wiser in their spending habits.

Occasionally, some of you stop to ask yourselves the disturbing question, "Where did my money go?" Then you try to figure out, rather unsuccessfully, what has happened to your money.

Do not get the impression that the important problem of trying to make your allowance take care of your expenses is something that only youth has to face. Parents have to meet the same problem. However, most of them learn how to do this by *careful advance planning*.

Most parents know approximately what their income will be each week. They are aware that their income must be distributed so that there is enough to provide for food, clothing, shelter, recreation, education, savings, gifts, charitable contributions, health, transportation, and taxes.

Living within a budget

When people plan in advance how to spend their money, we say that they are *living within a budget*. Naturally, the incomes of different people vary. Therefore, individuals plan their savings and expenses in line with their own earnings.

When people budget their income, they must keep records of their income and expenses so that they can compare the amounts spent with the amounts they had planned to spend. They do this to see if they are really living within their budgets and to see if their estimates were practical.

To learn how these records are kept, you will first keep the records of a student who has planned to budget an allowance and then in later jobs you will learn how to keep the records for an entire family.

SAMPLE PROBLEM

Ted Evans, a high school student, is given an allowance of $10.00 weekly which is to cover all his expenses except clothing. Ted decides to budget his allowance so he can meet his needs without overspending on one item to the neglect of others. Here is how he would do this:

Step 1: Estimate the receipts.

Ted knows that he can depend on getting the allowance of $10.00 a week from his parents. He also feels confident that he can earn about $5.00 a week by doing small jobs for his neighbors like mowing lawns in the summer or shoveling snow in the winter or doing some errands. Therefore, Ted feels that he can count on *receipts* of $15.00 a week.

Weekly allowance	=	$10.00
Additional estimated income	=	$ 5.00
Total estimated receipts	=	$15.00

Step 2: Estimate the payments.

Ted now makes a list of the payments that he can reasonably expect to make during a week. His list would look like this:

Carfare
Lunches
School expenses
Entertainment and recreation
Savings
Gifts and contributions

Notice that Ted has included the item "Savings." Ted knows that a wise and careful person takes part of his income and puts it into a savings account for two very important reasons:

A thrifty person provides for savings

1) An unexpected emergency
2) An expected large payment in the future

Ted has heard of the heavy expenses he will have in his senior year, and he wants to be prepared for them. Therefore, he is starting early in his school career to meet future needs. After Ted has made his list of expenses, he figures out how much he will need for each item.

Ted's final estimate appears as follows:

Item	Estimate for a Week
Carfare	$ 3.00
Lunches	3.75
School Expenses	1.00
Entertainment & Recreation	4.50
Savings	2.00
Gifts & Contributions	.75
Total estimated payments	$15.00

Step 3: Record all actual receipts and payments.

In order to keep a detailed record of what he receives and pays out, Ted rules a sheet of loose leaf paper to look like this:

RECEIPTS AND PAYMENTS			
DATE	EXPLANATION	RECEIPTS	PAYMENTS

Illustration 28a — Headings for a Budget

Ted had receipts and payments as follows during the week beginning Monday, December 1, 19--:

Dec. 1   Received an allowance of $10.00 for the week.

1   Paid 50¢ for carfare, 75¢ for lunch.

2   Paid 50¢ for carfare, 70¢ for lunch, 75¢ for school supplies, 40¢ for a magazine.

3   Paid 50¢ for carfare, 80¢ for lunch. Earned $6.00 shoveling snow.

4   Paid 50¢ for carfare, 65¢ for lunch, $1.00 for class dues, 15¢ for a newspaper; put $2.00 in the bank.

5   Paid 50¢ for carfare, 85¢ for lunch.

6   Paid 35¢ for a birthday card, $1.50 for movies, 40¢ for popcorn.

7   Gave 50¢ as a church contribution and paid $1.25 for admission to a football game.

Ted's completed record is illustrated below. Examine this record carefully so that you can prepare a Record of Receipts and Payments similar to it.

RECEIPTS AND PAYMENTS

DATE		EXPLANATION	RECEIPTS	PAYMENTS
Dec. 19—	1	Allowance for week	10 00	
	1	Carfare		50
	1	Lunch		75
	2	Carfare		50
	2	Lunch		70
	2	School supplies		75
	2	Magazine		40
	3	Carfare		50
	3	Lunch		80
	3	Shoveling snow	6 00	
	4	Carfare		50
	4	Lunch		65
	4	Class dues		1 00
	4	Newspaper		15
	4	Savings-bank		2 00
	5	Carfare		50
	5	Lunch		85
	6	Birthday card		35
	6	Movies		1 50
	6	Popcorn		40
	7	Church contribution		50
	7	Football game		1 25
			16 00	14 55
			16 00	14 55
	8	Balance of Cash	1 45	

Only one line is used for year, month, day

Receipts — Payments =

Illustration 28b — Record of Receipts and Payments for a Student

Date Columns — Notice that Ted followed the usual business practice for recording dates, just the way you learned in the Petty Cash Unit. Notice, too, that it is customary to use only one line to record the year and month.

Of course, when there was more than one receipt or payment on the same day, Ted repeated the date of the month. That is the reason you see the number "1" repeated three times on December 1.

Explanation Column — This gives Ted enough room to explain each entry. For example, he can now read that on December 1 he got his allowance for the week.

Receipts Column — Ted enters all receipts in this column. Looking down the column, he can see that he received money on two different days during the week.

Payments Column — Ted enters the amount of each individual payment in this column. Notice that a new line is used for each payment.

Step 4: Rule the book at the end of the week.

If Ted has kept his records accurately, the amount of cash he actually has left at the end of the week ($1.45) should equal the answer he gets for this simple arithmetic problem:

Total receipts:	$16.00
minus	
Total payments:	14.55
equals	
Total cash remaining:	$ 1.45
(Balance on hand)	

To show this in his records, Ted follows these steps:

a) He rules a line under the *Receipts* and *Payments* columns. This means he is ready to add each money column.

b) He pencil foots each column. Do you remember why it is a good idea to pencil foot the columns before inking in the totals? The figures are entered in pencil so Ted can erase easily if he finds he added incorrectly.

c) He inks in the totals. Once Ted has re-added his pencil totals and has found them correct, he enters the totals in ink.

d) He rules a double line across the *Date* and *Money* columns. This shows that he has checked his work and found it correct and complete.

e) He records the new balance. To show the amount of cash he has on hand to begin the next week, Ted enters "8" in the *Date* column, writes "Balance of Cash" in the *Explanation* column, and enters $1.45 in the *Receipts* column.

Step 5: Compare the budget with the actual receipts and payments.

It is now possible for Ted to see how much has been spent for carfare, lunches, school expenses, entertainment and recreation, savings, and gifts and contributions by examining his *Record of Receipts and Payments*. For instance, Ted can find out how much he spent for carfare by adding together all the payments labeled *carfare*. He does this and finds he spent $2.50 for carfare. He repeats this arithmetic problem for each classification in his budget. He discovers that the $14.55 he actually spent was divided as shown below.

Carfare	$ 2.50
Lunches	3.75
School expenses	1.75
Entertainment and recreation	3.70
Savings	2.00
Gifts and contributions	.85
Total payments	$14.55

Ted is now ready to compare his actual receipts and payments with the budget figures he had estimated in advance.

This is how the comparison would look:

	Estimated	Actual
Receipts	$15.00	$16.00
Payments:		
Carfare	3.00	2.50
Lunches	3.75	3.75
School Expenses	1.00	1.75
Entertainment & Recreation	4.50	3.70
Savings	2.00	2.00
Gifts & Contributions	.75	.85
Total	$15.00	$14.55

Ted can now decide whether he is living within his budget. He can also decide whether he has to change his estimated budget amounts.

Since you have seen how Ted keeps a record of his receipts and payments, see if you can do the same in the following practice problems.

PRACTICE PROBLEMS

Problem 1

Wendy Meyers, a high school student, estimates her receipts and payments for the week as follows:

Estimated Receipts		Estimated Payments	
From allowance	$ 9.00	Carfare	$ 3.00
From possible earnings	4.00	Lunches	3.50
		School expenses	1.50
		Entertainment and recreation	3.00
		Savings	1.50
		Gifts and contributions	.50
Total estimated receipts	$13.00	Total estimated payments	$13.00

In order to compare her estimated receipts and payments with the actual receipts and payments for the week, Wendy decides to keep a Record of Receipts and Payments as shown in Illustration 28b on page 176.

Directions:

a) Rule a sheet of paper like the one shown in Illustration 28b.

b) Record the following receipts and payments made during the week beginning Monday, April 14, 19--:

April 14   Received an allowance of $9.00 for the week.
  14   Paid 60¢ for carfare, 75¢ for lunch, 35¢ for a notebook.
  15   Paid 60¢ for carfare, 65¢ for lunch, 15¢ for a newspaper.
  16   Paid 60¢ for carfare, 70¢ for lunch, $1.00 for roller skating.
  17   Paid 60¢ for carfare, 80¢ for lunch, 75¢ for school dues. Earned $4.50 by baby sitting.
  18   Paid 60¢ for carfare, 55¢ for lunch; put $1.00 in the bank.
  19   Paid 60¢ for carfare, $1.25 admission to a movie, 25¢ for candy.
  20   Paid 30¢ as a church contribution, 45¢ for ice cream.

Enter the amount of each receipt and each payment

c) Rule the book and enter the totals for each column.

d) Find the new balance and record it in the Receipts column. If your work is correct, the new balance should be $.95.

e) Answer the following questions on a sheet of paper:
   1) What amount was spent for carfare?
   2) Did Wendy spend *more* or *less* for carfare than she had estimated? How much?
   3) What amount was spent for lunches?
   4) Did Wendy spend *more* or *less* for lunches than she had estimated? How much?
   5) What amount was spent for entertainment and recreation? (Include newspapers, magazines, and refreshments with payments for entertainment and recreation.)
   6) Did Wendy spend *more* or *less* for entertainment and recreation than she had estimated? How much?
   7) What amount was put in the savings bank?
   8) Did Wendy put *more* or *less* in the savings bank than she had estimated? How much?
   9) What amount was spent for gifts and contributions?
   10) Did Wendy spend *more* or *less* for gifts and contributions than she had estimated? How much?
   11) Did Wendy receive *more* or *less* income than she had estimated? How much?

Problem 2

Tony Demeo, a high school student, estimated his receipts and payments for a week as shown on page 180.

Estimated Receipts		Estimated Payments	
From allowance	$ 7.50	Carfare	$ 2.25
From possible earnings	5.00	Lunches	2.75
		School expenses	.50
		Entertainment and recreation	3.50
		Savings	2.50
		Gifts and contributions	1.00
Total estimated receipts	$12.50	Total estimated payments	$12.50

In order to compare his estimated receipts and payments with the actual receipts and payments for the week, Tony decided to keep a Record of Receipts and Payments as shown in Illustration 28b on page 176.

Directions:
a) Rule a sheet of paper like the one shown in Illustration 28b.
b) Record the following receipts and payments made during the week beginning on Monday, Sept. 22, 19––:

Sept. 22   Received an allowance of $7.50 for the week.
   22   Paid 45¢ carfare, 55¢ for lunch, 10¢ for a newspaper.
   23   Paid 45¢ carfare, 60¢ for lunch, 85¢ for a ticket to the school concert. Earned $3.75 for delivering packages.
   24   Paid 45¢ carfare, 70¢ for lunch, 65¢ for school supplies.
   25   Paid 45¢ carfare, 50¢ for lunch; put $2.00 in the bank.
   26   Paid 45¢ carfare, 40¢ for lunch, 25¢ for a donation to the Red Cross.
   27   Paid 45¢ carfare, $1.00 for a movie, 35¢ for candy.
   28   Paid 25¢ as a church contribution.

c) Rule the book and enter the totals for each column.
d) Find the new balance and record it in the receipts column. If your work is correct, the new balance should be $.35.
e) Answer the following questions on a sheet of paper.
   1) What amount was spent for carfare?
   2) Did Tony spend *more* or *less* for carfare than he had estimated? How much?
   3) What amount was spent for lunches?
   4) Did Tony spend *more* or *less* for lunches than he had estimated? How much?
   5) What amount was spent for entertainment and recreation?
   6) Did Tony spend *more* or *less* for entertainment and recreation than he had estimated? How much?
   7) What amount was put in the savings bank?
   8) Did Tony put *more* or *less* in the savings bank than he had estimated? How much?
   9) What amount was spent for gifts and contributions?
   10) Did Tony spend *more* or *less* for gifts and contributions than he had estimated? How much?

11) Did Tony receive *more* or *less* income than he had estimated? How much?

Problem 3

Ed James, a high school student, estimated his receipts and payments for a week as follows:

Estimated Receipts		**Estimated Payments**	
From allowance	$11.00	Carfare	$ 2.75
From possible earnings	5.00	Lunches	3.00
		School expenses	.75
		Entertainment and	
		recreation	5.00
		Savings	3.00
		Gifts and contributions	1.50
Total estimated		Total estimated	
receipts	$16.00	payments	$16.00

In order to compare his estimates with the actual receipts and payments for the week, Ed decides to keep a Record of Receipts and Payments as shown in Illustration 28b on page 176.

Directions:
a) Rule a sheet of paper like the one shown in Illustration 28b.
b) Record the following receipts and payments made during the week beginning Monday, Nov. 17, 19––:

Nov. 17 Received an allowance of $11.00 for the week.
17 Paid 55¢ for carfare, 65¢ for lunch, 40¢ for a notebook.
18 Earned $3.50 delivering packages. Paid 55¢ carfare, 80¢ for lunch, 75¢ for school dues, $1.75 for a gift.
19 Paid 55¢ carfare, 45¢ for lunch, 35¢ for a magazine.
20 Earned $2.75 delivering packages. Paid 55¢ carfare, 70¢ for lunch, 30¢ for a birthday card.
21 Paid 55¢ carfare, 50¢ for lunch; put $3.00 in the savings bank.
22 Paid $1.75 for a movie, 55¢ for ice cream.
23 Paid $2.00 for a ticket to a concert.

c) Rule the book and enter the totals for each column.
d) Find the new balance and record it in the receipts column. If your work is correct, the new balance should be $.55.
e) Answer the following questions on a sheet of paper:
1) What amount was spent for carfare?
2) Did Ed spend *more* or *less* for carfare than he had estimated? How much?
3) What amount was spent for lunches?
4) Did Ed spend *more* or *less* for lunches than he had estimated? How much?
5) What amount was spent for entertainment and recreation?
6) Did Ed spend *more* or *less* for entertainment and recreation than he had estimated? How much?

7) What amount was put in the savings bank?
8) Did Ed put *more* or *less* in the savings bank than he had estimated? How much?
9) What amount was spent for gifts and contributions?
10) Did Ed spend *more* or *less* for gifts and contributions than he had estimated? How much?
11) Did Ed receive *more* or *less* income than he had estimated? How much?

JOB 29 | BUDGETING FOR A STUDENT

	Copy these problems on a sheet of paper and find the answers. (Crossfoot and then add down.)

Practicing Related Arithmetic

1) $ 1.85 + $ 2.30 + $ 5.75 + $ 3.40 = $_____
2)   4.70 +   8.65 +   6.60 +   9.85 = $_____
3)   7.75 +   5.50 +   4.25 +   8.90 = $_____
4)   13.50 + 44.35 + 11.85 + 31.25 = $_____

5) $_____ + $_____ + $_____ + $_____ = $_____

AIM

To learn how to simplify the keeping of a Record of Receipts and Payments so that information can be easily found.

EXPLANATION

"Got to cut down on expenses!"

At the end of each week you need to know how much income you have received. You also need to know how this income has been spent. In the previous job, you learned that a daily record of receipts and payments would give this information. It was very tedious, however, to go through the whole list of payments to find out how much had been spent on a certain item.

If you recall, you had the same problem when you studied the "Petty Cash System" in Unit 4. As you remember, you opened separate columns where you wanted separate totals. You will learn now that instead of using only two money columns, you can add a special column for each item for which you want a separate total and thus get information very easily.

The first Record of Receipts and Payments illustrated on page 176 shows a two-column record without special columns. On page 184 is a form showing the same information with special distribution columns.

SAMPLE PROBLEM

Examine the record with distribution columns (Illustration 29 on page 184) so that you can keep similar records when you do the practice problems.

Each amount in the payments column must be shown in a distribution column

RECEIPTS AND PAYMENTS

DATE	EXPLANATION	RECEIPTS ($15.00)	PAYMENTS ($15.00)	DISTRIBUTION					
				Carfare ($3.00)	Lunches ($3.75)	School exp. ($1.00)	Ent. & Rec. ($4.50)	Savings ($2.00)	Gifts & Contrib. (.8%)
Dec. 1	Allowance for week	10 00							
1	Carfare		50	50					
1	Lunch		75		75				
2	Carfare		50	50					
2	Lunch		70		70				
2	School supplies		75			75			
2	Magazine		40				40		
3	Carfare		50	50					
3	Lunch		80		80				
3	Shoveling snow	6 00							
4	Carfare		50	50					
4	Lunch		65		65				
4	Class dues		1 00			1 00			
4	Newspaper		15				15		
4	Savings-bank		2 00					2 00	
5	Carfare		50	50					
5	Lunch		85		85				
6	Birthday card		35						35
6	Movies		1 50				1 50		
6	Popcorn		40				40		
7	Church contribution		50						50
7	Football game		1 25				1 25		
	Totals for week	16 00	14 55	2 50	3 75	1 75	3 70	2 00	85
8	Balance of Cash	1 45							

Illustration 29 — Record of Receipts and Payments for a Student, Showing Distribution Columns

Step 1: Record the estimated budget figures.

To help you remember the amounts which you had set up in your budget, you wrote the items for which you wanted separate totals in the column headings and below them wrote the estimated amount for each column.

The $15.00 under the heading "Receipts" means that you *hope* to have $15.00 to spend for the week. Of course, only future events will tell you whether you were correct in your guess. If you receive more than $15.00 during the week, you will be happy to receive more than you had planned on. If you receive less than $15.00, you will have to *reduce your spending* in order to live within your means.

The $15.00 under the heading "Payments" means that you plan to spend $15.00. The $3.00 under the heading "Carfare" means that you plan on spending $3.00 of this $15.00 for this purpose. If you add all the amounts appearing under each of the headings in the distribution columns, you will get a total of $15.00, which equals the $15.00 in the "Payments" column.

Step 2: Record amount of payment in "Payments" column.

Notice that you first recorded the December 1 payment of 50¢ for carfare in the "Payments" column, just as you did in Job 28.

Step 3: Repeat the amount in the correct distribution column.

After you recorded the 50¢ in the "Payments" column, you recorded the same 50¢ in the column headed "Carfare." Therefore, the 50¢ was shown twice: the first time to show that you had paid out 50¢ and the second time to show the purpose for which it had been paid. When you spent the 75¢ for lunch, you again first wrote it in the "Payments" column to show that 75¢ had been paid out and then you recorded it in the column headed "Lunches." Again, the amount was entered twice: once, in the "Payments" column to show that you had paid out 75¢ and then in the column headed "Lunches" to show the purpose for which it had been paid. On December 2, when you again spent money for carfare, you repeated what you had done on December 1 when you first spent money for carfare. If you look in the "Carfare" column you will now find two 50¢ entries. You can now easily see that you have spent $1.00 for carfare in two days. It is most important to remember that *any amount shown in the "Payments" column must be shown again in one of the distribution columns.*

Distribution column shows purpose of payment

Step 4: Rule a single line across all money columns.

At the end of the week you rule a single line across all money columns to show that you are ready to total each of the columns.

Step 5: Pencil foot each column.

Total each money column and write the totals of each column in small pencil figures.

Step 6: Prove totals.

There is a very simple way to check the total of $14.55 spent.

If every amount recorded in the "Payments" column was also recorded in the distribution columns, the total of all the distribution columns must be $14.55, which is the total of the Payments column. Therefore, to test your addition, add all the totals in the distribution columns on a scratch pad as shown below:

Total payments = total of distribution columns

Carfare	$ 2.50
Lunches	3.75
School expenses	1.75
Entertainment and recreation	3.70
Savings	2.00
Gifts and contributions	.85
Total payments	$14.55

This shows that you added correctly. Compare what you just did with what you had to do in the related drill problems and you will notice that you did the same kind of arithmetic problem when you crossfooted.

Locating errors

Unfortunately, people are sometimes careless when they record numbers or add them. Suppose you found that when you added the distribution columns you did not get the total of $14.55. What would you do? The first step would be to check the additions in all columns. If you still did not find the error, then the next step would be to see if each number written in the "Payments" column was correctly copied in the distribution column. For example, you might find that when you entered $1.50 for the movie on December 6 in the "Payments" column, you incorrectly entered the amount as $1.05 in the "Entertainment and Recreation" column. Naturally, this would give you an incorrect total.

Step 7: Ink in the totals.

After you have checked the totals and found that they are correct, enter them in ink.

Step 8: Double rule the Date column and all money columns.

To show that your work is correct, rule a double line across the Date column and all the money columns.

Step 9: Record the new balance.

To find the new balance you follow the same steps that you did in the practice problems in Job 28.

How to find the balance of cash

a) On a scratch pad do this arithmetic:

Total receipts:	$16.00
Total payments:	− 14.55
Balance of cash	=$ 1.45

b) Enter the next date ("8") in the Date column. Write the words "Balance of cash" in the Explanation column and enter the $1.45 in the Receipts column.

Accuracy is rewarding

Experienced record keepers find that it pays to be careful. They know that if they are careless in their record keeping, they will spend many needless hours trying to find their errors.

Under your new system of recording your receipts and payments, you can now easily get the answers to the questions which took you much more time in Job 28. To find how much was spent for school expenses, you can now refer to your record and see that $1.75 was spent. That amount now appears as the total for the "School Expenses" column for the week.

Now see how you can use this new method of keeping records. Of course, one of the most important decisions you will have to make is in which distribution column you will enter an amount after you have first shown it in the "Payments" column.

PRACTICE PROBLEMS

Problem 1

Sue Fiske, a high school student, estimates her receipts and payments for a week as follows:

Estimated Receipts		Estimated Payments	
From allowance	$6.50	Carfare	$ 2.00
From possible earnings	4.50	Lunches	3.00
		School expenses	1.00
		Entertainment and recreation	2.50
		Savings	1.75
		Gifts and contributions	.75
Total estimated receipts	$11.00	Total estimated payments	$11.00

In order to compare her estimated receipts and payments with the actual receipts and payments for the week, Sue keeps a Record of Receipts and Payments as shown in Illustration 29 on page 184.

Directions:
a) Use a ruled sheet of paper containing space for 8 money columns.
b) Head the paper "Receipts and Payments."
c) Refer to the model on page 184 and enter the same headings for:

1. Date
2. Explanation
3. Receipts
4. Payments
5. Carfare
6. Lunches
7. School expenses
8. Entertainment and recreation
9. Savings
10. Gifts and contributions

d) Enter the estimated income and payment figures just the way they are shown in the model. For example:

RECEIPTS AND PAYMENTS

RECEIPTS	PAYMENTS	DISTRIBUTION					
		Carfare	Lunches	School Exp.	Ent. & Rec.	Savings	Gifts & Contrib
($11.00)	($11.00)	($2.00)	($3.00)	($1.00)	($2.50)	($1.75)	($.75)

e) Record the receipts and payments shown on page 188 made during the week beginning Feb. 13, 19—.

Feb. 13   Received an allowance of $6.50 for the week.
    13   Paid 40¢ for carfare, 50¢ for lunch, 60¢ for class dues, 15¢ for a newspaper.
    14   Paid 40¢ for carfare, 55¢ for lunch; put $2.00 in the bank.
    15   Paid 40¢ for carfare, 60¢ for lunch. Earned $3.50 as a baby sitter.
    16   Paid 40¢ for carfare, 70¢ for lunch, 45¢ for a magazine. Earned $2.75 as a baby sitter.
    17   Paid 40¢ for carfare, 45¢ for lunch, $1.00 for admission to a roller skating rink.
    18   Paid 40¢ for carfare, 75¢ for admission to a basketball game, 65¢ for a slice of pizza and a soda.
    19   Gave 30¢ as a church contribution.

f) Rule the book and enter the totals for each column.

g) Find the new balance and record it in the Receipts column. If your work is correct, the new balance should be $1.65.

h) Answer the following questions on a sheet of paper:

1) Did Sue spend *more* or *less* for lunches than she had estimated? How much?

2) Did Sue spend *more* or *less* for carfare than she had estimated? How much?

3) Did Sue spend *more* or *less* for school expenses than she had estimated? How much?

4) Did Sue spend *more* or *less* for entertainment and recreation than she had estimated? How much?

5) Did Sue put *more* or *less* in the bank than she had estimated? How much?

6) Did Sue spend *more* or *less* for gifts and contributions than she had estimated? How much?

7) Did Sue receive *more* or *less* income than she had estimated? How much?

Problem 2

Vito Nova, a high school student, estimates his receipts and payments for a week as follows:

Estimated Receipts		Estimated Payments	
From allowance	$ 6.00	Carfare	$ 4.00
From possible earnings	12.00	Lunches	3.50
		School expenses	1.25
		Entertainment and recreation	5.50
		Savings	2.00
		Gifts and contributions	1.75
Total estimated receipts	$18.00	Total estimated payments	$18.00

In order to compare his estimated receipts and payments with the actual receipts and payments for the week, Vito decides to keep a Record of Receipts and Payments as shown in Illustration 29, page 184.

Directions:

a) Use a ruled sheet of paper with room for 8 money columns.

b) Head the paper "Receipts and Payments."

c) Refer to the model on page 184 and enter the same headings for:

1. Date	6. Lunches
2. Explanation	7. School expenses
3. Receipts	8. Entertainment and recreation
4. Payments	9. Savings
5. Carfare	10. Gifts and contributions

d) Enter the estimated receipts and payment figures which Vito had estimated under each heading as shown in the model on page 184.

e) Record the following receipts and payments made during the week beginning March 3, 19––:

March 3 Received an allowance of $6.00 for the week.

3 Paid 70¢ for carfare, 75¢ for lunch, $1.50 for a gift.

4 Paid 70¢ for carfare, 80¢ for lunch, $1.05 for school supplies. Earned $5.00 shoveling snow.

5 Paid 70¢ for carfare, 60¢ for lunch, $2.00 for bowling, 45¢ for a soda.

6 Paid 70¢ for carfare, 85¢ for lunch. Earned $8.00 delivering newspapers.

7 Paid 70¢ for carfare, 55¢ for lunch; put $3.00 in the bank.

8 Paid 40¢ for a magazine, $1.50 admission to a skating rink.

9 Gave 50¢ as a church contribution. Paid 35¢ for a ballpoint pen.

Enter each payment twice on the same line

f) Rule the book and enter the totals for each column.

g) Find the new balance and record it in the Receipts column. If your work is correct, the new balance should be $1.20.

h) Answer the following questions on a sheet of paper.

1) Did Vito spend *more* or *less* for carfare than he had estimated? How much?

2) Did Vito spend *more* or *less* for lunches than he had estimated? How much?

3) Did Vito spend *more* or *less* for school expenses than he had estimated? How much?

4) Did Vito spend *more* or *less* for entertainment and recreation than he had estimated? How much?

5) Did Vito put *more* or *less* in the bank than he had estimated? How much?

6) Did Vito spend *more* or *less* for gifts and contributions than he had estimated? How much?

7) Did Vito receive *more* or *less* income than he had estimated? How much?

Problem 3

Lucy Grant, a high school student, estimates her receipts and payments for a week as shown on page 190.

Estimated Receipts   **Estimated Payments**

From allowance	$10.00	Carfare	$ 3.75
From possible earnings	7.00	Lunches	4.25
		School expenses	1.00
		Entertainment and	
		recreation	3.50
		Savings	3.00
		Gifts and contributions	1.50
Total estimated		Total estimated	
receipts	$17.00	payments	$17.00

In order to compare her estimated receipts and payments with the actual receipts and payments for the week, Lucy keeps a Record of Receipts and Payments as shown in Illustration 29 on page 184.

Directions:

a) Use a ruled sheet of paper with space for 8 money columns.

b) Head the paper "Receipts and Payments."

c) Refer to the model on page 184 and enter the same headings for:

1. Date
2. Explanation
3. Receipts
4. Payments
5. Carfare
6. Lunches
7. School expenses
8. Entertainment and recreation
9. Savings
10. Gifts and contributions

d) Enter the estimated receipts and payment figures as shown just the way you entered the figures in Problems 1 and 2.

e) Record the following receipts and payments made during the week beginning May 19, 19--:

May 19 Received an allowance of $10.00 for the week.

19 Paid 75¢ for carfare, 80¢ for lunch, 50¢ as a contribution to the Heart Fund.

20 Paid 75¢ for carfare, 65¢ for lunch, 55¢ for school supplies.

21 Paid 75¢ for carfare, 85¢ for lunch, $1.00 for class dues. Earned $4.50 as a baby sitter.

22 Paid 75¢ for carfare, 70¢ for lunch; put $3.00 in the bank.

23 Paid 75¢ for carfare, 90¢ for lunch, 15¢ for a newspaper. Earned $5.00 as a baby sitter.

24 Paid $1.75 for admission to the school concert, 80¢ for pizza and soda.

25 Paid $2.00 for a birthday gift, $1.50 for bowling.

f) Rule the book and enter the totals for each column.

g) Find the new balance and record it in the Receipts column. If your work is correct, your new balance should be $.60.

h) Answer the following questions on a sheet of paper.

1) Did Lucy spend *more* or *less* for carfare than she had estimated? How much?

2) Did Lucy spend *more* or *less* for lunches than she had estimated? How much?

3) Did Lucy spend *more* or *less* for school expenses than she had estimated? How much?

4) Did Lucy spend *more* or *less* for entertainment and recreation than she had estimated? How much?

5) Did Lucy put *more* or *less* in the bank than she had estimated? How much?

6) Did Lucy spend *more* or *less* for gifts and contributions than she had estimated? How much?

7) Did Lucy receive *more* or *less* income than she had estimated? How much?

Problem 4

Don Ennis, a high school student, estimates his receipts and payments for a week as follows:

Estimated Receipts		**Estimated Payments**	
From allowance	$ 5.00	Carfare	$ 5.00
From possible earnings	15.00	Lunches	4.50
		School expenses	1.50
		Entertainment and	
		recreation	6.00
		Savings	2.00
		Gifts and contributions	1.00
Total estimated		Total estimated	
receipts	$20.00	payments	$20.00

In order to compare his estimated receipts and payments with the actual receipts and payments for the week, Don keeps a Record of Receipts and Payments as shown in Illustration 29 on page 184.

Directions:
a) Use a ruled sheet of paper containing 8 money columns.

b) Head the paper "Receipts and Payments."

c) Refer to the model on page 184 and enter the same headings for:

1. Date	6. Lunches
2. Explanation	7. School expenses
3. Receipts	8. Entertainment and recreation
4. Payments	9. Savings
5. Carfare	10. Gifts and contributions

d) Enter the estimated receipts and payments figures in the proper spaces in the "Receipts and Payments" record.

e) Record the following receipts and payments made during the week beginning October 6, 19—:

Oct. 6   Received an allowance of $5.00 for the week.

      6   Paid 80¢ for carfare, 75¢ for lunch, 60¢ for school supplies, $1.00 for class dues.

      7   Paid 80¢ for carfare, 70¢ for lunch. Earned $7.00 delivering packages.

Oct. 8　Paid 80¢ for carfare, 90¢ for lunch, $1.75 for admission to a movie, $1.05 for a hamburger and soda.

9　Paid 80¢ for carfare, 85¢ for lunch, 25¢ as a contribution for the Cancer Fund. Earned $8.50 delivering packages.

10　Paid 80¢ for carfare, 75¢ for lunch; put $2.00 in the bank.

11　Paid $2.25 for bowling, 60¢ for an ice cream soda.

12　Gave 35¢ as a church contribution.

f) Rule the book and enter the totals for each column.

g) Find the new balance and record it in the Receipts column. If your work is correct, the new balance should be $2.70.

h) Answer the following questions on a sheet of paper.

1) Did Don spend *more* or *less* for carfare than he had estimated? How much?

2) Did Don spend *more* or *less* for lunches than he had estimated? How much?

3) Did Don spend *more* or *less* for school expenses than he had estimated? How much?

4) Did Don spend *more* or *less* for entertainment and recreation? How much?

5) Did Don put *more* or *less* in the bank than he had estimated? How much?

6) Did Don spend *more* or *less* for gifts and contributions than he had estimated? How much?

7) Did Don receive *more* or *less* income than he had estimated? How much?

Practicing Related Arithmetic

Copy these problems on a sheet of paper and find the answers. (Crossfoot and then add down.)

1) $ 9.00 + $12.55 + $20.40 + $50.15 = $_____
2)   5.33 +   13.83 +   35.43 +   .63 = $_____
3)   8.26 +   40.66 +   10.16 +   30.56 = $_____
4)   10.08 +   7.28 +   25.18 +   9.48 = $_____

5) $_____ + $_____ + $_____ + $_____ = $_____

AIMS

1. To give you additional practice in keeping the budget records of a student.

2. To learn another method of recording daily payments.

EXPLANATION

In the previous job you were shown how to set up distribution columns in a "Receipts and Payments" record so that you can easily find the amounts spent for each item in your budget.

You will note from the Record of Receipts and Payments shown in Illustration 30a on the next page that on December 1 you spent money two times. Each time, you made two entries in your records. First, you recorded the amount in the Payments column. Then you entered the same amount in the correct distribution column. This method of recording is used by some record keepers.

Other record keepers find it saves time to enter the *total amount of each day's payments* on one line and to distribute this amount in the distribution columns on the same line according to the individual payments for the day. With this method the items in Illustration 30a would be entered as shown in Illustration 30b on the next page.

Compare Illustration 30a with Illustration 30b and see how they are alike and how they differ.

Headings — There is no difference in the headings.

Dates — In Illustration 30a the day of the month is written every time you receive or spend money. Since three events took place on December 1, the "1" was repeated three times.

RECEIPTS AND PAYMENTS

DATE	EXPLANATION	RECEIPTS ($15.00)	PAYMENTS ($15.00)	DISTRIBUTION Carfare ($3.00)	Lunches ($3.75)	School Exp. ($1.00)	Ent. & Rec. ($4.50)	Savings ($2.00)	Gifts & Contrib. ($.75)
Dec 1	Allowance for week	10 00							
1	Carfare		50	50					
1	Lunch		75		75				
2	Carfare		50	50					
2	Lunch		70		70				
2	School Supplies		75			75			
2	Magazine		40				40		
3	Carfare		50	50					
3	Lunch		80		80				
3	Shoveling snow	6 00							
4	Carfare		50	50					
4	Lunch		65		65				
4	Class dues		1 00			1 00			
4	Newspaper		15				15		
4	Savings-bank		2 00					2 00	
5	Carfare		50	50					
5	Lunch		85		85				
6	Birthday card		35						35
6	Movies		1 50				1 50		
6	Popcorn		40				40		
7	Church contribution		50						50
7	Football game		1 25				1 25		
	Totals for week	16 00	14 55	2 50	3 75	1 75	3 70	2 00	85
8	Balance of cash	1 45							

Illustration 30a — Record of Receipts and Payments

RECEIPTS AND PAYMENTS

DATE	EXPLANATION	RECEIPTS ($15.00)	PAYMENTS ($15.00)	DISTRIBUTION Carfare ($3.00)	Lunches ($3.75)	School Exp. ($1.00)	Ent. & Rec. ($4.50)	Savings ($2.00)	Gifts & Contrib. ($.75)
Dec 1	Allowance for week	10 00							
1			1 25	50	75				
2			2 35	50	70	75	40		
3			1 30	50	80				
3	Shoveling snow	6 00							
4			4 30	50	65	1 00	15	2 00	
5			1 35	50	85				
6			2 25				1 90		35
7			1 75				1 25		50
		16 00	14 55	2 50	3 75	1 75	3 70	2 00	85
8	Balance of cash	1 45							

You add together $1.50 for movies
+   .40 for popcorn
=$1.90 Remember: before you write any amount in a distribution column, be sure to add together all the payments for that particular heading.

Illustration 30b — Record of Receipts and Payments

In Illustration 30b the day of the month is only written when you receive money or when you total all the money spent on a particular day. Since you received money once on December 1 and spent $1.25 for the entire day, you show "1" only twice in the Date column.

Explanation Column — In Illustration 30a an explanation is written for every receipt and payment made.

In Illustration 30b an explanation is written only for the money you received.

Receipts Column — There is no difference in the illustrations.

Payments and Distributions Columns — In Illustration 30a you enter *separately each payment* of money in the Payments column and immediately record it in the proper distribution column. That is why you see two amounts in the Payments column on December 1.

Distribution columns show breakdown of payments

In Illustration 30b, you enter the *total* of all the money spent in one day and then show the breakdown of this total in each of the distribution columns. Therefore, you spent a total of $1.25 on December 1, of which 50¢ was spent for carfare and 75¢ was spent for lunch. Note that only one line was used to enter all this information.

Ruling the book and entering the new balance — There is no difference in the method of ruling the book and entering the new balance in either of these illustrations.

Deciding which method to use — If you want to explain each individual item of your spending, keep a record like the one in Illustration 30a. If you need only the information given in the distribution column headings, record your payments as shown in Illustration 30b.

From this point on, record your payments as shown in Illustration 30b.

PRACTICE PROBLEMS

Problem 1

Sue Fiske, a high school student, estimates her receipts and payments for a week as follows:

Estimated Receipts		Estimated Payments	
From allowance	$ 6.50	Carfare	$ 2.00
From possible earnings	4.50	Lunches	3.00
		School expenses	1.00
		Entertainment and	
		recreation	2.50
		Savings	1.75
		Gifts and contributions	.75
Total estimated		Total estimated	
receipts	$11.00	payments	$11.00

To compare her estimated receipts and payments with the actual receipts and payments for the week Sue keeps a Record of Receipts and Payments as shown in Illustration 30b on page 194.

Directions:
a) Use a ruled sheet of paper containing 8 money columns.
b) Head the paper "Receipts and Payments."
c) Refer to the model on page 194 and enter the same headings for:

1. Date	6. Lunches
2. Explanation	7. School expenses
3. Receipts	8. Entertainment and recreation
4. Payments	9. Savings
5. Carfare	10. Gifts and contributions

d) Enter the estimated receipt and payment figures which Sue had estimated under each heading as shown in the model on page 194.
e) Record the following receipts and payments made during the week beginning Feb. 13, 19--:

Feb. 13   Received an allowance of $6.50 for the week.
13   Paid 40¢ for carfare, 50¢ for lunch, 60¢ for class dues, 15¢ for a newspaper.
14   Paid 40¢ for carfare, 55¢ for lunch; put $2.00 in the bank.
15   Paid 40¢ for carfare, 60¢ for lunch. Earned $3.50 as a baby sitter.
16   Paid 40¢ for carfare, 70¢ for lunch, 45¢ for a magazine. Earned $2.75 as a baby sitter.
17   Paid 40¢ for carfare, 45¢ for lunch, $1.00 for admission to a roller skating rink.
18   Paid 40¢ for carfare, 75¢ for admission to a basketball game, 65¢ for a slice of pizza and a soda.
19   Gave 30¢ as a church contribution.

Add together similar payments

f) Rule the book and enter the totals for each column.
g) Find the new balance and record it in the Receipts column. If your work is correct, the new balance should be $1.65.
h) Answer the following questions on a sheet of paper:
   1) Did Sue spend *more* or *less* for carfare than she had estimated? How much?
   2) Did Sue spend *more* or *less* for lunches than she had estimated? How much?
   3) Did Sue spend *more* or *less* for school expenses than she had estimated? How much?
i) Compare this problem with Problem 1, page 187, for which you used the method shown in Illustration 30a. Note that it is the identical problem. If you compare the totals with the new balance you will see that they are still the same. Also you will see that the answers to each of the questions are alike.

Problem 2

Vito Nova, a high school student, estimates his receipts and payments for a week as follows:

Estimated Receipts		Estimated Payments	
From allowance	$ 6.00	Carfare	$ 4.00
From possible earnings	12.00	Lunches	3.50
		School expenses	1.25
		Entertainment and recreation	5.50
		Savings	2.00
		Gifts and contributions	1.75
Total estimated receipts	$18.00	Total estimated payments	$18.00

To compare his estimated receipts and payments with the actual receipts and payments for the week, Vito decides to keep a Record of Receipts and Payments as shown in Illustration 30b on page 194.

Directions:

a) Use a ruled sheet of paper containing 8 money columns.

b) Head the paper "Receipts and Payments."

c) Refer to Illustration 30b and enter the same headings for:

1. Date
2. Explanation
3. Receipts
4. Payments
5. Carfare
6. Lunches
7. School expenses
8. Entertainment and recreation
9. Savings
10. Gifts and contributions

d) Enter estimated receipts and payments figures which Vito estimated under each heading as shown in Illustration 30b, page 194.

e) Record the following receipts and payments made during the week beginning March 3, 19—:

March 3   Received an allowance of $6.00 for the week.
　　　3   Paid 70¢ for carfare, 75¢ for lunch, $1.50 for a gift.
　　　4   Paid 70¢ for carfare, 80¢ for lunch, $1.05 for school supplies. Earned $5.00 shoveling snow.
　　　5   Paid 70¢ for carfare, 60¢ for lunch, $2.00 for bowling, 45¢ for a soda.
　　　6   Paid 70¢ for carfare, 85¢ for lunch. Earned $8.00 delivering newspapers.
　　　7   Paid 70¢ for carfare, 55¢ for lunch; put $3.00 in the bank.
　　　8   Paid 40¢ for a magazine, $1.50 admission to a skating rink.
　　　9   Gave 50¢ as a church contribution. Paid 35¢ for a ballpoint pen.

f) Rule the book and enter the totals for each column.

g) Find the new balance and record it in the Receipts column. If your work is correct, the new balance should be $1.20.

h) Answer the following questions on a sheet of paper:

1) Did Vito spend *more* or *less* for carfare than he had estimated? How much?

2) Did Vito spend *more* or *less* for entertainment and recreation than he had estimated? How much?

3) Did Vito receive *more* or *less* income than he had estimated? How much?

i) Compare this problem with Problem 2, page 188, for which you used the method shown in Illustration 30a. Note that it is the identical problem. If you compare the totals with the new balance you will see that they are again the same. Also, you will see that the answers to each of the questions are alike.

Problem 3

Pattie Welan, a high school student, estimates her receipts and payments for a week as follows:

Estimated Receipts		Estimated Payments	
From allowance	$ 7.00	Carfare	$ 3.50
From possible earnings	12.00	Lunches	4.00
		School expenses	1.50
		Entertainment and	
		recreation	5.00
		Savings	3.00
		Gifts and contributions	2.00
Total estimated		Total estimated	
receipts	$19.00	payments	$19.00

To compare her estimated receipts and payments with the actual receipts and payments for the week, Pattie keeps a Record of Receipts and Payments as shown in Illustration 30b, page 194.

Directions:
a) Use a ruled sheet of paper containing 8 money columns.
b) Head the paper "Receipts and Payments."
c) Refer to the model on page 194 and enter the same headings for:

1. Date	6. Lunches
2. Explanation	7. School expenses
3. Receipts	8. Entertainment and recreation
4. Payments	9. Savings
5. Carfare	10. Gifts and contributions

d) Enter the estimated receipts and payments figures which Pattie had estimated under each heading as shown in Illustration 30b.
e) Record the following receipts and payments made during the week beginning May 12, 19––:

May 12   Received an allowance of $7.00 for the week.
     12   Paid 60¢ for carfare, 70¢ for lunch, 90¢ for school supplies. Earned $5.50 tutoring.
     13   Paid 60¢ for carfare, 75¢ for lunch, $1.25 for a ticket to the school dance.
     14   Paid 60¢ for carfare, 65¢ for lunch, $1.50 for a gift. Earned $4.00 tutoring.
     15   Paid 60¢ for carfare, 85¢ for lunch; put $3.00 in the bank.
     16   Paid 60¢ for carfare, 75¢ for lunch, 50¢ for a magazine. Earned $4.25 as a baby sitter.

May 17   Paid 60¢ carfare, $2.00 for admission to a movie, $1.35 for a
          hamburger and a soda.
      18 Paid 35¢ for a birthday card and $1.75 for bowling.

f) Rule the book and enter the totals for each column.
g) Find the new balance and record it in the Receipts column. If your work is
correct, the new balance should be $.85.
h) Answer the following questions on a sheet of paper:

1) Did Pattie spend *more* or *less* for entertainment and recreation than
   she had estimated?
2) Did Pattie spend *more* or *less* for gifts and contributions than she had
   estimated? How much?
3) Did Pattie receive *more* or *less* income than she had estimated? How
   much?

Problem 4

Jules Robel, a high school student, estimates his receipts and payments
for a week as follows:

Estimated Receipts		Estimated Payments	
From allowance	$ 8.50	Carfare	$ 4.00
From possible earnings	10.00	Lunches	4.50
		School expenses	1.75
		Entertainment and	
		recreation	5.00
		Savings	2.00
		Gifts and contributions	1.25
Total estimated		Total estimated	
receipts	$18.50	payments	$18.50

To compare his estimated receipts and payments with the actual receipts
and payments for the week, Jules keeps a Record of Receipts and Payments as
shown in Illustration 30b.

Directions:
a) Use a ruled sheet of paper containing 8 money columns.
b) Head the paper "Receipts and Payments."
c) Refer to the model on page 194 and enter the same headings for:

1. Date
2. Explanation
3. Receipts
4. Payments
5. Carfare
6. Lunches
7. School expenses
8. Entertainment and recreation
9. Savings
10. Gifts and contributions

d) Enter the estimated receipts and payments figures which Jules had
estimated under each heading as shown in Illustration 30b.
e) Record the receipts and payments below and on page 200 made during
the week beginning Sept. 22, 19—:

Sept. 22   Received an allowance of $8.50 for the week.
      22   Paid 80¢ for carfare, 75¢ for lunch, $1.00 for class dues.

Sept. 23   Paid 80¢ for carfare, 65¢ for lunch, 40¢ for an anniversary card.

24   Paid 80¢ for carfare, 90¢ for lunch, $1.25 as admission to a tennis match. Earned $6.75 tutoring.

25   Paid 80¢ for carfare, 70¢ for lunch, $1.25 for a gift; put $2.00 in the bank.

26   Paid 80¢ for carfare, 85¢ for lunch, 70¢ for notebooks. Earned $5.00 tutoring.

27   Paid 80¢ for carfare, $2.00 for his share of the fee for a tennis court, 90¢ for pizza and soda.

28   Paid $1.75 for bowling.

f) Rule the book and enter the totals for each column.

g) Find the new balance and record it in the Receipts column. If your work is correct, the new balance should be $.35.

h) Answer the following questions on a sheet of paper:

1) Did Jules spend *more* or *less* for school expenses than he had estimated? How much?

2) Did Jules spend *more* or *less* for gifts and contributions than he had estimated? How much?

Practicing Related Arithmetic

Copy these problems on a sheet of paper and find the answers. (Crossfoot and then add down.)

1) $25.30 + $75.25 + $15.00 + $40.75 = $_____
2)   30.05 + 20.00 + 50.45 + 60.85 = $_____
3) 100.00 + 320.86 + 295.36 + 400.26 = $_____
4)   48.87 + 97.17 + 13.60 + 86.77 = $_____

5) $____ + $____ + $____ + $____ = $_____

AIM

To learn how to keep the budget records for a family.

EXPLANATION

In the preceding jobs you learned how to keep a detailed record of the receipts and payments of a high school student. Now, you will learn that you can use the same method to keep records for a family.

The small amount of time necessary to keep such household records will pay the record keeper great rewards by showing how to get the most benefit from the money that is available.

Of course, the headings of the distribution columns will be different from those used in the previous jobs because the payments of a high school student are different from those of an entire family unit. The average family spends its income (which is usually received from wages) on food, clothing, shelter, savings, health and personal needs, entertainment and education, traveling expenses, and gifts and contributions. Some of these expenses may be familiar to you and others may not. To understand these various headings, consider the items usually placed under them.

How a family spends its income

Food	Shelter
Meals eaten at home and away from home	Rent, mortgage payments, property taxes
	Gas, electricity, water
Clothing	Telephone
	Furniture
Wearing apparel for all members of the family; also, repairing of any wearing apparel	Utensils
	Maintenance of shelter

Health & Personal Needs	Entertainment & Education
Doctor and dental bills	Theaters
Drugs	Books, magazines, newspapers
Hospital expenses	Hobbies
Glasses and hearing aids	Vacation trips
Beauty parlor and barber shop	Tuition to schools
Toilet articles	School supplies
Health and accident insurance policies	

Gifts & Contributions

Charities
Church contributions
Personal gifts

Savings

Money put in a bank
Investments
Government bonds
Life insurance premiums

Traveling Expenses

Carfare
Car expenses

"I told you budget-ing would pay off"

Perhaps you are wondering why no heading has been set up for income taxes and social security taxes. You will learn in later jobs that before workers are given their wages, the employer deducts certain taxes which the employer then turns over to various branches of the government for the benefit of the workers.

With this brief picture of the various expenses of the average family, see how a family can keep records that will show whether they are living within a budget.

SAMPLE PROBLEM

Mr. and Mrs. Russ Layne have found that, although Mr. Layne brings home wages totaling an average of $12,000.00 a year, they have difficulty meeting all their expenses. They decided, therefore, to prepare a budget to see if they could spend their money more wisely.

Here are the steps they followed:

Step 1: Prepare an estimate of receipts and payments.

Based upon past experiences they tried to decide how the $12,000.00 would be spent for food, clothing, shelter, savings, health and personal needs, entertainment and education, gifts and contributions, and traveling expenses.

Here is what they finally decided upon as a reasonable and workable budget for a year:

Estimated Receipts		Estimated Payments		
From wages	$12,000.00	Food	$ 3,300.00	Breakdown on a yearly basis
		Clothing	1,000.00	
		Shelter	3,120.00	
		Savings	1,040.00	
		Health and personal needs	860.00	
		Entertainment and education	1,200.00	
		Traveling expenses	1,000.00	
		Gifts and contributions	480.00	
Total estimated receipts	$12,000.00	Total estimated payments	$12,000.00	

Since Mr. and Mrs. Layne will be keeping their records on a weekly basis, they need to know how much money to budget for each item for a week. To learn this, they divide each yearly estimated payment by 52 to get the weekly estimated payment for each item in their budget. They decide to "round off" the resulting figures to the nearest half dollar, so their *weekly* estimated payments are:

Food	$63.50	Breakdown on a weekly basis
Clothing	19.00	
Shelter	60.00	
Savings	20.00	
Health and personal needs	16.50	
Entertainment and education	23.00	
Traveling expenses	19.00	
Gifts and contributions	9.00	
	$230.00	

Some of the items listed will require almost the same amount of money each week (*shelter* and *food*, for example). Others, like *clothing*, will vary from week to week. If a member of the family will soon need an expensive item of clothing, such as a winter coat, for several weeks they must spend less than the usual clothing allowance, so that money for the coat will be available when needed. Successful budgeting requires looking ahead to plan for these unusually large payments.

Successful budgeting = planning ahead

Step 2: Record receipts and payments.

Now that the budget had been prepared, the next job was to record all the receipts and payments so that a comparison could be made between the estimated and actual figures. To record all the facts properly, they used a columnar sheet containing 10 money columns like the one on page 204.

RECORD OF RECEIPTS AND PAYMENTS											
DATE	EXPLANATION	RECEIPTS	PAYMENTS	Food	Clothing	Shelter	Savings	Health & Personal Needs	Entertainment & Education	Traveling expenses	Gifts & Contributions

Illustration 31a — Record of Receipts and Payments for a Family

Once the record has been set up, a decision must be made. Shall the Layne family record the facts on a daily basis, or on one definite day each week? They will probably do what many record keepers have found to be most practical:

a) Record all receipts of money on the day received.

b) Record all payments on a weekly basis. (Mrs. Layne selected Saturday because she felt most of her marketing was done on this day.)

c) Find the balance on the last day of the month. (Of course, if the last day of the month did not fall on a Saturday, Mrs. Layne would have to record all the payments made between the last Saturday of the month and the end of the month.)

Here are the events which took place during the month of April beginning with April 1, 19--:

April	1	There was a balance of $190.00 left from the previous week's salary.
	4	Mr. Layne brought home his pay of $230.75.
	5	Made payments since March 31, as follows:

Food	$ 51.50
Pants	16.00
Rent	200.00
Bank deposit	20.00
Barber shop and beauty parlor	14.75
Newspapers and theater	16.25
Traveling	17.00
Church	3.00
Birthday gift	19.50

	11	Mr. Layne brought home his pay of $230.75.
	12	Made payments during the previous week as follows:

Food	$ 60.25
Shoes	10.00
Pots and pans	41.75
Bank deposit	20.00
Newspapers and concert tickets	19.50
Traveling	17.75
Church	3.00

	18	Mr. Layne brought home his pay of $230.75.

April 19   Made payments during the previous week as follows:

Food	$ 65.28
Dress	28.60
Telephone, gas, and electricity	31.25
Bank deposit	20.00
Doctor and medication	29.75
Newspapers, magazine, and golf course fees	15.95
Traveling	16.80
Church	3.00

    25   Mr. Layne brought home his pay of $230.75.

    26   Made payments during the previous week as follows:

Food	$ 57.62
Sports jacket	43.95
Bank deposit	20.00
Beauty parlor and cosmetics	10.20
Newspapers and records	22.70
Traveling	20.40
Church	3.00

    30   The payments made since the 26th were as follows:

Food	$ 45.25
Newspapers and bowling	13.40
Traveling	10.60
Anniversary gift	10.00

Examine Illustration 31b carefully so that you can keep similar records. Here is how the completed record would look at the end of the month:

RECORD OF RECEIPTS AND PAYMENTS

DATE	EXPLANATION	RECEIPTS	PAYMENTS	Food	Clothing	Shelter	Savings	Health & Personal Needs	Entertainment & Education	Traveling Expenses	Gifts & Contributions
19- April 1	Balance	190 00									
4	Wages	230 75									
5	Since Mar. 31		358 00	51 50	16 00	200 00	20 00	14 75	16 25	17 00	22 50
11	Wages	230 75									
12	For week		172 25	60 25	10 00	41 75	20 00		19 50	17 75	3 00
18	Wages	230 75									
19	For. week		210 63	65 28	28 60	31 25	20 00	29 75	15 95	16 80	3 00
25	Wages	230 75									
26	For week		177 87	57 62	43 95		20 00	10 20	22 70	20 40	3 00
30	To April 30		79 25	45 25					13 40	10 60	10 00
		1,113 00	998 00	279 90	98 55	273 00	80 00	54 70	87 80	82 56	41 56
		1,113 00	998 00	279 90	98 55	273 00	80 00	54 70	87 80	82 55	41 50
May 1	Balance	115 00									

Illustration 31b – Completed Record of Receipts and Payments

Entering the Balance — Since the Layne family had unspent money at the close of March, this amount is shown in the "Receipts" column as the balance on April 1.

Entering the Receipts — Receipts are recorded every time they are received. Since wages were received 4 times during the month, you will note that there were 4 entries made for wages.

Entering Payments —

a) Total all the amounts spent during the week and enter the sum in the Payments column. For example, in Illustration 31b, on April 5, $358.00 was entered in the Payments column. This figure was found by adding the figures below:

$$\begin{array}{r} \$\ 51.50 \\ 16.00 \\ 200.00 \\ 20.00 \\ 14.75 \\ 16.25 \\ 17.00 \\ \underline{22.50} \\ \$358.00 \end{array}$$

Using distribution columns

b) Show in the distribution columns how this $358.00 was spent. For example:

$\ 51.50 of the $358.00 was spent for Food.
$\ 16.00 of the $358.00 was spent for Clothing.
$200.00 of the $358.00 was spent for Shelter.
$\ 20.00 of the $358.00 was put in the Savings Bank.
$\ 14.75 of the $358.00 was spent for Health and Personal Needs.
$\ 16.25 of the $358.00 was spent for Entertainment and Education.
$\ 17.00 of the $358.00 was spent for Traveling Expenses.
$\ 22.50 of the $358.00 was spent for Gifts and Contributions.

Perhaps you are wondering why we have entered $22.50 for Gifts and Contributions since this figure did not appear as one of the payments on April 5 on page 205.

We found this amount as follows:

Similar payments are added together

Since the birthday gift	$19.50
and the Church contribution	3.00
are both considered to be part of Gifts and Contributions, we add the two items together and get:	
Gifts and Contributions	$22.50

Remember! Before you write any amount in the distribution column, be sure to add together all the payments for that particular heading.

Ruling the Book and Entering the New Balance — It is customary on the last day of the month to total each money column, to rule the columns, and to enter the new balance. Notice that the method of totaling, ruling and entering the new balance is the same as the method you used in Job 30 on page 194.

Step 3: Comparison of budget estimates with actual figures.

At the end of the year, the Layne family will be able to compare their actual receipts and payments with their budget estimates. They will be able to use this comparison as a guide in preparing their new budget for the next year.

Planning a new budget

PRACTICE PROBLEMS

Problem 1

Mr. and Mrs. Floyd Scott decide to keep a Record of Receipts and Payments as shown in Illustration 31b on page 205.

Directions:
a) Use a ruled sheet of paper containing 10 money columns.
b) Head the paper "Record of Receipts and Payments."
c) Refer to the model on page 204 for the headings and enter similar headings for:

1. Date	7. Shelter
2. Explanation	8. Savings
3. Receipts	9. Health and Personal Needs
4. Payments	10. Entertainment and Education
5. Food	11. Traveling Expenses
6. Clothing	12. Gifts and Contributions

d) Record the following receipts and payments made during the month of December, 19—:

Dec. 1   Balance of cash $159.28.
  5   Mr. Scott brought home his wages of $254.85.
  6   The payments made since November 30 were:

Food	$ 57.80
Gas, electricity, and telephone	39.40
Savings bank deposit	25.00
Dentist	38.00
Newspapers and records	18.60
Carfare and car expenses	15.30
Church contribution	4.00
Birthday gift	15.00

Reminder: Similar payments are added together

  12   Mr. Scott brought home his wages of $254.85.
  13   The payments made for the previous week were:

Food	$ 64.95
Rent	225.00
Savings bank deposit	25.00
Beauty parlor and cosmetics	13.25
Newspapers and books	14.70
Carfare and car expenses	18.10
Church contribution	4.00

  19   Mr. Scott brought home his wages of $254.85.
  20   The payments made for the previous week were:

Dec. 20	Food..	$ 71.42
	Shirts and ties..	18.75
	Window shades	56.85
	Savings bank deposit	25.00
	Barber shop and toilet articles........................	17.50
	Newspapers, magazines, and theater tickets	21.15
	Carfare and car expenses	17.25
	Church contribution	4.00
	Anniversary card	.35

26 Mr. Scott brought home his wages of $254.85.

27 The payments made for the previous week were:

	Food..	$ 61.13
	Sweaters	36.45
	Lamp	29.95
	Savings bank deposit	25.00
	Beauty parlor...	9.50
	Medication	11.20
	Newspapers, magazines, and theater tickets	24.40
	Carfare and car expenses	19.60
	Church contribution	4.00
	Cancer Fund contribution	5.00

31 The payments since the 27th were:

	Food..	$ 48.57
	Toilet articles	3.91
	Newspapers, books, and bowling	12.30
	Carfare and car expenses	14.75
	Heart Fund contribution	3.00

e) Rule the book, enter the totals, and record the new balance. If your work is correct, your total payments should be *$1,119.13* and your new balance should be *$59.55*.

Problem 2

Mr. and Mrs. Manuel Orez keep a record of receipts and payments as shown in Illustration 31b, on page 205.

Directions:

a) Use a ruled sheet of paper containing 10 money columns.

b) Head the paper "Record of Receipts and Payments."

c) Refer to the model on page 204 for the headings and enter similar headings for:

1. Date	7. Shelter
2. Explanation	8. Savings
3. Receipts	9. Health and Personal Needs
4. Payments	10. Entertainment and Education
5. Food	11. Traveling Expenses
6. Clothing	12. Gifts and Contributions

d) Record the receipts and payments on the next page made during the month of June, 19--.

June 1   Balance $61.92.

6   Mr. Orez brought home his wages of $270.10.

7   The payments since May 31 were as follows:

Food	$ 70.19
Gas, electricity, and telephone	40.80
Savings bank deposit	30.00
Cosmetics	4.20
Newspapers and tennis court fees	11.70
Carfare and car expenses	13.25
Church contribution	5.00

13   Mr. Orez brought home his wages of $270.10.

14   The payments for the previous week were as follows:

Food	$ 65.97
Pants and shoes	31.60
Rent	195.00
Savings bank deposit	15.00
Dentist	60.00
Newspapers, magazines, and theater tickets	14.45
Carfare and car expenses	15.10
Church contribution	5.00
Girl Scouts contribution	3.00

20   Mr. Orez brought home his wages of $270.10.

21   The payments for the previous week were as follows:

Food	$ 62.58
Dishes	38.50
Savings bank deposit	20.00
Beauty parlor and barber shop	12.50
Newspapers, books, and baseball tickets	19.05
Carfare and auto expenses	14.90
Church contribution	5.00

27   Mr. Orez brought home his wages of $270.10.

28   The payments for the previous week were as follows:

Food	$ 73.05
Dress	18.75
Sports jacket	32.60
Savings bank deposit	25.00
Hair spray	1.95
Newspapers, magazines, and golf course fees	15.90
Carfare and car expenses	12.30
Church contribution	5.00
Birthday gift	19.20

30   The payments since the 28th were:

Food	$ 28.66
Newspapers and books	6.25
Carfare and car expenses	4.55
Heart Fund contribution	4.00

e) Rule the book, enter the totals, and record the new balance. If your work is correct, your total payments should be *$1,000.00* and your new balance should be *$142.32*.

Problem 3

Mr. and Mrs. Gerry Rath keep a record of receipts and payments as shown in Illustration 31b on page 205.

Directions:
a) Use a ruled sheet of paper containing 10 money columns.
b) Head the paper "Record of Receipts and Payments."
c) Refer to the model on page 204 for the headings and enter similar headings for:

1. Date	7. Shelter
2. Explanation	8. Savings
3. Receipts	9. Health and Personal Needs
4. Payments	10. Entertainment and Education
5. Food	11. Traveling Expenses
6. Clothing	12. Gifts and Contributions

d) Record the following receipts and payments made during the month of April, 19--:

April 1   Balance of cash $182.69.

4   Mr. Rath brought home his wages of $201.30.

5   The payments since March 31 were as follows:

Food	$ 49.73
Rent	215.00
Newspapers and books	6.50
Carfare and car expenses	9.20
Church contribution	2.50

11   Mr. Rath brought home his wages of $201.30.

12   The payments for the previous week were as follows:

Food	$ 61.18
Gas, electricity, and telephone	42.20
Savings bank deposit	20.00
Newspapers and tennis court fees	10.90
Church contribution	2.50
Doctor and medication	28.50
Carfare and car expenses	11.40

18   Mr. Rath brought home his wages of $201.30.

19   The payments for the previous week were as follows:

Food	$ 68.59
Suit	51.25
Savings bank deposit	25.00
Newspapers and magazines	2.25
Blouse and skirt	23.55
Carfare and car expenses	10.60
Theater tickets	15.00
Church contribution	2.50

25   Mr. Rath brought home his wages of $201.30.

26   The payments for the previous week were as follows:

Food	$ 56.07
Desk and chair	48.35
Savings bank deposit	25.00

Barber shop and toilet articles............................	8.29
Newspapers, magazines, and concert tickets........	22.45
Church contribution	2.50
Carfare and car expenses	12.70
Gift	5.00

30 The payments since the 26th were as follows:

Food...	$ 40.31
Shoes and underwear	37.75
Newspapers and tennis court fees	8.80
Carfare and car expenses	7.40

e) Rule the book, enter the totals, and record the new balance. If your work is correct, your total payments should be *$932.97* and your new balance should be *$54.92*.

Problem 4

Mr. and Mrs. Ottis Parry keep a record of receipts and payments as shown in Illustration 31b, on page 205.

Directions:
a) Use a ruled sheet of paper containing 10 money columns.
b) Head the paper "Record of Receipts and Payments."
c) Refer to the model on page 204 for the headings and enter similar headings for the same items you used in Problem 3.
d) Record the following receipts and payments made during the month of September, 19––:

Sept. 1 Balance of cash $81.28.
     5 Mr. Parry brought home his wages of $294.65.
     6 The payments since August 31 were as follows:

Food	$ 74.19
Barber shop and toilet articles	11.25
Newspapers and admission fees to the ball games	21.55
Carfare and car expenses	16.90
Church contribution	3.50

   12 Mr. Parry brought home his wages of $294.65.
   13 The payments made for the previous week were:

Food	$ 68.51
Mortgage payment for mortgage, interest, and taxes on house	265.80
Carfare and car expenses	18.20
Gas and electricity	40.70
Church contribution	3.50
Telephone	18.10
Newspapers and magazines	2.35

   19 Mr. Parry brought home his wages of $294.65.
   20 The payments made for the previous week were:

Food	$ 60.76
Savings bank deposit	40.00
Dentist	25.00
Newspapers, books, and movies	15.40

Hair spray	2.18
Church contribution	3.50
Carfare and car expenses	13.15
Engagement gift	21.75

26 Mr. Parry brought home his wages of $294.65.

27 The payments made for the previous week were:

Food	$ 58.09
Savings bank deposit	30.00
Lamps	60.25
Newspapers, magazines, and theater tickets	23.90
Carfare and car expenses	15.45
Dresses	49.75
Church contribution	3.50

30 The payments made since the 27th were:

Food	$ 37.83
Newspapers and movies	11.25
Carfare and car expenses	7.30
Suit	82.50

e) Rule the book, enter the totals, and record the new balance. If your work is correct, your total payments should be *$1,106.11* and your new balance should be *$153.77*.

UNIT 6

RECORD KEEPING FOR RETAIL SALESCLERKS

UNIT 6

Practicing Related Arithmetic

Copy and answer the following problems:

1) $2 \times \$3.18 = \$$ _____   6) $7 \times \$6.83 = \$$ _____
2) $4 \times \$2.35 = \$$ _____   7) $6 \times \$5.22 = \$$ _____
3) $3 \times \$1.64 = \$$ _____   8) $5 \times \$6.17 = \$$ _____
4) $5 \times \$2.25 = \$$ _____   9) $3 \times \$7.69 = \$$ _____
5) $4 \times \$4.71 = \$$ _____   10) $2 \times \$3.96 = \$$ _____

AIM

To learn how to prepare a sales slip for a retail store.

EXPLANATION

In Unit 2 you learned the duties of a cashier employed in a retail store. You remember that each sale was rung up on a cash register so that the owner could find the total sales for the day.

Many retail store owners need to know more than the total sales for the day. They may need a detailed written record of each individual sale. To get this information, salesclerks prepare a *sales slip* for each sale.

If you were a salesclerk in a retail store, it might be part of your job to prepare a sales slip for each sale you made. The blank sales slips are printed in booklet form with an original and duplicate copy for each sale. The original copy is detached and given to the customer and the duplicate copy serves as a record of the sale.

Sales slips usually have a printed number with the original and duplicate slip having the same number. The sales slips are printed in numerical order so that any missing slip can be accounted for.

Instead of a booklet of sales slips, some retailers prefer to use a simple mechanical device called a *sales slip register* which is shown on the next page.

A supply of attached numbered blank sales slips are stored inside the locked register. After a sales slip is filled out the salesclerk turns the handle of the register and the completed sales slip rolls out and the next numbered blank slip replaces it in the machine. The completed carbon copies remain in the locked register in numerical order. You can see that by using this machine

Moore Business Forms

Sales slip register prevents loss of sales slips

there is less chance of losing any blank sales slips or completed carbon copies.

You have probably seen sales slips that are similar to the illustration shown here:

Sales slips are prepared in duplicate

NO. 21565	Dale's Sport Shop 1302 Chestnut Street Philadelphia, PA 19107

Sold To _____ _____19____

Street _____

City, State, Zip _____

Sold by	Cash	Charge	Amt. Rec'd
Quantity	Description		Amount

Please keep this slip for future reference

Customer's Signature for charge sales

Illustration 32a — Sales Slip

The copy of the sales slip given to the customer provides a record of the sale. This copy becomes most important if the store permits customers to return merchandise. In most cases, the customer must have the copy of the sales slip in order to return merchandise.

Many retail businesses keep an up-to-date record of the names and addresses of their customers. The businesses use these lists of names and addresses whenever they wish to mail advertising circulars to their customers. For this reason the clerks are instructed to write the name and address of each customer to whom merchandise is sold.

Other businesses, however, may not be interested in getting this information. The salesclerks in these stores need not bother to write the name and address of a cash customer on the sales slip.

Of course, if the sale is a charge sale, that is, the customer does not have to pay until a later date, it will be important to keep an accurate record of the customer's name and address. You will learn more about charge sales in Job 37.

Charge sales — customer pays later

In your work you will assume that the owner has told you to write the name and address of each customer on the sales slip.

After the name and address of the customer have been recorded on the sales slip, it is necessary to record the other information called for, such as:

Sold by — the salesperson's initials or number.
Cash or *Charge* — a check mark in one of these boxes.
Amount Received — the amount received from the customer. For example, $10.00 would be recorded if the customer gave $10.00 to pay for a $7.50 sale.
Quantity — the total number of each item sold.
Description — the kind of item sold and the price of that item.
Amount — the answer you get by multiplying the quantity sold by the selling price of each item. For example, $20.00 would be entered in this column if you sold 2 tennis rackets at $10.00 each since 2 times $10.00 equals $20.00.
Customer's Signature — the signature of the customer if it is a charge sale.

In many businesses, the selling price is shown on each item either by means of a tag of some sort or by a notation on the outside of the package or container. There are other businesses, however, where the selling price is not shown on each article because of frequent changes in price. In these businesses, the salesclerk has to refer to a price list in order to find the amount of the sale.

SAMPLE PROBLEM

Jane Frank was employed as a salesclerk for the Union Office Supply Co. Her employer gave her a book of sales slips and a copy of a price list which contained the items on the next page.

Price list

Item	Unit	Unit Price
Copy paper	ream (rm.)	$1.30
Order books	dozen (dz.)	3.20
Pencil sharpeners	each (ea.)	6.10
Petty cash pads	dozen (dz.)	1.60
Postal scale	each (ea.)	5.35
Typing paper	ream (rm.)	4.15

On October 5, Jane made the following cash sale to a customer, Sam Owens, 110 Park Avenue, Raleigh, NC 27605:

1 postal scale
3 dozen order books
2 reams copy paper

The customer gave Jane $20.00 in payment and Jane prepared the sales slip shown below:

Original to customer

Duplicate for our records

Illustration 32b — Completed Sales Slip

Jane followed these steps in preparing the sales slip:

Step 1: Record the date of the sale and the customer's name and address.

In the proper places, Jane wrote: October 5, 19--, Sam Owens, 110 Park Avenue, Raleigh, NC 27605.

Step 2: Record the initials of the salesclerk and whether the sale was for cash or credit.

Jane wrote her initials under "Sold by" and placed a check mark under "Cash."

Step 3: Find the unit price for each item.

The *unit price* is the selling price, which Jane found by referring to the price list. It is important to notice that the items listed in the price list are sold in different quantities. For example, the postal scales are sold individually ($5.35 *each*); the order books are sold by the dozen ($3.20 per *dozen*); the copy paper is sold by the package ($1.30 per *ream*, which is a package of paper containing 480 to 500 sheets of paper). The symbol "@" shown in Illustration 32b is the business way of writing "at." It indicates that the price shown represents the cost of each *unit of measure*, that is each item, or dozen, or ream.

> Unit price = price for each unit of measure (each, dozen, etc.)

Step 4: Extend the amount for each item.

The total amount due for each item sold is called the *extension* of the sales slip. Since the unit price of 1 dozen order books was listed @ $3.20, Jane found the extension of 3 dozen order books by doing the following multiplication:

> Extension = quantity × unit price

$$3 \times \$3.20 = \$9.60$$

Since the unit price of a ream of copy paper was listed @ $1.30, the extension for two reams of copy paper was found by doing the following multiplication:

$$2 \times \$1.30 = \$2.60$$

Step 5: Total the sales slip.

Jane added the three amounts on the sales slip. The total was $17.55. When she mentioned this amount to the customer, Mr. Owens gave her $20.00 in payment. To avoid any possible question about this amount, Jane immediately wrote this amount on the sales slip, as shown in Illustration 32b on page 218. At this point, Jane rang up the amount of the sale, $17.55, on the cash register and took out $2.45 in change. Here is the way Jane returned the change to Mr. Owens: She started with the amount of the sale and said, "$17.55"; then she handed Mr. Owens two dimes and said, "$17.75"; then she handed Mr. Owens a quarter and said "$18.00"; and then she handed Mr. Owens two one-dollar bills, saying "$19.00, $20.00."

If Mr. Owens had paid by check Jane would have written the word "check" in the space for the amount received.

PRACTICE PROBLEM

You have been employed as a salesclerk by the Silver Stationery Co. of New York City. Your employer has given you a book of sales slips and you are

to prepare a sales slip for each sale you make. It is important to check all your arithmetic since the amount each customer will pay you is based on the sales slip. Your employer gives you a price list that contains the following items:

Price list

Item	Unit	Unit Price
Book rings	dozen (dz.)	$ .70
Copy paper	ream (rm.)	1.30
Desk tray — large (lg.)	each (ea.)	2.80
Desk tray — small (sm.)	each (ea.)	2.40
Mimeograph paper	ream (rm.)	1.90
Order books	dozen (dz.)	3.20
Pencil sharpener	each (ea.)	6.10
Petty cash pads	dozen (dz.)	1.60
Postal scale	each (ea.)	5.35
Typing paper	ream (rm.)	4.15

Directions: On November 8, you made the ten cash sales shown below and on page 221. Prepare a separate sales slip for each sale using the price list you have been given. If necessary, use two lines for an item.

Sale #1
Customer's name: Louise Wilson
Address: 155 Chambers Street
         New York, NY 10007
Items sold: 2 reams typing paper
         3 reams copy paper
Amount received: $15.00
(If your work is correct, your total should be $12.20.)

Sale #2
Customer's name: Cromwell & Ross
Address: 221 W. 47th Street
         New York, NY 10036
Items sold: 5 dozen order books
         2 pencil sharpeners
Amount received: $30.00
(If your work is correct, your total should be $28.20.)

Sale #3
Customer's name: Lopez & Co., Inc.
Address: 1846 Broadway
         New York, NY 10023
Items sold: 4 dozen petty cash pads
         5 reams mimeo. paper
         2 desk trays (lg.)
Amount received: Paid by check
(If your work is correct, your total should be $21.50.)

Sale #4
Customer's name: Max Cohen
Address: 17 Duane Street
         New York, NY 10038
Items sold: 1 postal scale
         3 desk trays (sm.)
         4 reams copy paper
Amount received: $20.00
(If your work is correct, your total should be $17.75.)

Sale #5
Customer's name: Grand Corporation
Address: 220 Grand Street
         New York, NY 10013
Items sold: 5 dozen book rings
         2 pencil sharpeners
         6 reams typing paper
Amount received: Paid by check
(If your work is correct, your total should be $40.60.)

Sale #6
Customer's name: John West & Sons
Address: 507 Fifth Avenue
         New York, NY 10017
Items sold: 2 desk trays (lg.)
         2 dozen order books
         3 reams mimeo. paper
Amount received: $20.00.
(If your work is correct, your total should be $17.70.)

Sale #7	**Sale #8**
Customer's name: Gloria Payson	*Customer's name:* Madison Bros.
Address: 99 Washington Place New York, NY 10014	*Address:* 59 Lenox Avenue New York, NY 10026
Items sold: 6 reams copy paper 2 dozen book rings 1 pencil sharpener 3 reams typing paper	*Items sold:* 4 desk trays (lg.) 10 reams mimeo. paper 5 dozen order books 2 pencil sharpeners
Amount received: $30.00 (If your work is correct, your total should be $27.75.)	*Amount received:* Paid by check (If your work is correct, your total should be $58.40.)
Sale #9	**Sale #10**
Customer's name: Empire Sales Company	*Customer's name:* Evergreen Lawn Corporation
Address: 436 Greenwich Street New York, NY 10013	*Address:* 265 Fort Washington Avenue New York, NY 10032
Items sold: 9 reams copy paper 5 dozen petty cash pads 2 postal scales 7 reams typing paper	*Items sold:* 6 dozen book rings 4 desk trays (sm.) 5 reams mimeo. paper 2 pencil sharpeners
Amount received: Paid by check (If your work is correct, your total should be $59.45.)	*Amount received:* Paid by check (If your work is correct, your total should be $35.50.)

JOB 33 | PREPARING SALES SLIPS

Practicing Related Arithmetic	Copy and answer these problems:

Copy and answer these problems:

1) ½ × $ 6.22 = $ _____
2) ⅓ × $ 3.45 = $ _____
3) ¼ × $ 8.64 = $ _____
4) ½ × $36.28 = $ _____

5) ⅔ × $ 6.45 = $ _____
6) ¾ × $ 8.84 = $ _____
7) ⅔ × $35.10 = $ _____
8) ¾ × $16.80 = $ _____

AIM

To practice preparing sales slips when fractional parts of a unit are sold.

EXPLANATION

"Would it be easier if I bought 2 Dozen instead of 2½ Dozen?"

Pens #2.44 DOZ.

The ability to do arithmetic accurately is very important in preparing sales slips. In certain businesses you may find it necessary to multiply the unit price by a fraction. For example, you may sell 2½ dozen pens selling for $2.44 per dozen. In order to complete the sales slip for this sale it will be necessary to multiply $2.44 by 2½.

SAMPLE PROBLEM

You are asked to complete a sales slip that contains the following information:

2½ dozen pens at $2.44 per dozen

Many businesspeople think of this problem in two steps:

Step 1   ½ (dozen) × $2.44 = $1.22
Step 2   2 (dozen) × $2.44 = 4.88
                          Total = $6.10

When you combine these two steps you have this multiplication problem:

$2.44
  2½
 122   (½ × 244)
 488   (2 × 244)
$6.10

The decimal point was placed in the answer by moving the decimal point two places to the left. This follows the rule that you count off as many places in the answer of a multiplication problem as there are decimal places in the numbers in the problem itself. Since there were two decimal places in the number $2.44, we counted off two decimal places in the answer.

Occasionally you may have an extension such as 2½ dozen at $4.67 which presents an additional problem.

$$\begin{array}{r} \$\ 4.67 \\ 2\frac{1}{2} \\ \hline 233\frac{1}{2} \\ 934 \\ \hline \$11.67\frac{1}{2} \end{array}$$

Since the answer must be expressed in dollars and cents it is necessary to *round off* the answer to $11.68. Whenever the third place after the decimal point is ½ or more, the third place is changed to an extra cent. Whenever the third place is less than ½, it is dropped. For example:

Rounding off numbers

$$\begin{array}{rcl} \$15.47\frac{1}{2} &=& \$15.48 \\ 1.12\frac{1}{3} &=& 1.12 \\ 3.10\frac{1}{4} &=& 3.10 \\ 6.05\frac{2}{3} &=& 6.06 \\ 4.01\frac{3}{4} &=& 4.02 \end{array}$$

PRACTICE PROBLEMS

Problem 1

You are the salesclerk for the Olympic Men's Shop, San Francisco, California. On March 6, you sold the following merchandise to Nick Grasso, 189 Fillmore Street, San Francisco, CA 94117. (Mr. Grasso gave you $40.00.)

1 sweater	@	$14.50 each
2 ties	@	3.90 each
4 pairs socks	@	1.60 per pair
1½ dozen handkerchiefs	@	4.80 per dozen

Directions:
a) Prepare the sales slip. (If your work is correct, your answer should be $35.90.)
b) How much change should Mr. Grasso receive?

Problem 2

You are the salesclerk for the Federal Drug Store, Jacksonville, Florida. On January 12, you sold the following merchandise to R. Kyle, 2114 Pearce Street, Jacksonville, FL 32209. (Ms. Kyle gave you $15.00.)

2 tubes of toothpaste	@	$ .85 each
1 pair scissors	@	5.60 each
2½ dozen emery boards	@	.40 per dozen
3 toothbrushes	@	1.20 each

Directions:

a) Prepare the sales slip. (If your work is correct, your total should be $11.90.)

b) How much change should Ms. Kyle receive?

Problem 3

You are the salesclerk for the Commerce Supply Co., Boston, Massachusetts. On July 26, you sold the following merchandise to Johnson & Co., 159 State Street, Boston, MA 02109. (Johnson & Co. gave you $30.00.)

2⅓ dozen memo pads	@	$ .90 per dozen
3 reams typing paper	@	4.80 each
4 dozen manila folders	@	.60 per dozen
1 pencil sharpener	@	8.50 each

Directions:

a) Prepare the sales slip. (If your work is correct, your total should be $27.40.)

b) How much change should Johnson & Co. receive?

Problem 4

You are the salesclerk for the Today Ladies Store, Chicago, Illinois. On April 27, you sold the following merchandise to Linda Washington, 321 South Clark Street, Chicago, IL 60604. (Ms. Washington gave you $30.00.)

2¼ dozen handkerchiefs	@	$3.20 per dozen
4 pairs hose	@	1.45 per pair
2 slips	@	3.75 each
1 pair gloves	@	4.98 per pair

Directions:

a) Prepare the sales slip. (If your work is correct, your total should be $25.48.)

b) How much change should Ms. Washington receive?

Problem 5

You are the salesclerk for the Wilson Sport Store, Brooklyn, New York. On February 17, you sold the following merchandise to the Bath Beach Club, 2620 Benson Avenue, Brooklyn, NY 11214. (The Bath Beach Club gave you a check for the exact amount.)

Round off

7 sweat suits	@	$ 8.90 each
3 pairs track shoes	@	11.40 per pair
1½ dozen "T" shirts	@	7.25 per dozen
4 dozen sweat socks	@	6.10 per dozen

Directions: Prepare the sales slip. (If your work is correct, your total should be $131.78.)

Problem 6

You are the salesclerk for the Manor Office Supply House, Newark, New Jersey. On May 29, you sold the following merchandise to Jackson & Hansen, 212 Broad Street, Newark, NJ 07102. (Jackson & Hansen gave you a check for the exact amount.)

2⅓ dozen looseleaf rings	@	$ .70	per dozen
3 sales binders	@	8.35	each
1 bulletin board	@	11.60	each
1½ dozen memo books	@	10.00	per dozen

Round off

Directions: Prepare the sales slip. (If your work is correct, your total should be $53.28.)

Problem 7

You are the salesclerk for the Viking Athletic Co., Oakland, California. On June 9, you sold the following merchandise to the Lincoln Community Center, 2325 Valdez Street, Oakland, CA 94612. (The Lincoln Community Center gave you a check for the exact amount.)

1½ dozen tennis balls	@	$7.60	per dozen
6 pairs sneakers	@	8.70	per pair
4¼ dozen ping pong balls	@	2.85	per dozen
1 table tennis net	@	5.10	each

Round off

Directions: Prepare the sales slip. (If your work is correct, your total should be $80.81.)

JOB 34 | DETERMINING SALES TAXES

Practicing Related Arithmetic

Copy and answer the following problems:

1) 4 × $5.27 = $ _____
2) 6 × $8.24 = $ _____
3) 8 × $3.98 = $ _____
4) 3½ × $4.52 = $ _____
5) 5¼ × $7.24 = $ _____
6) 2⅓ × $5.11 = $ _____

AIM

To learn how to find the sales tax on sales of merchandise.

EXPLANATION

"But the tag is marked $30.00."

There are many communities where the retailer is required to collect a sales tax from each customer. The tax is based on the selling price of the items sold. The amount of the tax varies from state to state as do the sales tax regulations. In some communities, the sales tax is a state tax, which means that all retailers in the state must collect money for the sales tax from each customer and turn it over to the state. In other communities, the sales tax is a local tax. The money collected for local taxes must be turned over to the local government.

Where both state and local sales taxes are charged, the taxes are usually combined so that the retailer need collect only one amount. The state of New York, for example, requires all retailers to collect a sales tax of 4% on taxable items. However, since New York City has its own sales tax, retailers who do business in New York City must collect a sales tax of 8% from all customers, 4% for the state and 4% for the city.

Sales slips must show sales tax

Each sales slip must show not only the amount of the sale, but also the amount of the sales tax. To help the salesclerk compute the sales tax, tables are published showing the amount of tax due on sales of $1 or less. Tables for Indiana, New Jersey, Pennsylvania, California, and New York (city and state) appear below and on page 227.

Tables for Indiana's 4% Sales Tax

Indiana 4% tax

Table A — Sale of $1.00 or Less		Table B — Sale of $1.01 or More	
Amount of Sale	**Tax**	**Amount of Sale**	**Tax**
1¢ – 15¢	No tax	1¢ – 12¢	—
16¢ – 37¢	1¢	13¢ – 37¢	1¢
38¢ – 62¢	2¢	38¢ – 62¢	2¢
63¢ – 87¢	3¢	63¢ – 87¢	3¢
88¢ – $1.00	4¢	88¢ – to next even dollar	4¢

On a sale over $1.00, take 4¢ on each full dollar plus the tax given in Table B for the amount over an even dollar.

Table for New Jersey's 5% Sales Tax	
Amount of Sale	Tax
1¢ – 10¢	No tax
11¢ – 25¢	1¢
26¢ – 46¢	2¢
47¢ – 67¢	3¢
68¢ – 88¢	4¢
89¢ – $1.00	5¢

On a sale over $1.00, take 5¢ for each full dollar plus the tax given in the chart above for the amount over an even dollar.

Table for Pennsylvania's 6% Sales Tax	
Amount of Sale	Tax
1¢ – 10¢	No tax
11¢ – 17¢	1¢
18¢ – 34¢	2¢
35¢ – 50¢	3¢
51¢ – 67¢	4¢
68¢ – 84¢	5¢
85¢ – $1.00	6¢

On a sale over $1.00, take 6¢ for each full dollar plus the tax given in the chart above for the amount over an even dollar.

Tables for California's 6% Sales Tax

Table A — Sale of $1.00 or Less		Table B — Sale of $1.01 or More	
Amount of Sale	Tax	Amount of Sale	Tax
1¢ – 10¢	No tax	1¢ – 8¢	—
11¢ – 22¢	1¢	9¢ – 24¢	1¢
23¢ – 39¢	2¢	25¢ – 41¢	2¢
40¢ – 56¢	3¢	42¢ – 58¢	3¢
57¢ – 73¢	4¢	59¢ – 74¢	4¢
74¢ – 90¢	5¢	75¢ – 91¢	5¢
91¢ – $1.00	6¢	92¢ – to next even dollar	6¢

On a sale over $1.00, take 6¢ on each full dollar plus the tax given in Table B for the amount over an even dollar.

Tables for Combined New York State and City Sales Tax — 8%
(4% state; 4% city)

Table A — Sale of $1.00 or Less		Table B — Sale of $1.01 or More	
Amount of Sale	Tax	Amount of Sale	Tax
1¢ – 10¢	No tax	1¢ – 6¢	—
11¢ – 17¢	1¢	7¢ – 18¢	1¢
18¢ – 29¢	2¢	19¢ – 31¢	2¢
30¢ – 42¢	3¢	32¢ – 43¢	3¢
43¢ – 54¢	4¢	44¢ – 56¢	4¢
55¢ – 67¢	5¢	57¢ – 68¢	5¢
68¢ – 79¢	6¢	69¢ – 81¢	6¢
80¢ – 92¢	7¢	82¢ – 93¢	7¢
93¢ – $1.00	8¢	94¢ – to next even dollar	8¢

On a sale over $1.00, take 8¢ on each full dollar plus the tax given in Table B for the amount over an even dollar.

New Jersey 5% tax

Pennsylvania 6% tax

California 6% tax

New York City 8% tax

Test your skill in using this table by seeing if you agree with the sales tax shown in these examples:

Amount of Sale	Tax
$ .12 (Indiana)	0¢
.35 (New Jersey)	2¢
.54 (Pennsylvania)	4¢
.78 (California)	5¢
.96 (New York City)	8¢
1.20 (Indiana)	5¢
1.54 (New Jersey)	8¢
1.09 (Pennsylvania)	6¢
1.22 (California)	7¢
1.37 (New York City)	11¢

SAMPLE PROBLEM

You are a sales clerk for the Royal Jewelry Store in New York City, and you sold a bracelet for $16.90 and a watch band for $3.97. Both items are subject to the New York City sales tax. The completed sales slip would look like this:

NO. 00161	Royal Jewelery Store
	165 Madison Avenue
	New York, NY 10016

Sold To: *A. Stacy* — December 20, 19 ——

Street: *59 Fulton Street*

City, State, Zip: *New York, NY 10038*

Sold by *T. H.*	Cash ✓	Charge	Amt. Rec'd $25.00
Quantity	Description		Amount
1	bracelet		16 90
1	watch band		3 97
	Amount of sale		20 87
	8% sales tax		1 67
	Total		22 54

Please keep this slip for future reference

Customer's Signature
for charge sales

The sales tax of $1.67 on the sale of $20.87
was found as follows:

Tax on $20.00 (20 × 8¢) $1.60
Tax on .87 (Tax Table B — Between
    82¢ and 93¢)   .07
Total tax $1.67

PRACTICE PROBLEMS

Problem 1

Directions:
a) Copy the form shown below and the amounts shown in the *Sales* column.
b) Find the sales tax and the total amount of the sale for each sale shown below. Use the tax tables on pages 226 and 227 to find the sales tax. Here is a sample based on the New York City tax to use as a guide:

Sample:	Sales	Sales Tax	Total
	$ .45	$ .04	$ .49

State or City	Sales	Amount of Sales Tax	Total
a) Indiana	15		
b) Pennsylvania	45		
c) New Jersey	80		
d) New York City	90		
e) Pennsylvania	1 05		
f) California	2 15		
g) New Jersey	1 75		
h) New York City	3 06		
i) Indiana	5 60		
j) California	6 60		
k) Pennsylvania	12 45		
l) New York City	50 40		
m) California	70 92		
n) New Jersey	123 10		
o) New York City	216 30		

Problem 2

Directions:
a) Copy the form and the amounts shown in the *Sales* column on the next page.

b) Find the sales tax and the total amount of the sale for each sale shown. Use the tax tables on pages 226 and 227 to find the sales tax.

State or City	Sales		Amount of Sales Tax		Total	
a) Indiana		35				
b) California		08				
c) New Jersey		45				
d) New York City		85				
e) Pennsylvania	1	40				
f) California	2	25				
g) New Jersey	2	75				
h) New York City	4	62				
i) Indiana	8	03				
j) California	6	30				
k) Pennsylvania	14	61				
l) New York City	30	36				
m) Pennsylvania	45	58				
n) New Jersey	124	30				
o) New York City	256	10				

Problem 3

Directions: Copy and complete the four sales slips prepared by salesclerks at Grand Department Store, New York, New York, that appear on page 231. Use the table for New York shown on page 227.

Problem 4

Directions: Copy and complete the four sales slips prepared by salesclerks at Barclay's Department Store, Sacramento, California, that appear on page 232. Use the table for California shown on page 227.

Sales Slip # 1

NO. 3066	*GRAND DEPARTMENT STORE* *29 Fifth Avenue* *New York, NY 10003*		
M. Braff *June 20,* 19——			
Sold To			
125 Park Avenue			
Street			
New York, NY 10017			
City, State, Zip			

Sold by S 610	Cash ✓	Charge	Amt. Rec'd $15.00
Quantity	Description		Amount
1 pr.	*sneakers @ $8.65*		8 65
2 pr.	*socks @ $1.25*		2 50
	Amount of sale		
	Sales tax		
	Total		

Please keep this slip for future reference

_____
Customer's Signature
for charge sales

Sales Slip # 2

NO. 3067	*GRAND DEPARTMENT STORE* *29 Fifth Avenue* *New York, NY 10003*		
J. Cohen *June 20,* 19——			
Sold To			
62 West 50th Street			
Street			
New York, NY 10020			
City, State, Zip			

Sold by J 221	Cash ✓	Charge	Amt. Rec'd $40.00
Quantity	Description		Amount
1	*gold pin*		25 50
1	*link bracelet*		8 25
	Amount of sale		
	Sales tax		
	Total		

Please keep this slip for future reference

_____
Customer's Signature
for charge sales

Sales Slip #3

NO. 3068	*GRAND DEPARTMENT STORE* *29 Fifth Avenue* *New York, NY 10003*		
P. Mason *June 20,* 19——			
Sold To			
641 Second Avenue			
Street			
New York, NY 10016			
City, State, Zip			

Sold by ST 15	Cash ✓	Charge	Amt. Rec'd $20.00
Quantity	Description		Amount
2 bx.	*stationery @ $5.75*		
5	*ball point pens @ $.48*		
	Amount of sale		
	Sales tax		
	Total		

Please keep this slip for future reference

_____
Customer's Signature
for charge sales

Sales Slip # 4

NO. 3069	*GRAND DEPARTMENT STORE* *29 Fifth Avenue* *New York, NY 10003*		
A. Ludwig *June 20,* 19——			
Sold To			
726 College Avenue			
Street			
Bronx, NY 10451			
City, State, Zip			

Sold by D 76	Cash ✓	Charge	Amt. Rec'd $5.00
Quantity	Description		Amount
2	*toothbrushes @ $.89*		
3	*combs @ $.46*		
	Amount of sale		
	Sales tax		
	Total		

Please keep this slip for future reference

_____
Customer's Signature
for charge sales

Sales Slip # 1

NO. 6750	BARCLAY'S DEPARTMENT STORE 1905 BROADWAY SACRAMENTO, CA 95818

Sold To: *B. Dawer*   Sept. 29, 19--
Street: *495 Baxter Street*
City, State, Zip: *Sacramento, CA 95815*

Sold by H 315	Cash ✓	Charge	Amt. Rec'd $20.00
Quantity	Description		Amount
2 dz.	cups @ $4.80		
1	punch bowl @ $7.65		
	Amount of sale		
	Sales tax		
	Total		

Please keep this slip for future reference

_____
Customer's Signature
for charge sales

Sales Slip # 2

NO. 6751	BARCLAY'S DEPARTMENT STORE 1905 BROADWAY SACRAMENTO, CA 95818

Sold To: *M. Roseman*   Sept. 29, 19--
Street: *1508 Grand Avenue*
City, State, Zip: *Sacramento, CA 95838*

Sold by S 172	Cash ✓	Charge	Amt. Rec'd check
Quantity	Description		Amount
2 bx.	staples @ $1.05		
4 bx.	stationery @ $6.20		
	Amount of sale		
	Sales tax		
	Total		

Please keep this slip for future reference

_____
Customer's Signature
for charge sales

Sales Slip # 3

NO. 6752	BARCLAY'S DEPARTMENT STORE 1905 BROADWAY SACRAMENTO, CA 95818

Sold To: *K. Peterson*   Sept. 29, 19--
Street: *1137 Cypress Street*
City, State, Zip: *Sacramento, CA 95814*

Sold by F 622	Cash ✓	Charge	Amt. Rec'd Check
Quantity	Description		Amount
1	desk set @ $15.80		
2	lamps @ $8.15		
	Amount of sale		
	Sales tax		
	Total		

Please keep this slip for future reference

_____
Customer's Signature
for charge sales

Sales Slip # 4

NO. 6753	BARCLAY'S DEPARTMENT STORE 1905 BROADWAY SACRAMENTO, CA 95818

Sold To: *B. Miller*   Sept. 29, 19--
Street: *780 Oxford Street*
City, State, Zip: *Sacramento, CA 95814*

Sold by D 314	Cash ✓	Charge	Amt. Rec'd check
Quantity	Description		Amount
2 pr.	earrings @ $4.65		
1	wrist watch @ $23.10		
	Amount of sale		
	Sales tax		
	Total		

Please keep this slip for future reference

_____
Customer's Signature
for charge sales

Practicing Related Arithmetic

Copy and answer the following problems:

1) $317.30 × .01 = $ _____
2) $426.20 × .03 = $ _____
3) $275.40 × .05 = $ _____
4) $528.90 × .06 = $ _____
5) $372.25 × .04 = $ _____
6) $463.70 × .08 = $ _____

AIM

To practice finding the sales tax on retail sales when both labor and materials are to be taxed.

EXPLANATION

In the preceding job you learned that in certain communities the retailer is required to collect a sales tax from his customers.

In many communities, this tax applies not only to goods sold, but also to certain services sold by retailers. For example, to have your automobile repaired in the State of New York, you must pay a sales tax not only on the parts used in repairing your car, but also on the labor charged for the repairs.

Sales tax on parts and labor

SAMPLE PROBLEM

As an employee in the office of the Atlas Auto Repair Shop in New York City, you are asked to prepare a sales slip (often called a *bill*) for Harry Grant. Mr. Grant had his car repaired and is to be charged for materials and labor. You are to include the necessary sales tax based on this table:

Table for Combined New York State and City Sales Tax — 8%
(4% state; 4% city)

Table A — Sales of $1.00 or Less		Table B — Sales of $1.01 or More	
1¢–10¢	No tax	1¢– 6¢	—
11¢–17¢	1¢	7¢–18¢	1¢
18¢–29¢	2¢	19¢–31¢	2¢
30¢–42¢	3¢	32¢–43¢	3¢
43¢–54¢	4¢	44¢–56¢	4¢
55¢–67¢	5¢	57¢–68¢	5¢
68¢–79¢	6¢	69¢–81¢	6¢
80¢–92¢	7¢	82¢–93¢	7¢
93¢–$1.00	8¢	94¢–to next even dollar	8¢

On a sale of more than $1.00, take 8¢ on each full dollar plus the tax shown in Table B for the amount over an even dollar.

The completed sales slip or bill would look like this:

NO. *19900*

Atlas Auto Repair Shop
38 Broad Street
New York, NY 10004

NAME *Harry Grant*
ADDRESS *175 Baxter Street*
New York, NY 10013

YEAR	MAKE	LICENSE NO.	MILEAGE	DATE	
1974	*Ford*	*321NLY*	*9,430*	*October 8, 19--*	
DESCRIPTION				MATERIALS	LABOR
Install wind deflectors				12 00	10 00
Replace right window				38 00	20 00
TOTALS				50 00	30 00
MATERIALS FORWARD				▷	50 00
SUB-TOTAL					80 00
8% SALES TAX					6 40
FINAL TOTAL					86 40

The sales tax of $6.40 was based upon the total charge for materials and labor as follows: Tax on $80.00 (80 × 8¢) = $6.40.

"My dad comes home at five. Can you fix it by then?.."

PRACTICE PROBLEMS

Problem 1

Directions:

a) Copy the form on page 235 including the amounts shown in the "Labor" column and the "Materials" column.

b) Find the sales tax and the final total for each bill. Here is a sample to use as a guide, based on the New York City sales chart on page 233:

	Labor	Materials	Total Labor and Materials (Sub-total)	Sales Tax	Final Total
Sample:	$5.00	$15.00	$20.00	$1.60	$21.60

	Labor	Materials	Total Labor and Materials (Sub-total)	Sales Tax	Final Total
a	10 00	20 00			
b	6 00	14 00			
c	8 50	10 00			
d	16 00	30 25			
e	25 50	50 90			
f	38 60	60 45			
g	40 00	76 85			
h	23 50	48 15			
i	70 00	123 95			
j	57 50	152 65			

Problem 2

Directions:
a) Copy the form shown below including the amounts shown in the "Labor" column and the "Materials" column.

b) Find the sales tax and the final total for each bill.

	Labor	Materials	Total Labor and Materials (Sub-total)	Sales Tax	Final Total
a	8 00	40 00			
b	10 00	30 00			
c	12 00	24 50			
d	26 00	30 30			
e	42 60	60 45			
f	18 70	50 25			
g	30 00	86 80			
h	41 00	72 20			
i	70 50	130 35			
j	63 40	129 25			

Problem 3

Directions: Copy and complete the four bills on pages 236–237.

Bill # 1

NO. 19901

Atlas Auto Repair Shop
38 Broad Street
New York, NY 10004

NAME *Roberto Hernandez*

ADDRESS *739 Boston Road*

Bronx, NY 10456

YEAR	MAKE	LICENSE NO.	MILEAGE	DATE		
1973	Chrysler	217 BXX	25,315	October 9, 19--		
DESCRIPTION				MATERIALS	LABOR	
Replace fan belt				3 50	6 00	
Replace left front fender				54 00	25 00	
Motor tune-up					24 95	
Spark plugs				7 20		
TOTALS						
MATERIALS FORWARD ——————				⟶		
SUB-TOTAL						
8% SALES TAX						
FINAL TOTAL						

Bill # 2

NO. 19902

Atlas Auto Repair Shop
38 Broad Street
New York, NY 10004

NAME *Helen Lucas*

ADDRESS *877 Church Avenue*

Brooklyn, NY 11218

YEAR	MAKE	LICENSE NO.	MILEAGE	DATE		
1974	Chev.	786 BKL	15,110	October 9, 19--		
DESCRIPTION				MATERIALS	LABOR	
Replace rear brake shoes				30 02	16 00	
Balance front wheels					6 50	
Anti-freeze				3 80		
Replace thermostat				5 25	3 50	
TOTALS						
MATERIALS FORWARD ——————				⟶		
SUB-TOTAL						
8% SALES TAX						
FINAL TOTAL						

Bill # 3

NO. *19903*

Atlas Auto Repair Shop
38 Broad Street
New York, NY 10004

NAME *James Ross*
ADDRESS *38 Jane Street*
New York, NY 10014

YEAR	MAKE	LICENSE NO.	MILEAGE	DATE		
1973	*Plymouth*	*546NGE*	*20,614*	*October 9, 19--*		
DESCRIPTION				MATERIALS		LABOR
Replace tube and fix flat				4	50	1	50
Paint left front door						14	00
Replace left front molding				8	75	
Replace shocks				42	55	21	00
TOTALS						
MATERIALS FORWARD				➤		
SUB-TOTAL						
8 % SALES TAX						
FINAL TOTAL						

Bill # 4

NO. *19904*

Atlas Auto Repair Shop
38 Broad Street
New York, NY 10004

NAME *William Kelly*
ADDRESS *139 East 27th Street*
New York, NY 10016

YEAR	MAKE	LICENSE NO.	MILEAGE	DATE		
1973	*Dodge*	*828NUY*	*24,630*	*October 9, 19--*		
DESCRIPTION				MATERIALS		LABOR
Repair and repaint trunk lid						56	00
Replace gas filter				5	85	5	50
Replace window washer motor				45	43	5	50
Replace oil filter				4	95	2	50
TOTALS						
MATERIALS FORWARD				➤		
SUB-TOTAL						
8 % SALES TAX						
FINAL TOTAL						

JOB 36 | DETERMINING SALES TAXES

Practicing Related Arithmetic

Copy and answer the following problems:

1) $463.00 × 1% = $ _____
2) $792.80 × 1% = $ _____
3) $536.35 × 1% = $ _____
4) $ 37.00 × 8% = $ _____
5) $ 84.92 × 5% = $ _____

6) $635.90 × 10% = $ _____
7) $458.23 × 10% = $ _____
8) $ 62.71 × 10% = $ _____
9) $124.60 × 4% = $ _____
10) $215.48 × 6% = $ _____

AIM

To practice finding the sales tax on retail sales when only materials are taxed.

"We charge tax only on parts."

AUTO REPAIRS

EXPLANATION

Sales tax regulations vary from state to state. Most states will not tax such items as medicine and food. There are some states where basic articles of clothing are not taxed. In the previous job you practiced completing bills in which both labor and materials were subject to a sales tax. In some states, Indiana for example, labor and services are not taxed. In such states it is necessary to separate on a sales slip the charges for labor from the charges for materials. The sales tax then would be figured only on the charges for materials.

In this job you will practice preparing bills in which only the materials used are taxable.

You work for the Lion Auto Repair Shop. Paul Kaspar, of 53 Fairfield Avenue, Indianapolis, Indiana, has his car repaired and you are asked to prepare the bill. The completed bill is shown on page 239.

Sales tax on materials only

The sales tax of 80¢ was based only on the charge for materials as follows: Tax on $20.00 (20 × 4¢) = 80¢.

NO. 56100

LION AUTO REPAIR SHOP
2525 Ralston Avenue
Indianapolis, IN 46218

NAME *Paul Kaspar*

ADDRESS *53 Fairfield Avenue*

Indianapolis, IN 46205

YEAR	MAKE	LICENSE NO.	MILEAGE	DATE	
1974	Lincoln	93A3114	8,156	March 26, 19--	
DESCRIPTION				MATERIALS	LABOR
Replace fan belt				3 00	3 50
Repair right rear door				17 00	31 00
TOTALS				20 00	34 50
MATERIALS FORWARD ⎯⎯⎯⎯⎯⎯⎯⎯⎯⎯ ▷					20 00
4% SALES TAX IN MATERIALS					80
FINAL TOTAL					55 30

PRACTICE PROBLEMS

Problem 1

Directions:

a) Copy the form below and the amounts shown in the "Labor" column and the "Materials" column.

b) Find the sales tax and the final total for each bill. (You may use the sales tax table on page 226.)

	Labor	Materials	Indiana Sales Tax	Final Total
Example	5 00	10 00	40	15 40
a	9 50	20 00		
b	4 70	30 00		
c	25 60	14 20		
d	15 40	34 04		
e	19 50	43 40		
f	34 15	71 90		
g	42 25	126 50		
h	56 80	173 60		
i	81 75	212 15		
j	76 30	187 65		

Problem 2

Directions:

a) Copy the form shown below including the amounts shown in the "Labor" column and the "Materials" column.

b) Find the sales tax and the final total for each bill. (You may use the sales tax table on page 226.)

	Labor	Materials	Indiana Sales Tax	Final Total
a	25 00	10 00		
b	8 30	50 00		
c	5 60	25 50		
d	18 15	31 06		
e	27 80	84 75		
f	48 40	63 88		
g	81 25	126 30		
h	52 50	239 20		
i	65 10	182 65		
j	71 75	256 25		

Problem 3

You are employed by the Lion Auto Repair Shop, Indianapolis, Indiana.

Directions: Copy and complete the six bills shown on pages 241–243. Record the sales tax on all charges for materials.

Bill # 1

NO. 56101

LION AUTO REPAIR SHOP
2525 Ralston Avenue
Indianapolis, IN 46218

NAME *Norman Klein*

ADDRESS *1616 N. Gale Street*

Indianapolis, IN 46218

YEAR	MAKE	LICENSE NO.	MILEAGE	DATE		
1973	Chev.	93A5912	26,309	March 27, 19--		
DESCRIPTION				MATERIALS		LABOR
Replace battery				30 40		
Install bumper guards				34 00		6 00
Replace oil filter				4 10		2 50
Replace wheel bearings						8 00
TOTALS						
MATERIALS FORWARD				▷		
4% SALES TAX ON MATERIALS						
FINAL TOTAL						

Bill # 2

NO. 56102

LION AUTO REPAIR SHOP
2525 Ralston Avenue
Indianapolis, IN 46218

NAME *Tom Rock*

ADDRESS *3630 Penway Street*

Indianapolis, IN 46222

YEAR	MAKE	LICENSE NO.	MILEAGE	DATE		
1972	Lincoln	93A 171	45,820	March 29, 19--		
DESCRIPTION				MATERIALS		LABOR
Replace transmission bracket				2 10		10 00
Points				5 35		
Spark plugs				9 60		
Tune-up						34 95
TOTALS						
MATERIALS FORWARD				▷		
4% SALES TAX ON MATERIALS						
FINAL TOTAL						

Bill # 3

NO. 56103

LION AUTO REPAIR SHOP
2525 Ralston Avenue
Indianapolis, IN 46218

NAME *Jim Slattery*

ADDRESS *1100 Milburn Street*

Indianapolis, IN 46202

YEAR	MAKE	LICENSE NO.	MILEAGE	DATE		
1974	Ford	93A2915	10,817	March 29, 19--		
DESCRIPTION				MATERIALS	LABOR	
Front end alignment					14	95
Change oil				.5 40		
Grease				4 20	3	00
Install trailer hitch				19 15	8	50
TOTALS						
MATERIALS FORWARD _____				▷		
4 % SALES TAX ON MATERIALS						
FINAL TOTAL						

Bill # 4

NO. 56104

LION AUTO REPAIR SHOP
2525 Ralston Avenue
Indianapolis, IN 46218

NAME *Charles Johnson*

ADDRESS *415 Hudson Street*

Indianapolis, IN 46204

YEAR	MAKE	LICENSE NO.	MILEAGE	DATE		
1974	Dodge	93A2383	6,917	March 29, 19--		
DESCRIPTION				MATERIALS	LABOR	
Replace oil filter				3 95	2	50
Install auxiliary speaker				9 25	9	00
Tune-up					32	95
Change oil				5 40		
TOTALS						
MATERIALS FORWARD _____				▷		
4 % SALES TAX ON MATERIALS						
FINAL TOTAL						

Bill # 5

NO. 56105

LION AUTO REPAIR SHOP
2525 Ralston Avenue
Indianapolis, IN 46218

NAME *Judy Justman*
ADDRESS *929 Broadway*
Indianapolis, IN 46202

YEAR	MAKE	LICENSE NO.	MILEAGE	DATE		
1973	Ford	93A2792	25,906	*March 29,19--*		
DESCRIPTION				MATERIALS	LABOR	
Wiper blades				3 95		
Replace right rear fender				48 00	23 50	
Install water hose				1 75	3 00	
Balance wheels					8 75	
TOTALS						
MATERIALS FORWARD				▷		
4 % SALES TAX ON MATERIALS						
FINAL TOTAL						

Bill # 6

NO. 56106

NAME *Donald Hamburg*
ADDRESS *410 Cameron Street*
Indianapolis, IN 46225

LION AUTO REPAIR SHOP
2525 Ralston Avenue
Indianapolis, IN 46218

YEAR	MAKE	LICENSE NO.	MILEAGE	DATE		
1973	Pontiac	93A4672	31,612	*March 29, 19--*		
DESCRIPTION				MATERIALS	LABOR	
Spark plugs				7 20		
Points				4 75		
Tune-up					24 85	
Change oil				5 30		
TOTALS						
MATERIALS FORWARD				▷		
4 % SALES TAX ON MATERIALS						
FINAL TOTAL						

Copy and answer the following addition problems:

	(1)	(2)	(3)	(4)	(5)
	$ 61.43	$ 87.15	$ 49.23	$172.54	$258.60
	28.77	136.85	86.58	219.46	119.55
	43.65	92.20	32.91	38.17	86.45
	59.26	175.98	128.65	157.68	274.78
	72.98	67.53	237.45	92.35	63.12
	37.82	44.72	159.84	84.79	192.86

AIM

To understand how to keep records of charge customers in a retail business.

EXPLANATION

Charge accounts

Have you noticed that in the previous lessons all the sales to customers were made for cash? As you must know, not all retail sales are made for cash. Many retail stores, particularly department stores, encourage their customers to open charge accounts.

"That's only a dollar a week for 100 years."

$5200.00

When customers are permitted to open charge accounts, they do not have to pay for their purchases at the time the purchases are made. Instead, the customers can pay a certain amount towards the purchases each week or each month, depending upon the policy of the store.

Not all customers are allowed to open charge accounts. The customer must be a safe credit risk before being given the privilege of starting a charge account. In order to determine whether or not a customer is a good credit risk, the store owner or credit manager will get information from the customer's employer and bank, and from other people in the community whose names are submitted by the customer as references.

Having decided that the customer is a good credit risk, some large department stores give the customer an identification card or metal disc in order to help the salesclerks identify those customers who are entitled to credit.

The businesses which sell on credit must keep careful records in order to know how much each customer owes. There are many types of records used by businesses. The simplest form used to keep a record of the amount owed by a customer is called an *account*. An account is a sheet of paper divided in half so that the sales to the customer can be recorded on one side and the cash received from the customer in payment can be recorded on the other side.

CUSTOMER'S ACCOUNT

Charge sales are recorded on this side	Cash received in payment is recorded on this side

---

In business, a printed form of the account is used which contains special columns for the date and for the amount.

DATE			AMOUNT	DATE			AMOUNT

debit — left side of account   credit — right side of account

Illustration 37a — An Account

Businesspeople, accountants, and bookkeepers call the left side of the account the *debit* side and the right side of the account the *credit* side.

The information for the account will be taken from a duplicate copy of the sales slip and from a record made of the payments received from charge customers.

Large retailers with many thousands of charge customers, such as major department stores, use automated data processing equipment to help keep records of the amounts due from customers. When this happens special forms of sales slips are used. One such form of sales slip has a data processing card as the carbon copy. The data processing card is sent to a special operator who punches holes in the card to correspond with the information written on the card.

Using automated data processing to prepare customers' accounts

All punched cards can now be processed through special electronic equipment to give the business a record of the amount each customer owes as well as information about the amount of merchandise sold and the amount of merchandise left in stock.

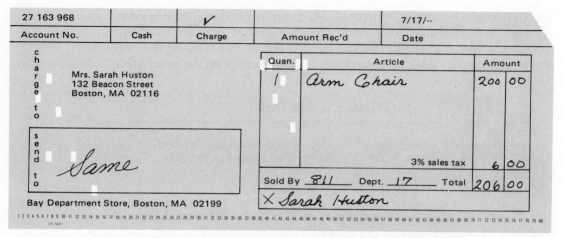

| 27 163 968 | | ✓ | | 7/17/-- |
| Account No. | Cash | Charge | Amount Rec'd | Date |

	Quan.	Article	Amount
Mrs. Sarah Huston 132 Beacon Street Boston, MA 02116	1	Arm Chair	200 00

charge to

send to — *Same*

Bay Department Store, Boston, MA 02199

| | 3% sales tax | 6 00 |

Sold By _811_   Dept. _17_   Total | 206 00

X *Sarah Huston*

1 2 3 4 5 6 7 8 9 10 11 12 13 14 15 16 17 18 19 20 21 22 23 24 25 26 27 28 29 30 31 32 33 34 35 36 37 38 39 40 41 42 43 44 45 46 47 48 49 50 51 52 53 54 55 56 57 58 59 60 61 62 63 64 65 66 67 68 69 70 71 72 73 74 75 76 77 78 79 80

Illustration 37b — Punched Sales Slip for Automated Data Processsing

Instead of using punched cards, some automated data processing systems use punched tape.

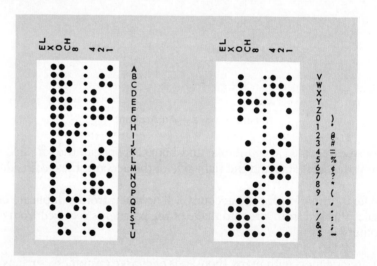

The punched tape can be produced either by the salesclerk using special equipment attached to the cash register, or by data processing operators who take the information from the sales slip.

Whether the record of charge customers is done manually (by hand), or electronically by machines, the same recording principles that you will practice in this job are used.

SAMPLE PROBLEM

The United Department Store opened a charge account for Mrs. Harriet Grover of Newark, New Jersey. The following information for the month of

April was taken from the duplicate sales slips and from the record of cash received from Mrs. Grover.

April	5	Sold to Mrs. Grover merchandise amounting to $35.00.
	11	Sold to Mrs. Grover merchandise amounting to $20.00.
	25	Received a check from Mrs. Grover for $25.00.
	27	Sold to Mrs. Grover merchandise amounting to $30.00.
	30	Received a check from Mrs. Grover for $40.00.

Here is the way the United Department Store would record this information in the charge account kept for Mrs. Grover:

NAME	Mrs. Harriet Grover						
ADDRESS	86 Camden Street, Newark, NJ 07107						

DATE		ITEM		DEBIT	DATE	ITEM	CREDIT
April '9--	5	Mdse.		35 00	April '9-- 25	Cash	25 00
	11	Mdse.	85.00 65.00	20 00	30	Cash	40 00
	27	Mdse.	20.00	30 00			65 00
				85 00			

Illustration 37c — Charge Account

These steps were followed in preparing the account:

Step 1: Record account heading.

At the time Mrs. Grover became a charge customer an account was opened for her by carefully copying her name and address at the top of an account. This account is used as a continuous record of all the business Mrs. Grover does with the United Department Store.

Step 2: Record charge sales.

The date and amount of each charge sale was copied from the store's duplicate sales slip and recorded on the *left*, or *debit*, side of the account.   Left side = debit

Step 3: Record payments received.

The date and amount of each payment received was recorded on the *right*, or *credit*, side of the account. Notice that although the date of each sale and each payment received was recorded, the month and year were recorded only once on each side.   Right side = credit

The year is recorded only at the top of the "Date" column and the month is written only once until the month changes. Then the new month is recorded.

Step 4: Find the total sales.

The total sales were found by pencil footing the charge sales on the debit side of the account. Notice that the pencil footing $85.00 was written with a well-sharpened pencil so that the numbers could be written in small yet legible figures.

Step 5: Find the total payments received.

The total of payments received ($65.00) was found by pencil footing the amounts on the credit side of the account. Notice again that the pencil footing of $65.00 was written in small, legible figures. (If there is only one amount in a column, it is not necessary to pencil foot.)

Step 6: Find the balance of the account.

Total debits
− Total credits
= Balance

The amount Mrs. Grover still owes the United Department Store is called the *balance of the account*. At the end of the month of April, Mrs. Grover owes the United Department Store a balance of $20.00. This amount was found by means of the following subtraction problem:

Total sales (total debits)	$85.00
Total cash received (total credits)	− 65.00
Balance of the account	= $20.00

Notice that this subtraction problem was done in small, penciled figures on the debit side of the account. (If the total debits equal the total credits, there is no balance. You would show only the pencil footings.)

PRACTICE PROBLEM

You are employed as an assistant to the bookkeeper by the Royce Department Store and it is your job to keep the accounts for charge customers. The information on the following pages was taken from the duplicate sales slips and from the record of payments received from the charge customers.

Directions:
a) Open an account for each charge customer listed on pages 248–250. (This means you are to write each customer's name and address at the top of an account.)
b) Record in each customer's account the charge sales and the money collected.
c) Find the total charge sales (pencil foot the debit side).
d) Find the total amount received in payment (pencil foot the credit side).
e) Find the balance of the account by subtracting the credits from the debits. (Do the arithmetic on the debit side.)

Account #1
Customer's Name: Mrs. T. H. Chang
Address: 119 N. Franklin Street, Chicago, IL 60606

Nov. 5   Sold to Mrs. Chang merchandise amounting to $128.35.

      13   Sold to Mrs. Chang merchandise amounting to $85.10.

      19   Received from Mrs. Chang a check for $80.00 in part payment of her account.

      27   Received from Mrs. Chang a check for $45.00 in part payment of her account.

      30   Received from Mrs. Chang a check for $25.00 in part payment of her account. (If your work is correct, the balance should be $63.45.)

Account #2

Customer's Name: Miss Lois Costa

Address: 914 S. Bishop Street, Chicago, IL 60607.

Nov. 2   Sold to Miss Costa merchandise amounting to $83.55.

      15   Received from Miss Costa a check for $50.00 in part payment of her account.

      16   Sold to Miss Costa merchandise amounting to $69.70.

      26   Received from Miss Costa a check for $33.55 in payment of the balance due on the sale of November 2.

      28   Sold to Miss Costa merchandise amounting to $18.65. (If your work is correct, the balance should be $88.35.)

Account #3

Customer's Name: Miss Marie Dunn

Address: 502 W. School Street, Chicago, IL 60657

Nov. 1   Sold to Miss Dunn merchandise amounting to $72.95.

      2   Sold to Miss Dunn merchandise amounting to $93.20.

      16   Received from Miss Dunn a check for $60.00 in part payment of her account.

      21   Sold to Miss Dunn merchandise amounting to $68.75.

      29   Received from Miss Dunn a check for $75.00 in part payment of her account. (If your work is correct, the balance should be $99.90.)

Account #4

Customer's Name: Miss Judith Levenson

Address: 488 S. Hamlin Avenue, Chicago, IL 60624

Nov. 5   Sold to Miss Levenson merchandise amounting to $75.70.

      15   Received from Miss Levenson a check for $35.00 in part payment of her account.

      16   Sold to Miss Levenson merchandise amounting to $85.25.

      23   Sold to Miss Levenson merchandise amounting to $53.40.

      28   Received from Miss Levenson a check for $40.70 in payment of the balance due on the sale of November 5. (If your work is correct, the balance should be $138.65.)

Account #5

Customer's Name: Mrs. Diane Malloy

Address: 1126 S. Keeler Avenue, Chicago, IL 60624

Nov. 6   Sold to Mrs. Malloy merchandise amounting to $92.46.

9   Sold to Mrs. Malloy merchandise amounting to $122.75.

23   Received from Mrs. Malloy $125.00 in part payment of her account.

26   Sold to Mrs. Malloy merchandise amounting to $58.90.

30   Received from Mrs. Malloy $80.00 in part payment of her account. (If your work is correct, the balance should be $69.11.)

Account #6

Customer's Name: Mrs. Alice Ogden

Address: 737 S. Austin Avenue, Chicago, IL 60644

Nov. 7   Sold to Mrs. Ogden merchandise amounting to $43.85.

9   Sold to Mrs. Ogden merchandise amounting to $67.30.

22   Received from Mrs. Ogden a check for $43.85 in payment of the sale of November 7.

23   Sold to Mrs. Ogden merchandise amounting to $27.45.

26   Received from Mrs. Ogden a check for $67.30 in payment of the sale of November 9. (If your work is correct, the balance should be $27.45.)

Account #7

Customer's Name: Mrs. Edna Rhodes

Address: 5631 S. Lafayette Avenue, Chicago, IL 60621

Nov. 2   Sold to Mrs. Rhodes merchandise amounting to $82.65.

12   Sold to Mrs. Rhodes merchandise amounting to $91.70.

22   Received from Mrs. Rhodes a check for $82.65 in payment of the sale of November 2.

26   Sold to Mrs. Rhodes merchandise amounting to $61.35.

30   Received from Mrs. Rhodes a check for $91.70 in payment of the sale of November 12. (If your work is correct, the balance should be $61.35.)

Account #8

Customer's Name: Mrs. Clara Sorensen

Address: 1211 S. Indiana Avenue, Chicago, IL 60605

Nov. 7   Sold to Mrs. Sorensen merchandise amounting to $73.15.

9   Sold to Mrs. Sorensen merchandise amounting to $89.60.

20   Received from Mrs. Sorensen a check for $43.00 in part payment of her account.

27   Received from Mrs. Sorensen a check for $30.15 in payment of the balance due on the sale of November 7.

30   Received from Mrs. Sorensen a check for $45.00 in part payment of her account. (If your work is correct, the balance should be $44.60.)

Copy and answer the following problems:

(1)	(2)	(3)	(4)
Add:	Add:	Subtract:	Subtract:
$162.79	$ 74.35	$4,378.75	$2,389.20
85.65	142.86	931.85	1,463.61
318.45	47.92		
36.38	253.88	(5)	(6)
49.12	56.71	Subtract:	Subtract:
27.84	95.63	$3,746.18	$1,731.80
		837.29	875.35

Practicing Related Arithmetic

AIM

To practice preparing accounts for charge customers.

"Cash? What's that? I just charge it"

PRACTICE PROBLEM

You are employed in the office of the Apollo Department Store. Your job is to keep the accounts for charge customers. The following information is taken from the duplicate sales slips and from the record of payments received from the charge customers.

Directions:

a) Open accounts for charge customers on pages 252–253.

b) Record in each customer's account the charge sales and the money collected.

c) Find the total charge sales and total amount received in payment by pencil footing the debit column and the credit column. (Remember, it is not necessary to pencil foot a column having only one entry.)

d) Find the balance of each account by subtracting the credits from the debits. (Remember, if the total debits equal the total credits, there is no balance. You would show only the pencil footings.)

Account #1

Customer's Name: Miss Sylvia DeWolf
Address: 1416 Eddy Street, San Francisco, CA 94115
May 3   Sold merchandise amounting to $39.10.
     8   Sold merchandise amounting to $10.35.
   16   Sold merchandise amounting to $23.50.
   21   Sold merchandise amounting to $46.80.
   31   Received a check for $75.00 to apply on account. (In part payment of her account.) (Did you get a balance of $44.75?)

Do not pencil foot columns having only one entry

Account #2

Customer's Name: Mrs. Esther Jones
Address: 129 Scott Street, San Francisco, CA 94117
May 1   Sold merchandise amounting to $59.55.
    3   Sold merchandise amounting to $41.38.
   11   Sold merchandise amounting to $6.19.
   25   Received a check for $107.12 in settlement of the account.
   30   Sold merchandise amounting to $36.42. (Did you get a balance of $36.42?)

Account #3

Customer's Name: Miss Margaret Kirby
Address: 718 Diamond Street, San Francisco, CA 94114
May 2   Sold to Miss Kirby merchandise amounting to $73.25.
    3   Sold merchandise amounting to $69.80.
   22   Received from Miss Kirby $80.00 to apply on account. (In part payment of her account.)
   24   Sold merchandise amounting to $26.96.
   31   Received a check for $50.00 to apply on account. (Did you get a balance of $40.01?)

Account #4

Total debits
− Total credits
= Balance

Customer's Name: Miss Nellie Lester
Address: 18 Diaz Avenue, San Francisco, CA 94132
May 1   Sold merchandise amounting to $48.70.
    8   Sold merchandise amounting to $12.95.
   25   Received a check for $25.00 to apply on account.
   30   Received a check for $36.65 in settlement of the balance due.
   31   Sold merchandise amounting to $31.10. (Did you get a balance of $31.10?)

Account #5

Customer's Name: Miss Rose Mackey
Address: 1115 Elm Street, San Francisco, CA 94115
May 4   Sold merchandise amounting to $92.30.
    8   Sold merchandise amounting to $75.80.
   23   Received a check for $125.00 to apply on account.
   25   Sold merchandise amounting to $51.45.
   31   Received a check for $94.55 in settlement of the balance due. (Did you find that no balance was due?)

Account #6

Customer's Name: Mrs. Lillian Marone
Address: 261 Chestnut Street, San Francisco, CA 94133

May 7	Sold merchandise amounting to $78.78.
9	Sold merchandise amounting to $46.25.
21	Received a check for $75.00 to apply on account.
24	Sold merchandise amounting to $39.45.
29	Received a check for $50.03. (Did you get a balance of $39.45?)

Account #7

Customer's Name: Mrs. Florence Nardo
Address: 766 Baker Street, San Francisco, CA 94115

May 4	Sold merchandise to Mrs. Nardo amounting to $161.88.
17	Received a check from Mrs. Nardo for $75.00 to apply on account.
18	Sold merchandise amounting to $85.30.
24	Received a check for $60.00 to apply on account.
31	Received a check for $112.18 in full settlement of the account. (Did you find that no balance was due?)

Account #8

Customer's Name: Miss Alice Perkins
Address: 76 Day Street, San Francisco, CA 94110

May 2	Sold merchandise amounting to $175.25.
22	Received a check for $65.00 to apply on account.
29	Received a check for $50.00 to apply on account.
30	Sold merchandise amounting to $89.45.
31	Received a check for $60.25 for balance due on sale of May 2. (Did you get a balance of $89.45?)

Copy and answer the following problems:

Practicing
Related
Arithmetic

(1)	(2)	(3)	(4)
Add:	Add:	Subtract:	Subtract:
$146.83	$207.85	$4,372.09	$5,036.87
254.27	64.15	2,165.94	1,672.78
89.76	172.91		
310.25	186.43	(5)	(6)
78.42	95.58	Subtract:	Subtract:
137.64	238.24	$3,625.12	$2,947.34
		2,073.87	1,788.17

AIM

To learn how to record merchandise returns in accounts for charge customers.

EXPLANATION

You may have had the experience of buying merchandise, taking it home, and after more careful consideration, deciding to return it.

If you had originally paid cash for the merchandise (and if the retailer permitted merchandise to be returned), the retailer's usual procedure would be to return the cash to you.

However, if you were a charge customer who had not yet paid for the merchandise, the procedure for handling the return would not be quite so simple. Obviously, since you had not as yet paid for the merchandise, the retailer would not give you cash in exchange for it. Instead of returning cash, the retailer would give you a slip of paper called a *credit slip*, shown in Illustration 39 on the next page, indicating that you owe less money than before. The retailer would keep the duplicate copy of the credit slip so that the amount of the credit could be recorded on your account.

Record returns on the credit side

In the previous lesson you learned that when a retailer receives a payment from a charge customer, this fact is recorded on the right (or *credit*) side of the account to show that the customer owes less. Since a return of merchandise also means that the customer owes less to the retailer, it too is recorded on the credit side of the account.

CREDIT SLIP

Customer's Name: *Mrs Emily Murray*   Account No: *216-07-211*

Address: *856 Ridge Avenue, Philadelphia*   Date: *October 8, 19--*

THIS IS A CREDIT FOR MERCHANDISE RETURNED		
1 coat - style M-312	38	00

R. Appleton
Approved by

C & M Department Store

Illustration 39 — Credit Slip

This means that when you examine all the facts recorded in a charge account, you find the charge sales recorded on the debit side (left side) and the "cash received" and the "merchandise returned" recorded on the credit side (right side).

CUSTOMER'S ACCOUNT	
Debits	**Credits**
1. Charge sales	1. Cash received in payment
	2. Merchandise returned

SAMPLE PROBLEM

The C & M Department Store opened a charge account for Mrs. Emily Murray, 856 Ridge Avenue, Philadelphia, PA 19107.

The following information for the month of October was taken from the duplicate sales slips, the duplicate credit slips, and from the records of cash received from Mrs. Murray:

Oct. 2 Sold to Mrs. Murray merchandise amounting to $38.00.
     5 Sold to Mrs. Murray merchandise amounting to $80.00.
     8 Received merchandise returned by Mrs. Murray amounting to $38.00. We sent her the credit slip shown above in Illustration 39.
     11 Received a check from Mrs. Murray for $30.00 in part payment of the balance due.
     15 Sold to Mrs. Murray merchandise amounting to $70.00.
     31 Received a check from Mrs. Murray for $40.00 to apply on account.

Here is how the C & M Department Store would record this information in the charge account kept for Mrs. Murray.

NAME	Mrs. Emily Murray					
ADDRESS	856 Ridge Avenue, Philadelphia, PA 19107					

DATE	ITEM	DEBIT	DATE	ITEM	CREDIT
19-- Oct. 2	Mdse.	38 00	19-- Oct. 8	Return	38 00
5	Mdse. 188.00	80 00	11	Cash	30 00
15	Mdse. 108.00	70 00	31	Cash	40 00
	80.00	1 98 00			1 08 00

Notice that the credit side of Mrs. Murray's account contains both the returns of merchandise and the checks the store has received in payment.

PRACTICE PROBLEM

You are employed as a clerk in the bookkeeping department of the Owens Department Store, and your job is to keep the accounts for charge customers. The information on the following pages was taken from the duplicate sales slips, the duplicate credit slips, and from the record of cash received from the charge customers.

Directions:

a) Open an account for each charge customer listed below and on the following pages.

b) Record in each customer's account the charge sales, the money collected, and the merchandise returned.

c) Find the balance of each account by subtracting the credits from the debits. (Show all pencil footings in each account.)

Account #1

Customer's Name: Miss Mary Blum
Address: 610 Beverly Road, Brooklyn, NY 11218
Dec. 4   Sold merchandise amounting to $84.22.
     6   Sold merchandise amounting to $115.85.
    10   Sent a credit slip for $32.15 to Miss Blum for merchandise she had returned.
    20   Received a check for $52.07 to apply on account.
    21   Sold merchandise amounting to $38.90.
    28   Sent a credit slip for $12.65 to Miss Blum for merchandise she had returned.
    31   Received a check for $75.00 to apply on account. (Is the balance $67.10?)

Account #2

Customer's Name: Mrs. Dora Carson
Address: 1415 Church Avenue, Brooklyn, NY 11226

Dec. 3   Sold merchandise amounting to $92.05.
    6   Sold merchandise amounting to $136.80.
  12   Sent a credit slip for $41.60 to Mrs. Carson for merchandise she had returned.
  20   Received a check for $50.45 to apply on account.
  27   Received a check for $80.00 to apply on account.
  28   Sold merchandise amounting to $41.55.
  31   Sent a credit slip to Mrs. Carson for $18.35 for merchandise she had returned. (Is the balance $80.00?)

Account #3

Customer's Name: Ms. Sue Caruso
Address: 3305 Foster Avenue, Brooklyn, NY 11203

Dec. 3   Sold merchandise amounting to $86.25.
    5   Sold merchandise amounting to $51.50.
    6   Received merchandise amounting to $35.90 which had been returned by Ms. Caruso. We sent her a credit slip for that amount.
  21   Received a check for $50.35 to apply on account.
  26   Sold merchandise amounting to $73.20.
  31   Received a check for $40.00 to apply on account. (Is the balance $84.70?)

Account #4

Customer's Name: Miss Ruth Levin
Address: 1116 E. 34th Street, Brooklyn, NY 11234

Dec. 5   Sold merchandise amounting to $73.92.
    6   Sold merchandise amounting to $58.10.
  10   Sent a credit slip for $12.15 to Miss Levin for merchandise she had returned.
  21   Received a check for $61.77.
  24   Sold merchandise for $61.25.
  27   Sent a credit slip for $9.86 to Miss Levin for merchandise she had returned.
  28   Received a check for $65.00. (Is the balance $44.49?)

Account #5

Customer's Name: Mrs. J. Martinez
Address: 722 Fort Hamilton Pkwy., Brooklyn, NY 11218

Dec. 5   Sold merchandise amounting to $141.60.
    7   Sent a credit slip for $27.50 to Mrs. Martinez for merchandise she had returned.
  10   Sold merchandise amounting to $34.85.
  12   Sent a credit slip for $18.25 to Mrs. Martinez for merchandise she had returned.
  20   Received a check for $85.00.
  28   Received a check for $30.00. (Is the balance $15.70?)

Account #6

Customer's Name: Mrs. Amy McBride
Address: 178 Meeker Avenue, Brooklyn, NY 11211

Dec.	7	Sold merchandise amounting to $81.10.
	10	Sold merchandise amounting to $63.85.
	12	Sent a credit slip for $25.45 to Mrs. McBride for merchandise she had returned.
	21	Received a check for $50.00.
	24	Sold merchandise amounting to $42.90.
	27	Sent a credit slip for $9.95 to Mrs. McBride for merchandise she had returned.
	28	Received a check for $60.00. (Is the balance $42.45?)

Account #7

Customer's Name: Miss Joan Rogers
Address: 87 E. 92nd Street, Brooklyn, NY 11212

Dec.	6	Sold merchandise amounting to $69.24.
	11	Sent a credit slip for $17.30 to Miss Rogers for merchandise she had returned.
	14	Sold merchandise amounting to $57.50.
	17	Sent a credit slip for $23.19 to Miss Rogers for merchandise she had returned.
	24	Received a check for $35.00.
	31	Received a check for $25.00. (Is the balance $26.25?)

Account #8

Customer's Name: Ms. Cora Smith
Address: 63 Classon Avenue, Brooklyn, NY 11211

Dec.	3	Sold merchandise amounting to $131.80.
	7	Sold merchandise amounting to $51.65.
	12	Sent a credit slip for $21.10 to Ms. Smith for merchandise she had returned.
	17	Received a check for $75.00.
	20	Received a check for $40.00.
	26	Sold merchandise amounting to $84.15.
	28	Sent a credit slip for $31.20 to Ms. Smith for merchandise she had returned.
	31	Sold merchandise amounting to $41.75. (Is the balance $142.05?)

Copy and answer the following problems:

	(1)	(2)	(3)	(4)
Practicing Related Arithmetic	Add:	Add:	Subtract:	Subtract:
	$238.36	$187.42	$4,258.15	$2,918.80
	172.64	56.80	1,867.82	1,385.89
	87.58	238.75		
	315.07	81.38	(5)	(6)
	63.82	275.27	Subtract:	Subtract:
	124.91	29.91	$1,915.47	$2,872.51
			1,284.56	1,604.38

AIM

To learn how to prepare statements of account.

EXPLANATION

In the previous lessons you learned how to keep a record of the amount owed by charge customers in a form called an *account*. At the close of each month, it is a common practice for retailers to send to their customers a copy of this account record so that the customers can compare the store's record against their own.

The copy of the customer's account that the retailer mails to charge customers at the close of the month is called a *statement of account*. The statement of account will show the charge sales, the payments, the returns, and the balance due.

"Nobody can spend *that* much money!"

Statement of account

SAMPLE PROBLEM

On March 1, the Ames Department Store opened a charge account for John Rivera, Boston, MA.

On March 31, Mr. Rivera's account appeared as follows:

NAME   *John Rivera*

ADDRESS   *316 Commonwealth Avenue, Boston, MA 02115*

DATE	ITEM	DEBIT	DATE	ITEM	CREDIT
Mar. 1	*Mdse.*	35 00	*Mar.* 9	*Return*	15 00
7	*Mdse.* 150.00	40 00	18	*Cash*	20 00
21	*Mdse.* 80.00 70.00	25 00	28	*Cash*	45 00
29	*Mdse.*	50 00			80 00
		150 00			

The Ames Department Store prepared the statement of account shown on page 261 and mailed it to Mr. Rivera.

These are the steps in preparing Mr. Rivera's statement of account:

Step 1: Record statement heading.

Businesses usually date the statement as of the last day of the month, or the first day of the next month. This statement was dated March 31. The customer's name and address were copied from the account heading.

Step 2: Record the charge sales.

Charges = Debits   The charge sales were copied from the debit side of the account. The amounts were then totaled, neatly ruled, and the total charge sales of $150.00 extended into the second money column. Notice that when an amount is entered in the second money column, its "explanation" (in this case, the words *total debits*) is indented.

Some retailers prefer to use the heading *CHARGES* instead of the heading *DEBITS* shown in the statement of the account. You should become familiar with both words and you should understand that they have the same meaning when used on a statement of account.

Step 3: Record the payments and returns.

The cash received in payment and the merchandise returned were copied from the credit side of the account. These amounts were then totaled and this total of $80.00 was extended into the second money column.

Step 4: Find the balance due.

The second money column now contains the total debits of $150.00 and the total credits of $80.00. The balance due was found by subtracting the total credits of $80.00 (which represents the cash received in payment and the price of any merchandise returned) from the total debits of $150.00 which represents the total charge sales. In other words, the following arithmetic problem was done:

STATEMENT OF ACCOUNT

AMES DEPARTMENT STORE
35 Broad Street
Boston, MA 02109

March 31, 19--

TO: John Rivera
     316 Commonwealth Avenue
     Boston, MA 02115

19--			DEBITS				
March	1	Mdse.		35	00		
	7	Mdse.		40	00		
	21	Mdse.		25	00		
	29	Mdse.		50	00		
			Total debits			150	00
			CREDITS				
March	9	Return		15	00		
	18	Cash		20	00		
	28	Cash		45	00		
			Total credits			80	00
			Balance due			70	00

Illustration 40 — Statement of Account

Total debits	$150.00
Total credits	−80.00
Balance due	$ 70.00

Step 5: Check the balance due.

Compare the balance due of $70.00 with the balance of the account as shown by the pencil footings in the account. Notice that the balance shown in Mr. Rivera's account of $70.00 agrees with the amount shown in the statement of account.

When Mr. Rivera receives this statement of account he will examine it and compare it with his records to see whether it is correct. In addition to helping him check his records, the statement of account also reminds Mr. Rivera of the amount he owes to the Ames Department Store.

PRACTICE PROBLEM

You are employed by the Alpha Department Store, Gary, Indiana. It is your job to prepare statements of account from the accounts kept for charge customers.

Directions: Prepare a statement of account for each customer whose account appears below and on the next page. Date all statements January 31.

Account #1

Miss J. Clay, 1661 Maine St., Gary, IN 46407

19--			19--		
Jan. 8	Mdse.	$41.90	Jan. 26	Cash	$45.00
16	Mdse.	68.45	31	Cash	35.00
29	Mdse.	37.27			

Account #2

Mrs. S. Eagen, 17 Colfax St., Gary, IN 46406

19--			19--		
Jan. 3	Mdse.	$ 39.55	Jan. 8	Return	$16.50
18	Mdse.	46.30	17	Cash	23.05
22	Mdse.	123.83	29	Cash	35.00
30	Mdse.	51.10			

Account #3

Mrs. T. Hess, 991 Willard St., Gary, IN 46404

19--			19--		
Jan. 3	Mdse.	$147.15	Jan. 8	Return	$ 27.84
11	Mdse.	51.20	25	Cash	119.31
16	Mdse.	15.75	30	Cash	45.00
26	Mdse.	29.84			

Account #4

Mrs. T. Howard, 1210 Tyler St., Gary, IN 46407

19--			19--		
Jan. 9	Mdse.	$68.54	Jan. 24	Cash	$68.54
12	Mdse.	47.85	31	Cash	40.00
23	Mdse.	31.30			

Account #5

Mrs. M. Jarvis, 2917 Forrest St., Gary, IN 46405

19--			19--		
Jan. 5	Mdse.	$ 81.20	Jan. 16	Cash	$50.00
10	Mdse.	115.42	17	Return	21.15
25	Mdse.	39.65	31	Cash	85.00
26	Mdse.	43.70			

Account #6

Miss O. Johnson, 316 Monroe St., Gary, IN 46402

19--			19--		
Jan. 2	Mdse.	$75.38	Jan. 22	Cash	$65.00
11	Mdse.	67.25	24	Cash	50.00
24	Mdse	91.60	29	Return	19.72

Account #7

Mrs. M. Kane, 481 Noble St., Gary, IN 46406

19--			19--		
Jan. 5	Mdse.	$73.94	Jan. 9	Return	$18.65
8	Mdse.	41.35	25	Cash	55.29
26	Mdse.	27.80	30	Cash	35.00

Account #8

Mrs. K. Northcott, 866 Lincoln St., Gary, IN 46402

19--			19--		
Jan. 3	Mdse.	$ 74.56	Jan. 8	Return	$15.45
10	Mdse.	39.75	10	Return	8.76
25	Mdse.	163.40	26	Cash	50.35
			31	Cash	30.00

Practicing Related Arithmetic

Copy and answer the following problems:

	(1)	(2)	(3)	(4)
	Add:	Add:	Subtract:	Subtract:
	$316.25	$291.52	$5,138.60	$4,681.07
	83.73	164.87	2,957.85	2,185.31
	127.32	57.39		
	61.47	283.48	(5)	(6)
	48.98	39.20	Subtract:	Subtract:
	285.56	48.76	$6,805.82	$2,861.54
			3,178.53	1,785.95

AIM

To gain more experience in preparing statements of account.

EXPLANATION

Purposes of statement of account:
1. Check records
2. Reminder to pay

You have learned that it is common practice for the retailer to mail a statement of account to charge customers at the end of each month. The information on the statement of account makes it easy for the customers to check their records against the retailer's records. There is another reason for sending statements of account to charge customers. The retailer hopes that when the customers see the statement of account they will be prompted to pay the balance that is due.

PRACTICE PROBLEM

You are employed as an assistant in the bookkeeping department of the Main Department Store, Akron, Ohio. It is your job to prepare statements of account from the accounts kept for charge customers.

Directions: Prepare a statement of account for each customer whose account appears on pages 264–266. Date all statements October 31.

Account #1

Mrs. M. Altman, 1215 Sunset Dr., Akron, OH 44301

19--				19--		
Oct.	2	Mdse.	$ 64.15	Oct.	5	Return	$ 9.25
	4	Mdse.	138.60		23	Cash	54.90
	15	Mdse.	37.05		29	Return	8.65
	26	Mdse.	15.80				

Account #2

Mrs. Y. Berris, 1166 Linden Ave., Akron, OH 44310

19--			19--		
Oct. 4	Mdse.	$161.80	Oct. 9	Return	$ 31.60
12	Mdse.	31.45	24	Cash	130.20
15	Mdse.	63.52	31	Cash	50.00
19	Mdse.	48.94			

Account #3

Mrs. R. Doyle, 176 Henry St., Akron, OH 44305

19--			19--		
Oct. 1	Mdse.	$143.75	Oct. 5	Return	$ 32.45
3	Mdse.	36.19	23	Cash	111.30
17	Mdse.	51.45	31	Cash	50.00
23	Mdse.	27.80			

Account #4

Miss H. Eastman, 1712 Smith Rd., Akron, OH 44313

19--			19--		
Oct. 5	Mdse.	$93.45	Oct. 25	Cash	$93.45
11	Mdse.	56.17	29	Cash	50.00
19	Mdse.	81.80	30	Return	11.75
26	Mdse.	30.15			

Account #5

Miss L. Huff, 501 Stanley Rd., Akron, OH 44312

19--			19--		
Oct. 9	Mdse.	$ 86.14	Oct. 19	Cash	$86.14
16	Mdse.	117.35	23	Return	41.20
19	Mdse.	75.50	26	Cash	76.15
24	Mdse.	36.70			

Account #6

Miss S. Jordan, 83 N. High St., Akron, OH 44308

19--			19--		
Oct. 1	Mdse.	$186.70	Oct. 4	Return	$ 37.15
10	Mdse.	92.85	23	Cash	149.55
18	Mdse.	43.60	30	Cash	75.00
25	Mdse.	56.95			

Account #7

Miss A. Logan, 76 Glendale Ave., Akron, OH 44308

19--				19--			
Oct.	2	Mdse.	$ 86.55	Oct.	19	Cash	$ 65.00
	9	Mdse.	54.70		23	Return	11.76
	17	Mdse.	131.65		29	Cash	125.00
	26	Mdse.	42.90				

Account #8

Mrs. E. Nelson, 1170 Jefferson Ave., Akron, OH 44313

19--				19--			
Oct.	2	Mdse.	$78.40	Oct.	5	Return	$ 8.16
	11	Mdse.	47.96		26	Cash	115.00
	15	Mdse.	53.10		31	Cash	50.00
	29	Mdse.	32.85				

Account #9

Miss C. Wilson, 110 Berry Ave., Akron, OH 44307

19--				19--			
Oct.	5	Mdse.	$ 91.35	Oct.	10	Return	$23.75
	9	Mdse.	160.15		13	Return	39.17
	16	Mdse.	31.20		25	Cash	28.43
	20	Mdse.	26.40				

Account #10

Mrs. P. Wolf, 920 Victory St., Akron, OH 44311

19--				19--			
Oct.	5	Mdse.	$ 56.25	Oct.	15	Cash	$56.25
	10	Mdse.	83.60		16	Return	12.90
	17	Mdse.	47.35		30	Cash	70.70
	23	Mdse.	61.42				

Copy and answer the following problems. (Try to solve all the problems mentally.)

1) 30 + 10 = _____
2) 20 + 30 = _____
3) 35 + 20 = _____
4) 25 + 15 = _____
5) 35 + 25 = _____
6) 45 + 25 = _____
7) 18 + 12 = _____
8) 26 + 14 = _____
9) 17 + 35 = _____
10) 85 + 25 = _____
11) 80 − 30 = _____
12) 45 − 14 = _____
13) 38 − 15 = _____
14) 47 − 18 = _____
15) 32 − 14 = _____

AIM

To learn about a new form of customer's account.

EXPLANATION

You have already learned how to keep a record of the amount owed by charge customers in a form called an account. There are two forms of accounts commonly used in business.

One form of the account is the form you have practiced using in which the debits are placed on the left half of the page and the credits on the right half. An example is shown below:

NAME   Robert Kahn

ADDRESS 841 Market Street, Oakland, CA 94607

DATE		ITEM		DEBIT		DATE		ITEM		CREDIT	
19-- June	4	Mdse.		40	00	19-- June	8	Return		10	00
	7	Mdse.	150.00 / 40.00	50	00		25	Cash		30	00
	28	Mdse.	10.00	60	00					90	00
				150	00						

Account Title

Debit | Credit

"T" Account

Illustration 42a — "T" Account Form

Since the basic form of this account resembles a large capital "T," this account is often referred to as the *"T" account form*.

The second form of account used by many businesses has three money columns: a debit column, a credit column, and a balance column.

The information in the account shown on page 267 would appear in the three-column form of the account as shown below.

Three-column account

NAME	Robert Kahn				
ADDRESS	841 Market Street, Oakland, CA 94607				

DATE		ITEM	DEBIT	CREDIT	BALANCE
19-- June	4	Mdse.	40 00		40 00
	7	Mdse	50 00		90 00
	8	Return		10 00	80 00
	25	Cash		30 00	50 00
	28	Mdse.	60 00	40 00	110 00
			150 00		

Illustration 42b — Three-column Account Form

The advantage of this form of a customer's account is that there is a special column for the balance of the account. Each time a *debit* is recorded it is *added* to the balance. Each time a *credit* is recorded it is *subtracted* from the balance. As a result, the account always shows an up-to-date balance. (Notice that the debit column is still at the *left* of the credit column, just as it was in the "T" account form, only here the columns are side-by-side.) Let us examine the steps followed by the clerk.

Step 1: Record the date.

The year is recorded only at the top of the "Date" column. The month is written only once until the month changes, at which time the new month is recorded. The day is written each time an entry is recorded.

Step 2: Record the amount.

Add debits

After the date is recorded, the amount is written in the proper "Debit" or "Credit" column. On June 4, the $40.00 was recorded in the "Debit" column to show the amount of the sale of merchandise and to show that Mr. Kahn owes $40.00 more than he did before.

Step 3: Record the new balance.

As soon as the amount is recorded in the *Debit* or *Credit* column, the total amount the customer owes at that time is written in the *Balance* column.

On June 4, after the $40.00 sale was recorded in the Debit column, it was added to the amount Mr. Kahn owed before the sale was made. (Remember: *debits* are always *added* to the old balance to find the new balance.) Since Mr. Kahn owed nothing before this sale, the total amount he now owes is $40.00.

(Zero + $40.00 = $40.00)

Now look at the entry on June 7. Again, merchandise was sold to Mr. Kahn and this time the sale amounted to $50.00. The $50.00 sale was recorded in the Debit column to show that Mr. Kahn owes more than he did before this sale was made. The new balance was then recorded in the Balance column. Do you know how the new balance was found? The debit of $50.00 was added to the old balance of $40.00 and the new balance was $90.00.

Add debits to old balance

($40.00 + $50.00 = $90.00)

On June 8, $10.00 was recorded in the Credit column to show that Mr. Kahn had returned some merchandise and to show that Mr. Kahn owed less than he did before. As soon as this amount was recorded the new balance of $80.00 was found by subtracting the $10.00 from the old balance of $90.00.

Subtract credits from old balance

($90.00 − $10.00 = $80.00)

Remember: *credits* are always *subtracted* from the old balance to find the new balance. All remaining debits and credits would be handled in the same way.

Step 4: Prove the balance.

On June 30, Mr. Kahn's account shows that he owes $110.00. It is important to check this amount to make sure that it is the correct amount owed.

Here is how you can prove that the final balance is correct. Start with the opening balance at the beginning of the month. Since Mr. Kahn owed nothing before the first sale was made, the opening balance is zero. Now pencil foot the Debit and Credit columns and get the total debits for the month and the total credits for the month. You would then do the following problem:

Balance to start with	$ 0.00
total debits	+ 150.00
Total	=$150.00
total credits	− 40.00
Balance	=$110.00

Proving the balance

PRACTICE PROBLEM

You are employed as an assistant in the bookkeeping department of the Miller's Men's Shop and your job is to keep the accounts for charge customers. The information shown on pages 270–271 was taken from the duplicate sales slips, the duplicate credit slips, and from the record of money received from charge customers.

Directions:

a) Open a *three-column* account for each charge customer.

b) Record in each customer's account the charge sales, the money collected, and the merchandise returned.

c) Find the new balance after each debit or credit is recorded.

d) Prove the balance at the end of the month. Show all pencil footings in each account.

Account #1

Customer's Name: Jacob Berman
Address: 510 Cypress Street, St. Paul, MN 55106
May   1   Sold merchandise amounting to $84.00.
     4   Sold merchandise amounting to $115.30.
     7   Sent a credit slip for $30.00 to Mr. Berman for merchandise he had returned.
   11   Sold merchandise amounting to $24.90.
   23   Sold merchandise amounting to $47.60.
   31   Received a check for $169.30 to apply on account.

Account #2

Customer's Name: William Colvin
Address: 961 Hudson Rd., St. Paul, MN 55106
May   3   Sold merchandise amounting to $74.00.
     8   Sold merchandise amounting to $35.95.
   10   Sold merchandise amounting to $52.60.
   11   Issued a credit slip for $18.00 for merchandise returned.
   15   Sold merchandise amounting to $67.40.
   18   Issued a credit slip for $36.75 for merchandise returned.
   24   Sold merchandise amounting to $29.80.
   30   Received a check for $91.95 to apply on account.

Account #3

Customer's Name: Frank Davis
Address: 891 Ohio Street, St. Paul, MN 55118
May   2   Sold merchandise amounting to $92.70.
     4   Sold merchandise amounting to $38.95.
     9   Issued a credit slip for $10.65 for merchandise returned.
   16   Sold merchandise amounting to $16.25.
   18   Sold merchandise amounting to $41.40.
   21   Sold merchandise amounting to $29.15.
   25   Issued a credit slip for $12.35 for merchandise returned.
   31   Received a check for $120.80 to apply on account.

Account #4

Customer's Name: Alfred Hansen

Address: 119 Edward Street, St. Paul, MN 55107

May 4   Sold merchandise amounting to $131.50.

     7   Sold merchandise amounting to $59.20.

     9   Received merchandise amounting to $39.00 which had been returned by Mr. Hansen. We sent him a credit slip for that amount.

   14   Sold merchandise amounting to $45.70.

   30   Received a check from Mr. Hansen for $92.50 to apply on account.

Account #5

Customer's Name: Adam Hudson

Address: 306 Cedar Dr., St. Paul, MN 55112

May 7   Sold merchandise amounting to $85.80.

    8   Sold merchandise amounting to $61.50.

   10   Sold merchandise amounting to $27.30.

   14   Issued a credit slip for $11.70 for merchandise returned by Mr. Hudson.

   17   Sold merchandise amounting to $46.90.

   21   Issued a credit slip for $21.60 for merchandise returned by Mr. Hudson.

   29   Received a check for $135.60 to apply on account.

Account #6

Customer's Name: Tom Petersen

Address: 2220 Lake Street, St. Paul, MN 55113

May 8   Sold merchandise amounting to $64.30.

   11   Sold merchandise amounting to $46.75.

   14   Sent Mr. Petersen a credit slip for $19.45 for merchandise returned to us.

   17   Sold merchandise amounting to $28.60.

   22   Sent Mr. Petersen a credit slip for $5.90 for merchandise returned to us.

   29   Received a check for $91.60 to apply on account.

Practicing Related Arithmetic

Copy and answer the following problems. (Try to solve all the problems mentally.)

1) 40 + 30 = _____
2) 35 + 20 = _____
3) 25 + 15 = _____
4) 45 + 15 = _____
5) 25 + 35 = _____
6) 42 + 26 = _____
7) 27 + 24 = _____
8) 18 + 37 = _____

9) 34 + 28 = _____
10) 68 + 15 = _____
11) 90 − 40 = _____
12) 65 − 24 = _____
13) 58 − 31 = _____
14) 62 − 15 = _____
15) 78 − 29 = _____

AIM

To learn how to use customers' three-column accounts for more than one month.

EXPLANATION

In the jobs you have completed, you were usually asked to record the transactions for only one month in a customer's account. This was done to save time and space. However, it is important for you to know that the same account is used for a customer, month after month.

Since you have learned how to record the transactions for one month, you should have no trouble recording the transactions for the months to follow.

SAMPLE PROBLEM

On June 1, the Jay Style Shop opened a charge account for Mrs. Selma Barton of Jamaica, NY. The following information was taken from the records for the months of June and July:

June	1	Sold to Mrs. Barton merchandise amounting to $72.00.
	4	Sent Mrs. Barton a credit slip for $12.00 for merchandise she had returned.
	20	Sold to Mrs. Barton merchandise amounting to $40.00.
July	9	Sold to Mrs. Barton merchandise amounting to $30.00.
	16	Received a check from Mrs. Barton for $100.00 for the balance due at the end of June.

The Jay Style Shop would record this information in Mrs. Barton's account as follows:

NAME   *Mrs. Selma Barton*
ADDRESS *80-09 Utopia Parkway, Jamaica, NY 11432*

DATE		ITEM	DEBIT	CREDIT	BALANCE
June	1	*Mdse.*	72 00		72 00
	4	*Return*		12 00	60 00
	20	*Mdse.*	40 00		100 00
July	9	*Mdse.*	30 00		130 00
	16	*Cash*		100 00	30 00

PRACTICE PROBLEM

You are employed in the office of the West Department Store and your job is to keep accounts for charge customers. The following information for the months of January and February was taken from the duplicate sales slips, the duplicate credit slips, and from the record of money received from charge customers.

Reminder:
Add debits,
subtract credits

Directions:

a) Open a three-column account for each charge customer.

b) Record in each customer's account the charge sales, the money collected, and the merchandise returned for the months of January and February.

c) Find the new balance after each debit or credit is recorded.

Account #1

Customer's Name: Mrs. Doris Bauer
Address: 3816 Red River Street, Austin, TX 78751

Jan.	4	Sold Mrs. Bauer merchandise amounting to $68.60.
	9	Sold merchandise amounting to $51.70.
	12	Sold merchandise amounting to $39.25.
	16	Sent Mrs. Bauer a credit slip for $9.60 for merchandise she had returned.
Feb.	1	Received a check for $59.00 to apply on account.
	14	Sold merchandise amounting to $16.80.
	20	Sold merchandise amounting to $41.35.
	27	Sent a credit slip for $15.85 to Mrs. Bauer for merchandise she had returned.

Record the new
month when it
has changed

Account #2

Customer's Name: Mrs. Mae Glenn
Address: 627 Gunter Street, Austin, TX 78702

Jan. 9 Sold Mrs. Glenn merchandise amounting to $81.10.
     12 Sold merchandise amounting to $50.75.
     15 Sent Mrs. Glenn a credit slip for $26.00 for merchandise she had returned.
     26 Sold merchandise amounting to $25.00.
Feb. 9 Sold merchandise amounting to $41.70.
     14 Received a check for $105.85 from Mrs. Glenn.
     16 Sold merchandise amounting to $68.00.

Account #3

Customer's Name: Miss Helen Grove
Address: 4140 Richland Street, Austin, TX 78745

Jan. 8 Sold to Miss Grove merchandise amounting to $46.80.
     10 Sent to Miss Grove a credit slip for $18.50 for merchandise she had returned.
     15 Sold merchandise amounting to $51.10.
     31 Sold merchandise amounting to $27.90.
Feb. 2 Sent a credit slip for $11.70 to Miss Grove for merchandise she had returned.
     15 Received a check for $79.40.
     22 Sold merchandise amounting to $61.25.
     28 Sold merchandise amounting to $19.50.

Account #4

Customer's Name: Mrs. Sarah Marcos
Address: 1115 Redwood Ave., Austin, TX 78721

Jan. 5 Sold to Mrs. Marcos merchandise amounting to $63.80.
      8 Sold merchandise amounting to $45.25.
     11 Sent Mrs. Marcos a credit slip for $15.80 for merchandise she had returned.
     22 Sold merchandise amounting to $38.00.
Feb. 2 Sold merchandise amounting to $41.30.
      8 Received a check for $93.25 from Mrs. Marcos.
      9 Issued a credit slip for $8.75 for merchandise returned.
     21 Sold merchandise amounting to $22.25.

Account #5

Customer's Name: Mrs. Polly Reese
Address: 5330 Link Ave., Austin, TX 78751

Jan. 2 Sold Mrs. Reese merchandise amounting to $53.35.
      8 Sent Mrs. Reese a credit slip for $12.25 for merchandise she had returned.
     16 Sold merchandise amounting to $36.15.
     30 Sold merchandise amounting to $49.20.
Feb. 6 Sent a credit slip for $12.90 to Mrs. Reese for merchandise returned.
     14 Received a check for $77.25.
     20 Sold merchandise amounting to $26.50.
     27 Sold merchandise amounting to $41.75.

Account #6

Customer's Name: Miss Anne Rogers
Address: 775 Clermont Ave., Austin, TX 78701

Jan. 3 Sold Miss Rogers merchandise amounting to $87.15.
     8 Sent Miss Rogers a credit slip for $15.30 for merchandise she had returned.
    19 Sold merchandise amounting to $31.80.
    25 Sold merchandise amounting to $47.50.
Feb. 5 Sold merchandise amounting to $29.55.
    13 Received a check for $103.65 from Miss Rogers.
    26 Sold merchandise amounting to $72.20.
    28 Issued a credit slip for $25.60 for merchandise returned to us.

Account #7

Customer's Name: Miss Rita Sanchez
Address: 1715 Pearl Street, Austin, TX 78701

Jan. 3 Sold to Miss Sanchez merchandise amounting to $57.65.
     5 Sent a credit slip for $8.40 to Miss Sanchez for merchandise she had returned.
    11 Sold merchandise amounting to $31.50.
    29 Sold merchandise amounting to $64.15.
Feb. 5 Received a check for $80.75.
    16 Sold merchandise amounting to $16.30.
    20 Sent a credit slip for $6.90 to Miss Sanchez for merchandise she had returned.
    23 Sold merchandise amounting to $19.80.

Practicing Related Arithmetic

Copy and answer the following problems. (Try to solve all the problems mentally.)

1) 60 + 20 = _____	9) 24 + 19 = _____
2) 45 + 30 = _____	10) 35 + 17 = _____
3) 35 + 15 = _____	11) 50 − 20 = _____
4) 65 + 25 = _____	12) 63 − 32 = _____
5) 15 + 45 = _____	13) 88 − 45 = _____
6) 32 + 26 = _____	14) 52 − 28 = _____
7) 27 + 32 = _____	15) 63 − 16 = _____
8) 19 + 18 = _____	

AIM

To learn a new form of statement of account.

EXPLANATION

In Job 40 you learned that a form called a statement of account is sent to each charge customer at the end of each month. You also learned that this statement of account is really a copy of the information recorded in the customer's account during the month and that the statement of account serves two purposes:

1. It enables customers to check their own records against the store's record.
2. It serves as a reminder to the customers of the amount owed.

You have learned that there are two basic forms of customer's accounts: the "T" account form shown here and the three-column form shown on page 277.

"T" account

NAME *Ben Soper*

ADDRESS *81 Post Avenue, Paterson, NJ 07506*

DATE	ITEM	DEBIT	DATE	ITEM	CREDIT
19--			*19--*		
Jan. 2	Mdse.	35 00	Jan. 6	Return	5 00
10	Mdse. 125.00 35.00	50 00	26	Cash	30 00
22	Mdse. 20.00	40 00			35 00
		125 00			

DATE		ITEM	DEBIT	CREDIT	BALANCE
Jan.¹⁹⁻⁻	2	Mdse.	35 00		35 00
	6	Return		5 00	30 00
	10	Mdse.	50 00		80 00
	22	Mdse.	40 00		1 20 00
	26	Cash		30 00	90 00

NAME Ben Soper
ADDRESS 81 Post Avenue, Paterson, NJ 07506

Three-column account

There are also two basic forms of statements of account. The first form which you learned in Job 40, is usually prepared when the "T" account form is used. It is prepared in the form of a report and is called the *report form* of statement of account.

A different form of statement of account is usually prepared when the three-column customer's account is used. It is a three-column statement of account. In this job you will practice preparing the three-column form of statement of account shown below:

Three-column statement of account

STATEMENT OF ACCOUNT
ROWAN RETAIL STORE
155 Belmont Avenue   Paterson, NJ 07506

TO: Ben Soper
     81 Post Avenue   January 31, 19--
     Paterson, NJ 07506

DATE		ITEM	DEBIT	CREDIT	BALANCE
Jan.¹⁹⁻⁻	2	Mdse.	35 00		35 00
	6	Return		5 00	30 00
	10	Mdse.	50 00		80 00
	22	Mdse.	40 00		1 20 00
	26	Cash		30 00	90 00

PLEASE PAY LAST AMOUNT IN THIS COLUMN ⬏

Illustration 44a — Three-column Statement of Account

SAMPLE PROBLEM

You are employed in the office of the Rowan Retail Store. It is the practice of the store to send statements of account to their charge customers at the end of each month. Statements of account were sent to all customers at the end of January. It is now the end of February and you are asked to prepare a statement of account for the *month of February* from the following account. The completed statement appears below the account.

NAME Ben Soper

ADDRESS 81 Post Avenue, Paterson, NJ 07506

Three-column account

DATE		ITEM	DEBIT	CREDIT	BALANCE
19-- Jan.	2	Mdse.	35 00		35 00
	6	Return		5 00	30 00
	10	Mdse.	50 00		80 00
	22	Mdse.	40 00		120 00
	26	Cash		30 00	90 00
Feb.	3	Mdse.	20 00		110 00
	7	Mdse.	10 00		120 00
	10	Cash		90 00	30 00
	14	Return		10 00	20 00
	27	Mdse.	25 00		45 00

STATEMENT OF ACCOUNT

ROWAN RETAIL STORE
155 Belmont Avenue   Paterson, NJ 07506

TO: Ben Soper
81 Post Avenue   February 28, 19 --
Paterson, NJ 07506

Three-column statement of account

DATE		ITEM.	DEBIT	CREDIT	BALANCE
19-- Feb.	1	Previous balance			90 00
	3	Mdse.	20 00		110 00
	7	Mdse.	10 00		120 00
	10	Cash		90 00	30 00
	14	Return		10 00	20 00
	27	Mdse.	25 00		45 00

PLEASE PAY LAST AMOUNT IN THIS COLUMN ▲

Illustration 44b — Three-column Statement of Account with Previous Balance

Here are the steps that were followed:

Step 1: Record previous balance.

The balance of $90.00 at the end of the month of January was recorded on the first line of the statement of account in the "Balance" column. If you examine the statement of account for the month of January (Illustration 44a on page 277), you will see that the last amount on that statement was this same amount, $90.00. Since this was the balance due at the end of January, it becomes the opening balance in the statement of account for the month of February (Illustration 44b on page 278).

Notice that the balance of $90.00 in the customer's account is dated January 26 because that is the date of the last transaction for the month of January. However, this amount is dated February 1 when written on the statement of account for the month of February to show it is the balance due at the beginning of that month.

Step 2: Copy the amounts for the month.

After the opening balance of $90.00 has been recorded, all the amounts in the account for the month of February starting with February 3 are copied from the account. The last amount in the balance column — $45.00 — is the balance due at the end of February.

In Job 37 you learned that retailers with many thousands of charge customers use a form of sales slip, shown below, that can be processed by electronic equipment to record information into customers' accounts.

27 163 968		✓		7/17/--
Account No.	Cash	Charge	Amount Rec'd	Date

charge to

Mrs. Sarah Huston
132 Beacon Street
Boston, MA 02116

send to *Same*

Bay Department Store, Boston, MA 02199

Quan.	Article	Amount	
1	*Arm Chair*	200	00
	3% sales tax	6	00
Sold By __811__ Dept. __17__ Total		206	00

X *Sarah Huston*

1 2 3 4 5 6 7 8 9 10 11 12 13 14 15 16 17 18 19 20 21 22 23 24 25 26 27 28 29 30 31 32 33 34 35 36 37 38 39 40 41 42 43 44 45 46 47 48 49 50 51 52 53 54 55 56 57 58 59 60 61 62 63 64 65 66 67 68 69 70 71 72 73 74 75 76 77 78 79 80

The same punched cards used to get information into customers' accounts are used to automatically prepare statements of accounts for all charge customers at the end of the month.

Using automatic
data processing
to prepare
statements of
account

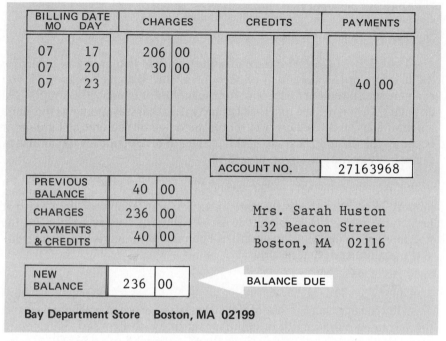

BILLING DATE MO DAY		CHARGES		CREDITS		PAYMENTS	
07	17	206	00				
07	20	30	00				
07	23					40	00

PREVIOUS BALANCE	40	00
CHARGES	236	00
PAYMENTS & CREDITS	40	00

NEW BALANCE	236	00

ACCOUNT NO.   27163968

Mrs. Sarah Huston
132 Beacon Street
Boston, MA   02116

BALANCE DUE

Bay Department Store   Boston, MA 02199

Illustration 44c — Electronically Prepared Statement of Account

Using
bookkeeping
machines to
prepare
statements of
account

Three-column accounts and three-column statements of account are also used in bookkeeping machines. When these machines are used, the statement of account, along with the customer's account, is placed in the machine together with a carbon backing so that whatever is printed on one form is also printed on the second form. In this way, by the end of the month the statement of account contains everything that was recorded in the customer's account and can be promptly mailed to the customer.

In this job you will put to practice the principles used in preparing a three-column statement of account whether it is prepared *manually* (by hand), *electronically* (by data processing equipment), or *mechanically* (by bookkeeping machines).

PRACTICE PROBLEM

You are employed by the S & M Department Store, Jacksonville, Florida. Your job is to prepare statements of account for charge customers. Statements of account were sent to all charge customers at the end of March and it is now the end of April.

Directions:
a) Prepare a statement of account for the *month of April* for each of the customers whose account appears on pages 281–282. Use the three-column form.
b) Date all statements April 30.
c) Remember: Start each statement with the opening balance on April 1.

Account #1

Date	Item	Debit	Credit	Balance
Miss Mary Hayes, 901 Prospect St., Jacksonville, FL 32205				
19--				
Mar. 2	Mdse.	$41.80		$41.80
5	Return		$ 9.00	32.80
28	Mdse.	22.00		54.80
Apr. 5	Mdse.	15.30		70.10
9	Cash		50.00	20.10
11	Return		5.00	15.10
30	Mdse.	38.00		53.10

Account #2

Date	Item	Debit	Credit	Balance
Mrs. Joan Jamison, 816 Spearing St., Jacksonville, FL 32206				
19--				
Mar. 5	Mdse.	$36.15		$36.15
8	Return		$ 8.50	27.65
Apr. 9	Mdse.	24.00		51.65
12	Cash		27.65	24.00
19	Mdse.	41.60		65.60
23	Return		10.20	55.40

Account #3

Date	Item	Debit	Credit	Balance
Mrs. Sophie Kalish, 59 Morgan Ave., Jacksonville, FL 32205				
19--				
Mar. 1	Mdse.	$47.00		$47.00
14	Mdse.	21.40		68.40
19	Return		$15.00	53.40
Apr. 6	Mdse.	14.85		68.25
11	Cash		53.40	14.85
12	Return		6.10	8.75
27	Mdse.	56.50		65.25

Account #4

Date	Item	Debit	Credit	Balance
Miss Marcia Lyons, 851 North St., Jacksonville, FL 32211				
19--				
Mar. 7	Mdse.	$25.30		$25.30
12	Return		$ 5.10	20.20
31	Mdse.	39.30		59.50
Apr. 11	Mdse.	31.90		91.40
13	Cash		59.50	31.90
24	Mdse.	46.00		77.90
27	Return		16.40	61.50

Account #5

Miss Olga Martin, 3750 Sommers St., Jacksonville, FL 32205				
Date	**Item**	**Debit**	**Credit**	**Balance**
19--				
Mar. 6	Mdse.	$56.00		$56.00
12	Mdse.	32.60		88.60
15	Return		$21.50	67.10
Apr. 4	Mdse.	27.75		94.85
16	Cash		60.00	34.85
17	Return		10.20	24.65
30	Mdse.	71.30		95.95

Account #6

Mrs. Sue Mellon, 3401 Taylor St., Jacksonville, FL 32207				
Date	**Item**	**Debit**	**Credit**	**Balance**
19--				
Mar. 1	Mdse.	$43.70		$43.70
9	Mdse.	26.50		70.20
14	Return		$12.00	58.20
Apr. 2	Cash		58.20	—
10	Mdse.	38.20		38.20
13	Return		3.60	34.60
25	Mdse.	19.10		53.70

Account #7

Miss Helen Pacetti, 3212 Duane Ave., Jacksonville, FL 32218				
Date	**Item**	**Debit**	**Credit**	**Balance**
19--				
Mar. 6	Mdse.	$51.80		$51.80
13	Mdse.	46.30		98.10
16	Return		$31.00	67.10
Apr. 4	Mdse.	18.30		85.40
6	Cash		67.10	18.30
25	Mdse.	37.60		55.90
27	Return		12.00	43.90

UNIT 7

RECORD KEEPING FOR A PURCHASING DEPARTMENT

UNIT 7

Copy these problems on a sheet of paper and find the correct answers. (Pay close attention to the + and − signs.)

Practicing Related Arithmetic

	(1)		(2)		(3)		(4)		(5)
+	25	+	53	+	243	+	705	+	3,064
+	20	+	84	+	146	+	850	+	2,515
+	55	−	37	+	308	−	225	−	2,435
−	15	+	79	−	425	+	409	+	5,070
+	43	+	168	+	656	−	206	+	4,213
+	85	−	46	−	53	+	1,350	−	3,124
+	117	+	78	+	97	+	2,086	+	4,257

AIMS

1. To learn the importance of keeping an accurate stockroom record of merchandise received and issued.

2. To learn how to enter the receipt and issuance of merchandise on a stockroom record.

EXPLANATION

You know from your personal experience as a customer that you like to shop in stores with a large variety or selection of merchandise, which is commonly called *stock*.

Keeping track of merchandise

Have you ever wondered how businesspeople keep a record of the merchandise they have on hand? How they know which merchandise moves rapidly and should be reordered? How they know which merchandise moves slowly and should be reduced in price for quick clearance? In this lesson and in the following ones, you will learn that successful businesspeople find it advantageous to keep accurate records of their stock so that the above questions can be answered quickly and accurately. In order to do this, businesspeople make use of a form known as a *stock record card*. A stock record card may look like the one shown on the next page.

"How many hammers do we have in stock?"

It is customary to print this form on a card instead of on paper because a card stands up much better under constant use.

STOCK RECORD CARD

ITEM _____ Maximum_____

STOCK No._____ Minimum_____

UNIT _____

Date	Quantity Received	Quantity Issued	Balance
19--			

Illustration 45a — Stock Record Card

To enable you to understand clearly how information is recorded, study the following sample problem.

SAMPLE PROBLEM

You have been employed as a clerk by the Atlas Office Supplies & Equipment Co., a wholesaler, to handle their stock record cards. You are sent to their stockroom where they store all the merchandise received. You are handed a number of stock record cards. Each of these cards is for a different item (like staplers, pencils, clips, fans, and so forth), because each item stored in the stockroom requires its own card. The first one you look at is shown on page 287.

Now study this card and learn the meaning of each heading and number.

As you can see, this card relates only to staplers. Since the company may handle a variety of staplers made by different manufacturers, each type is given a stock number to identify it. If the company handles *six different* types

Separate cards are prepared for each item

of staplers, there will be *six different* stock record cards, each with a different stock number.

STOCK RECORD CARD

ITEM *Staplers*   Maximum *200*

STOCK No. *51*   Minimum *50*

UNIT *Each*

Date		Quantity Received	Quantity Issued	Balance
19-- Apr.	1	100		100
	7		30	70
	9		10	60
	14	80		140

The balance changes after each entry

Illustration 45b — Completed Stock Record Card

Merchandise is sold in different units of measure. Some is sold individually (each); some is sold by the dozen (12); some is sold by the gross (144); etc. Therefore, each card must show what the unit of measure is. You can see that the unit above is "each." **Units of measure**

Businesspeople need to have *on hand* the merchandise their customers require. They know that it takes time to get the merchandise from their suppliers. Therefore, they cannot afford to wait until they are almost out of a particular item before they reorder. From past experience, successful businesspeople have learned that they must have a certain amount of a particular item to tide them over until their new shipment arrives. This amount of stock, below which it is unbusinesslike to go, is known as the *minimum* or the *least* amount that must be on hand to meet present needs. By looking at the card shown in Illustration 45b above, you can see that your employer needs at least 50 staplers in stock at all times to meet the needs of customers. Also, from past **Minimum = the least**

Maximum = the most

Balance = the amount on hand

experience, your employer feels that there will hardly ever be a need for having more than 200 staplers on hand at any one time. This is known as the *maximum* or the *most* that should be on hand.

Examine the numbers appearing in the various columns. You can see that on April 1, 19--, your employer received 100 staplers which had been purchased for the first time. Notice that this amount was entered twice: once to show that it had been received, and again to show that it was the balance on hand.

On April 7, 30 staplers which had been sold were shipped out, or *issued*. This amount was entered in the *Quantity Issued* column. Then on a scratch pad this arithmetic problem was done:

Previous balance:	100
Quantity issued:	− 30
New balance	= 70

In the Balance column, 70 was entered below the old balance of 100.

Remember: Every time you receive merchandise your balance increases, and every time you issue merchandise your balance decreases.

On April 9, 10 staplers were issued. It was first entered in the *Quantity Issued* column, and on the scratch pad this problem was done:

Previous balance:	70
Quantity issued:	− 10
New balance	= 60

In the Balance column, 60 was entered below the old balance of 70.

On April 14, 80 staplers were received. First we entered it in the *Quantity Received* column to show how many had been received. Then on a scratch pad this problem was done:

Previous balance:	60
Quantity received:	+ 80
New balance	=140

In the Balance column, 140 was entered below the old balance of 60.

Total of the "Quantity Received" column = total amount purchased

Total of the "Quantity Issued" column = total amount sold

If you study the stock record card in Illustration 45b, page 287, you can see that much valuable information can be found on it. For example, when you compare the balance of 60 on April 9 with the minimum of 50 which had been set, you understand why it was necessary to order the merchandise which was received on April 14. If you add the numbers in the *Quantity Received* column, you can see that 180 staplers were purchased between April 1 and April 14. If you add the *Quantity Issued* column, you can see that 40 staplers were sold in the same period of time. If you look in the *Balance* column, you will note that you had the smallest quantity of staplers on April 9 and the largest quantity of staplers on April 14.

All this information is important to a successful businessperson who depends on the accuracy of your record keeping to help in making wise decisions. **It is very important, therefore, to be sure to check your addition and subtraction before you enter each new balance.**

In very large concerns, businesspeople have found it advantageous to use automated data processing equipment to do the same kind of arithmetic you would do by hand as a recordkeeper in a smaller business.

As an employee of a smaller firm, however, your records must be as accurate as those kept by the data processing equipment. Now that you understand each item and number found on the stock record card, see if you can act as a stock record clerk for the small office supplies business in the following problems.

PRACTICE PROBLEMS

Problem 1

Directions:
a) Enter the information shown on page 290 at the top of a stock record card.

1) The item is *staplers.*
2) The stock number is *S1.*
3) The unit is *each.*
4) The maximum is *200.*
5) The minimum is *50.*

b) Make a record of the following. (Be sure to *increase* the balance when merchandise is *received* and to *decrease* the balance when merchandise is *issued*.)

19--

April	1	Received	100
	7	Issued	30
	9	Issued	10
	14	Received	80

c) Compare your work with the stock record card, Illustration 45b, page 287. Your work should agree since the illustration shows the same information that you recorded.

d) Continue recording the following information on the same stock record card:

19--

April	16	Issued	20
	18	Issued	75
	22	Received	130
	24	Issued	110
	28	Received	150
	30	Issued	55

e) Check your work. If your work is correct, the final balance should be 160.

f) Answer the following questions on a sheet of paper:
   1) On what date did you have the largest quantity of staplers? (Look for the largest number in the balance column.)
   2) On what date did you have the smallest quantity? (Look for the smallest number in the balance column.)
   3) On what dates did you go above the maximum? (Compare each figure in the balance column with the 200 shown as the maximum.)
   4) On what dates did you go below the minimum? (Compare each figure in the balance column with the 50 shown as the minimum.)
   5) What amount was received during the month? (Pencil foot the figures in the "Received" column.)
   6) What amount was sold during the month? (Pencil foot the figures in the "Issued" column.)

Problem 2

Directions:

a) Enter the following information at the top of a stock record card:
   1) The item is *pens.*
   2) The stock number is *P2.*
   3) The unit is *gross.*
   4) The maximum is *100.*
   5) The minimum is *25.*

b) Make a record of the following:

19--

July	1	Received	70	Merchandise
	3	Issued	5	received
	7	Issued	15	increases the
	10	Issued	10	balance
	15	Received	75	
	18	Issued	95	
	22	Received	65	
	25	Issued	25	Merchandise
	29	Issued	20	issued decreases
	31	Received	55	the balance

c) Check your work. If your work is correct, the final balance should be 95.

d) Answer the following questions on a sheet of paper:

  1) On what date did you have the *largest* quantity of pens?
  2) On what date did you have the *smallest* quantity?
  3) On what dates did you go *above* the *maximum*?
  4) On what dates did you go *below* the *minimum*?
  5) What amount was *received* during the month?
  6) What amount was *sold* during the month?

Problem 3

Directions:

a) Enter the following information at the top of a stock record card:

  1) The item is *pencils*.
  2) The stock number is *PE3*.
  3) The unit is *gross*.
  4) The maximum is *300*.
  5) The minimum is *75*.

b) Make a record of the following:

19--

Aug.	2	Received	250
	5	Issued	50
	9	Issued	35
	12	Issued	100
	16	Received	200
	19	Issued	124
	23	Issued	80
	25	Received	275
	27	Issued	130
	31	Issued	84

c) Check your work. If your work is correct, the final balance should be 122.

d) Answer the following questions on a sheet of paper:

  1) On what date did you have the *largest* quantity of pencils?
  2) On what date did you have the *smallest* quantity of pencils?
  3) On what dates did you go *above* the *maximum*?
  4) On what dates did you go *below* the *minimum*?
  5) What amount was *received* during the month?
  6) What amount was *sold* during the month?

Problem 4

Directions:

a) Enter the following information at the top of a stock record card:
1) The item is *envelopes*.
2) The stock number is *E7*.
3) The unit is *box*.
4) The maximum is *500*.
5) The minimum is *100*.

b) Make a record of the following:

19--

Dec.			
1	Received		400
6	Issued		45
10	Issued		72
14	Issued		150
17	Issued		36
20	Received		425
22	Issued		280
28	Issued		144
30	Received		375
31	Issued		288

c) Check your work. If your work is correct, the final balance should be 185.

d) Answer the following questions on a sheet of paper:
1) On what date did you have the *largest* quantity of envelopes?
2) On what date did you have the *smallest* quantity?
3) On what dates did you go *above* the *maximum*?
4) On what dates did you go *below* the *minimum*?
5) What amount was *received* during the month?
6) What amount was *sold* during the month?

Copy these problems on a sheet of paper and find the correct answers. (Pay close attention to the + and − signs.)

	(1)	(2)	(3)	(4)	(5)
Practicing	+ 125	+ 302	+ 1,213	+ 5,137	+ 18
Related	+ 270	+ 476	+ 3,142	− 2,014	+ 1,580
Arithmetic	+ 355	− 223	+ 4,534	+ 3,146	− 104
	− 115	+ 412	− 2,243	+ 561	+ 2,885
	+ 430	− 525	+ 6,051	− 4,170	− 2,312
	+ 585	+ 748	− 3,112	+ 5,243	+ 468
	+ 705	+ 631	+ 4,576	+ 2,452	+ 3,501

AIM

To give you practice in the use of stock record cards which have an opening or starting balance.

EXPLANATION

In Job 45 you learned how to record the receipt and the issuance of stock. In each of the problems, you first entered the amount purchased in the Receipt column; then you showed the same amount in the Balance column as shown in Illustration 46a on the next page.

Occasionally, however, you may have to open a stock record card where there is a quantity of merchandise already on hand. If, for example, you are told there are 50 toasters on hand on March 1 and you are to open a stock record card for the toasters, the card would look like Illustration 46b on the next page.

If you compare Illustration 46b with Illustration 46a you will note that in both cases you have a balance of 50. However, there is one difference. In Illustration 46a you purchased merchandise for the first time on March 1 and in Illustration 46b you were carrying forward the balance from a previous month. No additional merchandise has been purchased on March 1 in Illustration 46b.

Therefore, if you are informed that you have a balance on hand of a certain item, you need to enter that amount only *once* in the Balance column.

Date	Quantity Received	Quantity Issued	Balance
19-- *Mar* 1	50		50

Illustration 46a — Stock Record Card

Date	Quantity Received	Quantity Issued	Balance
19-- *Mar* 1			50

Illustration 46b — Stock Record Card with Opening Balance

You will then continue recording the receipt and issuance of merchandise as you did in Job 45.

SAMPLE PROBLEM

There are 30 tape recorders on hand on August 1, 19--. On Aug. 3, 100 additional tape recorders are received.

This is how the information would appear on the stock record card:

Date	Quantity Received	Quantity Issued	Balance
19-- *Aug* 1			30
3	100		130

PRACTICE PROBLEMS

Problem 1

Directions:
a) Enter this information on a stock record card:
   1) The item is *wallets*.
   2) The stock number is *WA1*.
   3) The unit is *dozen*.
   4) The maximum is *175*.
   5) The minimum is *30*.

b) Make a record of the following:

19--

Feb. 1   The balance on hand is 40. (Enter the 40 only in the *Balance column*.)

4	Received	120
9	Issued	25
11	Issued	48
15	Issued	66
17	Received	160
18	Issued	54
23	Issued	108
25	Received	150
26	Issued	72

Merchandise received increases the balance

Merchandise issued decreases the balance

c) Check your work. If your work is correct, the final balance should be 97.

d) Answer the following questions on a sheet of paper:

1) On what date did you have the *largest* quantity of wallets?
2) On what date did you have the *smallest* quantity of wallets?
3) On what dates did you go *above* the *maximum*?
4) On what dates did you go *below* the *minimum*?
5) What amount was *received* during the month?
6) What amount was *sold* during the month?

Problem 2

Directions:

a) Enter this information on a stock record card:

1) The item is *mattresses*.
2) The stock number is *M8*.
3) The unit is *each*.
4) The maximum is *70*.
5) The minimum is *10*.

b) Make a record of the following:

19--

May 1   The balance is 15. (Enter the 15 only in the *Balance column*.)

3	Issued	6
6	Received	40
10	Issued	18
14	Issued	24
19	Received	65
21	Issued	48
26	Issued	5
27	Received	56
28	Issued	32

c) Check your work. If your work is correct, the final balance should be 43.

d) Answer the following questions on a sheet of paper:

1) On what date did you have the *largest* quantity of mattresses?
2) On what date did you have the *smallest* quantity?
3) On what dates did you go *above* the *maximum*?
4) On what dates did you go *below* the *minimum*?
5) What amount was *received* during the month?
6) What amount was *sold* during the month?

Problem 3

Directions:

a) Enter this information on a stock record card:
    1) The item is *flash cubes*.
    2) The stock number is *FC10*.
    3) The unit is *box*.
    4) The maximum is *275*.
    5) The minimum is *60*.
b) Make a record of the following:

19--

Nov.	1	The balance on hand is 73.	
	2	Issued	12
	5	Issued	8
	8	Received	144
	12	Issued	72
	17	Issued	96
	19	Received	250
	23	Issued	108
	26	Issued	55
	30	Issued	30

c) Check your work. If your work is correct, the final balance should be 86.
d) Answer the following questions on a sheet of paper:
    1) On what date did you have the *largest* quantity of flash cubes?
    2) On what date did you have the *smallest* quantity?
    3) On what dates did you go *above* the *maximum*?
    4) On what dates did you go *below* the *minimum*?
    5) What amount was *received* during the month?
    6) What amount was *sold* during the month?

Problem 4

Directions:

a) Enter the following on a stock record card:
    1) The item is *flight bags*.
    2) The stock number is *FB8*.
    3) The unit is *each*.
    4) The maximum is *120*.
    5) The minimum is *24*.
b) Make a record of the following:

19--

Sept.	1	The balance on hand is 90.	
	2	Issued	25
	6	Issued	12
	9	Issued	30
	13	Received	100
	20	Issued	42
	23	Issued	60
	27	Received	120
	29	Issued	72
	30	Issued	50

c) Check your work. If your work is correct, the final balance should be 19.
d) Answer the following questions on a sheet of paper:
   1) On what date did you have the *largest* quantity of flight bags?
   2) On what date did you have the *smallest* quantity?
   3) On what dates did you go *above* the *maximum*?
   4) On what dates did you go *below* the *minimum*?
   5) What amount was *received* during the month?
   6) What amount was *sold* during the month?

Problem 5

Directions:
a) Enter the following on a stock record card:
   1) The item is *alarm clocks*.
   2) The stock number is *AC5*.
   3) The unit is *each*.
   4) The maximum is *60*.
   5) The minimum is *12*.
b) Make a record of the following:
   19--

Aug.	1	The balance on hand is 18.	
	4	Received	32
	10	Issued	9
	11	Issued	12
	16	Issued	18
	18	Received	54
	24	Issued	21
	25	Issued	38
	30	Received	60
	31	Issued	27

c) Check your work. If your work is correct, the final balance should be 39.
d) Answer the following questions on a sheet of paper:
   1) On what date did you have the *largest* quantity of alarm clocks?
   2) On what date did you have the *smallest* quantity?
   3) On what dates did you go *above* the *maximum*?
   4) On what dates did you go *below* the *minimum*?
   5) What amount was *received* during the month?
   6) What amount was *sold* during the month?

JOB 47 | KEEPING STOCK RECORD CARDS

Practicing Related Arithmetic

Find the answer for each of the following:

Item	Balance on Aug. 1	+	Received during Aug.	−	Issued during Aug.	=	Balance on Sept. 1
1) Files	25	+	75	−	60	=	1)_____
2) Hair spray	45	+	90	−	115	=	2)_____
3) Nail polish	30	+	155	−	160	=	3)_____
4) Scissors	65	+	140	−	85	=	4)_____
5) Shavers	15	+	330	−	210	=	5)_____

AIM

To give you practice in keeping stock record cards for a number of different items.

EXPLANATION

In a large concern, a stock record clerk keeps records for many different items. You had some practice doing this in the various problems in the preceding jobs. However, you never handled several different items in the same problem and that is what you are going to do now.

Remember! Each item requires a separate card and you must be careful to use the correct card for that particular item.

PRACTICE PROBLEMS

Problem 1

Directions:
a) Take 6 stock record cards.
b) Open a separate record card for each item listed in the table on page 299.
c) Now that you have opened these 6 cards, record the following in the order in which they are shown in the columns. *Be sure that you are using the correct card before you enter the information.*

Item	Stock #	Unit	Maximum	Minimum	Bal. on Jan. 1
Band Saws	BS2	Doz.	300	50	65
Hack Saws	HS4	Doz.	400	75	90
Padlocks	P5	Doz.	500	100	203
Safety Goggles	SG1	Gross	150	40	57
Spray Guns	SG3	Each	50	15	18
Tool Pouches	TP8	Doz.	250	80	130

19--
Jan. 3 Received 200 dozen band saws
3 Received 275 dozen hack saws
3 Received 80 gross safety goggles
3 Received 35 spray guns
6 Issued 50 dozen padlocks
6 Issued 75 gross safety goggles
6 Issued 12 spray guns
6 Issued 96 dozen tool pouches
8 Received 48 gross safety goggles
8 Issued 24 spray guns
8 Issued 170 dozen band saws
16 Received 225 dozen tool pouches
16 Issued 90 dozen padlocks

19--
Jan. 16 Received 28 spray guns
20 Issued 21 gross safety goggles
20 Received 425 dozen padlocks
20 Issued 280 dozen hack saws
21 Received 150 dozen band saws
21 Issued 27 spray guns
21 Issued 108 dozen tool pouches
23 Received 168 dozen hack saws
23 Issued 132 dozen band saws
23 Issued 54 dozen tool pouches
27 Received 66 gross safety goggles
27 Issued 78 dozen band saws
29 Issued 210 dozen padlocks
29 Received 30 spray guns
31 Issued 56 gross safety goggles

Check your arithmetic after each entry

d) Check each card to see that it is correct. If your work is correct, the final balances should be:
band saws, 35; hack saws, 253; padlocks, 278; safety goggles, 99; spray guns, 48; tool pouches, 97.
e) Answer the following questions on a sheet of paper: (Remember that each stock card has a different *maximum* and *minimum*.)
1) Which items went *below* the *minimum*?
2) Which items went *above* the *maximum*?
3) Which item was the *fastest* moving (the item which had the *largest* total quantity issued)?
4) Which item was the *slowest* moving (the item which had the *smallest* total quantity issued)?

Problem 2

Directions:
a) Take 6 stock record cards.
b) Open a separate record card for items listed in the table at the top of page 300.
c) Now that you have opened these 6 cards, record the information on page 300 in the order in which they are shown in the columns. *Be sure that you are using the correct card before you enter the information.*

Item	Stock #	Unit	Maximum	Minimum	Bal. on March 1
Batteries	BA2	Each	100	20	25
Battery cables	BC1	Doz.	400	125	142
Oil filters	OF2	Doz	250	60	190
Regulators	R5	Each	75	10	18
Safety belts	SB3	Doz.	600	150	180
Testers	T6	Each	125	20	41

Check your arithmetic after each entry

19--
Mar. 4 Received 200 dozen battery cables
    4 Received 320 dozen safety belts
    4 Issued 25 testers
    7 Received 50 regulators
    7 Issued 80 dozen oil filters
    11 Received 66 batteries
    11 Issued 125 dozen battery cables
    12 Issued 136 dozen safety belts
    12 Received 90 testers
    14 Issued 27 dozen oil filters
    14 Issued 45 regulators
    18 Issued 88 safety belts
    18 Issued 64 testers

19--
Mar. 20 Received 178 dozen oil filters
    20 Issued 23 batteries
    24 Received 32 regulators
    24 Issued 75 dozen battery cables
    25 Issued 35 batteries
    25 Issued 128 dozen safety belts
    25 Issued 18 testers
    26 Received 260 dozen battery cables
    26 Received 432 dozen safety belts
    26 Issued 29 regulators
    28 Received 78 testers
    31 Issued 225 dozen battery cables
    31 Issued 115 dozen oil filters

d) Check each card to see that it is correct. If your work is correct, the final balances should be:

batteries, 33; battery cables, 177; oil filters, 146; regulators, 26; safety belts, 580; testers, 102.

e) Answer the following questions on a sheet of paper. (Remember that each stock card has a different *maximum* and *minimum*.)
1) Which items went *below* the *minimum*?
2) Which items went *above* the *maximum*?
3) Which item was the *fastest* moving?
4) Which item was the *slowest* moving?

Problem 3

Directions:
a) Take 5 stock record cards.
b) Open a separate record card for each of the items listed in the table at the top of page 301.
c) Now that you have opened these 5 cards, record the information on page 301 in the order in which they are shown.

Item	Stock #	Unit	Maximum	Minimum	Bal. on Oct. 1
Car wax	CW2	Doz.	325	70	73
Floor wax	FW4	Doz.	750	100	196
Napkins	NA3	Case	175	20	52
Soap powder	SP1	Case	450	80	106
Sponges	S7	Gross	275	35	145

19--
Oct. 2 Received 175 dozen car wax
2 Issued 100 dozen floor wax
2 Received 70 cases napkins
7 Issued 42 cases soap powder
7 Issued 56 gross sponges
9 Received 384 dozen floor wax
9 Issued 27 gross sponges
9 Received 180 cases soap powder
15 Issued 65 dozen car wax
15 Received 225 gross sponges
16 Issued 135 dozen floor wax
16 Issued 94 cases napkins
16 Issued 118 cases soap powder

19--
Oct. 20 Received 150 cases napkins
20 Issued 110 dozen car wax
20 Issued 196 gross sponges
22 Issued 140 dozen floor wax
22 Issued 105 cases napkins
24 Received 216 dozen car wax
24 Received 432 dozen floor wax
27 Issued 37 cases soap powder
27 Received 130 gross sponges
29 Issued 94 dozen car wax
29 Issued 58 cases napkins
31 Received 212 cases soap powder
31 Issued 128 dozen floor wax

d) Check each card to see that it is correct. If your work is correct, the final balances should be:
car wax, 195; floor wax, 509; napkins, 15; soap powder, 301; sponges, 221.

e) Answer the following questions on a sheet of paper: (Remember that each stock record has a different *maximum* and *minimum*.)
1) Which items went *below* the *minimum*?
2) Which items went *above* the *maximum*?
3) Which item was the *fastest* moving?
4) Which item was the *slowest* moving?

**Practicing
Related
Arithmetic**

Find the answers for each of the following:

Item	Balance on Oct. 1	+	Received during Oct.	−	Issued during Oct.	=	Balance on Nov. 1
1) Jeans	62	+	154	−	195	=	1)_____
2) Pajamas	43	+	132	−	163	=	2)_____
3) Pea jackets	31	+	96	−	108	=	3)_____
4) Shirts	56	+	260	−	267	=	4)_____
5) Slacks	18	+	84	−	79	=	5)_____

AIMS

1. To give you additional practice in keeping stock record cards.
2. To teach you how to check your work.

EXPLANATION

Illustrated on page 303 is a stock record card showing the receipt and issuance of cassettes for the month of April.

As you know from your previous jobs, each time you issued cassettes your balance decreased. For this reason you only had 200 as your balance on *April 5* although you originally had 900 on *April 1*. Every time you received cassettes your balance increased. It is for that reason that you had a balance of 800 on *April 10* after you had 200 on *April 5*.

If you worked carefully, you always checked your addition and subtraction before you entered each new balance. Careful stock record clerks (sometimes called simply "stock clerks") use another method to check the accuracy of their arithmetic. They use this method at the end of the month to check the final balance. It will be demonstrated in the sample problem.

SAMPLE PROBLEM

Checking the
accuracy of the
final balance

Refer to Illustration 48a on the next page.   To check the accuracy of the final balance of 500 on April 30, these are the steps you follow:

STOCK RECORD CARD

ITEM *Cassettes*   Maximum *1000*

STOCK No. *CA 3*   Minimum *100*

UNIT *Dozen*

Date		Quantity Received	Quantity Issued	Balance
19-- Apr.	1			900
	5		700	200
	10	600		800
	12		450	350
	18		225	125
	19	750		875
	24		625	250
	25	550		800
	30		300	500

Illustration 48a — Stock Record Card

Step 1: Start with the opening balance at the beginning of the month.

On a separate sheet of paper or on a scratch pad, enter the opening balance of 900 which appeared on April 1 on your stock record card.

Step 2: Total all the numbers in the Quantity Received column.

Pencil foot the numbers in the Quantity Received column and arrive at a total of 1,900.

Step 3: Total all the numbers in the Quantity Issued column.

Pencil foot the numbers in the Quantity Issued column and arrive at a total of 2,300.

Step 4: Find the balance for the month.

You would do the following:

Balance to start with (Step 1)	900
Quantity received (Step 2)	+1,900
Total	2,800
Quantity issued (Step 3)	−2,300
Balance	= 500

Notice that this final balance of 500 agrees with the balance of 500 on the card on April 30. Therefore, your work is correct. If you find the balances do not agree, you must recheck your four steps. If you find that they still do not agree, then you must recheck each new balance on your card.

Locating an error   For example, you start with April 5 and see if:

Previous balance	900
Less amount issued	−700
Equals new balance	=200

If it does, put a check mark (√) next to the 200 to show that it is correct.

Date	Quantity Received	Quantity Issued	Balance
19-- Apr. 1			900
5		700	200√

Then add 600 to 200 to see if you get 800.

Previous balance	200
Add amount received	+600
Equals new balance	=800

Correcting an error   If you do get 800, put a check mark next to the 800 just the way you did for the 200. If you keep on doing this, you will find your error and will be able to correct the balances. Assume that you do find an error. You would then put a *line* through the incorrect balance and change each balance after that, as shown at the top of page 305.

Notice that you found an error in the entry of *April 24*. That is the reason you put one line through the balance of *240* and put the correct figure of *250* above it. Naturally, if the balance on *April 24* was incorrect, each balance after that one would also be incorrect and would have to be changed. Note that changes were made in the balances from *April 24* through *April 30*.

This added work can be eliminated if the record keeper works carefully and checks the arithmetic before recording new balances.

Date	Quantity Received	Quantity Issued	Balance
19-- Apr. 1			900
5		700	200✓
10	600		800✓
12		450	350✓
18		225	125✓
19	750		875✓
24		625	~~240~~ 250
25	550		~~790~~ 800
30		300	~~490~~ 500
	1900	2300	

The first error required changes to be made in all the following balances

Illustration 48b — Corrected Stock Record Card

PRACTICE PROBLEMS

Problem 1

Directions:
a) Copy the stock record card shown below:

Avoid errors by checking daily balances

Date	Quantity Received	Quantity Issued	Balance
19-- May 1			400
2		100	300
6		175	125
8	875		1,000
12		520	480
19		315	165
22	725		890
26		288	602
28		152	450
29		125	325

b) Follow the four steps listed in the sample problem on pages 303–304 and check the accuracy of the final balance. *If the final balance is correct, then you are finished with this problem.* If the final balance is incorrect, then you must do *part c)* of this problem.

c) Check each daily balance. If it is correct, put a check mark (√) next to the balance. If it is incorrect, put a line through the incorrect balance and put the correct figure above it. (Look at Illustration 48b shown on page 305.)

Remember! When you find one incorrect balance, all the balances appearing after that one are incorrect.

Problem 2

Directions:

a) Copy the following stock record card:

Date		Quantity Received	Quantity Issued	Balance
19-- June	1			170
	3	330		500
	5		150	350
	10		200	150
	12	560		710
	17		310	400
	18		180	220
	23	476		686
	25		66	620
	30		230	390

b) Follow the four steps listed in the sample problem on pages 303–304 and check the accuracy of the final balance. *If the final balance is correct, then you are finished with this problem.* If the final balance is incorrect, then you must do *part c)* of this problem.

c) Check each daily balance. If it is correct, put a check mark (√) next to the balance. If it is incorrect, put a line through the incorrect balance and put the correct figure above it. (Look at Illustration 48b shown on page 305.)

Remember! When you find one incorrect balance, then all the balances appearing after that one are incorrect.

Problem 3

Directions:

a) Copy the stock record card at the top of page 307.

Date		Quantity Received	Quantity Issued	Balance
19--Sept	1			2 50
	4		150	1 00
	9		25	75
	12	525		6 00
	15		55	5 45
	18		260	2 85
	22	312		597
	24		168	3 29
	29		1 00	2 29
	30	400		6 29

b) Follow the four steps listed in the sample problem on pages 303–304 and check the accuracy of the final balance. *If the final balance is correct, then you are finished with this problem.* If the final balance is incorrect, then you must do *part c)* of this problem.

c) Check each daily balance. If it is correct, put a check mark (√) next to the balance. If it is incorrect, put a line through the incorrect balance and put the correct figure above it. (Look at Illustration 48b shown on page 305.)

Remember! When you find one incorrect balance, then all the balances appearing after that one are incorrect.

Problem 4

Directions:

a) Take 4 stock record cards.

b) Open a separate record card for each of the items listed in the following table:

Item	Stock #	Unit	Maximum	Minimum	Bal. on Oct. 1
Butter dish	BD3	Doz.	50	5	8
Cookie jar	CJ2	Each	75	18	53
Percolator	PE4	Each	60	12	17
Teakettle	TK1	Each	100	25	42

c) Now that you have opened these 4 cards, record the information on the next page in the order in which it is given.

19--

Oct. 2 Received 40 percolators

      2 Issued 21 cookie jars

      6 Received 32 dozen butter dishes

      6 Issued 27 teakettles

      8 Issued 14 cookie jars

      8 Issued 16 dozen butter dishes

   10 Received 75 teakettles

   10 Issued 22 percolators

   10 Issued 7 dozen butter dishes

   14 Received 55 cookie jars

19--

Oct. 14 Issued 38 teakettles

   17 Received 25 dozen butter dishes

   17 Issued 19 percolators

   17 Issued 23 teakettles

   21 Issued 49 cookie jars

   21 Received 68 teakettles

   27 Issued 33 dozen butter dishes

   27 Received 42 percolators

   31 Issued 59 teakettles

   31 Received 37 cookie jars

d) Check the accuracy of the final balance on each card by the method you used in Problems 1 through 3. If the balance is incorrect, make the necessary correction on the card.

Find the answers for each of the following:

Item	Balance on Feb. 1	+	Received during Feb.	–	Issued during Feb.	=	Balance on Mar. 1
1) Band saws	48	+	172	–	168	=	1)_____
2) Hack saws	27	+	308	–	259	=	2)_____
3) Padlocks	150	+	920	–	871	=	3)_____
4) Safety goggles	183	+	747	–	652	=	4)_____
5) Spray guns	114	+	568	–	487	=	5)_____

AIMS

1. To learn how to notify the purchasing agent (the buyer) that more merchandise is needed in the stockroom.

2. To practice making out requests for merchandise.

EXPLANATION

Here is a sample of a card you have been working on:

STOCK RECORD CARD

ITEM *Antifreeze*   Maximum *250*

STOCK No. *AF 2*   Minimum *40*

UNIT *Case*

Date		Quantity Received	Quantity Issued	Balance
19-- Dec.	1			95
	8		45	50

Compare the balance with the minimum to see if additional merchandise should be ordered

In previous jobs you learned to record information on this card and to check the accuracy of your work. This, however, is only one of your duties. You are also responsible for notifying a person known as the *buyer* or *purchasing agent* when you need more merchandise. If you study the illustration on page 309, you will note three very important numbers to which you must pay close attention: the number next to the word "maximum" — 250; the number next to the word "minimum" — 40; and the balance — 50. You must constantly compare the balance, 50, with the minimum, 40. When you see that you are approaching the minimum, you must notify the purchasing agent that more merchandise should be ordered. Once you have decided that you need more merchandise, you must decide *how much* is required. This is done by subtracting your balance of 50 from the maximum of 250. You can see that you ought not to order more than 200. (Since the company may get a favorable price if goods are ordered in certain quantities, the purchasing agent will make the final decision on the quantity to be ordered.) After deciding to notify the purchasing agent, you must fill out a form which looks like this:

PURCHASE REQUISITION		
	NO. *1*	
FOR DEPARTMENT *Auto Supplies*	DATE *Dec. 8, 19--*	
NOTIFY *Mel Hogan* ON DELIVERY	DATE WANTED *Dec. 15, 19--*	
QUANTITY	DESCRIPTION	REMARKS
200 cases	*Quart cans of Gaines antifreeze*	
ORDER FROM _____	APPROVED BY _____ PURCHASING AGENT	

A purchase requisition notifies the purchasing agent that merchandise is needed

Illustration 49 – A Purchase Requisition

Examine the completed form above so that you can prepare purchase requisitions.

The words "Auto Supplies" were written to indicate that the merchandise was needed by the auto supplies department. In your own high school you may find that the school has been organized on the basis of departments, such as the mathematics department, the English department, etc. In the same way, a company may be organized into departments, each with a person in charge whose job is to operate the department efficiently.

The name "Mel Hogan" appears after the word "Notify" to indicate the name of the stock clerk. You can see that it is important to notify the person who has ordered something that the request has been attended to.

Since this is the first requisition made out by Mel Hogan, he has numbered it "1." Naturally, the second request will be numbered "2," and so on.

"Dec. 8, 19--" shows the date on which this request was written.

"Dec. 15, 19--" shows that Mel Hogan will need the merchandise on that date. Giving this date guides the purchasing agent when an order is placed for the merchandise.

"200 cases" written in the *Quantity* column indicates the amount requested.

Since there are many grades and sizes of cans of antifreeze, the buyer must know the size and grade needed. Therefore, this information is written in the Description column so the buyer will know that the stock clerk needs *quart cans of Gaines antifreeze.*

If there is any other information that the stock clerk wants to call to the attention of the buyer, he will indicate it in the *Remarks* column.

Notice that no information was written after the words, "Order from _____" or "Approved by _____." These spaces will be used by the purchasing agent. You will learn about this in following jobs.

Mel Hogan prepared an original and a duplicate copy of the requisition and sent the original copy to the purchasing department. In the next job, you will learn what to do with the duplicate copy, which he has kept.

PRACTICE PROBLEMS

Problem 1

Date Made Out	Date Wanted	Item	Description	Unit of Measure	Quantity Needed
19-- Aug. 11	Aug. 21	Electronic Calculator	F & G 12 Digit	Each	20
Aug. 12	Aug. 22	Electronic Calculator	S & Y 10 Digit	Each	12
Aug. 19	Aug. 29	Mini Calculator	Gem 8 Digit	Each	24

Directions: Prepare purchase requisitions for each of the items needed for the office equipment department shown in the table on page 311. Since *you* are preparing the purchase requisitions, write *your* name in the space next to the word "Notify." Start with #1. (You will need 3 purchase requisitions.)

Problem 2

Directions: Find the answers for each of the following:

Maximum
−Balance at start
=Amount needed

	Balance November 1	Maximum	Amount Needed to Bring the Balance up to the Maximum
a)	100	2,100	
b)	335	1,835	
c)	72	400	
d)	69	150	
e)	257	1,100	
f)	164	800	
g)	306	2,700	
h)	148	620	

Problem 3

Directions:

a) In each of the items listed below, find the amount you must order *to bring the balance up to the maximum*. To do this, you must subtract the balance on July 1 from the maximum.

b) After you have determined the quantity needed, prepare purchase requisitions for the electrical goods department for those amounts. Start with #86 and date the requisitions as of July 2, 19—. (You will need 3 purchase requisitions.)

Item	Unit	Description	Maximum	Date Wanted On	Balance on July 1
Fuse	Dozen	AJ20 Amps	200	July 12	46
Mercury Switch	Each	MS #12	75	July 17	9
Outdoor Switch	Each	OS #5	40	July 12	13

Problem 4

Directions:

a) In each of the items listed below, find the amount you must order to bring the balance up to the maximum.

b) After you have determined the quantity needed, prepare purchase requisitions. Start with #132 and date all requisitions March 4, 19—. The merchandise is needed by the camping supply department and all the merchandise is wanted on March 15, 19—:

Item	Unit	Description	Maximum	Minimum	Balance on Mar. 1
Camp Cot	Each	CC10	85	15	28
Pup Tent	Each	PT1	100	10	13
Sleeping Bag	Each	SB2	250	50	41

JOB 50 | MAINTAINING A RECORD OF GOODS EXPECTED

Find the answers for each of the following:

		Balance February 1	Maximum	Amount Needed To Bring The Balance up to Maximum
Practicing Related Arithmetic	1)	30	200	_____
	2)	55	375	_____
	3)	105	2,000	_____
	4)	208	1,300	_____
	5)	79	450	_____
	6)	87	650	_____
	7)	143	725	_____
	8)	1,006	5,000	_____
	9)	321	1,400	_____
	10)	1,202	6,000	_____

AIM

To learn how the stock clerk keeps a record of purchase requisitions.

EXPLANATION

Keeping track of the requisitions issued and filled

You have learned that a duty of the stock clerk is to notify the purchasing agent when more merchandise is needed. You have learned that this is done by filling out purchase requisitions. In order to keep a record of the requisitions filled out, a form similar to the one shown below is used.

RECORD OF GOODS EXPECTED					
DATE OF REQUISITION	PURCHASE REQUISITION NO.	DATE WANTED	DATE OF RECEIPT		REMARKS

Illustration 50a — Record of Goods Expected

Notice that there is no place in this form to record the quantity or description of the merchandise requested. (This information is available on the duplicate copies of the requisitions, which have been filed in numerical sequence — #1, #2, #3, and so on.) The purpose of the *Record of Goods Expected* form is to show the stock clerk at a glance whether the requisitions have been filled.

SAMPLE PROBLEM

Kay Hodge, the stock record clerk in the A & W Co., made out the following requisitions:

PURCHASE REQUISITION

NO. *132*

FOR DEPARTMENT *Furniture*   DATE *May 6, 19--*

NOTIFY *Kay Hodge* ON DELIVERY   DATE WANTED *May 26, 19--*

QUANTITY	DESCRIPTION	REMARKS
36	Headboards HE 4	

ORDER FROM_____   APPROVED BY_____
PURCHASING AGENT

PURCHASE REQUISITION

NO. *133*

FOR DEPARTMENT *Furniture*   DATE *May 7, 19--*

NOTIFY *Kay Hodge* ON DELIVERY   DATE WANTED *May 27, 19--*

QUANTITY	DESCRIPTION	REMARKS
9	Night stands NS 2	

ORDER FROM_____   APPROVED BY_____
PURCHASING AGENT

The merchandise was received on the following days:

Requisition No.	Date of Receipt	Remarks
132	May 23	1 damaged
133	May 29	Only 8 received

RECORD OF GOODS EXPECTED

DATE OF REQUISITION		PURCHASE REQUISITION NO.	DATE WANTED	DATE OF RECEIPT	REMARKS
19--					
May	*6*	*132*	*May 26*	*May 23*	*1 damaged*
	7	*133*	*May 27*	*May 29*	*only 8 received*

Illustration 50b — Completed Record of Goods Expected

Kay Hodge entered the information in the first three columns when she made out the requisitions. When she received the merchandise she was able to fill in the last two columns. She will now notify the purchasing agent about the damage in requisition #132 and the shortage in #133. The purchasing agent will contact the sellers of the merchandise and arrange for an adjustment.

PRACTICE PROBLEMS

Problem 1

Directions:

a) You are to enter on a Record of Goods Expected form the information listed below and on the next page. This form is shown in Illustration 50b, above. Be sure to write plainly.

Requisition No.	Date of Requisition	Stock No.	Item Wanted	Date Wanted
51	Jan. 2	ET2 TR7	8 End tables — Lot #6 5 dozen Tie racks — Lot #3	Jan. 13
52	Jan. 7	CH1 CH3	16 Three-drawer chests — Lot #5 9 Four-drawer chests — Lot #2	Jan. 17
53	Jan. 9	BB4 M6	10 Bunk beds — Lot #11 20 Mirrors — Lot #15	Jan. 20

Requisition No.	Date of Requisition	Stock No.	Item Wanted	Date Wanted
54	Jan. 14	BB8	7 Bookcase beds — Lot #23	Jan. 24
		DC9	5 Desk chests — Lot #1	
55	Jan. 17	D5	18 Three-drawer desks — Lot #16	Jan. 27
56	Jan. 21	QM10	30 Queensize mattresses — Lot #19	Jan. 28
		HB17	15 Headboards — Lot #4	
57	Jan. 22	SC18	6 Side chairs — Lot #7	Jan. 30
58	Jan. 23	BC11	4 Bookcases — Lot #9	Jan. 31
		NS15	12 Nightstands — Lot #10	
59	Jan. 28	KM14	36 Kingsize mattresses — Lot #8	Feb. 10
60	Jan. 29	CT20	14 Coffee tables — Lot #18	Feb. 19

b) Stock was received on the following dates. Enter the information on your record.

Requisition No.	Date of Receipt	Remarks
51	Jan. 10	None
52	Jan. 16	None
55	Jan. 24	Only 17 three-drawer desks
57	Jan. 29	1 damaged side chair
58	Jan. 31	None

c) It is now February 1.
   1) List the requisition numbers of goods which have not been received by this date.

   2) List the requisition numbers of goods which are more than 10 days overdue from the date you wanted the merchandise. (Remember! January has 31 days.)

Problem 2

Directions:
a) You are to enter the information listed on page 318 on a Record of Goods Expected form. Write plainly!

Requisition No.	Date of Requisition	Stock No.	Item Wanted	Date Wanted
120	April 1	SW2 SW5	10 dozen Sweaters — Brown — Size 34 8 dozen Sweaters — Blue — Size 36	April 16
121	April 2	TS3 TS4	15 dozen Twin-set sweaters — White — Size 38 12 dozen Twin-set sweaters — White — Size 40	April 17
122	April 7	AV9	20 dozen Argyle plaid vests — Size 13	April 21
123	April 9	SC7 SC9	24 dozen Scarves — Lot #4 18 dozen Scarves — Lot #6	April 18
124	April 10	BL12 BL13	6 dozen Blouses — White — Size 12 9 dozen Blouses — White — Size 14	April 17
125	April 14	SJ8 SJ10	7 dozen Shirt jackets — Light gray — Size 16 5 dozen Shirt jackets — Red — Size 18	April 24
126	April 16	PO15 PO16	24 dozen Pullovers — Light pink — Size 34 18 dozen Pullovers — Light blue — Size 36	April 28
127	April 18	CR11	16 dozen Chenille robes — Blue — Size 16	April 29
128	April 23	NSR14	14 dozen Nylon satin robes — Mint — Size 12	May 7
129	April 28	CS19	22 dozen Cardigan sweaters — Black — Size 36	May 19

b) Stock was received on the dates shown below and on page 319. Enter the information on your record.

Requisition No.	Date of Record	Remarks
120	April 18	None
122	April 23	None

123	April 21	Only 23 doz. — Lot #4
127	April 30	None

c) It is now May 6.

1) List the requisition numbers of merchandise which have not been received by this date.

2) List the requisition numbers of merchandise which are more than 10 days overdue from the date you wanted the merchandise. (Remember! April has 30 days.)

Problem 3

Directions:

a) You are to enter the information listed below on a Record of Goods Expected form. Write plainly!

Requisition No.	Date of Requisition	Stock No.	Item Wanted	Date Wanted
185	July 2	EP3 EC5	10 dozen Earphones — Lot #8 12 gross Extension cords — Lot #6	July 11
186	July 3	D19	5 dozen Dimmers — Lot #2	July 14
187	July 7	CK15	6 dozen Computer kits — Lot #4	July 17
188	July 9	AN1 AN2	4 dozen FM Antennas — Lot #10 3 dozen UHF Antennas — Lot #11	July 24
189	July 10	AD7	8 dozen Four channel adapters — Lot #5	July 21
190	July 14	PL4 PL7	9 gross AC Plugs — Lot #17 15 gross Phono plugs — Lot #18	July 23
191	July 16	MP16	7 dozen Microphones — Lot #12	July 29
192	July 21	RS10	6 gross Reels — Lot #15	July 31
193	July 24	HP20	2 dozen Headphones — Lot #13	Aug. 8
194	July 30	WT11 WT13	16 Walkie-talkies — Lot #7 20 Walkie-talkie cases — Lot #9	Aug. 20

b) Stock was received on the dates listed on the next page. Enter the information on your record.

Requisition No.	Date of Receipt	Remarks
185	July 10	None
186	July 16	Only 4 dozen dimmers
188	July 22	None
190	July 23	Only 14 gross phono plugs
192	July 31	None

c) It is now August 1.
   1) List the requisition numbers of merchandise which have not been received by this date.
   2) List the requisition numbers of merchandise which are more than 10 days overdue from the date you wanted the merchandise. (Remember! July has 31 days.)

Problem 4

Directions:
a) You are to enter the information listed below and on page 321 on a Record of Goods Expected form. Write plainly!

Requisition No.	Date of Requisition	Stock No.	Item Wanted	Date Wanted
213	Dec. 1	RS1	3 dozen Roller sets — 7 inch — Lot #4	Dec. 10
		RS4	5 dozen Roller sets — 9 inch — Lot #15	
214	Dec. 3	DC2	36 Drop cloths — 9 x 12 feet — Lot #18	Dec. 12
215	Dec. 5	MT3	6 gross Masking tape — Lot #2	Dec. 15
216	Dec. 8	LF9	30 gallons Interior latex flat paint — Green — Lot #5	Dec. 19
217	Dec. 11	NB10	2 gross Three-inch nylon brushes — Lot #1	Dec. 22
		NB11	5 gross Four-inch nylon brushes — Lot #3	
218	Dec. 15	SP5	24 gallons Exterior spar varnish — Lot #8	Dec. 30
219	Dec. 17	VR8	18 quarts Varnish remover — Lot #10	Dec. 31
220	Dec. 18	BP13	9 gross Interior brush pads — Lot #6	Jan. 9
		BP14	12 gross Exterior brush pads — Lot #7	

Requisition No.	Date of Requisition	Stock No.	Item Wanted	Date Wanted
221	Dec. 22	AL20	48 gallons Acrylic latex white paint — Lot #11	Jan. 12
222	Dec. 29	SG22	60 quarts Semi-gloss blue paint — Lot #13	Jan. 15

b) Stock was received on the following dates. Enter the information on your record.

Requisition No.	Date of Receipt	Remarks
213	Dec. 8	None
214	Dec. 15	Only 35 drop cloths
216	Dec. 22	3 damaged cans
218	Dec. 29	None
219	Dec. 30	None

c) It is now January 8.
1) List the requisition numbers of merchandise which have not been received by this date.
2) List the requisition numbers of merchandise which are more than 3 days overdue from the date you wanted the merchandise. (Remember! December has 31 days.)

Practicing Related Arithmetic	Copy these problems on a sheet of paper and find the answers:				
	(1)	(2)	(3)	(4)	(5)
	213 ×$3.25	536 ×$2.93	708 ×$5.46	1007 ×$6.09	85 ×$24.00

AIM

To learn how to keep simple records of the prices that different companies charge for the same item.

EXPLANATION

"Imagine! same set and $35°° Cheaper. You're a smart Shopper."

In previous jobs, you learned how important it was for the stock clerk to compare constantly the balance on each stock record card with the minimum number required on each card. You learned how a purchase requisition was used to notify the purchasing agent that additional merchandise was needed.

Today you will learn how the purchasing agent has a clerk keep records that help the buyer make a wise purchase.

You and your parents have personally acted as buyers on many occasions. When your parents decided to purchase a television set, they visited a number of stores to compare the prices and merits of each brand of television set.

A purchasing agent for a large business works along these lines by getting information and prices from different sellers of merchandise. Then, based on experience and knowledge of merchandise, the agent decides from which company to buy. In order to make an intelligent decision, the purchasing agent has a clerk keep a record of important information about any item on a card like the one on page 323.

This is called a *price quotation card* because the clerk will list the prices charged by different sellers for the same article on this one card. If there are four different sellers of one item, the clerk will list the name of each seller, the address, the price, and the terms. In this way, the buyer can look at this one card and see the different businesses selling this item and can note the different prices charged by each one. If certain important information about

PRICE QUOTATION CARD

		STOCK NO. _____			
ITEM _____ UNIT _____					

DATE	FIRM AND ADDRESS	PRICE	TERMS	ADDITIONAL INFORMATION

Illustration 51a — Price Quotation Card

a seller is learned, this special information is written in the column headed "Additional Information."

SAMPLE PROBLEM

You are employed by the Carter Hardware Co. to act as a clerk in the purchasing department. The purchasing agent, Mr. Odell, asks you to open a separate price quotation card for each item on April 1, 19--, from the information below.

Firm Name & Address	Stock #	Item	Unit	Price	Terms
K. Jordan 648 Bleigh Ave. Philadelphia, PA 19111	P2 SG5	Padlocks Safety Goggles	Doz. Gross	$19.25 $16.10	30 days 30 days
M & R Co. 716 Fulton Ave. Brooklyn, NY 11238	SG5	Safety Goggles	Gross	$16.00	30 days
L. Noyes Co. 86 Lewis St. Trenton, NJ 08611	P2	Padlocks	Doz.	$19.20	30 days
A. Volpe Co. 103 Canal St. New York, NY 10002	P2	Padlocks	Doz.	$19.30	30 days

Here is how the completed cards would look:

PRICE QUOTATION CARD

ITEM _Padlocks_   STOCK NO. _P2_
                                                   UNIT _Dozen_

DATE		FIRM AND ADDRESS	PRICE		TERMS	ADDITIONAL INFORMATION
_19--_						
April	1	K. Jordan, 648 Bleigh Ave.,				
		Philadelphia, PA 19111	19	25	30 days	
	1	L. Noyes Co., 86 Lewis St.,				
		Trenton, NJ 08611	19	20	30 days	
	1	A. Volpe Co., 103 Canal St.				
		New York, NY 10002	19	30	30 days	

PRICE QUOTATION CARD

ITEM _Safety Goggles_   STOCK NO. _SG5_
                                                   UNIT _Gross_

DATE		FIRM AND ADDRESS	PRICE		TERMS	ADDITIONAL INFORMATION
_19--_						
April	1	K. Jordan, 648 Bleigh Ave.,				
		Philadelphia, PA 19111	16	10	30 days	
	1	M&R Co., 716 Fulton Ave.,				
		Brooklyn, NY 11238	16	60	30 days	

Illustration 51b — Completed Price Quotation Cards

Of course, in large concerns, instead of this information being recorded manually (by hand), it would have been handled by data processing equipment.

Here is how K. Jordan's price quotation of $19.25 for padlocks would appear after it had been punched into a computer card.

Since you were given prices for two different articles, it was necessary to open two separate cards.

Do you know why K. Jordon appears on both cards? If you refer to the information on the table on page 323, you will note that this company sells *padlocks* and *safety goggles*. Therefore, it is necessary to list this company on both cards.

Mr. Odell, the buyer, can now refer to the card headed "Padlocks" and readily see which companies sell them.

You may be thinking that Mr. Odell's job as the purchasing agent is an easy one. You may think that all he has to do is to look at the card and pick the lowest price. However, this may not be what he will do. It is quite possible that he may send his order to the A. Volpe Co. even though its price is higher than the other two. He may do this because past experience has taught him that their merchandise is superior to that of the others. Or, Mr. Odell may prefer the service he gets from the A. Volpe Co.

You know from your own experience that there are many reasons why you buy from one store instead of from another.

PRACTICE PROBLEMS

Problem 1

Directions:

a) You are to open separate price quotation cards for *each different article* from the information shown on the next page. Use February 1, 19–– as the date.

b) You will need 6 cards since you will keep records for 6 different items: chisels, hammers, planes, saws, screwdrivers and wrenches.

Remember! Each card will be used to record important information about *all the companies* which sell that *one particular item*.

Firm Name & Address	Stock #	Item	Unit	Price	Terms
T. Algosa Co. 186 Walnut St. Raleigh, NC 27603	CH2 HA4 SA3	Chisels Hammers Saws	Doz. Doz. Each	$54.30 $38.65 $ 8.90	30 days 30 days 30 days
M. Benit Co. 106 Bell Ave. Chicago, IL 60612	PL6 SA3 WR1	Planes Saws Wrenches	Each Each Doz.	$14.70 $ 9.00 $40.35	45 days 45 days 45 days
S. Jenks Co. 3102 West St. Newark, NJ 07103	CH2 SK7	Chisels Screwdrivers	Doz. Doz.	$53.96 $21.50	20 days 20 days
R & T Co. 32 New St. Boston, MA 02128	HA4 SA3 SK7	Hammers Saws Screwdrivers	Doz. Each Doz.	$37.84 $ 9.20 $20.75	30 days 30 days 30 days
A. Santi Co. 806 East Ave. Akron, OH 44307	CH2 PL6 SK7	Chisels Planes Screwdrivers	Doz. Each Doz.	$54.10 $14.50 $21.00	45 days 45 days 45 days
F. Zang Co. 368 Webster Ave. Bronx, NY 10456	HA4 PL6 WR1	Hammers Planes Wrenches	Doz. Each Doz.	$37.40 $15.00 $41.00	20 days 20 days 20 days

c) Answer the following questions on a sheet of paper:
1) Which concern sells chisels at the lowest price?
2) Which concern sells planes at the lowest price?
3) Which concern sells saws at the lowest price?

Problem 2

Directions:

a) You are to open separate price quotation cards for *each different article* from the information shown on the next page. Use May 1, 19— as the date.

b) You will need 5 cards since you will keep records for 5 different items: cuticle scissors, facial cream, hair spray, nail polish, and nail polish remover.

Remember! Each card will be used to record important information about *all the companies* which sell that *one particular item*.

Firm Name & Address	Stock #	Item	Unit	Price	Terms
B. Cumo Co. 53 Duane St. New York, NY 10007	CS2 NP8 NR5	Cuticle scissors Nail polish Nail polish remover	Doz. Doz. Doz.	$30.00 $18.30 $ 6.48	30 days 30 days 30 days
T. Foote Co. 89 River St. Paterson, NJ 07501	CS2 FC2	Cuticle scissors Facial cream	Doz. Doz.	$31.00 $15.20	20 days 20 days
G & S Co. 159 Jamaica Ave. Jamaica, NY 11418	HS6 NP8 NR5	Hair spray Nail polish Nail polish remover	Doz. Doz. Doz.	$20.80 $17.90 $ 6.60	45 days 45 days 45 days
C. Kenney Co. 176 Adams Ave. Scranton, PA 19603	FC2 HS6	Facial cream Hair spray	Doz. Doz.	$14.85 $20.40	30 days 30 days
D. Topp Co. 233 Hovey St. Gary, IN 46406	CS2 HS6	Cuticle scissors Hair spray	Doz. Doz.	$29.75 $21.00	30 days 30 days

c) Answer the following questions on a sheet of paper:
  1) Which concern sells cuticle scissors at the lowest price?
  2) Which concern sells hair spray at the lowest price?
  3) Which concern sells nail polish at the lowest price?
  4) Which concern sells nail polish remover at the lowest price?

Problem 3

Directions:
a) You are to open separate price quotation cards for each different article from the information shown below and on the next page. Use July 1, 19— as the date.
b) You will need 5 cards since you will keep records for 5 different items: FM antennas, headphones, phono plugs, TV picture tubes, and video tape.

Remember! Each card will be used to record important information about *all the companies* which sell that *one particular item*.

Firm Name & Address	Stock #	Item	Unit	Price	Terms
H & K Co. 938 Dunns Ave. Jacksonville, FL 32218	HP2 PP4	Headphones Phono plugs	Doz. Gross	$ 48.50 $ 8.40	30 days 30 days

Firm Name & Address	Stock #	Item	Unit	Price	Terms
A. James Co. 102 Smith St. Providence, RI 02903	PT10 VT6	TV picture tubes Video tape	Each Each	$ 50.10 $ 8.75	45 days 45 days
W. Pace Co. 80 Grand Ave. Springfield, OH 45506	AN3 HP2 PP4	FM antennas Headphones Phono plugs	Doz. Doz. Gross	$186.00 $ 49.25 $ 8.00	30 days 30 days 30 days
Q & W Co. 620 Wilson St. Macon, GA 31201	AN3 PT10 VT6	FM antennas TV picture tubes Video tape	Doz. Each Each	$178.40 $ 51.00 $ 8.35	20 days 20 days 20 days
F. Stark Co. 73 Broadway Oakland, CA 94607	AN3 HP2 VT6	FM antennas Headphones Video tape	Doz. Doz. Each	$180.00 $ 47.80 $ 8.00	30 days 30 days 30 days

    c) Answer the following questions on a sheet of paper:
       1) Which concern sells FM antennas at the lowest price?
       2) Which concern sells phono plugs at the lowest price?
       3) Which concern sells video tapes at the lowest price?

Problem 4

Directions:

a) You are to open separate price quotation cards for each separate article from the information shown below and on the next page. Use October 1, 19— as the date.

b) You will need 5 cards since you will keep records for 5 different items: bicycles, bicycle mirrors, bicycle pumps, kick stands, and tool bags.

Remember! Each card will be used to record important information about *all the companies* which sell that *one particular item*.

Firm Name & Address	Stock #	Item	Unit	Price	Terms
J. Brett Co. 849 Spring St. Philadelphia, PA 19107	BY3 KS6 TB1	Bicycles Kick stands Tool bags	Each Doz. Doz.	$87.50 $17.75 $31.80	30 days 30 days 30 days
C. Carey Co. 290 Myrtle Ave. Brooklyn, NY 11205	BY3 BM2 BP5	Bicycles Bicycle mirrors Bicycle pumps	Each Doz. Doz.	$86.00 $33.80 $50.25	20 days 20 days 20 days
E. Porter Co. 3280 Barr Ave. Oklahoma City, OK 73122	BM2 BP5 KS6	Bicycle mirrors Bicycle pumps Kick stands	Doz. Doz. Doz.	$34.15 $51.00 $18.30	45 days 45 days 45 days

Firm Name & Address	Stock #	Item	Unit	Price	Terms
S & Y Co. 824 Marshall Ave. Norfolk, VA 23504	BM2 BP5 TB1	Bicycle mirrors Bicycle pumps Tool bags	Doz. Doz. Doz.	$32.95 $50.70 $30.40	30 days 30 days 30 days

c) Answer the following questions on a sheet of paper:
1) Which concern sells bicycle mirrors at the lowest price?
2) Which concern sells bicycle pumps at the lowest price?
3) Which concern sells kick stands at the lowest price?

Practicing Related Arithmetic

Copy these problems on a sheet of paper and find the answers.

(1)	(2)	(3)	(4)
152	46	95	4308
×$8.03	×$.12½	×$.37½	×$5.62½

AIMS

1. To learn how the purchasing agent informs companies that merchandise is needed.

2. To give you an opportunity to make out purchase orders.

EXPLANATION

In a previous job you learned how the purchasing agent keeps a detailed record of the prices and kinds of merchandise that can be purchased. After it is decided from whom merchandise will be purchased, an order is sent. Today you will become acquainted with this order, known as a *purchase order*. Here is a blank purchase order:

AA PHOTO SUPPLY CO.
3305 Pearl Street Philadelphia, PA 19104

PURCHASE ORDER

MARK OUR ORDER NO. ON ALL INVOICES, PACKAGES, AND SHIPPING PAPERS

TO

ORDER NO. _____
DATE _____
SHIP VIA _____
SHIP TO _____
DATE WANTED _____
TERMS _____

QUANTITY	DESCRIPTION	UNIT PRICE

BY _____
PURCHASING AGENT

A purchase order for merchandise is sent by the buyer to the seller

Illustration 52a — Purchase Order

SAMPLE PROBLEM

You are employed as a clerk in the purchasing department of the A A Photo Supply Co., located at 3305 Pearl St., Philadelphia, PA 19104.

Your job is to act as an assistant to the purchasing agent, Ms. Agnes Healy. Ms. Healy decides to place orders for the following:

> 15 Exposure meters #EM6 @ $20.15
> 18 Slide projectors #SP2 @ $71.25
> 36 Wall screens #WS1 @ $24.00

She asks you to prepare the purchase order and to place the order with the D. Grace Co., 97 Market Street, Newark, NJ 07102.

Here is how your completed order would look:

Illustration 52b — Completed Purchase Order

Notice that Ms. Healy has asked you to indicate clearly when she needs the merchandise and the method of shipment to be used.

PRACTICE PROBLEMS

Problem 1

Directions: You are working for the L & T Paint Supply Co., located at 1108 Barry Avenue, Los Angeles, CA 90049. You are to prepare purchase orders from the following information for your boss, Lester Fain. (Sign Lester Fain's name as the purchasing agent.)

a) Purchase order #51
Dated — Jan. 7, 19—
Date Wanted — Jan. 17, 19—
To: M. Chase Co.
     4970 Fir St.
     Los Angeles, CA 90016
Terms: 30 days
You want — 40 gallons Hard gloss gray enamel — Lot #2   @ $10.85
               25 quarts Varnish remover — Lot #1   @ $ 2.08
The merchandise is to be shipped to the stockroom by truck.

b) Purchase order #52
Dated — Jan. 7, 19—
Date Wanted — Jan. 20, 19—
To: R. Hill Co.
    3812 Globe Ave.
    Los Angeles, CA 90066
Terms: 20 days
You want — 50 gallons Acrylic latex blue — Lot #10   @ $ 9.10
          45 gallons Interior flat latex green — Lot #3 @ $11.20
The merchandise is to be shipped to the stockroom by truck.

c) Purchase order #53
Dated — Jan. 10, 19—
Date Wanted — Jan. 23, 19—
To: E. Howard Co.
    1361 Seward Ave.
    Los Angeles, CA 90028
Terms: 30 days
You want — 24 dozen Two-inch nylon brushes — Lot #14 @ $43.35
          30 dozen Three-inch nylon brushes — Lot #17@ $68.70
The merchandise is to be shipped to the stockroom by truck.

Problem 2

Directions: You are working for the H. Wade Co., located at 342 Coles Street, El Paso, TX 79901. You are to prepare purchase orders from the following information for your boss, Sally Davis. (Sign Sally Davis' name as the purchasing agent.)

a) Purchase order #609
Dated — May 13, 19—
Date Wanted — May 26, 19—
To: B & E Co.
    1751 Carver Ave.
    Fort Worth, TX 76102
Terms: 30 days
You want —   6 dozen Tweed patterned skirts —
          Off-white — size 14 — Lot #35   @ $156.00
          5 dozen Skirts — Medium gray — size 16
          — Lot #17   @ $163.80
The merchandise is to be shipped by truck to the stockroom.

b) Purchase order #610
Dated — May 13, 19—
Date Wanted — May 23, 19—
To: J. Danci Co.
    109 Bowie St.
    El Paso, TX 79905
Terms: 20 days
You want — 15 dozen Argyle plaid vests — True red — size
          12 — Lot #6   @ $114.75
          9 dozen Argyle plaid vests — Cream — size
          14 — Lot #7   @ $117.50
The merchandise is to be shipped by truck to the stockroom.

c) Purchase order #611
   Dated — May 15, 19—
   Date Wanted — June 25, 19—
   To: E. R. W. Co.
       139 Arizona Ave.
       El Paso, TX 79902
   Terms: 30 days
   You want —   4 dozen Trench coats — Bright blue — size
                13 — Lot #22   @ $266.00
                3 dozen Trench coats — Bright red — size 16
                — Lot #23   @ $280.00
   The merchandise is to be shipped by truck to the stockroom.

Problem 3
Directions: You are working for the Hy-Style Watch Co. located at 84 West 45th Street, New York, NY 10036. You are to prepare purchase orders from the following information for your boss, Jose Yordeo. (Sign Jose Yordeo's name as the purchasing agent.)

a) Purchase order #534
   Dated — Feb. 3, 19—
   Date Wanted — March 3, 19—
   To: C & T Co.
       1519 Tibbitts Ave.
       Troy, NY 12180
   Terms: 45 days
   You want —   2 dozen Stop watch timers — Black case —
                Lot #4   @ $304.00
                3 dozen Digital watches — Blue dials — Lot
                #1   @ $362.00
   The merchandise is to be shipped by air freight to the stockroom.

b) Purchase order #535
   Dated — Feb. 7, 19—
   Date Wanted — Feb. 28, 19—
   To: I. Leff Co.
       58 Essex St.
       Lynn, MA 01902
   Terms: 45 days
   You want —   7 dozen Calendar watches — Lot #3   @ $368.00
                4 dozen Pendants — Lot #5   @ $142.00
   The merchandise is to be shipped by air freight to the stockroom.

c) Purchase order #536
   Dated — Feb. 17, 19—
   Date Wanted — March 17, 19—
   To: M. Fleck Co.
       37 Hill St.
       Newark, NJ 07102
   Terms: 30 days
   You want —   5 dozen Nurse's style watches — Lot #16   @ $392.00
                2 dozen Combination watch & cameo — Lot
                #22   @ $308.00
   The merchandise is to be shipped by express to the stockroom.

Problem 4

Directions: You are working for the R. Baines Co., located at 25 Blake Avenue, New Haven, CT 06511. You are to prepare purchase orders from the following information for your boss, Nancy Speer. (Sign Nancy Speer's name as the purchasing agent.)

a) Purchase order #1032

Dated — June 2, 19—

Date Wanted — June 17, 19—

To: T. Kass

    40 Pine St.

    Waterbury, CT 06710

Terms: 30 days

You want — 3 dozen Knapsacks — Yellow — Lot #1   @ $216.00

                1 dozen Duffel bags — Black — Lot #4   @ $152.80

The merchandise is to be shipped by truck to the stockroom.

b) Purchase order #1033

Dated — June 2, 19—

Date Wanted — June 20, 19—

To: S. Klein

    122 Bridge St.

    Lowell, MA 01852

Terms: 20 days

You want — 15 dozen Tote bags — Red — Lot #5   @ $235.75

              2 dozen Attache cases — Gray — Lot #9   @ $186.20

The merchandise is to be shipped by truck to the stockroom.

c) Purchase order #1034

Dated — June 4, 19—

Date Wanted — June 23, 19—

To: J. Regan Co.

    214 Post Rd.

    Warwick, RI 02888

Terms: 30 days

You want — 7 dozen Pullman cases — Beige — Lot #11   @ $368.30

          10 dozen Roll bags — Red — Lot #14   @ $206.00

The merchandise is to be shipped by truck to the stockroom.

JOB 53 | CHECKING PURCHASE INVOICES

Practicing Related Arithmetic

Copy these problems on a sheet of paper and find the answers:

(1)	(2)	(3)	(4)	(5)
204	173	96	48	132
×$13.70	×$3.08½	×$.12¼	×$.05¼	×$.90¼

AIM

To learn how to check the invoices received from companies from whom merchandise is purchased.

EXPLANATION

In previous jobs you learned that the purchasing agent sends a purchase order to the company from whom merchandise is purchased. After shipping the merchandise, the seller sends a bill to the buyer which the buyer calls a *purchase invoice*. The same form is a *sales invoice* to the *seller* and a *purchase invoice* to the *buyer*. You will learn about sales invoices in the next unit. Here is how a blank invoice looks:

K. Tobin Auto Supply Co.
1412 Leers Street
South Bend, IN 46613

SOLD TO _____

INVOICE NO. _____

DATE _____ 19 _____

OUR ORDER NO. _____

CUSTOMER'S ORDER NO. _____

TERMS _____   SHIPPED VIA _____

QUANTITY	DESCRIPTION	UNIT PRICE	TOTAL AMOUNT

Illustration 53a — Purchase Invoice

The procedure for handling an incoming purchase invoice may differ in various companies. The important point to bear in mind is that the buyer must have some system of checking this purchase invoice before it is paid.

In order to understand the procedure clearly, let us consider the following problem.

SAMPLE PROBLEM

You are employed in the bookkeeping department of the H. Reo Co., located at 1109 King Street, South Bend, IN 46616. Here is a purchase invoice you have received.

The seller (creditor)

K. Tobin Auto Supply Co.
1412 Leers Street
South Bend, IN 46613

The buyer (debtor)

SOLD TO *H. Reo Co.*
1109 King Street
South Bend, IN 46616

INVOICE NO. *197*
DATE *May 6,* 19 --
OUR ORDER NO. *205*
CUSTOMER'S ORDER NO. *648*

TERMS *30 days*   SHIPPED VIA *Truck*

QUANTITY	DESCRIPTION	UNIT PRICE	TOTAL AMOUNT
24	*Batteries - 12 Volt - Lot # BA2*	28 25	678 00
10 doz.	*Booster cables - Lot # BC4*	30 00	300 00
			978 00

Approved Joan Galen

All facts have been checked and found to be correct

Illustration 53b — Completed Purchase Invoice

These are the steps you would follow in checking this invoice:

Step 1: Compare invoice with the purchase order.

The invoice is compared with the purchase order to see if the quantity, description, and unit prices agree. If not, the purchasing agent is notified.

Step 2: Check to see if the quantities have been received.

According to Illustration 53b, you should have received 24 batteries and 10 dozen booster cables. You now check with the clerk who received the merchandise (the receiving clerk in the stockroom) to see if the quantities were actually received. If they were not, the purchasing agent must contact the supplier (K. Tobin Auto Supply Co.) and register a complaint.

Step 3: Check extensions.

$
\begin{array}{r}
\$\ 28.25 \text{ (Unit price)}\\
\times\quad 24 \text{ (Quantity)}\\
\hline
11300\\
5650\\
\hline
\$678.00 \text{ (Extension)}
\end{array}
$

According to Illustration 53b, 24 × $28.25 = $678.00. But, does it? Your job is to check the arithmetic to see if it does.

The word *extension* as used in business means the answer you get when you multiply the unit price (cost of one unit of measure) by the quantity (number of units purchased).

Once you have determined that the first extension of $678.00 is correct, check the second extension of $300.00 by multiplying $30.00 by 10 to see if it is $300.00.

Many companies find it advisable to use calculators similar to the one shown below to check calculations.

"We simply must get him one of those new electronic calculators"

Step 4: Check totals.

If both of the extensions are correct, add the extensions to see if they total $978.00. If they do, you are ready for the next step.

Step 5: Approve the invoice for payment.

Now that you have checked the entire invoice and found it to be correct, write "approved" and sign your name. This means that you are giving your stamp of approval for payment. In business, it is said that you have "vouched" the invoice, that the invoice can be paid when it is due without any further investigation.

Vouched = checked

PRACTICE PROBLEMS

Directions:
a) You are working as a clerk in the bookkeeping department of the M. Thomas Auto Supply Co. Your job is to check purchase invoices.

b) You have checked and found that the quantities have been received.

c) Check the extensions and the totals. If you locate an error, show the correct extensions and the correct totals.

Problem 1

Quantity	Description	Unit Price	Extension
5	8-Ampere chargers — Lot #4	34 80	174 00
6	10-Ampere chargers — Lot #6	39 35	236 10
			410 10

Problem 2

Quantity	Description	Unit Price	Extension
10	Siren alarms — Lot #2	23 48	234 80
√ 23	Extra-loud siren alarms — Lot #5	30 96	712 08
			946 88

Problem 3

Quantity	Description	Unit Price	Extension
9	Steering wheel locks — Lot #SW1	9 57	86 13
32	Seat cushions — Lot #SC2	2 89	92 48
			178 61

Problem 4

Quantity	Description	Unit Price	Extension
85 gallons	Antifreeze and summer coolant — Lot #9	2|46	209|10 ✗
26 dozen	Oil filters — Lot #8	28|56	742|56
13	Adjustable jack stands — Lot #3	12|07	156|91 ✗
			1,118|57

Problem 5

Quantity	Description	Unit Price	Extension
29 dozen	Air filters — Lot #12	30|95	897|55
70 dozen	Spark plugs — Lot #11	9|84	688|80
			1,686|35

Problem 6 ✓

Quantity	Description	Unit Price	Extension
43	Alternators — Lot #AL2	40|62	1,746|66
25	Voltage regulators — Lot #VR3	7|06	166|50
			1,913|16

Problem 7

Quantity	Description	Unit Price	Extension
30	Solenoid switches — Lot #S015	6|12	183|60
8	Water pumps — Lot #WP4	23|60	188|80
			372|40

Problem 8

Quantity	Description	Unit Price	Extension
2	Ring overhaul kits — Lot #RO1	29|83	59|66
15	Ignition coils — Lot #IC2	16|00	250|00
50	Condensers — Lot #CS4	3|24	161|00
			470|66

Problem 9

Quantity	Description	Unit Price	Extension
12	Portable engine analyzers — Lot #EA6	59 40	812 80
4	Tune-up testing kits — Lot #TT1	143 57	574 28
			1,387 08

Problem 10

Quantity	Description	Unit Price	Extension
7	Ignition testers — Lot #IT5	45 12	315 84
12	A-C powered timing lights — Lot #TL9	18 63	223 56
3	Alternator-generator testers — Lot #AJ1	51 40	154 20
			693 60

Problem 11

Quantity	Description	Unit Price	Extension
36 dozen	Auto safety belts — Lot #7	50 00	1,800 00
20	Child's safety harnesses — Lot #14	10 15	203 00
			2,003 00

Problem 12

Quantity	Description	Unit Price	Extension
16 dozen	Hydrometers — Lot #19	28 70	459 20
11 dozen	5-gallon gas cans — Lot #24	109 50	1,095 00
			1,554 20

Problem 13

Quantity	Description	Unit Price	Extension
35 dozen	Tire gauges — Lot #TG3	49 00	1,715 00
18	Dry chemical fire extinguishers —		
	Lot #FE2	25 00	440 00
14 dozen	Oil filter wrenches — Lot #OF5	20 60	288 40
			2,443 40

Problem 14

Quantity	Description	Unit Price	Extension
21 cases	Dry gas — Lot #7	4 37	91 77
17 dozen	Wash brushes — Lot #WB10	96 70	1,633 90
			1,725 67

Problem 15

Quantity	Description	Unit Price	Extension
24	Batteries — 6 volt — Lot #BA3	14 05	337 20
38 boxes	Sealed beam fog lights — Lot #SB1	16 00	608 00
			945 20

Practicing Related Arithmetic	Copy these problems on a sheet of paper and find the answers:				
	(1)	(2)	(3)	(4)	(5)
	409 ×$7.63	307 ×$5.08	620 ×$.14½	1520 ×$.67½	524 ×$.10¼

AIMS

1. To understand the need for recording purchase invoices in a Purchases Journal.

2. To practice using a Purchases Journal.

3. To learn how to file the approved purchase invoices.

EXPLANATION

In the previous job, you learned how important it was to check each purchase invoice. Perhaps you wondered what happens to this invoice after it is checked. Today you will trace its course until payment is made to the *creditor* (the one to whom money is owed). Naturally, different companies have various ways of recording facts. In this job, you will learn one method of recording the invoices; namely, in a book known as a *Purchases Journal* (some record keepers call it a *Purchases Register*). Here is a sample of a Purchases Journal.

PURCHASES JOURNAL

DATE OF ENTRY	CREDITOR'S NAME	INVOICE NO.	DATE OF INVOICE	TERMS	AMOUNT

Illustration 54a — Purchases Journal

To understand the meaning of each column, consider the following problem:

SAMPLE PROBLEM

You are employed as a clerk in the D & R Office Equipment Co., located at 165 Fulton St., New York, NY 10038. Your job is to check the purchase invoices and then enter them in a Purchases Journal. The following invoices have been approved and are ready for entry on Dec. 5, 19—:

A. TAYLOR CO.
208 Flatbush Ave.
Brooklyn, NY 11217

SOLD TO D & R Office Equipment
165 Fulton St.
New York, NY 10038

TERMS 30 days

INVOICE NO. 102
DATE Dec. 1, 19--
OUR ORDER NO.113
CUSTOMER'S ORDER NO. 52
SHIPPED VIA Truck

QUANTITY	DESCRIPTION	UNIT PRICE	AMOUNT
10	12 Digit electronic calculators-Lot #EC1	203 00	$ 2,030 00
20	8 Digit electronic calculators-Lot #EC7	150 00	3,000 00
			$ 5,030 00

Approved
Jan Olsen

F. NORTON CO.
126 HUDSON ST.
NEW YORK, NY 10013

SOLD TO D & R Office Equipment Co.
165 Fulton St.
New York, NY 10038

TERMS 45 days

INVOICE NO. 290
DATE Dec. 3, 19--
OUR ORDER NO.301
CUSTOMER'S ORDER NO. 53
SHIPPED VIA Truck

QUANTITY	DESCRIPTION	UNIT PRICE	AMOUNT
6	Checkwriters M & O-Lot #CW3	70 00	$ 420 00
30	Floor safes-Lot #FS9	100 00	3,000 00
			$ 3,420 00

Approved
Jan Olsen

Here is how the Purchases Journal would look after these invoices had been entered:

PURCHASES JOURNAL

DATE OF ENTRY		CREDITOR'S NAME	INVOICE NO.	DATE OF INVOICE	TERMS	AMOUNT
19-- Dec.	5	A. Taylor Co.	102	Dec. 1	30 days	5 030 00
	5	F. Norton Co.	290	Dec. 3	45 days	3 420 00
						8 450 00
						8 450 00

Illustration 54b — Purchases Journal with Entries

To understand the meaning of each column and entry, trace the steps you would follow after the invoices have been checked.

Step 1: Enter the invoices in the Purchases Journal.

Compare A. Taylor's invoice with the entry recorded in Illustration 54b, the Purchases Journal. You will note that certain selected information has been recorded. Your employer's bookkeeper needs this information. You will learn more about how it is used in future units of work.

Date of Entry = date you recorded the entry

Perhaps you are wondering why it is necessary to have two columns to record dates. The first column, "Date of Entry," represents the date on which you made a record in the Purchases Journal. The second date column, "Date of Invoice," is the date from which your company is given a period of time (like 30 days, 45 days, etc.) in which to pay A. Taylor the $5,030.00. Although your company may not have received this invoice until Dec. 5, it legally became the owner of the merchandise on Dec. 1; therefore, your employer owes the money from that date on. According to the invoice, your employer has *30 days from Dec. 1* to make payment; that is until *Dec. 31*.

Date of Invoice = date from which you count to find the due date of the invoice

You can see that the "Date of Invoice" column is the more important of the two date columns.

Due date = date invoice should be paid

It was easy to find the *due date* of the invoice because the terms were *30 days*; *30 days* after *Dec. 1* (the date of the invoice) would be Dec. 1:

$$\text{Dec. 1} \quad + \quad 30 \text{ days} \quad = \quad \text{Dec. 31}$$

(Date of Invoice)   (Due Date)

Sometimes it is not this easy to find the due date. For example, look at the second entry in the Purchases Journal, Illustration 54b above, which shows that merchandise was bought from F. Norton Co. on Dec. 3. You will note that the terms are *45 days*. The *due date* is *Jan. 17*. This due date is found as follows:

a) Find the number of days left in the month in which the invoice is dated. Since this invoice is dated Dec. 3 and there are 31 days in December, there will be *28 days* left in the month of *December*.

31 (days in December)
− 3 (date of invoice, Dec. 3)
=28 (days from Dec. 3 to Dec. 31)

b) Add the days in the following month or months until the total equals the terms of the invoice. Since you found that there are *28 days left in December*, you need *an additional 17 days* in the next month of January to get the required total of *45 days* as shown below.

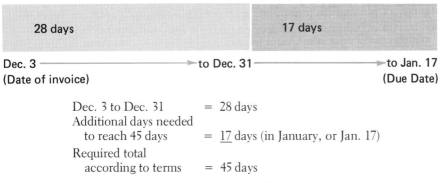

28 days	17 days

Dec. 3 ——————→ to Dec. 31 ——————→ to Jan. 17
(Date of invoice)   (Due Date)

Dec. 3 to Dec. 31 = 28 days
Additional days needed
to reach 45 days = 17 days (in January, or Jan. 17)
Required total
according to terms = 45 days

As you can see, in order to find the correct due date it is necessary to know the exact number of days in each month. You may remember the following rhyme which will help you to learn the days of the month:

Thirty days hath September
April, June, and November.
All the rest have thirty-one
Except February alone
To which we twenty-eight assign,
But leap year gives it twenty-nine.

Now test yourself and see if you agree with the due dates in the following examples:

Date of Invoice	Terms of Invoice	Due Date
July 7	20 days	July 27
April 25	20 days	May 15
September 10	30 days	October 10
January 16	30 days	February 15
October 1	45 days	November 15
March 1	60 days	April 30
March 21	60 days	May 20

If you refer to the "Amount" column you will notice that $5,030.00 has been entered. This figure is the *total* of the *amount* owed to A. Taylor Co. (*the creditor)* according to the invoice. You do not enter each individual extension shown on the invoice but only the final total. If there is any question about an item on the invoice, the actual invoice can be referred to.

Step 2: File the invoice.

Vouched invoices are usually filed by due date

Once the invoice has been recorded in the Purchases Journal, it is ready for filing. Just as companies have different methods of recording invoices, they also have different methods of filing invoices. A common method is to file the invoices according to the date the invoice is due. If this method is used in your office, A. Taylor's invoice would be put in a folder dated Dec. 31. Every purchase invoice which is due on Dec. 31 would be put in this folder. This system enables the bookkeeper to pay bills promptly. Under this system, at least 31 folders would be opened up, one for each day of the month.

Step 3: Total the Journal periodically.

At certain stated periods of time you will be asked to find the total amount purchased. As you can see, your company purchased merchandise worth $8,450.00 during the month of December. (Note that the column was pencil footed before the total was entered in ink.)

PRACTICE PROBLEMS

Problem 1

Directions: Find the date each invoice is due (the due date) in the following examples. (In order to find the correct due date, you must know the exact number of days in each month.)

30 days:
April
June
September
November

31 days:
January
March
May
July
August
October
December

28 or 29 days:
February

Date of Invoice	Terms of Invoice	Due Date
a) Jan. 3	20 days	
b) Jan. 21	20 days	
c) April 25	20 days	
d) Nov. 5	30 days	
e) Dec. 21	30 days	
f) Aug. 1	45 days	
g) July 16	45 days	
h) Sept. 10	45 days	
i) March 6	45 days	
j) May 1	60 days	
k) May 21	60 days	
l) Oct. 6	60 days	
m) Oct. 1	90 days	
n) June 20	90 days	
o) April 28	90 days	

Problem 2

You are employed as a clerk in the Dailey Audio-Visual Co., located at 21 Merrick Rd., Valley Stream, NY 11580. Your job is to check the purchase invoices and enter them in a Purchases Journal.

Directions:

a) Use a Purchases Journal like the one shown in Illustration 54a, page 342.

b) Check the extensions of the purchase invoices on the following pages. If they are correct, enter them in the Purchases Journal. If they are incorrect, find the correct totals but do not enter them in the Purchases Journal. Call them to your teacher's attention when you are asked for a list of the incorrect invoices and their corrected totals.

c) You received these invoices on June 9, 19—:

M. DOBBS CO.
100 Lafayette St.
New York, NY 10013

SOLD TO Dailey Audio-Visual Co.
21 Merrick Rd.
Valley Stream, NY 11580

INVOICE NO. 356
DATE June 4, 19--
OUR ORDER NO. 370
CUSTOMER'S ORDER NO. 133
SHIPPED VIA Truck

TERMS 20 days

QUANTITY	DESCRIPTION	UNIT PRICE	AMOUNT
4	Tape recorders-Lot #TR3	170 00	$ 680 00
25	Walkie-Talkies-Lot #WT10	24 00	600 00
			$ 1,280 00

D & T Co. 89 CLINTON ST. WHITE PLAINS, NY 10603

SOLD TO Dailey Audio-Visual Co.
21 Merrick Rd.
Valley Stream, NY 11580

INVOICE NO. 506
DATE June 6, 19--
OUR ORDER NO. 515
CUSTOMER'S ORDER NO. 134
SHIPPED VIA Truck

TERMS 20 days

QUANTITY	DESCRIPTION	UNIT PRICE	AMOUNT
9 doz.	Exposure meters-Lot #EM20	100 00	$ 900 00
16	Wall screens-Lot #WS17	25 00	400 00
			$1,300 00

Remember! Only correct invoices are to be entered.

d) You received the following invoices on June 17, 19—:

C. Ashe Co.
375 Emery St.
Philadelphia, PA 19125

SOLD TO Dailey Audio-Visual Co.
21 Merrick Rd.
Valley Stream, NY 11580

TERMS 30 days

INVOICE NO. 612
DATE June 11, 19--
OUR ORDER NO. 623
CUSTOMER'S ORDER NO. 135
SHIPPED VIA Truck

QUANTITY	DESCRIPTION	UNIT PRICE	AMOUNT
7	Movie editors-Lot #ME12	35 00	$ 245 00
14	Cassette projectors-Lot #CP15	110 00	1,530 00
			$1,775 00

B. Harper Co.
200 State St.
New Haven, CT 06510

SOLD TO Dailey Audio-Visual Co.
21 Merrick Rd.
Valley Stream, NY 11580

TERMS 45 days

INVOICE NO. 198
DATE June 12, 19--
OUR ORDER NO. 211
CUSTOMER'S ORDER NO. 136
SHIPPED VIA Truck

QUANTITY	DESCRIPTION	UNIT PRICE	AMOUNT
8	Turn tables-Lot #TT1	125 00	$ 1,004 00
2	4 Channel stereo phone system-Lot #SP3	220 80	441 60
			$ 1,445 60

Remember: only correct invoices are to be entered

---

e) You received this invoice on June 20, 19—:

J. Okun Co.   1120 Wilson Ave.   Baltimore, MD 21207

SOLD TO Dailey Audio-Visual Co.
21 Merrick Rd.
Valley Stream, NY 11580

TERMS 45 days

INVOICE NO. 49
DATE June 17, 19--
OUR ORDER NO. 54
CUSTOMER'S ORDER NO. 137
SHIPPED VIA Truck

QUANTITY	DESCRIPTION	UNIT PRICE	AMOUNT
3 doz.	Microphones-Lot #M12	196 00	$ 588 00
5 doz.	Mike stands-Lot #MS13	107 50	537 50
			$ 1,125 50

f) You received these invoices on June 25, 19—:

W. Paine Co.
140 Tremont Street
Boston, MA 02111

SOLD TO Dailey Audio-Visual Co.
21 Merrick Rd.
Valley Stream, NY 11580

INVOICE NO. 1502
DATE June 23, 19--
OUR ORDER NO. 1517
CUSTOMER'S ORDER NO. 138
SHIPPED VIA Truck

TERMS 60 days

QUANTITY	DESCRIPTION	UNIT PRICE	AMOUNT
14	100-Watt portable P. A. systems- Lot #PS21	203 25	$ 2,845 50
10	Paging/Talkback speakers-Lot #PTS1	276 00	2,760 00
			$ 5,605 50

A. & Y. CO.   20 IVY ST.   PERTH AMBOY, NJ 08863

SOLD TO Dailey Audio-Visual Co.
21 Merrick Rd.
Valley Stream, NY 11580

INVOICE NO. 2135
DATE June 24, 19--
OUR ORDER NO. 2148
CUSTOMER'S ORDER NO. 139
SHIPPED VIA Truck

TERMS 60 days

QUANTITY	DESCRIPTION	UNIT PRICE	AMOUNT
12	Zoom movie outfits-Lot #ZM11	162 45	$ 1,949 40
21	Tripods-Lot #T14	31 20	655 20
			$ 2,605 60

Remember: only correct invoices are to be entered

g) You received this invoice on June 30, 19—:

E. BAER CO.   16 BECK STREET   BRONX, NY 10455

SOLD TO Dailey Audio-Visual Co.
21 Merrick Rd.
Valley Stream, NY 11580

INVOICE NO. 3260
DATE June 27, 19--
OUR ORDER NO. 3283
CUSTOMER'S ORDER NO. 140
SHIPPED VIA Truck

TERMS 60 days

QUANTITY	DESCRIPTION	UNIT PRICE	AMOUNT
11 doz.	Slide viewers- Lot #SV19	140 15	$ 1,541 65
24 doz.	Slide trays- Lot #ST6	23 68	568 32
			$ 2,109 97

h) Total your Purchases Journal, using pencil footings only. If your work is correct, the total should be $11,420.97.

i) On a sheet of paper, list any incorrect invoices and their correct amounts.

j) On the same paper, list the due dates for all the invoices in the order in which they are given.

Problem 3

You are employed as a clerk in the K. Calvo Co., located at 1410 Fox St., Detroit, MI 48220. Your job is to check the purchase invoices, enter them in a Purchases Journal, and file them according to the due date.

Directions:

a) Use a Purchases Journal as shown in Illustration 54a, page 342.

b) Check the extensions of these purchase invoices. If they are correct, enter them in the Purchases Journal. If they are incorrect, find the correct totals but do not enter them in the Purchases Journal. Call them to your teacher's attention when you are asked for a list of the incorrect invoices and their corrected totals.

c) You received these invoices on July 7, 19—:

S. WEISS CO.
2160 Banner St.
Dearborn, MI 48124

SOLD TO K. Calvo Co.
1410 Fox St.
Detroit, MI 48220

INVOICE NO. 122
DATE July 2, 19--
OUR ORDER NO.136
CUSTOMER'S ORDER NO. 40

TERMS 45 days

SHIPPED VIA Truck

QUANTITY	DESCRIPTION	UNIT PRICE	AMOUNT
6 doz.	Knapsacks-brown-Lot #KS2	218 00	$ 1,308 00
2 doz.	Pullman cases-red-Lot #PC3	372 90	745 80
			$ 2,053 80

N. GABEL
23 MARCUS ST.
LANSING, MI 48912

SOLD TO K. Calvo Co.
1410 Fox St.
Detroit, MI 48220

INVOICE NO. 703
DATE July 3, 19--
OUR ORDER NO 715
CUSTOMER'S ORDER NO 41

TERMS 60 days

SHIPPED VIA Truck

QUANTITY	DESCRIPTION	UNIT PRICE	AMOUNT
13 Doz.	Duffel bags- yellow- Lot #D1315	161 20	$ 2,095 60
4 Doz.	Totebags- beige- Lot #TB8	238 40	953 60
			$ 3,049 20

d) You received these invoices on July 11, 19—:

H. LEWIS
551 Whitney Ave.
Flint, MI   48503

SOLD TO K. Calvo Co.
1410 Fox St.
Detroit, MI 48220

INVOICE NO. 1505
DATE July 7, 19--
OUR ORDER NO. 1527
CUSTOMER'S ORDER NO. 42
SHIPPED VIA Truck

TERMS   30 days

QUANTITY	DESCRIPTION	UNIT PRICE	AMOUNT
3 doz.	Attache cases-black Lot #AC5	187 65	$ 562 95
5 doz.	Roll bags-green-Lot #RB11	191 70	958 50
			$ 1,521 45

L. Carle Co.
81 Greene St.
Ann Arbor, MI 48104

SOLD TO K. Calvo Co.
1410 Fox St.
Detroit, MI 48220

INVOICE NO. 2004
DATE July 9, 19--
OUR ORDER NO. 2029
CUSTOMER'S ORDER NO. 43
SHIPPED VIA Truck

TERMS 60 days

QUANTITY	DESCRIPTION	UNIT PRICE	AMOUNT
15 doz.	Flight bags-yellow-Lot #FB19	143 00	$ 2,154 00
20 doz.	Wallets-black-Lot #W14	51 80	1,036 00
			$ 3,190 00

e) You received these invoices on July 30, 19—:

C & F Co.
1970 Martin St.
Warren, MI 48092

SOLD TO K. Calvo Co.
1410 Fox St.
Detroit, MI 48220

INVOICE NO. 59
DATE July 24, 19--
OUR ORDER NO. 70
CUSTOMER'S ORDER NO. 44
SHIPPED VIA Truck

TERMS 20 days

QUANTITY	DESCRIPTION	UNIT PRICE	AMOUNT
11 doz.	Men's underseat bags-brown- Lot #MU5	147 38	$ 1,621 18
25 doz.	Club bags-plaid-Lot #CB17	85 92	2,148 00
			$ 3,769 18

T. Uddell Co.   19 Main St.   Battle Creek, MI 49017

SOLD TO K. Calvo Co.
         1410 Fox St.
         Detroit, MI 48220

TERMS 30 days

INVOICE NO. 807
DATE July 28, 19--
OUR ORDER NO. 818
CUSTOMER'S ORDER NO. 45
SHIPPED VIA Truck

QUANTITY	DESCRIPTION	UNIT PRICE		AMOUNT	
52	Garment bags-blue-Lot #GB8	23	08	$ 1,200	16
36	Two-suiter case-charcoal grey-				
	Lot #TS20	41	50	1,491	00
				$ 2,691	16

f) Total your Purchases Journal, using pencil footings only. If your work is correct, the total should be $10,393.63.

g) On a sheet of paper, list any incorrect invoices and their correct amounts.

h) On the same paper, list the due dates for the invoices in the order in which they are given.

Problem 4

You are employed as a clerk in the E. Horton Co., located at 255 Madison Ave., New York, NY 10016. Your job is to check the purchase invoices, enter them in a Purchases Journal, and file them according to the due date.

Directions:

a) Use a Purchases Journal as shown in Illustration 54a, page 342.

b) Check the extensions of the following purchase invoices. If they are correct, enter them in your Purchases Journal. If they are incorrect, find the correct totals but do not enter them in the Purchases Journal. Call them to your teacher's attention when you are asked for a list of the incorrect invoices and their corrected totals.

c) You received the following invoices on March 6, 19—:

W. SOHL CO.
66 King St.
Charleston, SC 29401

SOLD TO E. Horton Co.
         255 Madison Ave.
         New York, NY 10016

TERMS 45 days

INVOICE NO. 904
DATE March 3, 19--
OUR ORDER NO. 919
CUSTOMER'S ORDER NO. 1092
SHIPPED VIA Express

QUANTITY	DESCRIPTION	UNIT PRICE		AMOUNT	
9 doz.	Twin-set sweaters-blue-				
	size 34-Lot #TS3	194	25	$ 1,748	25
12 doz.	Sweaters-green-size 36-				
	Lot #SW5	135	00	1,620	00
				$ 3,368	25

H L R Co.   793 Spring St., Richmond, VA 23220

SOLD TO E. Horton Co.
         255 Madison Ave.
         New York, NY 10016

TERMS 30 days

INVOICE NO. 2317
DATE March 4, 19--
OUR ORDER NO. 2354
CUSTOMER'S ORDER NO. 1043
SHIPPED VIA Express

QUANTITY	DESCRIPTION	UNIT PRICE	AMOUNT
27 doz.	Cardigan sweaters-red-size 34-Lot #CS20	93 00	$ 2,501 00
30 doz.	Pullovers-beige-size 32-Lot #P8	110 00	3,300 00
			$ 5,801 00

d) You received these invoices on March 18, 19--:

M & T co.   304 Union Ave.
              Paterson, NJ 07502

SOLD TO E. Horton Co.
         255 Madison Ave.
         New York, NY 10016

TERMS 60 days

INVOICE NO. 7012
DATE March 15, 19--
OUR ORDER NO. 7053
CUSTOMER'S ORDER NO. 1094
SHIPPED VIA Truck

QUANTITY	DESCRIPTION	UNIT PRICE	AMOUNT
6 doz.	Tweed patterned skirts-yellow-size 10-Lot #TW6	182 50	$ 1,095 00
7 doz.	Argyle plaid vests-size 11-Lot #AP9	124 35	870 45
			$ 1,965 45

E. Vaccaro Co.
20 West St.
Utica, NY 13501

SOLD TO E. Horton Co.
         225 Madison Ave.
         New York, NY 10016

TERMS 45 days

INVOICE NO. 79
DATE March 16, 19--
OUR ORDER NO. 42
CUSTOMER'S ORDER NO. 1095
SHIPPED VIA Truck

QUANTITY	DESCRIPTION	UNIT PRICE	AMOUNT
3 doz.	Trench coats-brown-size 16-Lot #TC10	275 00	$ 825 00
4 doz.	Raincoats-black-size 18-Lot #RC7	253 60	1,015 40
			$ 1,840 00

e) You received these invoices on March 30, 19—:

G. Witt Co.
5803 Warring Ave.
Los Angeles, CA 90038

SOLD TO E. Horton Co.
255 Madison Ave.
New York, NY 10016

INVOICE NO. 177
DATE March 28, 19--
OUR ORDER NO. 200
CUSTOMER'S ORDER NO. 1096
SHIPPED VIA Air Cargo

TERMS 30 days

QUANTITY	DESCRIPTION	UNIT PRICE		AMOUNT	
16 doz.	Blouses-light pink-size 14 Lot #B5	117	40	$ 1,878	40
10 doz.	Button-front jumpers-forest green- size 10-Lot #J8	113	70	1,137	00
				$ 3,015	40

P. Archer Co.
73 RUGBY ST.
ORLANDO, FL 32804

SOLD TO E. Horton Co.
255 Madison Ave.
New York, NY 10016

INVOICE NO. 1309
DATE March 28, 19--
OUR ORDER NO. 1362
CUSTOMER'S ORDER NO. 1097
SHIPPED VIA Air Cargo

TERMS 45 days

QUANTITY	DESCRIPTION	UNIT PRICE		AMOUNT	
2 doz.	Nylon satin robes-lilac- size 16- Lot #SR1	243	15	$ 486	30
8 doz.	Quilted robes-mint-size 32- Lot #QR2	265	70	2,127	60
				$ 2,613	90

f) Total your Purchases Journal, using pencil footings only. If your work is correct, the total should be $8,349.10.

g) On a sheet of paper, list any incorrect invoices and their correct amounts.

h) On the same paper, list the due dates for the invoices in the order in which they are given.

UNIT 8

RECORD KEEPING FOR A WHOLESALE SALES DEPARTMENT

UNIT 8

JOB 55 | PREPARING SALES INVOICES

Practicing Related Arithmetic

Copy and answer the following problems:

1) 10 × $ 94.50 = $_____
2) 10 × 118.90 = $_____
3) 10 × 73.42 = $_____
4) 100 × 7.15 = $_____
5) 100 × .89 = $_____
6) 100 × .07 = $_____

7) 50 × $ 4.60 = $_____
8) 25 × 86.40 = $_____
9) 20 × 16.21 = $_____
10) 30 × 7.58 = $_____
11) 150 × 26.20 = $_____
12) 125 × 16.80 = $_____

AIMS

1. To learn how sales orders are used in business.
2. To learn how to prepare sales invoices for a wholesale trading business.

EXPLANATION (SALES ORDER)

In earlier jobs you learned how to prepare sales slips for a retail store, where merchandise is sold over the counter. As you know, the merchandise the retailer sells is obtained from businesspeople called *jobbers*, or wholesalers, who sell in large quantities. In this job you will learn about the sales records of a wholesale business.

Wholesale Records

Retail Records

Consumer

Although the sales records of a wholesale business are similar to the records of a retail business, there are some important differences. When a sale is made in a retail store, a sales slip may be prepared. In the sales records of a wholesale business, *two* forms may be used. The first form is a *sales order*; the second form is a *sales invoice*, or *bill*. These forms will be considered separately.

The wholesaler receives orders for merchandise from the retailer by mail, by telephone, or through the wholesaler's sales representative. Most wholesale businesses make a written record of all merchandise ordered by the retailer to avoid errors and to record all the information needed for the invoice. The special form used is called a *sales order*.

SAMPLE PROBLEM (SALES ORDER)

You are employed as a clerk in the *sales department* of the Omega Wholesale Drug Company. Your employer gives you a pad of blank sales order forms, and asks you to prepare sales order forms when customers order merchandise.

Mr. George Tompkins, who owns a retail drug store, orders 4 dozen jars of Atlas vitamin tablets and 2 dozen cans of Super hair spray. The completed sales order form is shown below.

Sales Order
no extensions
no totals

Sales Order
OMEGA WHOLESALE DRUG CO.
110 MARKET STREET
TOPEKA, KS 66607

TO: George Tompkins
      1955 Madison Street
      Topeka, KS 66607

Date March 1, 19--
Our Order No. SO 1512
Cust. Order No. 834

Terms Net 30 Days

Ship Via Parcel Post

Quantity	Stock No.	Description	Unit Price
4 doz.	V121	Jars Atlas Vitamin Tablets	10 20
2 doz.	HS217	Cans Super Hair Spray	18 00

Illustration 55a — Sales Order

The following steps were taken in preparing the sales order:

Step 1: Record the date.

The date the order was received, March 1, was shown on the form.

Step 2: Record our order number.

Each sales order is numbered in consecutive order. The form used for Mr. Tompkins was numbered SO 1512. The next sales order will be numbered SO 1513, etc.

Step 3: Record customer's order number.

The customer's order number, 834, is copied from the purchase order received in the mail from Mr. Tompkins. It is important to make a record of the number because Mr. Tompkins will refer to his purchase order number in any correspondence about the merchandise ordered.

Step 4: Record customer's name and address.

Mr. Tompkins' name and address are carefully recorded on the sales order.

Step 5: Record terms.

The terms of the sale are *Net 30 Days*. This means that the customer, Mr. Tompkins, is expected to pay the total amount shown on the bill within 30 days from the date of the invoice (which will be sent to him later from a different department). If the invoice is dated March 1, it will be due 30 days later on March 31.

Step 6: Record method of shipment.

Mr. Tompkins wants the merchandise shipped by parcel post. This fact is shown on the sales order.

Step 7: Record description of merchandise.

The quantity, stock number, description, and unit price of the merchandise are recorded. Notice, however, that no extensions or totals are shown. Since this is only an *order* of merchandise and not a *sale* of merchandise, it is not necessary to extend or total this form.

EXPLANATION (SALES INVOICE)

After the sales order for Mr. Tompkins has been completed, it is sent to the credit department to find out whether or not Mr. Tompkins is a safe credit risk. If the credit department decides Mr. Tompkins is not a good risk, Mr. Tompkins will be asked to pay cash or the order will be canceled. If the credit department decides Mr. Tompkins is a good credit risk, a copy of the sales order will be sent to the billing department, where the sales invoice will be prepared for the customer.

The information for the sales invoice is copied directly from the sales order. **In addition, the unit prices are extended (quantity × unit price) and the amounts are totaled.**

Usually, at least three copies of the sales invoice are prepared. The original copy is mailed to the customer, the second copy is sent to the bookkeeping department as a record of the amount the customer owes and the third copy is sent to the shipping department to be used in selecting and

Sales Invoice copies to:

1) customer
2) bookkeeping dept.
3) shipping dept.

shipping the merchandise. The copy that goes to the shipping department does not show the unit prices or the extensions.

SAMPLE PROBLEM (SALES INVOICE)

You are employed in the *billing department* of the Omega Wholesale Drug Company. You are given a copy of the sales order prepared for a customer, Mr. Tompkins, shown on page 358. Your job is to prepare the sales invoice from the information shown on the sales order.

The completed sales invoice is shown below.

Sales Invoice extensions and totals are shown

OMEGA WHOLESALE DRUG CO.
110 MARKET STREET
TOPEKA, KS 66607

SOLD TO: George Tompkins
1955 Madison Street
Topeka, KS 66607

Invoice No. 1406
Date March 1, 19--
Our Order No. SO 1512
Cust. Order No. 834

Terms Net 30 days

Shipped Via Parcel Post

Quantity	Description	Unit Price	Total Amount
4 doz.	Atlas vitamin tablets V121	10 20	40 80
2 doz.	Super hair spray HS217	18 00	36 00
			76 80

Illustration 55b — Completed Sales Invoice

This form should look familiar to you. Actually, it is the same type of form you studied in Unit 7 when you learned to check purchase invoices. The seller (in this case, the Omega Wholesale Drug Co.) calls this form a *sales invoice* and the customer, Mr. Tompkins, calls the same form a *purchase invoice*.

Check all calculations

Notice that each invoice is numbered in consecutive order and the invoice prepared for the customer, Mr. Tompkins, is numbered 1406. Notice also that the unit prices are extended and the total of the invoice is $76.80. It is important to check the multiplication and addition shown in each invoice because any error in the total means that you are asking the customer to pay an amount which is not correct.

It is customary in most businesses to type invoices. There are many job openings for billing clerks who have had training in typing and who are accurate in arithmetic.

Some companies find it practical to use billing machines similar to the one pictured below to type and extend the invoices.

Burroughs Corporation

There are also more modern electronic billing systems made to automate billing operations of large companies. These machines print and compute an invoice at rapid speeds and also produce punched tape that is used to electronically prepare customers' records.

Electronic billing systems

In Step 5 on page 359, you learned that the terms of the sale are "Net 30 Days." This means that the customer has 30 days from the date of the invoice to pay the amount, which makes it due on March 31 (March 1 + 30 days = March 31).

Date of invoice
+Terms
—————————
=Due date

The date on which the invoice is due is called the *due date.* You learned in Job 54 how to find the due date of a purchase invoice. You can now use this same method to find the due dates for sales invoices.

Test yourself and see if you agree with the due dates in the examples below and on the next page:

Date of Invoice	Terms of Invoice	Due Date
January 21	30 days	February 20
March 11	30 days	April 10

April 25	30 days	May 25
June 23	30 days	July 23
August 4	30 days	September 3
September 5	60 days	November 4

PRACTICE PROBLEMS

Problem 1

Directions: Find the date each invoice is due (the due date) in the following examples. (To find the correct due date you must know the exact number of days in each month.)

Sept.
April } 30 days
June
Nov.

All the } 31 days
rest

except

Feb. } 28 days

Date of Invoice	Terms of Invoice	Due Date	Date of Invoice	Terms of Invoice	Due Date
a) March 14	10 days		i) July 1	15 days	
b) June 8	20 days		j) Nov. 9	20 days	
c) Jan. 1	30 days		k) Dec. 1	30 days	
d) April 1	30 days		l) June 5	30 days	
e) July 6	30 days		m) March 16	30 days	
f) Aug. 11	60 days		n) May 11	75 days	
g) April 20	60 days		o) April 10	90 days	
h) Oct. 1	90 days		p) July 27	90 days	

Problem 2

You are employed in the billing department of the Tiger Sporting Goods Co., Flint, Michigan. Your job is to prepare sales invoices from copies of sales orders that are given to you.

Directions: Prepare a sales invoice for each order below and on the following page. Date each invoice May 4, terms allowed each customer are 30 days, and all merchandise is to be shipped by truck.

Sales Invoice #1

Sold to: Buffalo Athletic Shop
         15 Beach Street, Flint, MI 48502
Our Order No. 101
Customer's Order No. 416

8 pairs baseball shoes, BH17	@	$ 9.80
3 dozen sweat shirts, SS3	@	14.30

(Did you get a total of $121.30?)

Sales Invoice #2

Sold to: Bollenger Bros.
         1505 Dakota Ave., Flint, MI 48505
Our Order No. 102
Customer's Order No. 351

10 tennis rackets, TRK03	@	$12.45
7 dozen tennis balls, TBL9	@	7.60

(Did you get a total of $177.70?)

Sales Invoice #3

Sold to: Pilgrim Stores
        1720 Oren Ave., Flint, MI 48505
Our Order No. 103
Customer's Order No. 716

7 catcher's mitts, CT91	@ $12.80
5 dozen baseball bats, BLB4	@ 46.50

(Did you get a total of $322.10?)

Sales Invoice #4

Sold to: Rand Athletic Stores
        1431 Avenue A, Flint, MI 48503
Our Order No. 104
Customer's Order No. 392

25 team jackets, TJ20	@ $14.75
12 warmup suits, WP15	@ 18.60
4 dozen sweat socks, SSK4	@ 6.35

(Did you get a total of $617.35?)

Sales Invoice #5

Sold to: S. & J. Sporting Goods, Inc.
        510 South Saginaw St., Flint, MI 48502
Our Order No. 105
Customer's Order No. 712

15 pairs sneakers, SN31	@ $ 8.40
9 dozen gym shorts, GS11	@ 14.60
6 dozen "T" shirts, TH7	@ 12.90
4 dozen handballs, HB25	@ 6.85

(Did you get a total of $362.20?)

Sales Invoice #6

Sold to: Cooper Sport Shop
        3561 Whitney Ave., Flint, MI 48503
Our Order No. 106
Customer's Order No. 975

5 golf bags, GFB21	@ $16.70
11 dozen golf balls, GFL7	@ 8.85
9 pairs golf shoes, GFS4	@ 12.50
2 dozen sweaters, SW11	@ 44.45

(Did you get a total of $382.25?)

Sales Invoice #7

Sold to: Tom Scott & Co.
        376 Root Street, Flint, MI 48503
Our Order No. 107
Customer's Order No. 461

4 dozen swim trunks, SW5	@ $46.00
3 surf boards, SBD12	@ 85.00
8 tennis rackets, TRK03	@ 12.45
5 dozen tennis balls, TBL9	@ 7.60

(Did you get a total of $576.60?)

Practicing Related Arithmetic	Copy and answer the following problems:

1)	100 × $ 7.45 = $ _____		7)	50 × $24.40 = $ _____
2)	100 × 12.65 = $ _____		8)	20 × 31.20 = $ _____
3)	100 × .08 = $ _____		9)	25 × 84.40 = $ _____
4)	1,000 × 3.72 = $ _____		10)	150 × 10.38 = $ _____
5)	1,000 × .91 = $ _____		11)	120 × 12.65 = $ _____
6)	1,000 × .05 = $ _____		12)	125 × 44.80 = $ _____

AIM

To gain experience in preparing sales invoices.

EXPLANATION

The purpose of this job is to provide you with additional practice in the important job of preparing sales invoices.

PRACTICE PROBLEMS

Problem 1

Directions: Find the date each invoice is due in the following examples:

Sept.
April
June } 30 days
Nov.

All the
rest } 31 days

except

Feb { 28 days

Date of Invoice	Terms of Invoice	Due Date		Date of Invoice	Terms of Invoice	Due Date
a) April 19	10 days		i) Feb. 10	15 days	
b) Jan. 1	30 days		j) Mar. 17	30 days	
c) June 1	30 days		k) Sept. 5	30 days	
d) Nov. 14	30 days		l) June 10	45 days	
e) Aug. 22	30 days		m) Oct. 3	60 days	
f) May 21	60 days		n) April 29	75 days	
g) July 11	90 days		o) July 1	90 days	
h) Sept. 5	90 days		p) May 24	90 days	

Problem 2

You are employed in the billing department of the Royce Drug Sales Co., Hempstead, New York. Your job is to prepare sales invoices from copies of sales orders.

Directions: Prepare a sales invoice for each order listed below and on the next page. Date each invoice March 20. Terms allowed each customer are 30 days, and all merchandise is to be shipped by truck.

Sales Invoice #1

Sold to: Ethic Drug Store
         76 Davis Ave., Albany, NY 12203
Our Order No. 111
Customer's Order No. 409
   8 Halent vaporizers   @ $ 6.70
   3 dozen Spree hair tonic   @   11.26
   1½ dozen Lady skin cream   @   8.84

(Did you get a total of $100.64?)

Sales Invoice #2

Sold to: Adelphi Clinic
         892 Old Country Road, Hicksville, NY 11803
Our Order No. 112
Customer's Order No. 1217
   3½ dozen Sea sponges   @ $ 4.80
   15 dozen Tru thermometers   @   10.50
   20 Ace bandages, 2″ wide   @   1.45

(Did you get a total of $203.30?)

Sales Invoice #3

Sold to: Clearview Drug Store
         12–15 Bell Blvd., Flushing, NY 11360
Our Order No. 113
Customer's Order No. 317
   7⅓ dozen Kleen toothbrushes   @ $ 9.60
   10 Spot heating pads   @   4.55
   6 dozen Dawn hair spray   @   18.90

(Did you get a total of $229.30?)

Sales Invoice #4

Sold to: Tulip Drugs
         110 Hillside Ave., Floral Park, NY 11001
Our Order No. 114
Customer's Order No. 1216
   7 Rapid electric toothbrushes   @ $14.35
   5 dozen Bronze sun tan oil   @   12.80
   4⅓ dozen Faun bath talc   @   9.15

(Did you get a total of $204.10?)

Sales Invoice #5

Sold to: Atlantic Drug Sales
           215 Atlantic Ave., Rochester, NY 14607
Our Order No. 115
Customer's Order No. 572

25 dozen Edge blades, #10 pack	@	$ 8.75
12½ dozen Dip cotton swab packs	@	5.12
6 Halent vaporizers	@	6.70
10 Ensign electric shavers	@	12.45

(Did you get a total of $447.45?)

Sales Invoice #6

Sold to: Palmer Shopping Center
           516 McLean Ave., Yonkers, NY 10705
Our Order No. 116
Customer's Order No. 4439

5½ dozen Royal shampoo	@	$ 7.90
6 dozen Lady skin cream	@	8.84
9 Tru scales	@	10.16
16 dozen Kleen toothbrushes	@	9.60

(Did you get a total of $341.53?)

Sales Invoice #7

Sold to: Lake Drug Store
           88–11 Merrick Blvd., Jamaica, NY 11432
Our Order No. 117
Customers'Order No. 618

12 ISO camera kits	@	$24.70
6⅓ dozen Beach sun glasses	@	15.36
2 dozen Dawn hair spray	@	18.90
3 Rapid electric toothbrushes	@	14.35

(Did you get a total of $474.53?)

Sales Invoice #8

Sold to: DeWitt Pharmacy
           1105 Broad St., Syracuse, NY 13210
Our Order No. 118
Customer's Order No. 3916

8 Spot heating pads	@	$ 4.55
3 dozen Bronze sun tan oil	@	12.80
6½ dozen Tru thermometers	@	10.50
5 Tru scales	@	10.16

(Did you get a total of $193.85?)

Copy and answer the following problems:

1) ½ × $7.84 = $ _____
2) ⅓ × 8.49 = $ _____
3) ¼ × 4.72 = $ _____
4) ⅔ × 5.73 = $ _____
5) ¾ × 9.24 = $ _____

6) 1½ × $26.42 = $ _____
7) 2⅓ × 7.26 = $ _____
8) 5¼ × 8.60 = $ _____
9) 4⅔ × 15.09 = $ _____
10) 3¾ × 6.08 = $ _____

AIM

To learn how to keep records of amounts owed to a wholesale business by customers.

EXPLANATION

Sales on credit

Did you know that almost all merchandise in a wholesale business is sold on credit? Of course, before selling merchandise on credit, a wholesaler must know whether or not the customer pays bills on time. The wholesaler will get this information from the customer's bank and from other businesses which have sold merchandise to the customer.

Since most merchandise sold in a wholesale business is sold on credit, you can understand how important it is for the wholesaler to keep careful records of the amount owed by each customer. This is done by keeping an account for each customer in the same way you learned to keep accounts for retail charge customers in Unit 6. All the customers' accounts are usually kept together in a book which is called a *ledger*.

Accounts
Receivable
Ledger

Since this book, or ledger, contains all the accounts for customers from whom money will be received, it is called an *Accounts Receivable Ledger*.

On page 368, as a reminder, is the form of the account.

Notice that the left side of the account is called the *debit* side and the right side of the account is called the *credit* side. The sales are recorded on the debit side and cash received from the customer is recorded on the credit side.

The information for the debit side of the account comes from the duplicate sales invoices, and the information for the credit side of the account comes from a list of the cash received from customers.

NAME	CUSTOMER'S ACCOUNT				TERMS	
ADDRESS						
DATE	ITEM	DEBIT	DATE	ITEM	CREDIT	
	Sales are recorded on this side.			Cash received in payment is recorded on this side.		

SAMPLE PROBLEM

You are employed by the Van Wholesale Co. Your job is to keep a record in the customers' accounts of merchandise sold and cash received. In order to get this information, you are given the duplicate sales invoices and a list of the cash collected.

Here is a list of the duplicate sales invoices you received:

Record sales on debit side

Date	Invoice Number	Customer	Amount
June 4	201	J. Perez & Co.	$330.00
8	202	Reilly & Son	600.00
11	203	R. Smith, Inc.	420.00
14	204	Reilly & Son	745.00
19	205	J. Perez & Co.	560.00
24	206	Reilly & Son	280.00

Here is a list of the cash received from customers:

Record cash received on credit side

Date	Customer	Amount	For
June 14	J. Perez & Co.	$330.00	Invoice of June 4
18	Reilly & Son	600.00	Invoice of June 8
21	R. Smith, Inc.	420.00	Invoice of June 11
24	Reilly & Son	700.00	On account

The illustration at the top of page 369 shows how the customers' accounts would look after the sales and the collections were recorded.

A separate account was prepared for each customer to whom merchandise was sold. In the problem shown there were three customers and, therefore, three accounts were opened. In an actual business situation there would be many more credit customers, and each of these customers would have a separate account.

At the end of the month, your employer would want a list of all the customers and the amount each customer owed. The word *schedule* is often used in business to mean a list. Since the form used is a list of customers or accounts receivable, it is often called a *Schedule of Accounts Receivable*.

NAME	J. Perez & Co.			TERMS	10 days		
ADDRESS	170 Capital Avenue , Norfolk VA 23506						
DATE	ITEM	DEBIT	DATE	ITEM		CREDIT	
19-- June 4	Mdse. 89000 33000 560	330 00	19-- June 14	Cash		330 00	
19	Mdse.	560 00 890 00					

NAME	Reilly & Son			TERMS	10 days		
ADDRESS	615 Gary Street, Richmond, VA 23234						
DATE	ITEM	DEBIT	DATE	ITEM		CREDIT	
19-- June 8	Mdse.	600 00	19-- June 18	Cash		600 00	
14	Mdse. 1625 00 1300 00 325 00	745 00	24	Cash		700 00 1 300 00	
24	Mdse.	280 00 1 625 00					

NAME	R. Smith, Inc.			TERMS	10 days		
ADDRESS	924 Brighton Street, Portsmouth, VA 23704						
DATE	ITEM	DEBIT	DATE	ITEM		CREDIT	
19-- June 11	Mdse.	420 00	19-- June 21	Cash		420 00	

No balance when debits and credits are equal

Illustration 57a — Customers' Accounts

Shown below is the Schedule of Accounts Receivable you would prepare for the accounts in Illustration 57a above.

Van Wholesale Co. Schedule of Accounts Receivable June 30, 19--		
J. Perez & Co.	560 00	
Reilly & Son	325 00	
Total		885 00

Illustration 57b — Schedule of Accounts Receivable

The steps you would follow in preparing the schedule shown above are listed on the following page.

Step 1: Pencil foot accounts.

Debits
−Credits
=Balance

In order to prepare the Schedule of Accounts Receivable you must first know how much each customer owes. This important fact is found by pencil footing the debit and credit sides of each account and subtracting the total credits from the total debits. If you examine the J. Perez & Co. account shown on page 369, you will see that this procedure was followed as shown by the following arithmetic problem:

Total debits	$890.00	
Total credits	− 330.00	
Balance due	=$560.00	

Step 2: Record heading.

Most business reports are headed to answer three questions: who?, what?, and when? When you prepare the Schedule of Accounts Receivable you must supply the answers to these questions. In this case, for instance:

Who?	Van Wholesale Co.
What?	Schedule of Accounts Receivable
When?	June 30, 19--

The Van Wholesale Co., of course, is the name of your employer for whom you are preparing the form. The Schedule of Accounts Receivable is the name of the form and, finally, the last day of the month is used to date the schedule. Notice that three separate lines are used for the heading.

Step 3: List balances due.

The balance due in each account is listed in the schedule. The R. Smith, Inc. account was not listed because there was no balance due.

Step 4: Find total.

Add all the balances listed. The total of $885.00 is the total amount due from all customers on June 30.

PRACTICE PROBLEMS

Problem 1

You are employed by the Hobart Wholesale Co. as an accounts receivable clerk. Your job is to record the duplicate sales invoices and the list of cash collections in the customers' accounts.

Directions:

a) Open a new account for each of the following customers. (To "open a new account" means to write the name and address of the customer at the top of a new account form.) (Terms: 10 days)

Carter & Cohen, 533 Lincoln Rd., Miami Beach, FL 33139
United Stores, Inc., 911 N.E. Second Ave., Miami, FL 33132
West & Co., 1506 Miami Dr., Miami, FL 33162

b) Record the sales and collections in the customers' accounts.
c) Pencil foot all accounts.
d) Prepare a Schedule of Accounts Receivable on October 31.

List of Duplicate Sales Invoices:

Date	Invoice Number	Customer	Amount
Oct. 1	101	Carter & Cohen	$315.00
5	102	United Stores, Inc.	290.00
8	103	West & Co.	435.00
16	104	United Stores, Inc.	670.00
19	105	Carter & Cohen	565.00
22	106	United Stores, Inc.	340.00
24	107	Carter & Cohen	455.00

Record sales on debit side

List of Cash Received:

Date	Customer	Amount	For
Oct. 11	Carter & Cohen	$315.00	Invoice of Oct. 1
15	United Stores, Inc.	290.00	Invoice of Oct. 5
18	West & Co.	435.00	Invoice of Oct. 8
26	United Stores, Inc.	500.00	On account
29	Carter & Cohen	225.00	On account

Record cash received on credit side

Problem 2

You are employed by the Auburn Wholesale Co. as an accounts receivable clerk. Your job is to record the duplicate sales invoices and the list of cash collections in the customers' accounts.

Directions:

a) Open accounts for the following customers: (Terms: 10 days)

Genovese Bros., 498 Chestnut Ave., Baltimore, MD 21204
Scott & Benson, 1207 Allison St., N.E., Washington, DC 20017
Trump Corporation, 4816 Clifton Ave., Baltimore, MD 21207

b) Record the sales and collections shown on the next page in the customers' accounts.
c) Pencil foot the accounts.
d) Prepare a Schedule of Accounts Receivable on July 31.

List of Duplicate Sales Invoices:

Date	Invoice Number	Customer	Amount
July 3	501	Genovese Bros.	$316.40
6	502	Scott & Benson	270.30
10	503	Trump Corporation	429.65
12	504	Scott & Benson	515.90
18	505	Genovese Bros.	486.50
24	506	Scott & Benson	193.25
30	507	Genovese Bros.	252.70

List of Cash Received:

Date	Customer	Amount	For
July 13	Genovese Bros.	$316.40	Invoice of July 3
16	Scott & Benson	270.30	Invoice of July 6
20	Trump Corporation	429.65	Invoice of July 10
22	Scott & Benson	250.00	On account
28	Genovese Bros.	300.00	On account

Problem 3

You are employed by the Pacific Wholesale Co. as an accounts receivable clerk. Your job is to record the duplicate sales invoices and the list of cash collections in the customers' accounts.

Directions:
a) Open accounts for the following customers: (Terms: 10 days)

T. Hanson & Co., 612 Cascade St., Erie, PA 16502
Jackson & Miller, 1107 Center St., Bethlehem, PA 18018
Lafferty, Inc., 235 Wayne St., Erie, PA 16507

b) Record the sales and collections shown below and on page 373 in the customers' accounts.
c) Pencil foot all accounts.
d) Prepare a Schedule of Accounts Receivable on November 30.

List of Duplicate Sales Invoices:

Date	Invoice Number	Customer	Amount
Nov. 5	411	T. Hanson & Co.	$521.80
6	412	Jackson & Miller	374.60
12	413	Lafferty, Inc.	293.75
14	414	Jackson & Miller	618.25
16	415	T. Hanson & Co.	482.40
21	416	Jackson & Miller	540.70
26	417	T. Hanson & Co.	186.55

List of Cash Received:

Date	Customer	Amount	For
Nov. 15	T. Hanson & Co.	$521.80	Invoice of Nov. 5
16	Jackson & Miller	374.60	Invoice of Nov. 6
22	Lafferty, Inc.	293.75	Invoice of Nov. 12
24	Jackson & Miller	450.00	On account
26	T. Hanson & Co.	280.00	On account

JOB 58 | HANDLING SALES RETURNS AND ALLOWANCES

Practicing Related Arithmetic

Find the dates on which the following invoices are due:

	Date of Invoice	Terms		Date of Invoice	Terms
1)	March 12	10 days	6)	April 15	45 days
2)	January 29	10 days	7)	May 21	60 days
3)	May 11	30 days	8)	July 7	60 days
4)	June 24	30 days	9)	March 9	90 days
5)	September 1	30 days	10)	August 23	90 days

AIM

To review the way to record merchandise returned by customers.

"Bend your Knees!"

Merchandise Return

EXPLANATION

Occasionally, customers must return merchandise because it was damaged in shipment or the wrong merchandise was shipped.

In Unit 6 you learned how retailers recorded merchandise returned by their customers. The wholesaler follows a similar procedure when customers return merchandise.

Obviously, since the customer has not yet paid for the merchandise, the wholesaler will not give cash for the returned merchandise. Instead, a form called a *credit memorandum* is issued which gives the customer a record of the returned merchandise and shows how much less is owed to the wholesaler.

Credit memorandum

The credit memorandum is prepared in duplicate so that one copy can be sent to the customer and the other copy can be used to complete the record in the customer's account. A credit memorandum is illustrated on page 375.

In the previous job you recorded cash received from a customer on the credit side of the account in order to show a reduction in the amount owed. A return of merchandise also results in a reduction of the amount owed and,

Credit Memorandum

Tower Corporation
1605 S. Stewart Avenue
Chicago, IL 60616

Wholesalers of Sound Equipment

No. 301
Date April 10, 19--

TO   The Radio Shack
     115 N. Austin Avenue
     Chicago, IL 60644

WE HAVE CREDITED YOUR ACCOUNT TODAY AS FOLLOWS:

Description	Unit Price		Total	
Damaged goods: 2 short wave receivers, W77-109	80	00	160	00

Illustration 58a — Credit Memorandum

therefore, it too is recorded on the credit side of the customer's account. A customer's account then would contain the following information:

Record credit memorandums on credit side

CUSTOMER'S ACCOUNT

Debits	Credits
1) Sales (from duplicate sales invoices)	1) Cash received in payment (from record of cash collections) 2) Merchandise returned (from duplicate credit memorandums)

SAMPLE PROBLEM

The Tower Corporation, wholesalers of sound equipment, sold merchandise to a retail radio and television store, The Radio Shack. The following information for the month of April was taken from:

a) The duplicate sales invoices,
b) The duplicate credit memorandums, and
c) The record of cash received from the customer, The Radio Shack.

April 3   Sold merchandise to The Radio Shack amounting to $460.00, Terms: 20 days.

10   Issued a credit memorandum for $160.00 for damaged merchandise returned by The Radio Shack. (The credit memorandum is shown in Illustration 58a above.)

23   Received a check from The Radio Shack for $300.00 in payment of the balance due on the invoice of April 3.

29   Sold merchandise to The Radio Shack amounting to $525.00, terms: 20 days.

Here is how the Tower Corporation would record this information in the customer's account:

"T" account form

NAME	The Radio Shack				TERMS 20 days	
ADDRESS	115 N. Austin Avenue, Chicago, Il 60644					
DATE	ITEM	DEBIT	DATE	ITEM	CREDIT	
Apr. 19-- 3	Mdse.	460 00	Apr. 19-- 10	Return	160 00	
29	Mdse. 985.00 460.00 525.00	525 00 985 00	23	Cash	300 00 460 00	

As you learned in Unit 6, there is a second form of customer's account which contains three money columns: a debit column, a credit column, and a balance column. There is a special column for the balance of the account. Each time a *debit* is recorded it is *added* to the balance. Each time a *credit* is recorded it is *subtracted* from the balance. As a result, the account always shows an up-to-date balance. Many businesses prefer this form of account. Below is an illustration showing how the information shown above would be recorded if the Tower Corporation decided to use a three-column account.

Add debits
Subtract credits

Three-column
account form

NAME	The Radio Shack		TERMS 20days		
ADDRESS	115 N. Austin Avenue, Chicago, IL 60644				
DATE	ITEM	DEBIT	CREDIT	BALANCE	
Apr. 19-- 3	Mdse.	460 00		460 00	
10	Return		160 00	300 00	
23	Cash		300 00		
29	Mdse.	525 00 985 00	460 00	525 00	

Both forms of the customer's account show that The Radio Shack still owes $525.00. In the three-column account, the end-of-the-month balance of $525.00 can be checked by subtracting the total credits from the total debits as shown below:

Total debits	$985.00
Total credits	− 460.00
Balance	=$525.00

Just as there are different forms of accounts, there are different kinds of ledgers used in business. The ledger, as you know, is the book in which all the accounts are kept. You find it convenient to use a looseleaf notebook instead of a bound notebook, and many businessmen find it convenient to keep the customers' accounts in a looseleaf ledger so that the accounts may be

Looseleaf ledger

arranged in alphabetical order and new accounts inserted in alphabetical order.

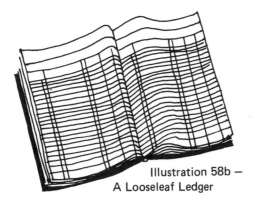

Illustration 58b —
A Looseleaf Ledger

Large companies use bookkeeping machines or automated data processing equipment to record sales and cash received in customers' accounts. Companies using bookkeeping machines keep their accounts on cards which can be inserted in a bookkeeping machine.

Card accounts

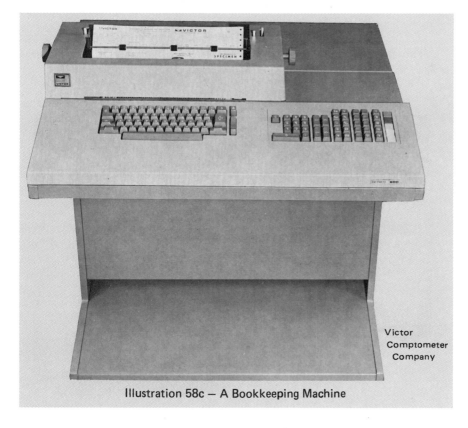

Victor
Comptometer
Company

Illustration 58c — A Bookkeeping Machine

Automated data
processing

Companies using automated data processing equipment may keep their customers' accounts in the form of punched cards such as the card shown below:

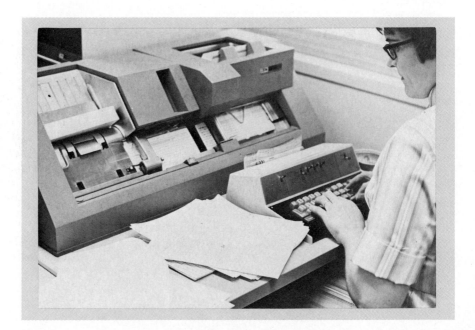

Punched card
accounts

The punched cards are prepared on a key punch machine shown below:

These cards are fed into automated data processing equipment to produce customer records very rapidly.

Automated data processing systems can use punched tape instead of cards.

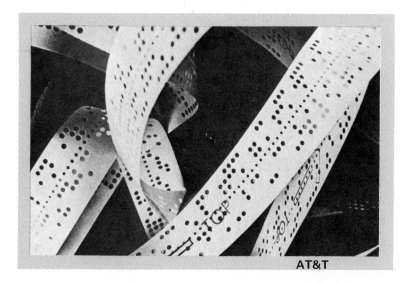

AT&T

Punched tape

High speed electronic systems use magnetic tape to store business information. Magnetic tape looks like the tape used in regular tape recorders. A chemical on the surface makes it possible to magnetize spots on the surface which are similar, in a way, to the holes in a punched card or punched tape. However, much more information can be crowded into a small area of magnetized tape and it can produce business records at much faster speeds than is possible with punched cards or punched tape.

Magnetic tape

PRACTICE PROBLEMS

You are employed as an accounts receivable clerk. Your job is to record the duplicate sales invoices, the list of cash received, and duplicate credit memorandums in the customers' accounts. Use the three-column form of account with a balance column as shown on page 376.

Problem 1

Directions:

a) Open accounts for the following customers: (Terms: 20 days)

Greenvale Shops, 3710 N. 27th St., Kansas City, KS 66104
Kessler & Sons, 639 N. Broadway, Wichita, KS 67214
R. & S. Co., Inc., 215 Gage Blvd., Topeka, KS 66606

b) Record the information shown on the next page in the customers' accounts.

c) Pencil foot the "Debit" and "Credit" columns at the end of the month to check the *final* balance of the account.

d) Prepare a Schedule of Accounts Receivable on September 30. (You are employed by Basin Wholesale Co.) Did you get a total of $667.00?

List of Duplicate Sales Invoices:

Record sales on debit side

Date	Invoice Number	Customer	Amount
Sept. 3	101	Greenvale Shops	$416.00
4	102	Kessler & Sons	372.00
5	103	R. & S. Co., Inc.	195.00
6	104	Greenvale Shops	248.00
9	105	Greenvale Shops	325.00
10	106	Kessler & Sons	284.00
23	107	Kessler & Sons	185.00

List of Duplicate Credit Memorandums:

Record credit memorandums and cash received on credit side

Date	Customer	Amount	Reason
Sept. 12	Greenvale Shops	$46.00	Damaged mdse.
16	R. & S. Co., Inc.	55.00	Damaged mdse.

List of Cash Received:

Date	Customer	Amount	For
Sept. 23	Greenvale Shops	$370.00	Balance of invoice of Sept. 3
24	Kessler & Sons	372.00	Invoice of Sept. 4
25	R. & S. Co., Inc.	140.00	Balance of invoice of Sept. 5
29	Greenvale Shops	250.00	On account
30	Kessler & Sons	125.00	On account

Problem 2

Directions:

a) Open accounts for the following customers: (Terms: 20 days)

J. Ackerman & Co., 2618 Arthur Ave., St. Louis, MO 63143
Danby & Sons, 310 W. Atlantic St., Springfield, MO 65803
Robinson Corporation, 922 Park Ave., Kansas City, MO 64127

b) Record the information shown on the next page in the customers' accounts.

c) Pencil foot the "Debit" and "Credit" columns at the end of the month to check the *final* balance of the account.

d) Prepare a Schedule of Accounts Receivable on June 30. (You are employed by Park Wholesale Shoe Co.) Did you get a total of $948.70?

List of Duplicate Sales Invoices:

Date	Invoice Number	Customer	Amount
June 1	351	J. Ackerman & Co.	$524.60
2	352	Danby & Sons	318.40
5	353	Robinson Corporation	276.50
6	354	Robinson Corporation	442.00
9	355	J. Ackerman & Co.	194.25
19	356	J. Ackerman & Co.	231.80
22	357	Robinson Corporation	305.65

List of Duplicate Credit Memorandums:

Date	Customer	Amount	Reason
June 20	J. Ackerman & Co.	$74.60	Damaged mdse.
21	Danby & Sons	65.00	Damaged mdse.

List of Cash Received:

Date	Customer	Amount	For
June 21	J. Ackerman & Co.	$450.00	Balance of invoice of June 1
22	Danby & Sons	253.40	Balance of invoice of June 2
25	Robinson Corporation	276.50	Invoice of June 5
26	Robinson Corporation	150.00	On account
29	J. Ackerman & Co.	75.00	On account

Problem 3

Directions:

a) Open accounts for the following customers: (Terms: 20 days)

D. Brock Stores, 126 Broad St., Charleston, SC 29401
Farley & Co., Inc., 5721 Edison Ave., Charleston, SC 29406
Heyman & Cole, 248 King St., Charleston, SC 29401

b) Record the information shown below and on the next page in the customers' accounts.

c) Pencil foot the "Debit" and "Credit" columns at the end of the month to check the *final* balance of the account.

d) Prepare a Schedule of Accounts Receivable on August 31. (You are employed by Superior Wholesale Fabric Co.) Did you get a total of $955.25?

List of Duplicate Sales Invoices:

Date	Invoice Number	Customer	Amount
Aug. 1	601	D. Brock Stores	$346.55
2	602	Farley & Co., Inc.	281.60
5	603	Heyman & Cole	417.35
6	604	Farley & Co., Inc.	198.25
8	605	D. Brock Stores	224.50
14	606	Farley & Co., Inc.	375.10
18	607	D. Brock Stores	163.30

List of Duplicate Credit Memorandums:

Date	Customer	Amount	Reason
Aug. 19	D. Brock Stores	$64.00	Overcharge allowance
20	Farley & Co., Inc.	30.00	Damaged mdse.

List of Cash Received:

Date	Customer	Amount	For
Aug. 21	D. Brock Stores	$282.55	Balance of invoice of Aug. 1
22	Farley & Co., Inc.	251.60	Balance of invoice of Aug. 2
25	Heyman & Cole	150.00	On account
26	Farley & Co., Inc.	198.25	Invoice of Aug. 6
28	D. Brock Stores	75.00	On account

Practicing
Related
Arithmetic

Find the dates on which the following invoices are due:

	Date of Invoice	Terms		Date of Invoice	Terms
1)	March 6	20 days	6)	July 9	60 days
2)	January 24	30 days	7)	August 12	60 days
3)	October 18	30 days	8)	May 21	90 days
4)	June 12	30 days	9)	March 11	90 days
5)	November 28	30 days	10)	June 15	90 days

AIM

To learn how to record sales in a Sales Journal.

EXPLANATION

In the previous job, you learned how to record sales in customers' accounts. You learned that these accounts are grouped together into an Accounts Receivable Ledger. You also learned that there are two different account forms used in business. Some businesspeople prefer the "T" account form:

NAME	Bering Bros.						TERMS 30 days	
ADDRESS	390 Bayshore Blvd., Tampa, FL 33606							
DATE	ITEM	DEBIT	DATE	ITEM	CREDIT			
Jan. 8	Mdse.	340 00						
16	Mdse.	400 00						
		740 00						

"T" account form

NAME	Bering Bros.				TERMS 30 days
ADDRESS	390 Bayshore Blvd., Tampa, FL 33606				
DATE	ITEM	DEBIT	CREDIT	BALANCE	
Jan. 8	Mdse.	340 00		340 00	
16	Mdse.	400 00		740 00	

Three-column account form

Duplicate sales
invoices are
recorded in
Sales Journal

In the work you have done so far, all the information for the debit side of the customers' accounts came directly from the duplicate sales invoices. Although this method is followed by many businesses, others prefer to record all the duplicate sales invoices for each month in a separate book called a *Sales Journal*.

	DATE		CUSTOMER'S NAME	INVOICE NO.	POST. REF.	AMOUNT
	19-- June	3	Jackson & Co.	101		280 00
		5	McGraw Stores	102		310 00

SALES JOURNAL — PAGE 1

Illustration 59a — Sales Journal

Posting from a
Sales Journal

Although the sales have been recorded in the Sales Journal, no record has been made as yet in the customers' accounts to show how much each customer owes. In order to do this it is necessary to transfer the amounts from the Sales Journal to the "Debit" column of the customers' accounts. The process of transferring amounts from a journal to the accounts receivable ledger is called *posting*. It means that two books are used to record sales. The first book that is used is the Sales Journal, where the duplicate sales invoices are first recorded. They are then posted to the customers' accounts in the Accounts Receivable Ledger.

Posting must be done with great care and accuracy to be sure that the correct amount is copied from the Sales Journal to the customers' accounts. Illustration 59b on page 385 shows how the first entry in the Sales Journal would be posted to the Jackson & Co. account.

Here are the four steps in posting shown in the illustration:

Step 1: Post the amount.

The amount, $280.00, was written in the "Debit" column of the account because, as you know, all sales are recorded in the Debit column.

Step 2: Copy the date.

The date, June 3, was copied from the Sales Journal. Since this was the first entry recorded in the Jackson & Co. account, the year was written at the top of the "Date" column and the month was written in the "Month" column. Record keepers usually post to customers' accounts at the end of each day to show the most up-to-date record of the balance owed.

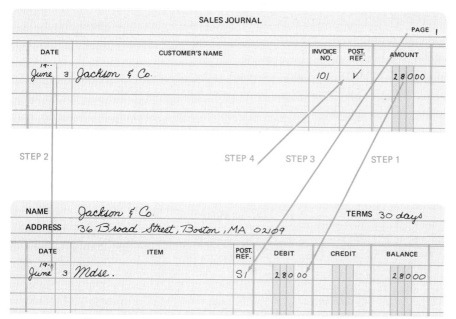

Illustration 59b — Customer's Account Showing Posting

Step 3: Record the posting reference.

The posting reference, S1, was recorded in the account in the narrow column just to the left of the money columns. This symbol, S1, indicates that the amount came from page 1 of the Sales Journal. When postings are made from the second page of the Sales Journal, the symbol S2 will be used. These symbols are called *posting references*, or *postmarks*, or *folio marks*. The narrow column in which the postmark is recorded is called the *"Posting Reference"* column, or the *"Folio"* column.

a) Posting references
b) Postmarks
c) Folio marks

Step 4: Enter the check mark.

The check mark was written in the "Posting Reference" column of the Sales Journal to show that the $280.00 had been posted to the customer's account. If you are interrupted while you are posting you can see how this check mark will help you to know which amounts in the Sales Journal were posted and which were not. Some record keepers number the customers' accounts to make it easier to find a particular account in the Accounts Receivable Ledger. When the customers' accounts are numbered, it is more convenient to write the number of the customer's account in the "Posting Reference" column of the Sales Journal instead of the check mark shown in Illustration 59b above. This kind of postmark would then serve two purposes. First, it would show the record keeper which accounts had been posted. Second, it would serve as a way of locating the customer's account quickly when the record keeper wanted to check the postings.

Check marks show that postings have been made

SAMPLE PROBLEM

According to the duplicate sales invoices, the Economy Wholesale Co. made the following sales during the month:

June	3	Sold merchandise to Jackson & Co. for $280.00.
	5	Sold merchandise to McGraw Stores for $310.00.
	11	Sold merchandise to Pride Bros. for $125.00.
	19	Sold merchandise to McGraw Stores for $420.00.
	26	Sold merchandise to Jackson & Co. for $110.00.
	29	Sold merchandise to McGraw Stores for $230.00.

After this information was recorded in the journal and posted to the accounts, the Sales Journal and customers' accounts showed the following:

Sales Journal

SALES JOURNAL

PAGE 1

DATE		CUSTOMER'S NAME	INVOICE NO.	POST. REF.	AMOUNT
June 19--	3	Jackson & Co.	101	✓	2 80 00
	5	McGraw Stores	102	✓	3 10 00
	11	Pride Bros.	103	✓	1 25 00
	19	McGraw Stores	104	✓	4 20 00
	26	Jackson & Co.	105	✓	1 10 00
	29	McGraw Stores	106	✓	2 30 00
					1 4 75 00
					1 4 75 00

Accounts Receivable Ledger (customers' accounts)

NAME   Jackson & Co.   TERMS 30 days
ADDRESS   36 Broad Street, Boston, MA 02109

DATE		ITEM	POST. REF.	DEBIT	CREDIT	BALANCE
June 19--	3	Mdse.	S1	2 80 00		2 80 00
	26	Mdse.	S1	1 10 00		3 90 00

NAME   McGraw Stores   TERMS 30 days
ADDRESS   3350 Watt Avenue, Sacramento, CA 95814

DATE		ITEM	POST. REF.	DEBIT	CREDIT	BALANCE
June 19--	5	Mdse.	S1	3 10 00		3 10 00
	19	Mdse.	S1	4 20 00		7 30 00
	29	Mdse.	S1	2 30 00		9 60 00

NAME   Pride Bros.   TERMS 30 days
ADDRESS   1615 Tremont Street, Denver, CO 80202

DATE		ITEM	POST. REF.	DEBIT	CREDIT	BALANCE
June 19--	11	Mdse.	S1	1 25 00		1 25 00

Here are the steps that were followed:

Step 1: Record sales in Sales Journal.

The sales were recorded in the Sales Journal from the information on the duplicate sales invoices.

Step 2: Post to the customers' accounts.

At the end of each day, the amounts in the Sales Journal were transferred, or posted, to the customers' accounts in the Accounts Receivable Ledger. Notice that in the illustration of the Sales Journal in the Sample Problem all the amounts have been checked to indicate that all the postings have been made.

Step 3: Total the Sales Journal.

At the end of the month, the Amount column was totaled to get the total sales for the month. You can see that the total sales for the month of June were $1,475.00. This amount was pencil footed and the column readded before the total was inked in. Notice that the *double* ruling is repeated on the same line in the Date column.

PRACTICE PROBLEMS

You are employed as an assistant bookkeeper and your job is to record the sales in a Sales Journal and to post to the customers' accounts.

Problem 1

Directions:

a) Open accounts for the customers shown below. Use the three-column account form. Use "Terms: 30 days" for all customers.

Customer	Address
J. Ervin & Co.	110 Pacific St., Omaha, NE 68108
Super Stores, Inc.	209 N. 9th St., St. Louis, MO 63101
Wolpert & Kenyon	4321 Grand Ave., Duluth, MN 55807

b) Record in a Sales Journal the sales shown below, using the form shown in Illustration 59a on page 384.

May 1   Sold merchandise for $580.00 to J. Ervin & Co. (Start with invoice #101.)

      9   Sold merchandise for $625.00 to Super Stores, Inc.

    21   Sold merchandise for $495.00 to Wolpert & Kenyon.

    25   Sold merchandise to Super Stores, Inc. for $735.00.

    31   Sold merchandise to J. Ervin & Co. for $220.00.

c) Post from the Sales Journal to the "Debit" column of the customers' accounts. Do not forget to enter a check mark in the Sales Journal and the postmark (S1) in the accounts as you post.

d) Find the total sales for the month by adding the Amount column in the Sales Journal. Be sure to pencil foot before inking in the totals.

e) Check the balance in the customers' accounts by pencil footing the "Debit" column in each account.

Problem 2

Directions:

a) Open accounts for the customers shown below. Use the three-column account form. Use "Terms: 30 days" for all customers.

Customer	Address
Baylor Enterprises	315 Washington Ave., Baltimore, MD 21225
Sheridan Corporation	801 Broad St., Newark, NJ 07102
Wilson & Co.	76 Hamilton Ave., Trenton, NJ 08611

b) Record in a Sales Journal (Page 4) the sales shown below:

Nov.　5　Sold merchandise for $270.00 to Baylor Enterprises. (Start with invoice #251.)

　　14　Sold merchandise for $385.00 to Sheridan Corporation.

　　19　Sold merchandise for $610.00 to Wilson & Co.

　　23　Sold merchandise to Sheridan Corporation for $160.00.

　　26　Sold merchandise to Wilson & Co. for $538.00.

　　27　Sold merchandise to Baylor Enterprises for $416.00.

c) Post from the Sales Journal to the "Debit" column of the customers' accounts. Use the postmark (S4) in the accounts.

d) Find the total sales for the month by adding the Amount column in the Sales Journal.

e) Check the balance in the customers' accounts by pencil footing the "Debit" column in each account.

Problem 3

Directions:

a) Open accounts for the customers shown below. Use the three-column account form. Use "Terms: 30 days" for all customers.

Customer	Address
Levin & Gross	86 Pine St., Cincinnati, OH 45216
Oxford Shops, Inc.	990 E. Market St., Akron, OH 44305
Palmer & Hernandez	165 E. Main St., Durham, NC 27701

b) Record in a Sales Journal (Page 10) the sales shown below:

Oct.　1　Sold merchandise for $134.50 to Levin & Gross. (Start with invoice #151.)

　　10　Sold merchandise for $356.10 to Oxford Shops, Inc.

　　12　Sold merchandise for $281.45 to Palmer & Hernandez.

　　19　Sold merchandise to Levin & Gross for $581.75.

　　25　Sold merchandise to Palmer & Hernandez for $419.50.

　　31　Sold merchandise to Oxford Shops, Inc. for $184.95.

c) Post from the Sales Journal to the "Debit" column of the customers' accounts. Use the postmark (S10) in the accounts.

d) Find the total sales for the month by adding the Amount column in the Sales Journal.

e) Check the balance in the customers' accounts by pencil footing the "Debit" column in each account.

Problem 4

Directions:

a) Open accounts for the customers shown below. Use the three-column account form. Use "Terms: 30 days" for all customers.

Customer	Address
Cutler Bros.	810 S.W. Broadway, Portland, OR 97205
Powell & Johnson	115 East Ave., Erie, PA 16507
Wilshire & Co., Inc.	435 Benson Ave., Philadelphia, PA 19111

b) Record in a Sales Journal (Page 8) the sales shown below:

Aug. 3   Sold merchandise for $251.60 to Cutler Bros. (Start with invoice #331.)
      6   Sold merchandise for $424.15 to Powell & Johnson.
     13   Sold merchandise for $192.35 to Wilshire & Co., Inc.
     24   Sold merchandise to Powell & Johnson for $378.10.
     27   Sold merchandise to Wilshire & Co., Inc. for $418.25.
     30   Sold merchandise to Cutler Bros. for $644.30.

c) Post from the Sales Journal to the "Debit" column of the customers' accounts. Use the postmark (S8) in the accounts.

d) Find the total sales for the month by adding the Amount column in the Sales Journal.

e) Check the balance in the customers' accounts by pencil footing the "Debit" column in each account.

Problem 5

Directions:

a) Open accounts for the customers shown below. Use the three-column account form. Use "Terms: 30 days" for all customers.

Customer	Address
Cortez & Chester	211 E. Bay St., Charleston, SC 29401
Patton & Sons	89 Cody St., Dallas, TX 75228
Union Shopping Center	1100 Central Ave., Tampa, FL 33602

b) Record in a Sales Journal (Page 3) the sales shown on the next page.

Mar. 5 Sold merchandise for $412.60 to Cortez & Chester. (Start with invoice #181.)
     13 Sold merchandise for $342.80 to Patton & Sons.
     15 Sold merchandise for $604.10 to Union Shopping Center.
     22 Sold merchandise to Cortez & Chester for $184.25.
     26 Sold merchandise to Union Shopping Center for $317.45.
     29 Sold merchandise to Patton & Sons for $556.75.

c) Post from the Sales Journal to the "Debit" column of the customers' accounts. Use the postmark (S3) in the accounts.

d) Find the total sales for the month by adding the Amount column in the Sales Journal.

e) Check the balance in the customers' accounts by pencil footing the "Debit" column in each account.

JOB 60 | USING A CASH RECEIPTS JOURNAL

Practicing
Related
Arithmetic

Find the dates on which the following invoices are due:

	Date of Invoice	Terms		Date of Invoice	Terms
1)	February 8	15 days	6)	April 10	60 days
2)	June 20	30 days	7)	August 21	60 days
3)	October 28	10 days	8)	May 1	90 days
4)	March 11	30 days	9)	March 12	90 days
5)	January 7	30 days	10)	July 17	90 days

AIM

To learn how to record cash received from customers in a Cash Receipts Journal.

Cash
Received

↓

Cash Receipts
Journal

↓

Customers'
Accounts

EXPLANATION

As you know, some businesspeople record all sales in a book called a Sales Journal for a permanent and systematic record of sales to customers. In the same way, cash received from customers is recorded in a separate book called a *Cash Receipts Journal*.

CASH RECEIPTS JOURNAL   PAGE 1

DATE		RECEIVED FROM	EXPLANATION	POST. REF.	AMOUNT
July	3	Jackson & Co.	Inv. of June 3		2 80 00
	5	McGraw Stores	Inv. of June 5		3 10 00

Illustration 60 — Cash Receipts Journal

After the cash received from customers has been recorded in the Cash Receipts Journal, the amounts are posted to the *credit* side of the customers' accounts. Then the page number is entered in the Posting Reference column (for instance, *CR1* for Cash Receipts Journal, page 1).

CR1 =
Cash Receipts
Journal, page 1

SAMPLE PROBLEM

The following customers' accounts show the sales made by the Economy Wholesale Co. during the month of June.

NAME	Jackson & Co			TERMS	30 days	
ADDRESS	36 Broad Street, Boston, MA 02109					

DATE	ITEM	POST. REF.	DEBIT	CREDIT	BALANCE
19--					
June 3	Mdse.	S1	280 00		280 00
26	Mdse.	S1	110 00		390 00

NAME	Mc Graw Stores			TERMS	30 days	
ADDRESS	3350 Walt Avenue, Sacramento, CA 95814					

DATE	ITEM	POST. REF.	DEBIT	CREDIT	BALANCE
19--					
June 5	Mdse.	S1	310 00		310 00
19	Mdse.	S1	420 00		730 00
29	Mdse.	S1	230 00		960 00

NAME	Pride Bros.			TERMS	30 days	
ADDRESS	1615 Tremont Street, Denver, CO 80202					

DATE	ITEM	POST. REF.	DEBIT	CREDIT	BALANCE
19--					
June 11	Mdse.	S1	125 00		125 00

Notice that according to the terms of each sale the customers are supposed to pay their bills within thirty days. Since the sales were made in the month of June you can expect to receive most of the money the customers owe in July, the following month.

This is exactly what happened, and here is a record of the money collected:

July 3　Received a check for $280.00 from Jackson & Co. for invoice of June 3.

5　Received a check for $310.00 from McGraw Stores for invoice of June 5.

11　Received a check for $125.00 from Pride Bros. for invoice of June 11.

19　Received a check for $100.00 from McGraw Stores to apply on account (part payment).

26　Received a check for $50.00 from Jackson & Co. to apply on account (part payment).

On the next page you can see how the Cash Receipts Journal and the customers' accounts looked with all this information recorded.

CASH RECEIPTS JOURNAL   PAGE 1

DATE		RECEIVED FROM	EXPLANATION	POST. REF.	AMOUNT
July	3	Jackson & Co.	Inv. of June 3	✓	280 00
	5	McGraw Stores	Inv. of June 5	✓	310 00
	11	Pride Bros.	Inv. of June 11	✓	125 00
	19	McGraw Stores	On account	✓	100 00
	26	Jackson & Co.	On account	✓	50 00
					865 00
					865 00

Post from cash receipts journal to credit side of customer accounts

NAME   Jackson & Co.   TERMS 30 days
ADDRESS   36 Broad Street, Boston, MA 02109

DATE		ITEM	POST. REF.	DEBIT	CREDIT	BALANCE
June	3	Mdse.	S1	280 00		280 00
	26	Mdse.	S1	110 00		390 00
July	3	Cash	CR1		280 00	110 00
	26	Cash	CR1		50 00	60 00
				390 00	330 00	

NAME   McGraw Stores   TERMS 30 days
ADDRESS   3350 Watt Avenue, Sacramento, CA 95814

DATE		ITEM	POST. REF.	DEBIT	CREDIT	BALANCE
June	5	Mdse.	S1	310 00		310 00
	19	Mdse.	S1	420 00		730 00
	29	Mdse.	S1	230 00		960 00
July	5	Cash	CR1		310 00	650 00
	19	Cash	CR1		100 00	550 00
				960 00	410 00	

NAME   Pride Bros.   TERMS 30 days
ADDRESS   1615 Tremont Street, Denver, CO 80202

DATE		ITEM	POST. REF.	DEBIT	CREDIT	BALANCE
June	11	Mdse.	S1	125 00		125 00
July	11	Cash	CR1		125 00	

Here are the steps that were followed:

Step 1: Record receipts in Cash Receipts Journal.

As money was received from each customer, the date, the customer's name, the explanation, and the amount were recorded in the Cash Receipts Journal. For example, you will notice that, according to the Cash Receipts Journal above, a check for $280.00 was received from Jackson & Co. for merchandise sold to them on June 3. The same information was recorded for all cash received from customers.

Step 2: Post to customers' accounts.

Old balance
−Credit
=New balance

After the receipts were recorded in the Cash Receipts Journal, the amounts were transferred, or posted, to the Credit column of the customers' accounts. For example, since $280.00 had been received from Jackson & Co. on July 3, this amount was posted to the Jackson & Co. account to show that this customer owes us less than he did before. If you refer to the Jackson & Co. account, you will notice that the $280.00 was recorded in the Credit column and then subtracted from the old balance of $390.00 to get the balance still due of $110.00.

As each posting was made, a check mark was entered in the Cash Receipts Journal and the postmark, CR1, was entered in the customer's account. The postmark, CR1, represents page 1 of the Cash Receipts Journal.

Step 3: Total the Cash Receipts Journal.

After all the postings for the month had been completed, the total amount of cash collected from customers for the month was found by adding all amounts in the Cash Receipts Journal. The Cash Receipts Journal shows that a total of $865.00 was collected from customers. This total was pencil footed and readded before it was inked in.

Notice that the double ruling is repeated on the same line in the *Date* column.

PRACTICE PROBLEMS

Problem 1

Directions:

a) Copy the accounts on page 395 which show sales recorded in the customers' accounts in March. Use the three-column account.

b) Record cash received from customers during the month of April in a Cash Receipts Journal. Use the form shown on page 391.

April 4   Received a check for $440.00 from Harrison & Co. for the invoice of March 5.

13   Received a check for $520.00 from Freeman Corporation for the invoice of March 14.

18   Received a check for $260.00 from Webster & Pierce for the invoice of March 19.

23   Received a check for $450.00 from Webster & Pierce to apply on account.

29   Received a check for $300.00 from Harrison & Co. to apply on account.

NAME	*Freeman Corporation*			TERMS	*30 days*	
ADDRESS	*1441 Miami Drive, Miami, FL 33162*					

DATE	ITEM	POST. REF.	DEBIT	CREDIT	BALANCE
19--					
Mar. 14	Mdse.	S1	520 00		520 00

Sales recorded in customers' accounts for month of March

NAME	*Harrison & Co.*			TERMS	*30 days*	
ADDRESS	*20 Fulton Avenue, Hempstead, NY 11550*					

DATE	ITEM	POST. REF.	DEBIT	CREDIT	BALANCE
19--					
Mar. 5	Mdse.	S1	440 00		440 00
29	Mdse.	S1	350 00		790 00

NAME	*Webster & Pierce*			TERMS	*30 days*	
ADDRESS	*6980 N. Clark Street, Chicago, IL 60626*					

DATE	ITEM	POST. REF.	DEBIT	CREDIT	BALANCE
19--					
Mar. 19	Mdse.	S1	260 00		260 00
23	Mdse.	S1	610 00		870 00
26	Mdse	S1	500 00		1370 00

c) Post from the Cash Receipts Journal to the Credit column of the customers' accounts. Enter a check mark in the Cash Receipts Journal and the postmark (CR1) in the accounts as you post.

d) Find the total cash received for the month by adding the Amount column in the Cash Receipts Journal.

e) Check the balance in the customers' accounts by pencil footing the Debit and Credit columns. Subtract the credit total from the debit total and the answer should agree with the final balance shown in the account.

Total debits
−Total credits
=Final balance

Problem 2

Directions:

a) Copy the accounts on page 396 which show the sales recorded in the customers' accounts in the month of November.

b) Record the cash received from customers during the month of December as shown below and on page 396 in a Cash Receipts Journal (Page 15):

Dec. 3   Received a check for $480.00 from Coronado Stores for the invoice of November 3.

      5   Received a check for $250.00 from Genovese & Sons for the invoice of November 5.

    12   Received a check for $625.00 from Sweeney & Co. for the invoice of November 12.

14 Received a check from Genovese & Sons for $200.00 to apply on account.

20 Received a check from Coronado Stores for $350.00 to apply on account.

NAME	Coronado Stores			TERMS	30 days	
ADDRESS	561 Commercial Street, San Francisco, CA 94111					

DATE		ITEM	POST. REF.	DEBIT	CREDIT	BALANCE
19-- Nov.	3	Mdse.	S11	480 00		480 00
	20	Mdse.	S11	510 00		990 00

Sales recorded in customers' accounts for month of November

NAME	Genovese & Sons			TERMS	30 days	
ADDRESS	215 Union Street, San Francisco, CA 94113					

DATE		ITEM	POST. REF.	DEBIT	CREDIT	BALANCE
19-- Nov.	5	Mdse.	S11	250 00		250 00
	14	Mdse.	S11	370 00		620 00
	28	Mdse.	S11	240 00		860 00

NAME	Sweeney & Co.			TERMS	30 days	
ADDRESS	1721 Sutter Street, San Francisco, CA 94115					

DATE		ITEM	POST. REF.	DEBIT	CREDIT	BALANCE
19-- Nov.	12	Mdse.	S11	625 00		625 00

c) Post from the Cash Receipts Journal to the Credit column of the customers' accounts. Use the postmark (CR15) in the accounts.

d) Find the total cash received for the month in the Cash Receipts Journal.

e) Check the balance in the customers' accounts by pencil footing the Debit and Credit columns. Subtract the credit total from the debit total and the answer should agree with the final balance shown in the account.

Problem 3

Directions:

a) Copy the accounts on page 397 which show the sales recorded in the customers' accounts in the month of May.

b) Record the cash receipts below and on page 397 from customers during the month of June in a Cash Receipts Journal (Page 9):

June 6 Received a check for $285.20 from Brooks & Mason for the invoice of May 7.

8 Received a check for $184.25 from Lexington Corporation for the invoice of May 9.

17 Received a check for $522.35 from Hudson Co., Inc. for the invoice of May 18.
20 Received a check from Lexington Corporation for $150.00 to apply on account.
22 Received a check from Brooks & Mason for $275.00 to apply on account.

NAME	Brooks & Mason			TERMS 30 days		
ADDRESS	2316 Broadway, New Orleans, LA 70125					
DATE	ITEM	POST. REF.	DEBIT	CREDIT	BALANCE	
19-- May 7	Mdse.	S5	285 20		285 20	
23	Mdse.	S5	425 30		710 50	
25	Mdse	S5	360 70		1071 20	

NAME	Hudson Co., Inc.			TERMS 30 days		
ADDRESS	940 Lewis Street, Shreveport, LA 71103					
DATE	ITEM	POST. REF.	DEBIT	CREDIT	BALANCE	
19-- May 18	Mdse.	S5	522 35		522 35	

Sales recorded in customers' accounts for month of May

NAME	Lexington Corporation			TERMS 30 days		
ADDRESS	404 North Blvd., Baton Rouge, LA 70801					
DATE	ITEM	POST. REF.	DEBIT	CREDIT	BALANCE	
19-- May 9	Mdse.	S5	184 25		184 25	
21	Mdse.	S5	276 80		461 05	
30	Mdse.	S5	450 00		911 05	

c) Post from the Cash Receipts Journal to the Credit column of the customers' accounts. Use the postmark (CR9) in the accounts.
d) Find the total cash received for the month in the Cash Receipts Journal.
e) Check the balance in the customers' accounts by pencil footing the Debit and Credit columns. Subtract the credit total from the debit total and the answer should agree with the final balance shown in the account.

Problem 4

Directions:
a) Copy the accounts on page 398 which show the sales recorded in the customers' accounts in the month of August.
b) Record the cash receipts on page 398 from customers during the month of September in a Cash Receipts Journal (Page 10).

NAME	Bond & Co., Inc.				TERMS 30 days	
ADDRESS	362 Dowd Avenue, Elizabeth, NJ 07206					

DATE	ITEM	POST. REF.	DEBIT	CREDIT	BALANCE
19-- Aug. 9	Mdse.	S8	2 07 52		2 07 52
16	Mdse.	S8	4 51 20		6 58 72
30	Mdse.	S8	2 64 60		9 23 32

Sales recorded in customers' accounts for month of August

NAME	Gates & Bergen				TERMS 30 days	
ADDRESS	73 Central Avenue, Jersey City, NJ 07306					

DATE	ITEM	POST. REF.	DEBIT	CREDIT	BALANCE
19-- Aug. 14	Mdse.	S8	8 26 40		8 26 40

NAME	Hawkins Bros.				TERMS 30 days	
ADDRESS	91 Clinton Avenue, Newark, NJ 07411					

DATE	ITEM	POST. REF.	DEBIT	CREDIT	BALANCE
19-- Aug. 6	Mdse.	S8	1 92 75		1 92 75
20	Mdse.	S8	3 81 20		5 73 95
28	Mdse.	S8	2 71 80		8 45 75

Sept. 5 Received a check for $192.75 from Hawkins Bros. for the invoice of August 6.

8 Received a check for $207.50 from Bond & Co., Inc. for the invoice of August 9.

13 Received a check for $826.40 from Gates & Bergen for the invoice of August 14.

15 Received a check from Bond & Co., Inc. for $350.00 to apply on account.

19 Received a check from Hawkins Bros. for $180.00 to apply on account.

c) Post from the Cash Receipts Journal to the Credit column of the customers' accounts. Use the postmark (CR10) in the accounts.

d) Find the total cash received for the month in the Cash Receipts Journal.

e) Check the balance in the customers' accounts by pencil footing the Debit and Credit columns. Subtract the credit total from the debit total and the answer should agree with the final balance shown in the account.

Copy and answer the following problems:

(1)	(2)
Add across	Subtract across

(1) Add across	(2) Subtract across
a) $45.00 + $15.00 = $	a) $85.00 − $60.00 = $
b) 130.00 + 75.00 = $	b) 104.00 − 30.00 = $
c) 61.20 + 30.40 = $	c) 70.00 − 15.00 = $
d) 55.10 + 70.80 = $	d) 180.00 − 35.00 = $
e) 60.50 + 81.70 = $	e) 160.00 − 25.00 = $
$____ + $____ = $____	$____ − $____ = $____

AIM

To practice using:

a) the Sales Journal,

b) the Cash Receipts Journal, and

c) the Accounts Receivable Ledger.

EXPLANATION

You are now using three books to keep a record of transactions with customers to whom merchandise is sold on credit. The three books are:

1. The Sales Journal in which you record all sales invoices.
2. The Cash Receipts Journal in which you record all collections from customers.
3. The Accounts Receivable Ledger in which you keep the customers' accounts. Debits in the customers' accounts come from or are posted from the Sales Journal. Credits in these accounts are posted from the Cash Receipts Journal.

Postings must follow the order of the dates

In this job you will make use of all three books. Since you will be posting from both the Sales Journal and the Cash Receipts Journal to the same accounts, it is important to remember that *postings are made at the end of the day and must follow the order of the dates.*

The order of recording sales invoices and cash collections in the journals and posting from the journals into customers' accounts is shown on page 400.

Shown on page 400 is an illustration of how to post when you are using both the Sales Journal and the Cash Receipts Journal.

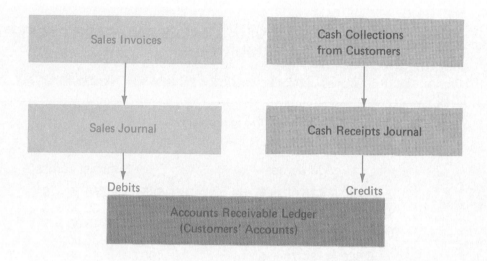

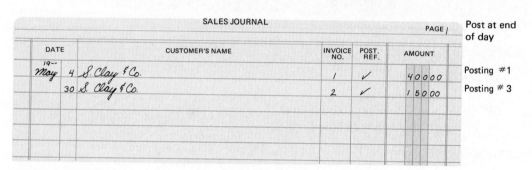

NAME	S. Clay & Co.			TERMS On account	
ADDRESS	1305 Church Avenue, Brooklyn, NY 11226				

DATE	ITEM	POST. REF.	DEBIT	CREDIT	BALANCE
19-- May 4	Mdse.	S1	400 00		400 00
24	Cash	CR1		300 00	100 00
30	Mdse.	S1	150 00		250 00

Illustration 61b — Method of Posting

Notice how the postings to S. Clay & Co.'s account followed the order of the dates:

First posting:	On May 4, the sale was posted from the Sales Journal
Second posting:	On May 24, the receipt was posted from the Cash Receipts Journal
Third posting:	On May 30, the sale was posted from the Sales Journal

PRACTICE PROBLEMS

Problem 1

You are employed by the Basic Wholesale Co. as an assistant to the bookkeeper.

Directions:
a) Open accounts for the three customers shown below. Use the three-column account form.

Customer	Address	Terms
Essex Co.	25 Beacon St., Boston, MA 02108	On account
Jenkins Bros.	406 Harding St., Detroit, MI 48214	20 days
Smith, Inc.	101 Chatham St., Lynn, MA 01902	10 days

Sales

Sales Journal

Cash Received

Cash Receipts Journal

b) Record the sales shown below in a Sales Journal and the cash collections in a Cash Receipts Journal. This means that as you read each transaction you must decide whether it is to be recorded in the Sales Journal or in the Cash Receipts Journal. *As soon as you have recorded each transaction you must post immediately to the customer's account.* Notice that in the workbook the customers' accounts are placed after the Sales Journal and Cash Receipts Journal, so that you can work *from* the journals *to* the accounts as you do the problems. Use page 1 for both journals.

Jan. 3   Sold merchandise to Essex Co. for $446.50 (Invoice #101). Since this is a sale it must be recorded in the Sales Journal.

     4   Sold merchandise to Jenkins Bros. for $286.40 (Invoice #102).

     6   Sold merchandise to Essex Co. for $528.70 (Invoice #103).

   12   Received a check for $400.00 from Essex Co. to apply on account. (This is a cash collection and it is the first transaction to be entered in the Cash Receipts Journal.)

   13   Sold merchandise to Smith, Inc. for $621.85 (Invoice #104).

   14   Sold merchandise to Smith, Inc. for $436.50 (Invoice #105).

   18   Sold merchandise to Jenkins Bros. for $372.90 (Invoice #106).

   23   Received a check for $621.85 from Smith, Inc. for the invoice of January 13.

   24   Received a check for $286.40 from Jenkins Bros. for the invoice of January 4.

   27   Sold merchandise to Jenkins Bros. for $362.20 (Invoice #107).

   31   Received a check for $150.00 from Essex Co. to apply on account.

Post after each transaction

c) Total the Sales Journal and the Cash Receipts Journal.

d) Prepare a Schedule of Accounts Receivable on January 31. (Refer to page 369 if necessary.) Did you get a total of $1,596.80?

Problem 2

You are employed by the Star Wholesale Co. as an assistant to the bookkeeper.

Directions:

a) Open accounts for the three customers shown below. Use the three-column account form.

Customer	Address	Terms
Beach Stores	732 Adams Ave., Cleveland, OH 44137	On account
Lyons & Bond	21 N. Wall St., Columbus, OH 43215	20 days
R. Preston Co.	315 Ridge Ave., Dayton, OH 45414	10 days

b) Record the following transactions using a Sales Journal and a Cash Receipts Journal. Be sure to post daily. Use page 1 for both journals.

Post daily

Mar. 1 Sold merchandise to Beach Stores for $723.80 (Invoice #301).

3 Sold merchandise to Lyons & Bond for $541.25 (Invoice #302).

6 Sold merchandise to Beach Stores for $635.50 (Invoice #303).

10 Received a check for $400.00 from Beach Stores to apply on account.

14 Sold merchandise to R. Preston Co. for $412.75 (Invoice #304).

15 Sold merchandise to R. Preston Co. for $538.40 (Invoice #305).

17 Sold merchandise to Lyons & Bond for $336.15 (Invoice #306).

23 Received a check for $541.25 from Lyons & Bond for the invoice of March 3.

24 Received a check for $412.75 from R. Preston Co. for the invoice of March 14.

27 Sold merchandise to Lyons & Bond for $185.35 (Invoice #307).

31 Received a check for $500.00 from Beach Stores to apply on account.

c) Total the Sales Journal and the Cash Receipts Journal.

d) Prepare the Schedule of Accounts Receivable on March 31. Did you get a total of $1,519.20?

Problem 3

You are employed by the Alpha Wholesale Co. as an assistant to the bookkeeper.

Directions:

a) Open accounts for the three customers shown on page 403. Use the three-column account form.

Customer	Address	Terms
Boggs & Co.	2200 Aster Rd., Knoxville, TN 37918	On account
McComb Bros.	332 Edith Ave., Memphis, TN 38126	20 days
Raynor, Inc.	87 North Pkwy., Memphis, TN 38103	10 days

b) Record the following transactions using a Sales Journal and a Cash Receipts Journal. Be sure to post daily. Use page 1 for both journals.

May 2	Sold merchandise to Boggs & Co. for $351.70 (Invoice #501).	
3	Sold merchandise to McComb Bros. for $192.80 (Invoice #502).	
5	Sold merchandise to Boggs & Co. for $584.25 (Invoice #503).	
12	Received a check for $300.00 from Boggs & Co. to apply on account.	
16	Sold merchandise to Raynor, Inc. for $907.35 (Invoice #504).	Post daily
18	Sold merchandise to McComb Bros. for $621.90 (Invoice #505).	
19	Sold merchandise to Raynor, Inc. for $574.25 (Invoice #506).	
23	Received a check for $192.80 from McComb Bros. for the invoice of May 3.	
26	Received a check for $907.35 from Raynor, Inc. for the invoice of May 16.	
29	Sold merchandise to McComb Bros. for $156.45 (Invoice #507).	
30	Received a check for $200.00 from Raynor, Inc. to apply on account.	
31	Received a check for $400.00 from Boggs & Co. to apply on account.	

c) Total the Sales Journal and the Cash Receipts Journal.

d) Prepare a Schedule of Accounts Receivable on May 31. Did you get a total of $1,388.55?

Copy and answer the following problems:

Practicing Related Arithmetic

	(1) Add across		(2) Subtract across
a)	$45.00 + $20.00 = $	a)	$85.00 − $20.00 = $
b)	65.00 + 15.00 = $	b)	40.00 − 15.00 = $
c)	70.00 + 22.40 = $	c)	65.50 − 30.10 = $
d)	25.60 + 80.25 = $	d)	45.25 − 15.15 = $
e)	40.70 + 75.50 = $	e)	130.00 − 75.00 = $
	$ + $ = $		$ − $ = $

AIM

To learn how to record merchandise returned by customers in a Sales Returns and Allowances Journal.

EXPLANATION

You now follow these steps in recording transactions with credit customers:

1. All sales are entered in a separate book called a *Sales Journal* and all cash collected from customers is entered in a separate book called a *Cash Receipts Journal*.

2. All recorded entries are *posted* from the Sales Journal and from the Cash Receipts Journal to the customers' accounts in the *Accounts Receivable Ledger*.

You record merchandise returned by customers in the same way:

Returns are posted as credits

1. Returns of merchandise are entered in a separate book called a *Sales Returns and Allowances Journal* shown on the next page.

2. The amounts of the returns are posted from the Sales Returns and Allowances Journal to the *credit* column of the customers' accounts.

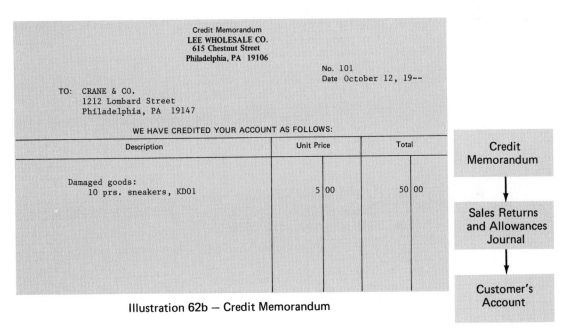

	DATE		CUSTOMER'S NAME	EXPLANATION	CREDIT MEMO NO.	POST. REF.	AMOUNT	
	19--							
Oct.	12	Crane & Co.	damaged mdse.	101		50 00	
	15	Owen Bros.	overcharge allowance	102		10 00	

SALES RETURNS AND ALLOWANCES JOURNAL   PAGE   1

Illustration 62a – Sales Returns and Allowances Journal

In Job 58, you learned that whenever a credit customer returns merchandise, the wholesaler prepares a form called a *credit memorandum*.

Credit Memorandum
LEE WHOLESALE CO.
615 Chestnut Street
Philadelphia, PA 19106

No. 101
Date October 12, 19--

TO: CRANE & CO.
      1212 Lombard Street
      Philadelphia, PA 19147

WE HAVE CREDITED YOUR ACCOUNT AS FOLLOWS:

Description	Unit Price		Total	
Damaged goods: 10 prs. sneakers, KD01	5	00	50	00

Illustration 62b – Credit Memorandum

Credit
Memorandum

↓

Sales Returns
and Allowances
Journal

↓

Customer's
Account

This form is prepared in duplicate. The original copy is sent to the customer to show that a record has been made of the return. The duplicate copy is kept by the wholesaler and used to record the information in the Sales Returns and Allowances Journal.

Occasionally, the customer may prefer to keep damaged merchandise if the amount of the sale is reduced by giving an allowance. In this case a credit memorandum is issued for the amount of the allowance. You may also send a credit memorandum to a customer as an allowance to correct an overcharge in the sales invoice.

Credit memorandums are issued, therefore, for two purposes:

> 1. To inform a customer that less is owed because of a *return* of merchandise.
> 2. To inform a customer that less is owed because of an *allowance*.

This is why the book in which we record credit memorandums is called a Sales Returns and Allowances Journal. After being recorded in the Sales Returns and Allowances Journal, each credit is posted to the *Credit* column of the Accounts Receivable Ledger. Then the check mark and postmark are made in the proper columns.

The following sample problem will show you how the Sales Returns and Allowances Journal is used.

SAMPLE PROBLEM

The following customers' accounts show the sales made by the Lee Wholesale Co. during the month:

NAME *Crane & Co.*   TERMS *30 days*
ADDRESS *1212 Lombard Street, Philadelphia, PA 19147*

DATE	ITEM	POST. REF.	DEBIT	CREDIT	BALANCE
19-- Oct. 3	*Mdse.*	S1	240 00		240 00
11	*Mdse.*	S1	410 00		650 00

NAME *Judson Stores*   TERMS *30 days*
ADDRESS *81 Arch Street, Philadelphia, PA 19106*

DATE	ITEM	POST. REF.	DEBIT	CREDIT	BALANCE
19-- Oct. 8	*Mdse.*	S1	120 00		120 00
18	*Mdse.*	S1	370 00		490 00

NAME *Owen Bros.*   TERMS *30 days*
ADDRESS *1926 Fuller Street, Philadelphia, PA 19152*

DATE	ITEM	POST. REF.	DEBIT	CREDIT	BALANCE
19-- Oct. 2	*Mdse.*	S1	530 00		530 00
10	*Mdse.*	S1	250 00		780 00

According to the duplicate credit memorandums, the sales returns and allowances listed on the next page were made during the month.

Oct. 12   Issued credit memorandum #101 for $50.00 to Crane & Co. for damaged merchandise they returned. (The credit memorandum is shown on page 405, Illustration 62b.)

15   Issued credit memorandum #102 for $10.00 to Owen Bros. as an allowance to correct an overcharge on invoice of October 10.

23   Issued credit memorandum #103 for $70.00 to Judson Stores for merchandise returned because the wrong styles were shipped.

26   Issued credit memorandum #104 for $30.00 to Crane & Co. for damaged merchandise they returned.

After this information was recorded, the Sales Returns and Allowances Journal and the customers' accounts showed the following:

SALES RETURNS AND ALLOWANCES JOURNAL   PAGE 1

DATE		CUSTOMER'S NAME	EXPLANATION	CREDIT MEMO NO.	POST. REF.	AMOUNT
Oct. 19--	12	Crane & Co.	damaged mdse.	101	✓	50 00
	15	Owen Bros.	overcharge allowance	102	✓	10 00
	23	Judson Stores	wrong style	103	✓	70 00
	26	Crane & Co.	damaged mdse.	104	✓	30 00
						160 00
						160 00

NAME   Crane & Co.   TERMS: 30 days
ADDRESS   1212 Lombard Street, Philadelphia, PA 19147

DATE		ITEM	POST. REF.	DEBIT	CREDIT	BALANCE
Oct. 19--	3	Mdse.	S1	240 00		240 00
	11	Mdse.	S1	410 00		650 00
	12	Return	SR1		50 00	600 00
	26	Return	SR1		30 00	570 00

NAME   Judson Stores   TERMS 30 days
ADDRESS   81 Arch Street, Philadelphia, PA 19106

DATE		ITEM	POST. REF.	DEBIT	CREDIT	BALANCE
Oct. 19--	8	Mdse.	S1	120 00		120 00
	18	Mdse.	S1	370 00		490 00
	23	Return	SR1		70 00	420 00

NAME   Owen Bros.   TERMS 30 days
ADDRESS   1926 Fuller Street, Philadelphia, PA 19152

DATE		ITEM	POST. REF.	DEBIT	CREDIT	BALANCE
Oct. 19--	2	Mdse.	S1	530 00		530 00
	10	Mdse.	S1	250 00		780 00
	15	Allowance	SR1		10 00	770 00

Here are the steps that were followed:

Step 1: Record credit memos in Sales Returns and Allowances Journal.

The returns and allowances were recorded in the Sales Returns and Allowances Journal from the information appearing on the duplicate credit memorandums.

Step 2: Post to customers' accounts.

Sales returns = Credits

After the returns and allowances were recorded in the Sales Returns and Allowances Journal, the amounts were transferred, or posted, to the *Credit* column of the customers' accounts and subtracted to find the new balance.

For example, since Crane & Co. returned $50.00 of damaged merchandise on October 12, this amount was posted to the Credit column in their account and subtracted from the old balance of $650.00 to get the new balance of $600.00 ($650 − $50 = $600.00).

SR1 = Page 1 of Sales Returns and Allowances Journal

As each posting was made, a check mark was entered in the Sales Returns and Allowances Journal to show that the posting had been made. At the same time the postmark, SR1, was entered in the customer's account to show that the amount came from page 1 of the Sales Returns and Allowances Journal.

Step 3: Total the Sales Returns and Allowances Journal.

At the end of the month, after all the postings had been made, the amounts in the Sales Returns and Allowances Journal were added to find the total returns and allowances for the month. The total was pencil footed, readded, and inked in.

As usual, the double ruling under the total is repeated on the same line in the *Date* column.

PRACTICE PROBLEMS

Problem 1

Directions:
a) Copy the customers' accounts shown on page 409.
b) Record the sales returns and allowances listed below and on page 409 in a Sales Returns and Allowances Journal: (Use the form shown in Illustration 62a on page 405.)

Aug. 13   Issued credit memorandum #71 for $50.00 to Jackson & Kelly for damaged merchandise returned.

15   Issued credit memorandum #72 for $25.00 to Westway Corporation for damaged merchandise returned.

16   Issued credit memorandum #73 for $45.00 to Mayfair & Co., Inc. as an allowance to correct an overcharge on the invoice of August 9.

20   Issued credit memorandum #74 for $80.00 to Jackson & Kelly as an allowance for an error in shipment.

27   Issued credit memorandum #75 for $65.00 to Mayfair & Co., Inc. for damaged merchandise returned.

NAME *Jackson & Kelly*   TERMS *30 days*
ADDRESS *59 Odell Avenue, Yonkers, NY 10701*

DATE	ITEM	POST. REF.	DEBIT	CREDIT	BALANCE	
19-- Aug. 2	Mdse.	S1	240 00		240 00	
10	Mdse.	S1	430 00		670 00	

NAME *Mayfair & Co., Inc.*   TERMS *30 days*
ADDRESS *182 Riverdale Avenue, Yonkers, NY 10705*

DATE	ITEM	POST. REF.	DEBIT	CREDIT	BALANCE	
19-- Aug. 3	Mdse.	S1	350 00		350 00	
9	Mdse.	S1	510 00		860 00	

NAME *Westway Corporation*   TERMS *30 days*
ADDRESS *414 Lake Avenue, Rochester, NY 14608*

DATE	ITEM	POST. REF.	DEBIT	CREDIT	BALANCE	
19-- Aug. 7	Mdse.	S1	270 00		270 00	
13	Mdse.	S1	120 00		390 00	

c) Post from the Sales Returns and Allowances Journal to the *Credit* column of the customers' accounts. Enter a check mark in the Sales and Returns and Allowances Journal and the postmark, SR1, in the accounts as you post.

d) Find the total returns and allowances for the month by adding the amounts in the Sales Returns and Allowances Journal.

Problem 2

Directions:

a) Copy the customers' accounts on page 410.

b) Record the sales returns and allowances listed on page 410 in a Sales Returns and Allowances Journal (Page 4).

NAME	*Abrams & Gerson*			TERMS	*30 days*	
ADDRESS	*175 Capitol Avenue, Norfolk, VA 23506*					

DATE	ITEM	POST. REF.	DEBIT	CREDIT	BALANCE
19-- Apr. 5	Mdse.	S6	510 00		510 00
7	Mdse.	S6	180 00		690 00

NAME	*Clarke Bros.*			TERMS	*30 days*	
ADDRESS	*319 Forest Avenue, Richmond, VA 23223*					

DATE	ITEM	POST. REF.	DEBIT	CREDIT	BALANCE
19-- Apr. 4	Mdse.	S6	420 00		420 00
10	Mdse.	S6	145 00		565 00

NAME	*Greenbrier Stores*			TERMS	*30 days*	
ADDRESS	*1105 N. Utah Street, Arlington, VA 22201*					

DATE	ITEM	POST. REF.	DEBIT	CREDIT	BALANCE
19-- Apr. 3	Mdse.	S6	235 00		235 00
12	Mdse.	S6	350 00		585 00

April 11 Issued a credit memorandum for $30.00 to Abrams & Gerson for damaged merchandise returned. (Start with credit memorandum #21.)

13 Issued a credit memorandum for $55.00 to Clarke Bros. as an allowance for an overcharge on the invoice of April 10.

17 Issued a credit memorandum for $35.00 to Greenbrier Stores for damaged merchandise returned.

19 Issued a credit memorandum for $60.00 to Clarke Bros. as an allowance for damaged merchandise which they kept.

26 Issued a credit memorandum for $15.00 to Abrams & Gerson as an allowance for a shortage in the shipment of April 7.

c) Post from the Sales Returns and Allowances Journal to the *Credit* column of the customers' accounts. Use the postmark (SR4).
d) Total the Sales Returns and Allowances Journal.

Problem 3

Directions:
a) Copy the customers' accounts at the top of page 411.
b) Record the sales returns and allowances on page 411 in a Sales Returns and Allowances Journal (Page 9).

NAME   Kimberly & Sons   TERMS 30 days
ADDRESS 1625 N. Elm Street, Spokane, WA 99205

DATE	ITEM	POST. REF.	DEBIT	CREDIT	BALANCE
19-- Sept. 6	Mdse.	S11	2 1 5 00		2 1 5 00
15	Mdse.	S11	1 5 4 00		3 6 9 00

NAME   Madison & Co.   TERMS 30 days
ADDRESS 120 S. Hudson Street, Seattle, WA 98134

DATE	ITEM	POST. REF.	DEBIT	CREDIT	BALANCE
19-- Sept. 1	Mdse.	S1	4 1 2 25		4 1 2 25
8	Mdse.	S1	1 6 3 50		5 7 5 75

NAME   J. Webster, Inc.   TERMS 30 days
ADDRESS 714 Alameda Avenue, Tacoma, WA 98466

DATE	ITEM	POST. REF.	DEBIT	CREDIT	BALANCE
19-- Sept. 8	Mdse.	S11	3 1 8 20		3 1 8 20
14	Mdse.	S11	2 4 0 00		5 5 8 20

Sept. 11   Issued a credit memorandum for $42.50 to Madison & Co. for
           damaged merchandise returned. (Start with credit memorandum
           #41.)
     18   Issued a credit memorandum for $26.10 to J. Webster, Inc. for
           damaged merchandise returned.
     21   Issued a credit memorandum for $19.30 to Kimberly & Sons as an
           allowance for an overcharge on the invoice of September 15.
     25   Issued a credit memorandum for $24.90 to J. Webster, Inc. for
           damaged merchandise returned.
     28   Issued a credit memorandum for $38.50 to Madison & Co. as an
           allowance for merchandise damaged in shipment.

c) Post from the Sales Returns and Allowances Journal to the *Credit* column
   of the customers' accounts. Use the postmark (SR9).
d) Total the Sales Returns and Allowances Journal.

Problem 4

Directions:
a) Copy the customers' accounts at the top of page 412.

NAME   *Corral Stores*   TERMS   *30 days*
ADDRESS   *2020 East Avenue, Austin, TX 78705*

DATE	ITEM	POST. REF.	DEBIT	CREDIT	BALANCE
19-- June 4	Mdse.	S9	325 00		325 00
12	Mdse.	S9	278 15		603 15

NAME   *Gallagher Bros.*   TERMS   *30 days*
ADDRESS   *4715 Denton Street, Dallas, TX 75219*

DATE	ITEM	POST. REF.	DEBIT	CREDIT	BALANCE
19-- June 6	Mdse.	S9	463 90		463 90
8	Mdse.	S9	151 00		614 90

NAME   *Sanchez & Wilson*   TERMS   *30 days*
ADDRESS   *217 Bowie Street, El Paso, TX 79905*

DATE	ITEM	POST. REF.	DEBIT	CREDIT	BALANCE
19-- June 5	Mdse.	S9	231 80		231 80
15	Mdse.	S9	187 15		418 95

b) Record the following sales returns and allowances in a Sales Returns and Allowances Journal (Page 6):

June 11   Issued a credit memorandum for $16.25 to Gallagher Bros. for damaged merchandise returned. (Start with credit memorandum #91.)

      18   Issued a credit memorandum for $32.70 to Sanchez & Wilson as an allowance for damaged merchandise.

      19   Issued a credit memorandum for $27.30 to Corral Stores as an allowance to correct an overcharge on an invoice.

      22   Issued a credit memorandum for $42.10 to Sanchez & Wilson for damaged merchandise returned.

      28   Issued a credit memorandum for $18.50 to Corral Stores as an allowance for damaged merchandise.

c) Post from the Sales Returns and Allowances Journal to the *Credit* column of the customers' accounts. Use the postmark (SR6).

d) Total the Sales Returns and Allowances Journal.

Practicing Related Arithmetic

Find the date on which the following invoices are due:

	Date of Invoice	Terms		Date of Invoice	Terms
1)	Feb. 3	20 days	6)	Oct. 3	60 days
2)	April 17	30 days	7)	March 18	60 days
3)	Sept. 29	20 days	8)	June 20	90 days
4)	July 24	30 days	9)	Aug. 5	90 days
5)	March 12	30 days	10)	May 26	90 days

AIM

To practice using the Sales Journal, the Cash Receipts Journal, the Sales Returns and Allowances Journal, and the Accounts Receivable Ledger.

EXPLANATION

You are now using four books to keep a record of transactions with customers to whom merchandise is sold on credit. The four books are:

1. The Sales Journal in which you redord all the duplicate sales invoices.
2. The Cash Receipts Journal in which you record all collections from customers.
3. The Sales Returns and Allowances Journal in which you record all the duplicate credit memorandums.
4. The Accounts Receivable Ledger in which you keep the customers' accounts.

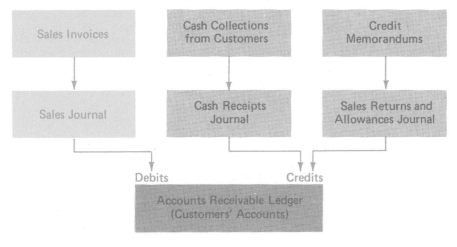

The debits in the customers' accounts are posted from the Sales Journal. The credits in these accounts are posted from the Cash Receipts Journal and from the Sales Returns and Allowances Journal.

You have learned that there are two different forms used for customers' accounts. As you know, some businesses prefer to use a three-column form as shown below:

Three-column account form

| NAME | Scott & De Carlo | | | TERMS | 20 days |

| NAME | Scott & De Carlo | TERMS 20 days |
| ADDRESS | 490 Broadway, New York, NY 10012 | |

DATE	ITEM	POST. REF.	DEBIT	CREDIT	BALANCE
Dec. 7	Mdse.	S1	400.00		400.00
14	Mdse.	S1	300.00		700.00
27	Cash	CR1		400.00	300.00
31	Return	SR1		20.00	280.00

In this three-column form of account the last amount in the Balance column represents the amount due at the end of the month.

Other businesses prefer the "T" form of account which you have used before.

"T" account form

| NAME | Scott & De Carlo | TERMS 20 days |
| ADDRESS | 490 Broadway, New York, NY 10012 | |

DATE	ITEM	POST. REF.	DEBIT	DATE	ITEM	POST. REF.	CREDIT
Dec. 7	Mdse.	S1	400.00	Dec. 27	Cash	CR1	400.00
14	Mdse. 700.00 420.00 280.00	S1	300.00 700.00	31	Return	SR1	20.00 420.00

You will recall that in this form of account, the balance due at the end of the month is found by pencil footing the account and subtracting the credits from the debits. It is for this reason that the debit side of the Scott & DeCarlo account shows the following subtraction problem:

$700.00
-420.00
$280.00

In this job you will make use of the Sales Journal, the Cash Receipts Journal, the Sales Returns and Allowances Journal, and the "T" form of customers' accounts. Inasmuch as you will be posting from more than one journal to the customers' accounts, it is important to remember that postings are made at the end of each day and must follow the order of the dates.

Postings must follow order of dates

PRACTICE PROBLEMS

Problem 1

You are the assistant bookkeeper for the Acme Wholesale Co.

Directions:

a) Open accounts for the three customers shown below. Use the "T" form of account.

Customer	Address	Terms
Benson, Inc.	64 Canal St., New York, NY 10002	On account
Gallo Bros.	128 Bowery, New York, NY 10013	20 days
McCoy & Roe	92 Park Ave., New York, NY 10017	20 days

b) Record the following transactions in the proper journal. This means that as you read each transaction you must decide whether to record it in the Sales Journal, the Cash Receipts Journal, or the Sales Returns and Allowances Journal. As soon as you have recorded the transaction in the proper journal you must post immediately to the customer's account. Use page 1 for all journals.

Oct. 1   Sold merchandise to Benson, Inc. for $635.00. (Enter this transaction in the Sales Journal. Start with invoice #101. Record all sales in the Sales Journal and number the invoices in order.)   *Post after each transaction*

3   Sold merchandise to Gallo Bros. for $520.00.

4   Sold merchandise to Benson, Inc. for $360.00.

11   Received a check for $250.00 from Benson, Inc. to apply on account. (This is a cash collection and it is the first transaction to be recorded in the Cash Receipts Journal.)

14   Received a check for $100.00 from Benson, Inc. to apply on account.   *Record postmarks*

17   Sent a credit memorandum for $40.00 to Gallo Bros. for damaged merchandise returned. (Enter this transaction in the Sales Returns and Allowances Journal. Start with credit memorandum #71. Record all other returns and allowances in a similar manner, numbering the credit memorandums in order.)

18   Sent a credit memorandum for $15.00 to Benson, Inc. for damaged merchandise returned.

19   Sold merchandise to McCoy & Roe for $755.00.

22   Sold merchandise to Gallo Bros. for $420.00.

23   Received a check for $480.00 from Gallo Bros. to settle the balance due on the invoice of October 3.

25   Sent a credit memorandum for $24.00 to McCoy & Roe as an allowance to correct an overcharge on the invoice of October 19.

26   Received a check for $450.00 from Benson, Inc. to apply on account.

30   Sold merchandise to Gallo Bros. for $645.00.

c) Total the Sales Journal, the Cash Receipts Journal, and the Sales Returns and Allowances Journal.

d) Pencil foot and find the balance in each account.

e) Prepare a Schedule of Accounts Receivable on October 31. Did you get a total of $1,976.00?

Problem 2

You are employed by the Opus Wholesale Co. as an assistant bookkeeper.

Directions:

a) Open accounts for the three customers shown below. Use the "T" account form.

Customer	Address	Terms
Bianco Bros.	410 W. Martin St., Raleigh, NC 27603	On account
E. Nesbit, Inc.	1225 Jackson St., Raleigh, NC 27605	10 days
O'Brien & Sons	552 Elm St., Raleigh, NC 27604	20 days

b) Record the following transactions using a Sales Journal, a Cash Receipts Journal, and a Sales Returns and Allowances Journal. Be sure to post daily. Use page 1 for all journals.

Aug. 1   Sold merchandise to Bianco Bros. for $710.00. (Start with invoice #401.)

3   Sold merchandise to E. Nesbit, Inc. for $485.00.

6   Sold merchandise to Bianco Bros. for $655.00.

11   Received a check for $350.00 from Bianco Bros. to apply on account.

13   Received a check for $275.00 from E. Nesbit, Inc. to apply on account.

16   Sent a credit memorandum for $35.00 to Bianco Bros. for damaged merchandise returned. (Start with credit memorandum #81.)

17   Sent a credit memorandum for $50.00 to E. Nesbit, Inc. as an allowance to correct an overcharge on the invoice of August 3.

20   Sold merchandise to O'Brien & Sons for $715.00.

22   Sold merchandise to E. Nesbit, Inc. for $430.00.

24   Received a check for $160.00 from E. Nesbit, Inc. to settle the balance due on the invoice of August 3.

27   Sent a credit memorandum for $65.00 to O'Brien & Sons for damaged merchandise returned.

29   Received a check for $650.00 from Bianco Bros. to apply on account.

31   Sold merchandise to E. Nesbit, Inc. for $385.00.

c) Total the Sales Journal, the Cash Receipts Journal, and the Sales Returns and Allowances Journal.

d) Pencil foot and find the balance in each account.

e) Prepare a Schedule of Accounts Receivable on August 31. Did you get a total of $1,795.00?

Problem 3

You are employed by the United Wholesale Co. as an assistant bookkeeper.

Directions:

a) Open accounts for the three customers shown on page 417. Use the "T" account form.

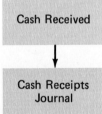
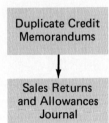

Duplicate Sales Invoices → Sales Journal → Cash Received → Cash Receipts Journal → Duplicate Credit Memorandums → Sales Returns and Allowances Journal

Customer	Address	Terms
Allen Shops	340 Chapel St., New Haven, CT 06511	On account
Lewis, Inc.	1102 Main St., Hartford, CT 06103	10 days
Scanlon & Co.	890 State St., Bridgeport, CT 06605	20 days

b) Record the following transactions using a Sales Journal, a Cash Receipts Journal, and a Sales Returns and Allowances Journal. Be sure to post daily. Use page 1 for all journals.

Mar. 1 Sold merchandise to Allen Shops for $765.00. (Start with invoice #301.)   *Post daily*

2 Sold merchandise to Lewis, Inc. for $490.00.

5 Sold merchandise to Allen Shops for $530.00.

12 Received a check for $350.00 from Lewis, Inc. to apply on account.

14 Sent a credit memorandum for $55.00 to Allen Shops for damaged merchandise returned. (Start with credit memorandum #41.)   *Record postmarks*

16 Sent a credit memorandum for $35.00 to Lewis, Inc. as an allowance for merchandise damaged in shipment.

20 Sold merchandise to Scanlon & Co. for $435.00.

22 Sold merchandise to Lewis, Inc. for $315.00.

23 Received a check for $105.00 from Lewis, Inc. for the balance due on the invoice of March 2.

26 Sent a credit memorandum for $75.00 to Scanlon & Co. for damaged merchandise returned.

28 Received a check for $850.00 from Allen Shops to apply on account.

30 Sold merchandise to Lewis, Inc. for $225.00.

c) Total the Sales Journal, the Cash Receipts Journal, and the Sales Returns and Allowances Journal.

d) Pencil foot and find the balance in each account.

e) Prepare a Schedule of Accounts Receivable on March 31. Did you get a total of $1,290.00?

Problem 4

You are employed by the Dow Wholesale Co. as an assistant bookkeeper.

Directions:

a) Open accounts for the three customers shown below. Use the "T" account form.

Customer	Address	Terms
Center Stores	15 La Paz Dr., Pasadena, CA 91107	On account
Grant & Sons	307 Market St., Oakland, CA 94607	10 days
Taylor, Inc.	121 Venice Blvd., Los Angeles, CA 90015	20 days

b) Record the transactions on page 418 using a Sales Journal, a Cash Receipts Journal, and a Sales Returns and Allowances Journal. Be sure to post daily. Use page 1 for all journals.

Post daily

June 1   Sold merchandise to Center Stores for $412.00. (Start with invoice #601.)

4   Sold merchandise to Grant & Sons for $846.00.

6   Sold merchandise to Center Stores for $471.00.

11   Received a check for $250.00 from Center Stores to apply on account.

14   Received a check for $175.00 from Grant & Sons to apply on account.

Record postmarks

15   Sent a credit memorandum for $32.00 to Grant & Sons for damaged merchandise returned. (Start with credit memorandum #21.)

18   Sent a credit memorandum for $18.00 to Center Stores as an allowance for an overcharge on the invoice of June 6.

21   Sold merchandise to Taylor, Inc. for $644.00.

22   Sold merchandise to Grant & Sons for $362.00.

25   Received a check for $639.00 from Grant & Sons to settle the balance due on the invoice of June 4.

26   Sent a credit memorandum for $57.00 to Taylor, Inc. for damaged merchandise they returned.

27   Received a check for $450.00 from Center Stores to apply on account.

29   Sold merchandise to Grant & Sons for $263.00.

c) Total the Sales Journal, the Cash Receipts Journal, and the Sales Returns and Allowances Journal.

d) Pencil foot and find the balance in each account.

e) Prepare a Schedule of Accounts Receivable on June 30. Did you get a total of $1,377.00?

Copy and find the balance of the following customers' accounts:

Practicing Related Arithmetic

Tom Abbott		Jane Brock	
Debit	Credit	Debit	Credit
506 40	35 30	274 25	150 00
2,183 20	471 10	526 30	124 25
1,417 85	2,183 20	412 75	526 30
732 15	450 00	1,345 05	15 90
354 90	167 85	2,631 50	396 85
265 75		179 20	

AIM

To practice preparing statements of account.

EXPLANATION

"They never forget to remind us what we owe"

In the unit entitled "Record Keeping for Retail Salesclerks" you learned that at the end of each month, the retailer mails a statement of account to each charge customer.

The wholesaler follows the same procedure. At the end of each month a statement of account is mailed to each customer. The statement of account serves two purposes:

1. Customers can check the statement of account against their own records for possible errors.

2. The customers are reminded of the amounts they owe the wholesaler.

SAMPLE PROBLEM

On February 28, Bristol Wholesale Co. sent a statement of account to Fenway & Co., a customer, whose account revealed the information shown on page 420.

NAME	*Fenway & Co.*						TERMS *10 days*	
ADDRESS	*718 Mission Street, San Francisco, CA 94103*							
DATE	ITEM	POST. REF.	DEBIT	DATE	ITEM	POST. REF.	CREDIT	
Feb. 19-- 5	*Mdse.*	S1	420 00	*Feb.* 19-- 15	*Cash*	CR1	420 00	
14	*Mdse.*	S1	250 00	20	*Return*	SR1	30 00	
23	*Mdse.*	S1	510 00	24	*Cash*	CR1	220 00	
26	*Mdse.*	S1	340 00				670 00	

Bristol Wholesale Co. mailed this statement of account to Fenway & Co.:

Balance in customer's account must agree with balance due on statement

STATEMENT OF ACCOUNT
BRISTOL WHOLESALE CO.
505 Lombard Street
San Francisco, CA 94133

TO: Fenway & Co.   February 28, 19--
    718 Mission Street
    San Francisco, CA 94103

DEBITS

Feb.	5	Mdse.	420 00	
	14	Mdse.	250 00	
	23	Mdse.	510 00	
	26	Mdse.	340 00	
		Total Debits		1,520 00

CREDITS

Feb.	15	Cash	420 00	
	20	Return	30 00	
	24	Cash	220 00	
		Total Credits		670 00
		Balance Due		850 00

The balance due of $850.00 agrees with the balance shown in the Fenway & Co. account. The balance was found by subtracting the total credits from the total debits as follows:

Total debits	$1,520.00
minus	
Total credits	− 670.00
equals	
Balance due	=$ 850.00

PRACTICE PROBLEM

You are employed by the Salem Wholesale Co., 210 Park Ave., Norfolk, Virginia. Your job as the assistant to the bookkeeper is to prepare statements of account from the Accounts Receivable Ledger.

Directions: Prepare a statement of account for each of the customers whose accounts appear below and on pages 422–423. Date all statements April 30.

Account #1

NAME *a. Bates, Inc.* TERMS *20 days*

ADDRESS *616 Cannon Street, Raleigh, NC 27603*

DATE	ITEM	POST. REF.	DEBIT	DATE	ITEM	POST. REF.	CREDIT
19-- Apr. 3	Mdse.	S4	1 8 6 20	19-- Apr. 23	Cash	CR7	1 8 6 20
17	Mdse.	S4	3 1 4 25	24	Return	SR3	2 5 00
26	Mdse.	S4	2 7 0 50				

Account #2

NAME *Carver & Benton* TERMS *20 days*

ADDRESS *23 Bragg Street, Raleigh, NC 27601*

DATE	ITEM	POST. REF.	DEBIT	DATE	ITEM	POST. REF.	CREDIT
19-- Apr. 7	Mdse.	S4	5 2 8 40	19-- Apr. 11	Allowance	SR3	5 0 00
12	Mdse.	S4	8 3 1 75	27	Cash	CR7	4 7 8 40
25	Mdse.	S4	3 7 2 50				

Total debits
−Total credits
=Balance due

Account #3

NAME *Derby Stores* TERMS *20 days*

ADDRESS *1572 Early Street, Norfolk, VA 23502*

DATE	ITEM	POST. REF.	DEBIT	DATE	ITEM	POST. REF.	CREDIT
19-- Apr. 4	Mdse.	S4	6 3 4 35	19-- Apr. 24	Cash	CR7	6 3 4 35
6	Mdse.	S4	1 1 6 2 15	25	Allowance	SR3	7 2 00
13	Mdse.	S4	4 8 5 70	26	Cash	CR7	6 9 0 15
27	Mdse.	S4	5 4 8 25				

Account #4

NAME	Lee & Co.						TERMS 20 days	
ADDRESS	468 Blanco Road, San Antonio, TX 78212							
DATE	ITEM	POST. REF.	DEBIT	DATE	ITEM	POST. REF.	CREDIT	
Apr. 19-- 6	Mdse.	S4	398 70	Apr. 19-- 9	Return	SR3	40 00	
10	Mdse.	S4	823 45	12	Return	SR3	35 00	
23	Mdse.	S4	1 461 50	26	Cash	CR7	323 70	
				30	Cash	CR7	500 00	

Account #5

NAME	McDonald Bros						TERMS 20 days	
ADDRESS	5304 Pardee Street, Houston, TX 77026							
DATE	ITEM	POST. REF.	DEBIT	DATE	ITEM	POST. REF.	CREDIT	
Apr. 19-- 2	Mdse	S4	714 65	Apr. 19-- 23	Cash	CR7	714 65	
5	Mdse	S4	1 272 10	24	Return	SR3	85 00	
17	Mdse	S4	308 55	25	Cash	CR7	1 187 10	
26	Mdse.	S4	231 20					

Total debits
−Total credits
=Balance due

Account #6

NAME	Pecos Corporation						TERMS 20 days	
ADDRESS	4816 Grove Street, Fort Worth, TX 76118							
DATE	ITEM	POST. REF.	DEBIT	DATE	ITEM	POST. REF.	CREDIT	
Apr. 19-- 5	Mdse.	S4	1 423 40	Apr. 19-- 12	Return	SR3	45 00	
9	Mdse.	S4	378 50	25	Cash	CR7	1 378 40	
20	Mdse.	S4	565 15	29	Cash	CR7	150 00	
30	Mdse.	S4	784 60					

Account #7

NAME	Renando Co., Inc.						TERMS 20 days	
ADDRESS	610 Castle Street, Memphis, TN 38107							
DATE	ITEM	POST. REF.	DEBIT	DATE	ITEM	POST. REF.	CREDIT	
Apr. 19-- 3	Mdse.	S4	608 95	Apr. 19-- 10	Allowance	SR3	80 00	
7	Mdse.	S4	1 752 30	23	Cash	CR7	528 95	
24	Mdse.	S4	537 25	24	Return	SR3	65 00	
				27	Cash	CR7	687 30	

Account #8

			POST. REF.	DEBIT	DATE		ITEM	POST. REF.	CREDIT
NAME	Taggert & Reed						TERMS	20 days	
ADDRESS	730 Merritt Avenue, Nashville, TN 37203								
DATE		ITEM	POST. REF.	DEBIT	DATE		ITEM	POST. REF.	CREDIT
Apr. ¹⁹⁻⁻	4	Mdse.	S4	472 55	Apr. ¹⁹⁻⁻	24	Cash	CR7	472 55
	10	Mdse.	S4	736 40		26	Return	SR3	70 00
	20	Mdse.	S4	1 651 25		30	Cash	CR7	666 40
	30	Mdse.	S4	395 15					

JOB 65 | PREPARING STATEMENTS OF ACCOUNT

Copy and find the balance of the following customers' accounts:

Bradley & Co.		J. Coburn & Sons	
Debit	**Credit**	**Debit**	**Credit**
461|35	461|35	1,572|15	85|70
2,583|20	184|70	689|20	550|00
710|45	2,398|50	346|85	936|45
1,127|60	710|45	2,264|30	25|50
342	85	194	95	517	05	663	70
668	25		730	00	

Practicing Related Arithmetic

AIM

To learn how to prepare a statement of account with a beginning balance.

EXPLANATION

You probably have noticed in previous jobs that when you pencil footed customers' accounts many customers had not paid the total amount due by the end of the month.

You can understand how this happens when you realize that if merchandise is sold to a customer for $100.00 on March 28 with terms of 10 days, the bill will not be due until sometime in April. This means that on April 1 the customer will still owe $100.00.

If you were asked to prepare a statement of account for this customer at the end of April, you would have to start with the balance of $100.00 due on April 1. As a result, the statement of account would show not only the amounts of merchandise sold during the month of April but also the balance due on April 1.

SAMPLE PROBLEM

On January 31, the Jet Wholesale Co. sent a statement of account to the Marine Co., Inc., a customer, whose account is shown at the top of the next page.

NAME	*Marine Co., Inc.*					TERMS *20 days*	
ADDRESS	*710 N. Michigan Street, Chicago, IL 60611*						

DATE	ITEM	POST. REF.	DEBIT	DATE	ITEM	POST. REF.	CREDIT
19-- Jan. 1	Balance	✓	400 00	*19--* Jan. 4	Return	SR31	50 00
24	Mdse. *1500.00*	S51	200 00	5	Cash	CR61	350 00
26	Mdse. *400.00 1100.00*	S51	900 00				400 00
			1500 00				

The Jet Wholesale Co. mailed the following statement of account to the Marine Co., Inc.

STATEMENT OF ACCOUNT

Jet Wholesale Co.
175 W. Madison Street
Chicago, IL 60602

TO: Marine Co., Inc.   January 31, 19--
    710 N. Michigan Street
    Chicago, IL 60611

		DEBITS				
Jan.	1	Previous balance			400	00
	24	Mdse.	200	00		
	26	Mdse.	900	00		
		Total debits			1,100	00
		Total			1,500	00
		CREDITS				
Jan.	4	Return	50	00		
	5	Cash	350	00		
		Total credits			400	00
		Balance due			1,100	00

Start with previous balance

The balance of $400.00 shown in the Marine Co., Inc. account on January 1 represents the balance carried forward from the previous month.

The additional debits of $200.00 and $900.00 represent the additional sales made during the month of January.

The balance due of $1,100.00 shown as the final balance on the statement of account was found in the following way:

Balance of Jan. 1	$ 400.00
plus	
Debits	+ 1,100.00
equals	
Total	= 1,500.00
minus	
Credits	− 400.00
equals	
Balance due on Jan. 31	=$1,100.00

Notice that all of these amounts starting with the balance of January 1 were recorded in the second column of the statement of account.

PRACTICE PROBLEM

You are employed by the Bella Wholesale Co., Brooklyn, NY. It is your job as the assistant to the bookkeeper to prepare statements of account from the customers' accounts in the Accounts Receivable Ledger.

Directions: Prepare a statement of account for each customer whose account appears below. Date all statements January 31 and follow the form shown in the illustration on page 425.

Account #1

NAME *Booth & Weiss* TERMS *20 days*
ADDRESS *1501 West End Avenue, Brooklyn, NY 11235*

DATE		ITEM	POST. REF.	DEBIT	DATE		ITEM	POST. REF.	CREDIT	
Jan. 19--	1	Balance	✓	6 3 0 00	Jan. 19--	2	Cash	CR41	4 5 0 00	
	3	Mdse.	S31	4 4 5 25		4	Cash	CR41	1 8 0 00	
	22	Mdse.	S31	5 0 7 70		23	Cash	CR41	4 4 5 25	
	29	Mdse.	S31	2 8 1 80						

Account #2

NAME *Clark Bros.* TERMS *20 days*
ADDRESS *110 E. Tremont Avenue, Bronx, NY 10453*

DATE		ITEM	POST. REF.	DEBIT	DATE		ITEM	POST. REF.	CREDIT	
Jan. 19--	1	Balance	✓	7 2 5 00	Jan. 19--	4	Return	SR11	2 8 40	
	4	Mdse.	S31	8 1 9 85		5	Cash	CR41	6 9 6 60	
	15	Mdse.	S31	6 4 1 05		24	Cash	CR41	5 0 0 00	
	26	Mdse.	S31	5 8 2 30						

Account #3

NAME	Easton, Inc.							TERMS 20 days	
ADDRESS	117 E. Ferry Street, Buffalo, NY 14209								
DATE	ITEM	POST. REF.	DEBIT	DATE	ITEM	POST. REF.		CREDIT	
Jan. 19-- 1	Balance	✓	982 50	Jan. 19-- 5	Cash	CR41		450 00	
8	Mdse.	S31	479 15	8	Cash	CR41		532 00	
16	Mdse.	S31	810 95	28	Cash	CR41		250 00	
31	Mdse.	S31	1264 10						

Account #4

NAME	Grand Stores							TERMS 20 days	
ADDRESS	659 Madison Avenue, New York, NY 10021								
DATE	ITEM	POST. REF.	DEBIT	DATE	ITEM	POST. REF.		CREDIT	
Jan. 19-- 1	Balance	✓	715 40	Jan. 19-- 3	Cash	CR41		200 00	
5	Mdse.	S31	1460 70	5	Allowance	SR11		28 60	
12	Mdse.	S31	591 25	8	Cash	CR41		486 80	
25	Mdse.	S31	324 60	25	Cash	CR41		960 70	

Previous balance
+Total debits
=Total
−Total credits
=Balance due

Account #5

NAME	Hudson & Co.							TERMS 20 days	
ADDRESS	19 Lyell Avenue, Rochester, NY 14608								
DATE	ITEM	POST. REF.	DEBIT	DATE	ITEM	POST. REF.		CREDIT	
Jan. 19-- 1	Balance	✓	726 50	Jan. 19-- 9	Cash	CR41		726 50	
2	Mdse.	S31	483 35	11	Return	SR11		47 70	
17	Mdse.	S31	818 40	22	Cash	CR41		435 65	
19	Mdse.	S31	562 15	23	Return	SR11		26 25	

Account #6

NAME	Kirby Bros.							TERMS 20 days	
ADDRESS	1107 Burnet Avenue, Syracuse, NY 13203								
DATE	ITEM	POST. REF.	DEBIT	DATE	ITEM	POST. REF.		CREDIT	
Jan. 19-- 1	Balance	✓	830 40	Jan. 19-- 3	Return	SR11		56 10	
9	Mdse.	S31	581 65	8	Cash	CR41		774 30	
17	Mdse.	S31	362 75	11	Return	SR11		38 60	
				29	Cash	CR41		543 05	

Account #7

NAME	Knox Co., Inc.					TERMS	20 days	
ADDRESS	190 S. Broadway, Yonkers, NY 10705							

DATE		ITEM	POST. REF.	DEBIT	DATE		ITEM	POST. REF.	CREDIT
19-- Jan.	1	Balance	✓	610 30	19-- Jan.	5	Cash	CR41	610 30
	10	Mdse.	S31	846 95		10	Allowance	SR11	52 50
	11	Mdse.	S31	571 40		30	Cash	CR41	794 45
	22	Mdse.	S31	622 45		31	Cash	CR41	250 00

Account #8

NAME	Park Shops & Co.					TERMS	20 days	
ADDRESS	733 Merrick Avenue, Hempstead, NY 11554							

DATE		ITEM	POST. REF.	DEBIT	DATE		ITEM	POST. REF.	CREDIT
19-- Jan.	1	Balance	✓	843 60	19-- Jan.	5	Allowance	SR11	82 40
	4	Mdse.	S31	597 25		10	Cash	CR41	761 20
	18	Mdse.	S31	915 80		24	Cash	CR41	597 25
	25	Mdse.	S31	765 45		26	Return	SR11	68 60

Previous balance
+Total debits
=Total
−Total credits
=Balance due

Account #9

NAME	Reed & Olsen					TERMS	20 days	
ADDRESS	429 Henry Street, Brooklyn, NY 11231							

DATE		ITEM	POST. REF.	DEBIT	DATE		ITEM	POST. REF.	CREDIT
19-- Jan.	1	Balance	✓	786 50	19-- Jan.	4	Cash	CR41	786 50
	5	Mdse.	S31	521 85		11	Return	SR11	115 20
	9	Mdse.	S31	458 25		25	Cash	CR41	406 65
	30	Mdse.	S31	814 10		29	Cash	CR41	350 00

Account #10

NAME	Troy Products, Inc.					TERMS	20 days	
ADDRESS	255 Broadway, Albany, NY 12202							

DATE		ITEM	POST. REF.	DEBIT	DATE		ITEM	POST. REF.	CREDIT
19-- Jan.	1	Balance	✓	1562 30	19-- Jan.	8	Cash	CR41	562 30
	3	Mdse.	S31	721 25		15	Cash	CR41	1000 00
	23	Mdse.	S31	289 70		17	Return	SR11	75 90
	26	Mdse.	S31	470 15		23	Cash	CR41	645 35

UNIT 9

RECORD KEEPING FOR A PAYROLL DEPARTMENT

UNIT 9

JOB 66 | HANDLING TIME CARDS

Practicing
Related
Arithmetic

Copy the following problems on a sheet of paper and find the answers:

	(1)	(2)	(3)	(4)	(5)
	7	8	6½	7¼	5¼
	6	7½	5¼	6¾	8½
	6½	5¼	8¼	8	7¾
	8½	7¼	7	8¼	8½
	+5	+4½	+8	+7¾	+4¾

AIMS

1. To become acquainted with the information on time cards.
2. To learn how to find the exact number of hours for which a worker should be paid.

EXPLANATION

Businesses find it helpful to install time clocks like the one below for keeping accurate records of the hours worked by each employee.

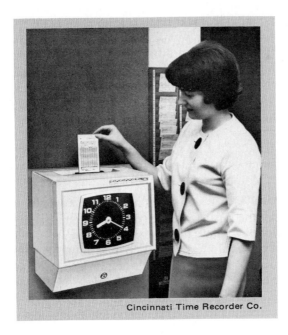

Cincinnati Time Recorder Co.

Each employee is given a time card like the one shown below. The information recorded on the card will be whatever the employer requires and will vary for different employers. On the next page is a time card that has been completed by an employee named Maria Romez.

Week Ending _____

No.

Name _____

DAY	IN	OUT	IN	OUT	IN	OUT	TOTAL
M							
TU							
W							
TH							
F							

TOTAL TIME _____ HOURS

RATE PER HOUR _____

TOTAL WAGES _____

Illustration 66a — A Time Card

Near the time clock, two racks are provided to hold the time cards, an "OUT" rack and an "IN" rack. Each employee's card is numbered. At the beginning of each week, the payroll clerk arranges the time cards in numerical sequence (1, 2, 3, and so forth) in the "OUT" rack. As you can see in Illustration 66b on page 433, Maria Romez has been given #23. Each morning when Maria Romez arrives, she goes to the "OUT" rack, removes her card (which is in numerical order), and inserts it in the opening in the time clock. She pushes the card down and the time clock automatically stamps it. In business, this is known as *punching* the time card. As you can see, the time clock has registered 8:00 a.m. for Monday. After punching the card, Maria takes it out of the clock and puts it in the "IN" rack, in the slot numbered 23. This shows that Maria has checked in for the day's work.

At lunchtime, Maria goes to the "IN" rack, removes her card, and inserts it into the clock. She pushes the card down, printing *12:00* for "OUT" after 8:00 a.m. for Monday. Maria then puts the card in the "OUT" rack slot #23. This shows that she has gone out to lunch. Returning from lunch, she repeats the same process she went through in the morning. She punches the time card and puts it in the "IN" rack. (As you can see, she returned from lunch at 1:00 p.m.) When Maria goes home, she punches her card and puts it in the "OUT" rack. According to the card, Maria left at 5:00 p.m.

	Week Ending _July 11, 19--_						
	No. _23_						
	Name _Maria Romez_						

DAY	IN	OUT	IN	OUT	IN	OUT	TOTAL
M	8⁰⁰	12⁰⁰	1⁰⁰	5⁰⁰			8
TU	7⁵⁷	12⁰³	1⁰⁰	5⁰⁰			8
W	7⁵⁹	12⁰⁴	12⁵⁶	5⁰⁴			8
TH	7⁵⁴	12⁰²	12⁵⁵	5⁰³			8
F	7⁵³	12⁰¹	12⁵⁴	5⁰¹			8

TOTAL TIME ____40____ HOURS

RATE PER HOUR _____

TOTAL WAGES _____

Illustration 66b — Completed Time Card

Notice that Maria has punched her card four times on Monday. This process is repeated daily for the rest of the week.

Cards are punched four times daily

At the end of the week, the payroll clerk will take out all the cards to figure the number of hours worked by each employee. She will then insert new cards so that on the following Monday, Maria will find a new card to record her time for that week.

Maria's employer has set certain rules as to the working hours. The employees must start working at 8:00 a.m., go out to lunch at 12:00 noon, return by 1:00 p.m., and work until 5:00 p.m.

It is a company rule that if a worker comes in any time *after 8:04 a.m.* she gets paid according the schedule below:

"Punching in" after 8:04 a.m.

Punches In From	Will Be Paid From
8:05 — 8:15	8:15
8:16 — 8:30	8:30
8:31 — 8:45	8:45
8:46 — 9:00	9:00
9:01 — 9:15	9:15
9:16 — 9:30	9:30
9:31 — 9:45	9:45
9:46 — 10:00	10:00
and so forth.	

"Punching in"
after 1:04 p.m.

Maria and all the other workers have their lunch hour between 12:00 noon and 1:00 p.m. Again, the employer expects the workers to return promptly. If Maria fails to return by 1:04 p.m., her time will be counted according to the schedule below:

Punches In From	Will Be Paid From
1:05 — 1:15	1:15
1:16 — 1:30	1:30
1:31 — 1:45	1:45
1:46 — 2:00	2:00
2:01 — 2:15	2:15
2:16 — 2:30	2:30
2:31 — 2:45	2:45
2:46 — 3:00	3:00
and so forth.	

This may seem to be a harsh regulation, but large companies lose a great deal of money when their machines are idle or workers have to wait for latecomers to arrive. You know how much you miss when you come late for class and how disturbing your late entrance is to the rest of the class. Naturally, continued lateness is a cause for dismissal in industry.

"Punching out"
for the day

Occasionally it may be necessary for Maria to leave before the end of her working day, which is 5:00 p.m. If that happens, she will be paid for the time she worked through the last quarter of an hour. For example:

Punches Out From	Will Be Paid To
3:00 — 3:14	3:00
3:15 — 3:29	3:15
3:30 — 3:44	3:30
3:45 — 3:59	3:45
4:00 — 4:14	4:00
4:15 — 4:29	4:15
4:30 — 4:44	4:30
and so forth.	

Now that you are aware of the regulations regarding being late and leaving early, you can see how the payroll clerk figured Maria's time. Since Maria was not late on Monday, the payroll clerk figures that Maria worked eight hours.

From 8:00 a.m. to 12:00 noon are four hours:	12:00 8:00 —— 4
From 1:00 p.m. to 5:00 p.m. are four hours:	5:00 1:00 —— 4

Therefore, the payroll clerk writes "8" in the "Total" column for Monday. (See Illustration 66b, page 433.)

On Tuesday, Maria came at 7:57 a.m. However, since she does not start working until 8:00 a.m., her time is counted from 8:00 a.m. You know that you like to arrive at school early so that you can start the day's work promptly in an orderly fashion. Maria likes to do the same thing; so she believes in getting to the place of business early.

You will notice that she punched out at 12:03 p.m. Naturally, in a large company many people will wait in line to punch out so that it may take her a few minutes until she reaches the machine.

If you figure her time for Tuesday, you will agree with the figure "8" in the "Total" column for Tuesday. Check each day and see if you agree with the total hours worked.

You can see how interested Maria and her employer will be in this time card. Both will have an accurate record of the hours she worked with which to calculate her wages. Besides being a basis for figuring Maria's wages, the time card will be useful in proving to various governmental representatives that Maria's employer is meeting the governmental regulations for hours of work and minimum pay scales. You will learn about this in future jobs.

SAMPLE PROBLEM

The payroll clerk has collected the time cards for the week. She is ready to compute the hours worked for each employee. She starts with the card below:

Week Ending _July 18, 19--_

No. _1_

Name _Clare Bigby_

DAY	IN	OUT	IN	OUT	IN	OUT	TOTAL
M	7^{57}	12^{00}	12^{55}	5^{03}			
TU	8^{25}	12^{01}	12^{54}	5^{01}			
W	7^{55}	12^{03}	1^{50}	5^{06}			
TH	7^{54}	11^{06}	1^{00}	5^{05}			
F	7^{53}	12^{04}	12^{57}	4^{47}			

TOTAL TIME _____ HOURS

RATE PER HOUR _____

TOTAL WAGES _____

The steps she follows to get the total number of hours worked are given below and on the following pages.

Step 1: Compute hours worked each day.

She would examine the four numbers appearing on the time card for each day to figure the hours worked. For example, on Monday, 7:57 means that Clare really started working at 8:00 a.m.

12:00	went to lunch
−8:00	started to work in morning
=4	hours worked until lunchtime

To determine the hours worked in the afternoon:

5:00	(although she left at 5:03, she is paid only until 5:00)
−1:00	(although she came back from lunch at 12:55, she is paid from 1:00)
=4	hours worked, afternoon

Therefore, she would be paid for 8 hours on Monday.

To figure the hours worked for Tuesday, she would do the following:

12:00	(although she went to lunch at 12:01, her time is figured from 12:00)
−8:30	(since she came in late at 8:25, she is given credit for starting at 8:30. See schedule on page 433.)
3:30	hours worked until lunchtime
=3½	hours

She worked 4 hours in the afternoon. To figure this the clerk would do the following:

5:00	(5:01 is really 5:00)
−1:00	(12:54 is really 1:00)
=4	hours worked, afternoon

She would be paid for 7½ hours.

3½	hours in the morning
+4	hours in the afternoon
=7½	the total for Tuesday

To figure the hours worked on Wednesday, she would also do the following:

12:00	(12:03 is really 12:00)
−8:00	(7:55 is really 8:00)
=4	hours worked until lunchtime

5:00	(5:06 is counted as 5:00)
−2:00	(since she came back from lunch at 1:50, her time begins on the next quarter of an hour which makes the time 2:00. See schedule on page 434.)
=3	hours worked, afternoon

She would be paid for 7 hours.

4	hours in the morning
+3	hours in the afternoon
=7	total hours for Wednesday

To figure the hours worked on Thursday, she would do the following:

11:00	(since she left at 11:06 she will lose 1 hour. Her time is figured until 11:00)
−8:00	(7:54 is counted as 8:00)
=3	hours worked until lunchtime

5:00	(5:05 is counted as 5:00)
−1:00	(came back from lunch)
=4	hours worked in the afternoon

She would be paid for 7 hours.

3	hours in the morning
+4	hours in the afternoon
=7	total hours for Thursday

To figure the hours worked on Friday, she would do the following:

12:00	(12:04 is counted as 12:00)
−8:00	(7:53 is counted as 8:00)
=4	hours worked until lunchtime

4:45	(since she left at 4:47, she is paid for the last ¼ hour which equals 4:45. See schedule on page 434.)
−1:00	(12:57 is counted as 1:00)
=3:45	(or 3¾ hours worked in the afternoon)

She would be paid for 7¾ hours.

4	hours in the morning
+3¾	hours in the afternoon
=7¾	total hours for Friday

Step 2: Enter in the proper column the total hours worked daily.

As soon as the payroll clerk determines the number of hours that Clare Bigby worked on Monday (8 hours), she puts the 8 in the "Total" column for Monday. She does the same for each day.

Step 3: Total the hours for the week.

You will notice that, in the illustration on the next page, the payroll clerk has entered 37¼ hours next to the "Total Time." She arrived at this total by adding all the numbers in the "Total" column. If you refer to your related arithmetic drill, you will understand why you were given practice in doing those problems. The illustration on page 438 is how the completed time card would look.

Week Ending *July 18, 19--*

No. *1*

Name *Clare Bigby*

DAY	IN	OUT	IN	OUT	IN	OUT	TOTAL
M	7⁵⁷	12⁰⁰	12⁵⁵	5⁰³			8
TU	8²⁵	12⁰¹	12⁵⁴	5⁰¹			7½
W	7⁵⁵	12⁰³	1⁵⁰	5⁰⁶			7
TH	7⁵⁴	11⁰⁶	1⁰⁰	5⁰⁵			7
F	7⁵³	12⁰⁴	12⁵⁷	4⁴⁷			7¾

TOTAL TIME ___37 ¼___ HOURS

RATE PER HOUR _____

TOTAL WAGES _____

PRACTICE PROBLEM

Directions: The time record sections of eight time cards are given below and on page 439 for the week ending May 19, 19--. You are to find how many hours each employee worked for each day. Once you have found the hours worked daily, you are then to find the total hours worked that week.

These employees start work at 8:00 a.m., leave for lunch at 12:00 noon, return at 1:00 p.m., and usually work until 5:00 p.m.

Workers arriving late 5 minutes or more are penalized according to the schedule shown on page 433.

If workers leave early, they are paid for the time they worked through the last quarter of an hour, as shown on page 434.

Card #1

M	8⁰¹	12⁰²	1⁰⁰	5⁰³
TU	7⁵⁷	12⁰³	12⁵⁸	5⁰¹
W	8³⁰	12⁰⁴	12⁵⁹	5⁰⁰
TH	8⁰²	12⁰¹	1⁰⁰	4³⁰
F	8⁰³	11²⁸	1⁰¹	5⁰⁰

Are your total hours 38¼?

Card #2

M	8⁰⁰	12⁰¹	1¹⁵	5⁰¹
TU	7⁵⁸	12⁰³	12⁵⁹	4⁰³
W	10⁰⁰	12⁰⁰	1⁰⁰	5⁰²
TH	7⁵⁴	11¹⁵	1⁰⁰	5⁰⁰
F	8⁰¹	12⁰⁰	12⁵⁷	3⁴⁸

Are your total hours 34¾?

Card #3

M	7^{58}	12^{01}	1^{55}	5^{00}
TU	8^{55}	12^{03}	1^{01}	5^{01}
W	7^{53}	12^{00}	12^{57}	4^{02}
TH	7^{58}	12^{04}	1^{28}	5^{02}
F	9^{20}	12^{00}	1^{00}	5^{04}

Are your total hours 35?

Card #4

M	8^{02}	12^{00}	2^{00}	5^{00}
TU	8^{19}	12^{01}	12^{57}	5^{04}
W	8^{00}	12^{02}	12^{56}	4^{11}
TH	8^{49}	12^{03}	1^{01}	5^{05}
F	7^{56}	10^{02}	12^{55}	5^{03}

Are your total hours 34½?

Card #5

M	7^{59}	11^{06}	12^{57}	5^{00}
TU	8^{00}	10^{45}	1^{00}	5^{03}
W	8^{21}	12^{00}	12^{56}	5^{04}
TH	7^{58}	12^{03}	1^{02}	4^{31}
F	7^{57}	12^{05}	2^{26}	5^{01}

Are your total hours 35¼?

Card #6

M	9^{00}	12^{04}	1^{00}	5^{03}
TU	8^{00}	11^{46}	1^{02}	5^{00}
W	7^{56}	12^{05}	1^{56}	5^{04}
TH	8^{33}	12^{02}	1^{01}	5^{01}
F	9^{20}	12^{00}	1^{00}	5^{02}

Are your total hours 35½?

Card #7

M	7^{56}	12^{00}	2^{10}	5^{00}
TU	8^{00}	10^{30}	1^{00}	4^{00}
W	8^{18}	12^{03}	12^{54}	3^{30}
TH	8^{47}	12^{04}	1^{01}	4^{08}
F	7^{50}	11^{19}	12^{55}	3^{06}

Are your total hours 29½?

Card #8

M	8^{00}	12^{03}	1^{01}	4^{06}
TU	8^{07}	12^{00}	1^{00}	4^{49}
W	9^{15}	12^{02}	12^{57}	4^{04}
TH	8^{35}	12^{05}	1^{02}	5^{00}
F	7^{59}	12^{01}	2^{02}	4^{45}

Are your total hours 34?

	Copy the following problems on a sheet of paper and find the answers.				
	(1)	(2)	(3)	(4)	(5)
Practicing Related Arithmetic	8	7½	6¾	7¾	$5.08
	6½	6¼	5	6¼	×31½
	5½	5	7¼	8½	
	7¼	6½	4¾	5¾	
	+6¼	+4¼	+8¾	+4½	

AIM

To give you additional practice in reading time cards and computing the total hours worked.

EXPLANATION

You have learned how to read a time card and how to find the total hours worked by each employee. Today you will try to increase your speed in finding the total hours worked.

PRACTICE PROBLEM

Directions: The time record sections of 12 time cards are given on the following pages for the week ending March 14, 19––. You are to find the total hours worked for each employee. Company employees start working at 8:00 a.m., go to lunch at 12:00 noon, return at 1:00 p.m., and usually work until 5:00 p.m.

Workers who are late 5 minutes or more are penalized according to the schedules shown on page 433. Workers leaving early are paid for the time they worked through the last quarter of an hour as shown on page 434.

Card #1

M	8^{06}	12^{03}	12^{56}	5^{00}
TU	8^{46}	12^{05}	1^{00}	5^{05}
W	10^{03}	12^{00}	12^{55}	5^{06}
TH	8^{00}	12^{01}	1^{00}	4^{04}
F	7^{55}	12^{02}	1^{01}	3^{34}

Are your total hours 34?

Card #2

M	8^{00}	11^{00}	1^{00}	5^{00}
TU	7^{57}	11^{48}	12^{56}	5^{03}
W	8^{00}	10^{10}	1^{00}	5^{04}
TH	7^{58}	12^{00}	2^{03}	5^{06}
F	10^{18}	12^{02}	12^{55}	5^{01}

Are your total hours 33?

Card #3

M	8^{00}	12^{00}	1^{00}	4^{19}
TU	8^{00}	12^{06}	12^{56}	3^{20}
W	9^{00}	12^{01}	12^{55}	5^{02}
TH	9^{19}	12^{00}	1^{00}	5^{00}
F	8^{01}	9^{50}	12^{54}	5^{03}

Are your total hours 32¾?

Card #5

M	7^{55}	12^{00}	12^{56}	3^{19}
TU	8^{00}	12^{02}	1^{40}	5^{03}
W	7^{56}	11^{09}	12^{57}	5^{00}
TH	8^{17}	12^{01}	1^{00}	5^{04}
F	9^{31}	12^{03}	1^{02}	5^{02}

Card #7

M	8^{00}	12^{01}	12^{57}	3^{25}
TU	8^{07}	12^{00}	12^{54}	5^{01}
W	7^{59}	12^{00}	1^{05}	5^{02}
TH	8^{42}	12^{04}	12^{56}	5^{00}
F	8^{00}	11^{38}	1^{00}	5^{03}

Card #9

M	7^{58}	12^{02}	12^{56}	5^{04}
TU	8^{00}	11^{01}	12^{55}	5^{00}
W	7^{57}	12^{04}	1^{50}	5^{03}
TH	9^{25}	12^{05}	1^{00}	5^{01}
F	7^{59}	12^{00}	12^{58}	3^{47}

Card #4

M	10^{00}	12^{00}	12^{56}	5^{00}
TU	9^{04}	12^{03}	12^{57}	5^{01}
W	8^{00}	11^{04}	1^{00}	5^{04}
TH	7^{59}	10^{56}	1^{01}	5^{05}
F	8^{00}	12^{00}	2^{02}	5^{06}

Are your total hours 33¼?

Card #6

M	7^{58}	12^{00}	2^{30}	5^{00}
TU	8^{00}	10^{46}	1^{00}	5^{01}
W	8^{01}	12^{02}	1^{03}	4^{01}
TH	8^{59}	12^{01}	12^{57}	5^{02}
F	7^{56}	11^{30}	12^{56}	5^{04}

Card #8

M	8^{00}	12^{00}	12^{56}	4^{32}
TU	7^{58}	12^{04}	12^{57}	4^{46}
W	8^{01}	12^{05}	1^{00}	2^{52}
TH	9^{03}	12^{02}	1^{02}	5^{00}
F	10^{04}	12^{00}	12^{55}	5^{02}

Card #10

M	8^{49}	12^{00}	12^{56}	5^{00}
TU	7^{55}	12^{03}	12^{57}	3^{06}
W	8^{00}	12^{02}	12^{55}	4^{48}
TH	9^{05}	12^{00}	12^{54}	5^{01}
F	8^{02}	12^{01}	1^{26}	5^{03}

Card #11

M	8^{03}	10^{30}	12^{56}	5^{00}
TU	7^{59}	12^{01}	2^{50}	5^{02}
W	8^{18}	12^{00}	1^{00}	5^{01}
TH	7^{57}	12^{02}	12^{55}	4^{37}
F	8^{04}	12^{04}	12^{59}	5^{05}

Card #12

M	7^{59}	12^{00}	12^{57}	4^{21}
TU	9^{01}	12^{04}	12^{56}	5^{00}
W	8^{00}	10^{26}	1^{00}	5^{01}
TH	8^{05}	12^{03}	1^{01}	5^{05}
F	7^{58}	12^{00}	12^{55}	3^{51}

JOB 68 | COMPUTING WAGES OF WORKERS

Copy the following problems on a sheet of paper and find the answers:

	(1)	(2)	(3)	(4)	(5)
Practicing Related Arithmetic	6	8¾	8¼	$4.28	$5.60
	7½	6	5¾	×37½	×38¼
	8	7¾	7¼		
	6¾	4½	4¾		
	+5¼	+8¾	+6¼		

AIM

To learn how to compute the wages due an employee at the end of a week.

EXPLANATION

In the previous jobs you learned how to read time cards and how to find the total hours for which an employee was to be paid. However, this was only the first step in computing a worker's wages. To find the worker's salary, the payroll clerk must know what salary the employer pays the employee.

"My favorite day—Pay day!"

Paymaster

There are various wage plans under which a worker may be hired. Some workers are hired at a certain wage per hour; others are hired at a fixed amount for a fixed number of hours worked in a week; and still others may be hired on a piecework basis (a fixed price paid for each item produced).

Wage plans:
a) per hour
b) per week
c) piecework

In this job, you will compute wages on an *hourly basis*.

SAMPLE PROBLEM

Todd Kent has been hired at the rate of $4.25 per hour. Todd worked 34 hours during the week. His total wages would be found by doing a problem in multiplication.

$$\begin{array}{r} \$\ 4.25 \ \text{(hourly rate)} \\ \times 34 \ \text{(hours worked)} \\ \hline 1700 \\ 1275 \\ \hline \$144.50 \ \text{(total wages)} \end{array}$$

PRACTICE PROBLEMS

Problem 1

Directions: Copy the following table on a sheet of paper and find the total wages for each worker. Check your work.

Name of Worker	Hours Worked	Rate Per Hour		Total Wages	
a) Wally Becke	37	4	15		
b) Pat Dann	32	5	30		
c) Marie Lauro	31	6	40		
d) Molly Haige	32½	3	76		
e) Anne Parry	38½	3	52		
f) Chuck Noone	30½	5	64		
g) Dale Veeck	36¼	7	20		
h) Ethel Solar	25¼	6	08		

Hourly rate
×Hours worked
=Total wages

Problem 2

Directions: Copy the following table on a sheet of paper and find the total wages for each worker. Check your work.

Name of Worker	Hours Worked	Rate Per Hour		Total Wages	
a) Glody Josel	31	4	85		
b) Gene Fenn	36	5	50		
c) Rick Alvo	29½	4	72		
d) Rita Ostre	23½	6	00		
e) Ted Gerth	19½	3	90		
f) Andy Catalo	27¼	7	00		
g) Kim Noy	16¼	5	28		
h) Rocco Tocci	35¼	4	08		

Problem 3

Directions: Copy the table on page 445 on a sheet of paper and find the total wages for each worker. Check your work.

Name of Worker	Hours Worked	Rate Per Hour		Total Wages	
a) Verne Jorge	21	5	37		
b) Sal Fazio	14	3	87		
c) Viola Alvino	31½	6	26		
d) Roy Steck	33½	5	42		
e) Owen Macely	26¼	7	36		
f) Marion Kalin	30¼	5	12		
g) Guy Ivone	34¾	3	72		
h) Keith Wide	20¾	6	20		

Problem 4

Directions: Copy the following table on a sheet of paper and find the total wages for each worker. Check your work.

Name of Worker	Hours Worked	Rate Per Hour		Total Wages	
a) Ed Palma	21	5	03		
b) Daisy Kale	20½	6	32		
c) Chris Forbert	10¼	3	92		
d) Cyril Guine	30¼	4	36		
e) Adde Winter	22¼	7	40		
f) Renee Zolti	32¾	6	48		
g) Mary Floro	23¾	5	36		
h) Percy Erhare	9¾	6	16		

Practicing Related Arithmetic	Copy the following problems on a sheet of paper and find the answers:				
	(1)	(2)	(3)	(4)	(5)
	7¼	8¾	5¾	$5.38	$6.76
	5¾	7	4¼	×30½	×31¼
	7¾	8¼	6¾		
	6½	5¾	8¾		
	+8	+4¾	+6½		

AIMS

1. To learn how to record time card information in a payroll book.
2. To find the total wages of workers paid on an hourly basis.

EXPLANATION

Entries are made in the payroll book each week

It is customary for payroll clerks to record certain time card information in a book known as a *payroll book*. This information is entered in the book at the end of each week after the payroll clerk has found the total hours worked each day by each employee. After the information has been recorded on the time card as you were taught to do in the preceding jobs, the payroll clerk enters the information in the payroll book. A simple form of a payroll book is shown below:

		WEEK ENDING							
CARD NO.	NAME OF EMPLOYEE	HOURS WORKED					TOTAL HRS. WORKED	PAY PER HOUR	TOTAL WAGES
		M	TU	W	TH	F			

Illustration 69a – Payroll Book

In order to learn how the information is recorded weekly by the payroll clerk, study the sample problem below.

SAMPLE PROBLEM

Jay Peters is a payroll clerk. At the end of the week, Jay took out all the cards from the payroll rack and totaled the hours for each employee. Here are two cards which he has just completed.

Week Ending *June 27, 19--*

No. *1*

Name *Roger Paige*

DAY	IN	OUT	IN	OUT	IN	OUT	TOTAL
M	8^{00}	12^{02}	1^{00}	5^{05}			8
TU	7^{57}	12^{04}	12^{56}	5^{00}			8
W	8^{02}	12^{00}	1^{03}	5^{06}			8
TH	7^{55}	12^{05}	12^{59}	5^{01}			8
F	8^{03}	12^{01}	12^{55}	5^{00}			8

TOTAL TIME _____40_____ HOURS

RATE PER HOUR _____$5.00_____

TOTAL WAGES _____$200.00_____

Week Ending *June 27, 19--*

No. *2*

Name *Perry Trayer*

DAY	IN	OUT	IN	OUT	IN	OUT	TOTAL
M	8^{02}	12^{04}	1^{01}	3^{00}			6
TU	9^{30}	12^{00}	12^{56}	5^{00}			6½
W	8^{00}	12^{05}	3^{30}	5^{00}			5½
TH	7^{58}	12^{01}	12^{59}	4^{00}			7
F	7^{56}	12^{00}	1^{00}	2^{09}			5

TOTAL TIME _____30_____ HOURS

RATE PER HOUR _____$6.00_____

TOTAL WAGES _____$180.00_____

Here is how the two cards would appear in the payroll book after Jay had entered them.

			WEEK ENDING				*June 27, 19--*			
CARD NO.	NAME OF EMPLOYEE	HOURS WORKED					TOTAL HRS. WORKED	PAY PER HOUR	TOTAL WAGES	
		M	TU	W	TH	F				
1	Roger Paige	8	8	8	8	8	40	5 00	200 00	
2	Perry Trayer	6	6½	5½	7	5	30	6 00	180 00	
	Total Wages for Week								380 00	

Illustration 69b – Payroll Book with Entries

Notice that Jay has entered all the information found on each time card.

Jay will use a new page in the payroll book for each succeeding week. Some payroll clerks do not enter the hours for each day in the payroll book, but enter only the total weekly hours for each employee. They rely on the time card as their source of information for the hours worked daily. However, the method shown in Illustration 69b on page 447 will give a payroll clerk a duplicate record.

PRACTICE PROBLEMS

Problem 1

Directions:

Pay per hour
×Total hours worked
=Total wages

a) Copy the following information on a payroll sheet. Date the sheet for the week ended March 7, 19--.

CARD NO.	NAME OF EMPLOYEE	HOURS WORKED					PAY PER HOUR	
		M	TU	W	TH	F		
1	Olga Aberte	7	8	8	6	8	4	72
2	Phil Early	6	8	7	5	6	5	20
3	Willie Ford	8	5½	6½	7	8	4	96
4	Nina Oliver	7¼	7¾	8	8	6½	6	80
5	Jean Rice	6	6¼	8	7	6¾	5	68
6	Peter Tadone	7½	7	8	8	8	6	40

b) Find the total hours worked for each employee and enter the information in the proper column.

c) Find the total wages for each employee and enter the answer in the proper column.

d) Find the total wages for the week. If your work is correct, the total should be $1,209.16.

Problem 2

Directions:

a) Copy the information on page 449 on another payroll sheet. Date the sheet for the week ended March 14, 19--.

b) Find the total hours worked for each employee and enter the information in the proper column.

c) Find the total wages for each employee and enter the answer in the proper column.

d) Find the total wages for the week. If your work is correct, the total should be $1,143.36.

CARD NO.	NAME OF EMPLOYEE	HOURS WORKED					PAY PER HOUR	
		M	TU	W	TH	F		
1	Olga Aberte	8	7½	6½	7	7	4	72
2	Phil Early	7	8½	7½	8	8	5	20
3	Willie Ford	6	7½	5½	6	5	4	96
4	Nina Oliver	7	7	8¼	6¼	6	6	80
5	Jean Rice	6	8	8½	7½	5½	5	68
6	Peter Tadone	5½	7½	6	5¼	4¾	6	40

Problem 3

Directions:
a) Copy the following information on a payroll sheet. Date the sheet for the week ended March 21, 19--.

CARD NO.	NAME OF EMPLOYEE	HOURS WORKED					PAY PER HOUR	
		M	TU	W	TH	F		
1	Olga Aberte	5	7½	5	6	4½	4	72
2	Phil Early	6	7	6½	5¼	7¼	5	20
3	Willie Ford	7	6½	5¼	6½	6¼	4	96
4	Nina Oliver	7	8	8½	8½	7½	6	80
5	Jean Rice	7	4½	5½	4¼	6	5	68
6	Peter Tadone	5	8	8½	8¾	6	6	40

b) Find the total hours worked for each employee and enter the information in the proper column.

c) Find the total wages for each employee and enter the answer in the proper column.

d) Find the total wages for the week. If your work is correct, the total should be $1,110.18.

Problem 4

Directions:
a) Copy the information on page 450 on a payroll sheet. Date the sheet for the week ended March 28, 19--.

b) Find the total hours worked for each employee and enter the information in the proper column.

c) Find the total wages for each employee and enter the answer in the proper column.

d) Find the total wages for the week. If your work is correct, the total should be $1,154.64.

CARD NO.	NAME OF EMPLOYEE	HOURS WORKED					PAY PER HOUR	
		M	TU	W	TH	F		
1	Olga Aberte	8½	8	7½	8	8	4	72
2	Phil Early	5	6	5½	6½	7½	5	20
3	Willie Ford	6½	5½	6	5	6½	4	96
4	Nina Oliver	4	6¾	5	6½	6	6	80
5	Jean Rice	6¼	7½	8½	7½	8	5	68
6	Peter Tadone	8¼	7½	8	8	8	6	40

Pay per hour
Total hours
× worked
= Total wages

Problem 5

Directions:

a) Copy the following information on a payroll sheet. Date the sheet for the week ended April 4, 19––.

CARD NO.	NAME OF EMPLOYEE	HOURS WORKED					PAY PER HOUR	
		M	TU	W	TH	F		
1	Olga Aberte	8	8½	5	8½	6½	4	72
2	Phil Early	8	6¼	7½	8	8½	5	20
3	Willie Ford	6½	5¼	5	7½	6½	4	96
4	Nina Oliver	7½	8½	7½	8	8½	6	80
5	Jean Rice	6	7	6	5¾	7	5	68
6	Peter Tadone	8	7¾	8	7	7	6	40

b) Find the total hours worked for each employee and enter the information in the proper column.

c) Find the total wages for each employee and enter the answer in the proper column.

d) Find the total wages for the week. If your work is correct, the total should be $1,217.64.

Copy the following problems on a sheet of paper and find the answers:

	(1)	(2)	(3)	(4)	(5)
Practicing Related Arithmetic	8¼	8¾	4½	$3.74	$7.40
	7½	4	6¾	×29½	×18¾
	6	7¾	8¼		
	4¾	6¾	5¼		
	+5½	+7¼	+7¾		

AIM

To learn how to determine the wages due an employee, using a wage computation book.

EXPLANATION

You have had practice in finding the wages of an employee hired on an hourly rate. Occasionally, employees are hired on a weekly rate. For example, Carl Allen is hired at a weekly rate of $200.00 for 40 hours' work. If he works only 35 hours, he will receive less than $200.00. Of course, you could find his wages by doing this arithmetic problem:

Step 1: Divide his weekly rate by the number of hours he is supposed to work to find the hourly rate.

$$\$200.00 \quad \div \quad 40 \quad = \quad \$5.00$$
(weekly rate)   (hours)   (hourly rate)

$$\frac{\$5.00}{40)\overline{\$200.00}}$$
$$\underline{200}$$

Step 2: Multiply hourly rate by number of hours worked.

$$\$5.00 \quad \times \quad 35 \quad = \quad \$175.00$$
(hourly rate)   (hours worked)   (total wages)

$$\$5.00 \text{ (hourly rate)}$$
$$\underline{\times 35} \text{ (actual hours worked)}$$
$$2500$$
$$\underline{1500}$$
$$\$175.00 \text{ (total wages)}$$

This method of computing wages requires that you do arithmetic problems. Of course, some payroll clerks use calculating machines to do the arithmetic and thereby save themselves lots of work.

But there is still another method of getting the total wages, and that is what you will learn to do today. There are a number of *wage computation books* published which enable payroll clerks to look at a table and determine the correct wages without doing any multiplication. These wage computation books are arranged so that there are pages for determining wages based on a 36-hour week, a 37-hour week, a 38-hour week, etc.

Page 453 is a sample page of a wage computation book based on a 40-hour week. Study the sample problem below to learn how to use this table.

SAMPLE PROBLEM

How to use a
wage
computation book

If an employee was hired at the rate of $200.00 for a *40-hour week* and only worked 35 hours, you would first look down the column headed "Hours Worked" until you came to the number "35." Then you would look across to the column headed "$200.00" where you would find $175.00. This means that the employee earned *$175.00* for *35 hours*. If you compare this answer to the one shown in Step 2 on page 451, you will note that this is the same answer. As you can see, using the table is certainly an easier way to get the answer.

Suppose an employee worked *10 hours* at the rate of $201.00 for a *40-hour week*. What would be the employee's wages? Again look at the column headed "Hours Worked" and find "10." Then look across to the column headed $201.00 and you will find the answer, $50.25. Your work will be speeded up if you use a ruler and place it under the number of hours you are looking for. This makes it easy to look across and locate the column you need. In addition, it prevents your eyes from shifting to the wrong column.

Suppose an employee worked 30¾ *hours* and earned $209.00 for a *40-hour week*. Here are the steps for finding the answer:

Step 1:   Find the wages for the part of the hour worked.

Look for the fraction ¾ in the "Hours Worked" column. Place your ruler underneath this number, across to the $209.00 column and you will find $3.92. This is what the employee earned for ¾ hour.

Step 2:   Find the wages earned for the whole number of hours.

Look for the number 30 in the "Hours Worked" column. Place your ruler underneath this number. Look in the column headed "$209.00" and you will find *$156.75*.

Step 3:   Add the answers in Steps 1 and 2 together.

Since ¾ hour	=	$ 3.92
and 30 hours	=	$156.75
Then 30¾ hours	=	$160.67

| WAGES TO BE PAID | | | | | | | | | |
Hours Worked	$200.00	$201.00	$202.00	$203.00	$204.00	$205.00	$206.00	$207.00	$208.00	$209.00
⅛	.63	.63	.63	.63	.64	.64	.64	.65	.65	.65
¼	1.25	1.26	1.26	1.27	1.28	1.28	1.29	1.29	1.30	1.31
⅜	1.88	1.88	1.89	1.90	1.91	1.92	1.93	1.94	1.95	1.96
½	2.50	2.51	2.53	2.54	2.55	2.56	2.58	2.59	2.60	2.61
⅝	3.13	3.14	3.16	3.17	3.19	3.20	3.22	3.23	3.25	3.27
¾	3.75	3.77	3.79	3.81	3.83	3.84	3.86	3.88	3.90	3.92
⅞	4.38	4.40	4.42	4.44	4.46	4.48	4.51	4.53	4.55	4.57
1	5.00	5.03	5.05	5.08	5.10	5.13	5.15	5.18	5.20	5.23
2	10.00	10.05	10.10	10.15	10.20	10.25	10.30	10.35	10.40	10.45
3	15.00	15.08	15.15	15.23	15.30	15.38	15.45	15.53	15.60	15.68
4	20.00	20.10	20.20	20.30	20.40	20.50	20.60	20.70	20.80	20.90
5	25.00	25.13	25.25	25.38	25.50	25.63	25.75	25.88	26.00	26.13
6	30.00	30.15	30.30	30.45	30.60	30.75	30.90	31.05	31.20	31.35
7	35.00	35.18	35.35	35.53	35.70	35.88	36.05	36.23	36.40	36.58
8	40.00	40.20	40.40	40.60	40.80	41.00	41.20	41.40	41.60	41.80
9	45.00	45.23	45.45	45.68	45.90	46.13	46.35	46.58	46.80	47.03
10	50.00	50.25	50.50	50.75	51.00	51.25	51.50	51.75	52.00	52.25
11	55.00	55.28	55.55	55.83	56.10	56.38	56.65	56.93	57.20	57.48
12	60.00	60.30	60.60	60.90	61.20	61.50	61.80	62.10	62.40	62.70
13	65.00	65.33	65.65	65.98	66.30	66.63	66.95	67.28	67.60	67.93
14	70.00	70.35	70.70	71.05	71.40	71.75	72.10	72.45	72.80	73.15
15	75.00	75.38	75.75	76.13	76.50	76.88	77.25	77.63	78.00	78.38
16	80.00	80.40	80.80	81.20	81.60	82.00	82.40	82.80	83.20	83.60
17	85.00	85.43	85.85	86.28	86.70	87.13	87.55	87.98	88.40	88.83
18	90.00	90.45	90.90	91.35	91.80	92.25	92.70	93.15	93.60	94.05
19	95.00	95.48	95.95	96.43	96.90	97.38	97.85	98.33	98.80	99.28
20	100.00	100.50	101.00	101.50	102.00	102.50	103.00	103.50	104.00	104.50
21	105.00	105.53	106.05	106.58	107.10	107.63	108.15	108.68	109.20	109.73
22	110.00	110.55	111.10	111.65	112.20	112.75	113.30	113.85	114.40	114.95
23	115.00	115.58	116.15	116.73	117.30	117.88	118.45	119.03	119.60	120.18
24	120.00	120.60	121.20	121.80	122.40	123.00	123.60	124.20	124.80	125.40
25	125.00	125.63	126.25	126.88	127.50	128.13	128.75	129.38	130.00	130.63
26	130.00	130.65	131.30	131.95	132.60	133.25	133.90	134.55	135.20	135.85
27	135.00	135.68	136.35	137.03	137.70	138.38	139.05	139.73	140.40	141.08
28	140.00	140.70	141.40	142.10	142.80	143.50	144.20	144.90	145.60	146.30
29	145.00	145.73	146.45	147.18	147.90	148.63	149.35	150.08	150.80	151.53
30	150.00	150.75	151.50	152.25	153.00	153.75	154.50	155.25	156.00	156.75
31	155.00	155.78	156.55	157.33	158.10	158.88	159.65	160.43	161.20	161.98
32	160.00	160.80	161.60	162.40	163.20	164.00	164.80	165.60	166.40	167.20
33	165.00	165.83	166.65	167.48	168.30	169.13	169.95	170.78	171.60	172.43
34	170.00	170.85	171.70	172.55	173.40	174.25	175.10	175.95	176.80	177.65
35	175.00	175.88	176.75	177.63	178.50	179.38	180.25	181.13	182.00	182.88
36	180.00	180.90	181.80	182.70	183.60	184.50	185.40	186.30	187.20	188.10
37	185.00	185.93	186.85	187.78	188.70	189.63	190.55	191.48	192.40	193.33
38	190.00	190.95	191.90	192.85	193.80	194.75	195.70	196.65	197.60	198.55
39	195.00	195.98	196.95	197.93	198.90	199.88	200.85	201.83	202.80	203.78
40	200.00	201.00	202.00	203.00	204.00	205.00	206.00	207.00	208.00	209.00

Use a ruler and place it under the hours you want to find

Sample Page of a Wage Computation Book

PRACTICE PROBLEMS

Problem 1

Directions:
a) Copy the following table on a sheet of paper:

Card No.	Wages for 40 Hours	Hours Actually Worked	Wages Earned	
1	200 00	15		
2	200 00	15½		
3	200 00	15¾		
4	204 00	25		
5	204 00	25¼		
6	206 00	21		
7	206 00	21¾		
8	209 00	39		
9	209 00	39½		
10	209 00	27¼		
Total Wages Earned				

b) Using the wage computation table found on page 453, find the wages earned by each employee. Enter the amount in the "Wages Earned" column.
c) Find the total wages earned by the ten employees. If your work is correct, the total should be $1,260.25.

Problem 2

Card No.	Wages for 40 Hours	Hours Actually Worked	Wages Earned	
1	201 00	27		
2	201 00	31¾		
3	203 00	26¼		
4	203 00	14¾		
5	205 00	36½		
6	205 00	28¼		
7	204 00	23½		
8	207 00	16¾		
9	202 00	32¼		
10	208 00	34¾		
Total Wages Earned				

Directions:
a) Copy the table shown on the bottom of page 454 on a sheet of paper.
b) Using the wage computation table on page 453, find the wages earned by each employee. Enter the amount in the "Wages Earned" column.
c) Find the total wages earned by the ten employees. If your work is correct, the total should be $1,385.24.

Problem 3

Directions:
a) Copy the table shown below on a sheet of paper:

Card No.	Wages for 40 Hours	Hours Actually Worked	Wages Earned
1	202 00	12¼	
2	207 00	20¾	
3	201 00	29½	
4	208 00	33¼	
5	203 00	34¾	
6	209 00	6¼	
7	205 00	18½	
8	200 00	38¼	
9	204 00	11¾	
10	206 00	24½	
Total Wages Earned			

b) Using the wage computation table found on page 453, find the wages earned by each employee. Enter the amount in the "Wages Earned" column.
c) Find the total wages earned by the ten employees. If your work is correct, the total should be $1,171.57.

Problem 4

Directions:
a) Copy the table shown on page 456 on a sheet of paper.
b) Using the wage computation table found on page 453, find the wages earned by each employee. Enter the amount in the "Wages Earned" column.
c) Find the total wages earned by the ten employees. If your work is correct, the total should be $903.46.

Card No.	Wages for 40 Hours		Hours Actually Worked	Wages Earned	
1	209	00	22¾		
2	204	00	19½		
3	200	00	13¼		
4	206	00	4¾		
5	203	00	28½		
6	208	00	26¾		
7	202	00	8¼		
8	207	00	17½		
9	205	00	25¾		
10	201	00	9¼		
Total Wages Earned					

JOB 71 | COMPUTING OVERTIME

Copy the following problems on a sheet of paper and find the answers:

	(1)	(2)	(3)	(4)	(5)
Practicing Related Arithmetic	9	7¼	10¾	a) ½ of 4 =	a) ½ of 4½ =
	10½	8½	9¼	b) ½ of 12 =	b) ½ of 8½ =
	8½	10	7¾	c) ½ of 3 =	c) ½ of 1½ =
	6¼	7¾	11½	d) ½ of 9 =	d) ½ of 7½ =
	+ 7¾	+ 9¼	+ 8¼		

AIMS

1. To learn the meaning of the expression "overtime."

2. To learn to figure the number of hours that a worker is entitled to be paid for overtime.

EXPLANATION

"And there is a chance of putting in a lot of overtime."

PERSONNEL MGR.

In 1938, Congress passed a law called the Fair Labor Standards Act. This law states that employers engaged in interstate commerce (the buying or selling of goods between states), or in the production of goods for interstate commerce, must pay their workers the regular rate of pay for 40 hours in any work week. If employees work one hour overtime, they must be paid a bonus of an additional ½ hour's pay. This means they will be paid for 1½ hours even though they have actually worked only one hour. That is the meaning of the expression "time and a half" as used by employers and employees. Of course, some businesses, by special agreement with workers or their labor organizations, pay "time and a half" if a person works beyond a certain time each day. However, in the problems you will solve, you will follow the Fair Labor Standards Act (U.S. rule). See what this paragraph actually means by doing a sample problem.

Workers are given a bonus for working overtime (above 40 hrs.)

SAMPLE PROBLEM

If Kate Colby worked 40 hours, obviously she is not entitled to be paid for more than 40 hours. If Kate Colby worked *48 hours*, she is entitled to be paid for the *48 hours plus a bonus of four hours*, or *52 hours*. Here is how the answer of 52 hours was found.

Step 1: Find the total hours actually worked.

The payroll clerk would examine the time card and find the total of the actual hours worked. In this case, it is 48 hours.

Step 2: Find the bonus hours to be paid for.

The payroll clerk would now do this problem:

$$\begin{array}{rl} 48 & \text{(hours actually worked)} \\ -40 & \text{(hours for which no overtime is paid)} \\ \hline 8 & \text{(hours above 40)} \end{array}$$

½ × 8 = 4 hours bonus for overtime

Step 3: Find the total hours to be paid for.

In order to find the total hours that the worker must be paid for, you do this arithmetic problem:

$$\begin{array}{rl} 48 & \text{(hours actually worked)} \\ +\ 4 & \text{(overtime bonus hours, Step 2)} \\ \hline 52 & \text{(hours that the worker must be paid for)} \end{array}$$

If Kate Colby worked 50 hours, she is entitled to be paid for 55 hours because:

$$\begin{array}{rl} 50 & \text{(hours actually worked)} \\ -40 & \text{(hours for which no overtime is paid)} \\ \hline 10 & \text{(hours on which you base the overtime bonus)} \end{array}$$

½ × 10 = 5 hours bonus for overtime

$$\begin{array}{rl} 50 & \text{(hours actually worked)} \\ +\ 5 & \text{(overtime bonus hours)} \\ \hline 55 & \text{(hours to be paid for)} \end{array}$$

If Kate Colby worked 45 hours, she is entitled to be paid for 47½ hours because:

$$\begin{array}{rl} 45 & \text{(hours actually worked)} \\ -40 & \text{(hours for which no overtime is paid)} \\ \hline 5 & \text{(hours on which you base the overtime bonus)} \end{array}$$

½ × 5 = 2½ hours bonus for overtime

$$\begin{array}{rl} 45 & \text{(hours actually worked)} \\ +\ 2½ & \text{(overtime bonus hours)} \\ \hline 47½ & \text{(hours to be paid for)} \end{array}$$

It is important that you always subtract 40 hours from the total hours worked to find the number of hours on which you figure ½ as a bonus.

PRACTICE PROBLEMS

Problem 1

Directions:
a) Copy the table below on a sheet of paper:

Card No.	Hours Actually Worked	Bonus Hours	Total Hours To Be Paid
Example	48	4	52
1	44		
2	46		
3	52		
4	56		
5	58		
6	43		
7	47		
8	51		
9	44½		
10	48½		

Bonus hours =
½ × hours over 40

b) Enter the bonus hours for each worker in the proper column.
c) Enter the total hours to be paid to each worker.

Problem 2

Directions:
a) Copy the following table on a sheet of paper:

Card No.	Hours Actually Worked	Bonus Hours	Total Hours To Be Paid
1	37½		
2	42		
3	49		
4	40½		
5	46½		
6	43½		
7	47½		
8	49½		
9	39¾		
10	41½		

b) Enter the bonus hours for each worker in the proper column.
c) Enter the total hours to be paid to each worker.

Problem 3

Directions:
a) Copy the following table on a sheet of paper:

Card No.	Hours Actually Worked	Bonus Hours	Total Hours To Be Paid
1	54		
2	53		
3	42½		
4	50½		
5	45½		
6	51½		
7	55½		
8	40¼		
9	44¼		
10	50¼		

b) Enter the bonus hours for each worker in the proper column.
c) Enter the total hours to be paid to each worker.

Problem 4

Directions:
a) Copy the following table on a sheet of paper:

Card No.	Hours Actually Worked	Bonus Hours	Total Hours To Be Paid
1	41		
2	42¼		
3	46¼		
4	48¼		
5	56¼		
6	41¼		
7	43¼		
8	42¾		
9	46¾		
10	56¾		

b) Enter the bonus hours for each worker in the proper column.
c) Enter the total hours to be paid to each worker.

**Practicing
Related
Arithmetic**

Copy the following problems on a sheet of paper and find the answers:

(1)	(2)	(3)	(4)
6¾	10¼	a) ½ of 10 =	a) ½ of 13½ =
8¼	11½	b) ½ of 14 =	b) ½ of ½ =
9	7¼	c) ½ of 11 =	c) ½ of 2¼ =
10½	9¼	d) ½ of 13 =	d) ½ of 4¼ =
+ 5¼	+ 8¾	e) ½ of 10½ =	e) ½ of 12¼ =

AIM

To practice finding the total hours for which employees must be paid when they work overtime.

EXPLANATION

Today you will review computing overtime. You will also combine the reading of time cards and the computation of bonus hours for working overtime.

PRACTICE PROBLEMS

Problem 1

Directions:
a) Copy the following table on a sheet of paper:

Card No.	Hours Actually Worked	Bonus Hours	Total Hours To Be Paid
1	42		
2	49		
3	45		
4	38¼		
5	42½		
6	44½		
7	43½		
8	47½		
9	40¼		
10	46¼		

Bonus hours =
½ × hours over 40

b) Enter the bonus hours for each worker in the proper column.

c) Enter the total hours to be paid to each worker.

Problem 2

Directions:

a) Copy the following table on a sheet of paper:

Card No.	Hours Actually Worked	Bonus Hours	Total Hours To Be Paid
1	45½		
2	49½		
3	51½		
4	42¼		
5	44¼		
6	58¼		
7	42¾		
8	44¾		
9	48¾		
10	50¾		

b) Enter the bonus hours for each worker in the proper column.

c) Enter the total hours to be paid to each worker.

Problem 3

Directions:

a) Find the total hours worked from each of the time record sections shown below and on the next page.

Workers who are late 5 minutes or more are penalized according to the schedules shown on page 433. If they leave before the time that they are supposed to, they are paid for the time they worked through the last quarter of an hour as shown on page 434.

Card #1

M	8^{00}	12^{01}	12^{57}	5^{08}
TU	7^{55}	12^{02}	12^{55}	3^{30}
W	7^{59}	12^{05}	1^{00}	6^{34}
TH	7^{57}	12^{00}	12^{56}	7^{06}
F	8^{03}	12^{03}	1^{00}	5^{02}

Card #2

M	9^{00}	12^{02}	1^{03}	5^{00}
TU	8^{00}	12^{05}	12^{56}	6^{39}
W	7^{57}	12^{00}	1^{00}	7^{02}
TH	8^{00}	12^{06}	12^{54}	6^{48}
F	7^{58}	12^{01}	1^{01}	5^{50}

Card #3

M	7^{54}	12^{05}	1^{01}	5^{32}
TU	7^{58}	12^{00}	1^{00}	5^{09}
W	8^{00}	12^{04}	12^{55}	3^{37}
TH	8^{02}	12^{06}	1^{02}	5^{36}
F	7^{59}	12^{01}	12^{55}	6^{05}

Card #4

M	8^{00}	12^{04}	1^{00}	5^{17}
TU	7^{56}	11^{03}	3^{00}	5^{07}
W	8^{01}	12^{02}	12^{59}	6^{46}
TH	8^{04}	12^{04}	12^{55}	4^{32}
F	7^{58}	12^{00}	12^{58}	4^{49}

b) Find the bonus hours. (Remember! An employee who works beyond 40 hours is entitled to a bonus for working overtime.)

c) Find the total hours to be paid. (Actual time worked plus bonus hours.) If your work is correct, Card #1 shows *43 total hours to be paid* and Card #2 shows *47½ total hours to be paid*.

Problem 4

Directions:

a) Find the total actual hours worked from each of the time record sections shown below. Remember, an employee who is late 5 minutes loses fifteen minutes' pay.

Card #1

M	8^{01}	12^{00}	12^{57}	4^{38}
TU	7^{57}	12^{02}	12^{56}	5^{45}
W	8^{04}	12^{00}	1^{00}	6^{20}
TH	7^{56}	12^{04}	1^{02}	6^{11}
F	8^{10}	12^{05}	1^{00}	5^{00}

Card #2

M	8^{00}	12^{02}	12^{57}	5^{53}
TU	8^{03}	12^{01}	1^{01}	6^{07}
W	7^{56}	12^{04}	1^{03}	7^{38}
TH	8^{04}	12^{03}	1^{05}	5^{00}
F	8^{01}	12^{00}	12^{56}	5^{31}

Card #3

M	8^{00}	12^{01}	1^{00}	6^{30}
TU	7^{53}	12^{00}	1^{03}	6^{08}
W	7^{58}	12^{05}	12^{57}	5^{32}
TH	7^{55}	12^{02}	12^{58}	7^{07}
F	8^{00}	12^{03}	12^{53}	5^{39}

Card #4

M	7^{56}	12^{00}	12^{58}	7^{45}
TU	8^{02}	12^{05}	1^{00}	8^{01}
W	7^{57}	12^{01}	12^{57}	7^{16}
TH	8^{58}	12^{06}	12^{55}	5^{00}
F	8^{00}	12^{00}	1^{10}	5^{05}

b) Find the bonus hours. (Remember! An employee who works beyond 40 hours is entitled to a bonus for working overtime.)

c) Find the total hours to be paid. (Actual time worked plus bonus hours.) If your work is correct, Card #1 shows *43⅜ total hours to be paid* and Card #2 shows *46¾ total hours to be paid*.

JOB 73 | RECORDING WAGES IN THE PAYROLL BOOK

Copy the following problems on a sheet of paper and find the answers:

	(1)	(2)	(3)	(4)
Practicing Related Arithmetic	10¼	6¼	a) ½ of 12 =	a) ½ of 1½ =
	6¾	5½	b) ½ of 19 =	b) ½ of 8¼ =
	8¼	10¾	c) ½ of 6½ =	c) ½ of 18¼ =
	7½	8½	d) ½ of 14½ =	d) ½ of 10¼ =
	+ 9¼	+ 7¼	e) ½ of 7½ =	e) ½ of 16¼ =

AIMS

1. To practice finding the total hours for which an employee should be paid.

2. To practice finding the total wages earned by an employee where overtime is involved.

3. To practice recording the information in a payroll book.

EXPLANATION

In previous jobs, you learned the importance of recording time card information in a payroll book. All those computations were based on actual time worked. You have since learned the need to pay workers for overtime. Perhaps you have been wondering how this information is shown in the payroll book. To meet this need, payroll books have additional columns to show separately regular wages, bonus wages for overtime, and total wages. A portion of one page of a payroll book is shown below.

WEEK ENDING										
CARD NO.	NAME OF EMPLOYEE	HOURS WORKED M TU W TH F	TOTAL HRS. WORKED	RATE PER HOUR	EARNINGS AT REGULAR RATE FOR TOTAL HOURS	BONUS FOR OVERTIME	TOTAL WAGES

Illustration 73a – Payroll Book

In order to see how information is entered, consider the sample problem below.

SAMPLE PROBLEM

Larry Beck is hired at the rate of $6.00 per hour in an industry requiring time and a half beyond 40 hours. Larry worked 42 hours. His wages would be figured as follows:

Step 1: Find wages earned for actual hours worked.

$6.00 (hourly rate)
× ___42 (hours worked)
$252.00 (wages for actual hours worked)

Since Larry worked 42 hours, you multiply the hourly rate of $6.00 by the number of hours worked.

Step 2: Find bonus paid for working overtime.

42   (hours actually worked)
−40   (hours on which no overtime bonus will be paid)
2   (hours on which bonus will be figured)

$\frac{1}{2} \times 2 = 1$ bonus hour

$6.00 (hourly rate)
× ___1 (bonus hour)
$6.00 (bonus payment)

Since there is 1 bonus hour, you multiply the hourly rate of $6.00 by this hour to find the wages paid for overtime bonus.

Step 3: Find total wages to be paid.

$252.00 (wages at regular rate = 42 hours × $6.00)
+ __6.00 (wages paid as an overtime bonus = 1 hour × $6.00)
$258.00

To do this, you add his pay at the regular rate (Step 1) and his overtime bonus wages (Step 2). The sum is Larry's total wages.

The information found in the three steps would be entered in the payroll book shown in Illustration 73b on the next page.

An inspector from the federal government checking to see if the employer is following the Fair Labor Standards Act can see that Larry Beck's employer complies with the law.

CARD NO.	NAME OF EMPLOYEE	HOURS WORKED					TOTAL HRS. WORKED	RATE PER HOUR		EARNINGS AT REGULAR RATE FOR TOTAL HOURS		BONUS FOR OVERTIME		TOTAL WAGES	
		M	TU	W	TH	F									
1	Larry Beck	9	8	9	11	5	42	6	00	2 5 2	00	6	00	2 5 8	00
										STEP 1		STEP 2		STEP 3	

Illustration 73b — Payroll Book with an Entry

PRACTICE PROBLEMS

Problem 1

Directions:
a) Copy the following information on a payroll sheet. (See Illustration 73b above.) Date the sheet for the week ending July 18, 19—.

CARD NO.	NAME OF EMPLOYEE	HRS. WORKED					RATE PER HOUR	
		M	TU	W	TH	F		
1	May Calo	8	8	9	10	9	5	30
2	Leo Feuer	7	5	7	8	5	6	25
3	Shirley Hart	9	9	10	8	10	6	50
4	Hugh Kahn	10	9	10	11	8	5	80
5	Craig Sealy	9	9	11	10	6	4	60
	Totals							

b) Find the total hours actually worked by each employee, and enter the information in the proper column.
c) Find the earnings at the regular rate for total hours, the bonus for overtime, and the total wages for each worker. Enter the figures in the proper columns.
d) Find the total earnings at the regular rate for the week for all the five employees and enter the figure. If your work is correct, the total should be $1,217.60.
e) Find the total overtime bonuses for all the five workers for the week, and enter the figure. If your work is correct, the total should be $64.80.

f) Find the total of all the wages paid to the five workers for the week, and enter the figure.

g) Check the answer in direction f) to see if it equals the total of the two answers you found in directions d) and e).

Problem 2

Directions:

a) Copy the following information on a payroll sheet. (See Illustration 73b.) Date the sheet for the week ending July 25, 19—.

CARD NO.	NAME OF EMPLOYEE	HRS. WORKED M	TU	W	TH	F	RATE PER HOUR	
1	May Calo	10	11	9	10	10	5	30
2	Leo Feuer	7½	7½	8	9	9	6	25
3	Shirley Hart	10½	10	7½	8	7	6	50
4	Hugh Kahn	8	8	7½	9½	8½	5	80
5	Craig Sealy	7	8	6½	8½	7	4	60
	Totals							

b) Find the total hours actually worked by each employee, and enter the information in the proper column.

c) Find the earnings at the regular rate for total hours, the bonus for overtime, and the total wages for each worker. Enter the figures in the proper columns.

d) Find the total earnings at the regular rate for the week for all employees and enter the figure. If your work is correct, the total should be $1,211.65.

e) Find the total bonus wages for all employees for the week, and enter the figure. If your work is correct, the total should be $43.73.

f) Find the total of all the wages paid to all the workers, and enter the total.

g) Check the answer in direction f) to see if it equals the total of the two answers you found in directions d) and e).

Problem 3

Directions:

a) Copy the table shown on page 469 on a sheet of paper.

CARD NO.	TOTAL HRS. WORKED	RATE PER HR.	EARNINGS AT REGULAR RATE FOR TOTAL HRS. WORKED	BONUS FOR OVERTIME	TOTAL WAGES
1	40	6 14			
2	52	4 72			
3	30½	5 68			
4	45½	5 24			
5	52½	4 90			
Totals					

b) Find the earnings at the regular rate, the bonus for overtime, and the total wages for *each worker*. Enter the figures in the proper columns.

c) Total each of the last 3 money columns. If your work is correct, the total wages for all employees should be $1,233.31.

Problem 4

Directions:

a) Copy the following table on a sheet of paper:

CARD NO.	TOTAL HRS. WORKED	RATE PER HR.	EARNINGS AT REGULAR RATE FOR TOTAL HRS. WORKED	BONUS FOR OVERTIME	TOTAL WAGES
1	28½	7 12			
2	49	5 06			
3	42½	5 48			
4	48½	4 50			
5	43½	6 70			
Totals					

b) Find the earnings at the regular rate, the bonus for overtime, and the total wages for *each worker*. Enter the figures in the proper columns.

c) Total each of the last 3 money columns. If your work is correct, the total wages should be $1,253.94.

COMPUTING WAGES INVOLVING OVERTIME

Copy the following problems on a sheet of paper and find the answers:

(1)	(2)	(3)	(4)
8¾	7½	a) ½ of 16 =	a) ½ of 9½ =
7¼	8¼	b) ½ of 3 =	b) ½ of 5½ =
5¾	10¾	c) ½ of 2½ =	c) ½ of 6¼ =
11¼	9½	d) ½ of 20½ =	d) ½ of 12¼ =
+ 9¾	+ 6¼	e) ½ of 3½ =	e) ½ of 3¼ =

AIMS

1. To give you additional practice in finding the total hours for which an employee should be paid when overtime is involved.

2. To give you additional practice in finding the total wages earned using a wage computation table.

EXPLANATION

In your previous job, you had practice in finding the wages of an employee who was paid on an hourly rate when overtime was involved. Today you will be given practice in figuring the wages of an employee who is paid at a weekly rate and has worked overtime.

SAMPLE PROBLEM

Neil Paget is a worker in an industry requiring time and a half beyond 40 hours. Neil is hired at a weekly rate of $206.00 for a 40-hour week. Neil worked 44 hours this week. His wages would be figured as follows:

Step 1: Find wages earned at the regular rate.

Look at the wage computation chart shown on page 453. With this chart you can find the wages for any employee who works no more than 40 hours. Do you know how to find his wages for 44 hours even though the chart only gives you the answers up to 40 hours? Here is what you do. You first put down the answer for 40 hours, which is $206.00. In order to find the answer for the additional hours, you look in the "Hours Worked" column for 4. Then you look across to the $206.00 column where you will find $20.60.

Therefore, at the regular rate, Neil gets:

$206.00 for 40 hours
+ 20.60 for 4 hours
$226.60 for 44 hours (at the regular rate)

Step 2: Find bonus paid for working overtime.

44	(hours actually worked)
−40	(hours for which no bonus is to be paid)
4	(hours on which bonus will be figured)

½ × 4 = 2 hours bonus

Since a *bonus* must be paid for *2 hours*, look at the wage computation chart to find what *2 hours* are worth at $206.00 *weekly*. The answer is $10.30. Neil is entitled to this amount as a bonus for overtime.

Step 3: Find total wages to be paid.

To do this, add his wages at the regular rate (Step 1) and his overtime bonus (Step 2) to get the total wages to be paid:

$226.60 (wages earned for 44 hours)
+ 10.30 (wages earned as a bonus for overtime)
$236.90 (total wages earned)

PRACTICE PROBLEMS

Problem 1

Directions:

a) Copy the following table on a sheet of paper:

CARD NO.	TOTAL HRS. WORKED	REGULAR RATE OF PAY PER WEEK FOR 40 HOURS	EARNINGS AT REGULAR RATE FOR TOTAL HRS. WORKED	BONUS FOR OVERTIME	TOTAL WAGES
1	48	200 00			
2	42	205 00			
3	43	209 00			
4	38	201 00			
5	49	208 00			
	Totals				

b) Use the wage computation table and find the earnings at the regular rate, the extra for overtime, and the total wages for *each worker*. Enter the figures in the proper columns.

c) Total each of the last 3 money columns. If your work is correct, the total wages should be $1,182.05.

Problem 2

Directions:
a) Copy the following table on a sheet of paper:

CARD NO.	TOTAL HRS. WORKED	REGULAR RATE OF PAY PER WEEK FOR 40 HOURS	EARNINGS AT REGULAR RATE FOR TOTAL HRS. WORKED	BONUS FOR OVERTIME	TOTAL WAGES
1	39	206 00			
2	46	202 00			
3	50	204 00			
4	45	203 00			
5	47	207 00			
	Totals				

b) Use the wage computation table and find the earnings at the regular rate, the bonus for overtime, and the total wages for *each worker*. Enter the figures in the proper columns.
c) Total each of the last 3 money columns. If your work is correct, the total wages should be $1,231.22.

Problem 3

Directions:
a) Copy the following table on a sheet of paper:

CARD NO.	TOTAL HRS. WORKED	REGULAR RATE OF PAY PER WEEK FOR 40 HOURS	EARNINGS AT REGULAR RATE FOR TOTAL HRS. WORKED	BONUS FOR OVERTIME	TOTAL WAGES
1	$32\frac{1}{2}$	209 00			
2	$40\frac{1}{2}$	200 00			
3	$48\frac{1}{2}$	203 00			
4	$54\frac{1}{2}$	208 00			
5	$43\frac{1}{2}$	201 00			
	Totals				

b) Use the wage computation table and find the earnings at the regular rate, the bonus for overtime, and the total wages for *each worker*. Enter the figures in the proper columns.

c) Total each of the last 3 money columns. If your work is correct, the total wages should be $1,189.76.

Problem 4

Directions:

a) Copy the following table on a sheet of paper:

CARD NO.	TOTAL HRS. WORKED	REGULAR RATE OF PAY PER WEEK FOR 40 HOURS	EARNINGS AT REGULAR RATE FOR TOTAL HRS. WORKED	BONUS FOR OVERTIME	TOTAL WAGES
1	42½	204 00			
2	46½	207 00			
3	49	202 00			
4	41½	206 00			
5	47½	205 00			
	Totals				

b) Use the wage computation table and find the earnings at the regular rate, the bonus for overtime, and the total wages for *each worker*. Enter the figures in the proper money columns.

c) Total each of the last 3 money columns.

Problem 5

Directions:

a) Copy the following table on a sheet of paper:

CARD NO.	TOTAL HRS. WORKED	REGULAR RATE OF PAY PER WEEK FOR 40 HOURS	EARNINGS AT REGULAR RATE FOR TOTAL HRS. WORKED	BONUS FOR OVERTIME	TOTAL WAGES
1	30½	203 00			
2	44½	201 00			
3	45½	208 00			
4	28¼	209 00			
5	42¼	200 00			
	Totals				

b) Use the wage computation table and find the earnings at the regular rate, the bonus for overtime, and the total wages for *each worker*. Enter the figures in the proper columns.

c) Total each of the last 3 money columns.

Problem 6

Directions:

a) Copy the following table on a sheet of paper:

CARD NO.	TOTAL HRS. WORKED	REGULAR RATE OF PAY PER WEEK FOR 40 HOURS	EARNINGS AT REGULAR RATE FOR TOTAL HRS. WORKED	BONUS FOR OVERTIME	TOTAL WAGES
1	40 ¼	2 0 6 00			
2	50 ¼	2 0 3 00			
3	31 ¾	2 0 7 00			
4	42 ¾	2 0 2 00			
5	44 ¾	2 0 5 00			
	Totals				

b) Use the wage computation table and find the earnings at the regular rate, the bonus for overtime, and the total wages for *each worker*.

c) Total each of the last 3 money columns.

JOB 75 | REVIEWING PAYROLL RECORDS

	(1)	(2)	(3)	(4)	(5)
Practicing Related Arithmetic	$6\frac{3}{4}$	$8\frac{1}{2}$	$6.20	a) $\frac{1}{2}$ of 8 =	a) $\frac{1}{2}$ of $4\frac{1}{4}$ =
	$11\frac{1}{4}$	9	$\times 18\frac{1}{4}$	b) $\frac{1}{2}$ of 5 =	b) $\frac{1}{2}$ of $8\frac{1}{4}$ =
	$9\frac{3}{4}$	$7\frac{3}{4}$		c) $\frac{1}{2}$ of $6\frac{1}{2}$ =	c) $\frac{1}{2}$ of $5\frac{1}{4}$ =
	$8\frac{1}{2}$	$10\frac{3}{4}$		d) $\frac{1}{2}$ of $22\frac{1}{2}$ =	d) $\frac{1}{2}$ of $6\frac{3}{4}$ =
	$+\ 7\frac{1}{4}$	$+\ 5\frac{1}{4}$		e) $\frac{1}{2}$ of $17\frac{1}{2}$ =	e) $\frac{1}{2}$ of $10\frac{3}{4}$ =

Copy the following problems on a sheet of paper and find the answers:

AIM

To review the information from previous jobs on the payroll.

EXPLANATION

In this job you will review:
- a) the reading of time cards,
- b) working with a wage computation table,
- c) recording information in a payroll book, and
- d) computing wages where overtime is involved.

PRACTICE PROBLEMS

Problem 1

Directions: Find the total hours worked for each employee from the time record sections of these time cards. Remember, an employee who is late 5 or more minutes loses a quarter of an hour's time. (See pages 433–434.)

Card #1					
M	7^{56}	12^{05}	1^{00}	5^{28}
TU	9^{00}	12^{00}	12^{55}	5^{03}
W	7^{57}	11^{07}	12^{57}	5^{01}
TH	8^{00}	12^{03}	12^{59}	3^{32}
F	7^{59}	12^{01}	1^{00}	7^{18}

Card #2	M	8^{00}	12^{00}	1^{26}	5^{06}
	TU	7^{58}	12^{01}	1^{00}	4^{38}
	W	8^{05}	12^{02}	12^{56}	5^{17}
	TH	7^{57}	10^{45}	1^{02}	5^{04}
	F	8^{02}	12^{03}	1^{04}	6^{51}

Problem 2

Directions:

a) Copy the following information on a payroll sheet. (See Illustration 73b on page 467.) Date the sheet for the week ending May 9, 19––.

CARD NO.	NAME OF EMPLOYEE	HRS. WORKED M	TU	W	TH	F	RATE PER HOUR	
1	Steve Behal	6	7½	10	11½	9	4	62
2	Muriel Day	8	10½	9½	8	7	5	40
3	Dennis Hoff	10¼	7¾	7½	8	7	6	00
4	Claire Rand	8½	6½	11	8½	8	4	84
5	Ray Vogel	9½	10½	9	9¾	8¾	5	00
	Totals							

b) Find the total hours worked by each employee, and enter the information in the proper column.

c) Find the earnings at the regular rate for the total hours actually worked for each employee, and enter the figures in the proper column.

d) Enter in the proper column the amount earned by each employee for the bonus given for overtime.

e) Enter the total wages earned by each employee in the proper column.

f) Total the wages earned at the regular rate, overtime bonus wages, and total wages. If your work is correct, the total wages for all employees should be $1,165.32.

Problem 3

Directions:

a) Copy the table shown on page 477 on a sheet of paper.

CARD NO.	TOTAL HRS. WORKED	REGULAR RATE OF PAY PER WEEK FOR 40 HOURS	EARNINGS AT REGULAR RATE FOR TOTAL HRS. WORKED	BONUS FOR OVERTIME	TOTAL WAGES
1	42	2 08 00			
2	45	2 00 00			
3	44 ½	2 06 00			
4	32 ¾	2 05 00			
5	47 ½	2 07 00			
Totals					

   b) Use the wage computation table on page 453, and find the earnings at the regular rate, the bonus for overtime, and the total wages for each worker. Enter the figures in the proper columns.

   c) Total each of the last 3 money columns. If your work is correct, the total wages for all employees should be $1,134.94.

Problem 4

Directions:

   a) Copy the following table on a sheet of paper:

CARD NO.	TOTAL HRS. WORKED	REGULAR RATE OF PAY PER WEEK FOR 40 HOURS	EARNINGS AT REGULAR RATE FOR TOTAL HRS. WORKED	BONUS FOR OVERTIME	TOTAL WAGES
1	39¼	2 02 00			
2	46½	2 04 00			
3	43 ½	2 09 00			
4	40 ¼	2 01 00			
5	42 ¼	2 03 00			
Totals					

   b) Use the wage computation table on page 453, and find the earnings at the regular rate, the bonus for overtime, and the total wages for each worker. Enter the figures in the proper columns.

   c) Total each of the last 3 money columns. If your work is correct, the total wages for all employees should be $1,111.40.

JOB 76 | DETERMINING SOCIAL SECURITY TAXES

Practicing Related Arithmetic

Copy the following problems on a sheet of paper and find the answers.

(1)	(2)	(3)	(4)	(5)
8¾	$ 23.45	$157.20	$ 98.56	$174.80
11¼	×.0585	×.0585	×.0605	×.0605
5¾				
10				
+ 9½				

AIMS

1. To learn why it is necessary to have social security legislation.

2. To learn how to obtain a social security card.

3. To learn how to figure deductions for social security.

EXPLANATION

In 1935, Congress passed a law known as the Federal Insurance Contributions Act (F.I.C.A.), commonly known as the Social Security Act.

Groups entitled to benefits

This law made provisions for various groups of people to receive monthly payments from the federal government provided they met certain conditions. Since 1935 there have been many changes in the law which have increased the amounts to be received by the worker, and there have been changes in the groups of people who are entitled to benefits. In general, workers may now retire at the age of 62 or thereafter. There are also provisions for payments to be made, under certain conditions, to widows, dependent children, and permanently disabled workers.

Since July 1, 1966, the law also provides medical care for persons over 65 years of age.

The important point to remember is that every person, regardless of wealth or lack of wealth, is entitled to receive payment if certain conditions have been satisfied. The United States Department of Health, Education, and Welfare prints a booklet known as *Your Social Security* which contains much valuable information as to the provisions of the Old-Age and Survivors Insurance Law which is one part of the Social Security Act. The United States Department of Health, Education, and Welfare has many offices throughout our country where information is given freely. You can find the office nearest your home by consulting a telephone book.

To be able to pay out these monthly benefits, the federal government taxes the employer and the employee equally. The rates are based on wages earned by the worker up to $14,100.00 a year. This means that only the first $14,100.00 of a worker's wages are subject to social security deductions by any *one* employer. Once an employee has reached $14,100.00 in wages for that year, the employer stops making deductions. This figure can be changed by Congress at any time.

Rates are based on wages up to $14,100.00

The rates are as follows:

Calendar Years	Employee Must Pay	Employer Must Pay
1975–77	5.85%	5.85%
1978–80	6.05%	6.05%
1981–85	6.3 %	6.3 %
1986–92	6.45%	6.45%
(These rates can be changed by Congress at any time.)		

When you compare the rates to be paid by the employees with those to be paid by the employer, you see they are the same.

The employer must deduct the social security contribution from the employee's wages each payday. This money is held by the employer and on certain dates this money, plus the employer's own share of the tax, is sent to the government. For example, if $50.00 has been collected from all of the employees, the employer must match this $50.00 and send $100.00 to the government.

To keep an accurate record of the wages and the deductions for each worker, the government has an individual record card for each worker. This record card is started when the government is notified that a person has become a member of the social security system. To become a member, any person working in any industry covered by the Social Security Act may apply to the nearest social security office for an application blank.

The government keeps a separate record card for each employee throughout the employee's lifetime

A Social Security application blank is shown in Illustration 76a on page 480.

APPLICATION FOR A SOCIAL SECURITY NUMBER

ID   CN   DO

See Instructions on Back.   *Print in Black or Dark Blue Ink or Use Typewriter.*   DO NOT WRITE IN THE ABOVE SPACE

1 *Print* FULL NAME YOU WILL USE IN WORK OR BUSINESS — *(First Name)* Martha *(Middle Name or Initial – if none, draw line ___)* O. *(Last Name)* Bateman

2 *Print* FULL NAME GIVEN YOU AT BIRTH — Martha O. Bateman

6 YOUR DATE OF BIRTH *(Month)* 6 *(Day)* 18 *(Year)* --

3 PLACE OF BIRTH *(City)* Augusta *(County if known)* *(State)* Georgia

7 YOUR PRESENT AGE *(Age on last birthday)* 17

4 MOTHER'S FULL NAME AT HER BIRTH *(Her maiden name)* Frances K. Ryder

8 YOUR SEX MALE ☐ FEMALE ☑

5 FATHER'S FULL NAME *(Regardless of whether living or dead)* Henry L. Bateman

9 YOUR COLOR OR RACE WHITE ☑ NEGRO ☐ OTHER ☐

10 HAVE YOU EVER BEFORE APPLIED FOR OR HAD A SOCIAL SECURITY, RAILROAD, OR TAX ACCOUNT NUMBER? NO ☑ DON'T KNOW ☐ YES ☐ *(If "YES" Print STATE in which you applied and DATE you applied and SOCIAL SECURITY NUMBER if known)*

11 YOUR MAILING ADDRESS *(Number and Street, Apt. No., P.O. Box, or Rural Route)* 609 Parker Street *(City)* Dallas *(State)* Texas *(Zip Code)* 75205

12 TODAY'S DATE April 11, 19--

NOTICE: Whoever, with intent to falsify his or someone else's true identity, willfully furnishes or causes to be furnished false information in applying for a social security number, is subject to a fine of not more than $1,000 or imprisonment for up to 1 year, or both.

13 TELEPHONE NUMBER 214-446-6910

14 Sign YOUR NAME HERE *(Do Not Print)* Martha O. Bateman

TREASURY DEPARTMENT Internal Revenue Service   ☐ RESCREEN   ☐ ASSIGN   ☐ DUP ISSUED   Return completed application to nearest SOCIAL SECURITY ADMINISTRATION OFFICE

FORM SS-5 (2-73)

Illustration 76a — Social Security Application

Every person should file for a social security card.

After this application blank is completed and sent in, the employee will receive a card which looks like this:

Illustration 76b — Social Security Card

Note that the card comes in two parts and that each part has the identification number of the holder of the card. You are well aware that there are many people who have identical names; therefore, the government has found it helpful to have identification numbers to distinguish one person from another. Since both a worker's name and account number are needed for the employer's payroll records, the card must be shown to the employer when the worker is hired. This enables the employer to send in a report of the name, identification number, total wages, and social security deduction for each employee. When the government receives this information, the employee's

The social security number is permanent throughout a person's lifetime

record is properly credited. Now that you have a little background information, you can do the arithmetic connected with social security deductions.

SAMPLE PROBLEM

Peter Waret earns $253.00 for the week. What amount will be deducted from his wages for social security? What amount will he receive (net pay)?

Step 1: Multiply the wages by the social security rate.

Since the social security rate is 5.85%, you must multiply the gross wages of $253.00 by 5.85%. You have learned that to multiply any number by a percent, you must first change the percent to its decimal equivalent. Therefore, to change 5.85% to a decimal, you drop the percent sign and divide by 100. The 5.85% becomes .0585. You can find the answer by any one of the two methods shown below:

Method #1

$$\begin{array}{r} \$253.00 \quad \text{(total wages)} \\ \times .0585 \quad \text{(5.85\% changed to its decimal equivalent)} \\ \hline 126500 \\ 202400 \\ 126500 \\ \hline \$14.800500 = \$14.80 \end{array}$$

Round off
final answer

Method #2 (eliminating the zeros in Method #1 which does not affect the answer)

$$\begin{array}{r} \$253 \\ \times .0585 \\ \hline 1265 \\ 2024 \\ 1265 \\ \hline \$14.8005 = \$14.80 \end{array}$$

Step 2: Deduct the social security charge from the total wages.

$$\begin{array}{r} \$253.00 \quad \text{(total wages)} \\ -14.80 \quad \text{(social security charge)} \\ \hline \$238.20 \quad \text{(net pay)} \end{array}$$

PRACTICE PROBLEMS

Problem 1

Directions:
a) Copy the table on page 482.

Week Ending June 6, 19--

Name	Total Wages		Social Security Tax		Net Pay	
B. Dart	203	00				
T. Forst	212	00				
M. Ivy	257	00				
S. Owen	186	00				
C. Palmer	192	70				
G. Renze	241	35				
Totals						

b) Find the net pay for each employee using the current social security tax rate. Enter the social security tax and the net pay for each worker in the proper column.

c) Find the total for each column. If your work is correct, the total "Net Pay" column should be $1,216.47.

d) Check your work by adding the total of the "Net Pay" column to the total of the "Social Security Tax" column to see if they equal the "Total Wages" column.

Problem 2

Directions:

a) Copy the following table:

Week Ending June 13, 19--

Name	Total Wages		Social Security Tax		Net Pay	
B. Dart	209	10				
T. Forst	213	45				
M. Ivy	254	60				
S. Owen	179	80				
C. Palmer	182	50				
G. Renze	235	16				
Totals						

b) Find the net pay for each employee using the current social security tax rate. Enter the social security tax and the net pay for each worker in the proper column.

c) Find the total for each column. If your work is correct, the total "Net Pay" column should be $1,200.04.

d) Check your work by adding the total of the "Net Pay" column to the total of the "Social Security Tax" column to see if they equal the "Total Wages" column.

Problem 3

Directions:

a) Copy the following table:

Week Ending June 20, 19--

Name	Total Wages		Social Security Tax		Net Pay	
B. Dart	207	43				
T. Forst	210	56				
M. Ivy	248	17				
S. Owen	193	20				
C. Palmer	175	40				
G. Renze	246	90				
Totals						

b) Find the net pay for each employee using the current social security tax rate. Enter the social security tax and the net pay for each worker in the proper column.

c) Find the total for each column. If your work is correct, the total "Net Pay" column should be $1,206.69.

d) Check your work by adding the total of the "Net Pay" column to the total of the "Social Security Tax" column to see if they equal the "Total Wages" column.

Problem 4

Directions:

a) Copy the following table:

Week Ending June 27, 19--

Name	Total Wages		Social Security Tax		Net Pay	
B. Dart	204	36				
T. Forst	215	75				
M. Ivy	239	08				
S. Owen	194	23				
C. Palmer	185	09				
G. Renze	240	56				
Totals						

b) Find the net pay for each employee using the current social security tax rate. Enter the social security tax and the net pay for each worker in the proper column.

c) Find the total for each column. If your work is correct, the total "Net Pay" column should be $1,204.24.

d) Check your work by adding the total of the "Net Pay" column to the total of the "Social Security Tax" column to see if they equal the "Total Wages" column.

Practicing
Related
Arithmetic

Copy the following problems on a sheet of paper and find the answers:

(1)	(2)	(3)	(4)	(5)
9¾	$ 64.70	$182.39	$205.40	$217.35
10¼	×.0585	×.0585	×.0605	×.0605
8½				
7¼				
+ 4½				

AIM

To learn how to use a table to find the social security tax deduction.

EXPLANATION

In your previous job, you learned to compute the deduction for social security by doing problems in multiplication. Since you had used a table profitably in Job 70 to compute wages and thus eliminate the need for multiplication, you may have asked yourself whether the same idea could be applied to finding the social security deduction. You showed clear thinking if that idea occurred to you because the government has done just that. A table for social security deductions can be found in a booklet known as *Employer's Tax Guide* issued by the Internal Revenue Service, United States Treasury Department. New tables are published whenever the tax rate changes. However, the method of using the table remains the same. A copy of the table appears on pages 486 and 487. Use this table to do some sample problems.

Tax tables are supplied by the Internal Revenue Service

SAMPLE PROBLEM 1

Phil Koff earned $177.70. Here is how his social security deduction of $10.40 was found.

You would first refer to the "Wages" column of the Social Security Tax Table (See page 486).

Notice that the word "Wages" appears above *two* columns. The figures in the "At Least" column are the ones to which you refer first to locate a certain wage figure.

SOCIAL SECURITY EMPLOYEE TAX TABLE — CONTINUED
5.85 percent employee tax deductions

(Tables from $.00 to $177.70 have been omitted)

Wages At least	Wages But less than	Tax to be withheld	Wages At least	Wages But less than	Tax to be withheld	Wages At least	Wages But less than	Tax to be withheld	Wages At least	Wages But less than	Tax to be withheld
$177.70	$177.87	$10.40	$188.81	$188.98	$11.05	$199.92	$200.09	$11.70	$211.03	$211.20	$12.35
177.87	178.04	10.41	188.98	189.15	11.06	200.09	200.26	11.71	211.20	211.37	12.36
178.04	178.21	10.42	189.15	189.32	11.07	200.26	200.43	11.72	211.37	211.54	12.37
178.21	178.38	10.43	189.32	189.49	11.08	200.43	200.60	11.73	211.54	211.71	12.38
178.38	178.55	10.44	189.49	189.66	11.09	200.60	200.77	11.74	211.71	211.89	12.39
178.55	178.72	10.45	189.66	189.83	11.10	200.77	200.95	11.75	211.89	212.06	12.40
178.72	178.89	10.46	189.83	190.00	11.11	200.95	201.12	11.76	212.06	212.23	12.41
178.89	179.06	10.47	190.00	190.18	11.12	201.12	201.29	11.77	212.23	212.40	12.42
179.06	179.24	10.48	190.18	190.35	11.13	201.29	201.46	11.78	212.40	212.57	12.43
179.24	179.41	10.49	190.35	190.52	11.14	201.46	201.63	11.79	212.57	212.74	12.44
179.41	179.58	10.50	190.52	190.69	11.15	201.63	201.80	11.80	212.74	212.91	12.45
179.58	179.75	10.51	190.69	190.86	11.16	201.80	201.97	11.81	212.91	213.08	12.46
179.75	179.92	10.52	190.86	191.03	11.17	201.97	202.14	11.82	213.08	213.25	12.47
179.92	180.09	10.53	191.03	191.20	11.18	202.14	202.31	11.83	213.25	213.42	12.48
180.09	180.26	10.54	191.20	191.37	11.19	202.31	202.48	11.84	213.42	213.59	12.49
180.26	180.43	10.55	191.37	191.54	11.20	202.48	202.65	11.85	213.59	213.77	12.50
180.43	180.60	10.56	191.54	191.71	11.21	202.65	202.83	11.86	213.77	213.94	12.51
180.60	180.77	10.57	191.71	191.89	11.22	202.83	203.00	11.87	213.94	214.11	12.52
180.77	180.95	10.58	191.89	192.06	11.23	203.00	203.17	11.88	214.11	214.28	12.53
180.95	181.12	10.59	192.06	192.23	11.24	203.17	203.34	11.89	214.28	214.45	12.54
181.12	181.29	10.60	192.23	192.40	11.25	203.34	203.51	11.90	214.45	214.62	12.55
181.29	181.46	10.61	192.40	192.57	11.26	203.51	203.68	11.91	214.62	214.79	12.56
181.46	181.63	10.62	192.57	192.74	11.27	203.68	203.85	11.92	214.79	214.96	12.57
181.63	181.80	10.63	192.74	192.91	11.28	203.85	204.02	11.93	214.96	215.13	12.58
181.80	181.97	10.64	192.91	193.08	11.29	204.02	204.19	11.94	215.13	215.30	12.59
181.97	182.14	10.65	193.08	193.25	11.30	204.19	204.36	11.95	215.30	215.48	12.60
182.14	182.31	10.66	193.25	193.42	11.31	204.36	204.53	11.96	215.48	215.65	12.61
182.31	182.48	10.67	193.42	193.59	11.32	204.53	204.71	11.97	215.65	215.82	12.62
182.48	182.65	10.68	193.59	193.77	11.33	204.71	204.88	11.98	215.82	215.99	12.63
182.65	182.83	10.69	193.77	193.94	11.34	204.88	205.05	11.99	215.99	216.16	12.64
182.83	183.00	10.70	193.94	194.11	11.35	205.05	205.22	12.00	216.16	216.33	12.65
183.00	183.17	10.71	194.11	194.28	11.36	205.22	205.39	12.01	216.33	216.50	12.66
183.17	183.34	10.72	194.28	194.45	11.37	205.39	205.56	12.02	216.50	216.67	12.67
183.34	183.51	10.73	194.45	194.62	11.38	205.56	205.73	12.03	216.67	216.84	12.68
183.51	183.68	10.74	194.62	194.79	11.39	205.73	205.90	12.04	216.84	217.01	12.69
183.68	183.85	10.75	194.79	194.96	11.40	205.90	206.07	12.05	217.01	217.18	12.70
183.85	184.02	10.76	194.96	195.13	11.41	206.07	206.24	12.06	217.18	217.36	12.71
184.02	184.19	10.77	195.13	195.30	11.42	206.24	206.42	12.07	217.36	217.53	12.72
184.19	184.36	10.78	195.30	195.48	11.43	206.42	206.59	12.08	217.53	217.70	12.73
184.36	184.53	10.79	195.48	195.65	11.44	206.59	206.76	12.09	217.70	217.87	12.74
184.53	184.71	10.80	195.65	195.82	11.45	206.76	206.93	12.10	217.87	218.04	12.75
184.71	184.88	10.81	195.82	195.99	11.46	206.93	207.10	12.11	218.04	218.21	12.76
184.88	185.05	10.82	195.99	196.16	11.47	207.10	207.27	12.12	218.21	218.38	12.77
185.05	185.22	10.83	196.16	196.33	11.48	207.27	207.44	12.13	218.38	218.55	12.78
185.22	185.39	10.84	196.33	196.50	11.49	207.44	207.61	12.14	218.55	218.72	12.79
185.39	185.56	10.85	196.50	196.67	11.50	207.61	207.78	12.15	218.72	218.89	12.80
185.56	185.73	10.86	196.67	196.84	11.51	207.78	207.95	12.16	218.89	219.06	12.81
185.73	185.90	10.87	196.84	197.01	11.52	207.95	208.12	12.17	219.06	219.24	12.82
185.90	186.07	10.88	197.01	197.18	11.53	208.12	208.30	12.18	219.24	219.41	12.83
186.07	186.24	10.89	197.18	197.36	11.54	208.30	208.47	12.19	219.41	219.58	12.84
186.24	186.42	10.90	197.36	197.53	11.55	208.47	208.64	12.20	219.58	219.75	12.85
186.42	186.59	10.91	197.53	197.70	11.56	208.64	208.81	12.21	219.75	219.92	12.86
186.59	186.76	10.92	197.70	197.87	11.57	208.81	208.98	12.22	219.92	220.09	12.87
186.76	186.93	10.93	197.87	198.04	11.58	208.98	209.15	12.23	220.09	220.26	12.88
186.93	187.10	10.94	198.04	198.21	11.59	209.15	209.32	12.24	220.26	220.43	12.89
187.10	187.27	10.95	198.21	198.38	11.60	209.32	209.49	12.25	220.43	220.60	12.90
187.27	187.44	10.96	198.38	198.55	11.61	209.49	209.66	12.26	220.60	220.77	12.91
187.44	187.61	10.97	198.55	198.72	11.62	209.66	209.83	12.27	220.77	220.95	12.92
187.61	187.78	10.98	198.72	198.89	11.63	209.83	210.00	12.28	220.95	221.12	12.93
187.78	187.95	10.99	198.89	199.06	11.64	210.00	210.18	12.29	221.12	221.29	12.94
187.95	188.12	11.00	199.06	199.24	11.65	210.18	210.35	12.30	221.29	221.46	12.95
188.12	188.30	11.01	199.24	199.41	11.66	210.35	210.52	12.31	221.46	221.63	12.96
188.30	188.47	11.02	199.41	199.58	11.67	210.52	210.69	12.32	221.63	221.80	12.97
188.47	188.64	11.03	199.58	199.75	11.68	210.69	210.86	12.33	221.80	221.97	12.98
188.64	188.81	11.04	199.75	199.92	11.69	210.86	211.03	12.34	221.97	222.14	12.99

SOCIAL SECURITY EMPLOYEE TAX TABLE — CONTINUED
5.85 percent employee tax deductions

Wages		Tax to be withheld	Wages		Tax to be withheld	Wages		Tax to be withheld	Wages		Tax to be withheld
At least	But less than		At least	But less than		At least	But less than		At least	But less than	
$222.14	$222.31	$13.00	$233.25	$233.42	$13.65	$244.36	$244.53	$14.30	$255.48	$255.65	$14.95
222.31	222.48	13.01	233.42	233.59	13.66	244.53	244.71	14.31	255.65	255.82	14.96
222.48	222.65	13.02	233.59	233.77	13.67	244.71	244.88	14.32	255.82	255.99	14.97
222.65	222.83	13.03	233.77	233.94	13.68	244.88	245.05	14.33	255.99	256.16	14.98
222.83	223.00	13.04	233.94	234.11	13.69	245.05	245.22	14.34	256.16	256.33	14.99
223.00	223.17	13.05	234.11	234.28	13.70	245.22	245.39	14.35	256.33	256.50	15.00
223.17	223.34	13.06	234.28	234.45	13.71	245.39	245.56	14.36	256.50	256.67	15.01
223.34	223.51	13.07	234.45	234.62	13.72	245.56	245.73	14.37	256.67	256.84	15.02
223.51	223.68	13.08	234.62	234.79	13.73	245.73	245.90	14.38	256.84	257.01	15.03
223.68	223.85	13.09	234.79	234.96	13.74	245.90	246.07	14.39	257.01	257.18	15.04
223.85	224.02	13.10	234.96	235.13	13.75	246.07	246.24	14.40	257.18	257.36	15.05
224.02	224.19	13.11	235.13	235.30	13.76	246.24	246.42	14.41	257.36	257.53	15.06
224.19	224.36	13.12	235.30	235.48	13.77	246.42	246.59	14.42	257.53	257.70	15.07
224.36	224.53	13.13	235.48	235.65	13.78	246.59	246.76	14.43	257.70	257.87	15.08
224.53	224.71	13.14	235.65	235.82	13.79	246.76	246.93	14.44	257.87	258.04	15.09
224.71	224.88	13.15	235.82	235.99	13.80	246.93	247.10	14.45	258.04	258.21	15.10
224.88	225.05	13.16	235.99	236.16	13.81	247.10	247.27	14.46	258.21	258.38	15.11
225.05	225.22	13.17	236.16	236.33	13.82	247.27	247.44	14.47	258.38	258.55	15.12
225.22	225.39	13.18	236.33	236.50	13.83	247.44	247.61	14.48	258.55	258.72	15.13
225.39	225.56	13.19	236.50	236.67	13.84	247.61	247.78	14.49	258.72	258.89	15.14
225.56	225.73	13.20	236.67	236.84	13.85	247.78	247.95	14.50	258.89	259.06	15.15
225.73	225.90	13.21	236.84	237.01	13.86	247.95	248.12	14.51	259.06	259.24	15.16
225.90	226.07	13.22	237.01	237.18	13.87	248.12	248.30	14.52	259.24	259.41	15.17
226.07	226.24	13.23	237.18	237.36	13.88	248.30	248.47	14.53	259.41	259.58	15.18
226.24	226.42	13.24	237.36	237.53	13.89	248.47	248.64	14.54	259.58	259.75	15.19
226.42	226.59	13.25	237.53	237.70	13.90	248.64	248.81	14.55	259.75	259.92	15.20
226.59	226.76	13.26	237.70	237.87	13.91	248.81	248.98	14.56	259.92	260.09	15.21
226.76	226.93	13.27	237.87	238.04	13.92	248.98	249.15	14.57	260.09	260.26	15.22
226.93	227.10	13.28	238.04	238.21	13.93	249.15	249.32	14.58	260.26	260.43	15.23
227.10	227.27	13.29	238.21	238.38	13.94	249.32	249.49	14.59	260.43	260.60	15.24
227.27	227.44	13.30	238.38	238.55	13.95	249.49	249.66	14.60	260.60	260.77	15.25
227.44	227.61	13.31	238.55	238.72	13.96	249.66	249.83	14.61	260.77	260.95	15.26
227.61	227.78	13.32	238.72	238.89	13.97	249.83	250.00	14.62	260.95	261.12	15.27
227.78	227.95	13.33	238.89	239.06	13.98	250.00	250.18	14.63	261.12	261.29	15.28
227.95	228.12	13.34	239.06	239.24	13.99	250.18	250.35	14.64	261.29	261.46	15.29
228.12	228.30	13.35	239.24	239.41	14.00	250.35	250.52	14.65	261.46	261.63	15.30
228.30	228.47	13.36	239.41	239.58	14.01	250.52	250.69	14.66	261.63	261.80	15.31
228.47	228.64	13.37	239.58	239.75	14.02	250.69	250.86	14.67	261.80	261.97	15.32
228.64	228.81	13.38	239.75	239.92	14.03	250.86	251.03	14.68	261.97	262.14	15.33
228.81	228.98	13.39	239.92	240.09	14.04	251.03	251.20	14.69	262.14	262.31	15.34
228.98	229.15	13.40	240.09	240.26	14.05	251.20	251.37	14.70	262.31	262.48	15.35
229.15	229.32	13.41	240.26	240.43	14.06	251.37	251.54	14.71	262.48	262.65	15.36
229.32	229.49	13.42	240.43	240.60	14.07	251.54	251.71	14.72	262.65	262.83	15.37
229.49	229.66	13.43	240.60	240.77	14.08	251.71	251.89	14.73	262.83	263.00	15.38
229.66	229.83	13.44	240.77	240.95	14.09	251.89	252.06	14.74	263.00	263.17	15.39
229.83	230.00	13.45	240.95	241.12	14.10	252.06	252.23	14.75	263.17	263.34	15.40
230.00	230.18	13.46	241.12	241.29	14.11	252.23	252.40	14.76	263.34	263.51	15.41
230.18	230.35	13.47	241.29	241.46	14.12	252.40	252.57	14.77	263.51	263.68	15.42
230.35	230.52	13.48	241.46	241.63	14.13	252.57	252.74	14.78	263.68	263.85	15.43
230.52	230.69	13.49	241.63	241.80	14.14	252.74	252.91	14.79	263.85	264.02	15.44
230.69	230.86	13.50	241.80	241.97	14.15	252.91	253.08	14.80	264.02	264.19	15.45
230.86	231.03	13.51	241.97	242.14	14.16	253.08	253.25	14.81	264.19	264.36	15.46
231.03	231.20	13.52	242.14	242.31	14.17	253.25	253.42	14.82	264.36	264.53	15.47
231.20	231.37	13.53	242.31	242.48	14.18	253.42	253.59	14.83	264.53	264.71	15.48
231.37	231.54	13.54	242.48	242.65	14.19	253.59	253.77	14.84	264.71	264.88	15.49
231.54	231.71	13.55	242.65	242.83	14.20	253.77	253.94	14.85	264.88	265.05	15.50
231.71	231.89	13.56	242.83	243.00	14.21	253.94	254.11	14.86	265.05	265.22	15.51
231.89	232.06	13.57	243.00	243.17	14.22	254.11	254.28	14.87	265.22	265.39	15.52
232.06	232.23	13.58	243.17	243.34	14.23	254.28	254.45	14.88	265.39	265.56	15.53
232.23	232.40	13.59	243.34	243.51	14.24	254.45	254.62	14.89	265.56	265.73	15.54
232.40	232.57	13.60	243.51	243.68	14.25	254.62	254.79	14.90	265.73	265.90	15.55
232.57	232.74	13.61	243.68	243.85	14.26	254.79	254.96	14.91	265.90	266.07	15.56
232.74	232.91	13.62	243.85	244.02	14.27	254.96	255.13	14.92	266.07	266.24	15.57
232.91	233.08	13.63	244.02	244.19	14.28	255.13	255.30	14.93	266.24	266.42	15.58
233.08	233.25	13.64	244.19	244.36	14.29	255.30	255.48	14.94	266.42	266.59	15.59

Your job is to find $177.70 in the column headed "At Least." When you do this, you will find the figures shown below:

Wages   **F.I.C.A.**

At Least (Column 1)	But Less Than (Column 2)	Social Security Tax To Be Withheld
$177.70	$177.87	$10.40
177.87	178.04	10.41

This means that any wages which fall between *$177.70* and *$177.87* will have the same tax of *$10.40*. If you tried to find the social security tax by multiplying *$177.70* by 5.85%, you would get an answer of *$10.40*. If you tried to multiply *$177.71* by 5.85%, you would again get a rounded off answer of *$10.40*. If you tried to multiply *$177.72* by 5.85%, you would again get a rounded off answer of *$10.40*. In fact, you would get the same answer of *$10.40* if you multiplied any number which *was at least $177.70 but less than $177.87 by 5.85%*. The rounded off amount would only change to *$10.41* when you tried to multiply *$177.87* by 5.85%. That is the reason the table is headed "At Least" and "But Less Than." Therefore, if you cannot find the exact amount you are looking for in Column 1, you see if the amount can be located between Columns 1 and 2.

Locating the tax on wages which do not appear in the table

For example, part of the table is shown below. If you were looking for *$178.00*, you would not find it in the chart. You know, however, *$178.00* falls between *$177.87* in Column 1 and *$178.04* in Column 2. Therefore, the tax is *$10.41*. If you were looking for *$178.25*, you would not find it in the chart. However, *$178.25* falls between *$178.21* in Column 1 and *$178.38* in Column 2. Therefore, the tax is *$10.43*.

Wages   **F.I.C.A.**

At Least (Column 1)	But Less Than (Column 2)	Social Security Tax To Be Withheld
$177.70	$177.87	$10.40
177.87	178.04	10.41
178.04	178.21	10.42
178.21	178.38	10.43
178.38	178.55	10.44

Suppose you had to find the tax on *$178.38*. Would you select *$10.43* or *$10.44*? You would select *$10.44*. Notice that although *$178.38* appears in Column 2, the column is headed "But Less Than." That means it *does not include $178.38*. Therefore, you must go to the next line and look at Column 1 where you again see $178.38, but this column is headed "At Least." Therefore, the tax is *$10.44*.

SAMPLE PROBLEM 2

To help you learn to use the table, here are a number of problems with the correct answers. Look at the F.I.C.A. (Federal Insurance Contributions Act, commonly called the Social Security Act) table found on pages 486 and 487, and see if you get the same answers.

Place a ruler underneath the proper wage column to prevent your eyes from shifting to the wrong columns in the table.

	Wages	Social Security Tax (F.I.C.A. Tax) Per Table
a)	$188 81	11 05
b)	199 92	11 70
c)	211 03	12 35
d)	188 75	11 04
e)	199 80	11 69
f)	210 25	12 30
g)	231 00	13 51
h)	250 00	14 63
i)	241 62	14 13
j)	225 00	13 16

PRACTICE PROBLEMS

Problem 1

Directions:
a) Copy the table below:

Card No.	Wages	Social Security Tax
1	187 78	
2	198 89	
3	227 95	
4	252 74	
5	248 64	
6	257 30	
7	260 25	
8	235 00	
9	247 00	
10	225 70	
Totals		

b) Enter the social security tax in the proper column. Use the tables on pages 486–487.

c) Total all money columns. If your work is correct, the total social security taxes should be $136.98.

Problem 2

Directions:
a) Copy the table below:

Card No.	Wages	Social Security Tax	
1	182 04		
2	193 00		
3	236 10		
4	221 05		
5	246 19		
6	249 00		
7	261 25		
8	216 16		
9	205 00		
10	180 95		
Totals			

b) Enter the social security tax in the proper column. Use the table on pages 486 and 487.
c) Total all money columns. If your work is correct, the total social security taxes should be $128.16.

Problem 3

Directions:
a) Copy the table below:

Card No.	Wages	Social Security Tax	
1	201 00		
2	240 95		
3	260 77		
4	211 25		
5	259 00		
6	196 00		
7	233 00		
8	206 07		
9	179 60		
10	195 00		
Totals			

b) Enter the social security tax in the proper column. Use the tables on pages 486 and 487.

c) Total all money columns. If your work is correct, the total social security taxes should be $127.71.

Problem 4

Directions:

a) Copy the table below:

Card No.	Wages	Social Security Tax	
1	189 23		
2	218 30		
3	208 47		
4	243 00		
5	224 70		
6	191 16		
7	202 50		
8	234 90		
9	251 65		
10	258 40		
Totals			

b) Enter the social security tax in the proper column. Use the tables on pages 486 and 487.

c) Total all money columns. If your work is correct, the total social security taxes should be $130.01.

Problem 5

Directions:

a) Copy the table below:

Card No.	Wages	Social Security Tax	
1	213 00		
2	214 00		
3	197 45		
4	178 89		
5	194 62		
6	205 56		
7	184 18		
8	234 79		
9	217 08		
10	241 00		
Totals			

b) Enter the social security tax in the proper column. Use the tables on pages 486 and 487.

c) Total all money columns. If your work is correct, the total social security taxes should be $121.73.

| **DETERMINING WITHHOLDING TAXES**

	Copy the following problems on a sheet of paper and find the answers:			
	(1)	(2)	(3)	(4)
Practicing Related Arithmetic	6¼	a) ½ × 8 =	\$140.28	\$213.53
	5¼	b) ½ × 12 =	×.0585	×.0605
	9	c) ½ × 4½ =		
	7½	d) ½ × 10½ =		
	+8¼	e) ½ × 7½ =		

AIMS

1. To understand the meaning of "withholding taxes."

2. To practice using a withholding tax table.

EXPLANATION

To pay for the expenses of operating the federal government, people earning beyond a certain amount of income are required to pay a federal income tax.

In general, the person who earns more than someone else will pay a larger tax, as our system of taxation is based upon the ability of people to pay the tax.

Income taxes formerly were paid on a yearly basis. To lighten the burden of paying income taxes, the government enacted a law known as the Withholding Tax Law. This law requires employers to deduct a certain sum of money from the wages of their employees each payday.

Deductions are made each payday

The amount that must be deducted can be found in the booklet mentioned in Job 77, known as the *Employer's Tax Guide*, published by the Internal Revenue Service, United States Treasury Department. Besides tables for social security taxes, it also has a set of tables known as the "Wage-Bracket Table Method of Income Tax Withholding."

There are tables for:

Separate tables can be found for making deductions from wages paid weekly, biweekly (every two weeks), semimonthly (every half month), monthly, and daily to single and married persons. Since businesses differ as to their pay periods, they need tables which can be used for these different pay periods.

a) different pay periods
b) single persons
c) married persons

On pages 495 and 496 you will find a table based on a weekly pay period for married persons. After you learn how to use this table, you will be able to use tables for any other pay period.

Exemptions

Notice that the numbers shown horizontally (straight across) read from 0 to 10 or more. Each of these figures shows the number of exemptions a worker expects to claim in figuring income tax at the end of the year. In general, a single worker has one exemption (himself or herself). A married worker with no children has two exemptions, one for the husband and one for the wife. A married worker with three children would claim five exemptions — one each for the husband and the wife and one for each of the three children. A worker who is single and who supports a widowed mother would be entitled to two exemptions, one for the worker and one for the mother. Occasionally a person may claim no exemptions because that person may be claimed as an exemption by someone else. For example, a husband may claim his working wife as an exemption; therefore, she would claim no exemption for herself.

Every time a worker is employed, the employer will ask the worker to fill out a form furnished by the Treasury Department known as "Form W-4," which looks like this:

Form **W-4**	**Employee's Withholding Allowance Certificate**	
(Rev. Aug. 1974) Department of the Treasury Internal Revenue Service	(This certificate is for income tax withholding purposes only; it will remain in effect until you change it.)	
Type or print your full name _John Brett_	Your social security number _512-03-6048_	
Home address (Number and street or rural route) _132 Hill Street_	Marital status ☐ Single ☑ Married	
City or town, State and ZIP code _Muncie, IN 47303_	(If married but legally separated, or wife (husband) is a nonresident alien, check the single block.)	
1 Total number of allowances you are claiming		_3_
2 Additional amount, if any, you want deducted from each pay (if your employer agrees)		$ _O_
I certify that to the best of my knowledge and belief, the number of withholding allowances claimed on this certificate does not exceed the number to which I am entitled.		
Signature ▶ _John Brett_	Date ▶ _April 21_ , 19_--_	

Illustration 78 — Form W-4

W-4 form shows how many exemptions are claimed

As you can see, this tells the employer how many exemptions a worker claims.

Once you know how many exemptions the worker claims, you refer to the withholding tax table on pages 495 and 496. Look at the first two vertical columns (read down instead of across) and you will note that the first column states "At least" and the second column reads "But less than." These columns are used when you know the worker's wages and you want to locate the withholding tax deduction. (You used the same process in working with the social security tax table in the previous job.)

MARRIED Persons — **WEEKLY** Payroll Period

And the wages are —		And the number of withholding allowances claimed is —										
At least	But less than	0	1	2	3	4	5	6	7	8	9	10 or more
		The amount of income tax to be withheld shall be —										
$0	$11	$0	$0	$0	$0	$0	$0	$0	$0	$0	$0	$0
11	12	.10	0	0	0	0	0	0	0	0	0	0
12	13	.30	0	0	0	0	0	0	0	0	0	0
13	14	.40	0	0	0	0	0	0	0	0	0	0
14	15	.50	0	0	0	0	0	0	0	0	0	0
15	16	.70	0	0	0	0	0	0	0	0	0	0
16	17	.80	0	0	0	0	0	0	0	0	0	0
17	18	1.00	0	0	0	0	0	0	0	0	0	0
18	19	1.10	0	0	0	0	0	0	0	0	0	0
19	20	1.20	0	0	0	0	0	0	0	0	0	0
20	21	1.40	0	0	0	0	0	0	0	0	0	0
21	22	1.50	0	0	0	0	0	0	0	0	0	0
22	23	1.70	0	0	0	0	0	0	0	0	0	0
23	24	1.80	0	0	0	0	0	0	0	0	0	0
24	25	1.90	0	0	0	0	0	0	0	0	0	0
25	26	2.10	.10	0	0	0	0	0	0	0	0	0
26	27	2.20	.20	0	0	0	0	0	0	0	0	0
27	28	2.40	.40	0	0	0	0	0	0	0	0	0
28	29	2.50	.50	0	0	0	0	0	0	0	0	0
29	30	2.60	.60	0	0	0	0	0	0	0	0	0
30	31	2.80	.80	0	0	0	0	0	0	0	0	0
31	32	2.90	.90	0	0	0	0	0	0	0	0	0
32	33	3.10	1.10	0	0	0	0	0	0	0	0	0
33	34	3.20	1.20	0	0	0	0	0	0	0	0	0
34	35	3.30	1.30	0	0	0	0	0	0	0	0	0
35	36	3.50	1.50	0	0	0	0	0	0	0	0	0
36	37	3.60	1.60	0	0	0	0	0	0	0	0	0
37	38	3.80	1.80	0	0	0	0	0	0	0	0	0
38	39	3.90	1.90	0	0	0	0	0	0	0	0	0
39	40	4.10	2.00	0	0	0	0	0	0	0	0	0
40	41	4.20	2.20	.20	0	0	0	0	0	0	0	0
41	42	4.40	2.30	.30	0	0	0	0	0	0	0	0
42	43	4.50	2.50	.40	0	0	0	0	0	0	0	0
43	44	4.70	2.60	.60	0	0	0	0	0	0	0	0
44	45	4.90	2.70	.70	0	0	0	0	0	0	0	0
45	46	5.00	2.90	.90	0	0	0	0	0	0	0	0
46	47	5.20	3.00	1.00	0	0	0	0	0	0	0	0
47	48	5.30	3.20	1.10	0	0	0	0	0	0	0	0
48	49	5.50	3.30	1.30	0	0	0	0	0	0	0	0
49	50	5.70	3.40	1.40	0	0	0	0	0	0	0	0
50	51	5.80	3.60	1.60	0	0	0	0	0	0	0	0
51	52	6.00	3.70	1.70	0	0	0	0	0	0	0	0
52	53	6.10	3.90	1.80	0	0	0	0	0	0	0	0
53	54	6.30	4.00	2.00	0	0	0	0	0	0	0	0
54	55	6.50	4.10	2.10	.10	0	0	0	0	0	0	0
55	56	6.60	4.30	2.30	.20	0	0	0	0	0	0	0
56	57	6.80	4.50	2.40	.40	0	0	0	0	0	0	0
57	58	6.90	4.60	2.50	.50	0	0	0	0	0	0	0
58	59	7.10	4.80	2.70	.70	0	0	0	0	0	0	0
59	60	7.30	4.90	2.80	.80	0	0	0	0	0	0	0
60	62	7.50	5.20	3.00	1.00	0	0	0	0	0	0	0
62	64	7.80	5.50	3.30	1.30	0	0	0	0	0	0	0
64	66	8.10	5.80	3.60	1.60	0	0	0	0	0	0	0
66	68	8.50	6.10	3.90	1.80	0	0	0	0	0	0	0
68	70	8.80	6.50	4.20	2.10	.10	0	0	0	0	0	0
70	72	9.10	6.80	4.50	2.40	.40	0	0	0	0	0	0
72	74	9.40	7.10	4.80	2.70	.70	0	0	0	0	0	0
74	76	9.70	7.40	5.10	3.00	.90	0	0	0	0	0	0
76	78	10.10	7.70	5.40	3.20	1.20	0	0	0	0	0	0
78	80	10.40	8.10	5.80	3.50	1.50	0	0	0	0	0	0
80	82	10.70	8.40	6.10	3.80	1.80	0	0	0	0	0	0
82	84	11.00	8.70	6.40	4.10	2.10	0	0	0	0	0	0
84	86	11.30	9.00	6.70	4.40	2.30	.30	0	0	0	0	0
86	88	11.70	9.30	7.00	4.70	2.60	.60	0	0	0	0	0
88	90	12.00	9.70	7.40	5.00	2.90	.90	0	0	0	0	0
90	92	12.30	10.00	7.70	5.40	3.20	1.20	0	0	0	0	0
92	94	12.60	10.30	8.00	5.70	3.50	1.40	0	0	0	0	0
94	96	12.90	10.60	8.30	6.00	3.70	1.70	0	0	0	0	0
96	98	13.30	10.90	8.60	6.30	4.00	2.00	0	0	0	0	0
98	100	13.60	11.30	9.00	6.60	4.30	2.30	.30	0	0	0	0

To use the tax table:

Step 1 — read down
Step 2 — read across

(Continued on next page)

MARRIED Persons — **WEEKLY** Payroll Period

And the wages are —		And the number of withholding allowances claimed is —										
		0	1	2	3	4	5	6	7	8	9	10 or more
At least	But less than	The amount of income tax to be withheld shall be —										
$100	$105	$14.10	$11.80	$9.50	$7.20	$4.90	$2.80	$.80	$0	$0	$0	$0
105	110	14.90	12.60	10.30	8.00	5.70	3.50	1.50	0	0	0	0
110	115	15.70	13.40	11.10	8.80	6.50	4.20	2.20	.10	0	0	0
115	120	16.50	14.20	11.90	9.60	7.30	5.00	2.90	.80	0	0	0
120	125	17.30	15.00	12.70	10.40	8.10	5.80	3.60	1.50	0	0	0
125	130	18.10	15.80	13.50	11.20	8.90	6.60	4.30	2.20	.20	0	0
130	135	18.90	16.60	14.30	12.00	9.70	7.40	5.10	2.90	.90	0	0
135	140	19.70	17.40	15.10	12.80	10.50	8.20	5.90	3.60	1.60	0	0
140	145	20.50	18.20	15.90	13.60	11.30	9.00	6.70	4.40	2.30	.30	0
145	150	21.30	19.00	16.70	14.40	12.10	9.80	7.50	5.20	3.00	1.00	0
150	160	22.50	20.20	17.90	15.60	13.30	11.00	8.70	6.40	4.10	2.00	0
160	170	24.10	21.80	19.50	17.20	14.90	12.60	10.30	8.00	5.70	3.40	1.40
170	180	26.00	23.40	21.10	18.80	16.50	14.20	11.90	9.60	7.30	5.00	2.80
180	190	28.00	25.20	22.70	20.40	18.10	15.80	13.50	11.20	8.90	6.60	4.30
190	200	30.00	27.20	24.30	22.00	19.70	17.40	15.10	12.80	10.50	8.20	5.90
200	210	32.00	29.20	26.30	23.60	21.30	19.00	16.70	14.40	12.10	9.80	7.50
210	220	34.40	31.20	28.30	25.40	22.90	20.60	18.30	16.00	13.70	11.40	9.10
220	230	36.80	33.30	30.30	27.40	24.50	22.20	19.90	17.60	15.30	13.00	10.70
230	240	39.20	35.70	32.30	29.40	26.50	23.80	21.50	19.20	16.90	14.60	12.30
240	250	41.60	38.10	34.60	31.40	28.50	25.60	23.10	20.80	18.50	16.20	13.90
250	260	44.00	40.50	37.00	33.60	30.50	27.60	24.70	22.40	20.10	17.80	15.50
260	270	46.40	42.90	39.40	36.00	32.50	29.60	26.70	24.00	21.70	19.40	17.10
270	280	48.80	45.30	41.80	38.40	34.90	31.60	28.70	25.80	23.30	21.00	18.70
280	290	51.20	47.70	44.20	40.80	37.30	33.90	30.70	27.80	25.00	22.60	20.30
290	300	53.60	50.10	46.60	43.20	39.70	36.30	32.80	29.80	27.00	24.20	21.90
300	310	56.00	52.50	49.00	45.60	42.10	38.70	35.20	31.80	29.00	26.10	23.50
310	320	58.40	54.90	51.40	48.00	44.50	41.10	37.60	34.10	31.00	28.10	25.20
320	330	60.80	57.30	53.80	50.40	46.90	43.50	40.00	36.50	33.10	30.10	27.20
330	340	63.60	59.70	56.20	52.80	49.30	45.90	42.40	38.90	35.50	32.10	29.20
340	350	66.40	62.40	58.60	55.20	51.70	48.30	44.80	41.30	37.90	34.40	31.20
350	360	69.20	65.20	61.10	57.60	54.10	50.70	47.20	43.70	40.30	36.80	33.40
360	370	72.00	68.00	63.90	60.00	56.50	53.10	49.60	46.10	42.70	39.20	35.80
370	380	74.80	70.80	66.70	62.70	58.90	55.50	52.00	48.50	45.10	41.60	38.20
380	390	77.60	73.60	69.50	65.50	61.50	57.90	54.40	50.90	47.50	44.00	40.60
390	400	80.40	76.40	72.30	68.30	64.30	60.30	56.80	53.30	49.90	46.40	43.00
400	410	83.20	79.20	75.10	71.10	67.10	63.00	59.20	55.70	52.30	48.80	45.40
410	420	86.30	82.00	77.90	73.90	69.90	65.80	61.80	58.10	54.70	51.20	47.80
420	430	89.50	84.80	80.70	76.70	72.70	68.60	64.60	60.50	57.10	53.60	50.20
430	440	92.70	88.00	83.50	79.50	75.50	71.40	67.40	63.30	59.50	56.00	52.60
440	450	95.90	91.20	86.60	82.30	78.30	74.20	70.20	66.10	62.10	58.40	55.00
450	460	99.10	94.40	89.80	85.20	81.10	77.00	73.00	68.90	64.90	60.90	57.40
460	470	102.30	97.60	93.00	88.40	83.90	79.80	75.80	71.70	67.70	63.70	59.80
470	480	105.50	100.80	96.20	91.60	87.00	82.60	78.60	74.50	70.50	66.50	62.40
480	490	108.70	104.00	99.40	94.80	90.20	85.60	81.40	77.30	73.30	69.30	65.20
490	500	112.20	107.20	102.60	98.00	93.40	88.80	84.20	80.10	76.10	72.10	68.00
500	510	115.80	110.60	105.80	101.20	96.60	92.00	87.40	82.90	78.90	74.90	70.80
510	520	119.40	114.20	109.10	104.40	99.80	95.20	90.60	86.00	81.70	77.70	73.60
520	530	123.00	117.80	112.70	107.60	103.00	98.40	93.80	89.20	84.50	80.50	76.40
530	540	126.60	121.40	116.30	111.10	106.20	101.60	97.00	92.40	87.70	83.30	79.20
540	550	130.20	125.00	119.90	114.70	109.50	104.80	100.20	95.60	90.90	86.30	82.00
550	560	133.80	128.60	123.50	118.30	113.10	108.00	103.40	98.80	94.10	89.50	84.90
560	570	137.40	132.20	127.10	121.90	116.70	111.50	106.60	102.00	97.30	92.70	88.10
570	580	141.00	135.80	130.70	125.50	120.30	115.10	109.90	105.20	100.50	95.90	91.30
580	590	144.60	139.40	134.30	129.10	123.90	118.70	113.50	108.40	103.70	99.10	94.50
590	600	148.20	143.00	137.90	132.70	127.50	122.30	117.10	111.90	106.90	102.30	97.70
600	610	151.80	146.60	141.50	136.30	131.10	125.90	120.70	115.50	110.30	105.50	100.90
610	620	155.40	150.20	145.10	139.90	134.70	129.50	124.30	119.10	113.90	108.70	104.10
620	630	159.00	153.80	148.70	143.50	138.30	133.10	127.90	122.70	117.50	112.30	107.30
630	640	162.60	157.40	152.30	147.10	141.90	136.70	131.50	126.30	121.10	115.90	110.70
		36 percent of the excess over $640 plus —										
$640 and over		164.40	159.20	154.10	148.90	143.70	138.50	133.30	128.10	122.90	117.70	112.50

SAMPLE PROBLEM 1

John Brett claims 3 exemptions and he earns $90.00 for the week. The payroll clerk can find the withholding tax deduction by following these steps.

Step 1: Locate the wages in Wages columns one and two.

The payroll clerk would look in the first vertical column entitled "At least" until the number $90.00 was found. When this number was found, the payroll clerk would be ready for the next step.

Step 2: Locate the Exemption column.

The payroll clerk would then look across until the column showing 3 *exemptions* was directly above. The amount of $5.40 would be seen. This means there must be a deduction of $5.40 from John Brett's wages for withholding tax.

SAMPLE PROBLEM 2

If John Brett earned wages which amounted to $91.00, how would you find his withholding tax? The process would still be the same. You would look for $91.00 in the first column. Since $91.00 falls between $90.00 and the $92.00 in the second column, you have located the correct wages column. Then you would look in the exemption column headed "3" and you would find the correct withholding tax of $5.40. Notice that the withholding tax was the same amount as it was in Sample Problem 1. This had to be so because both $90.00 and $91.00 fall between the columns "At least" $90.00 and "But less than" $92.00. In addition, 3 exemptions were mentioned in both sample problems.

SAMPLE PROBLEM 3

To help you use the table, here are some problems and their correct answers. Look at the table and see if you can find the same answers as illustrated.

To keep your eyes from shifting to the wrong columns in the table, place a ruler below the proper wages column and then locate the exemption column.

	Wages	Exemptions	Correct Federal Withholding Tax
a)	74 00	1	7 40
b)	200 00	6	16 70
c)	235 00	3	29 40
d)	251 85	7	22 40
e)	118 40	0	16 50

PRACTICE PROBLEMS

Problem 1

Directions:
a) Copy the table below on a sheet of paper:

Card No.	Number of Exemptions	Wages	Federal Withholding Tax
1	2	125 00	
2	6	261 00	
3	0	94 72	
4	1	136 20	
5	5	210 05	
6	3	169 00	
7	4	275 00	
8	2	208 15	
9	8	320 00	
10	5	286 00	

b) Enter the withholding tax in the appropriate column. Use the tables on pages 495 and 496.

Problem 2

Directions:
a) Copy the table below:

Card No.	Number of Exemptions	Wages	Federal Withholding Tax
1	1	150 00	
2	5	240 00	
3	0	80 00	
4	2	76 58	
5	4	193 10	
6	6	335 00	
7	3	229 65	
8	7	292 82	
9	1	66 00	
10	4	170 00	

b) Enter the withholding tax in the appropriate column. Use the tables on pages 495 and 496.

Problem 3

Directions:

a) Copy the table below:

Card No.	Number of Exemptions	Wages	Social Security Tax	Federal Withholding Tax
1	1	178 60		
2	4	188 90		
3	0	199 95		
4	3	226 12		
5	5	244 36		
6	2	202 48		
7	6	255 30		
8	3	216 84		
9	5	238 00		
10	7	265 56		

b) Enter the social security tax and withholding tax in the appropriate columns. Use the social security tax tables on pages 486 and 487. Use the withholding tax tables on pages 495 and 496. Bear in mind that the withholding tax is based on the *total wages*.

Problem 4

Directions:

a) Copy the following table:

Card No.	Number of Exemptions	Wages	Social Security Tax	Federal Withholding Tax
1	2	223 00		
2	3	192 05		
3	6	253 00		
4	5	266 54		
5	0	183 49		
6	1	236 00		
7	8	240 75		
8	3	203 28		
9	4	262 73		
10	2	179 00		

b) Enter the social security tax and withholding tax in the appropriate columns. Use the social security tax tables on pages 486 and 487. Use the withholding tax tables on pages 495 and 496. Bear in mind that the withholding tax is based on the *total wages*.

Practicing Related Arithmetic

Copy the following problems on a sheet of paper and find the answers:

(1)	(2)	(3)	(4)
11	$193.46	a) $\frac{1}{2} \times 5 =$	a) $60 \times .0585 =$
7¾	− 25.78	b) $\frac{1}{2} \times 3\frac{1}{2} =$	b) $84 \times .0585 =$
6¾		c) $\frac{1}{2} \times 9\frac{1}{2} =$	c) $210 \times .0585 =$
9¼		d) $\frac{1}{2} \times 4\frac{1}{4} =$	d) $198 \times .0605 =$
+ 8½		e) $\frac{1}{2} \times \frac{1}{4} =$	e) $237 \times .0605 =$

AIMS

1. To learn how to find a worker's "take home" pay after making social security and withholding tax deductions.

2. To learn how to enter the information in a payroll book.

EXPLANATION

In previous jobs, you learned that all information relating to a worker's "take home" pay is usually entered in a payroll book and you were given many opportunities to record information from time cards. In the last two jobs, you learned that the employee does not take home the total wages which are earned because deductions are made for social security and withholding taxes. This information must also be recorded in the payroll book. Payroll books contain the necessary columns to provide for this. Here is how a typical page of such a payroll book looks.

WEEK ENDING *August 8, 19--*

CARD NO.	NAME OF EMPLOYEE	NO. OF EXEMP-TIONS	HOURS WORKED M	TU	W	TH	F	S	TOTAL HOURS WORKED	REGULAR RATE OF PAY FOR 40 HR. WEEK	EARNINGS AT REG. RATE FOR TOTAL HRS. WORKED	BONUS FOR OVERTIME	TOTAL WAGES	SOCIAL SECURITY (F.I.C.A.)	FEDERAL WITH. TAX	TOTAL DEDUC.	NET PAY
1	Ken Hart	2	7	8	10	8	7		40	201 00	201 00		201 00	11 76	26 30	38 06	162 94
2	Carl Fealy	5	8	10	8	10	10		46	203 00	233 45	15 23	248 68	14 55	25 60	40 15	208 53
	Totals										434 45	15 23	449 68	26 31	51 90	78 21	371 47

Illustration 79 — Page from a Payroll Book

SAMPLE PROBLEM

Ken Hart's total deductions of $38.06 were found by adding his social security tax (F.I.C.A. tax) of $11.76 and his withholding tax of $26.30.

Social Security Tax (F.I.C.A. tax)	$11.76
+ Withholding Tax	26.30
= Total Deductions	$38.06

His net pay of $162.94 was found by subtracting his total deductions of $38.06 from his total wages of $201.00.

Total Wages	$201.00
Less:	
Total Deductions	38.06
Net Pay	$162.94

Carl Fealy's net pay of $208.53 was found by subtracting his total deductions of $40.15 from his total wages of $248.68.

Total Wages	$248.68
Less:	
Total Deductions	40.15
Net Pay	$208.53

You can check the totals for the week like this:

Step 1

Total Social Security Taxes	$ 26.31
+ Total Withholding Taxes	51.90
Must Equal Total Deductions	$ 78.21

Step 2

Total Wages for the Week	$449.68
− Total Deductions for the Week	78.21
Must Equal the Total Net Pay for the Week	$371.47

PRACTICE PROBLEMS

Problem 1

Directions:

a) Copy the table shown on page 502 on a sheet of paper.

b) Complete the payroll. Use the social security tax table on pages 486 and 487, and the withholding tax table on pages 495 and 496.

c) Check your totals. If your work is correct, the total of the "Net Pay" column should be $895.45.

CARD NO.	NO. OF EXEMP- TIONS	TOTAL WAGES	DEDUCTIONS			NET PAY
			SOCIAL SECURITY (F.I.C.A.)	FEDERAL WITH. TAX	TOTAL DEDUC.	
1	4	249 08				
2	3	177 85				
3	5	258 10				
4	1	185 00				
5	2	217 43				
TOTALS						

WEEK ENDING — *March 14, 19--*

Problem 2

Directions:

a) Copy the following table on a sheet of paper:

WEEK ENDING — *November 21, 19--*

CARD NO.	NO. OF EXEMP- TIONS	TOTAL WAGES	DEDUCTIONS			NET PAY
			SOCIAL SECURITY (F.I.C.A.)	FEDERAL WITH. TAX	TOTAL DEDUC.	
1	6	254 00				
2	2	195 60				
3	3	213 72				
4	0	239 88				
5	1	178 40				
TOTALS						

b) Complete the payroll. Use the social security tax table on pages 486 and 487, and the withholding tax table on pages 495 and 496.

c) Check your totals. If your work is correct, the total of the "Net Pay" column should be $881.33.

Problem 3

Directions:

a) Copy the table on page 503 on a sheet of paper.

WEEK ENDING			February 7, 19--				
			DEDUCTIONS				
CARD NO.	NO. OF EXEMP- TIONS	TOTAL WAGES	SOCIAL SECURITY (F.I.C.A.)	FEDERAL WITH. TAX	TOTAL DEDUC.	NET PAY	
1	2	20400					
2	0	18116					
3	6	26390					
4	1	18958					
5	3	22552					
	TOTALS						

b) Complete the payroll. Use the social security tax table on pages 486 and 487, and the withholding tax table on pages 495 and 496.

c) Check your totals. If your work is correct, the total of the "Net Pay" column should be $868.31.

Problem 4

Directions:

a) Copy the following table on a sheet of paper:

WEEK ENDING			May 9, 19--				
			DEDUCTIONS				
CARD NO.	NO. OF EXEMP- TIONS	TOTAL WAGES	SOCIAL SECURITY (F.I.C.A.)	FEDERAL WITH. TAX	TOTAL DEDUC.	NET PAY	
1	3	18600					
2	4	19406					
3	2	20541					
4	5	25269					
5	1	18035					
	TOTALS						

b) Complete the payroll. Use the social security tax table on pages 486 and 487, and the withholding tax table on pages 495 and 496.

c) Check your totals. If your work is correct, the total of the "Net Pay" column should be $839.73.

Problem 5

Directions:

a) Copy the following table on a sheet of paper:

			DEDUCTIONS			
WEEK ENDING *September 12, 19--*						
CARD NO.	NO. OF EXEMP- TIONS	TOTAL WAGES	SOCIAL SECURITY (F.I.C.A.)	FEDERAL WITH. TAX	TOTAL DEDUC.	NET PAY
1	7	264 09				
2	2	228 40				
3	6	250 90				
4	5	243 82				
5	2	217 63				
TOTALS						

b) Complete the payroll. Use the social security tax table on pages 486 and 487, and the withholding tax table on pages 495 and 496.

c) Check your totals. If your work is correct, the total of the "Net Pay" column should be $1,001.46.

JOB 80 | PREPARING THE PAYROLL

Practicing Related Arithmetic	Copy the following problems on a sheet of paper and find the answers:			
	(1)	(2)	(3)	(4)
	4¾	a) ½ of 14 =	a) ½ of 2¼ =	$210.28
	7½	b) ½ of 13 =	b) ½ of 12¼ =	×.0585
	8¼	c) ½ of 6½ =	c) ½ of 16¼ =	
	10½	d) ½ of 8½ =	d) ½ of 4¾ =	
	+ 6½	e) ½ of 11½ =	e) ½ of 10¾ =	

AIMS

1. To give you practice in computing a payroll.
2. To give you practice in recording in a payroll book.

EXPLANATION

In your previous job you had practice in completing a payroll book with the "Total Wages" column. Today you will get practice in preparing the entire page of a payroll book. In order to do this, you will need a payroll book with the following columnar headings:

CARD NO.	NAME OF EMPLOYEE	NO. OF EXEMP-TIONS	HOURS WORKED						TOTAL HOURS WORKED	REGULAR RATE OF PAY FOR 40 HR. WEEK	EARNINGS AT REG. RATE FOR TOTAL HRS. WORKED	BONUS FOR OVERTIME	TOTAL WAGES	DEDUCTIONS			NET PAY
			M	TU	W	TH	F	S						SOCIAL SECURITY (F.I.C.A.)	FEDERAL WITH. TAX	TOTAL DEDUC.	

WEEK ENDING

Illustration 80 — Headings for a Payroll Sheet

PRACTICE PROBLEMS

Problem 1

Directions:
a) Head a payroll sheet with the columnar headings shown in Illustration 80.

b) Enter the following information in the appropriate columns for the week ending January 24, 19--. (Note that you have been given the total hours worked so that you will not need to fill in the daily hours.)

Card No.	Name of Employee	Number of Exemptions	Total Hours Worked	Regular Rate of Pay for 40 Hours
1	L. Leda	5	40	208 00
2	R. Geraci	2	35	205 00
3	D. Baltor	1	44	200 00
4	O. Neer	4	42	206 00
5	M. Savoy	3	45	204 00

c) Use the wage computation table found on page 453, and compute the wages for each employee.

d) Complete the payroll sheet. Use the social security tax tables on pages 486 and 487, and the withholding tax table on pages 495 and 496.

e) Total all money columns and check your totals. If your work is correct, the total of the "Net Pay" column should be $886.14.

Problem 2

Directions:

a) Head a payroll sheet with the columnar headings shown in Illustration 80.

b) Enter the following information in the appropriate columns for the week ending October 10, 19--. (Note that you have been given the total hours worked so that you will not need to fill in the daily hours.)

Card No.	Name of Employee	Number of Exemptions	Total Hours Worked	Regular Rate of Pay for 40 Hours
1	N. Jenks	2	38½	207 00
2	K. Falb	1	46	201 00
3	I. Deere	6	43	209 00
4	G. Mage	0	44½	203 00
5	E. Kane	3	48½	202 00

c) Use the wage computation table found on page 453, and compute the wages for each employee.

d) Complete the payroll sheet. Use the social security tax tables on pages 486 and 487, and the withholding tax table on pages 495 and 496.

e) Total all money columns and check your totals. If your work is correct, the total of the "Net Pay" column should be $953.42.

Problem 3

Directions:

a) Head a payroll sheet with the columnar headings shown in Illustration 80.

b) Enter the following information in the appropriate columns for the week ending July 18, 19--. (Note that you have been given the total hours worked so that you will not need to fill in the daily hours.)

Card No.	Name of Employee	Number of Exemptions	Total Hours Worked	Regular Rate of Pay for 40 Hours
1	Y. Salz	4	37	208 00
2	P. Oliver	5	36¼	206 00
3	L. Hajek	1	47	200 00
4	A. Dicarl	6	42½	201 00
5	T. Jarvis	2	43½	205 00

c) Use the wage computation table found on page 453, and compute the wages for each employee.

d) Complete the payroll sheet. Use the social security tax tables on pages 486 and 487, and the withholding tax table on pages 495 and 496.

e) Total all money columns and check your totals. If your work is correct, the total of the "Net Pay" column should be $893.37.

Problem 4

Directions:

a) Head a payroll sheet with the columnar headings shown in Illustration 80.

b) Enter the following information in the appropriate columns for the week ending December 5, 19--. (Note that you have been given the total hours worked so that you will not need to fill in the daily hours.)

Card No.	Name of Employee	Number of Exemptions	Total Hours Worked	Regular Rate of Pay for 40 Hours
1	R. Samis	7	39½	207 00
2	N. Randy	0	34¾	209 00
3	B. Atwell	1	40½	202 00
4	C. Marsh	6	41½	204 00
5	J. Olse	2	47½	203 00

c) Use the wage computation table found on page 453, and compute the wages for each employee.

d) Complete the payroll sheet. Use the social security tax tables on pages 486 and 487, and the withholding tax table on pages 495 and 496.

e) Total all money columns and check your totals. If your work is correct, the total of the "Net Pay" column should be $875.62.

Practicing
Related
Arithmetic

Copy the following problems on a sheet of paper and find the answers:

(1)	(2)
a) $\frac{1}{2}$ of 10 $\quad=$	a) $7 + 9 + 8 + 11 + 6\frac{1}{2} =$
b) $\frac{1}{2}$ of $14\frac{1}{2} =$	b) $9 + 8 + 8\frac{1}{2} + 5\frac{1}{2} + 4 \quad=$
c) $\frac{1}{2}$ of $5\frac{1}{2} =$	c) $6\frac{1}{4} + 5\frac{1}{4} + 9 + 7\frac{1}{2} + 10 \quad=$
d) $\frac{1}{2}$ of $\frac{1}{2} =$	d) $8\frac{1}{2} + 9\frac{1}{4} + 3 + 7\frac{1}{4} + 11 \quad=$
e) $\frac{1}{2}$ of $12\frac{1}{2} =$	e) $8\frac{1}{4} + 5\frac{3}{4} + 7 + 9\frac{1}{4} + 4\frac{1}{2} =$

AIMS

1. To give you additional practice in calculating a payroll based on hourly rates.

2. To give you additional practice in recording information in a payroll book.

EXPLANATION

In your previous job, you had practice in completing a payroll after you had been given information as to the number of hours worked and as to the weekly rate to be paid each worker. Today you will have to calculate the total hours and will base each worker's pay on an hourly rate basis.

In order to enter this information in a payroll book, you will need the following columnar headings.

CARD NO.	NAME OF EMPLOYEE	NO. OF EXEMP-TIONS	HOURS WORKED						TOTAL HOURS WORKED	WAGES PER HOUR	EARNINGS AT REG. RATE FOR TOTAL HRS. WORKED	BONUS FOR OVERTIME	TOTAL WAGES	DEDUCTIONS			NET PAY
			M	TU	W	TH	F	S						SOCIAL SECURITY (F.I.C.A.)	FEDERAL WITH TAX	TOTAL DEDUC.	

WEEK ENDING

Illustration 81 — Payroll Sheet with Multiple Columns

PRACTICE PROBLEMS

Problem 1

Directions:

a) Head a payroll sheet with the columnar headings shown in Illustration 81, page 508.

b) Enter the following information in the appropriate columns for the week ending September 12, 19--.

Card No.	Name of Employee	Number of Exemptions	Hours Worked					Wages Per Hour
			M	TU	W	TH	F	
1	F. Parisi	0	5	4	8	3	6	7 20
2	H. Harpe	6	8	9	6	8	9	5 30
3	N. Essen	3	10	9	9	8	8	5 70
4	V. Banks	1	9	8	10	8	7	5 50
5	P. Rae	2	11	9	8	5½	9½	5 15

c) Compute the wages for each employee, and enter the information in the appropriate columns.

d) Complete the payroll sheet. Use the social security tax tables on pages 486 and 487, and the withholding table on pages 495 and 496.

e) Total all money columns, and check your totals. If your work is correct, the total of the "Net Pay" column should be $912.84.

Problem 2

Directions:

a) Head a payroll sheet with the columnar headings shown in Illustration 81, page 508.

b) Enter the following information in the appropriate columns for the week ending August 15, 19--.

Card No.	Name of Employee	Number of Exemptions	Hours Worked					Wages Per Hour
			M	TU	W	TH	F	
1	B. Norca	1	7	7	6½	6½	8	6 75
2	D. Arkin	7	8	8	9	9	5½	5 80
3	G. Fazio	4	10	10	7	9	10½	4 95
4	S. Olde	2	11	10	10	8½	9	4 85
5	I. Fean	3	9	9	8	10	9½	5 00

c) Compute the wages for each employee, and enter the information in the appropriate columns.

d) Complete the payroll sheet. Use the social security tax tables on pages 486 and 487, and the withholding table on pages 495 and 496.

e) Total all money columns, and check your totals. If your work is correct, the total of the "Net Pay" column should be $987.80.

Problem 3

Directions:

a) Head a payroll sheet with the columnar headings shown in Illustration 81, page 508.

b) Enter the following information in the appropriate columns for the week ending April 11, 19—.

Card No.	Name of Employee	Number of Exemptions	Hours Worked					Wages Per Hour
			M	TU	W	TH	F	
1	M. Gelsey	4	7	7	8	6½	9	5│10
2	T. Lauth	5	7¾	7½	6	9	8	6│80
3	W. Prior	2	6	8	7	6½	8¾	5│60
4	C. Baffi	0	8	8	8¼	9	7¾	5│48
5	E. Ittig	6	8½	9	8	7½	9½	6│00

c) Compute the wages for each employee, and enter the information in the appropriate columns.

d) Complete the payroll sheet. Use the social security tax tables on pages 486 and 487, and the withholding table on pages 495 and 496.

e) Total all money columns, and check your totals. If your work is correct, the total of the "Net Pay" column should be $938.22.

Problem 4

Directions:

a) Head a payroll sheet with the columnar headings shown in Illustration 81, page 508.

b) Enter the following information in the appropriate columns for the week ending November 21, 19—.

Card No.	Name of Employee	Number of Exemptions	Hours Worked					Wages Per Hour
			M	TU	W	TH	F	
1	O. Halpin	1	10	10	11	9	10	4│00
2	A. Mauer	8	11	9½	8	7½	8½	5│20
3	J. Kani	3	7	5	4½	5½	7	6│35
4	Y. Desarlo	7	9	9½	9	9½	10½	4│60
5	K. Roher	0	8	6	5	8¼	4½	6│24

c) Compute the wages for each employee, and enter the information in the appropriate columns.

d) Complete the payroll sheet. Use the social security tax tables on pages 486 and 487, and the withholding table on pages 495 and 496.

e) Total all money columns, and check your totals. If your work is correct, the total of the "Net Pay" column should be $896.48.

Copy the following problems on a sheet of paper and find the answers:

Practicing
Related
Arithmetic

(1)	(2)	(3)
$250.83	a) 240 × $.10 =	a) ½ × 5 =
167.29	b) 135 × $.05 =	b) ½ × 13 =
203.46	c) 196 × $.25 =	c) ½ × 15 =
175.90	d) 72 × $.50 =	d) ½ × 12½ =
241.87	e) 308 × $.25 =	e) ½ × 16½ =
186.30	f) 87 × $.10 =	f) ½ × 1½ =
98.05	g) 213 × $.05 =	g) ½ × 8¼ =
309.50	h) 142 × $.25 =	h) ½ × 10¼ =
+192.14	i) 39 × $.50 =	i) ½ × 14¼ =

"Not enough change.. again!"

Payroll Dept.

AIMS

1. To learn the meaning of the expression "currency breakup."

2. To learn why you prepare a currency breakup.

3. To learn how to prepare a currency breakup.

4. To learn how to prepare a currency memorandum.

EXPLANATION

As you know, employees may be paid by cash or check. If they are paid by check, the problem of payment is quite simple. The check is written, signed by the employer, and handed to the employee each payday. Paying wages by cash, however, becomes a bit more complicated for the employer. There must be sufficient bills and coins of various denominations to meet the payroll needs. For example, if a worker is to be paid $174.29, the employer must have bills and coins in the exact amount, without burdening the employee with too many single bills and coins. On the other hand, the employer cannot go to the other extreme and give the worker bills which are difficult to use. For instance, a worker with a $100 bill would have the problem of changing the bill into smaller denominations. Therefore, good judgment must be used in the selection of the denominations. To determine the number of bills and coins needed to pay each worker conveniently, people who prepare payrolls use a form like the one shown on the next page.

CURRENCY BREAKUP

FOR PAYROLL FOR WEEK ENDING _____

TIME CARD NO.	NAME OF EMPLOYEE	CASH TO BE PAID	BILLS				COINS				
			$20	$10	$5	$1	50c	25c	10c	5c	1c
TOTALS											

Illustration 82a — Currency Breakup Form

SAMPLE PROBLEM

Mary Romers is the payroll clerk for the W. Bay Co. Here is how the payroll book looked for the week ending February 7, 19--.

CARD NO.	NAME OF EMPLOYEE	TOTAL WAGES	DEDUCTIONS			NET PAY
			SOCIAL SECURITY (F.I.C.A.)	FEDERAL WITH. TAX	TOTAL DEDUC.	
	WEEK ENDING	February 7, 19--				
1	G. Forest	205 30	12 01	19 00	31 01	174 29
2	A. Galan	226 80	13 27	17 60	30 87	195 93
3	M. Romero	173 75	10 16	14 20	24 36	149 39
4	R. Paris	237 45	13 89	23 80	37 69	199 76
5	C. Wiles	251 70	14 22	32 50	47 22	204 48
	Totals	1 095 00	64 05	107 10	171 15	923 85
		1 095 00	64 05	107 10	171 15	923 85

Mary needs $923.85 to pay the five employees. Mary will make use of the form shown in Illustration 82a to determine the number of bills and coins to give each worker. The completed form is shown on the next page.

Mary had to go through the following steps to complete this currency breakup.

Step 1: Find the number of bills and coins needed to pay each employee.

The "currency breakup" shows the payroll clerk the numbers of bills and coins needed for each employee

TIME CARD NO.	NAME OF EMPLOYEE	CASH TO BE PAID	BILLS $20	$10	$5	$1	COINS 50c	25c	10c	5c	1c
1	G. Forest	1 7 4 29	8	1		4		1			4
2	A. Galan	1 9 5 93	9	1	1		1	1	1	1	3
3	M. Romero	1 4 9 39	7		1	4	1	1			4
4	R. Paris	1 9 9 76	9	1	1	4	1	1			1
5	C. Wilos	2 0 4 48	10			4		1	2		3
	TOTALS	9 2 3 85	43	3	3	16	2	5	4	1	15

CURRENCY BREAKUP

FOR PAYROLL FOR WEEK ENDING *February 7, 19--*

Illustration 82b — Completed Currency Breakup Form

Examine Illustration 82b carefully. In the case of the first employee, G. Forest, the largest number of $20 bills that could be used would be 8 (8 × $20 = $160.00).

The next largest bill that could be used would be a $10 bill. If you follow the same process, G. Forest's pay envelope should contain the following bills and coins:

8 twenty-dollar bills	$160.00
1 ten-dollar bill	10.00
4 one-dollar bills	4.00
1 quarter	.25
4 pennies	.04
Total take home pay	$174.29

The same process would be followed for all the workers.

Step 2: Total the currency breakup form.

After the payroll clerk has found the number of bills and coins needed for each employee, she will total all columns in the currency breakup form in Illustration 82b.

These totals show the payroll clerk that she needs the following denominations to meet the payroll of $923.85:

43 twenty-dollar bills	5 quarters
3 ten-dollar bills	4 dimes
3 five-dollar bills	1 nickel
16 one-dollar bills	15 pennies
2 half dollars	

To make sure that the above quantities equal $923.85, the payroll clerk does the next step.

Step 3: Multiply the quantity by the denominations to find the total cash to be paid out.

Mary multiplies each denomination by the quantity to find the total cash to be paid. The answer must agree with the $923.85, which equals the total cash to be paid, according to the total shown in Illustration 82b.

$20.00 × 43	$860.00
10.00 × 3	30.00
5.00 × 3	15.00
1.00 × 16	16.00
.50 × 2	1.00
.25 × 5	1.25
.10 × 4	.40
.05 × 1	.05
.01 × 15	.15
	$923.85

Mary knows that her work is correct because the total is in agreement with the cash required of $923.85. If the totals do not agree, Mary must recheck all her steps to locate the error.

Step 4: Prepare a currency memorandum.

To get the $923.85 she requires, the payroll clerk gets a check for this amount from her employer. At the bank, to get the proper amounts of the various denominations, she gives the bank teller the check and a currency memorandum like the one below. It is then a simple matter for the bank teller to give her exactly the denominations she needs.

The bank teller can now see the quantity of bills and coins required for the entire payroll

CURRENCY MEMORANDUM

DATE: _February 7, 19--_
DEPOSITOR: _W. Bay Co._

DENOMINATION	QUANTITY	VALUE
$20 bills	43	860 00
$10 bills	3	30 00
$5 bills	3	15 00
$1 bills	16	16 00
Half dollars	2	1 00
Quarters	5	1 25
Dimes	4	40
Nickels	1	05
Pennies	15	15
TOTAL		923 85

Illustration 82c — Currency Memorandum

Step 5: Prepare the pay envelope.

It is customary for the payroll clerk to put the money into pay envelopes for distribution each payday.

Deductions that have been made from wages are shown on the outside of the envelope like this:

Payroll envelope shows amount earned, deductions, and net amount paid

PAYROLL ENVELOPE	
PAYROLL RECORD DATA	
EMPLOYEE WILL PLEASE RETAIN THIS STATEMENT	
Name____G. Forest_____	
Pay Period Ending____February 7, 19--____	
Amount Earned	$205.30
Deductions:	
Social Security Tax (F. I. C. A.)	$12.01
Federal Withholding Tax	$19.00
Total Deductions	31.01
Net Amount Paid	$174.29

When you compare this envelope with G. Forest's payroll record on page 513, you will see that all the information recorded in the payroll book for him has been copied on his envelope.

PRACTICE PROBLEMS

Problem 1

Directions:

a) Copy the following information on a currency breakup form like Illustration 82a, page 513.

Week Ending May 2, 19--		
Card No.	Name of Employee	Cash To Be Paid
1	B. Cagle	203 86
2	R. Ellis	196 79
3	D. Lanzo	182 63
4	E. Packer	235 47
5	S. Welsh	179 18

b) Prepare the completed currency breakup.
c) Prepare a currency memorandum like the one shown in Illustration 82c, on page 515. You are working for the M. Fox Co.

Problem 2

Directions:
a) Copy the following information on a currency breakup form like Illustration 82a, page 513.

Week Ending May 9, 19--		
Card No.	Name of Employee	Cash To Be Paid
1	B. Cagle	234 27
2	R. Ellis	216 34
3	D. Lanzo	177 82
4	E. Packer	198 99
5	S. Welsh	159 43

b) Prepare the completed currency breakup.
c) Prepare a currency memorandum like the one shown in Illustration 82c, on page 515. You are working for the M. Fox Co.

Problem 3

Directions:
a) Copy the following information on a currency breakup form like Illustration 82a, page 513.

Week Ending May 16, 19--		
Card No.	Name of Employee	Cash To Be Paid
1	B. Cagle	217 18
2	R. Ellis	188 30
3	D. Lanzo	149 42
4	E. Packer	248 80
5	S. Welsh	175 25

b) Prepare the completed currency breakup.
c) Prepare a currency memorandum like the one shown in Illustration 82c, on page 515. You are working for the M. Fox Co.

Problem 4

Directions:
a) Copy the information on page 518 on a currency breakup form like Illustration 82a, page 513.

Week Ending May 23, 19--		
Card No.	Name of Employee	Cash To Be Paid
1	B. Cagle	219 69
2	R. Ellis	177 72
3	D. Lanzo	191 83
4	E. Packer	224 51
5	S. Welsh	132 14

b) Prepare the completed currency breakup.

c) Prepare a currency memorandum like the one shown in Illustration 82c, on page 515. You are working for the M. Fox Co.

Practicing Related Arithmetic	Copy the following problems on a sheet of paper and find the answers:	
	(1)	**(2)**
	$216.03	Crossfoot and then add down:
	98.72	
	182.56	a) 12 + 32 + 52 =
	307.25	b) 24 + 14 + 64 =
	86.37	c) 36 + 46 + 16 =
	240.18	d) 10 + 35 + 70 =
	+169.74	e) 63 + 83 + 26 = _____
		f) ___ ___ ___ = _____

AIM

To learn how to keep a record of each employee's earnings, withholding tax and social security tax deductions.

EXPLANATION

In preceding jobs, you have learned why you make salary deductions for social security and withholding taxes. You also learned that employers must pay the money to the federal government at stated times. In addition to paying the money, employers must also furnish information to federal and state agencies about the earnings and deductions of each employee. Information may be required at the end of each quarter (in the case of social security) and at the end of the year (in the case of withholding taxes). To have this information ready, payroll clerks keep individual records for each employee on forms similar to the one shown on page 520.

Reasons for keeping individual "Employee's Record" cards

The information for the upper portion of the card is recorded at the time the employee is hired.

Instead of recopying all the information about the employee found in the heading, some record keepers put this information on a separate card which is kept in the files and show only the following information at the top of the employee's record card:

    Last Name, First, Middle   **Time Card #**   **Soc. Sec. #**

At the end of each week, the payroll clerk enters the information found in the payroll book on the employee's record card.

EMPLOYEE'S RECORD

NAME_____   ADDRESS_____

SINGLE_____ MARRIED_____   _____

SOCIAL SECURITY NO._____   NUMBER OF EXEMPTIONS_____

DEPARTMENT_____   AGE_____

WAGES_____ CARD NO._____   JOB_____DATE HIRED_____

TERMINATION DATE_____   REASON FOR LEAVING_____

FIRST QUARTER

WEEK ENDING	TOTAL WAGES	SOC. SEC. TAX	FEDERAL WITH. TAX
1			
2			
3			
4			
5			
6			
7			
8			
9			
10			
11			
12			
13			
TOTAL			

SUMMARY

QUARTERS	TOTAL WAGES	SOC. SEC. TAX	FEDERAL WITH. TAX
FIRST			
SECOND			
THIRD			
FOURTH			
TOTAL FOR THE YEAR			

Illustration 83a — Employee's Record Card

SAMPLE PROBLEM

The payroll book shows the following information for the week ending on January 6, 19--.

| CARD NO. | NAME OF EMPLOYEE | TOTAL WAGES | DEDUCTIONS | | | NET PAY |
			SOCIAL SECURITY (F.I.C.A.)	FEDERAL WITH. TAX	TOTAL DEDUC.	
	WEEK ENDING *January 6, 19--*					
1	John Ellis	200 00	11 70	23 60	35 30	164 70
2	Sam Marel	170 00	9 95	16 50	26 45	143 55
3	Anne Reich	195 00	11 41	15 10	26 51	168 49
4	Maria Verga	216 00	12 64	28 30	40 94	175 06
		781 00	45 70	83 50	129 20	651 80
	Totals	781 00	45 70	83 50	129 20	651 80

Here is how the information would appear on the employee's card.

EMPLOYEE'S RECORD

NAME *John Ellis*   ADDRESS *45 Park Avenue*
SINGLE_____ MARRIED _✓_   *Newark, NJ 07104*
SOCIAL SECURITY NO. *108-06-4673*   NUMBER OF EXEMPTIONS _3_
DEPARTMENT *Appliances*   AGE *29*
WAGES $*200/wk* CARD NO. _1_   JOB *Repairman* DATE HIRED *1/2/--*
TERMINATION DATE_____   REASON FOR LEAVING_____

FIRST QUARTER

WEEK ENDING	TOTAL WAGES	SOC. SEC. TAX	FEDERAL WITH. TAX
1 *Jan. 6* 19--	200 00	11 70	23 60
2			
3			

Illustration 83b — One Week Recorded on a Record Card

The payroll clerk went through the following steps in order to record the above information.

Step 1: Record the upper section of the card at the time of employment.

An employee is hired with an agreement as to the number of hours to be worked in order to get a stated salary. John Ellis is hired at $200.00 a week for

40 hours. In addition to the salary agreement, John Ellis is asked a number of personal questions. His answers are entered on the upper section of his employee's card.

Naturally, a separate card is opened for each employee.

Step 2: Transfer information from the payroll book to the employees' cards each payday.

Each payday, the payroll clerk copies selected information from the payroll book, shown on page 521, to the employees' cards. John Ellis' card, shown in Illustration 83b, page 521, shows selected information copied from the payroll book for the week ending January 6. At the end of the second week, January 13, 19--, the information is again transferred to the individual employees' cards. At the end of the first quarter (13 weeks) John Ellis' card would look like this:

FIRST QUARTER			
WEEK ENDING	**TOTAL WAGES**	**SOC. SEC. TAX**	**FEDERAL WITH. TAX**
1 Jan. 6 (19--)	2 0 0 00	1 1 70	2 3 60
2 13	2 2 2 50	1 3 02	2 7 40
3 20	2 0 0 00	1 1 70	2 3 60
4 27	2 0 0 00	1 1 70	2 3 60
5 Feb. 3	2 3 0 00	1 3 46	2 9 40
6 10	2 0 0 00	1 1 70	2 3 60
7 17	2 0 0 00	1 1 70	2 3 60
8 24	1 9 5 00	1 1 41	2 2 00
9 March 3	2 0 0 00	1 1 70	2 3 60
10 10	2 0 0 00	1 1 70	2 3 60
11 17	2 4 5 00	1 4 33	3 1 40
12 24	1 8 5 00	1 0 82	2 0 40
13 31	2 0 0 00	1 1 70	2 3 60
TOTAL	2 6 7 7 50	1 5 6 64	3 1 9 40

Illustration 83c — One Quarter Completed on a Record Card

Notice that the total wages on January 13 in Illustration 83c differ from the total wages on January 6. John Ellis worked more than 40 hours (43 hours) and received wages for the extra three hours plus an overtime bonus.

Step 3: Total each money column on each employee's card at the end of the quarter.

Notice that the employee record card in Illustration 83c has been totaled at the end of the first quarter. The card of each employee is totaled like this.

After all cards have been totaled, the payroll clerk is ready with selected information for various government agencies.

PRACTICE PROBLEMS

Problem 1

Directions:

a) Use the model shown in Illustration 83a to open separate employee's record cards for the following people employed by the R. Lacey Co. You will need 4 cards.

Jack Carle lives at 403 Elm St., Toledo, OH 43604. He is married and claims 4 exemptions. He is 42 years of age and his social security number is 121-34-2983. He is employed in the service department as a mechanic. He was hired at $235.00 a week on January 2 and was given card #1.

Peter Raccio lives at 85 Opal St., Toledo, OH 43614. He is married and claims 5 exemptions. He is 39 years of age and his social security number is 132-41-3562. He is employed in the service department as a mechanic. He was hired at $275.00 a week on January 2 and was given card #2.

Grace Long lives at 230 Harvey St., Toledo, OH 43608. She is single and claims 1 exemption. She is 20 years of age and her social security number is 154-12-4216. She is employed in the office department as a record keeper. She was hired at $140.00 a week on January 2 and was given card #3.

Ralph Paley lives at 176 Grange St., Toledo, OH 43618. He is married and claims 2 exemptions. He is 30 years of age and his social security number is 146-05-2137. He is employed in the service department as a mechanic. He was hired at $180.00 a week on January 2 and was given card #4.

b) Transfer the information on the payroll sheets below and on page 524 for the first quarter to the proper cards:

WEEK ENDING — *January 6, 19--*

CARD NO.	NAME OF EMPLOYEE	TOTAL WAGES	SOCIAL SECURITY (F.I.C.A.)	FEDERAL WITH. TAX	TOTAL DEDUC.	NET PAY
1	Jack Carle	235 00	13 75	26 50	40 25	194 75
2	Peter Raccio	275 00	16 09	31 60	47 69	227 31
3	Grace Long	136 50	7 99	20 80	28 79	107 71
4	Ralph Paley	180 00	10 53	22 70	33 23	146 77
		826 50	48 36	101 60	149 96	676 54
	Totals	826 50	48 36	101 60	149 96	676 54

WEEK ENDING _____ January 13, 19--

CARD NO.	NAME OF EMPLOYEE	TOTAL WAGES	DEDUCTIONS			NET PAY
			SOCIAL SECURITY (F.I.C.A.)	FEDERAL WITH. TAX	TOTAL DEDUC.	
1	Jack Carle	235 00	13 75	26 50	40 25	194 75
2	Peter Raccio	275 00	16 09	31 60	47 69	227 31
3	Grace Long	140 00	8 19	21 80	29 99	110 01
4	Ralph Paley	207 00	12 11	26 30	38 41	168 59
		857 00	50 14	106 20	156 34	700 66
	Totals	857 00	50 14	106 20	156 34	700 66

WEEK ENDING _____ January 20, 19--

CARD NO.	NAME OF EMPLOYEE	TOTAL WAGES	DEDUCTIONS			NET PAY
			SOCIAL SECURITY (F.I.C.A.)	FEDERAL WITH. TAX	TOTAL DEDUC.	
1	Jack Carle	243 82	14 26	28 50	42 76	201 06
2	Peter Raccio	213 13	12 47	20 60	33 07	180 06
3	Grace Long	150 50	8 80	24 50	33 30	117 20
4	Ralph Paley	180 00	10 53	22 70	33 23	146 17
		787 45	46 06	96 30	142 36	645 09
	Totals	787 45	46 06	96 30	142 36	645 09

WEEK ENDING _____ January 27, 19--

CARD NO.	NAME OF EMPLOYEE	TOTAL WAGES	DEDUCTIONS			NET PAY
			SOCIAL SECURITY (F.I.C.A.)	FEDERAL WITH. TAX	TOTAL DEDUC.	
1	Jack Carle	229 12	13 40	24 50	37 90	191 22
2	Peter Raccio	285 32	16 69	33 90	50 59	234 73
3	Grace Long	140 00	8 19	21 80	29 99	110 01
4	Ralph Paley	171 00	10 00	21 10	31 10	139 90
		825 44	48 28	101 30	149 58	675 86
	Totals	825 44	48 28	101 30	149 58	675 86

c) Pencil foot each column on each of the 4 employee's record cards to show the totals for the month of January.

Problem 2

Directions:

a) Use the same cards you worked with in Problem 1.

b) Record the information below and on page 526.

c) Pencil foot each column on each of the 4 employee's record cards to show the *totals for January and February*.

WEEK ENDING _____ *February 3, 19--*

CARD NO.	NAME OF EMPLOYEE	TOTAL WAGES	DEDUCTIONS			NET PAY
			SOCIAL SECURITY (F.I.C.A.)	FEDERAL WITH. TAX	TOTAL DEDUC.	
1	Jack Carle	235 00	13 75	26 50	40 25	194 75
2	Peter Raccio	275 00	16 09	31 60	47 69	227 31
3	Grace Long	166 25	9 73	26 60	36 33	129 92
4	Ralph Paley	180 00	10 53	22 70	33 23	146 77
		856 25	50 10	107 40	157 50	698 75
	Totals	856 25	50 10	107 40	157 50	698 75

WEEK ENDING _____ *February 10, 19--*

CARD NO.	NAME OF EMPLOYEE	TOTAL WAGES	DEDUCTIONS			NET PAY
			SOCIAL SECURITY (F.I.C.A.)	FEDERAL WITH. TAX	TOTAL DEDUC.	
1	Jack Carle	235 00	13 75	26 50	40 25	194 75
2	Peter Raccio	275 00	16 09	31 60	47 69	227 31
3	Grace Long	140 00	8 19	21 80	29 99	110 01
4	Ralph Paley	180 00	10 53	22 70	33 23	146 77
		830 00	48 56	102 60	151 16	678 84
	Totals	830 00	48 56	102 60	151 16	678 84

WEEK ENDING — February 17, 19--

CARD NO.	NAME OF EMPLOYEE	TOTAL WAGES	SOCIAL SECURITY (F.I.C.A.)	FEDERAL WITH. TAX	TOTAL DEDUC.	NET PAY
1	Jack Carle	226 18	13 23	24 50	37 73	188 45
2	Peter Raccio	275 00	16 09	31 60	47 69	227 31
3	Grace Long	161 00	9 42	26 60	36 02	124 98
4	Ralph Paley	193 50	11 32	24 30	35 62	157 88
		855 68	50 06	107 00	157 06	698 62
	Totals	855 68	50 06	107 00	157 06	698 62

WEEK ENDING — February 24, 19--

CARD NO.	NAME OF EMPLOYEE	TOTAL WAGES	SOCIAL SECURITY (F.I.C.A.)	FEDERAL WITH. TAX	TOTAL DEDUC.	NET PAY
1	Jack Carle	235 00	13 75	26 50	40 25	194 75
2	Peter Raccio	206 25	12 07	19 00	31 07	175 18
3	Grace Long	140 00	8 19	21 80	29 99	110 01
4	Ralph Paley	180 00	10 53	22 70	33 23	146 77
		761 25	44 54	90 00	134 54	626 71
	Totals	761 25	44 54	90 00	134 54	626 71

Problem 3

Directions:

a) Use the same cards you worked with in Problem 2.

b) Record the payroll information on pages 527 and 528.

c) Record the totals for each column on each of the 4 employee's record cards to show the totals for the *entire 3 months*.

d) Transfer these totals to the summary section of each record card.

e) Prepare a list showing the name of each employee and the total wages earned for the quarter. Find the total wages to be reported to the District Director of Internal Revenue at the end of the first quarter for *all employees* by totaling this list. If your work is correct, the total should be $10,737.37.

f) Find the total security taxes taken from *all employees* for the first quarter. If your work is correct, the total should be $628.18.

g) Find the total withholding taxes taken from *all employees* for the first quarter. If your work is correct, the total should be $1,325.80.

WEEK ENDING _____ March 3, 19--

| CARD NO. | NAME OF EMPLOYEE | TOTAL WAGES | DEDUCTIONS | | | NET PAY |
			SOCIAL SECURITY (F.I.C.A.)	FEDERAL WITH. TAX	TOTAL DEDUC.	
1	Jack Carle	235 00	13 75	26 50	40 25	194 75
2	Peter Raccio	275 00	16 09	31 60	47 69	227 31
3	Grace Long	155 75	9 11	24 50	33 61	122 14
4	Ralph Paley	180 00	10 53	22 70	33 23	146 77
	Totals	845 75	49 48	105 30	154 78	690 97
		845 75	49 48	105 30	154 78	690 97

WEEK ENDING _____ March 10, 19--

| CARD NO. | NAME OF EMPLOYEE | TOTAL WAGES | DEDUCTIONS | | | NET PAY |
			SOCIAL SECURITY (F.I.C.A.)	FEDERAL WITH. TAX	TOTAL DEDUC.	
1	Jack Carle	270 25	15 81	34 90	50 71	219 54
2	Peter Raccio	254 38	14 88	27 60	42 48	211 90
3	Grace Long	140 00	8 19	21 80	29 99	110 01
4	Ralph Paley	210 38	12 31	28 30	40 61	169 77
	Totals	875 01	51 19	112 60	163 79	711 22
		875 01	51 19	112 60	163 79	711 22

WEEK ENDING _____ March 17, 19--

| CARD NO. | NAME OF EMPLOYEE | TOTAL WAGES | DEDUCTIONS | | | NET PAY |
			SOCIAL SECURITY (F.I.C.A.)	FEDERAL WITH. TAX	TOTAL DEDUC.	
1	Jack Carle	235 00	13 75	26 50	40 25	194 75
2	Peter Raccio	275 00	16 09	31 60	47 69	227 31
3	Grace Long	140 00	8 19	21 80	29 99	110 01
4	Ralph Paley	180 00	10 53	22 70	33 23	146 77
	Totals	830 00	48 56	102 60	151 16	678 84
		830 00	48 56	102 60	151 16	678 84

WEEK ENDING _____ *March 24, 19--*

CARD NO.	NAME OF EMPLOYEE	TOTAL WAGES	DEDUCTIONS			NET PAY
			SOCIAL SECURITY (F.I.C.A.)	FEDERAL WITH. TAX	TOTAL DEDUC.	
1	Jack Carle	235 00	13 75	26 50	40 25	194 75
2	Peter Raccio	280 16	16 39	33 90	50 29	229 87
3	Grace Long	122 50	7 17	17 60	24 77	97 73
4	Ralph Paley	142 88	8 36	15 90	24 26	118 62
	Totals	780 54	45 67	93 90	139 57	640 97
		780 54	45 67	93 90	139 57	640 97

WEEK ENDING _____ *March 31, 19--*

CARD NO.	NAME OF EMPLOYEE	TOTAL WAGES	DEDUCTIONS			NET PAY
			SOCIAL SECURITY (F.I.C.A.)	FEDERAL WITH. TAX	TOTAL DEDUC.	
1	Jack Carle	211 50	12 37	22 90	35 27	176 23
2	Peter Raccio	275 00	16 09	31 60	47 69	227 31
3	Grace Long	140 00	8 19	21 80	29 99	110 01
4	Ralph Paley	180 00	10 53	22 70	33 23	146 77
	Totals	806 50	47 18	99 00	146 18	660 32
		806 50	47 18	99 00	146 18	660 32

Copy the following problems on a sheet of paper and find the answers:

(1)	(2)

Practicing Related Arithmetic

(1)

$2,034.61
3,591.82
1,729.35
3,072.08
916.70
4,050.03
870.90
5,034.16
600.51
2,853.00
1,009.64
798.05
+3,540.10

(2)

Crossfoot and then add down:

a) 45 + 70 + 15 + 65 =

b) 60 + 18 + 12 + 30 =

c) 11 + 14 + 50 + 83 =

d) 37 + 80 + 18 + 26 =

e) 53 + 92 + 40 + 78 = _____

f) ___ + ___ + ___ + ___ = _____

AIMS

1. To learn why a withholding tax form (W-2) is prepared.
2. To learn how a W-2 form is prepared.

EXPLANATION

In the preceding job, you learned to keep payroll information for each employee on an employee's record card. You also learned that these cards are used to furnish government agencies with selected information at stated times. In this lesson, you will learn to use these cards to give both the government and the employee a record of the total wages, total social security deductions, and total withholding tax deductions for the year.

Withholding tax forms furnish information to governmental agencies and the employee

The record (which is given to the employee and to the District Director of Internal Revenue) is commonly known as a "W-2" form.

All the information on this form can be secured from the employee's record card. Refer to the summary section of the employee's record card in Illustration 83a, page 520. Note that the year's total wages, total social security tax, and total withholding tax can be obtained very easily.

The payroll clerk prepares four copies of the W-2 form for each employee. One copy is sent to the District Director of Internal Revenue, one copy is

Illustration 84a — Blank W-2 Form

retained by the employer for the files, and two copies are given to each employee. The employee attaches one of the copies to the income tax return and files the other copy.

If the employee works in a city or state which requires a copy of the W-2 form, then the payroll clerk prepares six instead of four copies of the form.

SAMPLE PROBLEM

Paul Taft lives at 183 Pacific St., Newark, NJ 07105. His social security number is 402-15-3640. He is married. He earns $203.00 a week. His record card shows the following summary section:

SUMMARY			
QUARTERS	TOTAL WAGES	SOC. SEC. TAX	FEDERAL WITH. TAX
FIRST	2 6 3 9 00	1 5 4 44	3 4 1 90
SECOND	2 6 8 4 68	1 5 7 11	3 4 9 90
THIRD	2 7 4 5 58	1 6 0 67	3 6 3 00
FOURTH	2 6 3 9 00	1 5 4 44	3 4 1 90
TOTAL FOR THE YEAR	10 7 0 8 26	6 2 6 66	1 3 9 6 70

His W-2 form would look like Illustration 84b at the top of the next page.

Illustration 84b — Completed W-2 Form

PRACTICE PROBLEMS

Problem 1

Directions:

a) Listed below and on page 532 are the summary sections for 3 employee's record cards. Copy each summary on a sheet of paper.

Card #1

SUMMARY			
QUARTERS	TOTAL WAGES	SOC. SEC. TAX	FEDERAL WITH. TAX
FIRST	2 4 7 0 00	1 4 4 56	2 5 6 10
SECOND	2 5 1 2 75	1 4 7 05	2 6 0 90
THIRD	2 4 7 0 00	1 4 4 56	2 5 6 10
FOURTH	2 5 3 4 13	1 4 8 30	2 6 4 10
TOTAL FOR THE YEAR			

Card #2

SUMMARY			
QUARTERS	TOTAL WAGES	SOC. SEC. TAX	FEDERAL WITH. TAX
FIRST	2 7 9 5 00	1 6 3 54	2 6 7 80
SECOND	2 8 9 9 91	1 6 9 68	2 8 6 10
THIRD	2 7 9 5 00	1 6 3 54	2 6 7 80
FOURTH	2 8 6 7 63	1 6 7 79	2 8 1 10
TOTAL FOR THE YEAR			

Card #3

QUARTERS	TOTAL WAGES					SOC. SEC. TAX				FEDERAL WITH. TAX			
				SUMMARY									
	TOTAL WAGES					SOC. SEC. TAX				FEDERAL WITH. TAX			
FIRST	2	5	6	4	28	1	5	0	07	3	2	1	90
SECOND	2	5	3	5	00	1	4	8	33	3	1	5	90
THIRD	2	6	3	7	48	1	5	4	35	3	3	7	00
FOURTH	2	5	3	5	00	1	4	8	33	3	1	5	90
TOTAL FOR THE YEAR													

    b) Total each column on each card.

    c) Find the total wages for all the employees (add the "Total Wages" column for all the 3 cards together).

    d) Find the total social security deductions for all the employees (add the "Social Security Tax" columns together).

    e) Find the total withholding tax deductions for all the employees (add the total withholding taxes for all three cards together).

Problem 2

Directions

    a) Listed below and on page 533 are the summary sections for 3 employee's record cards. Copy each summary on a sheet of paper.

Card #1

QUARTERS	TOTAL WAGES					SOC. SEC. TAX				FEDERAL WITH. TAX			
				SUMMARY									
	TOTAL WAGES					SOC. SEC. TAX				FEDERAL WITH. TAX			
FIRST	2	2	7	5	00	1	3	3	12	3	0	4	20
SECOND	2	2	7	5	00	1	3	3	12	3	0	4	20
THIRD	2	3	0	7	85	1	3	5	04	3	1	0	00
FOURTH	2	2	3	1	40	1	3	0	57	2	9	7	40
TOTAL FOR THE YEAR													

Card #2

QUARTERS	TOTAL WAGES					SOC. SEC. TAX				FEDERAL WITH. TAX			
				SUMMARY									
	TOTAL WAGES					SOC. SEC. TAX				FEDERAL WITH. TAX			
FIRST	2	8	9	6	68	1	6	9	43	3	4	6	20
SECOND	2	8	3	4	00	1	6	5	75	3	3	0	20
THIRD	2	8	3	4	00	1	6	5	75	3	3	0	20
FOURTH	2	8	9	9	40	1	6	9	58	3	4	5	60
TOTAL FOR THE YEAR													

Card #3

QUARTERS	TOTAL WAGES	SOC. SEC. TAX	FEDERAL WITH. TAX
	SUMMARY		
FIRST	2 7 1 7 00	1 5 8 99	3 4 1 90
SECOND	2 7 6 2 06	1 6 1 62	3 5 2 20
THIRD	2 7 1 7 00	1 5 8 99	3 4 1 90
FOURTH	2 7 2 7 86	1 5 9 62	3 4 7 40
TOTAL FOR THE YEAR			

b) Total each column on each card.
c) Find the total wages for all the employees (add the "Total Wages" column for all the three cards together).
d) Find the total social security deductions for all the employees (add the "Social Security Tax" columns for all the three cards together).
e) Find the total withholding tax deductions for all the employees (add the total withholding taxes for all the three cards together).

Problem 3

Directions:
a) Listed below and on page 534 are the summary sections for 4 employee's record cards. Copy each summary.

Card #1

QUARTERS	TOTAL WAGES	SOC. SEC. TAX	FEDERAL WITH. TAX
	SUMMARY		
FIRST	2 4 7 4 65	1 4 4 74	3 0 9 40
SECOND	2 4 0 5 00	1 4 0 66	2 9 5 10
THIRD	2 4 0 5 00	1 4 0 66	2 9 5 10
FOURTH	2 4 1 0 03	1 4 0 96	2 9 5 10
TOTAL FOR THE YEAR			

Card #2

QUARTERS	TOTAL WAGES	SOC. SEC. TAX	FEDERAL WITH. TAX
	SUMMARY		
FIRST	2 9 2 5 00	1 7 1 08	3 1 8 50
SECOND	2 8 5 7 64	1 6 7 14	3 0 7 30
THIRD	2 9 5 0 74	1 7 2 59	3 2 3 30
FOURTH	2 9 2 5 00	1 7 1 08	3 1 8 50
TOTAL FOR THE YEAR			

Card #3

QUARTERS	TOTAL WAGES				SOC. SEC. TAX				FEDERAL WITH. TAX			
SUMMARY												
FIRST	3 1	2 0	00		1	8 2	52		3 3	2	80		
SECOND	3 1	2 0	00		1	8 2	52		3 3	2	80		
THIRD	3 0	3 0	00		1	7 7	26		3 1	8	20		
FOURTH	2 9	9 1	00		1	7 4	97		3 1	0	60		
TOTAL FOR THE YEAR												

Card #4

QUARTERS	TOTAL WAGES				SOC. SEC. TAX				FEDERAL WITH. TAX			
SUMMARY												
FIRST	2 7	5 5	25		1	6 1	18		3 2	2	60		
SECOND	2 6	7 8	00		1	5 6	65		3 0	6	80		
THIRD	2 6	6 2	55		1	5 5	75		3 0	8	20		
FOURTH	2 6	6 7	70		1	5 6	05		3 0	5	20		
TOTAL FOR THE YEAR												

b) Total each column on each card.

c) Find the total wages for all the employees (add the "Total Wages" column for all the four cards together).

d) Find the total social security deductions for all the employees (add the "Social Security Tax" columns for all the cards together).

e) Find the total withholding tax deductions for all the employees (add the total withholding taxes for all the four cards together).

Copy the following problems on a sheet of paper and find the answers:

(1)   (2)

$ 91.76	Crossfoot and then add down:
257.38	
182.90	a) $30 + 43 + 27 + 80 =$
205.13	b) $19 + 31 + 20 + 59 =$
168.42	c) $28 + 50 + 62 + 98 =$
86.25	d) $74 + 16 + 35 + 41 =$
340.04	e) $\underline{60} + \underline{83} + \underline{92} + \underline{10} =$
+273.50	f) $\underline{} + \underline{} + \underline{} + \underline{} = \underline{}$

Practicing Related Arithmetic

AIMS

1. To learn about other deductions made from an employee's wages besides social security and withholding taxes.

2. To learn how to record these deductions in the payroll book.

EXPLANATION

You have learned that deductions are made from a worker's wages for federal withholding taxes and social security taxes. Perhaps you have wondered why the column in the payroll book has always been labeled "Federal Withholding Taxes" instead of just "Withholding Taxes." This was necessary because some states and cities require that employers withhold taxes for state or city income taxes. Separate tables are prepared by the state or city income tax department. Therefore, to separate the federal from the state withholding taxes, one column would be labeled "Federal Withholding Taxes" and the other would be "State Withholding Taxes" or "City Withholding Taxes." You would use these withholding tax tables in the same manner as the federal withholding tax table.

In addition to these deductions, some employers make deductions, with the consent of the worker, for a number of other reasons. They may be for union dues, for United States Savings Bonds, for hospital care, for life insurance premiums, for private pension plans, or for any one or a number of other things. These deductions may be made each payday or on certain selected paydays. Naturally, the payroll clerk must be careful to make these

Various deductions made from wages

deductions according to the plan agreed upon between the worker and the organization to whom the money is to be sent.

Typical payroll books have provision for columns for social security and withholding tax deductions and, in addition, usually have two or three columns with no headings. The payroll clerk may fill in the headings necessary for the deductions.

To acquaint you with the use of some of these other columns, let us work with deductions made monthly from workers' wages for union dues, hospital care, and United States Savings Bonds.

SAMPLE PROBLEM

Adele Keats is a worker in a state which does not require the withholding of state income taxes. She has earned $202.00 for the week ending March 7, 19--. Her time card shows the following:

Wages..	$202.00
Less:	
Social Security tax.....................................	$11.82
Federal withholding tax.............................	29.20
Union dues..	5.00
Hospitalization	6.25
Total deductions..	52.27
Net pay..	$149.73

Here is how this information would appear in a payroll book:

CARD NO.	NAME OF EMPLOYEE	NO. OF EXEMP- TIONS	TOTAL HOURS WORKED	REGULAR RATE OF PAY FOR 40 HR. WEEK	EARNINGS AT REG. RATE FOR TOTAL HRS. WORKED	BONUS FOR OVERTIME	TOTAL WAGES	SOCIAL SECURITY (F.I.C.A.)	FEDERAL WITH. TAX	UNION DUES	HOSPITALI- ZATION	TOTAL DEDUC.	NET PAY
1	Adele Keats	1	40	202 00	202 00		202 00	11 82	29 20	5 00	6 25	52 27	149 73

WEEK ENDING March 7, 19--

DEDUCTIONS

Illustration 85a — Payroll Book with an Entry

The payroll clerk enters the information found on each card in the same way. After all the cards have been entered, the payroll clerk then totals each money column and checks the totals just as you learned to do in previous jobs.

When all information has been recorded in the payroll book, the payroll clerk will transfer selected information to the employee's record card.

Can you think of a way that payroll clerks can record information in a payroll book just the way you see it in Illustration 85a and at the same time record information in the employee's record card and write separate pay checks for each employee?

If you thought of using carbon paper, you were on the right track; and you will find that you can save yourself a lot of work. In addition, since the information is *written only once and not re-copied*, errors occasionally made in recopying can be eliminated. However, if you try to write all of these forms at the same time, you may have some trouble placing each form on top of the other so that the *columns are lined up properly*.

The "One-Write" system reduces errors in recopying information

To make it easy for a record keeper to line up the columns, some manufacturers of business forms and machines have produced specially constructed *writing boards* which enable the record keeper to *line up* the *columns* conveniently and rapidly. These specially constructed boards are sometimes called "Peg Boards." They are called "Peg Boards" because pegs are located along the sides of the board as shown in Illustration 85b.

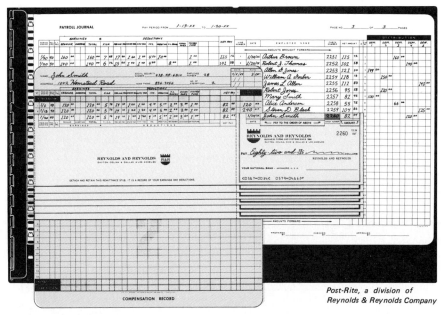

One writing prepares
1) payroll check
2) employee's record card
3) weekly payroll sheet

Post-Rite, a division of
Reynolds & Reynolds Company

Illustration 85b — The Payroll Check, the Employee's Record Card, and the Payroll Sheet Properly Lined Up

This system of writing all three forms at the same time is commonly called the "One-Write" system, and many concerns use specially treated business forms which permit duplication without the use of carbon paper.

"Peg Boards" and similar mechanical aids have been found to be useful not only in recording payroll information but also in other record-keeping activities such as handling stock records and accounts receivable.

Many large concerns find it advantageous to use computers to calculate wages, prepare checks and record all payroll information which you have learned to do manually (by hand).

Shown below is a punched card processed by a computer.

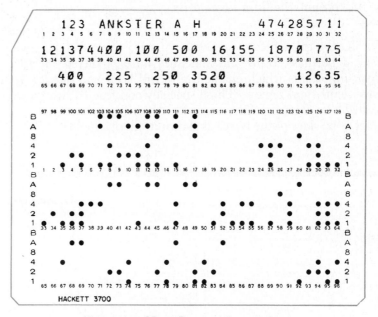

Illustration 85c — Punched Payroll Card

PRACTICE PROBLEMS

Problem 1

Directions:
a) Copy the following table:

CARD NO.	NO. OF EXEMP-TIONS	TOTAL WAGES	DEDUCTIONS					NET PAY
			SOCIAL SECURITY (F.I.C.A.)	FEDERAL WITH. TAX	UNION DUES	HOSPITALI-ZATION	TOTAL DEDUC.	
1	4	21612						
2	0	18314						
3	6	23490						
4	2	20087						
	Totals							

b) Complete the payroll. Deduct $5.00 for union dues from each worker's pay. Deduct $7.50 for hospital care from each worker's pay.

c) Check your totals. If your work is correct, the total of the "Net Pay" column should be $637.49.

Problem 2

Directions:

a) Copy the following table:

CARD NO.	NO. OF EXEMP- TIONS	TOTAL WAGES	DEDUCTIONS					NET PAY
			SOCIAL SECURITY (F.I.C.A.)	FEDERAL WITH. TAX	UNION DUES	HOSPITALI- ZATION	TOTAL DEDUC.	
1	1	223 60						
2	5	251 70						
3	3	249 55						
4	7	265 23						
5	2	178 04						
Totals								

b) Complete the payroll. Deduct $5.25 for union dues from each worker's pay. Deduct $6.75 for hospital care from each worker's pay.

c) Check your totals. If your work is correct, the total of the "Net Pay" column should be $902.38.

Problem 3

Directions:

a) Copy the following table:

CARD NO.	NO. OF EXEMP- TIONS	TOTAL WAGES	DEDUCTIONS					NET PAY
			SOCIAL SECURITY (F.I.C.A.)	FEDERAL WITH. TAX	UNION DUES	HOSPITALI- ZATION	TOTAL DEDUC.	
1	0	187 27						
2	6	232 05						
3	5	195 82						
4	3	208 98						
5	8	243 34						
6	1	185 73						
Totals								

b) Complete the payroll. Deduct $4.25 for union dues from each worker's pay. Deduct $9.00 for hospital care from the following workers: 2, 4, 5, and 6. Since workers #1 and #3 did not wish to join the plan, we do not make any deduction for hospital care from their pay.

c) Check your totals. If your work is correct, the total of the "Net Pay" column should be $984.16.

Problem 4

Directions:

a) Copy the following table:

CARD NO.	NO. OF EXEMP-TIONS	TOTAL WAGES	DEDUCTIONS					NET PAY
			SOCIAL SECURITY (F.I.C.A.)	FEDERAL WITH. TAX	UNION DUES	HOSPITALI-ZATION	TOTAL DEDUC.	
1	3	179 92						
2	7	257 03						
3	2	226 07						
4	4	218 41						
5	0	196 05						
Totals								

b) Complete the payroll. Deduct $6.00 for union dues from each worker's pay. Deduct $9.35 for hospital care from each worker's pay, *except cards #2 and #5*. They did not wish to join the plan.

c) Check your totals. If your work is correct, the total of the "Net Pay" column should be $831.98.

UNIT 10

RECORD KEEPING FOR SMALL RETAIL BUSINESSES

UNIT 10

JOB 86 | PREPARING AN INCOME STATEMENT

Copy and complete the following problems:

<table>
<tr><td></td><td>(1)</td><td>(2)</td><td>(3)</td></tr>
<tr><td rowspan="8">Practicing
Related
Arithmetic</td><td>$1,456.20</td><td>$ 876.50</td><td>$4,625.40</td></tr>
<tr><td>372.45</td><td>1,428.45</td><td>−1,871.82</td></tr>
<tr><td>825.83</td><td>532.15</td><td>$ _____</td></tr>
<tr><td>314.27</td><td>2,659.92</td><td></td></tr>
<tr><td>2,589.72</td><td>307.08</td><td>(4)</td></tr>
<tr><td>1,312.18</td><td>1,294.31</td><td>$3,841.25</td></tr>
<tr><td>426.34</td><td>468.64</td><td>−2,372.80</td></tr>
<tr><td>+ 201.70</td><td>+ 247.26</td><td>$ _____</td></tr>
<tr><td>$ _____</td><td>$ _____</td><td></td></tr>
</table>

AIM

To learn how to prepare an income statement for a retail business.

EXPLANATION

Many of you have worked after school or during the summer vacation and received a weekly salary.

Some of you, at some future time, may go into business for yourselves. Of course, when you are in business for yourself no one pays you a salary.

Here is how you can earn a living if you own and operate a small business such as a television repair shop. Each day you receive money from your customers for repairing their television sets. The money you receive from your customers is called your *income*. But not all of this money can be your earnings or profit. To operate the business, you must spend money for necessary business expenses such as rent for the building, the telephone bill, the electric bill, gasoline and repairs for the business automobile, and television parts and supplies. Since no one pays you a salary when you are in business for yourself, you earn money only if the amount you receive from your customers as your income is more than the money you spend for expenses. The amount of your earnings is found by subtracting your expenses from your income. This amount is called *net income*, or *net profit*.

Income
−Expenses
=Profit

Office Expenses 22¢   Rent 25¢

Salaries 41¢   Profit 12¢

For example, if during the month you received $2,200.00 from your customers for television repairs, and you spend $1,000.00 for expenses, your net income would amount to $1,200.00.

Income from repairs	$2,200.00
Less expenses	−1,000.00
Net income	=$1,200.00

The net income of $1,200.00 represents your earnings for the month. From month to month, the net income will vary as a result of changes in the amounts received from customers and changes in the amounts paid for expenses.

People in business find how much they have earned by preparing a form called an income statement. Here is how this form is prepared in an actual business situation.

SAMPLE PROBLEM

Joe Kern operates his own auto repair shop. He keeps separate records of the *income received for his repair services* and *income received from the sale of parts*.

During the month of May, Mr. Kern received $1,800.00 from his repair services and $900.00 from the sale of parts.

He paid the following expenses during the month: rent, $400.00; supplies and parts, $670.00; telephone, $30.00; insurance premium, $80.00; electricity, $20.00.

Mr. Kern found the amount he had earned for the month (his net income) by preparing the income statement shown on page 545.

Joe Kern Income Statement For The Month of May, 19--		
Income:		
Repairs	1800 00	
Parts	900 00	
Total Income		2700 00
Expenses:		
Rent	400 00	
Supplies & Parts	670 00	
Telephone	30 00	
Insurance	80 00	
Electricity	20 00	
Total Expenses		1200 00
Net Income		1500 00

Illustration 86 — Completed Income Statement

According to the statement, the net income or profit earned by Mr. Kern amounted to $1,500.00. If you examine the second column of the income statement, you can see that Mr. Kern found this amount by subtracting the total expenses for the month from the total income for the month as follows:

Total Income	$2,700.00
−Total Expenses	1,200.00
=Net Income	$1,500.00

PRACTICE PROBLEMS

Problem 1

Sal Monte operates his own auto repair shop. He keeps a separate record of the income received for his repair services and the income received from the sale of parts.

Directions: Prepare an income statement for the month of August from the following information (see Illustration 86 above):

During the month Mr. Monte received $1,620.00 for repair services and $510.00 from the sale of parts.

He paid the following expenses during the month: rent, $390.00; supplies and parts, $410.00; telephone, $75.00; insurance premium, $130.00; electricity, $30.00.

Problem 2

Gus Hansen operates his own painting and decorating business. He keeps a separate record of the income received from painting and the income received from hanging wallpaper.

Directions: Prepare an income statement for the month of March from the following information:

During the month Mr. Hansen received $1,240.00 for his painting services and $1,415.00 for his wallpapering services.

He paid the following expenses during the month: rent, $225.00; paints and supplies, $330.00; wallpaper, $275.00; truck expenses, $170.00; telephone, $40.00; advertising, $60.00; electricity, $24.00.

Problem 3

Janet Simons operates her own beauty shop. She keeps a separate record of the income received for beautician services and the income received from the sale of beauty preparations.

Directions: Prepare an income statement for the month of November from the following information:

During the month Ms. Simons received $1,803.00 for beautician services and $351.65 from the sale of beauty preparations.

She paid the following expenses during the month: rent, $520.00; beauty supplies, $163.40; laundry, $73.90; cleaning expenses, $95.00; telephone, $46.25; electricity, $24.80; stationery and stamps, $19.30.

Problem 4

Tom Scott is an electrician who is in business for himself. He keeps a separate record of the income received for his repair services and the income received from the sale of lighting fixtures.

Directions: Prepare an income statement for the month of April from the following information:

During the month Mr. Scott received $1,969.60 for repair services and $815.75 from the sale of lighting fixtures.

He paid the following expenses during the month: rent, $260.00; materials and supplies, $532.45; lighting fixtures, $416.30; office expenses, $31.20; truck expenses, $98.15; telephone, $48.10; miscellaneous expenses, $29.50.

Problem 5

Maria Castle owns and operates a dancing school. She keeps a separate record of the income received for dancing instruction and the income received from the sale of dancing costumes.

Directions: Prepare an income statement for the month of May from the following information:

During the month Miss Castle received $1,426.50 for dancing lessons and $251.35 from the sale of dance costumes.

She paid the following expenses during the month: rent, $270.00; dance costumes, $191.80; advertising, $95.00; stationery and stamps, $32.25; telephone, $41.30; electricity, $21.65; miscellaneous expenses, $19.20.

Problem 6

Joe Montez owns and operates a bowling alley. He keeps a separate record of income received from bowling fees and income received from the sale of bowling equipment.

Directions: Prepare an income statement for the month of December from the following information:

During the month Mr. Montez received $2,865.00 from bowling fees and $781.95 from the sale of bowling equipment.

He paid the following expenses during the month: rent, $910.00; bowling equipment, $431.65; insurance premiums, $338.00; telephone, $81.55; electricity, $73.15; advertising, $107.00; office expenses, $47.80.

JOB 87 | PREPARING AN INCOME STATEMENT

Practicing Related Arithmetic

Copy and solve the following problem:

	Jan.	Feb.	March	Totals
Income	$914.70	$992.85	$974.60	= $
− Expenses	346.80	193.40	215.75	=
= Net Income	$	$	$	= $

AIM

To give additional experience in preparing income statements.

EXPLANATION

In the preceding job, you learned that those in business prepare income statements in order to find the amount they have earned, which is called *net income* or *net profit*.

Internal Revenue Service (IRS) examines the income statement to check a businessperson's income tax

The businessperson is not the only one who is interested in the income statement. The income tax examiner from the federal government's Internal Revenue Service must see it in order to see whether or not the correct amount of income tax has been paid. In fact, the income tax return filed by a businessperson shows the income, expenses, and net profit for the year in the same way you will be asked to show these facts in the problems in this job.

In the unit on payroll, you learned that the federal income tax is collected from employees in the form of withholding tax by deducting a portion of the tax each week from the employee's salary.

As you know, those who own and operate a business do not earn a living by receiving a salary from anyone. Instead they earn a living only if their businesses show a profit. It is this profit, or net income, that is used as a basis for the businessperson's income tax.

Since it is difficult to know the profit at the end of each week, the federal government permits a businessperson to *estimate* the income tax for the year by estimating the net income for the year.

The estimated income tax must be paid in four installments on the following dates: April 15, June 15, September 15, and January 15. If an error is made in estimating the profit, the businessperson can correct the error by changing the estimated tax on any of the installment dates after April 15.

In the payroll work you have done, you learned that an employee's wage is not only subject to a federal income tax but that it is also subject to a social security tax.

In the same way, a businessperson's net income is subject not only to a federal income tax but also to a social security tax. The social security tax in this case is called a *self-employment tax* because it is based on earnings from self-employment.

Self-employment tax (social security tax for businesspersons)

Only the first $14,100.00 of the businessperson's net income for the year is subject to the social security or self-employment tax. This rule is similar to the rule you learned about employees' wages which limited the social security tax to the first $14,100.00 of each employee's annual wage. The limit of $14,100.00 can be changed by Congress at any time.

The rate of self-employment tax up to the year 1992 is scheduled as follows:

Year	Rate
1975–1977	7.9%
1978–1980	8.1%
1981–1985	8.35%
1986–1992	8.5%

(These rates can be changed by Congress at any time.)

PRACTICE PROBLEMS

Problem 1

Refer to the table above as a guide and find the self-employment tax for each of the following incomes.

Net Income	Tax	Net Income	Tax
a) $ 8,000.00	$_____	f) $ 7,400.00	$_____
b) 6,000.00	$_____	g) 9,500.00	$_____
c) 9,100.00	$_____	h) 13,600.00	$_____
d) 11,000.00	$_____	i) 15,800.00	$_____
e) 12,600.00	$_____	j) 21,600.00	$_____

Problem 2

Refer to the table above as a guide and find the self-employment tax for each of the following incomes.

Net Income	Tax	Net Income	Tax
a) $ 7,000.00	$_____	f) $ 6,800.00	$_____
b) 5,000.00	$_____	g) 7,400.00	$_____
c) 8,100.00	$_____	h) 13,500.00	$_____
d) 12,000.00	$_____	i) 16,700.00	$_____
e) 10,300.00	$_____	j) 19,200.00	$_____

Problem 3

Sam Wayne operates his own radio and television repair shop. He keeps a separate record of his income from repairs and his income from the sale of parts.

Directions: Prepare an income statement for the year ended December 31, 19— from the following information: (The date should be written — "For the year ended December 31, 19—.")

During the year, Mr. Wayne received $18,272.80 from repairs and $4,376.25 from the sale of parts.

He paid the following expenses during the year: rent, $3,420.00; parts and supplies, $3,175.30; truck expenses, $671.80; insurance premiums, $624.00; advertising, $210.00; telephone, $427.60; electricity, $364.90.

Problem 4

Ruth Johnson owns and operates a dry cleaning store. She receives income from dry cleaning and from tailoring and alterations.

Directions: Prepare an income statement for the year ended December 31, 19— from the following information:

During the year, Ruth Johnson received $16,734.65 from dry cleaning and $2,274.50 from tailoring.

She paid the following expenses during the year: rent, $3,780.00; cleaning supplies, $972.30; insurance premiums, $625.00; telephone, $348.75; advertising, $215.00; machinery repairs, $112.40; electricity, $641.70.

Problem 5

The business staff of the City High School Magazine receives income from its subscribers (people who buy the magazine) and from its advertisers.

Directions: Prepare an income statement for the year ended December 31, 19— for the City High School Magazine from the following information:

During the year the magazine staff received $960.75 from subscriptions and $291.50 from advertising.

The following expenses were paid during the year: printing, $832.00; photo supplies, $85.65; stationery, $42.90; postage, $72.00; telephone, $91.30; miscellaneous expenses, $63.15.

Problem 6

John Genovese operates his own moving and storage business. He keeps a separate record of the amount he receives from moving income and the amount he receives from storage income.

Directions: Prepare an income statement for the year ended December 31, 19— from the following information:

During the year, Mr. Genovese received $21,615.00 from moving income and $5,642.45 from storage income.

He paid the following expenses during the year: rent, $5,040.00; truck expenses, $2,381.35; advertising, $875.00; storage supplies, $624.75; telephone, $812.60; office expenses, $215.20; light and heat, $481.90.

Problem 7

Maureen Kean owns and operates a furniture upholstery business. She keeps a separate record of her income from labor and her income from the sale of fabrics.

Directions: Prepare an income statement for the year ended December 31, 19— from the following information:

During the year Ms. Kean received $20,310.00 for labor and $6,271.70 for fabrics.

She paid the following expenses during the year: rent, $4,680.00; fabrics and supplies, $4,190.30; auto expenses, $819.65; insurance, $621.00; telephone, $413.15; electricity, $398.75; office supplies, $207.40.

**Practicing
Related
Arithmetic**

Copy and solve the following problem:

	Jan.	Feb.	March	Totals
Income	$891.60	$912.70	$784.40 = $	
– Expenses	147.90	238.50	125.60 =	
= Net Income	$	$	$ = $	

AIM

To learn how businesspeople keep a record of their income.

EXPLANATION

You have learned that businesspeople must know their income and expenses so that they can prepare income statements and determine what their profit has been.

Up to this point when you were asked to prepare an income statement, the amounts of income and expenses were given to you in the problem. Of course, if you were in business for yourself, these figures would be found by adding up the amounts you actually received as income and by adding up the amounts that you actually paid out for expenses. In other words, you would need careful records so that you could find your total income and your total expenses at any time.

In this job you are going to keep a record of income received. Later you will learn how to keep a record of the money spent for expenses.

Using a cash register to record income

When you studied the work of the cashier, you learned that those who operate retail businesses keep a record of cash received by using a cash register or by issuing a receipt for the money received.

The method used to keep a record of cash received depends upon the nature of the business involved. When money is regularly received at a place of business, it is usually convenient to use a cash register. For example, if you operated a gasoline service station a cash register would be convenient.

At the end of each day you could find the total cash received from the cash register readings. If you wanted to keep a separate record of cash received for gas, oil, and repairs, you would be able to do this by depressing the appropriate key on the cash register.

On the other hand, if you were in the business of repairing appliances, you would probably collect your money in the homes of your customers. You would write out a sales slip, or invoice, which would serve as a written receipt for the money collected. This form would be prepared in duplicate and you would keep the duplicate copy as a record of your income.

TOM'S TELEVISION REPAIRS
8421 COLUMBIA STREET
DEARBORN, MI 48127

Customer *Mr. S Slocum*

Address *215 Drexel Street*
Dearborn, MI 48128

Invoice No. *835*

Date *June 23, 19--*

Quantity	Description	Price	Amount
2	*tubes, 7AT4*	3 30	6 60
	service charge	8 00	8 00
			14 60

*Rec'd payment
Tom Baker*

Illustration 88a — Sales Slip, or Invoice

Whether a cash register or duplicate invoices are used, income is recorded in a book called a *Cash Receipts Journal*.

This sample problem will demonstrate the use of a Cash Receipts Journal.

Income received is recorded in a Cash Receipts Journal

SAMPLE PROBLEM

Juleo Santos has a storage and moving business. He prepares a sales invoice for each customer, and keeps the duplicate copy for his records. As Mr. Santos wants to keep separate records of his storage income and his moving income, he lists the storage income separately from the moving income on each sales slip.

Here is how Mr. Santos' Cash Receipts Journal will look at the end of the month.

CASH RECEIPTS JOURNAL   PAGE *1*

INV. NO.	DATE	RECEIVED FROM	STORAGE INCOME	MOVING INCOME	TOTAL RECEIPTS	BANK DEPOSITS
101	*19--* *Aug. 2 B. Rubin*		65 00		65 00	
102	*5 T. Forest*			80 00	80 00	145 00
103	*14 A. Polansky*		30 00	100 00	130 00	
104	*23 Ed. Haley*		20 00	70 00	90 00	
105	*30 W. Horn*			210 00	210 00	430 00
			115 00	460 00	575 00	575 00
			115 00	460 00	575 00	575 00

Illustration 88b — Completed Page of a Cash Receipts Journal

Here are the steps that were followed in preparing the Cash Receipts Journal:

Step 1: Enter each invoice.

The number, date, customer's name, and amount were recorded in the Cash Receipts Journal from each duplicate invoice.

Notice that the date for the first entry includes the month and year as well as the day.

Step 2: Enter amounts in correct columns.

Each invoice was examined to determine the type of income. Invoice #101 was issued for storage income and as a result, the $65.00 was entered in the column headed "Storage Income" and again in the column headed "Total Receipts."

Invoice #102 was issued for moving income and the $80.00 was entered in the column headed "Moving Income" and again in the column headed "Total Receipts."

Invoice #103 totaled $130.00. Of this total, $30.00 was storage income and $100.00 was moving income. Notice how these amounts were entered in the journal.

Notice that the total amount of every invoice has been entered in the Total Receipts column. At the end of the month, you will be able to find the total receipts for the month.

Step 3: Enter bank deposits.

Mr. Santos deposited in a bank the money he collected. He made two deposits during the month. The first deposit of $145.00 included the $65.00 received from B. Rubin on August 2 and the $80.00 received from T. Forest on August 5. The deposit of $145.00 was entered in the Bank Deposits column on the same line with the $80.00 to show that it included all receipts up to that point. Notice that the two receipts add up to the amount of the deposit.

$$\$65.00 + \$80.00 = \$145.00$$

In the same way, the deposit of $430.00 included the receipts of $130.00, $90.00, and $210.00. Notice that these three receipts add up to the amount of the deposit.

$$\$130.00 + \$90.00 + \$210.00 = \$430.00$$

Step 4: Pencil foot columns.

All columns were added and the totals for the month were entered in small penciled amounts.

Step 5: Verify totals.

The pencil footings were checked by crossfooting. The total for storage and moving incomes should equal the total receipts.

$$\$115.00 + \$460.00 = \$575.00$$

The total receipts and the total of the Bank Deposits column should be equal.

Step 6: Ink in totals and rule journal.

After the pencil footings had been checked, the totals were written in ink and the Cash Receipts Journal was ruled in the usual way.

PRACTICE PROBLEMS

Problem 1

You are employed by George Wood who has a storage and moving business. It is part of your job to record the information from the duplicate invoices into a Cash Receipts Journal.

Directions:
a) Open a Cash Receipts Journal with these columnar headings:

		CASH RECEIPTS JOURNAL			PAGE 1	
INV. NO.	DATE	RECEIVED FROM	STORAGE INCOME	MOVING INCOME	TOTAL RECEIPTS	BANK DEPOSITS

b) Record the information from the following duplicate invoices into the Cash Receipts Journal.

Invoice Number	Date	Received From	Storage Income	Moving Income
101	May 1	R. Perez	$ 43.20	
102	4	L. Smith		$115.90
103	8	M. Cohen		320.00
	8	Deposited $479.10. (Enter in Bank Deposits column on the same line with the last receipt.)		
104	11	P. Kelly	65.00	270.00
105	16	C. Russo	38.00	310.00
106	21	B. Farley	124.50	
107	29	E. Pape	118.25	225.60
	29	Deposited $1,151.35. (Enter in Bank Deposits column on the same line with the last receipt.)		

c) Pencil foot all money columns.
d) Verify pencil footings by crossfooting totals. In addition, see if the totals of the Total Receipts and Bank Deposits columns agree.
e) Ink in totals and rule the journal.

Problem 2

You are employed by Charles Kovacs, a TV repairman, who is in business for himself. It is part of your job to record in a Cash Receipts Journal the information shown on the duplicate invoices.

Directions:

a) Open a Cash Receipts Journal with the following columnar headings:

		CASH RECEIPTS JOURNAL			PAGE 1	
INV. NO.	DATE	RECEIVED FROM	REPAIR INCOME	PARTS INCOME	TOTAL RECEIPTS	BANK DEPOSITS

b) Record the information from the list of duplicate invoices below into the Cash Receipts Journal.

Invoice Number	Date	Received From	Repair Income	Parts Income
411	Jan. 4	R. Anker	$64.00	
412	8	S. Marchi	38.00	$15.25
413	11	J. Ludwig	21.50	32.90
	11	Deposited $171.65		
414	15	M. Kahn	41.90	18.75
415	19	A. Ackley	28.50	15.30
	19	Deposited $104.45		
416	24	L. Stacy	56.25	37.15
417	29	P. Barton	43.00	
418	31	F. Hagan	61.50	27.80
	31	Deposited $225.70		

c) Pencil foot all money columns.
d) Verify pencil footings by crossfooting totals. (Are the total receipts and total bank deposits the same?)
e) Ink in totals and rule the journal.

Problem 3

You are employed by Oscar Jones, a plumber, who is in business for himself. It is part of your job to record in a Cash Receipts Journal the information shown on the duplicate invoices.

Directions:

a) Open a Cash Receipts Journal with these columnar headings:

		CASH RECEIPTS JOURNAL			PAGE 1	
INV. NO.	DATE	RECEIVED FROM	REPAIR INCOME	PARTS INCOME	TOTAL RECEIPTS	BANK DEPOSITS

b) Record the information from the list of duplicate invoices on page 557 into the Cash Receipts Journal.

Invoice Number	Date	Received From	Repair Income	Parts Income
231	July 6	G. Miller	$ 78.40	
232	10	H. Kern	52.80	$15.75
233	12	B. Graham	96.10	52.50
	12	Deposited $295.55		
234	17	K. Mason	85.00	29.30
235	23	J. Anders	124.70	48.85
	23	Deposited $287.85		
236	25	H. Larsen	68.50	57.15
237	27	M. Cody	227.00	42.35
238	31	T. Allen	72.10	35.95
	31	Deposited $503.05		

c) Pencil foot all money columns.
d) Verify pencil footings by crossfooting all totals.
e) Ink in totals and rule the journal.

Problem 4

You are employed by B. Gordon, a painter and decorator, who is in business for himself. Mr. Gordon receives income for his painting services and his wallpapering services. It is part of your job to copy the information shown on the duplicate invoices into a Cash Receipts Journal.

Directions:
a) Open a Cash Receipts Journal with these columnar headings:

		CASH RECEIPTS JOURNAL				PAGE 1

INV. NO.	DATE	RECEIVED FROM	PAINTING INCOME	WALLPAPER INCOME	TOTAL RECEIPTS	BANK DEPOSITS

b) Record the information from the following list of duplicate invoices into the Cash Receipts Journal.

Invoice Number	Date	Received From	Painting Income	Wallpaper Income
441	Nov. 2	H. Condon	$161.50	$ 52.10
442	8	W. Atlas	307.80	
443	12	A. Watson	86.40	92.25
	12	Deposited $700.05		
444	15	J. Perez	251.25	156.80
445	20	C. Greco	72.75	205.15
446	23	S. Orr	138.50	41.75
	23	Deposited $866.20		
447	26	P. Arson	238.90	164.25
448	30	M. Kenny	94.00	87.65
	30	Deposited $584.80		

c) Pencil foot all money columns.
d) Verify pencil footings by crossfooting totals.
e) Ink in totals and rule the journal.

Practicing Related Arithmetic	Copy and solve the following problem:				
		April	May	June	Totals
	Income	$1,384.65	$1,732.50	$1,652.20	= $
	− Expenses	605.80	871.75	738.25	=
	= Net Income	$	$	$	= $

AIM

To practice using a Cash Receipts Journal.

EXPLANATION

In the previous job, you learned how to use a Cash Receipts Journal for retail businesses where invoices were prepared for sales.

In this job, you will practice using a Cash Receipts Journal for businesses in which the sales for the day are found from the cash register readings.

The next time you go to a supermarket, watch the cashier at the cash register depress special keys to indicate the sale of meats, vegetables, dairy products, etc. In the same way, any businessperson can keep a separate record of each type of income by using special keys on the cash register.

"That's $5⁰⁰ for gas and $8⁰⁰ for repairs."

PRACTICE PROBLEMS

Problem 1

You are keeping the records for a gasoline service station owned and operated by Jack Burns. Each day you are given the total amount of cash received for the sale of gas and oil and for repairs.

Directions:

a) Open a Cash Receipts Journal with the columnar headings below:

CASH RECEIPTS JOURNAL					
					PAGE	
DATE			GAS & OIL	REPAIR INCOME	TOTAL RECEIPTS	BANK DEPOSITS

Note: Since the income for each day is taken from the cash register readings, there is no need to enter the customer's name in this Cash
Receipts Journal. As a result, the wide column in which you had
entered the name of the customer is usually left blank.

b) Record in the Cash Receipts Journal the daily receipts and the weekly
deposits shown below.

	Gas & Oil	Repair Income	Deposit
Oct. 1	$120.00	$65.50	Oct. 5 — Enter the total deposit of
2	110.25	42.40	$888.75 in the Bank Deposits
3	134.60	54.50	column
4	115.35	72.15	
5	122.10	51.90	

	Gas & Oil	Repair Income	Deposit
Oct. 8	$136.70	$50.60	Oct. 12 — Enter the total deposit of
9	124.25	61.35	$960.15 in the Bank Deposits
10	112.90	43.25	column
11	128.75	72.40	
12	149.45	80.50	

	Gas & Oil	Repair Income	Deposit
Oct. 15	$127.30	$40.80	Oct. 19 — Enter the total deposit of
16	122.55	50.70	$973.00 in the Bank Deposits
17	146.70	65.15	column
18	134.35	70.60	
19	151.65	63.20	

	Gas & Oil	Repair Income	Deposit
Oct. 22	$118.25	$50.60	Oct. 26 — Enter the total deposit of
23	136.70	63.25	$930.00 in the Bank Deposits
24	125.15	41.30	column
25	142.80	52.90	
26	137.60	61.45	

c) Pencil foot all money columns.
d) Verify totals by crossfooting. The total receipts and total bank deposits
should agree.
e) Ink in totals and rule the journal.

Problem 2

You are keeping records for Frank Marlow who operates his own dry
cleaning store. Each day you are given the total amount of cash received for
dry cleaning income and the total received for tailoring income.

Directions:

a) Open a Cash Receipts Journal with the following columnar headings:

CASH RECEIPTS JOURNAL					PAGE 1	
DATE			CLEANING INCOME	TAILORING INCOME	TOTAL RECEIPTS	BANK DEPOSITS

b) Record in the Cash Receipts Journal the daily receipts and the weekly deposits shown below.

	Cleaning Income	Tailoring Income	Deposit
April 2	$102.70	$21.20	April 6 — Enter the total deposit of
3	138.15	46.25	$814.20 in the Bank Deposits
4	146.25	38.10	column
5	124.00	26.35	
6	141.80	29.40	

	Cleaning Income	Tailoring Income	Deposit
April 9	$115.45	$32.80	April 13 — Enter the total deposit of
10	128.10	41.75	$850.25 in the Bank Deposits
11	143.95	24.25	column
12	136.30	37.50	
13	146.25	43.90	

	Cleaning Income	Tailoring Income	Deposit
April 16	$126.30	$35.75	April 20 — Enter the total deposit of
17	110.55	42.70	$836.45 in the Bank Deposits
18	131.60	31.85	column
19	129.40	50.80	
20	148.10	29.40	

	Cleaning Income	Tailoring Income	Deposit
April 23	$121.75	$42.20	April 27 — Enter the total deposit of
24	136.50	35.85	$865.70 in the Bank Deposits
25	112.25	51.75	column
26	148.60	39.65	
27	135.85	41.30	

c) Pencil foot all money columns.

d) Verify totals by crossfooting. The total receipts and total bank deposits should agree.

e) Ink in totals and rule the journal.

Practicing Related Arithmetic

Copy and solve the following problem:

	July	Aug.	Sept.		Total
Income	$1,537.65	$1,821.25	$1,672.55	= $	
− Expenses	641.38	704.80	693.40	=	
= Net Income $	$	$		= $	

AIM

To learn how businesspeople keep a record of their expenses.

EXPLANATION

In the same way that a payment received for an invoice is recorded in a Cash Receipts Journal, all payments of expenses are recorded in a book called a *Cash Payments Journal*. The information for the Cash Payments Journal is taken from the stubs of the checkbook.

You remember that when you learned to write checks you wrote the stub of the check before the check itself. It remained in the checkbook after the check had been issued. This job will show you how businesspeople use the check stubs to find their total expenses.

Record check stubs in the Cash Payments Journal

SAMPLE PROBLEM

Ed Nemo is a plumber who operates his own business. He deposits all his receipts in the bank and makes all payments by check. His checkbook contains the stubs shown below and on the next page:

No. 1 To: Bart's, Inc. For: Plumbing supplies	April 3	120|00
No. 2 To: Vic's Auto Shop For: Truck tune up	April 10	50|00
No. 3 To: ABC Gas For: Gas & oil for truck	April 16	30|00

No. 4 To: Topp Realty For: Rent for shop	April 20	300 | 00
No. 5 To: Bart's, Inc. For: Plumbing supplies	April 26	90 | 00
No. 6 To: Apex Tires For: Tire for truck	April 30	40 | 00

Here is how the information on the check stubs will be recorded in Mr. Nemo's Cash Payments Journal:

CASH PAYMENTS JOURNAL　　　　PAGE 1

CHECK NO.	DATE	PAID TO	FOR	AMOUNT OF CHECK	PLUMBING SUPPLIES	TRUCK EXPENSES	OTHER PAYMENTS
1	Apr. 3	Bart's, Inc.	supplies	120 00	120 00		
2	10	Vic's Auto Shop	truck tune-up	50 00		50 00	
3	16	ABC Gas	gas and oil	30 00		30 00	
4	20	Topp Realty	shop rent	300 00			300 00
5	26	Bart's, Inc.	supplies	90 00	90 00		
6	30	Apex Tires	truck tire	40 00		40 00	
				630 00	210 00	120 00	300 00
				630 00	210 00	120 00	300 00

Illustration 90 — Completed Page of a Cash Payments Journal

Here are the steps that were followed:

Step 1: Enter each payment.

The check number, the date, the name of the person or company to whom the check was issued, the reason for the payment, and the amount were copied from each check stub into the Cash Payments Journal.

Step 2: Enter amounts in correct columns.

Enter each amount twice

Each amount was entered twice. After an amount was entered in the first column, it was extended (entered a second time) to the appropriate expense column to enable Mr. Nemo to find the total amount spent for each type of expense during the month.

Expenses which rarely occur more than once during the month, such as the payment for rent on stub number 4, are extended to the column headed "Other Payments."

Step 3: Pencil foot columns.

All columns were added and the totals entered in small penciled figures.

Step 4: Verify totals.

The pencil footings were checked by crossfooting. Since the total of the column headed "Amount of Check" is $630.00, you would expect the totals of the three expense columns to equal this amount. To see if they do:

Plumbing supplies	$210.00
+ Truck expenses	120.00
+ Other payments	300.00
= Total amount of the checks	$630.00

After the totals were checked, the totals were inked in and the Cash Payments Journal was ruled.

PRACTICE PROBLEMS

Problem 1

You are employed by David Ricci, a plumber, who operates his own business. It is part of your job to copy the information from the check stubs into a Cash Payments Journal.

Directions:
a) Open a Cash Payments Journal with these columnar headings:

CASH PAYMENTS JOURNAL

PAGE 1

CHECK NO.	DATE	PAID TO	FOR	AMOUNT OF CHECK	PLUMBING SUPPLIES	TRUCK EXPENSES	OTHER PAYMENTS

b) Copy the information shown on the check stubs below and on page 564 into the Cash Payments Journal.

No. 1 To: Jay, Inc. For: Plumbing supplies	July 6	163 00
No. 2 To: Fred's Garage For: Truck repairs	July 10	84 00
No. 3 To: Low Realty For: Rent for shop	July 16	275 00

No. 4 To: Elm Gas, Inc. For: Gas & oil for truck	July 20		52|00
No. 5 To: Jay, Inc. For: Plumbing supplies	July 24		114|00
No. 6 To: Elm Gas, Inc. For: Gas & oil for truck	July 27		23|00
No. 7 To: Rex Supplies For: Plumbing supplies	July 30		98|00
No. 8 To: Bar Tire Co. For: Tires for truck	July 31		75|00

c) Pencil foot all money columns.

d) Verify totals by crossfooting. The total of the three expense columns should equal the total of the column headed "Amount of Check."

e) Ink in totals and rule the journal.

Problem 2

You are employed by Otis Jones who operates an automobile body repair shop. It is part of your job to copy the information from the check stubs into a Cash Payments Journal.

Directions:

a) Open a Cash Payments Journal with these columnar headings:

CASH PAYMENTS JOURNAL

PAGE 1

CHECK NO.	DATE	PAID TO	FOR	AMOUNT OF CHECK	PAINTS	PARTS	OTHER PAYMENTS

b) Copy the information shown on the check stubs below and on page 565 into the Cash Payments Journal.

No. 51 To: Sure Paint Co. For: Paint supplies	Jan. 3		83|00

No. 52 To: Fair Auto Co. For: Auto parts	Jan. 9		130 00
No. 53 To: Kelly, Inc. For: Rent for shop	Jan. 12		310 00
No. 54 To: J. K. Co. For: Fenders	Jan. 18		190 00
No. 55 To: Sure Paint Co. For: Paint supplies	Jan. 23		76 00
No. 56 To: Bell Telephone Co. For: Bill for Dec.	Jan. 25		59 00
No. 57 To: Fair Auto Co. For: Auto parts	Jan. 29		87 00
No. 58 To: Tex Paints For: Paint supplies	Jan. 31		114 00

c) Pencil foot all money columns.
d) Verify all totals by crossfooting.
e) Ink in totals and rule the journal.

Total of Amount
of Check column =
Total of expense
columns

Problem 3

You are employed by Don Palk, an electrician, who operates his own business.

Directions:
a) Open a Cash Payments Journal with these column headings:

		CASH PAYMENTS JOURNAL						PAGE 1
CHECK NO.	DATE	PAID TO	FOR	AMOUNT OF CHECK	ELEC. SUPPLIES	TRUCK EXPENSES	OTHER PAYMENTS	

b) Copy the information shown on the check stubs on page 566 into the Cash Payments Journal.

No. 101 To: Lane, Inc. For: Electrical supplies	June 1		67 | 25
No. 102 To: Mac's Shop For: Truck repair	June 7		121 | 30
No. 103 To: Town Bugle For: Advertisement	June 15		45 | 00
No. 104 To: Rio Service For: Gas & oil	June 20		29 | 65
No. 105 To: T. J. Casey For: Rent for shop	June 22		280 | 00
No. 106 To: Lane, Inc. For: Electrical supplies	June 26		138 | 50
No. 107 To: Cord Tires For: Tire for truck	June 28		42 | 00
No. 108 To: Acme Lights For: Electrical supplies	June 30		119 | 15

c) Pencil foot all money columns.
d) Verify all totals by crossfooting.
e) Ink in totals and rule the journal.

Problem 4

You are employed by Laura Stacy who operates a beauty parlor.

Directions:
a) Open a Cash Payments Journal with these columnar headings:

CASH PAYMENTS JOURNAL							
						PAGE	1
CHECK NO.	DATE	PAID TO	FOR	AMOUNT OF CHECK	BEAUTY SUPPLIES	ADVERTISING	OTHER PAYMENTS

    b) Copy the information shown on the check stubs on page 567 into the Cash Payments Journal.

No. 201 To: Beauty, Inc. For: Beauty supplies	Oct. 4		74	60
No. 202 To: Daily News For: Advertisement	Oct. 10		62	50
No. 203 To: Yellow Pages For: Advertisement	Oct. 18		53	40
No. 204 To: Opus, Inc. For: Rent	Oct. 19		275	00
No. 205 To: Beauty, Inc. For: Beauty supplies	Oct. 23		91	35
No. 206 To: Town Electric Co. For: Shop electric bill	Oct. 26		42	10
No. 207 To: Daily News For: Advertisement	Oct. 29		23	80
No. 208 To: Spray, Inc. For: Beauty supplies	Oct. 31		126	25

c) Pencil foot all columns.
d) Verify totals by crossfooting.
e) Ink in totals and rule the journal.

Practicing Related Arithmetic

Copy and solve the following problem:

	Oct.	Nov.	Dec.	Total
Income	$1,738.50	$1,946.60	$1,887.20	= $
− Expenses	627.85	782.90	591.25	=
= Net Income $	$	$	= $

AIM

To practice using a Cash Payments Journal in which payments for personal use are recorded.

EXPLANATION

Most self-employed businesspeople arrange to take a certain amount of money out of their business each week for their personal living expenses, such as rent, food, and life insurance.

Using business profits for personal living expenses

Businesspeople do this by drawing checks to themselves and cashing them. In addition to taking money out of the business this way, they may find it convenient to issue business checks for personal expenses, such as life insurance premiums.

However, they can continue to take money out of the business for personal expenses only if they are making a profit.

Consider Mr. Weber, a businessman whose income statement for the year shows these amounts:

Income	$35,000.00
− Expenses	20,000.00
= Net Income	$15,000.00

The largest amount available to Mr. Weber for his personal expenses is the net income of $15,000.00. Since many careful businesspeople *leave part of the net income in the business*, Mr. Weber does not withdraw the entire $15,000.00. In this way, his business will continue to grow from year to year.

It is important to be able to compare the amount taken out of the business for personal use against the net income, so all businesspeople must keep separate records of payments from the business for personal use. This can be done easily by adding a special column headed "Personal Payments" to the Cash Payments Journal.

SAMPLE PROBLEM

Jean Michel, a lawyer, deposits all her receipts in the bank and makes all payments by check. Her checkbook contains these stubs:

No. 1 To: Mays, Inc. For: Office supplies	Sept. 4	50 00
No. 2 To: Cash For: Personal use	Sept. 7	200 00
No. 3 To: Mays, Inc. For: Stationery	Sept. 12	30 00
No. 4 To: Lofts Co. For: Office rent	Sept. 21	240 00
No. 5 To: Cash For: Personal use	Sept. 24	300 00
No. 6 To: Bow Bros. For: Home rent	Sept. 28	280 00

Here is how these check stubs would appear in Miss Michel's Cash Payments Journal:

CASH PAYMENTS JOURNAL   PAGE /

CHECK NO.	DATE	PAID TO	FOR	AMOUNT OF CHECK	PERSONAL PAYMENTS	BUSINESS PAYMENTS	
						OFFICE EXPENSES	OTHER ITEMS
1	Sept. 4	Mays, Inc.	office supplies	50 00		50 00	
2	7	Cash	personal use	200 00	200 00		
3	12	Mays, Inc.	stationery	30 00		30 00	
4	21	Lofts Co.	office rent	240 00			240 00
5	24	Cash	personal use	300 00	300 00		
6	28	Bow Bros.	home rent	280 00	280 00		
				1100 00	780 00	80 00	240 00

Notice that there is a special column headed "Personal Payments" in which all payments for personal use are recorded.

Personal expense compared with business expense

It is important to compare check #4 with check #6. Although both checks were issued for rent, note that check #4 for $240.00 covered the rent for the office and was a business expense. On the other hand, check #6 covered rent for Miss Michel's residence, and therefore represents a payment for personal use.

You recall from your work in earlier jobs that the heading "Office Expenses" includes payments for stationery, stamps, business forms, and the like. A large expense like the payment of $240.00 for office rent is listed in the "Other Items" column, rather than in the "Office Expenses" column.

PRACTICE PROBLEMS

Problem 1

You are employed by Alfred Dodd, a public accountant. It is part of your job to record the information from his check stubs into a Cash Payments Journal.

Directions:
a) Open a Cash Payments Journal with the following headings:

| | | | | | | BUSINESS PAYMENTS | |
CHECK NO.	DATE	PAID TO	FOR	AMOUNT OF CHECK	PERSONAL PAYMENTS	OFFICE EXPENSE	OTHER ITEMS

CASH PAYMENTS JOURNAL — PAGE 1

b) Copy the information shown on the check stubs below and on page 571 into the Cash Payments Journal.

No. 41 To: Cash For: Personal use	June 1	325 00
No. 42 To: J. & K., Inc. For: Office supplies	June 5	65 00
No. 43 To: Salem Co. For: Office rent	June 11	210 00
No. 44 To: J. & K., Inc. For: Office stationery	June 14	42 70

No. 45 To: Homes, Inc. For: Home rent	June 20	240 00	
No. 46 To: N.Y. Telephone Co. For: Business bill	June 26	72 40	
No. 47 To: N.Y. Telephone Co. For: Home bill	June 28	29 80	
No. 48 To: Cash For: Personal use	June 29	300 00	

Check stubs
are recorded
in the Cash
Payments Journal

c) Pencil foot all columns.
d) Verify totals by crossfooting.
e) Ink in totals and rule the journal.

Problem 2

You are employed by Joe Dennis who operates an auto paint shop.

Directions:
a) Open a Cash Payments Journal with the following headings:

| | | | | | | BUSINESS PAYMENTS | |
CHECK NO.	DATE	PAID TO	FOR	AMOUNT OF CHECK	PERSONAL PAYMENTS	PAINTS & SUPPLIES	OTHER ITEMS

CASH PAYMENTS JOURNAL — PAGE 1

b) Copy the information shown on the check stubs below and on page 572 into the Cash Payments Journal.

No. 101 To: Tru Insurance Co. For: Personal life insurance	Sept. 1	246 50	
No. 102 To: Rex Corp. For: Paint supplies	Sept. 6	112 60	
No. 103 To: Bell Telephone Co. For: Business phone	Sept. 10	51 30	

No. 104
To: IRS (Internal Revenue
     Service)
For: Installment on personal
      income tax
	Sept. 13		450 00

No. 105 To: Beta Co. For: Shop rent	Sept. 19		340 00
No. 106 To: Rex Corp. For: Paint supplies	Sept. 24		97 20
No. 107 To: Cash For: Personal use	Sept. 27		400 00
No. 108 To: Halo, Inc. For: Paints	Sept. 28		81 90

c) Pencil foot all columns.
d) Verify totals by crossfooting.
e) Ink in totals and rule the journal.

Problem 3

You are employed by Peter Slade who operates his own plumbing business.

Directions:
a) Open a Cash Payments Journal with the following headings:

						BUSINESS PAYMENTS	
CHECK NO.	DATE	PAID TO	FOR	AMOUNT OF CHECK	PERSONAL PAYMENTS	PLUMBING SUPPLIES	OTHER ITEMS

CASH PAYMENTS JOURNAL — PAGE 1

b) Copy the information shown on the check stubs below and on page 573 into the Cash Payments Journal.

No. 91 To: Ram Corp. For: Shop rent	July 6		285 00
No. 92 To: Cash For: Personal use	July 10		150 00

No. 93 To: City Electric Co. For: Shop electric bill	July 12		36|75
No. 94 To: Jay, Inc. For: Plumbing supplies	July 17		91|30
No. 95 To: Dr. J. Weiss For: Personal medical bill	July 23		25|00
No. 96 To: Twin Co. For: Plumbing supplies	July 25		167|85
No. 97 To: Cash For: Personal use	July 30		225|00
No. 98 To: Jay, Inc. For: Plumbing supplies	July 31		86|15

c) Pencil foot all columns.
d) Verify totals by crossfooting.
e) Ink in totals and rule the journal.

Problem 4

You are employed by Al Lurio, an electrician, who is in business for himself.

Directions:
a) Open a Cash Payments Journal with the following headings:

						BUSINESS PAYMENTS	
CHECK NO.	DATE	PAID TO	FOR	AMOUNT OF CHECK	PERSONAL PAYMENTS	ELECTRICAL SUPPLIES	OTHER ITEMS

CASH PAYMENTS JOURNAL — PAGE 1

b) Copy the information shown on the check stubs below and on page 574 into the Cash Payments Journal.

No. 301 To: Cash For: Personal use	Nov. 2		260|00

No. 302 To: Ramp, Inc. For: Electrical supplies	Nov. 5	138	45
No. 303 To: Dow T.V. Co. For: Television set for home	Nov. 12	275	00
No. 304 To: Commerce, Inc. For: Shop rent	Nov. 16	320	00
No. 305 To: Ramp, Inc. For: Electrical supplies	Nov. 21	184	90
No. 306 To: Bell Telephone Co. For: Business phone	Nov. 26	67	85
No. 307 To: Bell Telephone Co. For: Home phone	Nov. 28	24	25
No. 308 To: Ohm Corp. For: Electrical supplies	Nov. 30	321	70

c) Pencil foot all money columns.
d) Verify all totals by crossfooting.
e) Ink in totals and rule the journal.

Practicing Related Arithmetic

Copy and solve the following problem:

	Jan.	Feb.	March		Total
Income	$1,964.30	$1,753.80	$1,827.40	=	$
− Expenses	872.50	815.95	906.75	=	
= Net Income	$	$	$	=	$

AIM

To practice using the Cash Receipts and Cash Payments Journals.

EXPLANATION

You have practiced using the Cash Receipts Journal and the Cash Payments Journal separately. In this job you will use both journals together as they are used in business. Of course, all receipts will be recorded in the Cash Receipts Journal and all payments will be recorded in the Cash Payments Journal.

PRACTICE PROBLEMS

Problem 1

You are employed by Roy Miller, who has an auto repair shop. Part of your job is to record the receipts in the Cash Receipts Journal and to record the payments in the Cash Payments Journal.

Directions:
a) Open a Cash Receipts Journal with the following headings:

CASH RECEIPTS JOURNAL					PAGE 1	
INV. NO.	DATE	RECEIVED FROM	REPAIR INCOME	PARTS INCOME	TOTAL RECEIPTS	BANK DEPOSITS

b) Open a Cash Payments Journal with the following headings:

CASH PAYMENTS JOURNAL					PAGE	BUSINESS PAYMENTS	
CHECK NO.	DATE	PAID TO	FOR	AMOUNT OF CHECK	PERSONAL PAYMENTS	PARTS & SUPPLIES	OTHER ITEMS

c) Record the following receipts and payments in the proper journal:

Record income received in the Cash Receipts Journal

April 3   Received $42.00 from B. Evans for repairs. (Start with invoice #101.)

4   Received $35.00 from L. Mandel for a new auto battery (Invoice #102).

6   Issued a check for $76.00 to the Moro Co. for auto parts. (Start with check #61.)

9   Received $245.00 from T. Casey; $200.00 was for repair work and $45.00 was for parts.

9   Deposited all the money received up to this date in the bank. The deposit amounted to $322.00. (Enter this amount in the Bank Deposits column on the same line with the last receipt.)

Record checks issued in the Cash Payments Journal

10   Issued a check for $325.00 to the New Co. for the shop rent for the month.

12   Mr. Miller, the owner, cashed a check for $125.00 to take home for his personal use. This check was made payable to "Cash."

13   Received $430.00 from T. Gomez; $320.00 was for repair work and $110.00 was for parts.

16   Received $89.00 from S. Cobb for repairs to his car.

18   Issued a check for $96.00 to the Tex Co. for parts and supplies.

19   Issued a check for $170.00 to the Able Insurance Co. for the premium due on the owner's personal life insurance.

20   Received $285.00 from T. Russo; $260.00 was for repair work and $25.00 was for parts.

20   Deposited all the money received from April 13 to this date. The deposit amounted to $804.00. (Enter this amount in the Bank Deposits column on the same line with the last receipt.)

24   Issued a check for $52.00 to the Penn Telephone Co. for the business telephone bill for the month.

25   Received $76.00 from R. Kahn for new tires.

26   Issued a check for $84.00 to the Tex Co. for auto parts.

27   Issued a check for $28.00 to the Penn Telephone Co. for Mr. Miller's home telephone bill.

30   Received $516.00 from K. Jarvis; $310.00 was for repair work and $206.00 was for parts.

30   Deposited the money received from April 25 to this date amounting to $592.00. (Enter this amount in the Bank Deposits column on the same line with the last receipt.)

d) Pencil foot money columns in both journals.

e) Verify totals by crossfooting.

f) Ink in totals and rule the journals.

Problem 2

You are employed by Ben Smith, who operates a landscape and fence business. Part of your job is to record the receipts in the Cash Receipts Journal and to record the payments in the Cash Payments Journal.

Directions:

a) Open a Cash Receipts Journal with the headings shown on page 577.

		CASH RECEIPTS JOURNAL			PAGE		
INV. NO.	DATE	RECEIVED FROM	LANDSCAPE INCOME	FENCE INCOME	TOTAL RECEIPTS	BANK DEPOSITS

b) Open a Cash Payments Journal with the following headings:

		CASH PAYMENTS JOURNAL				PAGE		
						BUSINESS PAYMENTS	
CHECK NO.	DATE	PAID TO	FOR	AMOUNT OF CHECK	PERSONAL PAYMENTS	LUMBER & SUPPLIES	OTHER ITEMS

c) Record the following receipts and payments in the proper journal:

June 1   Received $195.10 from L. Samson for gardening and landscape work. (Start with invoice #301.)   *Record income received in the Cash Receipts Journal*

4   Received $328.70 from C. Press for a redwood fence.

5   Issued a check for $180.00 to the Ax Lumber Co. for lumber for fences. (Start with check #121.)

7   Received a check for $421.25 from A. Jansen; $120.00 for landscape work and $301.25 for a cedar fence.

7   Deposited all the money received to this date in the bank. The deposit amounted to $945.05. (Enter this amount in the Bank Deposits column on the same line with the last receipt.)

8   Issued a check for $43.45 to the Pacific Telephone Co. for the business bill for the month.   *Record checks issued in the Cash Payments Journal*

11   Mr. Smith, the owner, cashed a check for $250.00 to take home for his personal use. The check was made payable to "Cash."

12   Received $296.20 from N. Santo; $141.00 was for landscape work and $155.20 was for a fence.

14   Received $153.00 from G. Carter for landscape work.

15   Issued a check for $307.30 to the Rose Co. for gardening supplies.

18   Issued a check for $184.90 to the East Insurance Co. for a fire insurance policy on Mr. Smith's home.

19   Received $471.80 from D. Hale; $210.00 was for landscape work and $261.80 was for a fence.

19   Deposited all the money received from June 12 to this date. The deposit amounted to $921.00. (Enter this amount in the Bank Deposits column on the same line with the last receipt.)

21   Received $341.75 from G. Callas for a split rail fence.

22   Issued a check for $270.00 to the Top Corp. for business rent.

25   Issued a check for $318.50 to the Coe Co. for lumber for fences.

26   Received $524.00 from L. Florio; $144.00 was for landscape work and $380.00 was for a fence.

26   Deposited the money received from June 21 to this date. The deposit amounted to $865.75. (Enter this amount in the Bank Deposits column on the same line with the last receipt.)

29   Issued a check for $60.00 to Dr. K. Dunn for the owner's personal medical bill.

d) Pencil foot money columns in both journals.

e) Verify totals by crossfooting.

f) Ink in totals and rule the journals.

Copy and complete the following problems:

Practicing Related Arithmetic

(1)

Balance, May 1	$ 381.40
+ Deposits	1,428.75
= Total	$
− Payments	1,247.10
= Balance, May 31	$

(2)

Balance, Feb. 1	$ 462.50
+ Deposits	1,816.60
= Total	$
− Payments	1,693.85
= Balance, Feb. 28	$

(3)

Balance, Nov. 1	$ 553.15
+ Deposits	1,681.50
= Total	
− Payments	1,379.45
= Balance, Nov. 30	$

(4)

Balance, Jan. 1	$ 816.65
+ Deposits	1,372.40
= Total	
− Payments	1,761.70
= Balance, Jan. 31	$

AIM

To practice keeping a checkbook with a Cash Receipts Journal and a Cash Payments Journal.

EXPLANATION

In small businesses, it is not unusual for one employee to take care of the Cash Receipts Journal, the deposit slips, the checkbook, and the Cash Payments Journal. In this job you will practice using all of these records.

In Unit 3 you learned that all checks should be written in ink and that all amounts must be written clearly. Do you remember that the check stub should be completed before the check itself is written? It may be a good idea to go back to Unit 3 (it starts on page 93) and spend a few minutes reviewing the steps in keeping a checkbook. It will also be helpful to examine the illustration of properly written checks and stubs on page 98.

Write the check stub first

In each of the practice problems you will be asked to do the important record-keeping jobs listed on page 580.

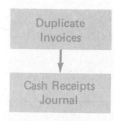

1) Record information from the duplicate invoices into a Cash Receipts Journal,
2) Prepare deposit slips,
3) Write stubs and checks,
4) Keep the checkbook balance up to date, and
5) Record information from the check stubs into a Cash Payments Journal.

PRACTICE PROBLEMS

Problem 1

You are employed by Frank Shaw who operates his own television and stereo repair business.

Directions:

a) Open a Cash Receipts Journal with the following headings:

CASH RECEIPTS JOURNAL					PAGE 1	
INV. NO.	DATE	RECEIVED FROM	REPAIR INCOME	PARTS INCOME	TOTAL RECEIPTS	BANK DEPOSITS

b) Open a Cash Payments Journal with the following headings:

CASH PAYMENTS JOURNAL					BUSINESS PAYMENTS	PAGE 1
CHECK NO.	DATE	PAID TO	FOR	AMOUNT OF CHECK	PERSONAL PAYMENTS	PARTS & SUPPLIES	OTHER ITEMS

c) Start the checkbook by recording the April 1 bank balance on the first check stub. On April 1, Mr. Shaw had a balance of $1,560.00 in the Frontier National Bank.

d) Record the transactions shown below and on page 581:

Subtract checks issued from checkbook balance

April 2 Received $48.00 from D. Post for repairs. Enter this transaction in the Cash Receipts Journal. Start with invoice #201. Record each cash receipt in a similar manner. Number the invoices in order.

3 Issued check #471 for $61.00 to the Lars Co. for television parts. Write the stub and the check. Find the new checkbook balance. Enter the payment in the Cash Payments Journal. Record each cash payment in a similar manner.

4 Issued check #472 for $225.00 to Bond Realty for rent for the store.

6 Received $140.00 from N. Soper; $50.00 was for repairs and $90.00 was for parts.

10 Received $127.00 from P. Mott; $42.00 was for repairs and $85.00 was for parts.

10 Mr. Shaw, the owner, decided to deposit the three receipts collected up to this date totaling $315.00. Prepare a deposit slip for the following bills, coins, and checks which should equal the $315.00 collected.

Bills	Coins	Checks
3 $10 bills	20 half dollars	$ 48.00
17 $ 5 bills	17 quarters	$127.00
9 $ 1 bills	17 dimes	
	5 pennies	

10   Record the total shown on the deposit slip on check stub #473. Find the new checkbook balance on stub #473. Enter the deposit in the Bank Deposits column of the Cash Receipts Journal.

Add deposits to checkbook balance

12   Mr. Shaw, the owner, cashed check #473 for $150.00 for his personal use. Make the check payable to "Cash."

13   Issued check #474 for $31.00 to Opus Corp. for television parts.

16   Received $82.00 from S. Hill for repairs.

19   Issued check #475 for $36.00 to the Bell Telephone Co. for Mr. Shaw's home telephone bill.

24   Received $124.00 from R. Ahern; $34.00 was for repairs and $90.00 was for parts.

27   Received $168.00 from E. Rock; $62.00 was for repairs and $106.00 was for parts.

27   Prepare a deposit slip for the following bills, coins, and checks which should equal $374.00, the total of the receipts since the previous deposit.

Bills	Coins	Checks
7 $10 bills	26 half dollars	$124.00
15 $ 5 bills	25 quarters	$ 82.00
3 $ 1 bills	15 nickels	

27   Record the deposit on check stub #476. Find the new checkbook balance on stub #476. Enter the deposit in the Bank Deposits column of the Cash Receipts Journal.

30   Issued check #476 for $47.95 to the Bell Telephone Co. for the business phone bill. (Your final checkbook balance should be $1,698.05.)

e) Pencil foot money columns in both journals.

f) Verify totals by crossfooting.

g) Ink in totals and rule the journals.

Problem 2

You are employed by Adam Rich who operates an auto repair shop.

Directions:

a) Open a Cash Receipts Journal with the following headings:

		CASH RECEIPTS JOURNAL			PAGE 1	
INV. NO.	DATE	RECEIVED FROM	REPAIR INCOME	PARTS INCOME	TOTAL RECEIPTS	BANK DEPOSITS

b) Open a Cash Payments Journal with the following headings:

						BUSINESS PAYMENTS	
CHECK NO.	DATE	PAID TO	FOR	AMOUNT OF CHECK	PERSONAL PAYMENTS	PARTS & SUPPLIES	OTHER ITEMS

CASH PAYMENTS JOURNAL — PAGE 1

c) Start the checkbook by recording the August 1 bank balance on the first check stub. On August 1, Mr. Rich had a balance of $1,840.00 in the Fulton National Bank.

d) Record the transactions shown below and on page 583:

Aug. 1   Received $181.40 from L. Simon for repairing his auto. Enter this transaction in the Cash Receipts Journal. Start with invoice #501. Record each cash receipt in a similar manner. Number the invoices in order.

Subtract checks issued from checkbook balance

3   Issued check #311 for $84.65 to the Ram Corp. for auto parts. Write the stub and check. Find the new checkbook balance. Enter the payment in the Cash Payments Journal. Record each payment in a similar manner.

6   Issued check #312 for $48.90 to the N.Y. Telephone Co. for the business telephone bill.

7   Received $401.50 from R. Stein; $240.00 was for repairs and $161.50 for parts.

10   Received $382.30 from E. Dell; $170.00 was for repairs and $212.30 for parts.

10   Mr. Rich, the owner, decided to deposit the three receipts collected up to this date totaling $965.20. Prepare a deposit slip for the following bills, coins, and checks which should equal the $965.20 collected.

Bills	Coins	Checks
18 $10 bills	41 half dollars	$401.50
31 $ 5 bills	30 quarters	$181.40
19 $ 1 bills	30 pennies	

Add deposits to checkbook balance

10   Record the deposit on check stub #313. Find the new checkbook balance on stub #313. Enter the deposit in the Bank Deposits column of the Cash Receipts Journal.

14   Mr. Rich, the owner, cashed check #313 for $350.00 for his personal use. Make the check payable to "Cash."

15   Issued check #314 for $286.00 to Star Co. for a television set for the owner's home.

20   Received $142.80 from S. Lombardi for repairing his car.

22   Issued check #315 for $217.25 to Cars, Inc. for auto parts.

24   Received $396.90 from P. Daub; $240.00 for repairs and $156.90 for parts.

27   Received $237.25 from T. Fenn; $165.00 for repairs and $72.25 for parts.

27 Prepare a deposit slip for the following bills, coins, and checks which should equal $776.95, the total of the receipts since the previous deposit.

Bills	Coins	Checks
28 $10 bills	35 half dollars	$237.25
14 $ 5 bills	40 quarters	$142.80
16 $ 1 bills	27 dimes	
	14 nickels	

27 Record the deposit on check stub #316. Find the new checkbook balance on stub #316. Enter the deposit in the Bank Deposits column of the Cash Receipts Journal.

31 Issued check #316 for $310.00 to Dow Realty for the business rent for the month. (Your final checkbook balance should be $2,285.35.)

e) Pencil foot money columns in both journals.

f) Verify totals by crossfooting.

g) Ink in totals and rule the journals.

JOB 94 | RECONCILING THE BANK STATEMENT

Practicing Related Arithmetic

Copy and solve the following problems:

	(1)	(2)	(3)	(4)
Balance, May 1	$1,538.70	$1,716.25	$1,240.35	$1,842.45
+Deposits	2,162.80	3,253.80	2,681.40	4,076.60
=Total	$	$	$	$
−Payments	1,657.10	2,589.15	1,852.65	3,258.65
=Balance, May 31	$_____	$_____	$_____	$_____

AIM

To practice recording receipts and payments and to review the use of a bank reconciliation statement.

EXPLANATION

In Unit 3 you learned that at the end of each month the bank sends a statement listing the deposits made during the month, the checks paid during the month, and the balance on deposit at the end of the month. Along with the bank statement, the bank returns all the checks paid out during the month. The bank stamps these checks "Paid." They are called *canceled* checks.

Reconciling the bank statement with the Cash Receipts and Cash Payments Journals

Refer back to Job 17 of Unit 3 to see how the bank statement and the canceled checks are used to verify the accuracy of the checkbook balance.

In this job, you will practice using the bank statement and the canceled checks to prove your work in the Cash Receipts and Cash Payments Journals.

PRACTICE PROBLEMS

Problem 1

You are a member of the business staff of the school magazine, "The Laguna Log." You receive money from the treasurer of each class and from advertisers. All receipts are deposited in a separate checking account in the Pacific National Bank. Part of your job will be the activities listed on the next page.

1) Recording information from duplicate receipts (the carbon copies) into a Cash Receipts Journal,
2) Writing checks and keeping the checkbook balance up-to-date, and
3) Recording information from the check stubs into a Cash Payments Journal.

Directions:

a) Open a Cash Receipts Journal with the following headings:

		CASH RECEIPTS JOURNAL			PAGE 1	
REC'T NO.	DATE	RECEIVED FROM	SALES INCOME	ADVERTISING INCOME	TOTAL RECEIPTS	BANK DEPOSITS

b) Open a Cash Payments Journal with the following headings:

		CASH PAYMENTS JOURNAL			PAGE 1		
CHECK NO.	DATE	PAID TO	FOR	AMOUNT OF CHECK	PRINTING COSTS	OFFICE EXPENSES	OTHER PAYMENTS

c) The bank balance on May 1 was $895.00. Record this amount on the first stub, check #341.

d) Record the transactions shown below and on the next page:

May 1   Received $61.50 from the junior class for magazine copies sold. Enter this transaction in the Cash Receipts Journal. Start with receipt #101. Record each cash receipt in a similar manner. Number the receipts in order.

2   Issued check #341 for $50.00 to the Rowe Co. as a part payment for printing costs. Write the stub and the check. Find the new checkbook balance. Enter the payment in the Cash Payments Journal. Record each payment in a similar manner.

Subtract checks issued from checkbook balance

4   Received $75.00 from the Team Athletic Co. for advertising.

4   Deposited $136.50, the total amount received to this date. Record the deposit on check stub #342. Find the new checkbook balance. Enter the deposit in the Bank Deposits column of the Cash Receipts Journal.

Add deposits to checkbook balance

8   Issued check #342 for $41.90 to the Gem Corp., for stationery and other office supplies.

10   Issued check #343 for $80.00 to Rowe Co. as a part payment for printing costs.

14   Received $72.50 from the freshman class for magazines sold.

18   Received $90.00 from the ABC Auto School for advertising.

21   Issued check #344 for $40.00 to the Spot Co. for photographic supplies. (Use "Other Payments" column.)

25   Received $91.00 from the senior class for magazines sold.

25   Deposited $253.50, the total amount received since the previous deposit. Record the deposit on check stub #345. Find the new checkbook balance. Enter the deposit in the Bank Deposits column of the Cash Receipts Journal.

31   Issued check #345 for $31.80 to the Gem Corp. for office supplies. (Your final checkbook balance should be $1,041.30.)

e) Pencil foot the money columns in both journals.
f) Verify the totals by crossfooting.
g) Ink in totals and rule the journals.

Problem 2

In Problem 1 you kept a record of the income received and the checks issued by the business staff of the school magazine. In this problem you will check the accuracy of those records by comparing them with the bank statement and the canceled checks received from the bank.

A few days after the close of the month of May you received the following bank statement (shown below) from the bank.

PACIFIC NATIONAL BANK

ACCOUNT OF
    The Laguna Log   Account Number: 0203 0217 7
    Laguna High School
    San Francisco, CA 94102   Statement Date: May 31, 19--

Total Deposits 390.00	Total Checks Cleared 211.90	Current Balance 1,073.10

Date	Checks Paid	Deposits	Balance
May 1	Balance Brought Forward		895.00
3	50.00		845.00
4		136.50	981.50
11	41.90		939.60
14	80.00		859.60
23	40.00		819.60
25		253.50	1,073.10

Directions:
a) Compare the two deposits listed on the bank statement with the amounts listed in the Bank Deposits column of the Cash Receipts Journal you prepared in Problem 1. If the amounts are correct, place a small check mark in the Cash Receipts Journal next to each deposit.
b) The following canceled checks were returned in the same envelope with the bank statement:

| Check #341 | $50.00 | Check #343 | $80.00 |
| Check #342 | 41.90 | Check #344 | 40.00 |

Find the outstanding checks by comparing the canceled checks with the Amount of Check column of the Cash Payments Journal.

c) Find out if the May 31 balance of the checkbook you prepared in Problem 1 agrees with the May 31 balance shown on the bank statement by making up a bank reconciliation statement using Illustration 17b on page 127 of the textbook as an example.

Problem 3

You are employed in the office of the Mary Kay Music and Dance School. Part of your job will be the following activities:

1) Recording information from duplicate receipts into a Cash Receipts Journal,
2) Writing checks and keeping the checkbook balance up-to-date, and
3) Recording information from the check stubs into a Cash Payments Journal.

Directions:
a) Open a Cash Receipts Journal with the following headings:

		CASH RECEIPTS JOURNAL				PAGE [
REC'T NO.	DATE	RECEIVED FROM	MUSIC INCOME	DANCE INCOME	TOTAL RECEIPTS	BANK DEPOSITS

b) Open a Cash Payments Journal with the following headings:

		CASH PAYMENTS JOURNAL				PAGE J	
						BUSINESS PAYMENTS	
CHECK NO.	DATE	PAID TO	FOR	AMOUNT OF CHECK	PERSONAL PAYMENTS	ADVER-TISING	OTHER ITEMS

c) The bank balance on July 1 was $1,415.00. Record this amount on the first check stub, check #201.

d) Record the transactions shown below and on page 588:

July 2   Received $68.50 from C. Emery for dance lessons for her daughter. Enter this transaction in the Cash Receipts Journal. Start with receipt #71. Record each cash receipt in a similar manner. Number the receipts in order.

      5   Issued check #201 for $57.00 to the Alba Co. for advertising circulars. Write the stub and the check. Find the new checkbook balance. Enter the payment in the Cash Payments Journal. Record each cash payment in a similar manner.

      6   Received $51.00 from V. MacDonald for music lessons.

      6   Deposited $119.50, the total amount received to this date. Record the deposit on check stub #202. Find the new checkbook balance. Enter the deposit in the Bank Deposits column of the Cash Receipts Journal.

      9   Mary Kay, the owner, cashed check #202 for $150.00 for her personal use. (Make the check payable to "Cash.")

12   Issued check #203 for $41.50 to the Cue Corp. for advertising posters.

17   Received $98.70 from G. Kaplan for music and dance lessons for his children. The music lessons amounted to $33.60 and the dance lessons amounted to $65.10.

20   Received $52.30 from W. Herman for music lessons.

24   Issued check #204 for $220.00 to Matt, Inc. for the business rent for the month. (Use the "Other Items" column.)

26   Received $29.50 from M. Rudd for dance lessons.

26   Deposited $180.50, the total amount received since the previous deposit. Record the deposit on check stub #205. Find the new checkbook balance. Enter the deposit in the Bank Deposits column of the Cash Receipts Journal.

31   Issued check #205 for $24.80 to the Bell Telephone Co. for the owner's home telephone bill. (Your final checkbook balance should be $1,221.70.)

e) Pencil foot the money columns in both journals.

f) Verify the totals by crossfooting.

g) Ink in totals and rule the journals.

Problem 4

In Problem 3 you kept a record of the income received and the checks issued by the Mary Kay Music and Dance School. In this problem, you will check the accuracy of those records by comparing them with the following bank statement received from the bank a few days after the close of the month of July.

Florida State Bank

Account of
Mary Kay Music and Dance School   Account Number: 0314 0526 9
8770 Dickens Avenue
Miami, FL   33154   Statement Date: July 31, 19--

Total Deposits	Total Checks Cleared	Service Charges	Current Balance
300.00	468.50	2.10	1,244.40

Date	Checks Paid	Deposits	Balance
July 1	Balance Brought Forward		1,415.00
5	57.00		1,358.00
6		119.50	1,477.50
9	150.00		1,327.50
16	41.50		1,286.00
25	220.00		1,066.00
26		180.50	1,246.50
30	2.10 SC		1,244.40

Directions:

a) Compare the two deposits listed on the bank statement with the amounts listed in the Bank Deposits column of the Cash Receipts Journal you prepared in Problem 3. If the amounts are correct, place a small check mark in the Cash Receipts Journal next to each deposit.

b) The following canceled checks were returned in the same envelope with the bank statement:

Check #201	$ 57.00	Check #203	$ 41.50
Check #202	150.00	Check #204	220.00

Find the outstanding checks by comparing the canceled checks returned with the Amount of Check column of the Cash Payments Journal.

c) Find out if the July 31 balance of the checkbook you prepared in Problem 3 agrees with the July 31 balance shown on the bank statement by making up a bank reconciliation statement using Illustration 19b on page 133 of the textbook as an example. (Notice that on July 30 the bank statement shows a service charge [SC] of $2.10.)

Practicing Related Arithmetic

Copy and find the balance of the following customers' accounts:

NAME *Gloria Parrell*   TERMS *net 20 days*
ADDRESS *2707 E. Towers Drive, Cincinnati, OH 45238*

DATE	ITEM	POST. REF.	DEBIT	DATE	ITEM	POST. REF.	CREDIT
Apr. 1			1930 62	Apr. 3			1930 62
7			3709 45	10			156 20
16			5281 13	17			3553 25
18			452 87	21			78 97
30			6345 21	23			5202 16

NAME *Ramon Vassale*   TERMS *net 20 days*
ADDRESS *1806 Westmont Lane, Cincinnati, OH 45205*

DATE	ITEM	POST. REF.	DEBIT	DATE	ITEM	POST. REF.	CREDIT
Apr. 1			7134 29	Apr. 2			7134 29
9			4615 13	11			308 12
16			720 65	18			4307 01
22			2863 50	21			16 08
29			8294 76	25			704 57

AIM

To learn how to keep separate records for cash and income accounts in a ledger.

EXPLANATION

In Jobs 88 and 89 you learned how to use a Cash Receipts Journal. In Unit 8 you also learned how information was transferred (posted) from journals to customers' accounts which were kept in a book known as an Accounts Receivable Ledger. Today you will learn that information other than information about customers is posted to accounts in a separate ledger. The ledger where *miscellaneous* accounts are kept is called a *General Ledger*.

Look at Illustration 95a on page 591. It is a record of the cash received by Bruce West, who has been in the commercial refrigeration business for the past three months.

CASH RECEIPTS JOURNAL PAGE 1

INV. NO.	DATE	RECEIVED FROM	POST. REF.	INCOME, CR. LABOR	INCOME, CR. PARTS	TOTAL RECEIPTS, DR.	BANK DEPOSITS
1	Jan. 6	D. Kruz	✓	1 0 0 0u		1 0 0 00	
2	9	M. Leaf	✓	1 2 0 00	9 0 00	2 1 0 00	3 1 0 00
3	17	L. & Y. Co.	✓	8 0 00	1 7 0 00	2 5 0 00	
4	20	A. Dune	✓	6 0 00	1 3 0 00	1 9 0 00	4 4 0 00
5	29	M & Z Co.	✓	2 4 0 00	3 1 0 00	5 5 0 00	5 5 0 00
				6 0 0 00	7 0 0 00	1 3 0 0 00	1 3 0 0 00

CASH RECEIPTS JOURNAL PAGE 2

INV. NO.	DATE	RECEIVED FROM	POST. REF.	INCOME, CR. LABOR	INCOME, CR. PARTS	TOTAL RECEIPTS, DR.	BANK DEPOSITS
6	Feb. 5	R. Aiken	✓	2 3 5 00	1 6 5 00	4 0 0 00	4 0 0 00
7	11	B. Shack	✓	1 1 0 00	1 5 5 00	2 6 5 00	2 6 5 00
8	19	I. & R. Co.	✓	5 0 00		5 0 00	
9	21	E. Hare	✓	3 0 0 00	3 4 0 00	6 4 0 00	6 9 0 00
10	24	T. Doyle	✓	1 7 5 00	1 9 5 00	3 7 0 00	3 7 0 00
11	28	F. & J. Co.	✓	1 3 0 00	4 5 00	1 7 5 00	1 7 5 00
				1 0 0 0 00	9 0 0 00	1 9 0 0 00	1 9 0 0 00

CASH RECEIPTS JOURNAL PAGE 3

INV. NO.	DATE	RECEIVED FROM	POST. REF.	INCOME, CR. LABOR	INCOME, CR. PARTS	TOTAL RECEIPTS, DR.	BANK DEPOSITS
12	Mar. 3	K. Howell	✓	4 5 0 00	2 0 0 00	6 5 0 00	6 5 0 00
13	10	N. Doure	✓	2 8 5 00	1 2 0 00	4 0 5 00	4 0 5 00
14	13	B. Alba	✓	2 7 0 00	8 0 00	3 5 0 00	3 5 0 00
15	26	A. & H. Co.	✓	1 9 5 00	7 5 00	2 7 0 00	
16	27	O. Sera	✓	2 5 0 00	1 2 5 00	3 7 5 00	6 4 5 00
				1 4 5 0 00	6 0 0 00	2 0 5 0 00	2 0 5 0 00

Illustration 95a – Cash Receipts Journal

If Mr. West asked you how much cash had been received during the past three months, you would refer to these three pages in the Cash Receipts Journal and list:

$1,300.00 (from page 1)
1,900.00 (from page 2)
2,050.00 (from page 3)
$5,250.00 Total

You could tell him that the total amount of cash received for the past three months amounted to $5,250.00.

If he had asked you how much had been received for *"Income from Labor"* for the past three months, you would list:

$$\begin{array}{l}
\$\ \ 600.00\ \text{(page 1)} \\
1,000.00\ \text{(page 2)} \\
\underline{1,450.00}\ \text{(page 3)} \\
\$3,050.00\ \text{Total}
\end{array}$$

You could tell him that the total amount received for *"Income from Labor"* for the past three months amounted to $3,050.00.

If he had asked you how much he had received for "Income from Parts," you would go through the same process to get an answer of $2,200.00. If these questions were asked at the end of a year, you would refer to each month's figures to get the required information.

Businesspeople use a record-keeping system which helps them get the information much more readily than the method just shown. Mr. West's records would look like Illustration 95b on page 593 at the end of January.

Now compare this Cash Receipts Journal in Illustration 95b with Illustration 95a appearing on page 591. The only differences between these two illustrations are the circled numbers and a circled check mark under the double rulings in Illustration 95b:

②	③	①	✓
below the double ruling in the Income from Labor column	below the double ruling in the Income from Parts column	below the double ruling in the Total Receipts column	below the double ruling in the Bank Deposits column

The circled notation "1" shows that you have transferred (posted) the $1,300.00 to an account called *Cash,* which can be found on page 1 of the General Ledger. The circled notation "1" is called a *postmark* or *posting reference number.* This postmark was recorded below the *Total Receipts* column in the Cash Receipts Journal when the $1,300.00 was posted to the Cash account in the General Ledger. It means that the $1,300.00 can be found on *page 1* of the General Ledger.

Now look at the Cash account in the General Ledger, Illustration 95b. Since the Cash account is on the first page of the ledger, *Page 1* appears on the right side of the page. You will also note that the year 19–– and the month and date *Jan. 31* appear in the Date column in the usual way. (You can see the date recorded in the same way in the Related Arithmetic Drill for this job.)

Postmarks show that information has been transferred (posted) from a journal to a ledger. They also are useful for cross-referencing purposes.

The date is January 31 for this reason: The record keeper must total the columns before the posting can be done, and the columns are always totaled on the *last day of the month.*

		CASH RECEIPTS JOURNAL					PAGE 1	
INV. NO.	DATE	RECEIVED FROM	POST. REF.	INCOME, CR.		TOTAL RECEIPTS, DR.	BANK DEPOSITS	
				LABOR	PARTS			
1	19-- Jan. 6	D. Kruz	✓	100 00		100 00		
2	9	M. Leaf	✓	120 00	90 00	210 00	310 00	
3	17	L. & Y. Co.	✓	80 00	170 00	250 00		
4	20	A. Dune	✓	60 00	130 00	190 00	440 00	
5	29	M & Z Co.	✓	240 00	310 00	550 00	550 00	
				600 00	700 00	1300 00	1300 00	
				②	③	①	✓	

GENERAL LEDGER

ACCOUNT *Cash*   PAGE 1

DATE	ITEM	POST. REF.	DEBIT	DATE	ITEM	POST. REF.	CREDIT
19-- Jan. 31		CR1	1300 00				

ACCOUNT *Income from Labor*   PAGE 2

DATE	ITEM	POST. REF.	DEBIT	DATE	ITEM	POST. REF.	CREDIT
				19-- Jan. 31		CR1	600 00

ACCOUNT *Income from Parts*   PAGE 3

DATE	ITEM	POST. REF.	DEBIT	DATE	ITEM	POST. REF.	CREDIT
				19-- Jan. 31		CR1	700 00

Illustration 95b — Cash Receipts Journal and General Ledger

The "CR 1" means that the $1,300.00 was posted from *page 1* of the Cash Receipts Journal. "CR" is the abbreviation for Cash Receipts.

The notation "2" shows that the $600.00 has been posted to the *Income from Labor* account on *page 2* of the General Ledger. Look at page 2 of the ledger, Illustration 95b, and you will see the $600.00 in that account, along with the year and date and the postmark, "CR 1." This means that the $600.00 was posted from page 1 of the Cash Receipts Journal.

The notation "3" shows that the $700.00 has been posted to the *Income from Parts* account on *page 3* of the General Ledger. If you look at page 3 of the ledger in Illustration 95b, you will see the $700.00 in that account. The record keeper has again recorded the year, month, date, and "CR 1," because the $700.00 was posted from page 1 of the Cash Receipts Journal on January 31, 19--.

You are probably wondering why the $1,300.00 was posted to the left-hand side of the Cash account (the *debit* side) and why both the $600.00 and the $700.00 were posted to the right-hand side of their respective accounts (the *credit* side). Examine the Cash Receipts Journal, Illustration 95b, and you will see that:

		Income from		Income from
Cash	=	Labor	+	Parts
$1,300	=	$600	+	$700

We post into the ledger this way to show that the cash debit of $1,300.00 equals the sum of the two credits of $600.00 and $700.00. What you have here is an *equation (something* equals *something else).*

Total debits must equal total credits in the journal and in the ledger

It is important to remember that the Total Receipts is always posted to the debit side of the Cash account and that the total of each Income column is posted to the credit side of its own Income account.

To help you to remember that *cash received* should be posted to the *debit side* of the ledger account, your heading for the Total Receipts column in the Cash Receipts Journal should include the word *debit*. (The abbreviation for debit is *Dr.*) Likewise, to help you remember that *Income* totals should be posted to the *credit* side of the ledger accounts, the headings of the Income columns should show the word *credit*. (The abbreviation for credit is *Cr.*) Therefore, the headings for the columns in Illustration 95b should be like this:

CASH RECEIPTS JOURNAL				PAGE I			
INV. NO.	DATE	RECEIVED FROM	POST. REF.	INCOME, CR.		TOTAL RECEIPTS, DR.	BANK DEPOSITS
				LABOR	PARTS		

Do not post from the Bank Deposits column since it is a memorandum column

Now that you have learned about the postmarks "1," "2," and "3," consider the postmark "√" which appears under the Bank Deposits column. The check mark "√" indicates that *the total is not to be posted* to the ledger. Of course, the reason is that the $1,300.00 has already been posted to the Cash account from the Total Receipts column in the Cash Receipts Journal. The Bank Deposits column in the Cash Receipts Journal serves to remind the record keeper that the actual money is not in the office but is now deposited in the bank. The column also provides a record of the amount of each bank deposit. Record keepers call this column a *memorandum column* since it merely helps them to remember important information.

Use a check mark (√) to show that no posting is made to an account

Record keepers make a check mark (√) in a journal as a reminder that no posting is to be made to any account in the ledger at that time. Check marks appear on Jan. 6, 9, 17, 20, and 29 in the Cash Receipts Journal to show that none of the individual income amounts are to be posted to the ledger during the month. These amounts are not posted individually because they will be *posted as one total at the end of the month.*

SAMPLE PROBLEM

Now return to the original problem of finding the total cash and income received for the three months ending March 31, 19-- by Bruce West, owner of the commercial refrigeration business.

CASH RECEIPTS JOURNAL — PAGE 1

INV. NO.	DATE	RECEIVED FROM	POST. REF.	INCOME, CR. LABOR	PARTS	TOTAL RECEIPTS, DR.	BANK DEPOSITS
1	Jan. 6	D. Kruz	✓	1000 00		100 00	
2	9	M. Leaf	✓	120 00	90 00	210 00	310 00
3	17	L. & Y. Co.	✓	80 00	170 00	250 00	
4	20	A. Dune	✓	60 00	130 00	190 00	440 00
5	29	M. & Z Co.	✓	240 00	310 00	550 00	550 00
				600 00	700 00	1300 00	1300 00
				(2)	(3)	(1)	(✓)

CASH RECEIPTS JOURNAL — PAGE 2

INV. NO.	DATE	RECEIVED FROM	POST. REF.	INCOME, CR. LABOR	PARTS	TOTAL RECEIPTS, DR.	BANK DEPOSITS
6	Feb. 5	R. Aiken	✓	235 00	165 00	400 00	400 00
7	11	B. Shack	✓	110 00	155 00	265 00	265 00
8	19	I. & R. Co.	✓	50 00		50 00	
9	21	E. Hare	✓	300 00	340 00	640 00	690 00
10	24	T. Doyle	✓	175 00	195 00	370 00	370 00
11	28	F. & J. Co.	✓	130 00	45 00	175 00	175 00
				1000 00	900 00	1900 00	1900 00
				(2)	(3)	(1)	(✓)

CASH RECEIPTS JOURNAL — PAGE 3

INV. NO.	DATE	RECEIVED FROM	POST. REF.	INCOME, CR. LABOR	PARTS	TOTAL RECEIPTS, DR.	BANK DEPOSITS
12	Mar. 3	K. Howell	✓	450 00	200 00	650 00	650 00
13	10	N. Doure	✓	285 00	120 00	405 00	405 00
14	13	B. Alba	✓	270 00	80 00	350 00	350 00
15	26	A. & H. Co.	✓	195 00	75 00	270 00	
16	27	O. Sera	✓	250 00	125 00	375 00	645 00
				1450 00	600 00	2050 00	2050 00
				(2)	(3)	(1)	(✓)

Illustration 95c — Cash Receipts Journals

Illustration 95c on page 595 shows how the Journals in Illustration 95a on page 591 would look at the end of three months with the necessary postmarks. The General Ledger to which the amounts were posted is shown below.

GENERAL LEDGER

ACCOUNT *Cash*   PAGE   1

DATE	ITEM	POST. REF.	DEBIT	DATE	ITEM	POST. REF.	CREDIT
19--							
Jan. 31		CR1	1 300 00				
Feb. 28		CR2	1 900 00				
Mar. 31		CR3	2 050 00				

ACCOUNT *Income from Labor*   PAGE   2

DATE	ITEM	POST. REF.	DEBIT	DATE	ITEM	POST. REF.	CREDIT
				19--			
				Jan. 31		CR1	600 00
				Feb. 28		CR2	1 000 00
				Mar. 31		CR3	1 450 00

ACCOUNT *Income from Parts*   PAGE   3

DATE	ITEM	POST. REF.	DEBIT	DATE	ITEM	POST. REF.	CREDIT
				19--			
				Jan. 31		CR1	700 00
				Feb. 28		CR2	900 00
				Mar. 31		CR3	600 00

Illustration 95d — General Ledgers

General ledger accounts help you to get important information easily

If Mr. West were to ask you how much cash had been received for the three months ending March 31, 19--, you would refer to the Cash account appearing on page 1 of the General Ledger, Illustration 95d, pencil foot the account, and tell him $5,250.00.

If he wanted to know how much had been received from labor for the three months ending March 31, 19--, you would look at the Income from Labor account, Illustration 95d, pencil foot the account, and tell him $3,050.00.

The same procedure would give you the answer for Income from Parts, and you would tell him $2,200.00.

Under this new system, by using a journal plus a ledger, you can readily get important information.

Here are the steps that the record keeper follows in *journalizing* (making journal entries) and posting the entries for three months for Mr. West:

Step 1: Journalize each transaction.

Refer to the Cash Receipts Journal for January, Illustration 95c, and you will note recorded the invoice number, date, name of customer, and the fact that Mr. West received $100.00. You will see that the *$100.00 is written twice*. It is first recorded in the Income from Labor column to show how Mr. West earned the $100.00. It is recorded a second time in the Total Receipts column to show that money has been received.

Each amount is written twice

Step 2: Record necessary check marks in the Posting Reference column.

The $100.00 will not be posted on this date to either the Income from Labor account or to the Cash account, but will be accumulated with other income that will be posted as totals to the respective accounts at the end of the month. Therefore, a check mark ($\sqrt{}$) is made in the Posting Reference column on January 6 when the $100.00 is entered in the journal. The same procedure is used for the remaining entries.

Amounts entered in special columns are posted as a total at the end of the month

Step 3: Record bank deposits in the Bank Deposits column. (Memorandum Entry)

When $310.00 is deposited in the bank on January 9, the amount is entered in the Bank Deposits column. This $310.00 is the accumulation of the $100.00 received on January 6 and the $210.00 on January 9. Note that the $310.00 is recorded on the same line as the $210.00.

Amounts are recorded in the Bank Deposits column on the date the deposit is made

Step 4: Pencil foot the Cash Receipts Journal.

On the last day of the month the columns are pencil footed and the total debits compared with the total credits to see if they agree:

Cash, Dr.		Income from Labor, Cr.		Income from Parts, Cr.
$1,300.00	=	$600.00	+	$700.00

Since the total debits equal the total credits, the record keeper can feel sure that the columns have been added correctly.

Total debits must always equal total credits

If they do not agree, it is necessary to recheck the addition and then recheck the entries to determine if the same amount has been entered in both the Cash Receipts column and also in an Income column.

Step 5: Enter totals in ink and rule columns.

If the debits and credits agree when the columns are pencil footed, the record keeper enters the totals in ink and rules the columns, as shown in Illustration 95c.

Step 6: Post the total cash and income received to their respective accounts.

The importance of the postmark

The postmarks under each column in the Cash Receipts Journal indicate the page number in the General Ledger to which the total amount in that column has been posted. The postmarks in the ledger show the page of the Cash Receipts Journal from which the amounts have been posted.

PRACTICE PROBLEMS

Problem 1

You are acting as the record keeper for Mr. Bruce West, who is in the commercial refrigeration business.

Directions:
a) Copy the Cash Receipts Journal for the month of April, 19—:

CASH RECEIPTS JOURNAL   PAGE 4

INV. NO.	DATE	RECEIVED FROM	POST. REF.	INCOME, CR. LABOR	PARTS	TOTAL RECEIPTS, DR.	BANK DEPOSITS
17	Apr. 4	A. Huce	✓	105 00	163 50	268 50	268 50
18	9	T. Esse	✓	37 00	86 00	123 00	
19	11	F. Cafaro	✓	145 00	214 75	359 75	482 75
20	18	R. Soble	✓	270 00	335 20	605 20	605 20
21	28	E & T9. Co.	✓	205 00	179 15	384 15	384 15

b) Copy the accounts below and on the next page which appear in the General Ledger and which show the postings for the past three months. Allow 6 lines for each account.
c) Rule a single line across all the money columns in the Cash Receipts Journal.
d) Pencil foot all money columns in the Cash Receipts Journal.
e) Verify pencil footings by seeing if the total debits equal the total credits. In addition, see if the totals of the Total Receipts and Bank Deposits columns agree.
f) Ink in totals and rule a double line as shown in Illustration 95c.
g) Post the totals to their respective accounts. Be sure to indicate the postmarks in the journal and in the ledger.
h) Pencil foot the accounts. Does the pencil footing in the Cash account amount to $6,990.60?

GENERAL LEDGER

ACCOUNT Cash   PAGE 1

DATE	ITEM	POST. REF.	DEBIT	DATE	ITEM	POST. REF.	CREDIT
Jan. 31		CR1	1 300 00				
Feb. 28		CR2	1 900 00				
Mar. 31		CR3	2 050 00				

ACCOUNT *Income from Labor*   PAGE 2

DATE	ITEM	POST. REF.	DEBIT	DATE	ITEM	POST. REF.	CREDIT
				19-- Jan. 31		CRI	60000
				Feb. 28		CR2	100000
				Mar. 31		CR3	145000

ACCOUNT *Income from Parts*   PAGE 3

DATE	ITEM	POST. REF.	DEBIT	DATE	ITEM	POST. REF.	CREDIT
				Jan. 31		CRI	70000
				Feb. 28		CR2	90000
				Mar. 31		CR3	60000

Problem 2

You are acting as the record keeper for Jeff Slater, who repairs and sells commercial sewing machines.

Directions:

a) Copy the Cash Receipts Journal for the month of October, 19—:

CASH RECEIPTS JOURNAL   PAGE 5

INV. NO.	DATE	RECEIVED FROM	POST. REF.	INCOME, CR. LABOR	INCOME, CR. MACHINES & PARTS	TOTAL RECEIPTS, DR.	BANK DEPOSITS
108	19-- Oct. 6	B. Fox Co.	✓	16000	54000	70000	70000
109	14	J. Kraile	✓	8500	60550	69050	
110	16	G. Tigre	✓	23000	179280	202280	271330
111	23	W. Prior Co.	✓	32000	261025	293025	293025
112	29	D. Manes	✓	14500	97630	112130	112130

b) Copy the General Ledger accounts which appear on page 600 and which show the postings for the past four months. Allow 6 lines for each account.

c) Rule a single line across all money columns in Cash Receipts Journal.

d) Pencil foot all money columns in the Cash Receipts Journal.

e) Verify pencil footings by seeing if the total debits equal the total credits. In addition, see if the totals of the Total Receipts and Bank Deposits columns agree.

f) Ink in totals and rule a double line as shown in Illustration 95c, page 595.

g) Post the totals to their respective accounts. Be sure to indicate the postmarks in the journal and in the ledger.

h) Pencil foot the accounts. Does the pencil footing in the Cash account amount to $30,651.34?

GENERAL LEDGER

ACCOUNT *Cash*   PAGE 1

DATE		ITEM	POST. REF.	DEBIT	DATE	ITEM	POST. REF.	CREDIT
19-- June	30		CR1	6 2 0 7 90				
July.	31		CR2	5 0 8 6 21				
Aug.	31		CR3	7 1 9 9 70				
Sept.	30		CR4	4 6 9 2 68				

ACCOUNT *Income from Labor*   PAGE 2

DATE	ITEM	POST. REF.	DEBIT	DATE		ITEM	POST. REF.	CREDIT
				19-- June	30		CR1	1 0 2 5 00
				July	31		CR2	8 1 0 00
				Aug.	31		CR3	1 1 9 0 00
				Sept.	30		CR4	7 6 5 00

ACCOUNT *Income from Sale of Sewing Machines and Parts*   PAGE 3

DATE	ITEM	POST. REF.	DEBIT	DATE		ITEM	POST. REF.	CREDIT
				19-- June	30		CR1	5 1 8 2 90
				July	31		CR2	4 2 7 6 21
				Aug.	31		CR3	6 0 0 9 70
				Sept.	30		CR4	3 9 2 7 68

Problem 3

You are acting as the record keeper for the A A Moving & Storage Co., which started in business September 1, 19--.

Directions:
a) Copy the Cash Receipts Journal for the month of December, 19—:

CASH RECEIPTS JOURNAL   PAGE 4

INV. NO.	DATE		RECEIVED FROM	POST. REF.	INCOME, CR.		TOTAL RECEIPTS, DR.	BANK DEPOSITS
					MOVING	STORAGE		
57	19-- Dec.	8	K. Demero	✓	4 8 0 00		4 8 0 00	
58		9	C. Albin	✓	3 4 5 00	1 7 5 00	5 2 0 00	1 0 0 0 00
59		15	H. Teiler	✓		8 3 4 50	8 3 4 50	8 3 4 50
60		19	O. Kayson	✓	5 6 0 50	9 5 8 25	1 5 1 8 75	1 5 1 8 75
61		30	P. Norge	✓	8 2 5 00		8 2 5 00	8 2 5 00

b) Copy the General Ledger accounts which appear on page 601 and which show the postings for the past three months. Allow 6 lines for each account.

c) Rule a single line across all the money columns in the Cash Receipts Journal.

GENERAL LEDGER

ACCOUNT *Cash*   PAGE 1

DATE	ITEM	POST. REF.	DEBIT	DATE	ITEM	POST. REF.	CREDIT
19-- *Sept.* 30		CR1	15 2 3 7 75				
Oct. 31		CR2	1 7 0 2 8 00				
Nov. 30		CR3	11 6 35 75				

ACCOUNT *Income from Moving*   PAGE 2

DATE	ITEM	POST. REF.	DEBIT	DATE	ITEM	POST. REF.	CREDIT
				19-- *Sept.* 30		CR1	9 8 6 5 25
				Oct. 31		CR2	10 5 9 0 00
				Nov. 30		CR3	7 3 85 75

ACCOUNT *Income from Storage*   PAGE 3

DATE	ITEM	POST. REF.	DEBIT	DATE	ITEM	POST. REF.	CREDIT
				19-- *Sept.* 30		CR1	5 3 7 2 50
				Oct. 31		CR2	6 4 3 8 00
				Nov. 30		CR3	4 2 5 0 00

d) Pencil foot all money columns in the Cash Receipts Journal.

e) Verify pencil footings by seeing if the total debits equal the total credits. In addition, see if the totals of the Total Receipts and Bank Deposits columns agree.

f) Ink in totals and rule a double line as shown in Illustration 95c.

g) Post the totals to their respective accounts. Be sure to indicate the postmarks in the journal and in the ledger.

h) Pencil foot the accounts. Does the pencil footing in the Cash account amount to $48,079.75?

Problem 4

You are acting as the record keeper for the C & Y Restaurant Equipment & Repair Co., which has operated its business since January 1, 19--.

Directions:

a) Copy from page 602 the Cash Receipts Journal for May, 19--.

b) Copy the General Ledger accounts which appear on page 602 and which show the postings for the past four months. Allow 6 lines for each account.

c) Rule a single line across all the money columns in the Cash Receipts Journal.

d) Pencil foot all money columns in the Cash Receipts Journal.

CASH RECEIPTS JOURNAL   PAGE 5

INV. NO.	DATE	RECEIVED FROM	POST. REF.	INCOME, CR. LABOR	INCOME, CR. EQUIPMENT	TOTAL RECEIPTS, DR.	BANK DEPOSITS	
143	19-- May 2	N & Q Co.	✓	1 150 00	5 893 75	7 043 75	7 043 75	
144	5	W. French Co.	✓	804 00	4 768 50	5 572 50	5 572 50	
145	12	I. Villa Co.	✓	230 00		230 00		
146	14	A & Y Co.	✓	910 50	6 173 20	7 083 70	7 313 70	
147	26	S. Gold	✓	582 25	3 905 00	4 487 25	4 487 25	

GENERAL LEDGER

ACCOUNT Cash   PAGE 1

DATE	ITEM	POST. REF.	DEBIT	DATE	ITEM	POST. REF.	CREDIT	
19-- Jan. 31		CR1	15 577 15					
Feb. 28		CR2	13 136 30					
Mar. 31		CR3	10 171 75					
Apr. 30		CR4	12 810 20					

ACCOUNT Income from Labor   PAGE 2

DATE	ITEM	POST. REF.	DEBIT	DATE	ITEM	POST. REF.	CREDIT	
				19-- Jan. 31		CR1	2 514 00	
				Feb. 28		CR2	3 008 50	
				Mar. 31		CR3	1 870 75	
				Apr. 30		CR4	732 00	

ACCOUNT Income from Sale of Equipment   PAGE 3

DATE	ITEM	POST. REF.	DEBIT	DATE	ITEM	POST. REF.	CREDIT	
				19-- Jan. 31		CR1	13 063 15	
				Feb. 28		CR2	10 127 80	
				Mar. 31		CR3	8 301 00	
				Apr. 30		CR4	12 078 20	

e) Verify pencil footings by seeing if the total debits equal the total credits. In addition see if the Total Receipts and Bank Deposits columns agree.

f) Ink in totals and rule a double line as shown in Illustration 95c.

g) Post the totals to their respective accounts. Be sure to indicate the postmarks in the journal and in the ledger.

h) Pencil foot the accounts.

Problem 5

You are acting as the record keeper for the Super Home Improvement Co., which has operated its business since August 1, 19--.

Directions:
a) Copy the Cash Receipts Journal for November, 19—:

CASH RECEIPTS JOURNAL   PAGE 4

INV. NO.	DATE	RECEIVED FROM	POST. REF.	INCOME, CR. LABOR	INCOME, CR. MATERIALS & SUPPLIES	TOTAL RECEIPTS, DR.	BANK DEPOSITS
176	Nov. 3	E. Skaro	✓	275 00	538 62	813 62	813 62
177	10	M. Grace	✓	420 00	714 35	1134 35	1134 35
178	12	C. Duffy	✓	315 00	604 10	919 10	919 10
179	18	M. Amato	✓	120 00	229 45	349 45	
180	20	S. Judge	✓	550 00	942 75	1492 75	1842 20
181	28	B. Pierce	✓	260 00	436 16	696 16	696 16

b) Copy the following accounts which appear in the General Ledger and which show the postings for the past three months. Allow 6 lines for each account.

GENERAL LEDGER

ACCOUNT Cash   PAGE 1

DATE	ITEM	POST. REF.	DEBIT	DATE	ITEM	POST. REF.	CREDIT
19-- Aug. 31		CR1	6570 58				
Sept. 30		CR2	8102 50				
Oct. 31		CR3	3926 82				

ACCOUNT Income from Labor   PAGE 2

DATE	ITEM	POST. REF.	DEBIT	DATE	ITEM	POST. REF.	CREDIT
				19-- Aug. 31		CR1	2378 00
				Sept. 30		CR2	3024 00
				Oct. 31		CR3	1605 00

ACCOUNT Income from Materials and Supplies   PAGE 3

DATE	ITEM	POST. REF.	DEBIT	DATE	ITEM	POST. REF.	CREDIT
				19-- Aug. 31		CR1	4192 58
				Sept. 30		CR2	5078 50
				Oct. 31		CR3	2321 82

c) Rule a single line across all the money columns in the Cash Receipts Journal.

d) Pencil foot all money columns in the Cash Receipts Journal.

e) Verify pencil footings by seeing if the total debits equal the total credits. In addition, see if the totals of the Total Receipts and Bank Deposits columns agree.

f) Ink in totals and rule a double line as shown in Illustration 95c.

g) Post the totals to their respective accounts. Be sure to indicate the postmarks in the journal and in the ledger.

h) Pencil foot the accounts.

USING A CASH RECEIPTS JOURNAL AND A GENERAL LEDGER

Copy and solve the following problems:

	(1)	(2)
Practicing Related Arithmetic	$3,165.72 4,080.93 5,276.39 900.08 2,054.21 1,418.56 + 709.47 $ _____	Crossfoot and then add down a) 13 + 20 + 56 + 34 = ___ b) 50 + 75 + 30 + 42 = ___ c) 45 + 18 + 27 + 70 = ___ d) 64 + 80 + 74 + 58 = ___ e) 7 + 49 + 10 + 63 = ___ f) ___ + ___ + ___ + ___ = ___

AIMS

1. To practice using the Cash Receipts Journal.
2. To practice posting to the General Ledger.

EXPLANATION

In this job you will record transactions in the Cash Receipts Journal on a daily basis and post to the General Ledger at the end of the month.

PRACTICE PROBLEMS

Problem 1

You are employed as a record keeper by Lloyd Erhart, an electrician, who started in business on June 1, 19--.

Directions:
a) Copy the Cash Receipts Journal shown below:

CASH RECEIPTS JOURNAL PAGE 4

INV. NO.	DATE	RECEIVED FROM	POST. REF.	INCOME, CR. LABOR	INCOME, CR. EQUIPMENT & SUPPLIES	TOTAL RECEIPTS, DR.	BANK DEPOSITS
87	Sept. 19-- 4	B. Durun	✓	75 00	2 1 8 25	2 9 3 25	
88	5	D. Azuto Co.	✓	55 00	9 6 75	1 5 1 75	4 4 5 00

b) Copy the General Ledger accounts which appear below and which show the postings for the past three months. Allow 6 lines for each account.

GENERAL LEDGER

ACCOUNT *Cash*   PAGE 1

DATE	ITEM	POST. REF.	DEBIT	DATE	ITEM	POST. REF.	CREDIT
19--							
June 30		CR1	3324 16				
July 31		CR2	2657 31				
Aug. 31		CR3	3788 78				

ACCOUNT *Income from Labor*   PAGE 2

DATE	ITEM	POST. REF.	DEBIT	DATE	ITEM	POST. REF.	CREDIT
				19--			
				June 30		CR1	81000
				July 31		CR2	76500
				Aug. 31		CR3	103200

ACCOUNT *Income from Equipment and Supplies*   PAGE 3

DATE	ITEM	POST. REF.	DEBIT	DATE	ITEM	POST. REF.	CREDIT
				19--			
				June 30		CR1	2514 16
				July 31		CR2	1892 31
				Aug. 31		CR3	2756 78

c) Record the information shown in the list of duplicate invoices below in the Cash Receipts Journal for the month of September. Since you have already entered invoices #87 and #88, continue with invoice #89.

Invoice Number	Date	Received From	Income from Labor	Income from Equipment & Supplies
89	11	O. Gorde	$ 82.00	
90	12	H. Alt Co.	43.00	$ 153.20
	12	Deposited $278.20 (Enter in Bank Deposits column)		
91	16	F. Flyn	68.00	49.17
92	17	T. Weill	190.00	1,241.36
	17	Deposited $1,548.53		
93	25	C. Rhode Co.	35.00	23.40
94	26	I. Mann Co.	100.00	710.65
	26	Deposited $869.05		
95	29	P. Fero	50.00	37.52
96	30	N. Sealy	220.00	803.95
	30	Deposited $1,111.47		

d) Pencil foot all money columns in the Cash Receipts Journal.

e) Verify pencil footings by seeing if the total debits equal the total credits. In addition, see if the totals of the Total Receipts and Bank Deposits columns agree.

f) Ink in totals and rule the journal.

g) Post the totals to their respective accounts. Be sure to indicate the postmarks in the journal and the ledger.

h) Pencil foot the accounts. Does the pencil footing in the Cash account amount to $14,022.50?

Problem 2

You are employed as a record keeper by the M Z Landscape & Fence Co., which has been in business since August 1, 19--.

Directions:

a) Copy the Cash Receipts Journal shown on the next page.

b) Copy the accounts which appear in the General Ledger on the next page and which show the postings for the past two months. Allow 6 lines for each account.

c) Record the information shown in the list of duplicate invoices for month of October in the Cash Receipts Journal just the way invoices #37 and #38 were recorded in the Cash Receipts Journal which you opened in Part a).

Invoice Number	Date	Received From	Income from Sale of Fences	Income from Sale of Gardening Supplies	Income from Landscaping
39	15	K. Panaro	$350.00	$ 86.72	
40	16	V. Kyle	195.25		$263.30
41	17	E. Gore		56.16	320.00
	17	Deposited $1,271.43 (Enter in Bank Deposits column)			
42	20	M. Dudley	623.50		
43	21	Q. Bayn		79.05	
	21	Deposited $702.55			
44	22	G. Aloceo	280.75		412.65
45	23	O. Flaks		61.10	
	23	Deposited $754.50			
46	29	W. Sisto	548.00		605.00
47	30	Y. Union		117.32	
48	31	S. Joyce	370.20	35.80	394.50
	31	Deposited $2,070.82			

d) Pencil foot all money columns in the Cash Receipts Journal.

e) Verify pencil footings by seeing if the total debits equal the total credits. In addition, see if the totals of the Total Receipts and Bank Deposits columns agree.

f) Ink in totals and rule the journal.

CASH RECEIPTS JOURNAL   PAGE 3

INV. NO.	DATE	RECEIVED FROM	POST. REF.	FENCES	INCOME CR. GARDENING SUPPLIES	LANDSCAPE	TOTAL RECEIPTS, DR.	BANK DEPOSITS
37	Oct. 6	J. Keene	✓		1 0 3 25		1 0 3 25	
38	7	N. Horn	✓	4 0 0 00		5 0 0 00	9 0 0 00	1 0 0 3 25

GENERAL LEDGER

ACCOUNT *Cash*   PAGE 1

DATE	ITEM	POST. REF.	DEBIT	DATE	ITEM	POST. REF.	CREDIT
Aug. 31		CR1	4 7 0 7 25				
Sept. 30		CR2	6 3 7 0 90				

ACCOUNT *Income from Sale of Fences*   PAGE 2

DATE	ITEM	POST. REF.	DEBIT	DATE	ITEM	POST. REF.	CREDIT
				Aug. 31		CR1	2 0 3 1 80
				Sept. 30		CR2	2 5 1 8 25

ACCOUNT *Income from Sale of Gardening Supplies*   PAGE 3

DATE	ITEM	POST. REF.	DEBIT	DATE	ITEM	POST. REF.	CREDIT
				Aug. 31		CR1	6 7 1 28
				Sept. 30		CR2	7 4 2 14

ACCOUNT *Income from Landscaping*   PAGE 4

DATE	ITEM	POST. REF.	DEBIT	DATE	ITEM	POST. REF.	CREDIT
				Aug. 31		CR1	2 0 0 4 17
				Sept. 30		CR2	3 1 1 0 51

g) Post the totals to their respective accounts. Be sure to indicate the postmarks in the journal and in the ledger.

h) Pencil foot the accounts. Does the pencil footing in the Cash account amount to $16,880.70?

Problem 3

You are employed as a record keeper by Greg Lamia, a lawyer and real estate broker, who started business on May 1, 19--.

Directions:
a) Copy the Cash Receipts Journal shown at the top of page 609.

CASH RECEIPTS JOURNAL   PAGE 4

INV. NO.	DATE	RECEIVED FROM	POST. REF.	LEGAL FEES	INCOME, CR. MANAGEMENT FEES	REAL ESTATE COMM.	TOTAL RECEIPTS, DR.	BANK DEPOSITS
70	19-- Aug. 6	J. Altman	✓	300 00			300 00	
71	8	M. Crowley Co.	✓		480 00	1000 00	1480 00	1780 00

b) Copy the General Ledger accounts which appear below and which show the postings for the past three months. Allow 6 lines for each account.

GENERAL LEDGER

ACCOUNT Cash   PAGE 1

DATE	ITEM	POST. REF.	DEBIT	DATE	ITEM	POST. REF.	CREDIT
19-- May 31		CR1	11 705 00				
June 30		CR2	11 440 00				
July 31		CR3	13 690 00				

ACCOUNT Income from Legal Fees   PAGE 2

DATE	ITEM	POST. REF.	DEBIT	DATE	ITEM	POST. REF.	CREDIT
				19-- May 31		CR1	1 640 00
				June 30		CR2	2 135 00
				July 31		CR3	2 500 00

ACCOUNT Income from Management Fees   PAGE 3

DATE	ITEM	POST. REF.	DEBIT	DATE	ITEM	POST. REF.	CREDIT
				19-- May 31		CR1	2 475 00
				June 30		CR2	2 980 00
				July 31		CR3	3 120 00

ACCOUNT Income from Real Estate Commissions   PAGE 4

DATE	ITEM	POST. REF.	DEBIT	DATE	ITEM	POST. REF.	CREDIT
				19-- May 31		CR1	7 590 00
				June 30		CR2	6 325 00
				July 31		CR3	8 070 00

c) Record the information shown in the list of duplicate invoices on page 610 for the month of August in the Cash Receipts Journal just the way invoices #70 and #71 were recorded in the Cash Receipts Journal which you opened in Part a).

Invoice Number	Date	Received From	Income from Legal Fees	Income from Management Fees	Income from Real Estate Commissions
72	11	T. Millan	$275.00		$ 850.00
73	12	Y. Quione		$625.00	720.00
	12	Deposited $2,470.00 (Enter in Bank Deposits column)			
74	14	S. Ron	450.00		
75	15	P. Wolte Co.		935.00	
	15	Deposited $1,385.00			
76	18	K. Lynn	250.00		2,100.00
77	19	N. Rolfe Co.	180.00	540.00	
	19	Deposited $3,070.00			
78	21	G. Kent	325.00		2,580.00
	21	Deposited $2,905.00			
79	27	A. Craig Co.		395.00	
80	28	C. Robert	200.00		1,960.00
	28	Deposited $2,555.00			
81	29	F. Kenny		810.00	
	29	Deposited $810.00			

d) Pencil foot all money columns in the Cash Receipts Journal.
e) Verify pencil footings by seeing if the total debits equal the total credits. In addition, see if the totals of the Total Receipts and Bank Deposits columns agree.
f) Ink in totals and rule the journal.
g) Post the totals to their respective accounts. Be sure to indicate the postmarks in the journal and in the ledger.
h) Pencil foot the accounts.

Problem 4

You are employed as a record keeper by Eric Nicols, who sells and repairs motorcycles. He has been in business since March 1, 19--.

Directions:
a) Copy the Cash Receipts Journal below:

CASH RECEIPTS JOURNAL PAGE 4

INV. NO.	DATE	RECEIVED FROM	POST. REF.	INCOME, CR. LABOR	PARTS	MOTOR-CYCLES	TOTAL RECEIPTS, DR.	BANK DEPOSITS
154	June 2	D. Torbert	✓	63 00	102 85		165 85	
155	3	U. Sharli	✓			925 50	925 50	1091 35

b) Copy the accounts which appear in the General Ledger below and which show the postings for the past three months. Allow 6 lines for each account.

GENERAL LEDGER

ACCOUNT *Cash*   PAGE 1

DATE	ITEM	POST. REF.	DEBIT	DATE	ITEM	POST. REF.	CREDIT
19-- Mar. 31		CR1	5 8 7 3 63				
Apr. 30		CR2	9 3 1 8 46				
May 31		CR3	7 6 7 4 23				

ACCOUNT *Income from Labor*   PAGE 2

DATE	ITEM	POST. REF.	DEBIT	DATE	ITEM	POST. REF.	CREDIT
				19-- Mar. 31		CR1	5 2 7 50
				Apr. 30		CR2	6 0 8 25
				May 31		CR3	7 1 2 00

ACCOUNT *Income from Sale of Parts*   PAGE 3

DATE	ITEM	POST. REF.	DEBIT	DATE	ITEM	POST. REF.	CREDIT
				Mar. 31		CR1	7 1 6 83
				Apr. 30		CR2	5 9 2 71
				May 31		CR3	9 0 3 48

ACCOUNT *Income from Sale of Motorcycles*   PAGE 4

DATE	ITEM	POST. REF.	DEBIT	DATE	ITEM	POST. REF.	CREDIT
				19-- Mar. 31		CR1	4 6 2 9 30
				Apr. 30		CR2	8 1 1 7 50
				May 31		CR3	6 0 5 8 75

c) Record the information shown in the list of duplicate invoices on page 612 for the month of June in the Cash Receipts Journal just the way invoices #154 and #155 were recorded in the Cash Receipts Journal which you opened in Part a).

d) Pencil foot all money columns in the Cash Receipts Journal.

e) Verify pencil footings by seeing if the total debits equal the total credits. In addition, see if the totals of the Total Receipts and Bank Deposits columns agree.

f) Ink in totals and rule the journal.

g) Post the totals to their respective accounts. Be sure to indicate the postmarks in the journal and in the ledger.

h) Pencil foot the accounts.

Invoice Number	Date	Received From	Income from Labor	Income from Parts	Income from Sale of Motorcycles
156	9	W. Mittel	$ 56.00	$ 91.73	
157	10	Y. Sydna			$ 832.75
	10	Deposited $980.48 (Enter in Bank Deposits column)			
158	11	J. Veloze	103.00	156.32	
159	12	K. Harris			1,420.00
	12	Deposited $1,679.32			
160	17	B. Luga	49.00	87.64	
161	18	A. Gannon			1,740.25
	18	Deposited $1,876.89			
162	23	L. Cooper	72.00	125.15	
163	24	C. Boseck	87.00	113.90	
164	25	F. Ellis			1,290.80
	25	Deposited $1,688.85			
165	30	T. Marra			1,574.60
	30	Deposited $1,574.60			

Copy and solve the following problems:

	(1)	(2)

Practicing
Related
Arithmetic

(1)

$5,108.26
3,245.71
871.92
2,050.38
1,702.05
467.13
+6,389.27
$ _____

(2)

Crossfoot and then add down:

a) 25 + 35 + 60 + 15 =
b) 43 + 22 + 73 + 90 =
c) 14 + 56 + 24 + 42 =
d) 58 + 78 + 38 + 28 =
e) 39 + 19 + 59 + 69 = ___
f) ___ + ___ + ___ + ___ = ___

AIMS

1. To learn how to post from the Cash Payments Journal to the Cash account.

2. To learn how to post to expense accounts in the General Ledger.

EXPLANATION

In Jobs 95 and 96 you learned how to post from the Cash Receipts Journal to the Cash account and to various income accounts in the General Ledger. The illustration on the next page reviews the postings made from the Cash Receipts Journal to the General Ledger of Bruce West for the month of January as shown in Job 95.

Notice that all cash received was posted to the *debit* side of the Cash account and that the income amounts were posted to the *credit* side of the income accounts.

If you were keeping the records for Mr. West, you would record not only the cash he receives but also the cash he pays out. In addition, just as Mr. West needed to know the total amount of *income* he received, he would need to know the total amounts he spent for different types of business *expenses*. He could then compare his income with his expenses to determine whether he was making a profit, just as you learned to do this in Jobs 86 and 87.

CASH RECEIPTS JOURNAL   PAGE 1

INV. NO.	DATE	RECEIVED FROM	POST. REF.	INCOME, CR. LABOR	INCOME, CR. PARTS	TOTAL RECEIPTS, DR.	BANK DEPOSITS
1	Jan. 6	D. Kruz	✓	100 00		100 00	
2	9	M. Leaf	✓	120 00	90 00	210 00	310 00
3	17	L.S.Y. Co.	✓	80 00	170 00	250 00	
4	20	A. Dune	✓	60 00	130 00	190 00	440 00
5	29	M & Z Co.	✓	240 00	310 00	550 00	550 00
				600 00	700 00	1300 00	1300 00
				(2)	(3)	(1)	(✓)

ACCOUNT Cash   PAGE 1

DATE	ITEM	POST. REF.	DEBIT	DATE	ITEM	POST. REF.	CREDIT
Jan. 31		CR1	1300 00				

ACCOUNT Income from Labor   PAGE 2

DATE	ITEM	POST. REF.	DEBIT	DATE	ITEM	POST. REF.	CREDIT
				Jan. 31		CR1	600 00

ACCOUNT Income from Parts   PAGE 3

DATE	ITEM	POST. REF.	DEBIT	DATE	ITEM	POST. REF.	CREDIT
				Jan. 31		CR1	700 00

Illustration 97a — Review of Cash Receipts Journal and General Ledger

SAMPLE PROBLEM

Look at Illustration 97b below. It is a record of the cash *paid out* by Bruce West for the month of January.

CASH PAYMENTS JOURNAL   PAGE 1

CHECK NO.	DATE	PAID TO	FOR	POST. REF.	AMOUNT OF CHECK, CR.	PARTS & SUPPLIES, DR.	OTHER ITEMS, DR. ITEM	OTHER ITEMS, DR. AMOUNT
1	Jan. 3	Foley Co.	parts	✓	250 00	250 00		
2	6	Paris Realty Co.	store rent		400 00		Rent	400 00
3	10	B.S.E. Co.	stationery		30 00		Office Expenses	30 00
4	23	Worth Co.	supplies	✓	100 00	100 00		
5	28	A. Kane Co	stationery		20 00		Office Expenses	20 00
					800 00	350 00		450 00

Illustration 97b — Cash Payments Journal

In the same way that you posted from the Cash *Receipts* Journal to the General Ledger, you will post from the Cash *Payments* Journal to the General Ledger. Illustration 97c, on the next page, shows how Mr. West's Cash Payments Journal and General Ledger would appear at the end of January.

Compare the General Ledger in Illustration 97c with the General Ledger in Illustration 97a and you will see several differences.

1. The Cash account contains a *credit* posting of $800.00.
2. Three new accounts have been added to the ledger:
   a) The Parts and Supplies account (Page 4) with a *debit* posting of $350.00.
   b) The Rent account (Page 5) with a *debit* posting of $400.00.
   c) The Office Expenses account (Page 6) with *debit* postings of $30.00 and $20.00.

The circled postmark "1" shown in the Cash Payments Journal below the Amount of Check column shows that the *total* of $800.00 was posted from the Cash Payments Journal to the Cash account, page 1, in the General Ledger. In Job 95 you learned that cash *receipts* were posted to the *debit* side of the Cash account. Cash payments are the opposite of cash receipts and for this reason the $800.00 representing the total cash *payments* for January was posted to the opposite side of the Cash account which as you know is called the *credit* side of the Cash account. The total amount of *cash received* is always posted to the *debit* side of the Cash account and the total amount of *cash paid out* is always posted to the *credit* side of the Cash account.

Cash Account	
Debit	**Credit**
Cash Received	Cash Paid Out

Now look at the Cash account in the General Ledger. You will see that $800.00 has been posted to the credit side of the account. The date is January 31 because posting is done at the end of the month after the columns in the Cash Payments Journal have been totaled. The postmark "CP 1" shows that the $800.00 was posted from *page 1* of the Cash Payments Journal. The postmark "CP" is the abbreviation for Cash Payments.

The amount of cash received for the month of January is recorded on the debit side of the Cash account and the amount of cash paid out for the month of January is recorded on the credit side of the Cash account. To find the cash balance at the end of the month, subtract the credit total from the debit total:

Total debits in the Cash account (Cash Received)	$1,300.00
− Total credits in the Cash account (Cash Paid Out)	800.00
= Balance of Cash on January 31	$ 500.00

CASH PAYMENTS JOURNAL

PAGE 1

CHECK NO.	DATE	PAID TO	FOR	POST. REF.	AMOUNT OF CHECK, CR.	PARTS & SUPPLIES, DR.	OTHER ITEMS, DR. ITEM	AMOUNT
1	Jan. 3	Foley Co.	parts	✓	250 00	250 00		
2	6	Paris Realty Co.	store rent	5	400 00		Rent	400 00
3	10	B & E Co.	stationery	6	30 00		Office Expenses	30 00
4	23	Worth Co.	supplies	✓	100 00	100 00		
5	28	A. Kane Co.	stationery	6	20 00		Office Expenses	20 00
					800 00	350 00		450 00
					800 00	350 00		450 00
					①	④		✓

GENERAL LEDGER

ACCOUNT Cash — PAGE 1

DATE	ITEM	POST. REF.	DEBIT	DATE	ITEM	POST. REF.	CREDIT
Jan. 31		CR1	1300 00	Jan. 31		CP1	800 00

The balance of the Cash account is found by subtracting the total credits from the total debits.

ACCOUNT Income from Labor — PAGE 2

DATE	ITEM	POST. REF.	DEBIT	DATE	ITEM	POST. REF.	CREDIT
				Jan. 31		CR1	600 00

ACCOUNT Income from Parts — PAGE 3

DATE	ITEM	POST. REF.	DEBIT	DATE	ITEM	POST. REF.	CREDIT
				Jan. 31		CR1	700 00

ACCOUNT Parts and Supplies — PAGE 4

DATE	ITEM	POST. REF.	DEBIT	DATE	ITEM	POST. REF.	CREDIT
Jan. 31		CP1	350 00				

ACCOUNT Rent — PAGE 5

DATE	ITEM	POST. REF.	DEBIT	DATE	ITEM	POST. REF.	CREDIT
Jan. 6		CP1	400 00				

ACCOUNT Office Expenses — PAGE 6

DATE	ITEM	POST. REF.	DEBIT	DATE	ITEM	POST. REF.	CREDIT
Jan. 10		CP1	30 00				
28		CP1	20 00				

Illustration 97c — Cash Payments Journal and General Ledger

The circled postmark "4" shown in the Cash Payments Journal under the Parts & Supplies column shows that the total of $350.00 was posted to the Parts and Supplies account, *page 4* in the General Ledger.

Look at the Parts and Supplies account in the General Ledger and you will see that the total of $350.00 has been posted to the debit side of this account. Again, the date January 31 and the postmark "CP1" have been entered to show that the $350.00 was posted from the first page of the Cash Payments Journal at the end of the month.

On January 6 the Cash Payments Journal shows a payment for rent of $400.00 entered in the Other Items column. In the same way, the payments for office expenses of $30.00 and $20.00 on January 10 and January 28 were entered in the Other Items column. In earlier jobs you learned that the Other Items column is used whenever a separate column has not been provided for a particular type of payment. Separate columns are usually provided only for items which occur frequently during the month.

The $450.00 total of Other Items column is made up of three amounts:

Rent	$400.00
Office Expenses	30.00
Office Expenses	20.00
Total	$450.00

The $400.00 was posted separately to the Rent account and the $30.00 and $20.00 were posted separately to the Office Expenses account in the General Ledger. (You will notice that the names of the accounts to which the items were posted were written in the Other Items column along with the amounts.) By posting these amounts to separate accounts, at any time during the year Mr. West can find the total amount spent for rent and the total amount spent for office expenses. He can do this merely by pencil footing the Rent account and the Office Expenses account in the General Ledger.

Daily postings are made of amounts from the "Other Items, Dr." column. Monthly postings are made of totals from the columns with special headings.

In the transaction of January 6 in the Cash Payments Journal (Illustration 97c) you will see postmark "5" in the Posting Reference column to show that the $400.00 in the Other Items column was posted to the Rent account on *page 5* of the General Ledger. This amount was posted separately on January 6, and that is why this date is shown in the Rent account in the General Ledger. Of course, the postmark "CP1" in the Rent account shows that the $400.00 was posted from *page 1* of the Cash Payments Journal.

In the same way the payments of $30.00 and $20.00 for Office Expenses entered in the Cash Payments Journal on January 10 and January 28 were posted to the Office Expenses account on page 6 in the General Ledger. Notice the postmark "6" in the Cash Payments Journal for both of these entries. In the Office Expenses account, the dates January 10 and January 28 show that the postings were made on these days.

It is important to understand that all amounts shown in the Other Items column are posted separately to the ledger account. That is why the two payments shown for Office Expenses in the Other Items column are posted separately to the Office Expenses account in the ledger. Only accounts that have their own special columns in the journal are totaled, and only these *totals* are posted to the ledger as one amount. The separate entries in the special columns are marked with a memorandum "√" in the Posting Reference column, whereas the *total* of each special column is postmarked with the page number of its account in the General Ledger.

Special columns are opened for items that occur frequently

If payments for office expenses began to occur more frequently, you could reduce the number of times required to post to the Office Expenses account during the month by adding another column to the Cash Payments Journal headed "Office Expenses, Dr." All office expenses payments would then be recorded in this column instead of in the Other Items column, and the total of this column would be posted to the Office Expenses account only at the end of the month. In this way only one *total* posting would be made to the Office Expenses account each month.

You can see from the postings made from the Cash Payments Journal that the total cash paid out ($800.00) was posted to the *credit* side of the Cash account, while the postings to the various expense accounts were made to the *debit* side of these accounts.

When you compare the *debits* of $350.00, $400.00, $30.00 and $20.00 posted to the expense accounts with the *credit* of $800.00 posted to the Cash account, you will see that the *total debits equal the total credits*.

Postings from Cash Payments Journal			
Debits		**Credits**	
Parts & Supplies	$350.00	Cash	$800.00
Rent	400.00		
Office Expenses	30.00		
Office Expenses	20.00		
Total Debits	$800.00 =	Total Credits	$800.00

It is important to remember that expenses are always posted to the debit side of the various expense accounts and that the total cash payments is always posted to the credit side of the Cash account.

To help you remember that cash payments should be posted to the credit side of the cash account, the abbreviation "Cr." (for the word "credit") is included in the heading of the Amount of Check column in the Cash Payments Journal. In the same way, the headings of the Parts & Supplies column and the Other Items column in the Cash Payments Journal include the abbreviation "Dr." to show that these amounts are posted to the debit side of the expense accounts in the ledger.

As you know, a check mark shown in a journal indicates that no posting is to be made at that time. The check mark shown in the Posting Reference column of the Cash Payments Journal on January 3 indicates that the $250.00 debit in the Parts & Supplies column should not be posted to the ledger on that day because it will be included in the column's total posted to the Parts and Supplies account at the end of the month. In the same way, and for the same reason, a check mark was recorded in the Posting Reference column on January 23 for the $100.00 debit in the Parts & Supplies column. Remember that the only *numbers* in the Posting Reference column in the journal are the postmarks for the debits in the *Other Items* column, which are posted separately.

The check mark under the total $450.00 of Other Items column shows that this amount is not to be posted to the ledger. Remember that the three amounts, $400.00, $30.00, and $20.00, that make up this total were already posted separately during the month. The $400.00 was posted to the Rent account on January 6 as shown by the postmark "5" in the Posting Reference column. The $30.00 and $20.00 were posted to the Office Expenses account on January 10 and January 28 as shown by the postmark "6" in the Posting Reference column.

A check mark is recorded under a column to show that the total is not to be posted

Here are the steps the record keeper followed in recording the journal entries in the Cash Payments Journal and in posting to the accounts in the General Ledger.

Step 1: Journalize each transaction.

The information on each check stub is recorded in the Cash Payments Journal. Look at the Cash Payments Journal shown in Illustration 97c and you will see the check number, date, the name of the party to whom the check was issued, and a brief explanation of the reason for the payment. Notice that each amount is entered twice. On January 3, for example, the $250.00 is entered first in the Amount of Check column to show the amount paid out, and it is entered a second time in the Parts & Supplies column to show the amount has been paid for parts and supplies expenses. On January 6, the Other Items column is used because a separate column is not provided for payments of rent. Notice that the name of the account (Rent) is written in the Other Items column to show the ledger account to which this amount will be posted. A similar entry is made on January 10 for the payment of $30.00 for office expenses and again on January 28 for the payment of $20.00.

Step 2: Record necessary check marks.

On January 3 and January 23, check marks are made in the Posting Reference column to show that the amounts in the Parts & Supplies column are not to be posted at this time, because they will be posted at the end of the month in the total amount.

Step 3: Complete daily postings.

On January 6, the $400.00 that was recorded in the Other Items column is posted to the Rent account in the ledger. The postmark "5" is recorded in the

Posting Reference column of the journal, and the postmark "CP1" is recorded in the Rent account of the ledger. The Office Expenses account is posted in a similar manner on January 10 and January 28.

Step 4: Pencil-foot the Cash Payments Journal.

On the last day of the month, the columns in the Cash Payments Journal are pencil footed and the total debits compared with the total credits to see if they agree:

Total debits =
Total credits

Parts & Supplies, Dr.		Other Items, Dr.		Amount of Check, Cr.
$350.00	+	$450.00	=	$800.00

Since the total debits equal the total credits, the record keeper can feel sure that the columns have been added correctly. If they do not agree, it is necessary to re-check the addition and then re-check the entries to make certain that the same amount has been entered twice on each date.

Step 5: Enter total in ink and rule columns.

Since the debits and credits agreed when the columns were pencil footed, the totals are written in ink and the columns are ruled as shown in Illustration 97c.

Step 6: Complete end-of-month postings.

At the end of the month, the total of the Amount of Check column is posted to the credit side of the Cash account and the total of the Parts & Supplies column is posted to the debit side of the Parts and Supplies account. The postmarks under the totals of the Amount of Check column and the Parts & Supplies column show the page numbers in the General Ledger to which these totals have been posted. The postmark "CP 1" is recorded in the ledger account.

The check mark under the total of the Other Items column is recorded to show that the $450.00 is not to be posted at the end of the month, because the items in this column have been posted separately.

PRACTICE PROBLEMS

Problem 1

You are acting as the record keeper for Bruce West, who is in the commercial refrigeration business.

Directions:
a) Copy the Cash Payments Journal for the month of February, 19— on page 621.

CASH PAYMENTS JOURNAL   PAGE 2

CHECK NO.	DATE		PAID TO	FOR	POST. REF.	AMOUNT OF CHECK, CR.	PARTS & SUPPLIES DR.	OTHER ITEMS, DR.	
								ITEM	AMOUNT
6	feb	4	Foley Co.	parts	✓	525 00	525 00		
7		5	B & E Co.	office supplies		19 75		Office Expenses	19 75
8		7	Paris Realty Co.	store rent		400 00		Rent	400 00
9		20	Worth Co.	supplies	✓	240 00	240 00		
10		27	A. Kane Co.	office supplies		15 25		Office Expenses	15 25

b) Copy the General Ledger accounts below and on page 622. Include the amounts that have already been posted. Allow 6 lines for each account.

GENERAL LEDGER

ACCOUNT *Cash*   PAGE 1

DATE	ITEM	POST. REF.	DEBIT	DATE	ITEM	POST. REF.	CREDIT
19-- Jan. 31		CR1	1300 00	19-- Jan. 31		CP1	800 00
Feb. 28		CR2	1900 00				

ACCOUNT *Income from Labor*   PAGE 2

DATE	ITEM	POST. REF.	DEBIT	DATE	ITEM	POST. REF.	CREDIT
				19-- Jan. 31		CR1	600 00
				Feb. 28		CR2	1000 00

ACCOUNT *Income from Parts*   PAGE 3

DATE	ITEM	POST. REF.	DEBIT	DATE	ITEM	POST. REF.	CREDIT
				19-- Jan. 31		CR1	700 00
				Feb. 28		CR2	900 00

ACCOUNT *Parts and Supplies*   PAGE 4

DATE	ITEM	POST. REF.	DEBIT	DATE	ITEM	POST. REF.	CREDIT
19-- Jan. 31		CP1	350 00				

ACCOUNT *Rent*   PAGE 5

DATE	ITEM	POST. REF.	DEBIT	DATE	ITEM	POST. REF.	CREDIT
19-- Jan. 6		CP1	400 00				

ACCOUNT *Office Expenses*   PAGE *6*

DATE	ITEM	POST. REF.	DEBIT	DATE	ITEM	POST. REF.	CREDIT
19-- Jan. 10		CP1	30 00				
28		CP1	20 00				

c) Complete the daily postings by posting each item shown in the Other Items column of the journal. Be sure to record the necessary postmarks in the Posting Reference column of the Cash Payments Journal and in the General Ledger.

d) Pencil foot all money columns in the Cash Payments Journal.

e) Verify totals by crossfooting.

f) Ink in totals and rule the journal.

g) Complete the end-of-month postings by posting the totals to their respective accounts. Record the necessary postmarks in the journal and in the ledger. Record a check mark for any total that is not to be posted.

h) Pencil foot the ledger accounts.

Problem 2

You are the record keeper for Harry Gale, a house painter.

Directions: (Use the journal and ledgers shown on page 623.)
a) Copy the Cash Payments Journal for the Month of August, 19--.

b) Copy the General Ledger accounts on page 623. Include the amounts that have already been posted. Allow 6 lines for each account.

c) Complete the daily postings by posting each item shown in the Other Items column of the journal. Be sure to record the necessary postmarks in the Posting Reference column of the Cash Payments Journal and in the General Ledger.

d) Pencil foot all money columns in the Cash Payments Journal.

e) Verify totals by crossfooting.

f) Ink in totals and rule the journal.

g) Complete the end-of-month postings by posting the totals to their respective accounts. Record necessary postmarks in the journal and in the ledger. Record a check mark for any total not to be posted.

h) Pencil foot the ledger accounts.

CASH PAYMENTS JOURNAL   PAGE 3

CHECK NO.	DATE	PAID TO	FOR	POST. REF.	AMOUNT OF CHECK, CR.	PAINT & SUPPLIES, DR.	OTHER ITEMS, DR. ITEM	AMOUNT
21	Aug. 5	H. Carp Co.	paint	✓	307 91	307 91		
22	6	Gale Realty Co.	store rent		225 00		Rent	225 00
23	22	L. Sauer Co.	supplies	✓	84 06	84 00		
24	27	Bay Telephone Co.	for month		73 15		Telephone	73 15
25	29	F. Wyle Co.	paint	✓	261 53	261 53		

GENERAL LEDGER

ACCOUNT Cash   PAGE 1

DATE	ITEM	POST. REF.	DEBIT	DATE	ITEM	POST. REF.	CREDIT
June 30		CR1	1 960 00	June 30		CP1	768 42
July 31		CR2	2 135 00	July 31		CP2	669 33
Aug. 31		CR3	2 450 00				

ACCOUNT Income from Labor   PAGE 2

DATE	ITEM	POST. REF.	DEBIT	DATE	ITEM	POST. REF.	CREDIT
				June 30		CR1	1 960 00
				July 31		CR2	2 135 00
				Aug. 31		CR3	2 450 00

ACCOUNT Paint and Supplies   PAGE 3

DATE	ITEM	POST. REF.	DEBIT	DATE	ITEM	POST. REF.	CREDIT
June 30		CP1	491 82				
July 31		CP2	376 53				

ACCOUNT Rent   PAGE 4

DATE	ITEM	POST. REF.	DEBIT	DATE	ITEM	POST. REF.	CREDIT
June 2		CP1	225 00				
July 3		CP2	225 00				

ACCOUNT Telephone   PAGE 5

DATE	ITEM	POST. REF.	DEBIT	DATE	ITEM	POST. REF.	CREDIT
June 20		CP1	51 60				
July 25		CP2	67 80				

Problem 3

You are the record keeper for Lou Riggs, who repairs office machines.

Directions:

a) Copy the Cash Payments Journal for the month of April, 19—:

CASH PAYMENTS JOURNAL
PAGE 4

CHECK NO.	DATE	PAID TO	FOR	POST. REF.	AMOUNT OF CHECK, CR.	PARTS & SUPPLIES DR.	OTHER ITEMS, DR. ITEM	OTHER ITEMS, DR. AMOUNT
99	Apr. 3	A. Philips Co.	parts	✓	1 5 6 72	1 5 6 72		
100	4	Fine Realty Co.	month		2 8 5 00		Rent	2 8 5 00
101	11	E & J Co.	supplies	✓	1 0 2 93	1 0 2 93		
102	22	Penn Telephone Co.	month		7 3 45		Telephone	7 3 45
103	30	C. Wayne Co.	parts	✓	4 9 1 64	4 9 1 64		

b) Copy the General Ledger accounts shown below and on page 625. Include the amounts that have already been posted.

c) Complete the daily postings by posting each item shown in the Other Items column of the journal. Be sure to record the necessary postmarks in the Posting Reference column of the Cash Payments Journal and in the General Ledger.

d) Pencil foot all money columns in the Cash Payments Journal.

e) Verify totals by crossfooting.

f) Ink in totals and rule the journal.

g) Complete the end-of-month postings by posting the totals to their respective accounts. Record the necessary postmarks in the journal and in the ledger. Record a check mark for any total that is not to be posted.

h) Pencil foot the ledger accounts.

GENERAL LEDGER

ACCOUNT Cash
PAGE 1

DATE	ITEM	POST. REF.	DEBIT	DATE	ITEM	POST. REF.	CREDIT
19-- Jan. 31		CR1	2 40 6 30	19-- Jan. 31		CP1	7 5 2 48
Feb. 28		CR2	1 9 4 7 52	Feb. 28		CP2	1 0 2 9 22
Mar. 31		CR3	2 0 6 3 87	Mar. 31		CP3	8 1 7 01
Apr. 30		CR4	2 1 9 8 45				

ACCOUNT Income from Repairs
PAGE 2

DATE	ITEM	POST. REF.	DEBIT	DATE	ITEM	POST. REF.	CREDIT
				19-- Jan. 31		CR1	2 40 6 30
				Feb. 28		CR2	1 9 4 7 52
				Mar. 31		CR3	2 0 6 3 87
				Apr. 30		CR4	2 1 9 8 45

ACCOUNT *Parts and Supplies*   PAGE   3

DATE	ITEM	POST. REF.	DEBIT	DATE	ITEM	POST. REF.	CREDIT
19-- Jan. 31		CP1	402 18				
Feb. 28		CP2	673 97				
Mar. 31		CP3	485 31				

ACCOUNT *Rent*   PAGE   4

DATE	ITEM	POST. REF.	DEBIT	DATE	ITEM	POST. REF.	CREDIT
19-- Jan. 7		CP1	285 00				
Feb. 5		CP2	285 00				
Mar. 6		CP3	285 00				

ACCOUNT *Telephone*   PAGE   5

DATE	ITEM	POST. REF.	DEBIT	DATE	ITEM	POST. REF.	CREDIT
19-- Jan. 20		CP1	65 30				
Feb. 25		CP2	70 25				
Mar. 21		CP3	46 70				

Problem 4

You are the record keeper for the Jean Slater Employment Agency.

Directions: (Use the journal and ledgers on page 626.)

a) Copy the Cash Payments Journal for the month of July, 19—.

b) Copy the General Ledger accounts. Include the amounts that have already been posted. Allow 6 lines for each account.

c) Complete the daily postings by posting each item shown in the Other Items columns of the journal. Be sure to record the necessary postmarks in the Posting Reference column of the Cash Payments Journal and in the General Ledger.

d) Pencil foot all money columns in the Cash Payments Journal.

e) Verify totals by crossfooting.

f) Ink in totals and rule the journal.

g) Complete the end-of-month postings by posting the totals to their respective accounts. Record the necessary postmarks in the journal and in the ledger. Record a check mark for any total that is not to be posted.

h) Pencil foot the ledger accounts.

CASH PAYMENTS JOURNAL   PAGE 4

CHECK NO.	DATE	PAID TO	FOR	POST. REF.	AMOUNT OF CHECK CR.	ADVERTISING, DR.	OTHER ITEMS, DR. ITEM	AMOUNT
117	July 1	Lyle Co.	advertising	✓	1 85 50	1 85 50		
118	7	D&N Realty Co.	office rent		6 00 00		Rent	6 00 00
119	15	F. Jason Co.	advertising	✓	2 79 25	2 79 25		
120	28	RY Telephone Co.	month		1 05 60		Telephone	1 05 60
121	29	R. Manor Co.	advertising	✓	1 12 10	1 12 10		

GENERAL LEDGER

ACCOUNT Cash   PAGE 1

DATE	ITEM	POST. REF.	DEBIT	DATE	ITEM	POST. REF.	CREDIT
Apr. 30		CR1	3 10 8 50	Apr. 30		CP1	1 3 16 45
May 31		CR2	3 6 27 00	May 31		CP2	1 1 54 80
June 30		CR3	2 5 45 75	June 30		CP3	1 4 47 30
July 31		CR4	3 7 10 25				

ACCOUNT Income from Fees   PAGE 2

DATE	ITEM	POST. REF.	DEBIT	DATE	ITEM	POST. REF.	CREDIT
				Apr. 30		CR1	3 10 8 50
				May 31		CR2	3 6 27 00
				June 30		CR3	2 5 45 75
				July 31		CR4	3 7 10 25

ACCOUNT Advertising   PAGE 3

DATE	ITEM	POST. REF.	DEBIT	DATE	ITEM	POST. REF.	CREDIT
Apr. 30		CP1	6 04 30				
May 31		CP2	4 58 25				
June 30		CP3	7 23 40				

ACCOUNT Rent   PAGE 4

DATE	ITEM	POST. REF.	DEBIT	DATE	ITEM	POST. REF.	CREDIT
Apr. 3		CP1	6 00 00				
May 6		CP2	6 00 00				
June 2		CP3	6 00 00				

ACCOUNT Telephone   PAGE 5

DATE	ITEM	POST. REF.	DEBIT	DATE	ITEM	POST. REF.	CREDIT
Apr. 25		CP1	1 12 15				
May 26		CP2	9 65 5				
June 24		CP3	1 23 90				

JOB 98 | USING A CASH PAYMENTS JOURNAL AND A GENERAL LEDGER

Practicing Related Arithmetic

Copy and solve the following problems:

(1)

$ 128.39
2,816.81
3,405.58
781.90
5,060.02
1,257.65
+4,393.76

$ _____

(2)

Crossfoot and then add down:

a) 31 + 54 + 61 + 24 =
b) 27 + 33 + 47 + 13 =
c) 75 + 42 + 80 + 62 =
d) 16 + 65 + 25 + 56 =
e) 82 + 58 + 33 + 85 = ___
f) ___ + ___ + ___ + ___ = ___

AIMS

1. To practice recording payments for personal use into the Cash Payments Journal.

2. To practice posting to the General Ledger.

EXPLANATION

In Job 91 you learned that self-employed businesspeople withdraw a certain amount of money from their business each week to pay for their personal living expenses. They usually do this by writing checks to themselves and cashing them. In addition, they may occasionally issue a business check directly for certain personal expenses.

The careful businessperson knows that no more money should be drawn from the business than has been made in profit. For this reason, the business records must permit the businessperson to compare the total amount withdrawn for personal use with the net income of the business. To show the total amount withdrawn for personal use, a separate account is used in the General Ledger. The account used is called the owner's "drawing account." If the owner's name were Peter Lopez, the account would be called *Peter Lopez, Drawing*.

You have learned that it is a good practice to add an additional column to the Cash Payments Journal for any payment that occurs frequently. Since payments for the owner's personal use do occur frequently, most Cash Payments Journals will contain a separate column in which to record this type of payment.

A separate column for the owner's "drawing account"

SAMPLE PROBLEM

Peter Lopez, a doctor, deposits all his receipts in the bank and makes all payments by check.

He opened his office on May 1, and at the end of the month, his checkbook contains the following stubs:

Check #	To	For	Date	Amount
1	C. Doyle Co.	Medical supplies	May 5	$400.00
2	Wolfe Realty Co.	Office rent	May 6	650.00
3	Cash	Personal use	May 9	350.00
4	J & L Realty Co.	Personal home rent	May 12	375.00
5	M. King Co.	Medical supplies	May 27	125.00
6	Alpine Telephone Co.	Office telephone	May 28	60.00
7	Alpine Telephone Co.	Home telephone	May 29	40.00

Here is how these check stubs would be recorded in Mr. Lopez's Cash Payments Journal:

CASH PAYMENTS JOURNAL   **PAGE 1**

CHECK NO.	DATE	PAID TO	FOR	POST. REF.	AMOUNT OF CHECK, CR.	P. LOPEZ, DRAWING, DR.	MEDICAL SUPPLIES, DR.	OTHER ITEMS, DR. ITEM	OTHER ITEMS, DR. AMOUNT
1	May 5	C. Doyle Co.	medical supplies	✓	400 00		400 00		
2	6	Wolfe Realty Co.	office rent		650 00			Rent	650 00
3	9	Cash	personal use	✓	350 00	350 00			
4	12	J & L Realty Co.	personal home rent	✓	375 00	375 00			
5	27	M. King Co.	medical supplies	✓	125 00		125 00		
6	28	Alpine Telephone Co.	office telephone		60 00			Telephone	60 00
7	29	Alpine Telephone Co.	home telephone	✓	40 00	40 00			

Notice that there is a separate column headed *P. Lopez, Drawing* for recording all payments for personal use.

Record all payments for personal items in the special column "Drawing, Dr."

Compare the stub for check #6 with the stub for check #7. Both checks were issued to the Alpine Telephone Co. to pay monthly telephone bills. However, check #6 was issued to pay the *business* telephone bill while check #7 was issued to pay Dr. Lopez's *home* telephone bill. Check #7 therefore represents a payment for *personal use*. Check #6 for $60.00 was entered in the Other Items column (telephone account) as a *business expense*. Check #7 for $40.00 was listed in the P. Lopez, Drawing column as a personal payment.

On the next page, Dr. Lopez's Cash Payments Journal and General Ledger are shown on May 31 after all postings had been completed.

(Dr. Lopez's Cash Receipts Journal is not shown. However, the postings from this journal are included in the General Ledger.)

CASH PAYMENTS JOURNAL PAGE 1

CHECK NO.	DATE	PAID TO	FOR	POST. REF.	AMOUNT OF CHECK CR.	P. LOPEZ, DRAWING, DR.	MEDICAL SUPPLIES, DR.	OTHER ITEMS, DR. ITEM	AMOUNT
1	May 5	C. Doyle Co.	medical supplies	✓	400 00		400 00		
2	6	Wolfe Realty Co.	office rent	5	650 00			Rent	650 00
3	9	Cash	personal use	✓	350 00	350 00			
4	12	J & L Realty Co	personal home rent	✓	375 00	375 00			
5	27	M. King Co.	medical supplies	✓	125 00		125 00		
6	28	Alpine Telephone Co.	office telephone	6	60 00			Telephone	60 00
7	29	Alpine Telephone Co.	home telephone	✓	40 00	40 00			
					2000 00	765 00	525 00		710 00
					2000 00	765 00	525 00		710 00
					①	③	④		✓

GENERAL LEDGER

ACCOUNT Cash — PAGE 1

DATE	ITEM	POST. REF.	DEBIT	DATE	ITEM	POST. REF.	CREDIT
May 31		CR1	3500 00	May 31		CP1	2000 00

ACCOUNT Income from Fees — PAGE 2

DATE	ITEM	POST. REF.	DEBIT	DATE	ITEM	POST. REF.	CREDIT
				May 31		CR1	3500 00

ACCOUNT Peter Lopez, Drawing — PAGE 3

DATE	ITEM	POST. REF.	DEBIT	DATE	ITEM	POST. REF.	CREDIT
May 31		CP1	765 00				

ACCOUNT Medical Supplies — PAGE 4

DATE	ITEM	POST. REF.	DEBIT	DATE	ITEM	POST. REF.	CREDIT
May 31		CP1	525 00				

ACCOUNT Rent — PAGE 5

DATE	ITEM	POST. REF.	DEBIT	DATE	ITEM	POST. REF.	CREDIT
May 6		CP1	650 00				

ACCOUNT Telephone — PAGE 6

DATE	ITEM	POST. REF.	DEBIT	DATE	ITEM	POST. REF.	CREDIT
May 28		CP1	60 00				

PRACTICE PROBLEMS

Problem 1

You are employed by Dr. Peter Lopez who opened his office on May 1.

Directions:

a) Open a Cash Payments Journal with the headings shown:

CASH PAYMENTS JOURNAL   PAGE 2

CHECK NO.	DATE	PAID TO	FOR	POST. REF.	AMOUNT OF CHECK, CR.	P. LOPEZ, DRAWING, DR.	MEDICAL SUPPLIES, DR.	OTHER ITEMS, DR.	
								ITEM	AMOUNT

b) Copy the General Ledger accounts below and on page 631. Include the amounts that have already been posted. Allow six lines for each account.

GENERAL LEDGER

ACCOUNT Cash   PAGE 1

DATE	ITEM	POST. REF.	DEBIT	DATE	ITEM	POST. REF.	CREDIT
May 19-- 31		CR1	3500 00	May 19-- 31		CP1	200 00
June 30		CR2	3175 00				

ACCOUNT Income from Fees   PAGE 2

DATE	ITEM	POST. REF.	DEBIT	DATE	ITEM	POST. REF.	CREDIT
				May 19-- 31		CR1	3500 00
				June 30		CR2	3175 00

ACCOUNT Peter Lopez, Drawing   PAGE 3

DATE	ITEM	POST. REF.	DEBIT	DATE	ITEM	POST. REF.	CREDIT
May 19-- 31		CP1	765 00				

ACCOUNT Medical Supplies   PAGE 4

DATE	ITEM	POST. REF.	DEBIT	DATE	ITEM	POST. REF.	CREDIT
May 19-- 31		CP1	525 00				

ACCOUNT *Rent*   PAGE 5

DATE	ITEM	POST. REF.	DEBIT	DATE	ITEM	POST. REF.	CREDIT
19-- May 6		CPI	650 00				

ACCOUNT *Telephone*   PAGE 6

DATE	ITEM	POST. REF.	DEBIT	DATE	ITEM	POST. REF.	CREDIT
19-- May 28		CPI	60 00				

c) Enter the information shown in the list of check stubs below into the Cash Payments Journal. Record a check mark in the Posting Reference column for all items that are not to be posted at the end of the day.

Check #	To	For	Date	Amount
8	Cash	Personal use	June 2	$500.00
9	Wolfe Realty Co.	Office rent	June 5	650.00
10	C. Doyle Co.	Medical supplies	June 11	265.50
11	J & L Realty Co.	Personal home rent	June 13	375.00
12	Alpine Telephone Co.	Office telephone	June 24	73.95
13	Alpine Telephone Co.	Home telephone	June 27	51.75

d) Complete the daily postings of all items recorded in the Other Items column of the journal. Record the necessary postmarks in the journal and in the ledger.

e) Pencil foot all money columns in the Cash Payments Journal.

f) Verify totals by crossfooting.

g) Ink in totals and rule the journal.

h) Complete the end-of-month postings of the totals. Record all postmarks and record a check mark for any total that is not to be posted.

i) Pencil foot the ledger accounts.

Problem 2

You are employed in the office of Lewis Hodge, an investment counselor, who has been in business since February 1, 19--.

Directions:
a) Open a Cash Payments Journal with the headings shown on the next page.

CASH PAYMENTS JOURNAL   PAGE 3

CHECK NO.	DATE	PAID TO	FOR	POST. REF.	AMOUNT OF CHECK, CR.	L. HODGE, DRAWING, DR.	OFFICE EXPENSES, DR.	OTHER ITEMS, DR.	
								ITEM	AMOUNT

b) Copy the General Ledger accounts shown below and on page 633. Include the amounts that have already been posted. Allow six lines for each account.

GENERAL LEDGER

ACCOUNT *Cash*   PAGE 1

DATE	ITEM	POST. REF.	DEBIT	DATE	ITEM	POST. REF.	CREDIT
19-- Feb. 28		CR1	3982 25	19-- Feb. 28		CP1	2207 42
Mar. 31		CR2	4638 50	Mar. 31		CP2	2361 19
Apr. 30		CR3	3741 60				

ACCOUNT *Income from Fees*   PAGE 2

DATE	ITEM	POST. REF.	DEBIT	DATE	ITEM	POST. REF.	CREDIT
				19-- Feb. 28		CR1	3982 25
				Mar. 31		CR2	4638 50
				Apr. 30		CR3	3741 60

ACCOUNT *Lewis Hodge, Drawing*   PAGE 3

DATE	ITEM	POST. REF.	DEBIT	DATE	ITEM	POST. REF.	CREDIT
19-- Feb. 28		CP1	1209 15				
Mar. 31		CP2	1453 40				

ACCOUNT *Office Expenses*   PAGE 4

DATE	ITEM	POST. REF.	DEBIT	DATE	ITEM	POST. REF.	CREDIT
19-- Feb. 28		CP1	316 87				
Mar. 31		CP2	270 24				

ACCOUNT *Rent*   PAGE 5

DATE	ITEM	POST. REF.	DEBIT	DATE	ITEM	POST. REF.	CREDIT
19-- Feb. 5		CP1	545 00				
Mar. 6		CP2	545 00				

ACCOUNT *Telephone*   PAGE 6

DATE	ITEM	POST. REF.	DEBIT	DATE	ITEM	POST. REF.	CREDIT
19-- Feb. 26		CP1	136 40				
Mar. 25		CP2	92 55				

c) Record the information shown in the list of check stubs below into the Cash Payments Journal. Record a check mark for all items that are not to be posted at the end of the day.

Check #	To	For	Date	Amount
71	A & T Co.	Office supplies	April 1	$106.38
72	Judge Realty Co.	Office rent	April 4	545.00
73	Pearl Realty Co.	Home rent	April 8	430.00
74	Reno Telephone Co.	Home phone	April 17	43.80
75	F & G Co.	Office supplies	April 21	97.12
76	Bule Co.	Personal clothing	April 25	135.75
77	Reno Telephone Co.	Office phone	April 28	86.15
78	Cash	Personal use	April 29	560.00

d) Complete the daily postings of all items recorded in the Other Items column of the journal. Record the necessary postmarks in the journal and in the ledger.

e) Pencil foot all money columns in the Cash Payments Journal.

f) Verify totals by crossfooting.

g) Ink in totals and rule the journal.

h) Complete the end-of-month postings of the totals. Record all postmarks and record a check mark for any total that is not to be posted.

i) Pencil foot the ledger accounts.

Problem 3

You are employed in the office of Gloria Silver, an insurance broker, who has been in business since September 1, 19--.

Directions:

a) Open a Cash Payments Journal with the headings shown in the illustration on page 634.

CASH PAYMENTS JOURNAL
PAGE 4

CHECK NO.	DATE	PAID TO	FOR	POST. REF.	AMOUNT OF CHECK, CR.	G. SILVER, DRAWING, DR.	OFFICE EXPENSES, DR.	OTHER ITEMS, DR.	
								ITEM	AMOUNT

b) Copy the General Ledger accounts shown below and on page 635. Include the amounts that have already been posted. Allow six lines for each account.

GENERAL LEDGER

ACCOUNT **Cash**   PAGE 1

DATE	ITEM	POST. REF.	DEBIT	DATE	ITEM	POST. REF.	CREDIT
19-- Sept. 30		CR1	4138 45	19-- Sept. 30		CP1	2307 48
Oct. 31		CR2	3673 80	Oct. 31		CP2	2382 97
Nov. 30		CR3	4552 70	Nov. 30		CP3	2116 72
Dec. 31		CR4	3047 90				

ACCOUNT **Income from Premiums**   PAGE 2

DATE	ITEM	POST. REF.	DEBIT	DATE	ITEM	POST. REF.	CREDIT
				19-- Sept. 30		CR1	4138 45
				Oct. 31		CR2	3673 80
				Nov. 30		CR3	4552 70
				Dec. 31		CR4	3047 90

ACCOUNT **Gloria Silver, Drawing**   PAGE 3

DATE	ITEM	POST. REF.	DEBIT	DATE	ITEM	POST. REF.	CREDIT
19-- Sept. 30		CP1	1305 26				
Oct. 31		CP2	1628 49				
Nov. 30		CP3	1213 61				

ACCOUNT **Office Expenses**   PAGE 4

DATE	ITEM	POST. REF.	DEBIT	DATE	ITEM	POST. REF.	CREDIT
19-- Sept. 30		CP1	416 82				
Oct. 31		CP2	185 63				
Nov. 30		CP3	307 06				

ACCOUNT *Rent*   PAGE 5

DATE	ITEM	POST. REF.	DEBIT	DATE	ITEM	POST. REF.	CREDIT
19--							
Sept. 3		CP1	465 00				
Oct. 2		CP2	465 00				
Nov. 6		CP3	465 00				

ACCOUNT *Telephone*   PAGE 6

DATE	ITEM	POST. REF.	DEBIT	DATE	ITEM	POST. REF.	CREDIT
19--							
Sept. 29		CP1	1 20 40				
Oct. 23		CP2	1 03 85				
Nov. 25		CP3	1 31 05				

c) Record the information shown on the check stubs below into the Cash Payments Journal. Record a check mark for all items that are not to be posted at the end of the day.

Check #	To	For	Date	Amount
108	Cash	Personal use	Dec. 3	$600.00
109	M. C. Realty Co.	Office rent	Dec. 5	465.00
110	P. Lillo Co.	Office supplies	Dec. 9	156.14
111	N. J. Electric Co.	Home electricity	Dec. 12	40.35
112	N. J. Telephone Co.	Home phone	Dec. 15	39.20
113	D & I Co.	Office supplies	Dec. 19	85.31
114	N. J. Telephone Co.	Office phone	Dec. 24	114.70
115	King Furniture Co.	Home furniture	Dec. 31	312.83

d) Complete the daily postings of all items recorded in the Other Items column of the journal. Record the necessary postmarks in the journal and in the ledger.

e) Pencil foot all money columns in the Cash Payments Journal.

f) Verify totals by crossfooting.

g) Ink in totals and rule the journal.

h) Complete the end-of-month postings of the totals. Record all postmarks and record a check mark for any total that is not to be posted.

i) Pencil foot the ledger accounts.

Problem 4

You are employed in the office of Dennis Halse, an architect, who has been in business since May 1, 19--.

Directions:

a) Open a Cash Payments Journal with the headings shown on page 636.

CASH PAYMENTS JOURNAL

PAGE 4

CHECK NO.	DATE	PAID TO	FOR	POST. REF.	AMOUNT OF CHECK, CR.	D. HALSE, DRAWING, DR.	SUPPLIES, DR.	OTHER ITEMS, DR.	
								ITEM	AMOUNT

b) Copy the General Ledger accounts shown below and on page 637. Include the amounts that have already been posted. Allow six lines for each account.

GENERAL LEDGER

ACCOUNT Cash   PAGE 1

DATE	ITEM	POST. REF.	DEBIT	DATE	ITEM	POST. REF.	CREDIT
19-- May 31		CR1	5 1 9 0 75	19-- May 31		CP1	2 9 7 6 62
June 30		CR2	4 2 8 3 00	June 30		CP2	3 3 2 3 25
July 31		CR3	6 0 2 8 25	July 31		CP3	2 8 1 0 59
Aug. 31		CR4	3 7 4 0 00				

ACCOUNT Income from Fees   PAGE 2

DATE	ITEM	POST. REF.	DEBIT	DATE	ITEM	POST. REF.	CREDIT
				19-- May 31		CR1	5 1 9 0 75
				June 30		CR2	4 2 8 3 00
				July 31		CR3	6 0 2 8 25
				Aug. 31		CR4	3 7 4 0 00

ACCOUNT Dennis Halse, Drawing   PAGE 3

DATE	ITEM	POST. REF.	DEBIT	DATE	ITEM	POST. REF.	CREDIT
19-- May 31		CP1	1 5 1 7 81				
June 30		CP2	2 0 5 2 46				
July 31		CP3	1 4 6 0 92				

ACCOUNT Supplies   PAGE 4

DATE	ITEM	POST. REF.	DEBIT	DATE	ITEM	POST. REF.	CREDIT
19-- May 31		CP1	7 0 5 16				
June 30		CP2	5 5 3 29				
July 31		CP3	6 1 0 72				

ACCOUNT _Rent_ _____ PAGE _5_

DATE	ITEM	POST. REF.	DEBIT	DATE	ITEM	POST. REF.	CREDIT
May 19-- 1		CP1	575 00				
June 5		CP2	575 00				
July 2		CP3	575 00				

ACCOUNT _Telephone_ _____ PAGE _6_

DATE	ITEM	POST. REF.	DEBIT	DATE	ITEM	POST. REF.	CREDIT
May 19-- 16		CP1	178 65				
June 17		CP2	142 50				
July 15		CP3	163 95				

c) Record the information shown on the check stubs below into the Cash Payments Journal. Record a check mark for all items that are not to be posted at the end of the day.

Check #	To	For	Date	Amount
39	Dr. J. Meyers	Medical bill	Aug. 1	$ 65.00
40	H & O Realty Co.	Office rent	Aug. 4	575.00
41	Alese Realty Co.	Home rent	Aug. 7	320.00
42	R. Topp Co.	Supplies	Aug. 14	319.47
43	Arizona Telephone Co.	Office phone	Aug. 18	152.10
44	Cash	Personal use	Aug. 21	700.00
45	L. Cerf Co.	Supplies	Aug. 27	102.34
46	Arizona Electric Co.	Home electricity	Aug. 28	48.25

d) Complete the daily postings of all items recorded in the Other Items column of the journal. Record the necessary postmarks in the journal and in the ledger.

e) Pencil foot all money columns in the Cash Payments Journal.

f) Verify totals by crossfooting.

g) Ink in totals and rule the journal.

h) Complete the end-of-month postings of the totals. Record all postmarks and record a check mark for any total that is not to be posted.

i) Pencil foot the ledger accounts.

Practicing Related Arithmetic

Copy and solve the following problems:

(1)

$1,483.72
659.23
4,176.51
2,040.39
5,201.04
867.40
+3,592.68
$ _____

(2)

Crossfoot and then add down:

a) 50 + 95 + 30 + 75 =
b) 81 + 62 + 43 + 24 =
c) 68 + 24 + 14 + 48 =
d) 15 + 33 + 69 + 51 =
e) 20 + 59 + 86 + 92 = ___
f) ___ + ___ + ___ + ___ = ___

AIM

To practice using the Cash Receipts Journal, the Cash Payments Journal, and the General Ledger.

They balance when— total debits = total credits

EXPLANATION

You have learned that all cash received is first recorded in a Cash Receipts Journal and then posted to ledger accounts. All *cash receipts* are posted to the *debit* side of the Cash account while the *income amounts* are posted to the *credit* side of the income accounts.

You have also learned that all cash paid out is first recorded in a Cash Payments Journal and then posted to ledger accounts. All *cash payments* are posted to the *credit* side of the Cash account while the *expenses amounts* and *payments for personal use* are posted to the *debit* side of their respective accounts.

In each journal the total of the debit columns must equal the total of the credit columns.

In this job you will use the Cash Receipts Journal and the Cash Payments Journal at the same time, posting from both journals to the ledger accounts.

PRACTICE PROBLEMS

Problem 1

You are employed in the office of Mark Strong, who started in the roofing and aluminum siding business on May 1, 19--.

Directions:
a) Copy the Cash Receipts Journal for the month of July, 19—:

CASH RECEIPTS JOURNAL   PAGE 3

INV. NO.	DATE	RECEIVED FROM	POST. REF.	INCOME, CR. ALUMINUM SIDING	INCOME, CR. ROOFING	TOTAL RECEIPTS, DR.	BANK DEPOSITS
90	July 2	A. Jason	✓	1825 00	1740 00	3565 00	3565 00
91	8	S. Poceli	✓		527 25	527 25	
92	9	W. Graves	✓	2987 50	675 00	3662 50	4189 75
93	22	E. Cierta	✓	3108 00		3108 00	3108 00
94	30	M. Umans	✓	1565 25	910 00	2475 25	2475 25

b) Copy the Cash Payments Journal for the month of July, 19—:

CASH PAYMENTS JOURNAL   PAGE 3

CHECK NO.	DATE	PAID TO	FOR	POST. REF.	AMOUNT OF CHECK, CR.	M. STRONG, DRAWING, DR.	MATERIALS & SUPPLIES, DR.	OTHER ITEMS, DR. ITEM	OTHER ITEMS, DR. AMOUNT
53	July 1	Cash	personal	✓	845 00	845 00			
54	2	K&K Realty Co.	store rent		750 00			Rent	750 00
55	14	B. Taks Co.	materials	✓	5263 94		5263 94		
56	15	Mace Realty Co.	home rent	✓	357 50	357 50			
57	29	Albany Telephone Co.	business phone		129 45			Telephone	129 45

c) Copy the General Ledger accounts on page 640 which show the postings for the months of May and June. Allow six lines for each account.

d) Complete the daily postings from the Other Items column of the Cash Payments Journal. Record the necessary postmarks.

e) Pencil foot all money columns in both journals.

f) Verify totals in both journals by crossfooting.

g) Ink in totals and rule the journals.

h) Complete the end-of-month postings by posting the totals of both journals to the ledger. Record the necessary postmarks. Record a check mark for any total that is not to be posted.

i) Pencil foot the ledger accounts.

GENERAL LEDGER

ACCOUNT *Cash*　　　　　　　　　　　　　　　　　　　　　PAGE 1

DATE	ITEM	POST. REF.	DEBIT	DATE	ITEM	POST. REF.	CREDIT
19-- May 31		CR1	13019 25	19-- May 31		CP1	10523 73
June 30		CR3	17308 50	June 30		CP2	12470 17

ACCOUNT *Income from Aluminum Siding*　　　　　　　　　PAGE 2

DATE	ITEM	POST. REF.	DEBIT	DATE	ITEM	POST. REF.	CREDIT
				19-- May 31		CR1	11036 25
				June 30		CR2	14259 00

ACCOUNT *Income from Roofing*　　　　　　　　　　　　　PAGE 3

DATE	ITEM	POST. REF.	DEBIT	DATE	ITEM	POST. REF.	CREDIT
				19-- May 31		CR1	1983 00
				June 30		CR2	3049 50

ACCOUNT *Mark Strong, Drawing*　　　　　　　　　　　　PAGE 4

DATE	ITEM	POST. REF.	DEBIT	DATE	ITEM	POST. REF.	CREDIT
19-- May 31		CP1	1618 36				
June 30		CP2	2032 68				

ACCOUNT *Materials & Supplies*　　　　　　　　　　　　　PAGE 5

DATE	ITEM	POST. REF.	DEBIT	DATE	ITEM	POST. REF.	CREDIT
19-- May 31		CP1	8014 32				
June 30		CP2	9586 79				

ACCOUNT *Rent*　　　　　　　　　　　　　　　　　　　　　PAGE 6

DATE	ITEM	POST. REF.	DEBIT	DATE	ITEM	POST. REF.	CREDIT
19-- May 1		CP1	750 00				
June 4		CP2	750 00				

ACCOUNT *Telephone*　　　　　　　　　　　　　　　　　　PAGE 7

DATE	ITEM	POST. REF.	DEBIT	DATE	ITEM	POST. REF.	CREDIT
19-- May 28		CP1	141 05				
June 27		CP2	100 70				

Problem 2

You are employed in the office of Victor Knole, who sells and repairs restaurant equipment.

Directions:

a) Open a Cash Receipts Journal with the following headings:

CASH RECEIPTS JOURNAL   PAGE 3

INV. NO.	DATE	RECEIVED FROM	POST. REF.	INCOME, CR.		TOTAL RECEIPTS, DR.	BANK DEPOSITS
				LABOR	EQUIPMENT & MATERIALS		

b) Open a Cash Payments Journal with the following headings:

CASH PAYMENTS JOURNAL   PAGE 3

CHECK NO.	DATE	PAID TO	FOR	POST. REF.	AMOUNT OF CHECK, CR.	V. KNOLE, DRAWING, DR.	EQUIPMENT & MATERIALS, DR.	OTHER ITEMS, DR.	
								ITEM	AMOUNT

c) Copy the General Ledger accounts shown below and on page 642, which show the postings for the months of August and September. Allow six lines for each account.

GENERAL LEDGER

ACCOUNT *Cash*   PAGE 1

DATE	ITEM	POST. REF.	DEBIT	DATE	ITEM	POST. REF.	CREDIT
19-- Aug. 31		CR1	9 41 8 40	19-- Aug. 31		CP1	7 02 5 05
Sept. 30		CR2	8 06 7 95	Sept. 30		CP2	6 54 0 58

ACCOUNT *Income from Labor*   PAGE 2

DATE	ITEM	POST. REF.	DEBIT	DATE	ITEM	POST. REF.	CREDIT
				19-- Aug. 31		CR1	9 1 3 00
				Sept. 30		CR2	1 02 6 00

ACCOUNT *Income from Equipment and Materials*   PAGE 3

DATE	ITEM	POST. REF.	DEBIT	DATE	ITEM	POST. REF.	CREDIT
				19-- Aug. 31		CR1	8 505 40
				Sept. 30		CR2	7 041 95

ACCOUNT *Victor Knole, Drawing*   PAGE 4

DATE	ITEM	POST. REF.	DEBIT	DATE	ITEM	POST. REF.	CREDIT
19-- Aug. 31		CP1	738 68				
Sept. 30		CP2	1 057 35				

ACCOUNT *Equipment and Materials*   PAGE 5

DATE	ITEM	POST. REF.	DEBIT	DATE	ITEM	POST. REF.	CREDIT
19-- Aug. 31		CP1	5 407 52				
Sept. 30		CP2	4 629 18				

ACCOUNT *Rent*   PAGE 6

DATE	ITEM	POST. REF.	DEBIT	DATE	ITEM	POST. REF.	CREDIT
19-- Aug. 4		CP1	800 00				
Sept. 5		CP2	800 00				

ACCOUNT *Telephone*   PAGE 7

DATE	ITEM	POST. REF.	DEBIT	DATE	ITEM	POST. REF.	CREDIT
19-- Aug. 25		CP1	78 85				
Sept. 23		CP2	54 05				

d) Record the receipts and payments in the proper journal. Record a check mark in the Posting Reference column for all items that are not to be posted at the end of the day.

Oct. 1   Issued a check for $800.00 to the Gill Realty Co. for the store rent for the month. (Start with check #61.)

2   Issued a check for $2,916.30 to the M & Z Co. for equipment.

7   Received $524.72 from the J. Felt Co. Of this amount, $138.00 was for labor and $386.72 for materials. (Start with invoice #23.)

8   Received $2,675.00 from the Y. Carp Co. Of this amount, $417.00 was for labor and $2,258.00 was for equipment.

8   Deposited in the bank all the money received up to this date. The deposit amounted to $3,199.72. (Enter this amount in the Bank Deposits column on the same line with the last receipt.)

9   Issued a check for $210.65 to K. Woods Co. for clothing bought by Mr. Knole for his personal use.

14	Issued a check for $571.96 to the T. Doyle Co. for materials.
15	Received $165.48 from the D. Gasby Co. Of this amount, $63.00 was for labor and $102.48 for materials.
16	Issued a check for $26.85 to the Mobile Telephone Co. for Mr. Knole's personal home phone bill.
17	Received $3,620.00 from the S. Aigen Co. Of this amount, $345.00 was for labor and $3,275.00 was for equipment.
17	Deposited all the money received from Oct. 15 to this date. The deposited amount was $3,785.48. (Enter this amount in the Bank Deposits column on the same line with the last receipt.)
21	Mr. Knole, the owner, cashed a check for $685.00 to take home for his personal use. (The check was made payable to "Cash.")
22	Issued a check for $67.25 to the Mobile Telephone Co. for the business telephone bill.
28	Issued a check for $3,052.49 to the R. Ellis Co. for equipment.
29	Issued a check for $41.50 to the Mobile Electric Co. for electricity supplied to Mr. Knole's home.
30	Received $5,390.00 from the L. Rubin Co. Of this amount, $500.00 was for labor and $4,890.00 for equipment.
31	Received $305.80 from the H. Lang Co. Of this amount, $86.00 was for labor and $219.80 for materials.
31	Deposited all the money received from Oct. 30 to this date. The deposit amounted to $5,695.80. (Enter this amount in the Bank Deposits column on the same line with the last receipt.)

e) Complete the daily postings of all items recorded in the Other Items column of the Cash Payments Journal. Record the necessary postmarks in the journal and in the ledger.

f) Pencil foot the money columns in the Cash Receipts Journal and in the Cash Payments Journal.

g) Verify totals in both journals by crossfooting.

h) Ink in totals and rule both journals.

i) Complete the end-of-month postings of the totals in both journals. Record all postmarks and record a check mark for any total that is not to be posted.

j) Pencil foot the ledger accounts.

Problem 3

You are employed in the office of Henry Sears, who sells and repairs alarm systems.

Directions:

a) Open a Cash Receipts Journal with the headings shown at the top of the next page.

CASH RECEIPTS JOURNAL — PAGE 3

INV. NO.	DATE	RECEIVED FROM	POST. REF.	INCOME, CR. LABOR	INCOME, CR. ALARMS & MATERIALS	TOTAL RECEIPTS, DR.	BANK DEPOSITS

b) Open a Cash Payments Journal with the following headings:

CASH PAYMENTS JOURNAL — PAGE 3

CHECK NO.	DATE	PAID TO	FOR	POST. REF.	AMOUNT OF CHECK, CR.	H. SEARS, DRAWING, DR.	EQUIPMENT & MATERIALS, DR.	OTHER ITEMS, DR. ITEM	OTHER ITEMS, DR. AMOUNT

c) Copy the General Ledger accounts shown below and on page 645 which show the postings for the months of October and November, 19—. Allow six lines for each account.

GENERAL LEDGER

ACCOUNT **Cash**   PAGE 1

DATE	ITEM	POST. REF.	DEBIT	DATE	ITEM	POST. REF.	CREDIT
Oct. 19-- 31		CR1	9531 72	Oct. 19-- 31		CP1	7782 71
Nov. 30		CR2	10516 63	Nov. 30		CP2	8820 54

ACCOUNT **Income from Labor**   PAGE 2

DATE	ITEM	POST. REF.	DEBIT	DATE	ITEM	POST. REF.	CREDIT
				Oct. 19-- 31		CR1	1136 00
				Nov. 30		CR2	1078 00

ACCOUNT **Income from Alarms and Materials**   PAGE 3

DATE	ITEM	POST. REF.	DEBIT	DATE	ITEM	POST. REF.	CREDIT
				Oct. 19-- 31		CR1	8395 72
				Nov. 30		CR2	9438 63

ACCOUNT *Henry Sears, Drawing*   PAGE 4

DATE		ITEM	POST. REF.	DEBIT	DATE	ITEM	POST. REF.	CREDIT
19--								
Oct.	31		CP1	1 01 6 20				
Nov.	30		CP2	9 83 58				

ACCOUNT *Alarms & Materials*   PAGE 5

DATE		ITEM	POST. REF.	DEBIT	DATE	ITEM	POST. REF.	CREDIT
19--								
Oct.	31		CP1	6 07 4 81				
Nov.	30		CP2	7 1 9 2 46				

ACCOUNT *Rent*   PAGE 6

DATE		ITEM	POST. REF.	DEBIT	DATE	ITEM	POST. REF.	CREDIT
19--								
Oct.	2		CP1	5 4 8 00				
Nov.	3		CP2	5 4 8 00				

ACCOUNT *Telephone*   PAGE 7

DATE		ITEM	POST. REF.	DEBIT	DATE	ITEM	POST. REF.	CREDIT
19--								
Oct	28		CP1	1 43 70				
Nov.	25		CP2	9 6 50				

d) Record the following receipts and payments in the proper journal. Record a check mark in the Posting Reference column for all items that are not to be posted at the end of the day.

Dec. 1 Issued a check for $548.00 to the Kelly Realty Co. for the store rent for the month. (Start with check #100.)

3 Received $374.27 from B. Wiggs Co. Of this amount, $64.00 was for labor and $310.27 for materials. (Start with invoice #117.)

4 Received $1,024.50 from H. Pacente Co. Of this amount, $86.00 was for labor and $938.50 was for alarm equipment.

4 Deposited in the bank all the money received up to this date. The deposit amounted to $1,398.77. (Enter this amount in the Bank Deposits column on the same line with the last receipt.)

10 Issued a check for $265.37 to the A. Lilly Co. for materials.

11 Received $2,127.00 from F. Emmery. Of this amount, $235.00 was for labor and $1,892.00 for alarm equipment.

12 Received $2,923.85 from T. Dumas. Of this amount, $308.00 was for labor and $2,615.85 was for alarm equipment.

12 Deposited in the bank all the money received up to this date. The deposit amounted to $5,050.85. (Enter this amount in the Bank Deposits column on the same line with the last receipt.)

15 Issued a check for $287.00 to S. Parks Realty Co. for Mr. Sears' personal home rent.

17 Issued a check for $3,139.68 to C. Spaer Co. for alarm equipment.

18 Mr. Sears, the owner, cashed a check for $840.00 to take home for his personal use. (The check was made payable to "Cash.")

22 Received $1,180.60 from K. Veit Co. Of this amount, $157.00 was for labor and $1,023.60 was for alarm equipment.

23 Issued a check for $2,003.70 to the G & J Co. for alarm equipment.

24 Received $838.93 from N. Holly. Of this amount, $92.00 was for labor and $746.93 was for alarm equipment.

24 Deposited in the bank all the money received up to this date. The deposit amounted to $2,019.53. (Enter this amount in the Bank Deposits column on the same line with the last receipt.)

29 Issued a check for $612.45 to the Russ Furniture Co. for furniture delivered to Mr. Sears' home.

31 Issued a check for $106.80 to the N. E. Telephone Co. for the business telephone bill.

e) Complete the daily postings of all items recorded in the Other Items column of the Cash Payments Journal. Record the necessary postmarks in the journal and in the ledger.

f) Pencil foot the money columns in the Cash Receipts Journal and in the Cash Payments Journal.

g) Verify the totals in both journals by crossfooting.

h) Ink in totals and rule both journals.

i) Complete the end-of-month postings of the totals in both journals. Record all postmarks and record a check mark for any total that is not to be posted.

j) Pencil foot the ledger accounts.

INDEX